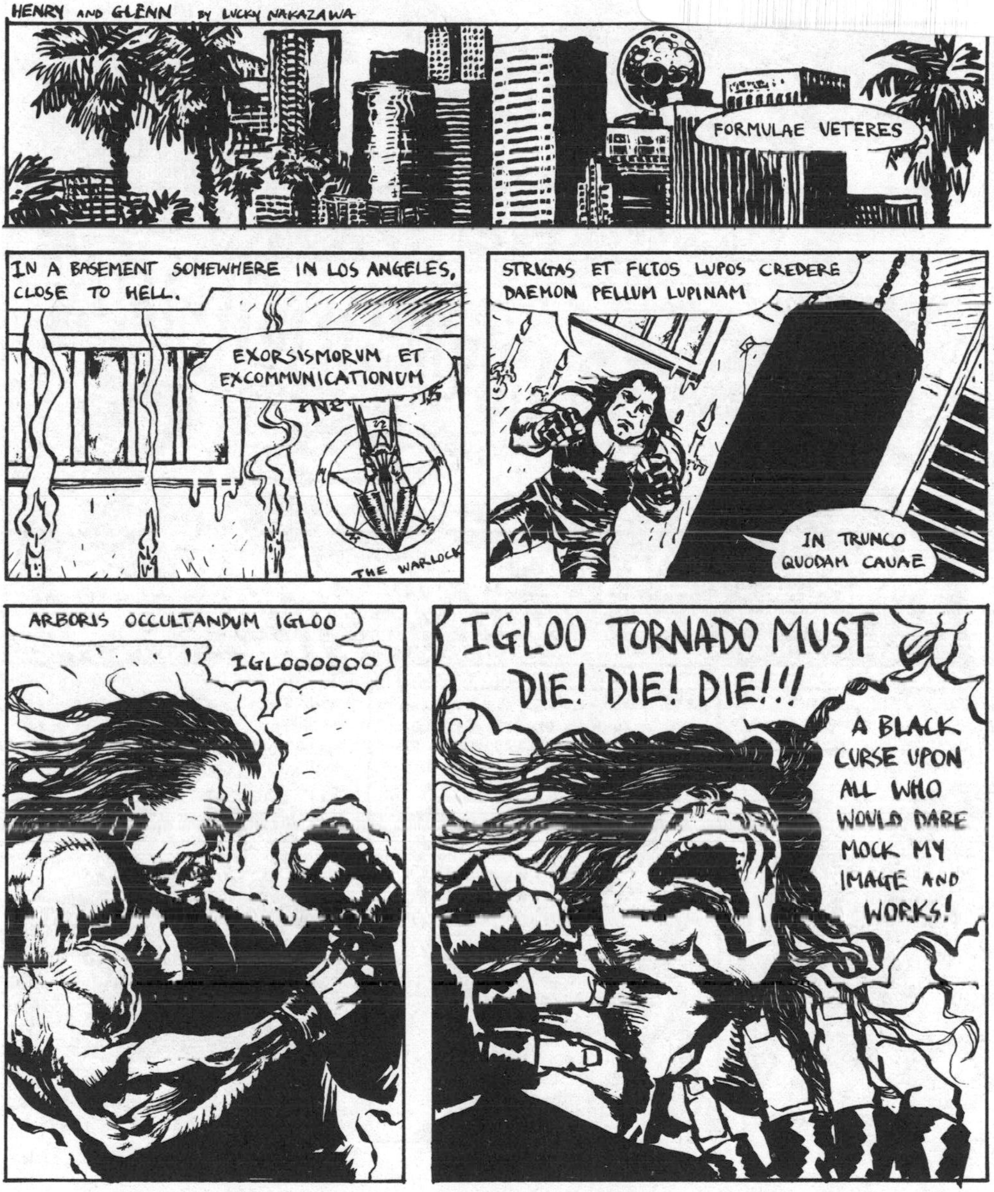
HENRY AND GLENN BY LUCKY NAKAZAWA
FORMULAE VETERES
IN A BASEMENT SOMEWHERE IN LOS ANGELES, CLOSE TO HELL.
EXORSISMORUM ET EXCOMMUNICATIONUM
THE WARLOCK
STRIGAS ET FICTOS LUPOS CREDERE DAEMON PELLUM LUPINAM
IN TRUNCO QUODAM CAUAE
ARBORIS OCCULTANDUM IGLOO
IGLOOOOOO
IGLOO TORNADO MUST DIE! DIE! DIE!!!
A BLACK CURSE UPON ALL WHO WOULD DARE MOCK MY IMAGE AND WORKS!

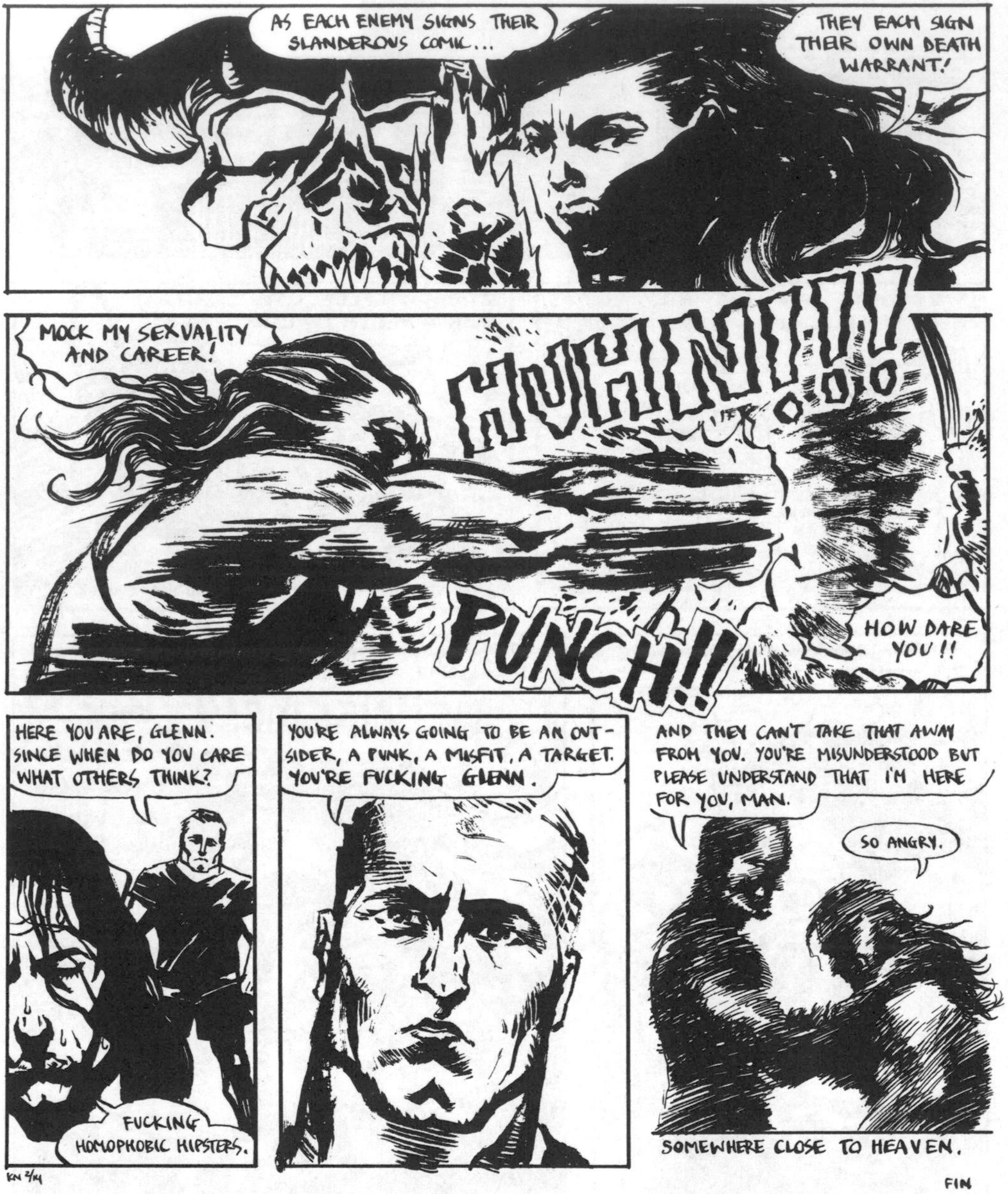
AS EACH ENEMY SIGNS THEIR SLANDEROUS COMIC...
THEY EACH SIGN THEIR OWN DEATH WARRANT!
MOCK MY SEXUALITY AND CAREER!
PUNCH!!
HOW DARE YOU!!
HERE YOU ARE, GLENN. SINCE WHEN DO YOU CARE WHAT OTHERS THINK?
FUCKING HOMOPHOBIC HIPSTERS.
YOU'RE ALWAYS GOING TO BE AN OUT-SIDER, A PUNK, A MISFIT, A TARGET. YOU'RE FUCKING GLENN.
AND THEY CAN'T TAKE THAT AWAY FROM YOU. YOU'RE MISUNDERSTOOD BUT PLEASE UNDERSTAND THAT I'M HERE FOR YOU, MAN.
SO ANGRY.
SOMEWHERE CLOSE TO HEAVEN.

KN 2/14

FIN

IGLOO TORNADO'S
HENRY & GLENN
FOREVER & EVER

Tom Neely & Friends

Microcosm Publishing
Portland, OR

I Will Destroy You Comics
Los Angeles, CA

HENRY & GLENN FOREVER & EVER
The Completely Ridiculous Edition

© 2007, 2009, 2012, 2013, 2014, 2017 the respective creators
Permission to reprint must be obtained from artist or publisher
© This edition I will Destroy You / Microcosm Publishing 2022
First edition - 3,000 copies - March 23, 2022
ISBN 9781648411441
This is Microcosm #154
Cover by Tom Neely

To join the ranks of high-class stores that feature Microcosm titles, talk to your local rep: In the U.S. **COMO** (Atlantic), **FUJII** (Midwest), **BOOK TRAVELERS WEST** (Pacific), **TURNAROUND** (Europe), **UTP/MANDA** (Canada), **NEW SOUTH** (Australia/New Zealand), **GPS** in Asia, Africa, India, South America, and other countries, or **FAIRE** in the gift trade.

For a catalog, write or visit:
Microcosm Publishing
2752 N Williams Ave.
Portland, OR 97227
https://microcosm.pub/Henry-Glenn

For a catalog, write or visit:
I Will Destroy You
Los Angeles, CA
IWillDestroyYou.com

Did you know that you can buy our books directly from us at sliding scale rates? Support a small, independent publisher and pay less than Amazon's price at **www.Microcosm.Pub**

Global labor conditions are bad, and our roots in industrial Cleveland in the 70s and 80s made us appreciate the need to treat workers right. Therefore, our books are MADE IN THE USA.

Library of Congress Cataloging-in-Publication Data

Names: Neely, Tom, editor. | Halford, Rob, writer of foreword.
Title: Henry & Glenn forever & ever / edited and designed by Tom Neely ; foreword by Rob Halford.
Other titles: Henry and Glenn forever and ever
Description: Ridiculously complete edition. | Portland, OR : Microcosm Publishing, 2022. | Summary: "Two men. Two myths. One Legend. The greatest love story every told has finally been released in graphic novel form. This epic tome features twenty short stories about the domestic life of "Henry" and "Glenn" and sometimes their neighbors "Daryl" and "John." Digging beneath Glenn's bricks in the front yard, Henry uncovers Glenn's mother. Freshly unearthed, she moves in with him and Henry. Glenn's issues come to the surface as she critiques his art, replaces his wardrobe, scrubs their dungeon, and recalls his childhood. Later, Glenn tries to sell his signature to a UPS driver, takes a punch, and has some daydreaming adventures with a plunger. Henry, "a loud guy with a good work ethic," shows his darker side and indifference to a fan as he drinks black coffee and bonds with Glenn over their distaste for their own bands. These are two men who truly suffer best alone together. Among other hijinks, Henry and Glenn go to therapy together, battle an evil cult in the forest, and profess their love for each other, all while dealing with jealousy and other normal relationship problems and trying to figure out if their soft-rocking neighbors are actually Dungeons and Dragons playing Satanists. The saga of Henry and Glenn is a true testament to the power of love to overcome even the biggest, manliest egos of our time. The hardcover edition collects four serialized comics, the trade paperback, the original 6x6" book, and adds 16 never-before published pages, including new stories, pin up art, and full color covers from the original series"-- Provided by publisher.
Identifiers: LCCN 2021059329 | ISBN 9781648411441 (paperback)
Subjects: LCSH: Rollins, Henry, 1961---Comic books, strips, etc. | Danzig, Glenn--Comic books, strips, etc. | LCGFT: Humorous comics. | Romance comics. | Short stories. | Graphic novels.
Classification: LCC PN6728.H388 H46 2022 | DDC 741.5/973--dc23/eng/20211228
LC record available at https://lccn.loc.gov/2021059329

TABLE OF CONTENTS

With Pin-ups by:

Gabe Martinez (82), Sean Stepanoff (84), Katie Skelly (85), Willow Dawson (88), Rafer Roberts (89)
Zak Sally (100), Tom Forget (101), Alex Chiu (132), Beth Dean (133), Matt Crabe (142)
Keenan Marshall Keller (143), Mikey Wetzel (158), Nate Powell (186), Chuck BB (187), Grant Reynolds (188)
Dennis Halbritter (189), Tim Sievert (192), Trevor Alixopulos (193), Ed Luce (194) Fred Noland (197)
Eric Yahnker (214), Coop (215), Jeff Ward (216), Andy Belanger (217), Ken Garduno (218)

End paper illustrations by Dave Davenport and Gin Stevens
Completely Ridiculous Edition cover by Jim-muthuh-fuhkin-Rugg!!!
Back Cover "Henri devant un miroir endommagé" by Tom Neely

ROB HALFORD
LEANS FOREWORD

Oh, how transparent of you Tom Neely... you deluded fool... thinking you can reel me in on some ruse about: "Hey, wouldn't it be cool if we could get Rob Halford to foreword this collection of *Henry and Glenn Forever and Ever*?!" HA!

I know how your sick and twisted mind works... laying awake at night in your hovel... sweating and gasping as you rewind me one more time off of your so-called hidden VHS collection that displays the full oasis of my male masculinity on stage! You even have the nerve to half heartedly ink me in at some sex boutique when you full well know I worked at a porno shop. Was your hand trembling with the urge to go further? I know it was. Yet somehow your mad plan just about held together. You thought that just because you had heard a so-called rumor that I was already sucked into the (cough) genius of your work and by using your "talent" of combining satire... pathos... wit... absurdity... and other variables on a theme so... OUT THERE MAN... that I would jump at the chance to give you a moment of my mind to grovel at your twinky feet! Then you go one step further and rope in other people convincing them to use their gifts to amp up your sham and making it all even more addictive...

Well, now it crumbles around you! Like a boy on a beach whose sand castle gets swept away by the unforgiving tide of truth. Of exposure. I expose you Tom Neely! Yes, I expose myself to you that this Henry and Glenn thing is really about... Tom and Rob! There! It's out in the open for all the world to see at last... I'm doing this for you Tom. I'm setting you free from the shame and the guilt of your dirty closet. No, no don't thank me... You just keep thinking and inking your way into the hall of what ever it is you guys go into... by your..."fuck you world" aesthetic!

But listen... Hear me now Tom Neely! One day our paths will cross... not in your vivid imaginings... it will be a bar or diner or bathhouse... and then... THEN THE SPARKS WILL FLY!

- Rob Halford
April, 2014

For Kristina
the best friend I will ever have!

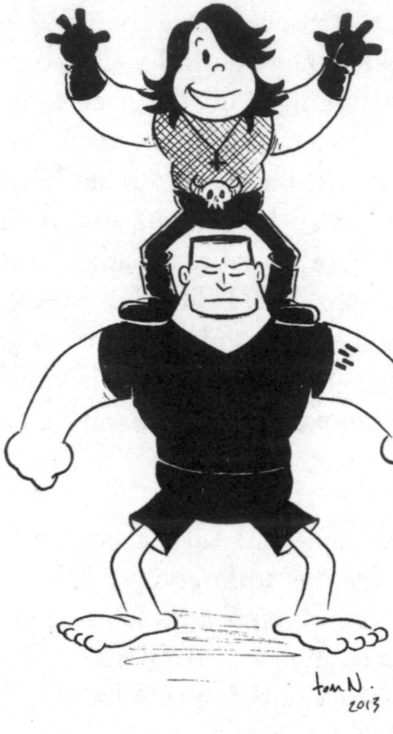
tom N.
2013

Thank you to the Igloo Tornado
for giving me the reins to this stoopid beast!

Special thanks to Joe, Ed, J and all my friends
for encouraging me to beat this dead horse a few more times.

And to my Mother, who will never "get it,"
but bless her for trying.

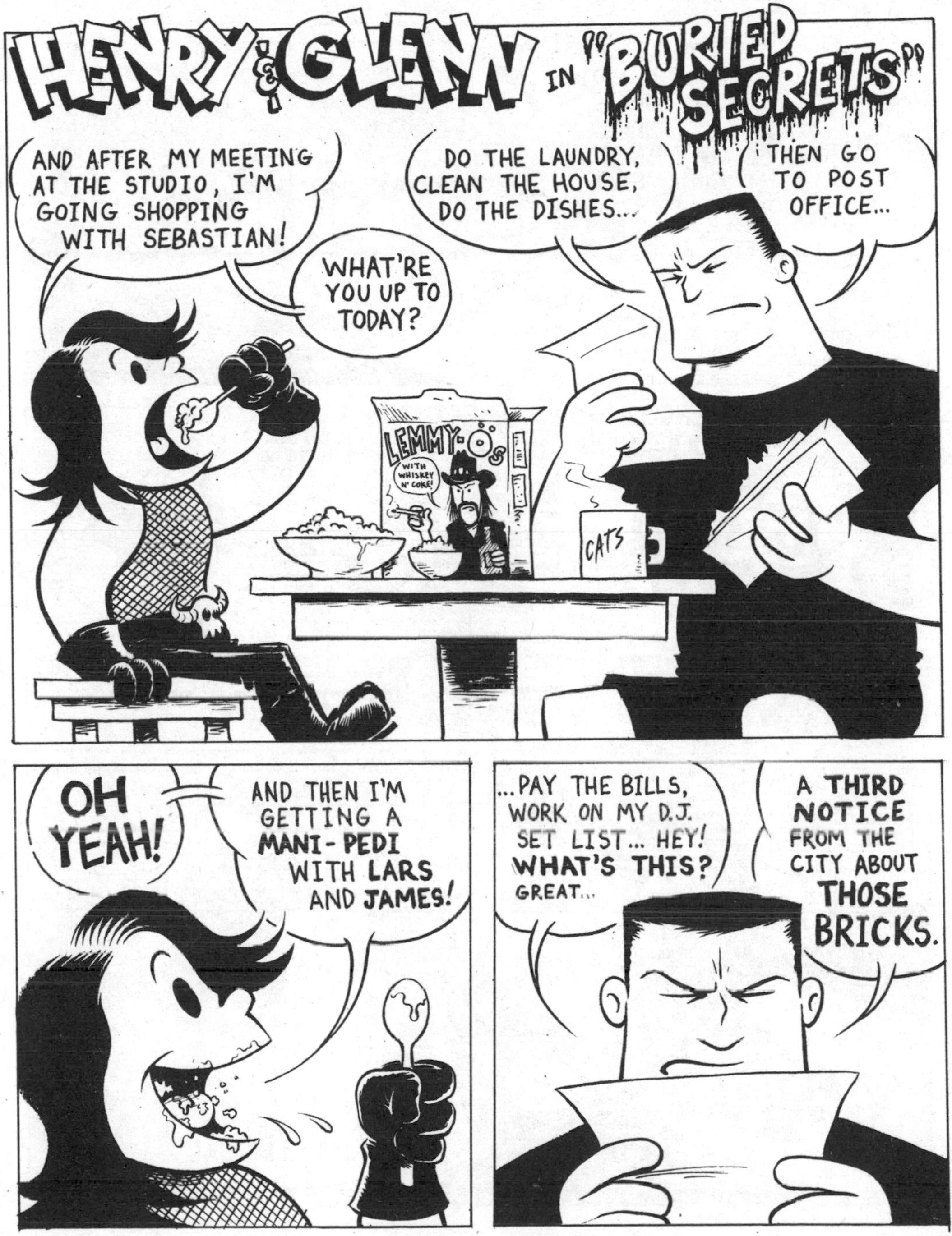
HENRY & GLENN IN "BURIED SECRETS"
AND AFTER MY MEETING AT THE STUDIO, I'M GOING SHOPPING WITH SEBASTIAN!
WHAT'RE YOU UP TO TODAY?
DO THE LAUNDRY, CLEAN THE HOUSE, DO THE DISHES...
THEN GO TO POST OFFICE...
LEMMY-O'S
WITH WHISKEY N' COKE!
CATS
OH YEAH!
AND THEN I'M GETTING A MANI-PEDI WITH LARS AND JAMES!
...PAY THE BILLS, WORK ON MY D.J. SET LIST... HEY! WHAT'S THIS? GREAT...
A THIRD NOTICE FROM THE CITY ABOUT THOSE BRICKS.

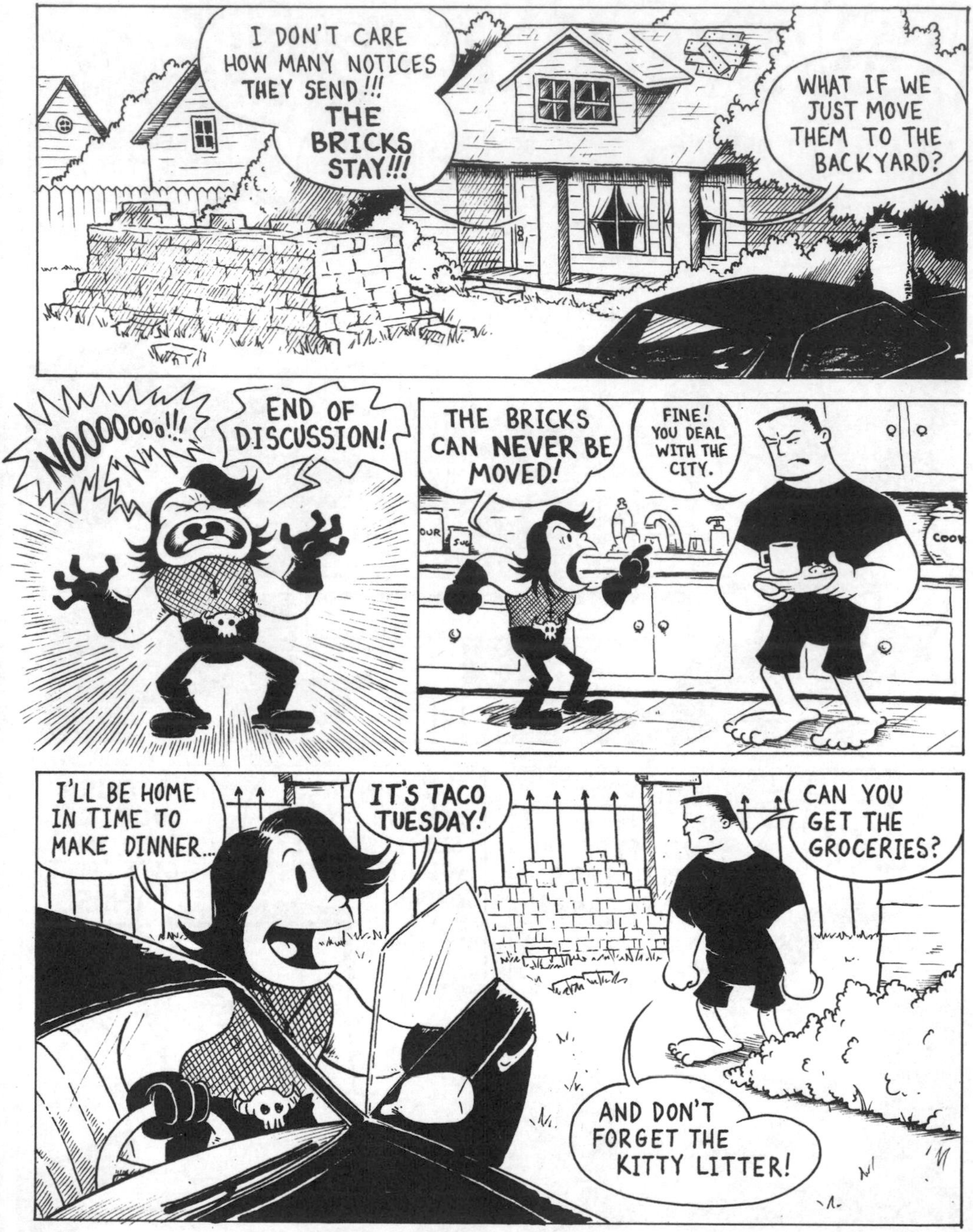
I DON'T CARE HOW MANY NOTICES THEY SEND!!! THE BRICKS STAY!!!
WHAT IF WE JUST MOVE THEM TO THE BACKYARD?
NOOOOOoo!!!
END OF DISCUSSION!
THE BRICKS CAN NEVER BE MOVED!
FINE! YOU DEAL WITH THE CITY.
I'LL BE HOME IN TIME TO MAKE DINNER...
IT'S TACO TUESDAY!
CAN YOU GET THE GROCERIES?
AND DON'T FORGET THE KITTY LITTER!

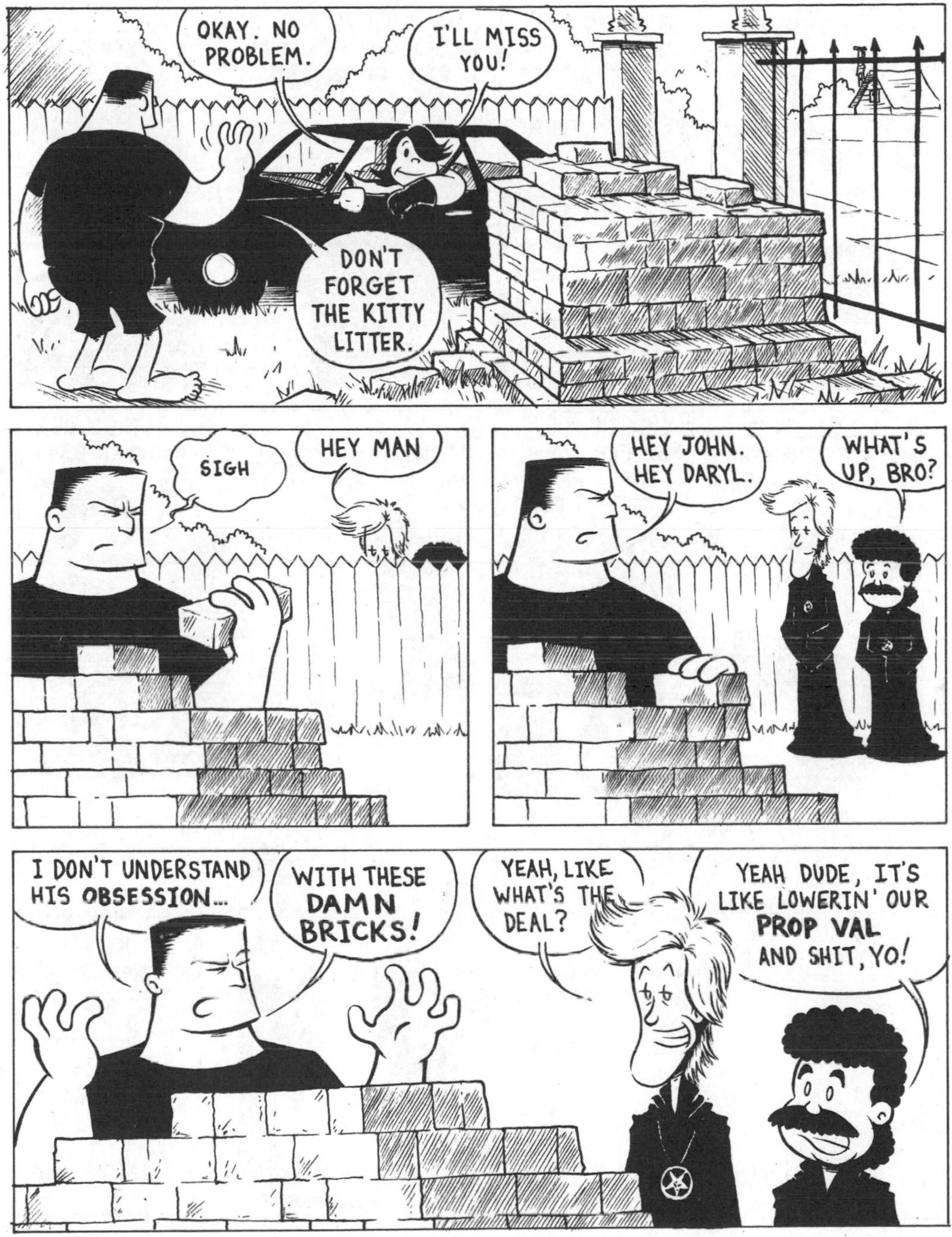
OKAY. NO PROBLEM.
I'LL MISS YOU!
DON'T FORGET THE KITTY LITTER.
SIGH
HEY MAN
HEY JOHN. HEY DARYL.
WHAT'S UP, BRO?
I DON'T UNDERSTAND HIS OBSESSION...
WITH THESE DAMN BRICKS!
YEAH, LIKE WHAT'S THE DEAL?
YEAH DUDE, IT'S LIKE LOWERIN' OUR PROP VAL AND SHIT, YO!

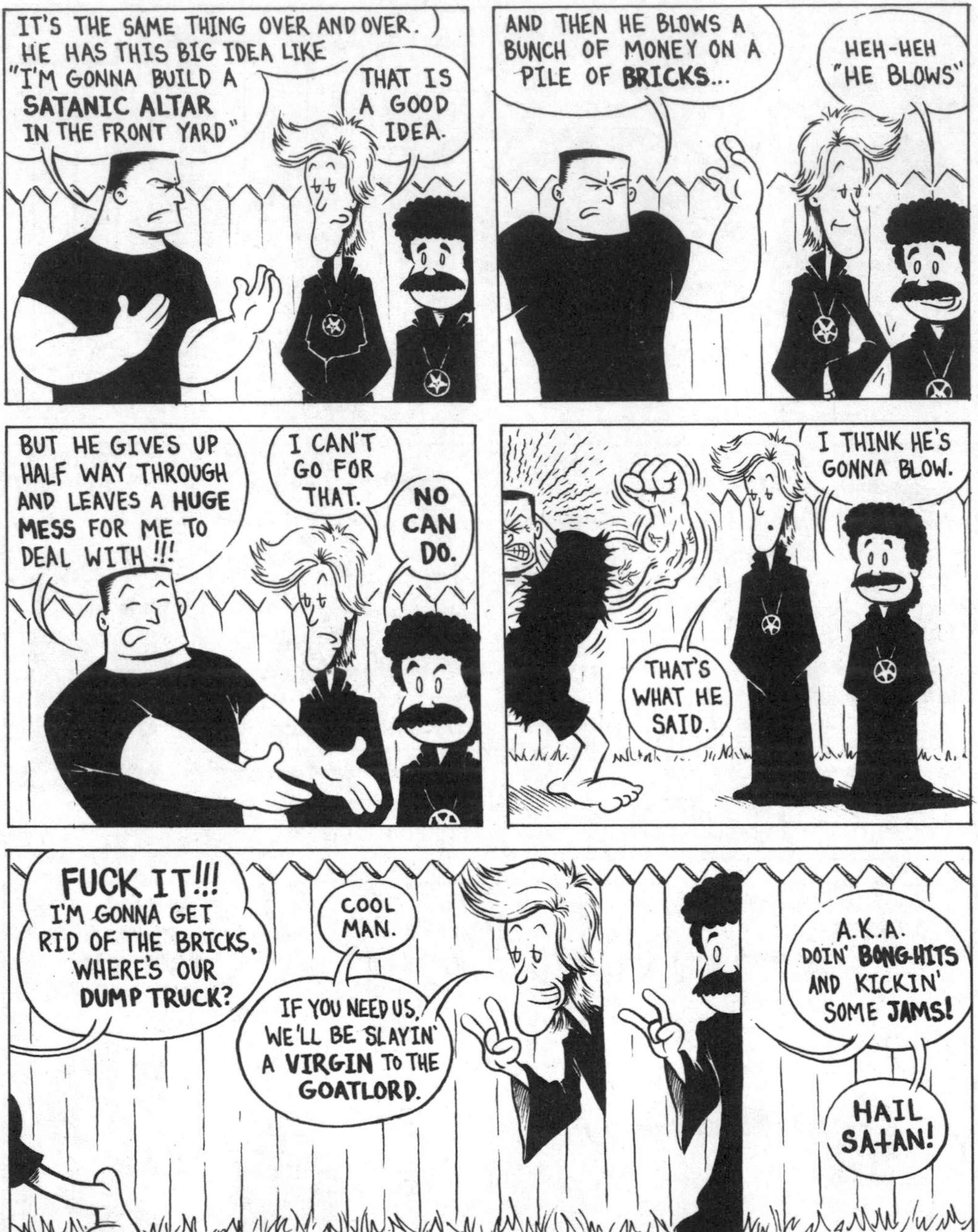
IT'S THE SAME THING OVER AND OVER. HE HAS THIS BIG IDEA LIKE "I'M GONNA BUILD A SATANIC ALTAR IN THE FRONT YARD"
THAT IS A GOOD IDEA.
AND THEN HE BLOWS A BUNCH OF MONEY ON A PILE OF BRICKS...
HEH-HEH "HE BLOWS"
BUT HE GIVES UP HALF WAY THROUGH AND LEAVES A HUGE MESS FOR ME TO DEAL WITH!!!
I CAN'T GO FOR THAT.
NO CAN DO.
I THINK HE'S GONNA BLOW.
THAT'S WHAT HE SAID.
FUCK IT!!! I'M GONNA GET RID OF THE BRICKS. WHERE'S OUR DUMP TRUCK?
COOL MAN.
IF YOU NEED US, WE'LL BE 'SLAYIN' A VIRGIN TO THE GOATLORD.
A.K.A. DOIN' BONG-HITS AND KICKIN' SOME JAMS!
HAIL SATAN!

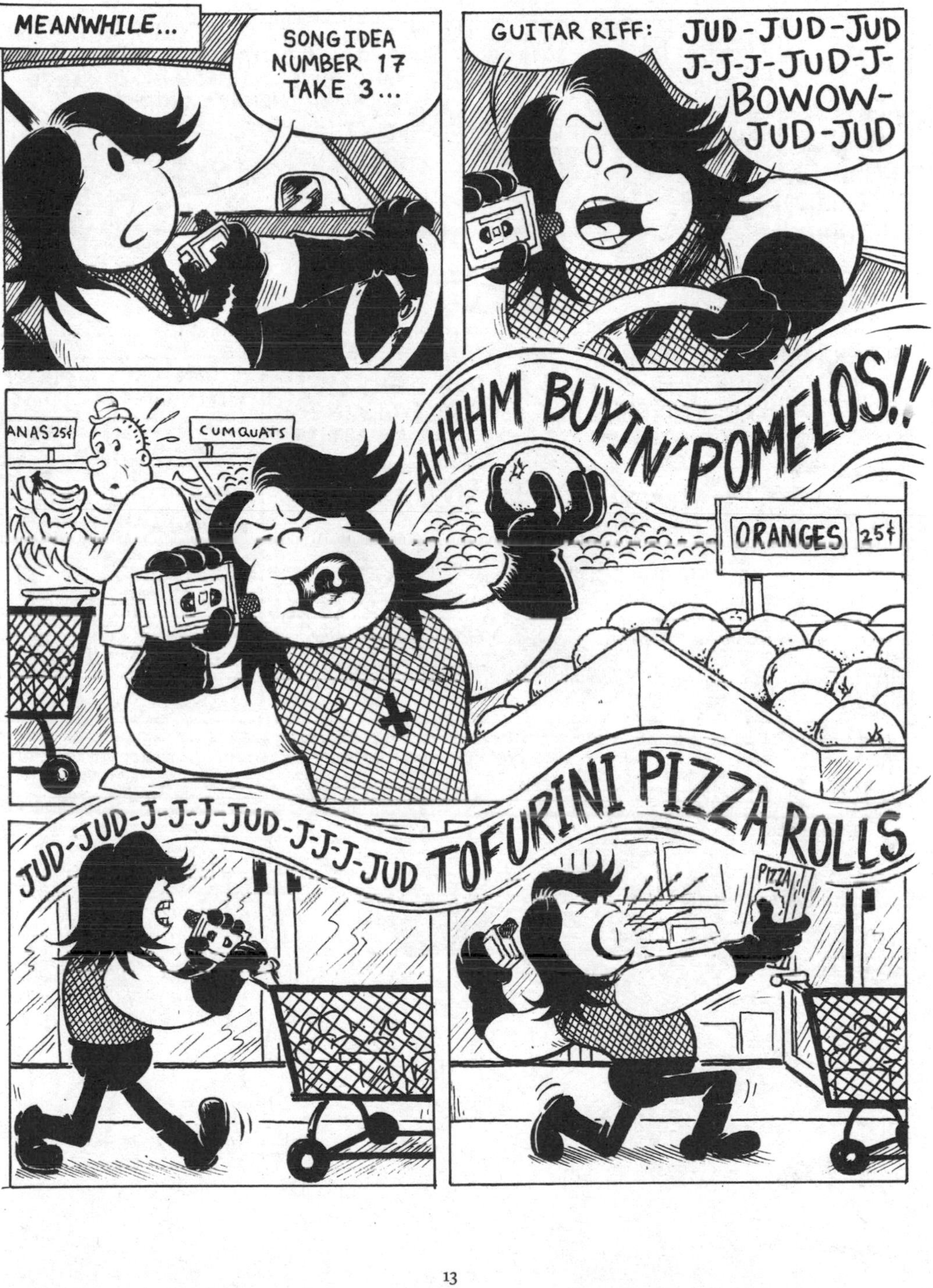
MEANWHILE...
SONG IDEA NUMBER 17 TAKE 3...
GUITAR RIFF: JUD-JUD-JUD J-J-J-JUD-J-BOWOW-JUD-JUD
ANAS 25¢
CUMQUATS
AHHHM BUYIN' POMELOS!!
ORANGES 25¢
JUD-JUD-J-J-J-JUD-J-J-J-JUD TOFURINI PIZZA ROLLS
PIZZA

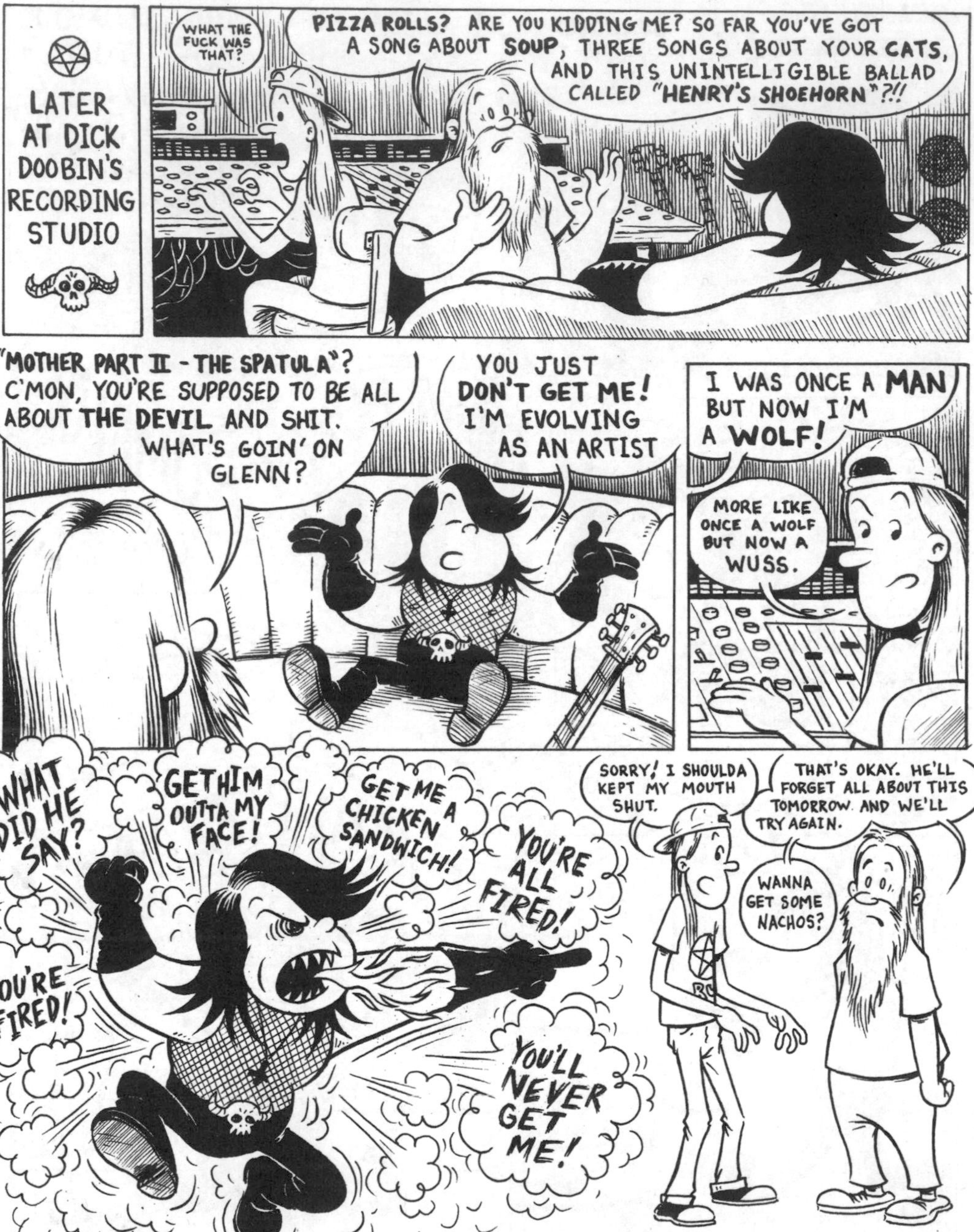
LATER AT DICK DOOBIN'S RECORDING STUDIO
WHAT THE FUCK WAS THAT?
PIZZA ROLLS? ARE YOU KIDDING ME? SO FAR YOU'VE GOT A SONG ABOUT SOUP, THREE SONGS ABOUT YOUR CATS, AND THIS UNINTELLIGIBLE BALLAD CALLED "HENRY'S SHOEHORN"?!!
"MOTHER PART II - THE SPATULA"? C'MON, YOU'RE SUPPOSED TO BE ALL ABOUT THE DEVIL AND SHIT. WHAT'S GOIN' ON GLENN?
YOU JUST DON'T GET ME! I'M EVOLVING AS AN ARTIST
I WAS ONCE A MAN BUT NOW I'M A WOLF!
MORE LIKE ONCE A WOLF BUT NOW A WUSS.
WHAT DID HE SAY?
GET HIM OUTTA MY FACE!
GET ME A CHICKEN SANDWICH!
YOU'RE ALL FIRED!
YOU'RE FIRED!
YOU'LL NEVER GET ME!
SORRY! I SHOULDA KEPT MY MOUTH SHUT.
THAT'S OKAY. HE'LL FORGET ALL ABOUT THIS TOMORROW. AND WE'LL TRY AGAIN.
WANNA GET SOME NACHOS?

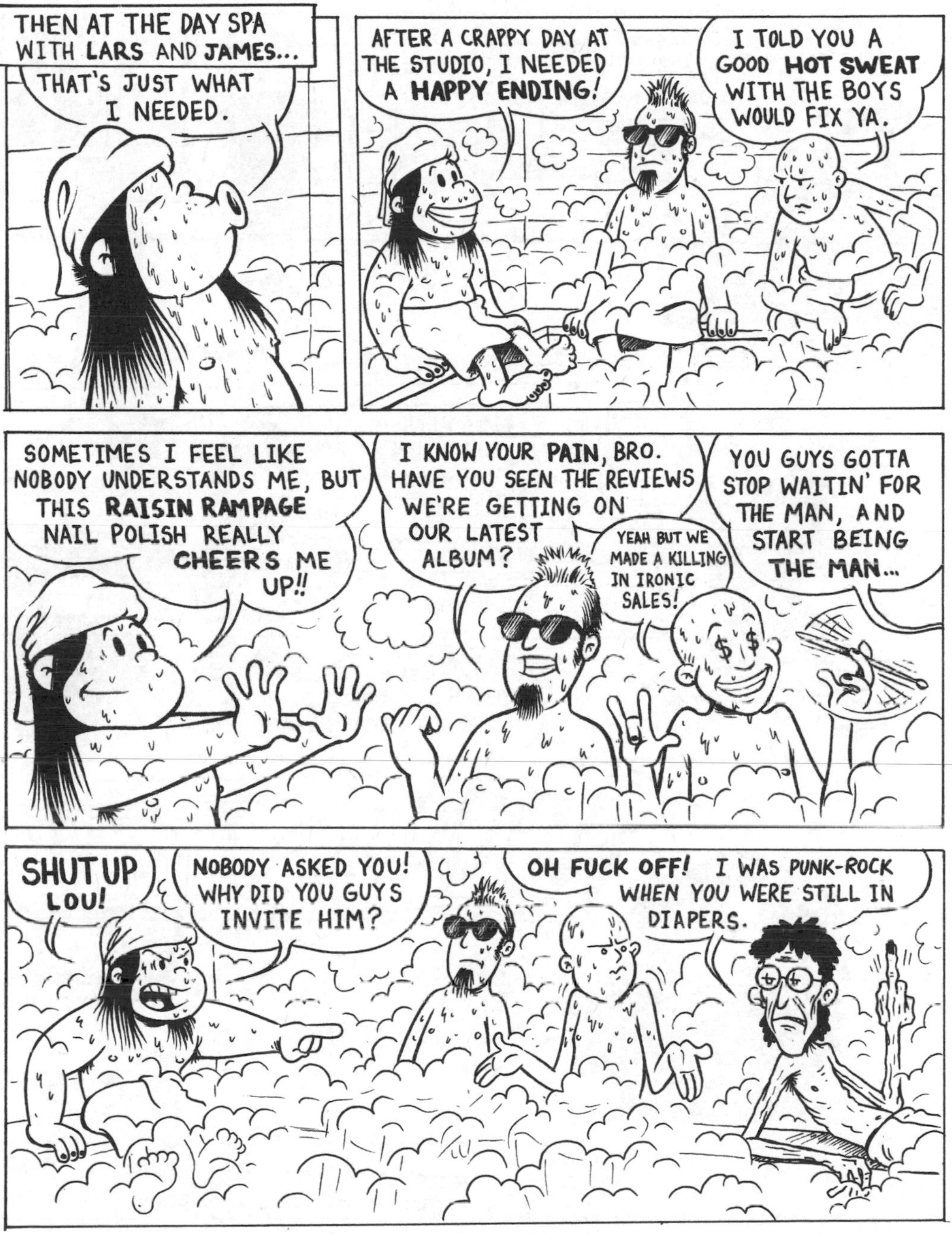
THEN AT THE DAY SPA WITH **LARS** AND **JAMES**...
THAT'S JUST WHAT I NEEDED.
AFTER A CRAPPY DAY AT THE STUDIO, I NEEDED A **HAPPY ENDING**!
I TOLD YOU A GOOD **HOT SWEAT** WITH THE BOYS WOULD FIX YA.
SOMETIMES I FEEL LIKE NOBODY UNDERSTANDS ME, BUT THIS **RAISIN RAMPAGE** NAIL POLISH REALLY **CHEERS** ME UP!!
I KNOW YOUR **PAIN**, BRO. HAVE YOU SEEN THE REVIEWS WE'RE GETTING ON OUR LATEST ALBUM?
YEAH BUT WE MADE A KILLING IN IRONIC SALES!
YOU GUYS GOTTA STOP WAITIN' FOR THE MAN, AND START BEING **THE MAN**...
SHUT UP LOU!
NOBODY ASKED YOU! WHY DID YOU GUYS INVITE HIM?
OH FUCK OFF! I WAS PUNK-ROCK WHEN YOU WERE STILL IN DIAPERS.

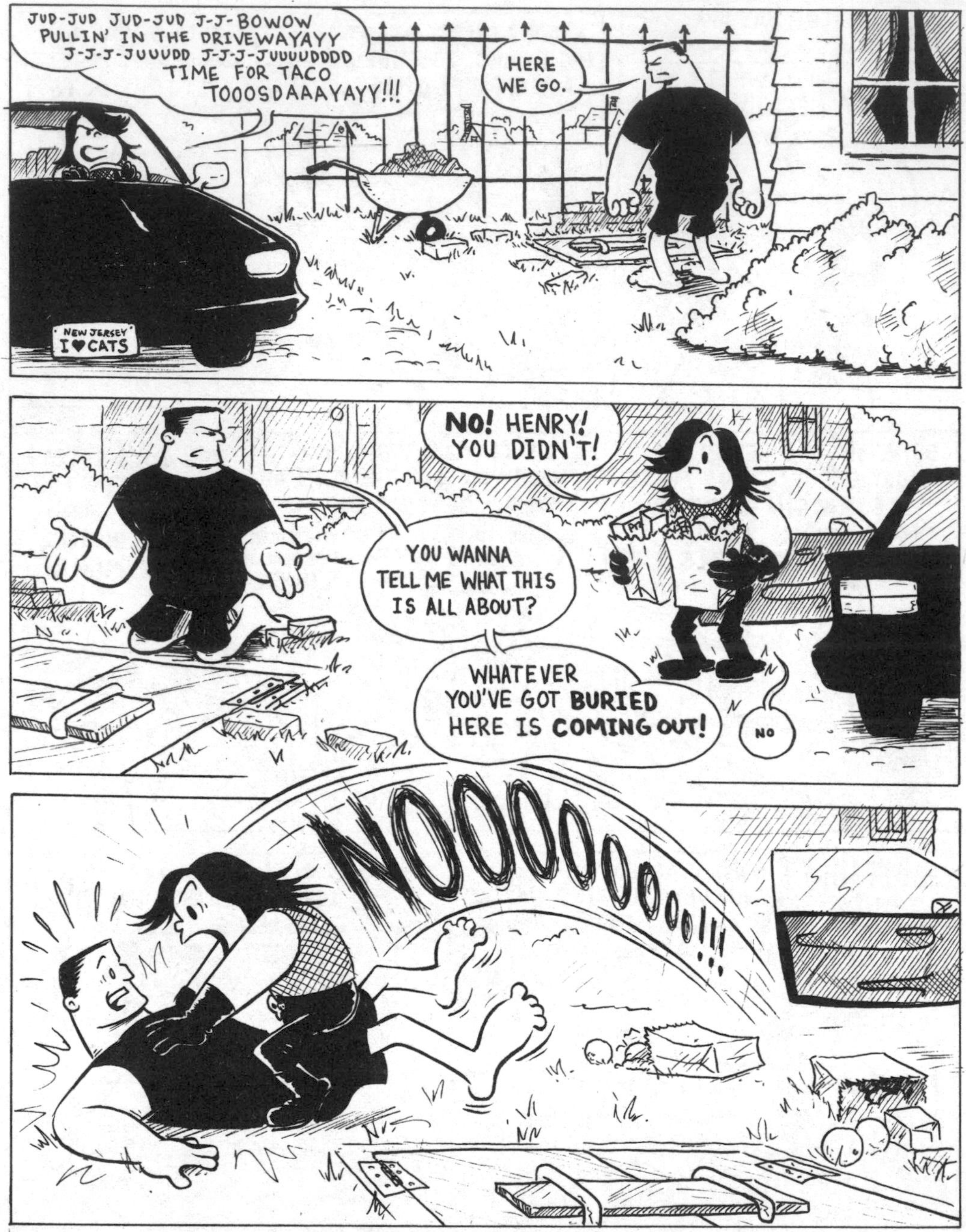
JUD-JUD JUD-JUD J-J-BOWOW
PULLIN' IN THE DRIVEWAYAYY
J-J-J-JUUUDD J-J-J-JUUUUDDDD
TIME FOR TACO
TOOOSDAAAYAYY!!!
HERE WE GO.
NEW JERSEY
I ♥ CATS
NO! HENRY! YOU DIDN'T!
YOU WANNA TELL ME WHAT THIS IS ALL ABOUT?
WHATEVER YOU'VE GOT BURIED HERE IS COMING OUT!
NO
NOOOOOOoo!!!

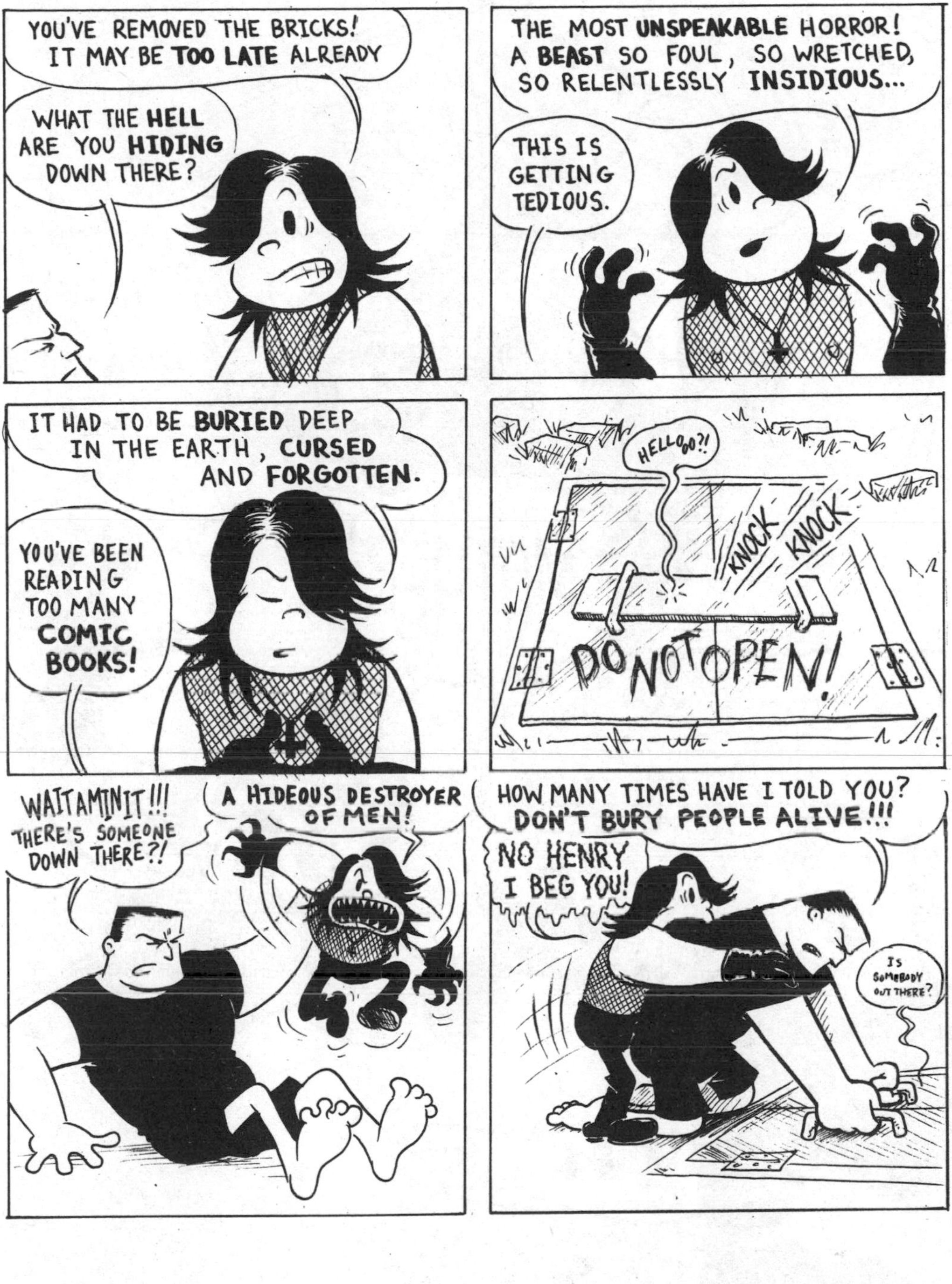
YOU'VE REMOVED THE BRICKS! IT MAY BE TOO LATE ALREADY
WHAT THE HELL ARE YOU HIDING DOWN THERE?
THE MOST UNSPEAKABLE HORROR! A BEAST SO FOUL, SO WRETCHED, SO RELENTLESSLY INSIDIOUS...
THIS IS GETTING TEDIOUS.
IT HAD TO BE BURIED DEEP IN THE EARTH, CURSED AND FORGOTTEN.
YOU'VE BEEN READING TOO MANY COMIC BOOKS!
HELLOoo?!
KNOCK
KNOCK
DO NOT OPEN!
WAITAMINIT!!! THERE'S SOMEONE DOWN THERE?!
A HIDEOUS DESTROYER OF MEN!
HOW MANY TIMES HAVE I TOLD YOU? DON'T BURY PEOPLE ALIVE!!!
NO HENRY I BEG YOU!
IS SOMEBODY OUT THERE?

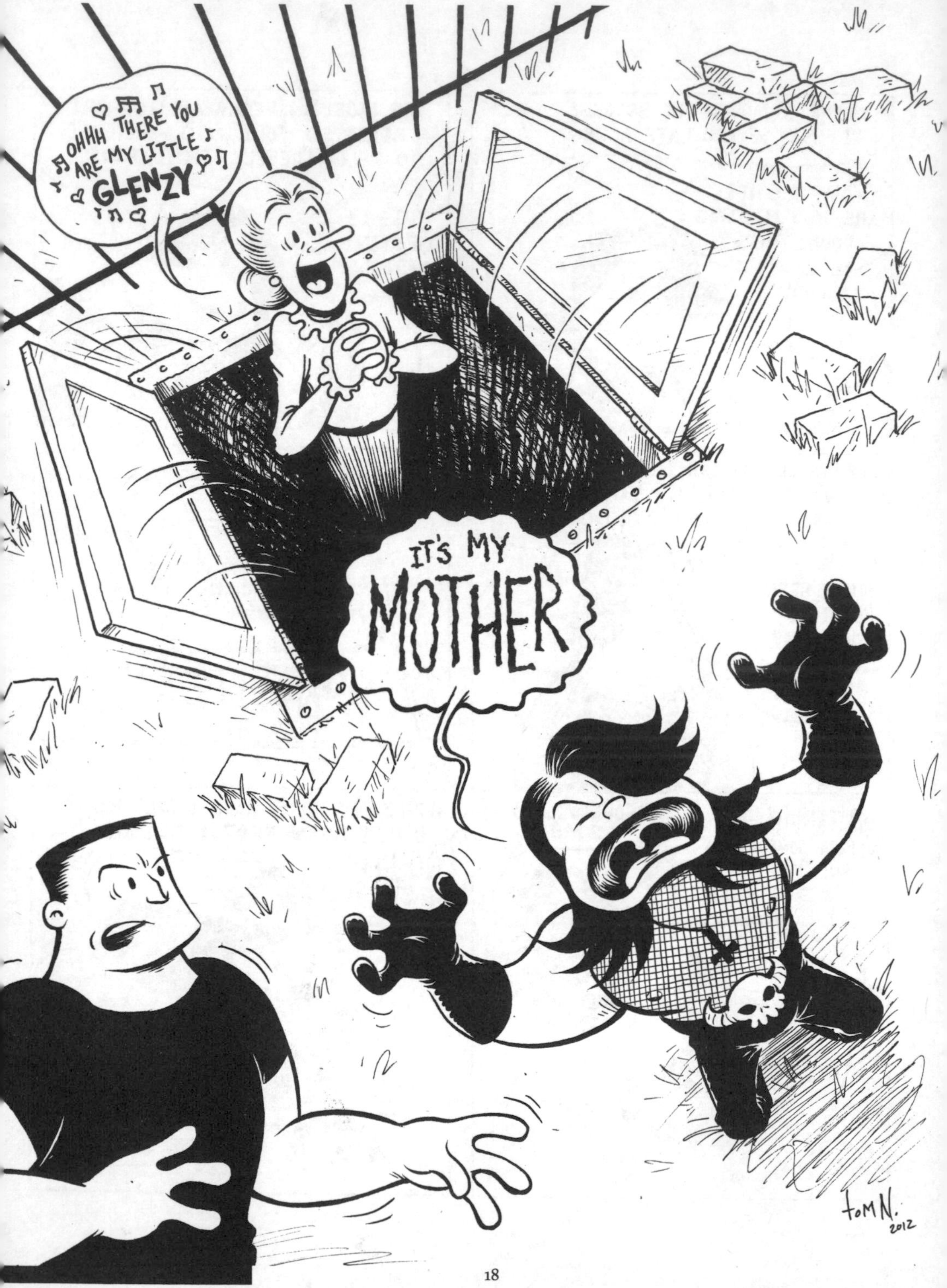
OHHH THERE YOU ARE MY LITTLE GLENZY
IT'S MY MOTHER
tom N. 2012

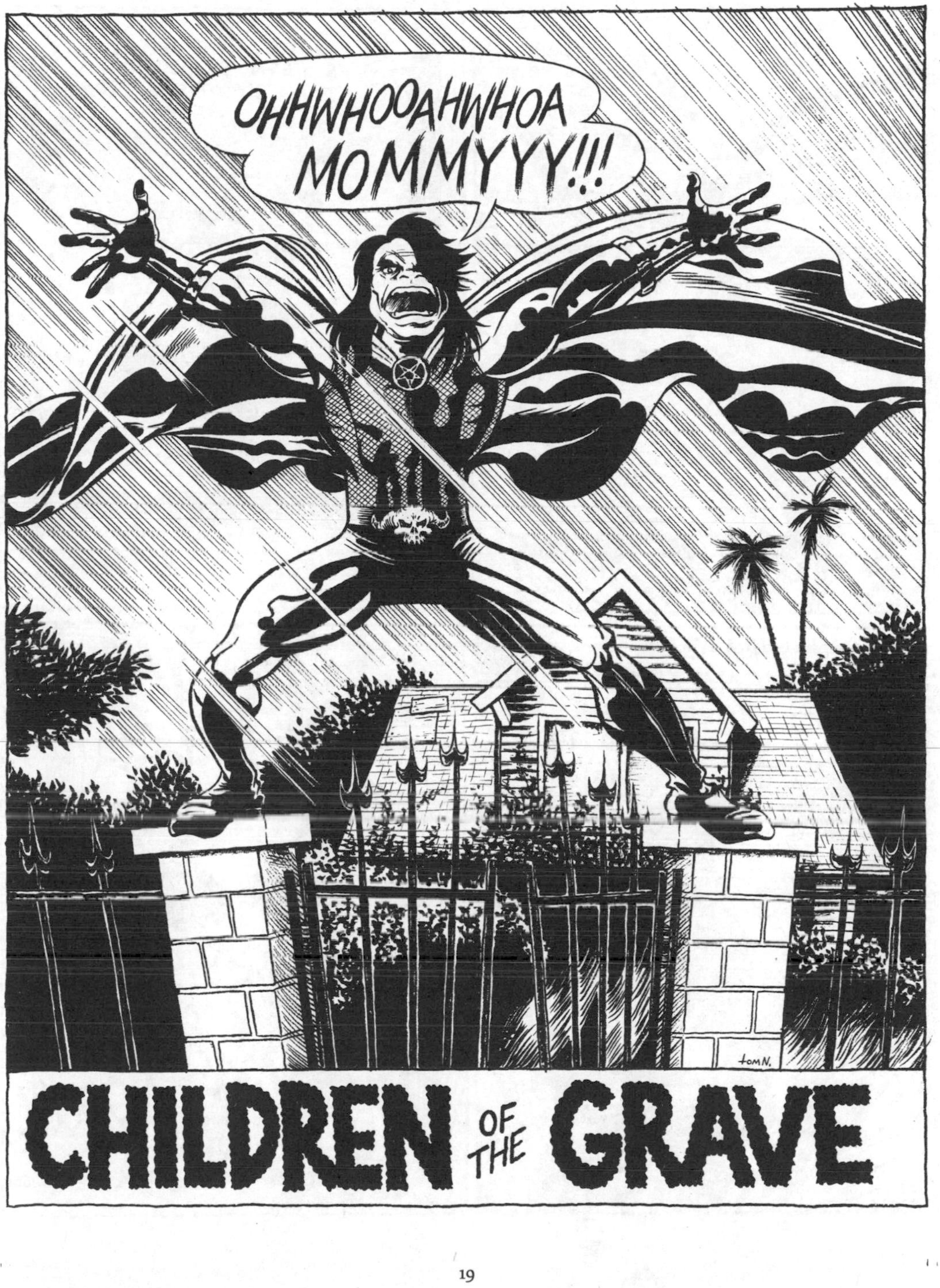
OHHWHOOAHWHOA MOMMYYY!!!

CHILDREN OF THE GRAVE

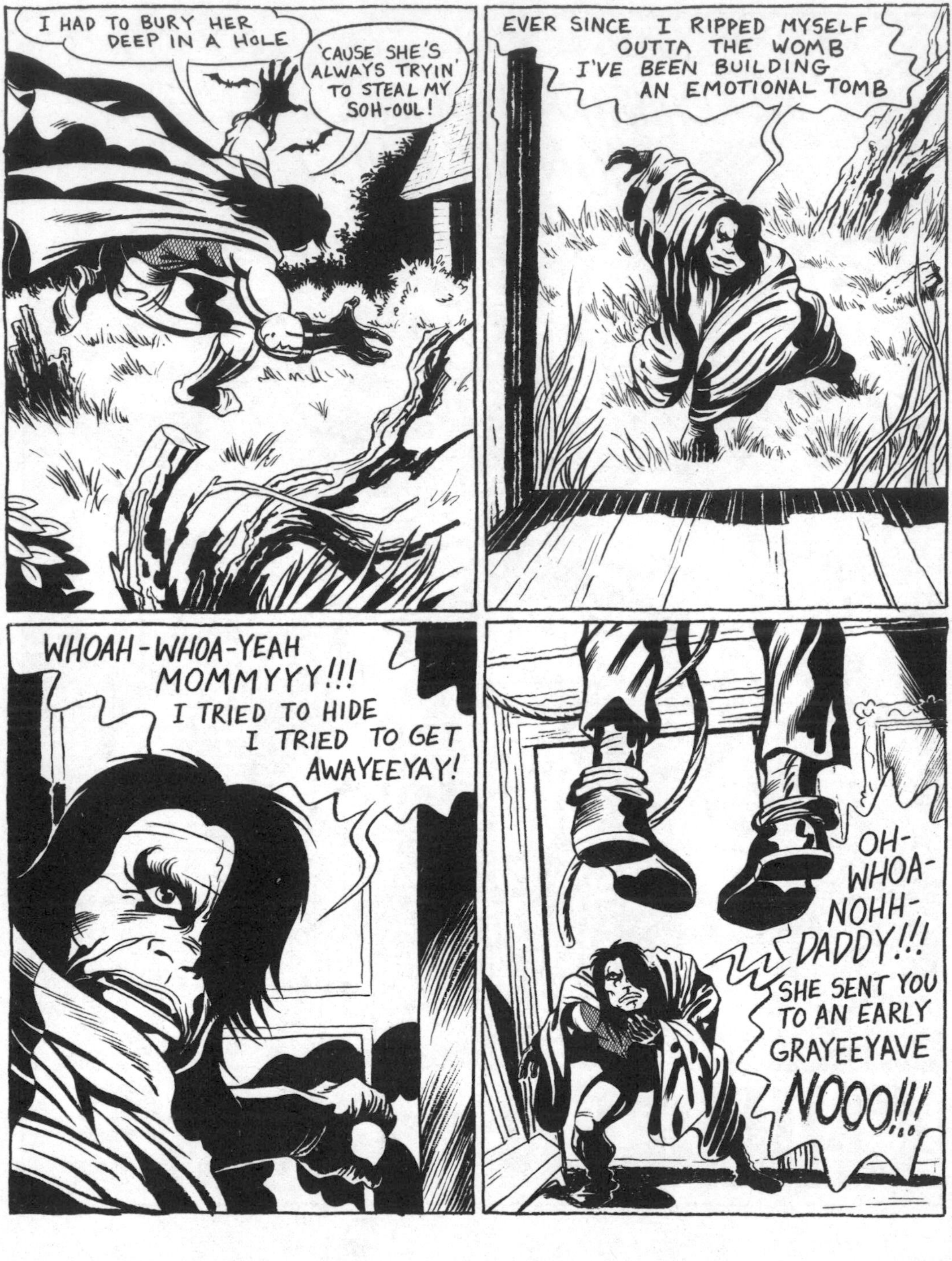
I HAD TO BURY HER DEEP IN A HOLE
'CAUSE SHE'S ALWAYS TRYIN' TO STEAL MY SOH-OUL!
EVER SINCE I RIPPED MYSELF OUTTA THE WOMB I'VE BEEN BUILDING AN EMOTIONAL TOMB
WHOAH-WHOA-YEAH MOMMYYY!!! I TRIED TO HIDE I TRIED TO GET AWAYEEYAY!
OH-WHOA-NOHH-DADDY!!! SHE SENT YOU TO AN EARLY GRAYEEYAVE
NOOO!!!

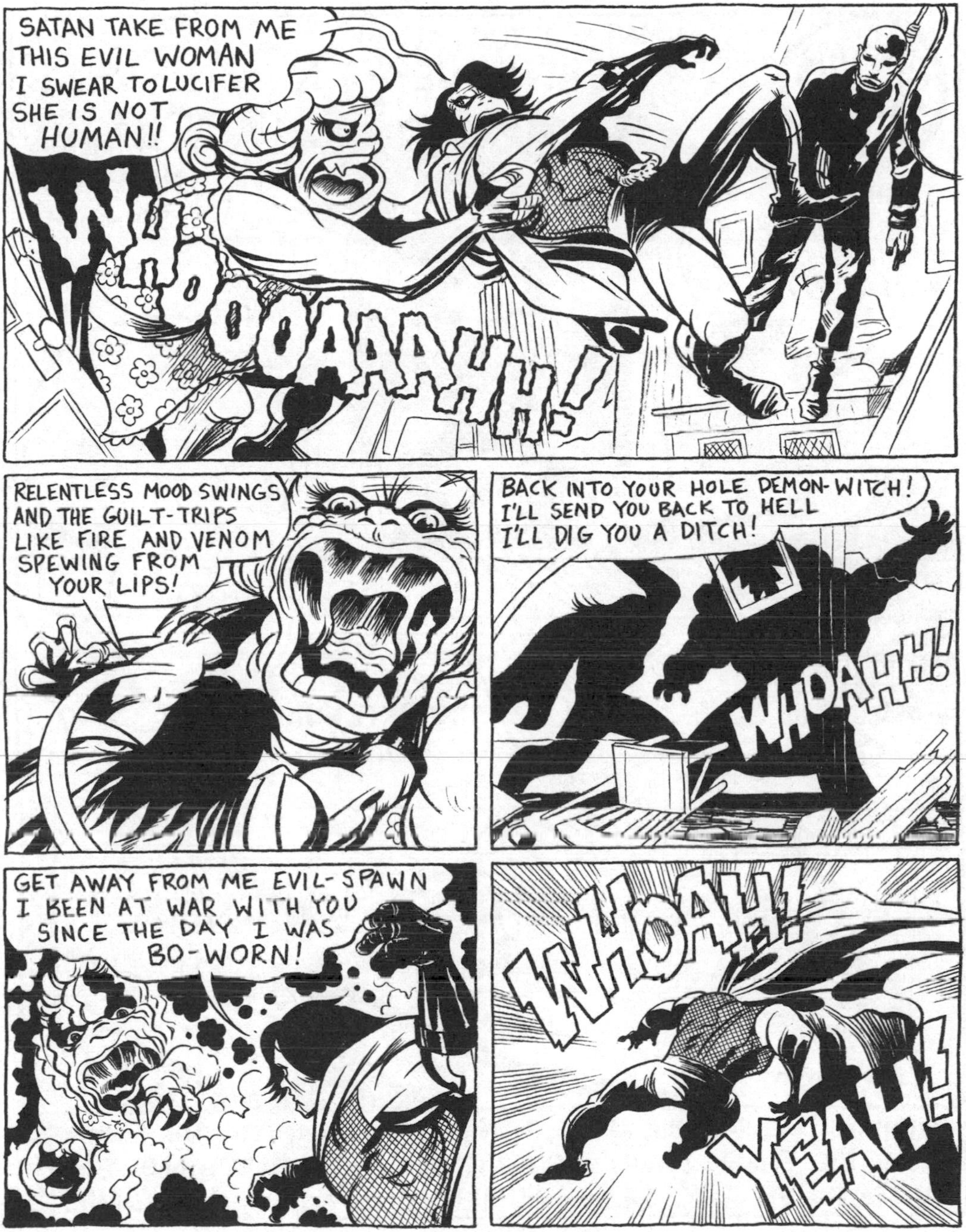
SATAN TAKE FROM ME THIS EVIL WOMAN I SWEAR TO LUCIFER SHE IS NOT HUMAN!!
WHOOOAAAHH!
RELENTLESS MOOD SWINGS AND THE GUILT-TRIPS LIKE FIRE AND VENOM SPEWING FROM YOUR LIPS!
BACK INTO YOUR HOLE DEMON-WITCH! I'LL SEND YOU BACK TO HELL I'LL DIG YOU A DITCH!
WHOAHH!
GET AWAY FROM ME EVIL-SPAWN I BEEN AT WAR WITH YOU SINCE THE DAY I WAS BO-WORN!
WHOAH!
YEAH!

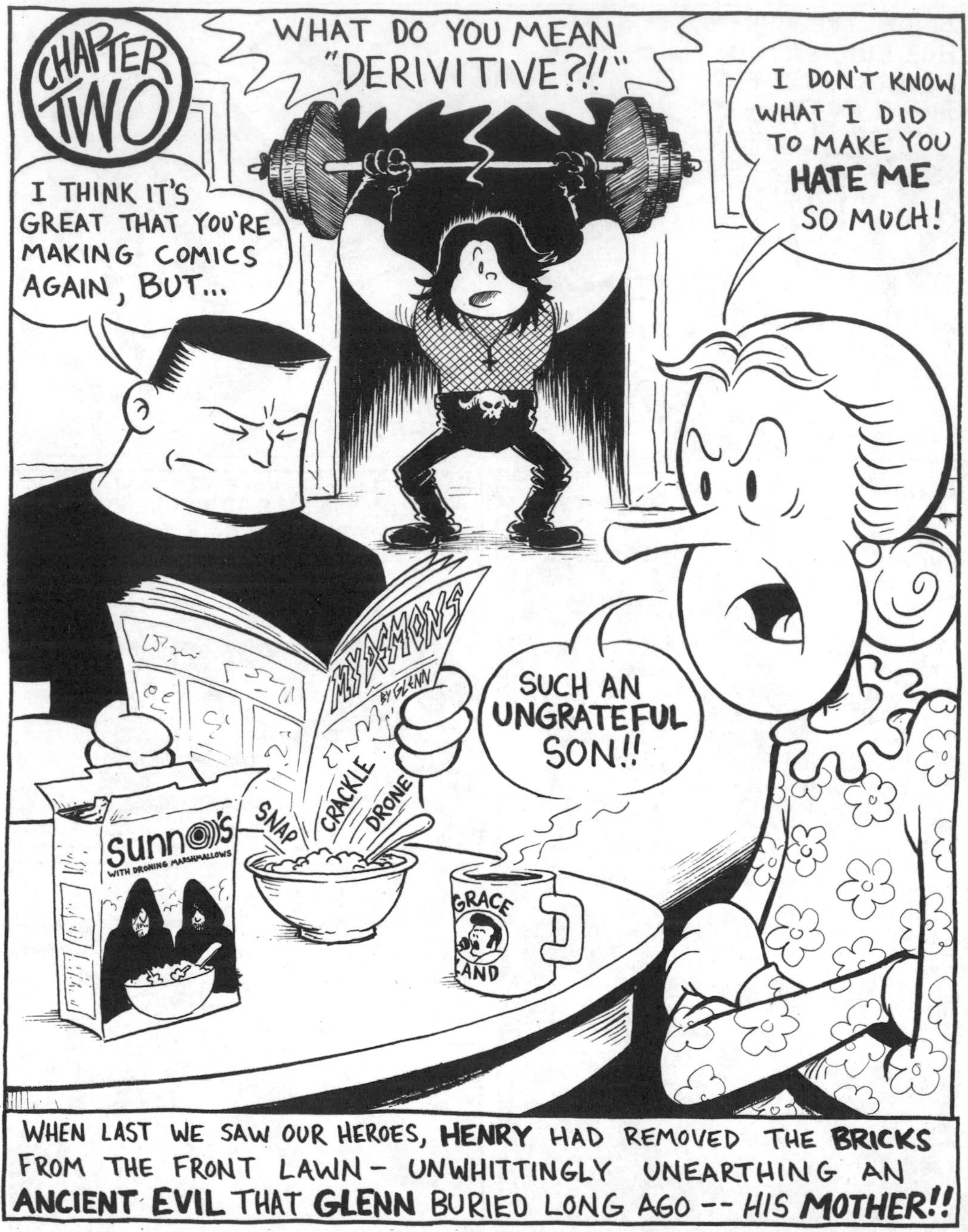
CHAPTER TWO
I THINK IT'S GREAT THAT YOU'RE MAKING COMICS AGAIN, BUT...
WHAT DO YOU MEAN "DERIVITIVE?!!"
I DON'T KNOW WHAT I DID TO MAKE YOU HATE ME SO MUCH!
SUCH AN UNGRATEFUL SON!!
MY DEMONS
BY GLENN
SNAP
CRACKLE
DRONE
sunn O)))'s
WITH DRONING MARSHMALLOWS
GRACE LAND
WHEN LAST WE SAW OUR HEROES, HENRY HAD REMOVED THE BRICKS FROM THE FRONT LAWN - UNWHITTINGLY UNEARTHING AN ANCIENT EVIL THAT GLENN BURIED LONG AGO -- HIS MOTHER!!

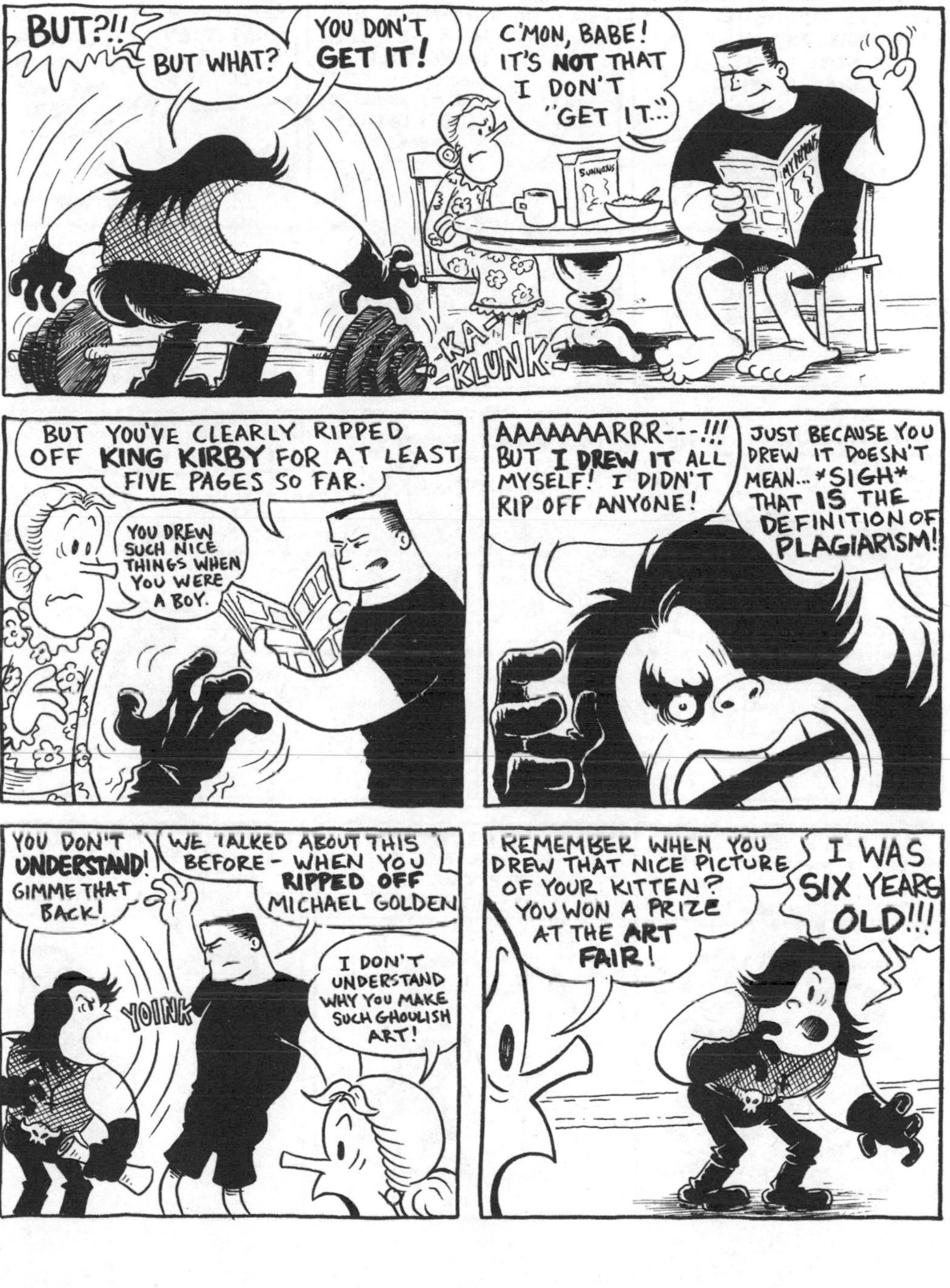

BUT?!!
BUT WHAT?
YOU DON'T GET IT!
C'MON, BABE! IT'S NOT THAT I DON'T "GET IT..."
-KA-KLUNK-
BUT YOU'VE CLEARLY RIPPED OFF KING KIRBY FOR AT LEAST FIVE PAGES SO FAR.
YOU DREW SUCH NICE THINGS WHEN YOU WERE A BOY.
AAAAAAARRR---!!! BUT I DREW IT ALL MYSELF! I DIDN'T RIP OFF ANYONE!
JUST BECAUSE YOU DREW IT DOESN'T MEAN... *SIGH* THAT IS THE DEFINITION OF PLAGIARISM!
YOU DON'T UNDERSTAND! GIMME THAT BACK!
WE TALKED ABOUT THIS BEFORE- WHEN YOU RIPPED OFF MICHAEL GOLDEN
YOINK
I DON'T UNDERSTAND WHY YOU MAKE SUCH GHOULISH ART!
REMEMBER WHEN YOU DREW THAT NICE PICTURE OF YOUR KITTEN? YOU WON A PRIZE AT THE ART FAIR!
I WAS SIX YEARS OLD!!!

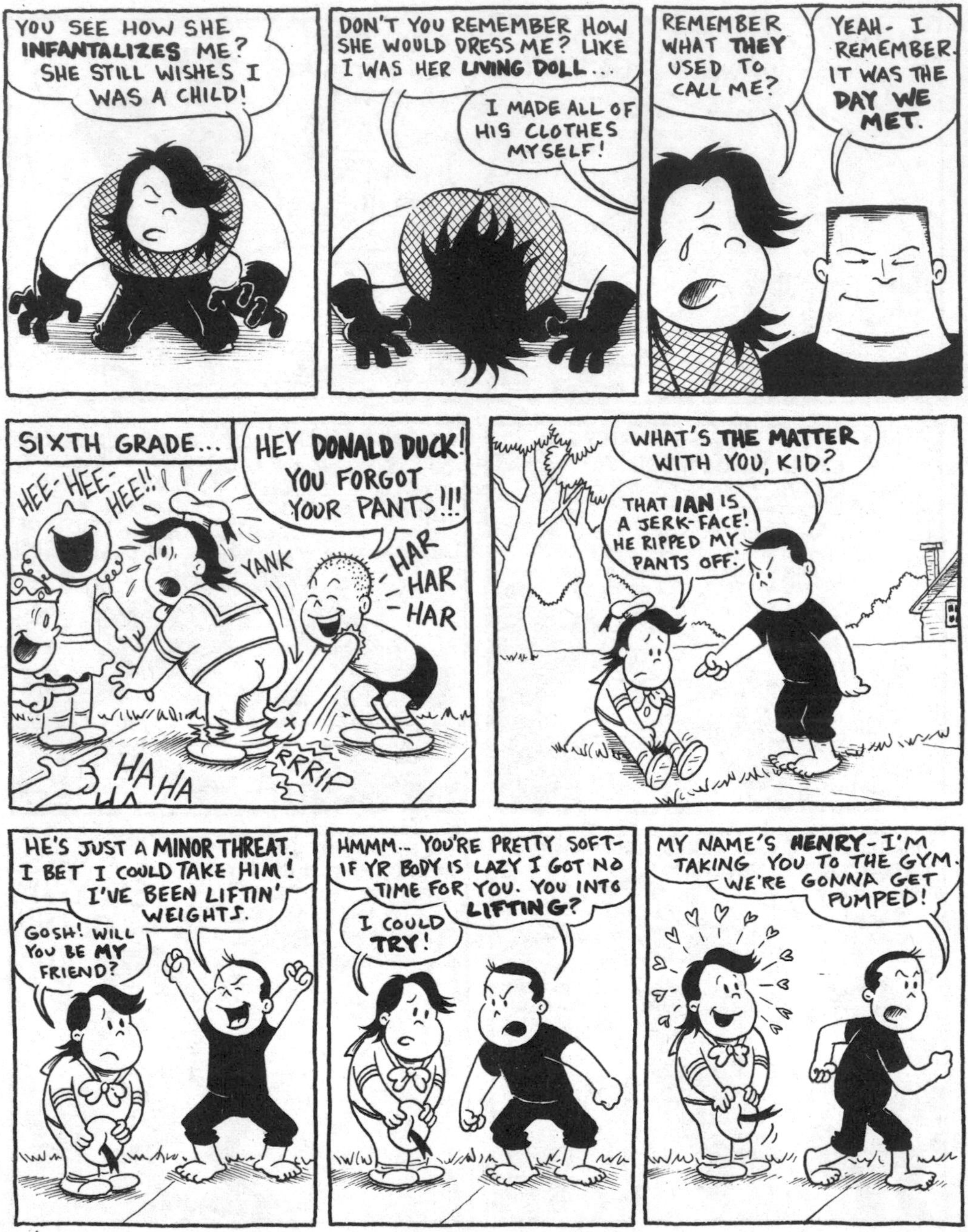
YOU SEE HOW SHE INFANTALIZES ME? SHE STILL WISHES I WAS A CHILD!
DON'T YOU REMEMBER HOW SHE WOULD DRESS ME? LIKE I WAS HER LIVING DOLL...
I MADE ALL OF HIS CLOTHES MYSELF!
REMEMBER WHAT THEY USED TO CALL ME?
YEAH- I REMEMBER. IT WAS THE DAY WE MET.
SIXTH GRADE...
HEY DONALD DUCK! YOU FORGOT YOUR PANTS!!!
HEE-HEE-HEE!!
YANK
HAR HAR HAR
HA HA HA
RRRIP
WHAT'S THE MATTER WITH YOU, KID?
THAT IAN IS A JERK-FACE! HE RIPPED MY PANTS OFF.
HE'S JUST A MINOR THREAT. I BET I COULD TAKE HIM! I'VE BEEN LIFTIN' WEIGHTS.
GOSH! WILL YOU BE MY FRIEND?
HMMM... YOU'RE PRETTY SOFT- IF YR BODY IS LAZY I GOT NO TIME FOR YOU. YOU INTO LIFTING?
I COULD TRY!
MY NAME'S HENRY- I'M TAKING YOU TO THE GYM. WE'RE GONNA GET PUMPED!

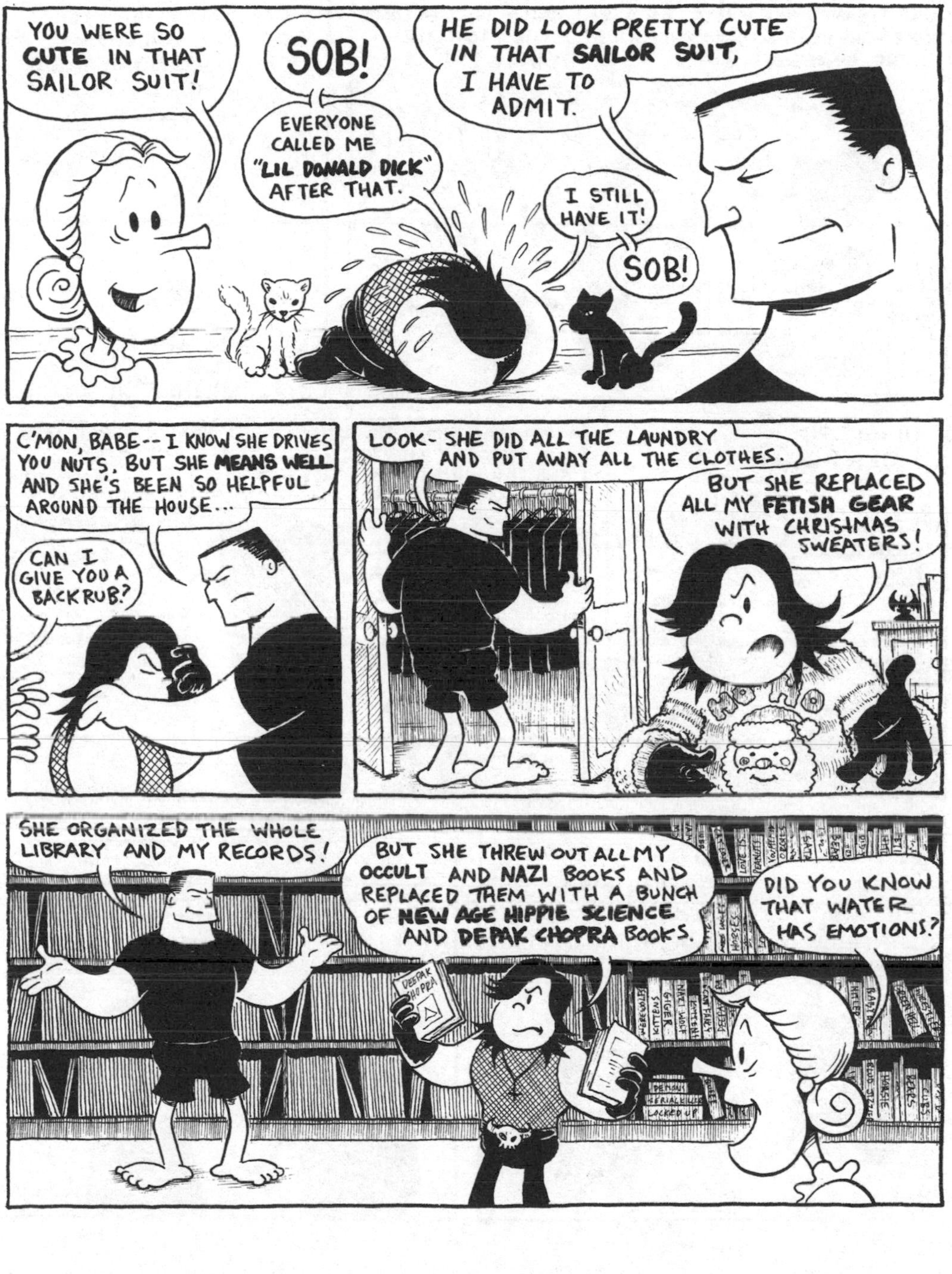
YOU WERE SO CUTE IN THAT SAILOR SUIT!
SOB!
EVERYONE CALLED ME "LIL DONALD DICK" AFTER THAT.
HE DID LOOK PRETTY CUTE IN THAT SAILOR SUIT, I HAVE TO ADMIT.
I STILL HAVE IT!
SOB!
C'MON, BABE-- I KNOW SHE DRIVES YOU NUTS, BUT SHE MEANS WELL AND SHE'S BEEN SO HELPFUL AROUND THE HOUSE...
CAN I GIVE YOU A BACKRUB?
LOOK- SHE DID ALL THE LAUNDRY AND PUT AWAY ALL THE CLOTHES.
BUT SHE REPLACED ALL MY FETISH GEAR WITH CHRISTMAS SWEATERS!
SHE ORGANIZED THE WHOLE LIBRARY AND MY RECORDS!
BUT SHE THREW OUT ALL MY OCCULT AND NAZI BOOKS AND REPLACED THEM WITH A BUNCH OF NEW AGE HIPPIE SCIENCE AND DEPAK CHOPRA BOOKS.
DID YOU KNOW THAT WATER HAS EMOTIONS?
DEEPAK CHOPRA

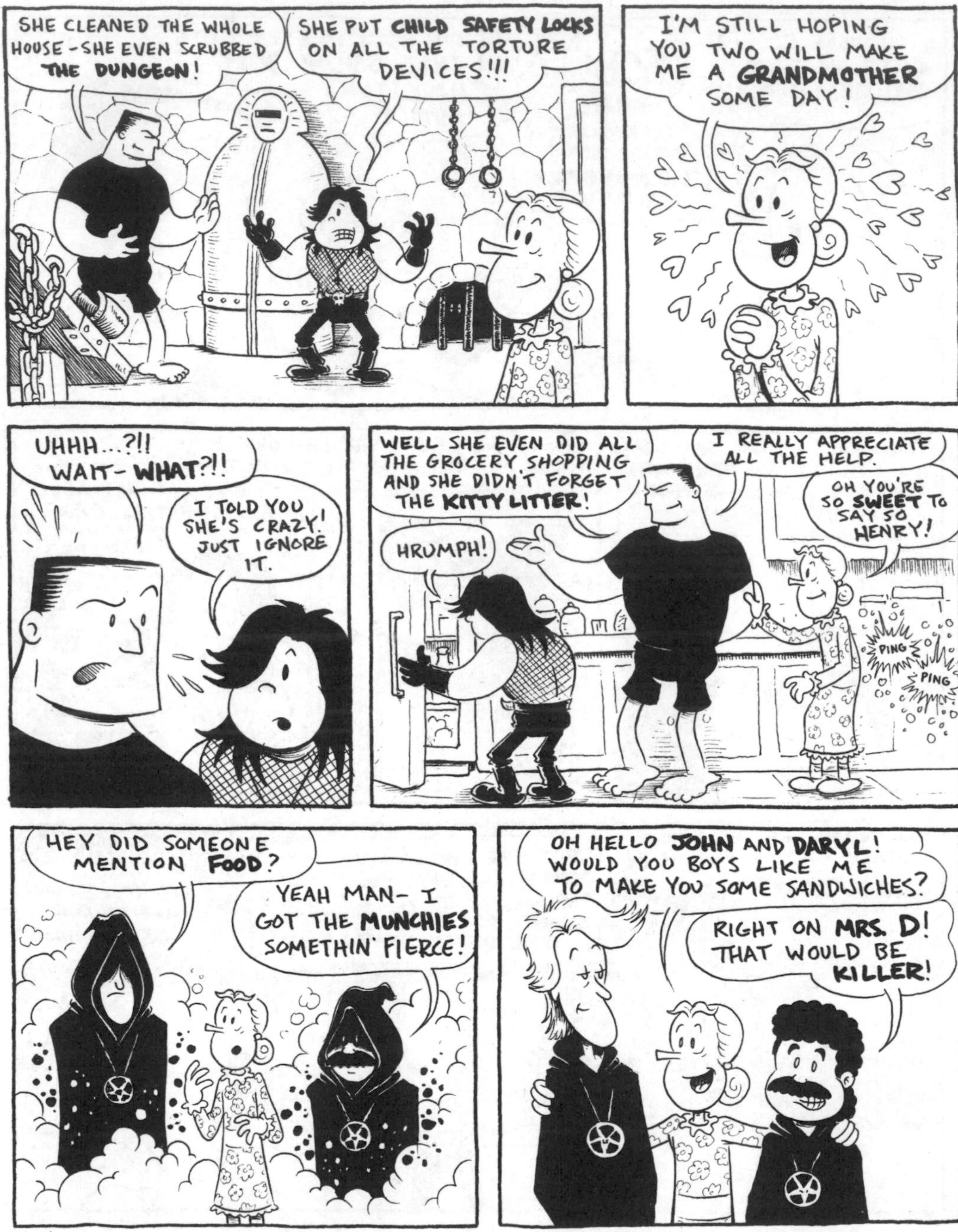
SHE CLEANED THE WHOLE HOUSE - SHE EVEN SCRUBBED THE DUNGEON!
SHE PUT CHILD SAFETY LOCKS ON ALL THE TORTURE DEVICES!!!
I'M STILL HOPING YOU TWO WILL MAKE ME A GRANDMOTHER SOME DAY!
UHHH...?!! WAIT- WHAT?!!
I TOLD YOU SHE'S CRAZY! JUST IGNORE IT.
WELL SHE EVEN DID ALL THE GROCERY SHOPPING AND SHE DIDN'T FORGET THE KITTY LITTER!
I REALLY APPRECIATE ALL THE HELP.
OH YOU'RE SO SWEET TO SAY SO HENRY!
HRUMPH!
PING
PING
HEY DID SOMEONE MENTION FOOD?
YEAH MAN- I GOT THE MUNCHIES SOMETHIN' FIERCE!
OH HELLO JOHN AND DARYL! WOULD YOU BOYS LIKE ME TO MAKE YOU SOME SANDWICHES?
RIGHT ON MRS. D! THAT WOULD BE KILLER!

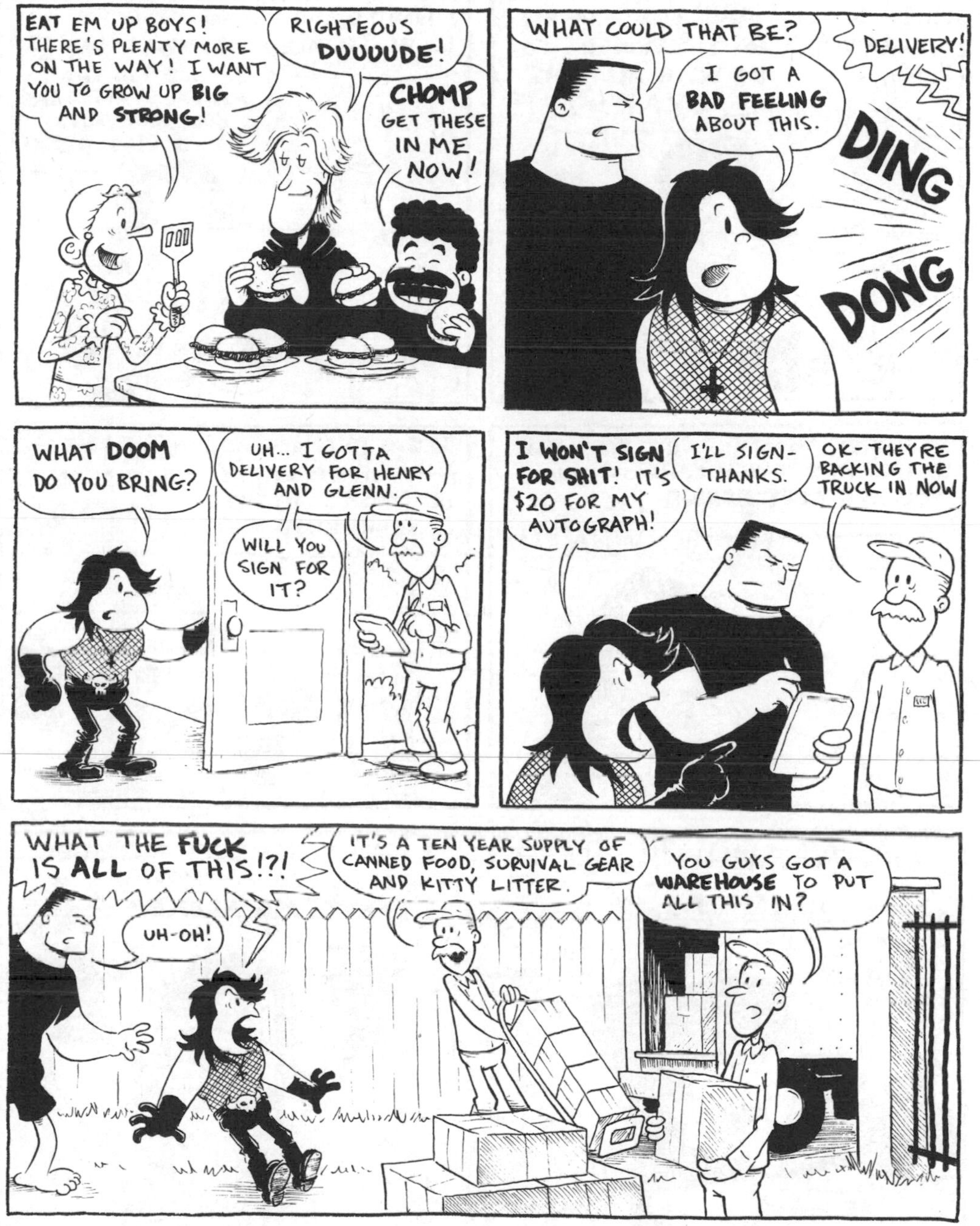
EAT EM UP BOYS! THERE'S PLENTY MORE ON THE WAY! I WANT YOU TO GROW UP BIG AND STRONG!
RIGHTEOUS DUUUUDE!
CHOMP GET THESE IN ME NOW!
WHAT COULD THAT BE?
I GOT A BAD FEELING ABOUT THIS.
DELIVERY!
DING
DONG
WHAT DOOM DO YOU BRING?
UH... I GOTTA DELIVERY FOR HENRY AND GLENN.
WILL YOU SIGN FOR IT?
I WON'T SIGN FOR SHIT! IT'S $20 FOR MY AUTOGRAPH!
I'LL SIGN- THANKS.
OK- THEYRE BACKING THE TRUCK IN NOW
WHAT THE FUCK IS ALL OF THIS!?!
UH-OH!
IT'S A TEN YEAR SUPPLY OF CANNED FOOD, SURVIVAL GEAR AND KITTY LITTER.
YOU GUYS GOT A WAREHOUSE TO PUT ALL THIS IN?

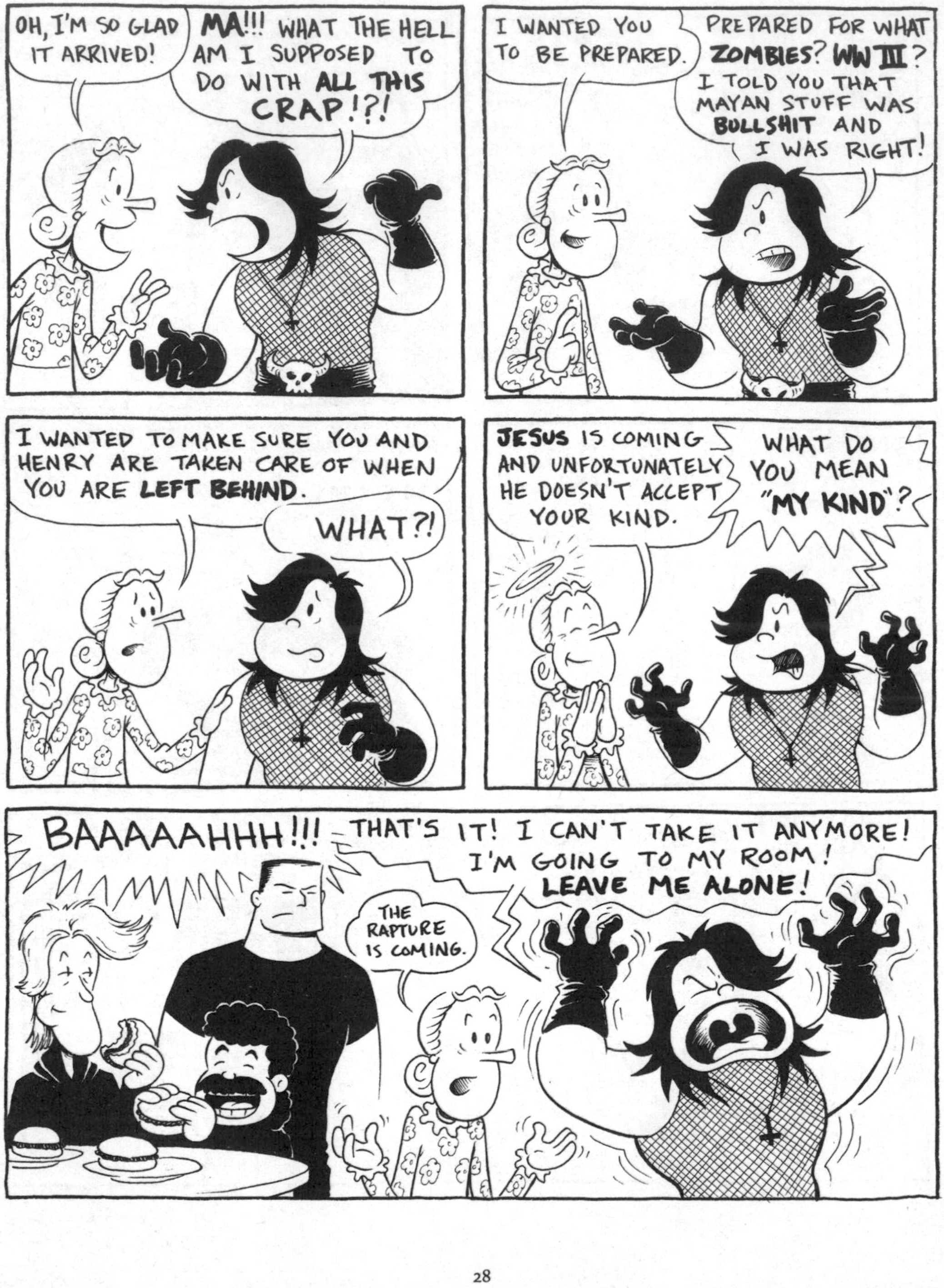

OH, I'M SO GLAD IT ARRIVED!
MA!!! WHAT THE HELL AM I SUPPOSED TO DO WITH ALL THIS CRAP!?!
I WANTED YOU TO BE PREPARED.
PREPARED FOR WHAT ZOMBIES? WW III? I TOLD YOU THAT MAYAN STUFF WAS BULLSHIT AND I WAS RIGHT!
I WANTED TO MAKE SURE YOU AND HENRY ARE TAKEN CARE OF WHEN YOU ARE LEFT BEHIND.
WHAT?!
JESUS IS COMING AND UNFORTUNATELY HE DOESN'T ACCEPT YOUR KIND.
WHAT DO YOU MEAN "MY KIND"?
BAAAAAHHH!!!
THAT'S IT! I CAN'T TAKE IT ANYMORE! I'M GOING TO MY ROOM! LEAVE ME ALONE!
THE RAPTURE IS COMING.

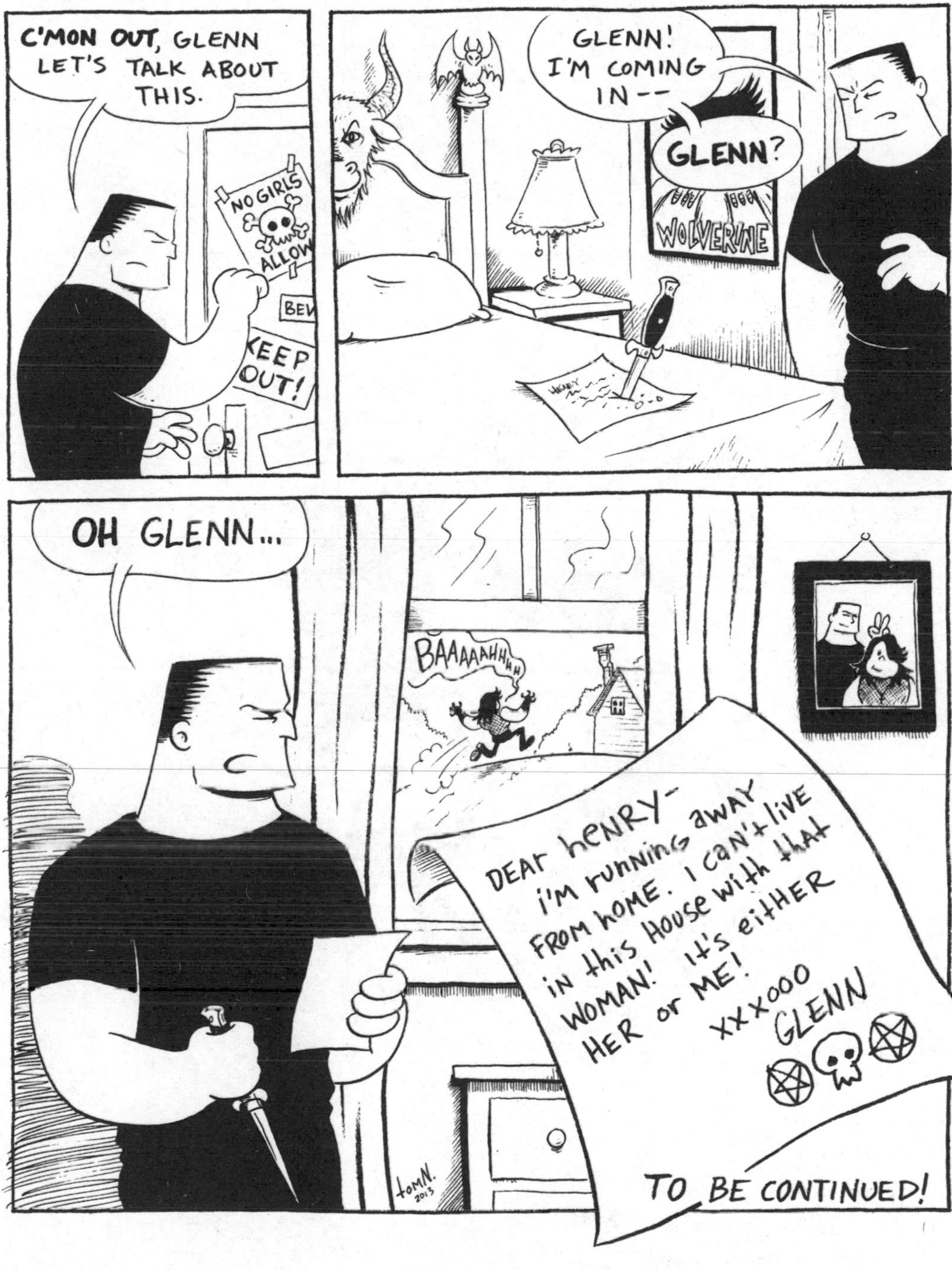
C'MON OUT, GLENN
LET'S TALK ABOUT THIS.
NO GIRLS ALLOW
BEV
KEEP OUT!
GLENN! I'M COMING IN--
GLENN?
WOLVERINE
OH GLENN...
BAAAAAHHhh
DEAR HENRY-
i'M running away FROM HOME. I CAN'T live in this House with that WOMAN! it's either HER or ME!
XXXOOO
GLENN
tomN. 2013
TO BE CONTINUED!

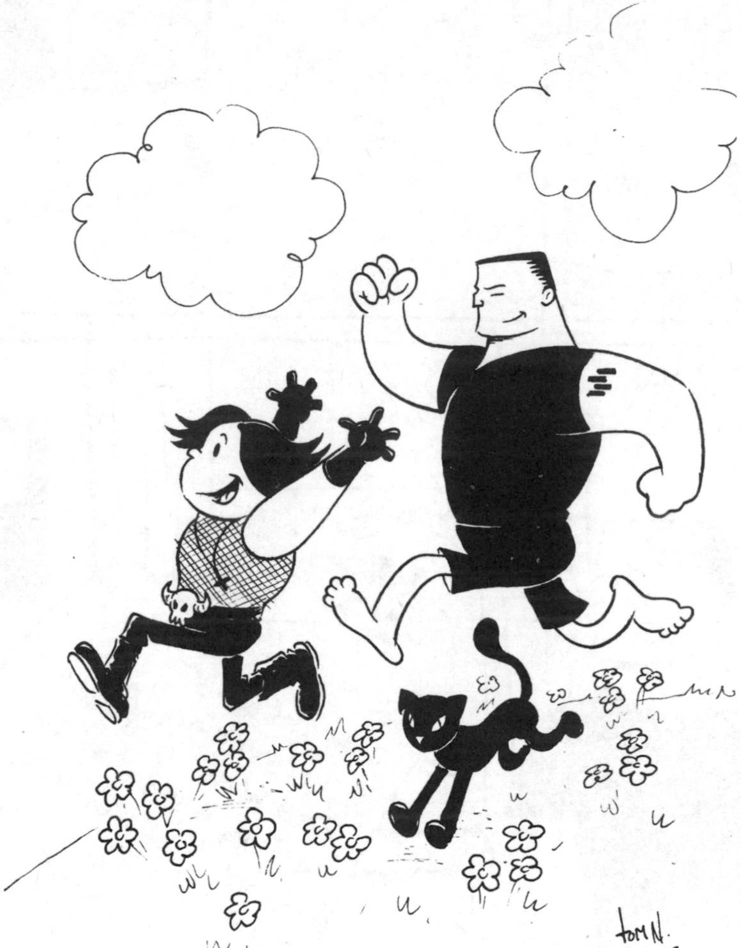
tom N.
2013

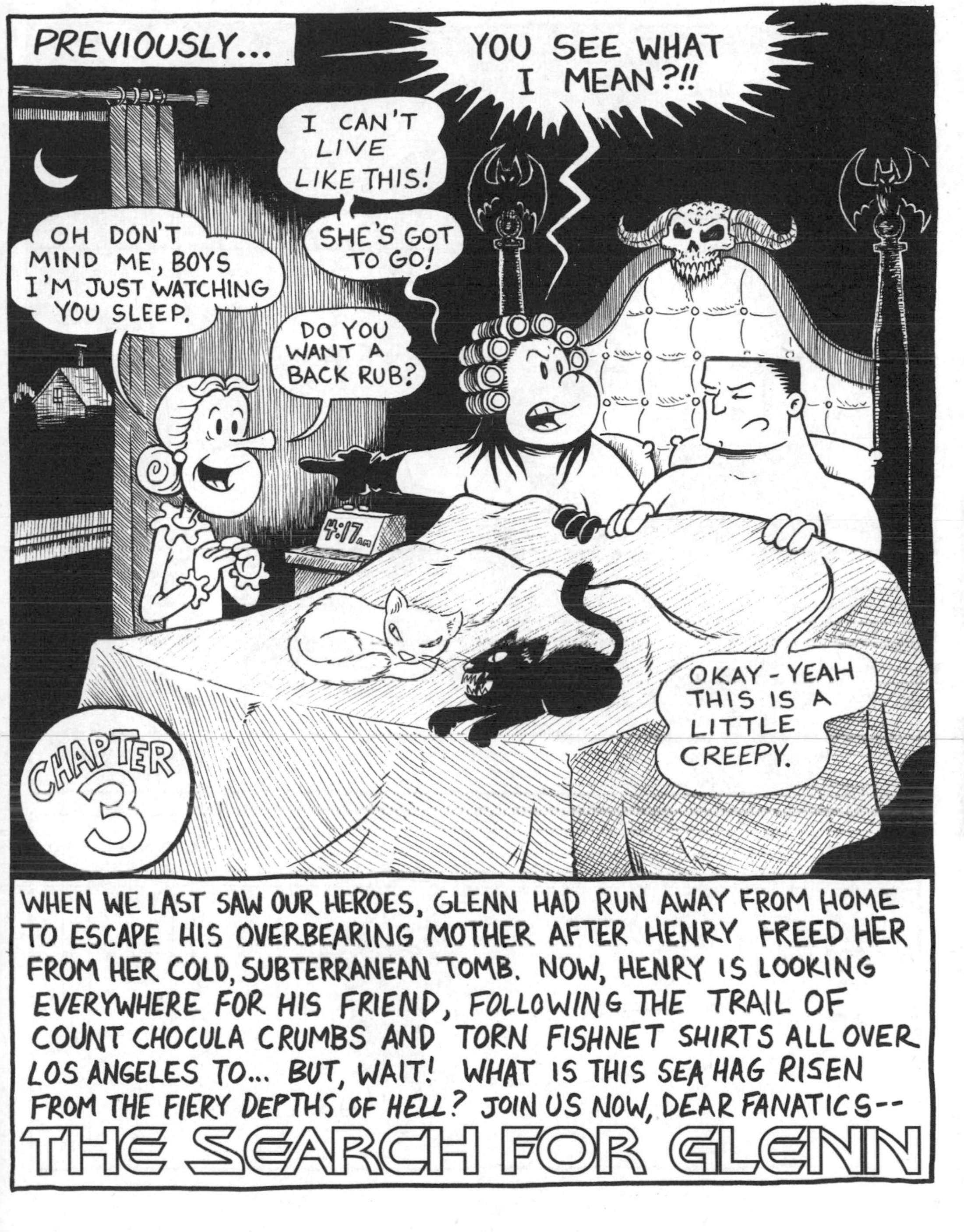
PREVIOUSLY...
YOU SEE WHAT I MEAN?!!
I CAN'T LIVE LIKE THIS!
SHE'S GOT TO GO!
OH DON'T MIND ME, BOYS I'M JUST WATCHING YOU SLEEP.
DO YOU WANT A BACK RUB?
4:17AM
OKAY - YEAH THIS IS A LITTLE CREEPY.
CHAPTER 3
WHEN WE LAST SAW OUR HEROES, GLENN HAD RUN AWAY FROM HOME TO ESCAPE HIS OVERBEARING MOTHER AFTER HENRY FREED HER FROM HER COLD, SUBTERRANEAN TOMB. NOW, HENRY IS LOOKING EVERYWHERE FOR HIS FRIEND, FOLLOWING THE TRAIL OF COUNT CHOCULA CRUMBS AND TORN FISHNET SHIRTS ALL OVER LOS ANGELES TO... BUT, WAIT! WHAT IS THIS SEA HAG RISEN FROM THE FIERY DEPTHS OF HELL? JOIN US NOW, DEAR FANATICS--
THE SEARCH FOR GLENN

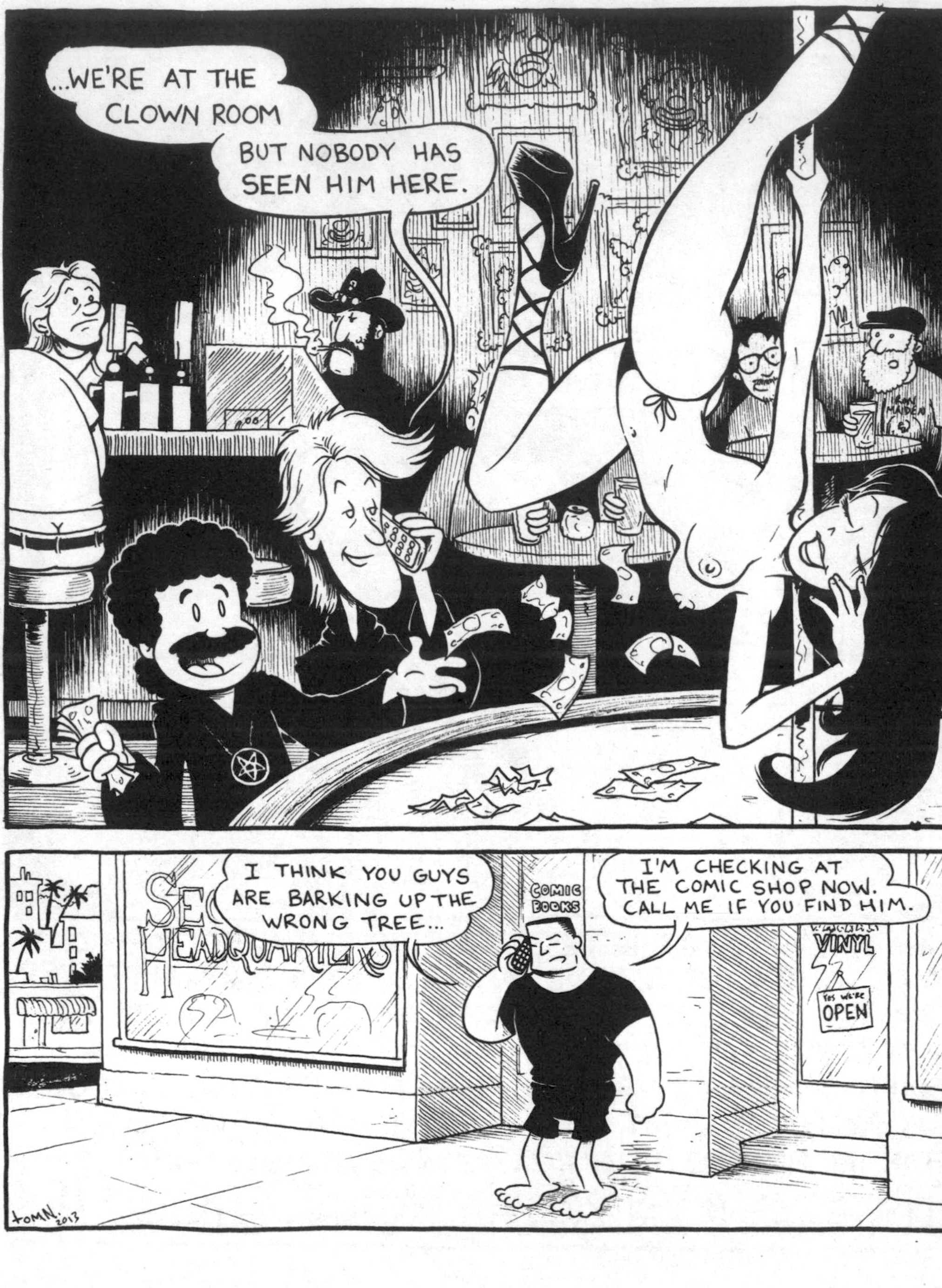
...WE'RE AT THE CLOWN ROOM
BUT NOBODY HAS SEEN HIM HERE.
I THINK YOU GUYS ARE BARKING UP THE WRONG TREE...
COMIC BOOKS
I'M CHECKING AT THE COMIC SHOP NOW. CALL ME IF YOU FIND HIM.
VINYL
YES WE'RE OPEN
tomN. 2013

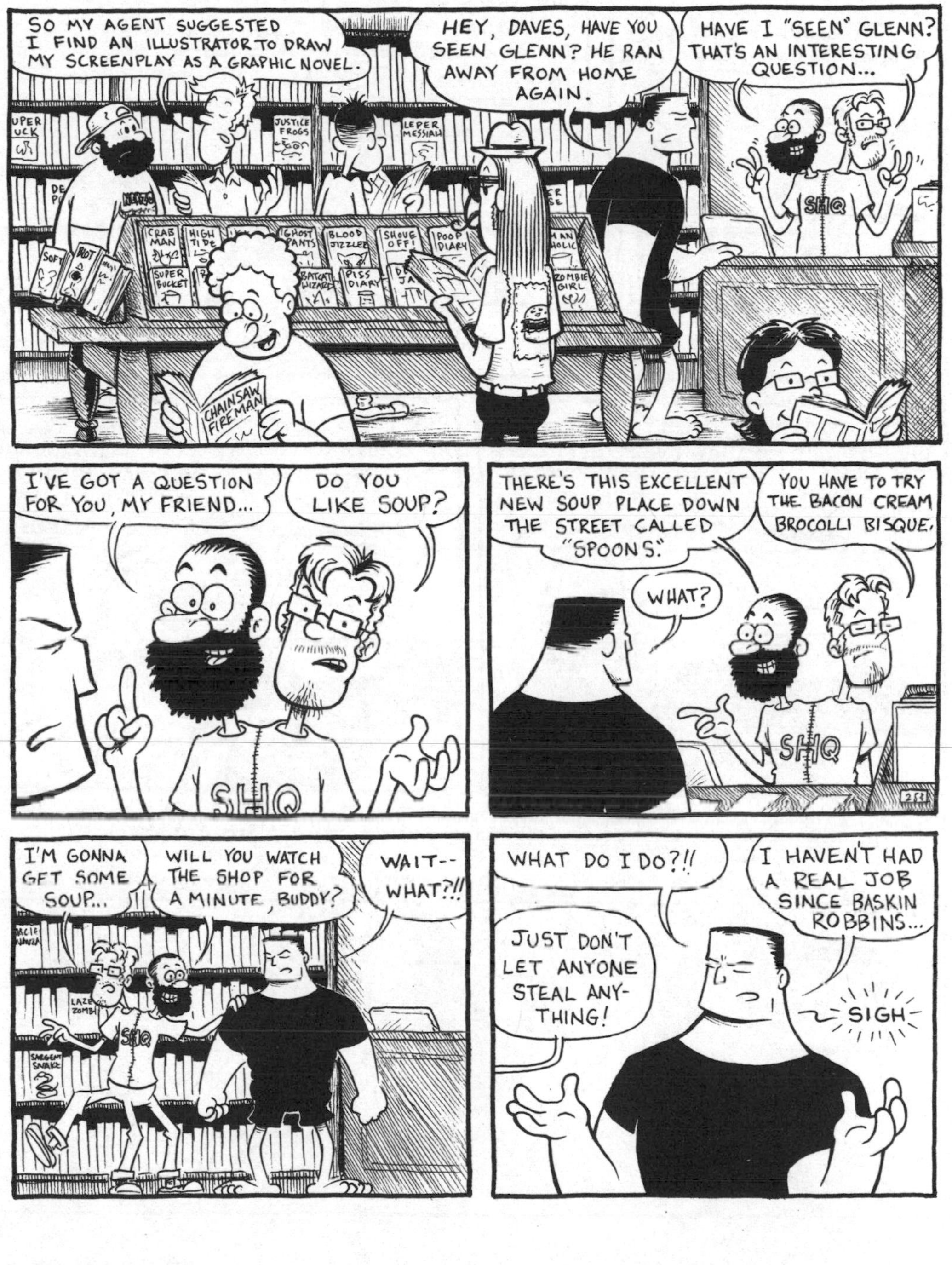
SO MY AGENT SUGGESTED I FIND AN ILLUSTRATOR TO DRAW MY SCREENPLAY AS A GRAPHIC NOVEL.
HEY, DAVES, HAVE YOU SEEN GLENN? HE RAN AWAY FROM HOME AGAIN.
HAVE I "SEEN" GLENN? THAT'S AN INTERESTING QUESTION...
JUSTICE FROGS
LEPER MESSIAH
CRAB MAN
HIGH TIDE
GHOST PANTS
BLOOD JIZZLER
SHOVE OFF!
POOP DIARY
SUPER BUCKET
BATCAT WIZARD
PISS DIARY
ZOMBIE GIRL
CHAINSAW FIREMAN
SHQ
I'VE GOT A QUESTION FOR YOU, MY FRIEND...
DO YOU LIKE SOUP?
SHQ
THERE'S THIS EXCELLENT NEW SOUP PLACE DOWN THE STREET CALLED "SPOONS."
YOU HAVE TO TRY THE BACON CREAM BROCOLLI BISQUE.
WHAT?
SHQ
I'M GONNA GET SOME SOUP...
WILL YOU WATCH THE SHOP FOR A MINUTE, BUDDY?
WAIT-- WHAT?!!
SHQ
WHAT DO I DO?!!
I HAVEN'T HAD A REAL JOB SINCE BASKIN ROBBINS...
JUST DON'T LET ANYONE STEAL ANYTHING!
SIGH

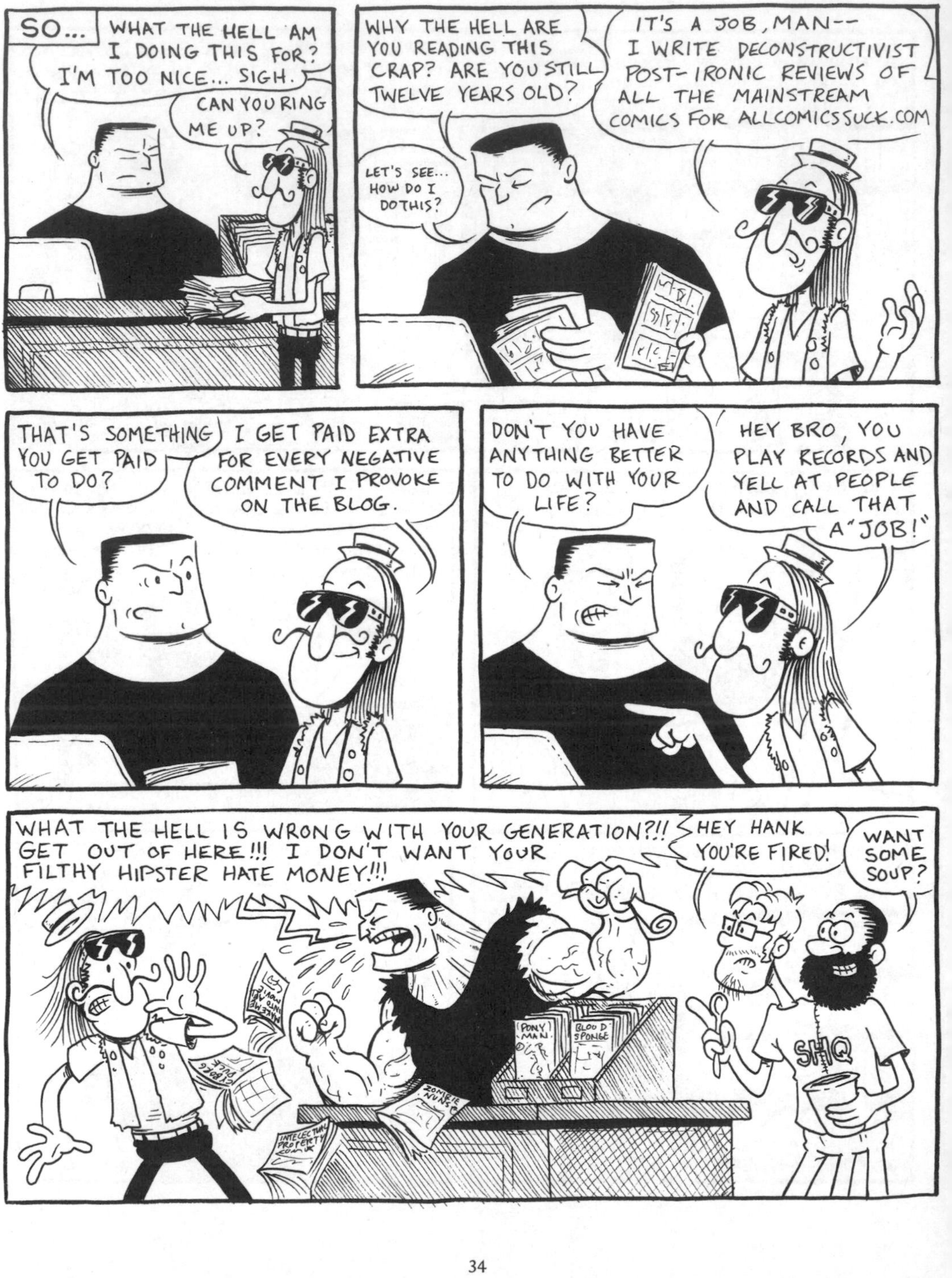
SO...
WHAT THE HELL AM I DOING THIS FOR? I'M TOO NICE... SIGH.
CAN YOU RING ME UP?
WHY THE HELL ARE YOU READING THIS CRAP? ARE YOU STILL TWELVE YEARS OLD?
LET'S SEE... HOW DO I DO THIS?
IT'S A JOB, MAN-- I WRITE DECONSTRUCTIVIST POST-IRONIC REVIEWS OF ALL THE MAINSTREAM COMICS FOR ALLCOMICSSUCK.COM
THAT'S SOMETHING YOU GET PAID TO DO?
I GET PAID EXTRA FOR EVERY NEGATIVE COMMENT I PROVOKE ON THE BLOG.
DON'T YOU HAVE ANYTHING BETTER TO DO WITH YOUR LIFE?
HEY BRO, YOU PLAY RECORDS AND YELL AT PEOPLE AND CALL THAT A "JOB!"
WHAT THE HELL IS WRONG WITH YOUR GENERATION?!! GET OUT OF HERE!!! I DON'T WANT YOUR FILTHY HIPSTER HATE MONEY!!!
HEY HANK YOU'RE FIRED!
WANT SOME SOUP?
PONY MAN
BLOOD SPONGE
ZOMBIE NUNS
SHQ

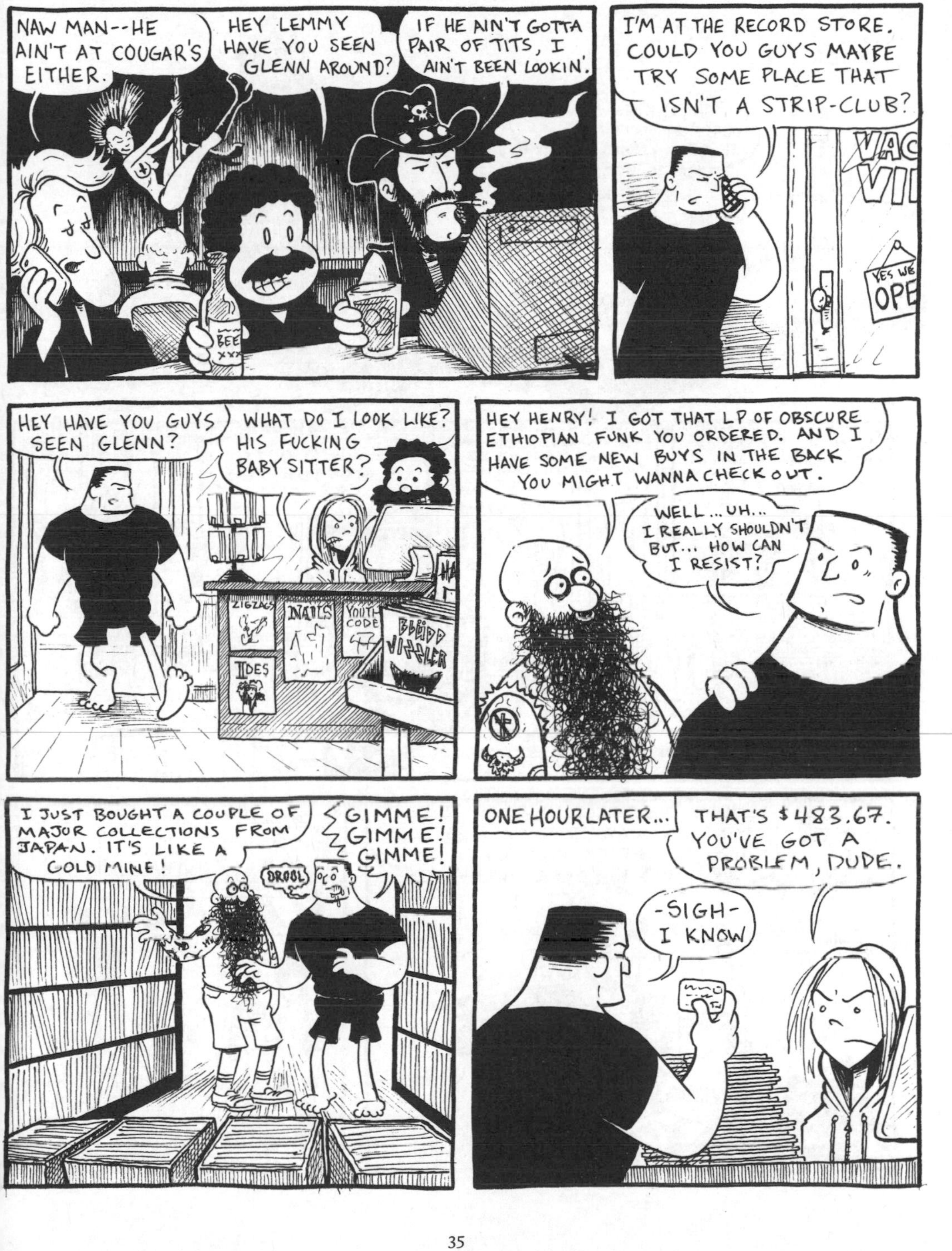
NAW MAN--HE AIN'T AT COUGAR'S EITHER.
HEY LEMMY HAVE YOU SEEN GLENN AROUND?
IF HE AIN'T GOTTA PAIR OF TITS, I AIN'T BEEN LOOKIN'.
I'M AT THE RECORD STORE. COULD YOU GUYS MAYBE TRY SOME PLACE THAT ISN'T A STRIP-CLUB?
YES WE OPE
HEY HAVE YOU GUYS SEEN GLENN?
WHAT DO I LOOK LIKE? HIS FUCKING BABY SITTER?
ZIGZAGS
NAILS
YOUTH CODE
IDES
HEY HENRY! I GOT THAT LP OF OBSCURE ETHIOPIAN FUNK YOU ORDERED. AND I HAVE SOME NEW BUYS IN THE BACK YOU MIGHT WANNA CHECK OUT.
WELL... UH... I REALLY SHOULDN'T BUT... HOW CAN I RESIST?
I JUST BOUGHT A COUPLE OF MAJOR COLLECTIONS FROM JAPAN. IT'S LIKE A GOLD MINE!
DROOL
GIMME! GIMME! GIMME!
ONE HOUR LATER...
THAT'S $483.67. YOU'VE GOT A PROBLEM, DUDE.
-SIGH- I KNOW

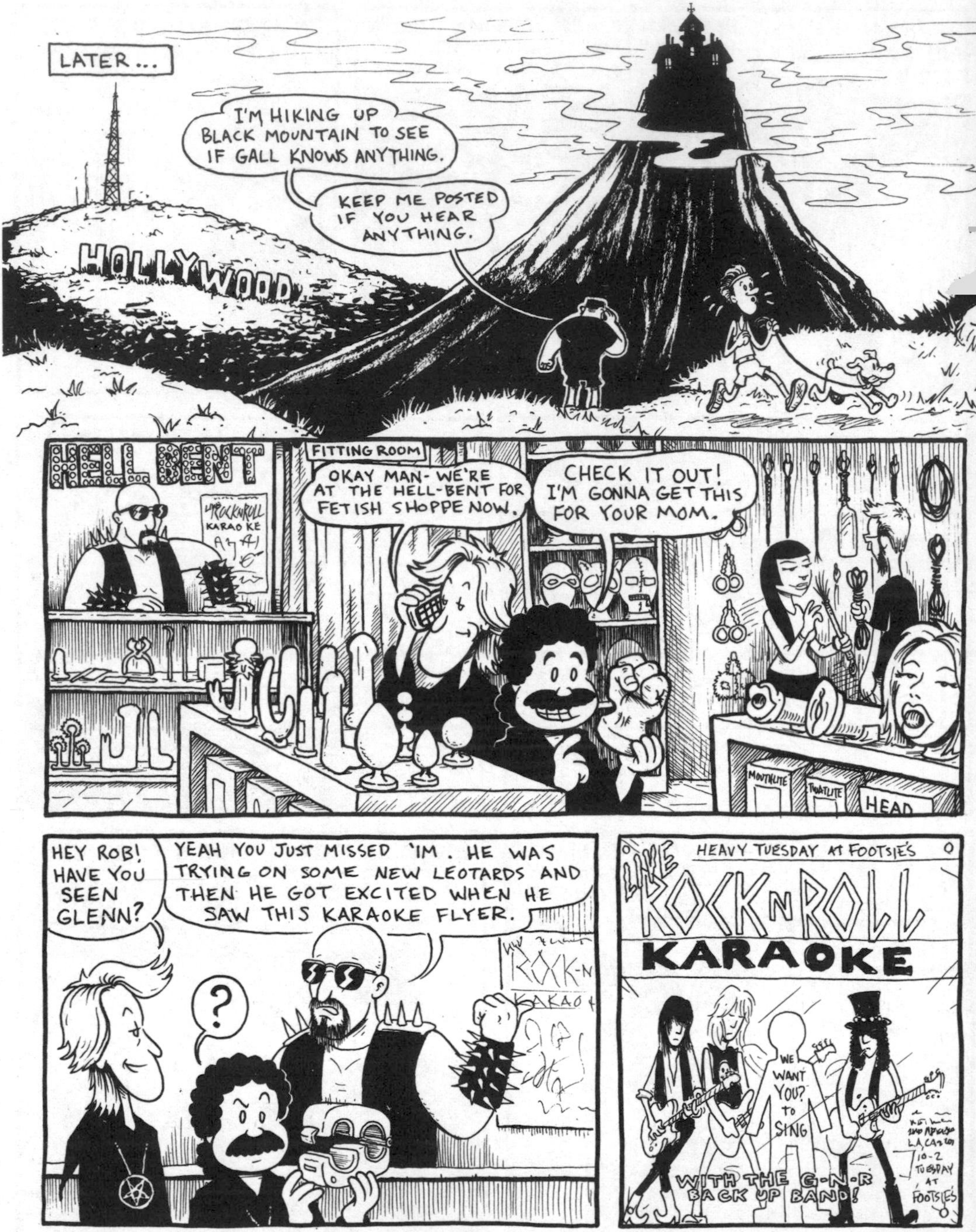
LATER...
I'M HIKING UP BLACK MOUNTAIN TO SEE IF GALL KNOWS ANYTHING.
KEEP ME POSTED IF YOU HEAR ANYTHING.
HOLLYWOOD
HELL BENT
FITTING ROOM
OKAY MAN- WE'RE AT THE HELL-BENT FOR FETISH SHOPPE NOW.
CHECK IT OUT! I'M GONNA GET THIS FOR YOUR MOM.
MOUTHLITE
TWATLITE
HEAD
HEY ROB! HAVE YOU SEEN GLENN?
YEAH YOU JUST MISSED 'IM. HE WAS TRYING ON SOME NEW LEOTARDS AND THEN HE GOT EXCITED WHEN HE SAW THIS KARAOKE FLYER.
?
HEAVY TUESDAY AT FOOTSIE'S
LIVE ROCK N ROLL
KARAOKE
WE WANT YOU? TO SING
WITH THE G-N-R BACK UP BAND!
10-2 TUESDAY AT FOOTSIE'S

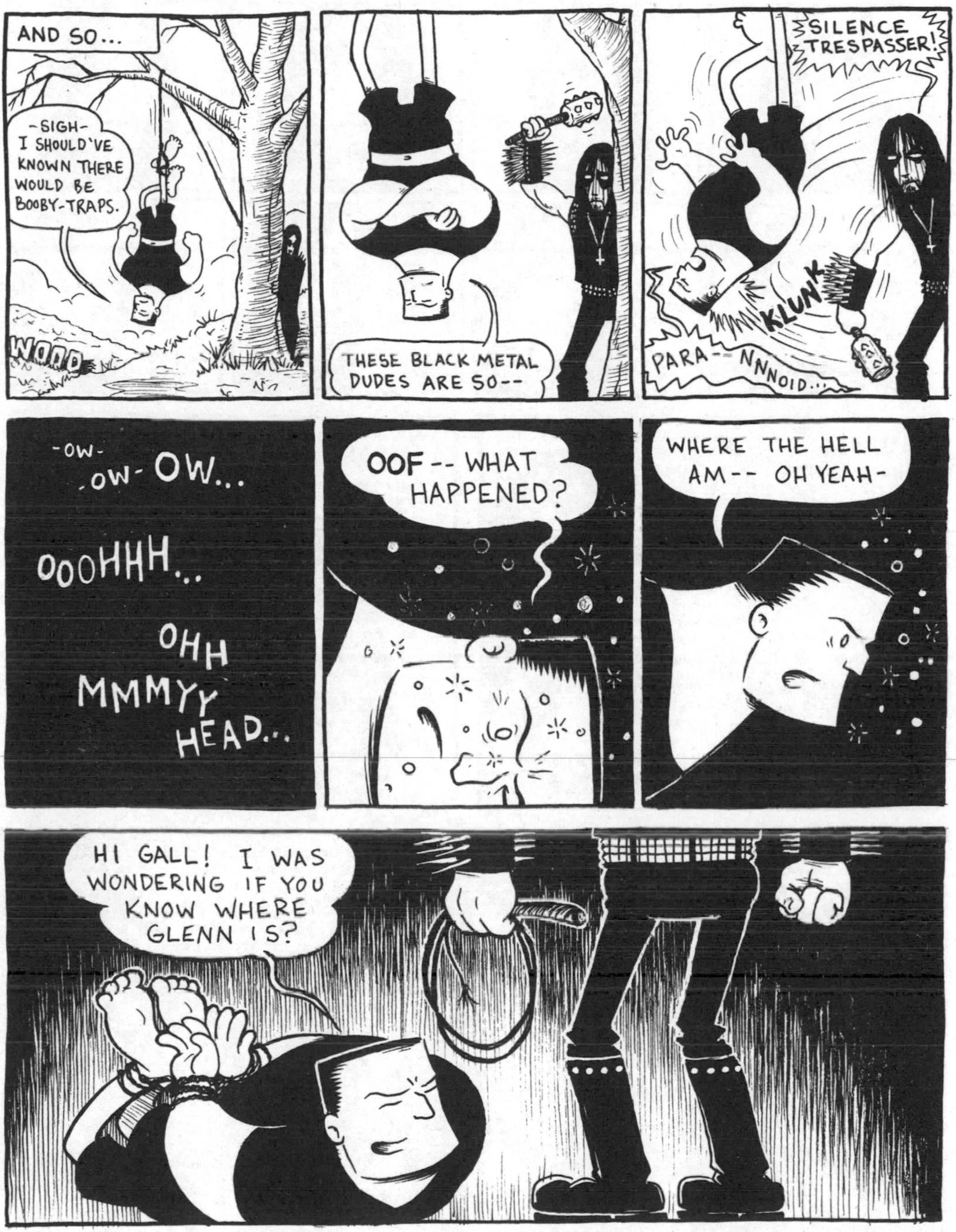
AND SO...
-SIGH- I SHOULD'VE KNOWN THERE WOULD BE BOOBY-TRAPS.
WOOD
THESE BLACK METAL DUDES ARE SO--
SILENCE TRESPASSER!
KLUNK
PARA--NNNOID...
-OW- -OW- OW...
OOOHHH...
OHH MMMYY HEAD...
OOF -- WHAT HAPPENED?
WHERE THE HELL AM-- OH YEAH-
HI GALL! I WAS WONDERING IF YOU KNOW WHERE GLENN IS?

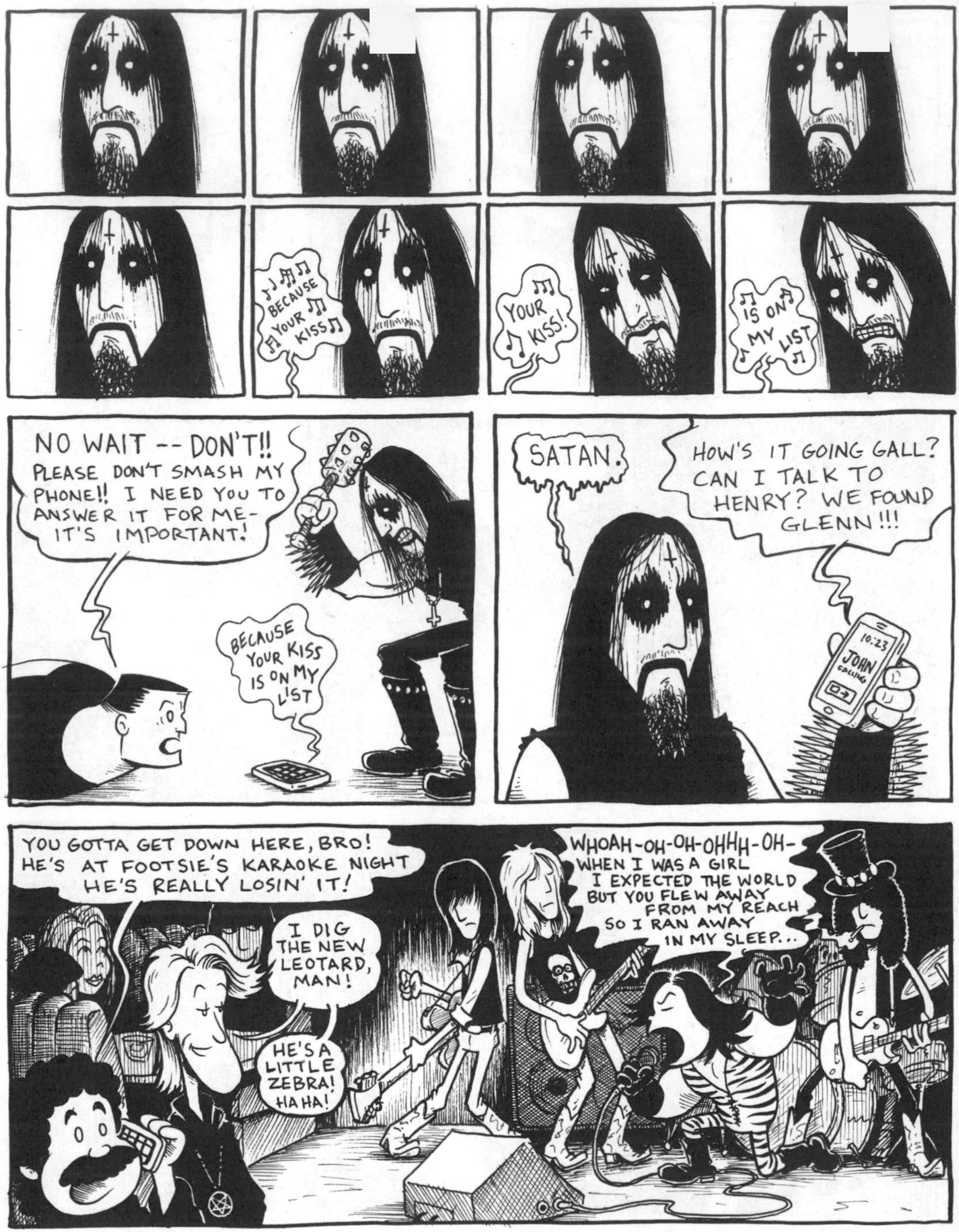
BECAUSE YOUR KISS
YOUR KISS!
IS ON MY LIST
NO WAIT -- DON'T!! PLEASE DON'T SMASH MY PHONE!! I NEED YOU TO ANSWER IT FOR ME- IT'S IMPORTANT!
BECAUSE YOUR KISS IS ON MY LIST
SATAN.
HOW'S IT GOING GALL? CAN I TALK TO HENRY? WE FOUND GLENN!!!
10:23
JOAN CALLING
YOU GOTTA GET DOWN HERE, BRO! HE'S AT FOOTSIE'S KARAOKE NIGHT HE'S REALLY LOSIN' IT!
I DIG THE NEW LEOTARD, MAN!
HE'S A LITTLE ZEBRA! HA HA!
WHOAH-OH-OH-OHHH-OH- WHEN I WAS A GIRL I EXPECTED THE WORLD BUT YOU FLEW AWAY FROM MY REACH SO I RAN AWAY IN MY SLEEP...

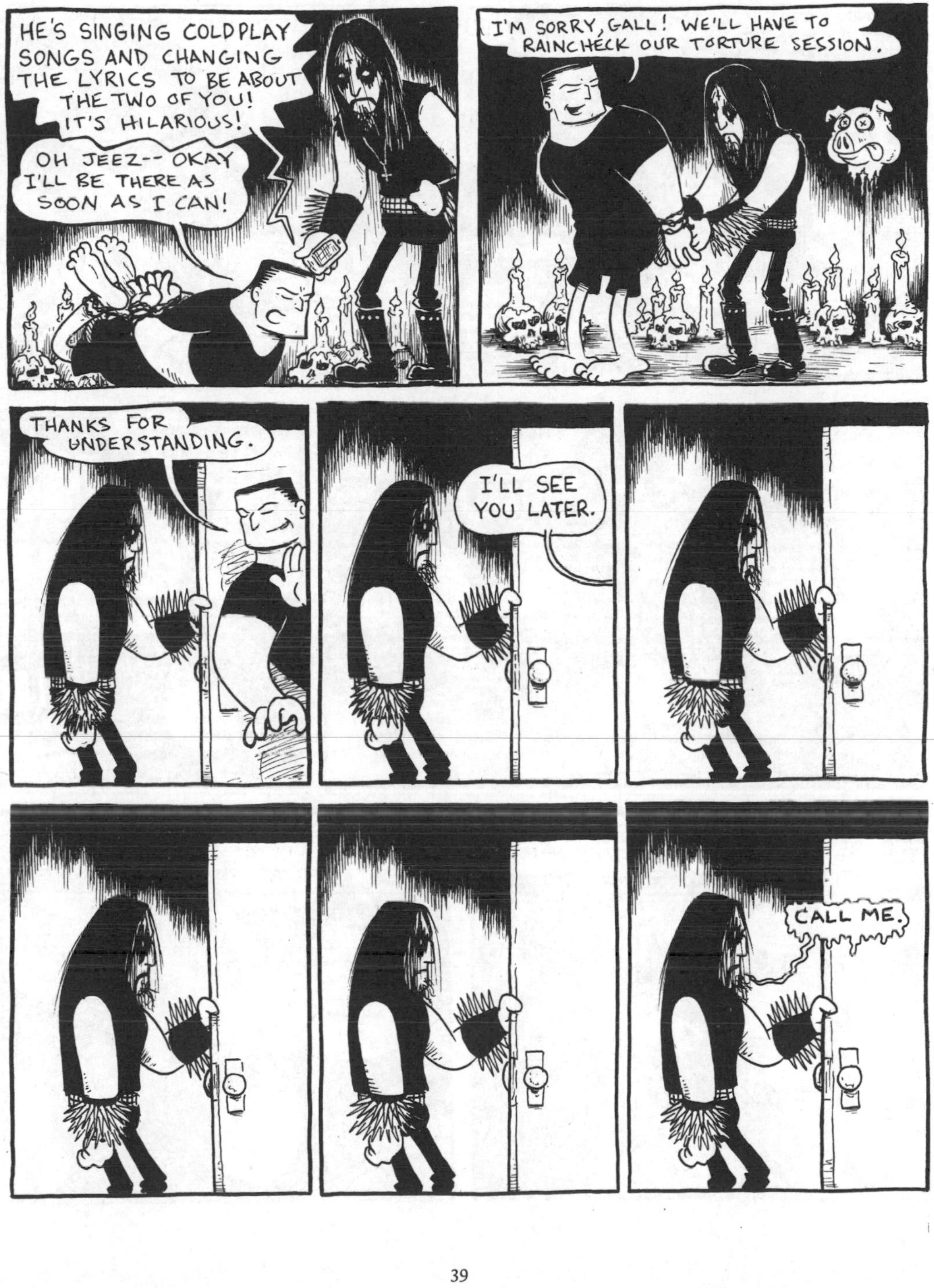
HE'S SINGING COLDPLAY SONGS AND CHANGING THE LYRICS TO BE ABOUT THE TWO OF YOU! IT'S HILARIOUS!
OH JEEZ-- OKAY I'LL BE THERE AS SOON AS I CAN!
I'M SORRY, GALL! WE'LL HAVE TO RAINCHECK OUR TORTURE SESSION.
THANKS FOR UNDERSTANDING.
I'LL SEE YOU LATER.
CALL ME.

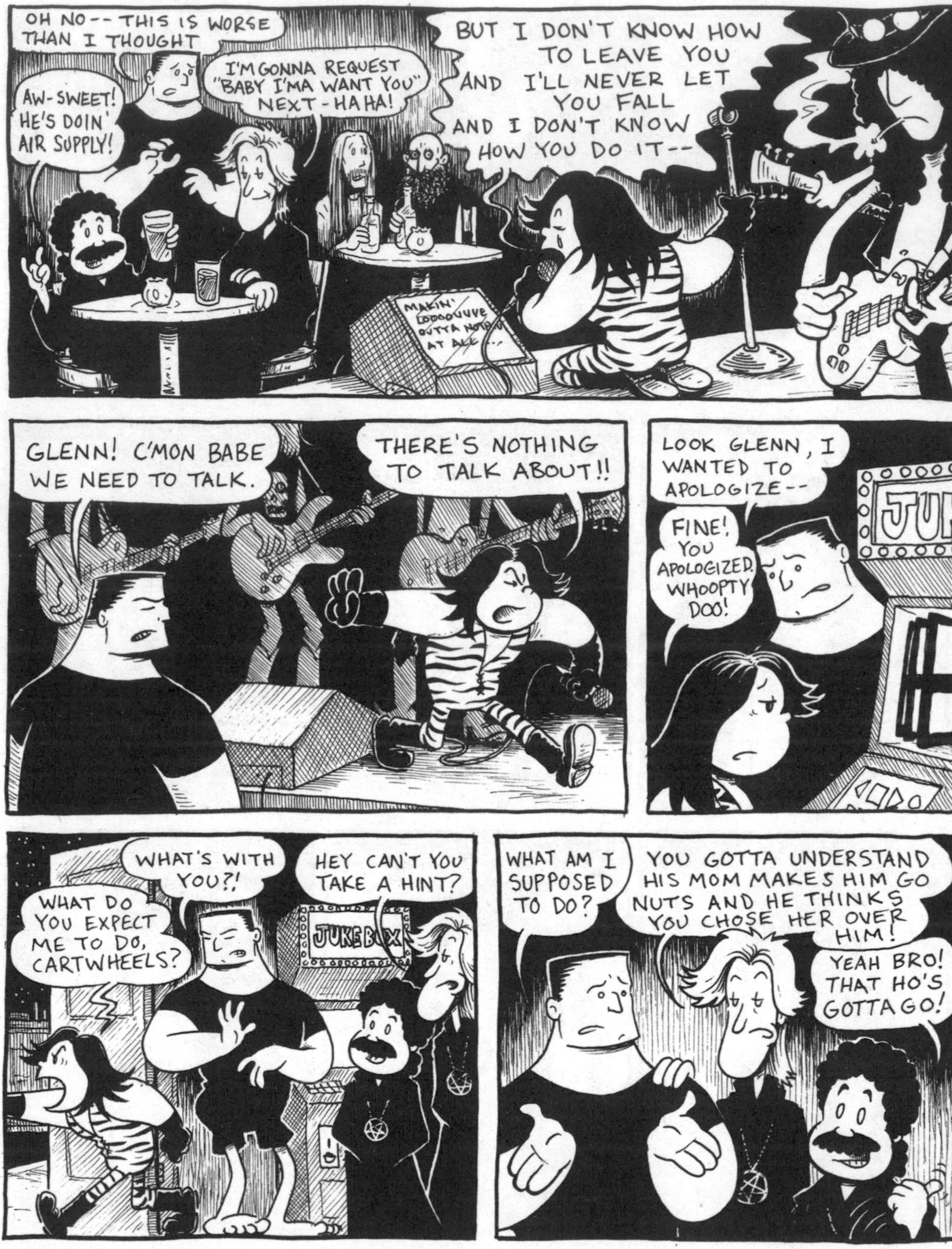
OH NO-- THIS IS WORSE THAN I THOUGHT
AW-SWEET! HE'S DOIN' AIR SUPPLY!
I'M GONNA REQUEST "BABY I'MA WANT YOU" NEXT-HAHA!
BUT I DON'T KNOW HOW TO LEAVE YOU AND I'LL NEVER LET YOU FALL AND I DON'T KNOW HOW YOU DO IT--
MAKIN' LOOOOUUVE OUTTA NOTH
AT ALL...
GLENN! C'MON BABE WE NEED TO TALK.
THERE'S NOTHING TO TALK ABOUT!!
LOOK GLENN, I WANTED TO APOLOGIZE--
FINE! YOU APOLOGIZED. WHOOPTY DOO!
WHAT'S WITH YOU?!
WHAT DO YOU EXPECT ME TO DO, CARTWHEELS?
HEY CAN'T YOU TAKE A HINT?
JUKEBOX
WHAT AM I SUPPOSED TO DO?
YOU GOTTA UNDERSTAND HIS MOM MAKES HIM GO NUTS AND HE THINKS YOU CHOSE HER OVER HIM!
YEAH BRO! THAT HO'S GOTTA GO!

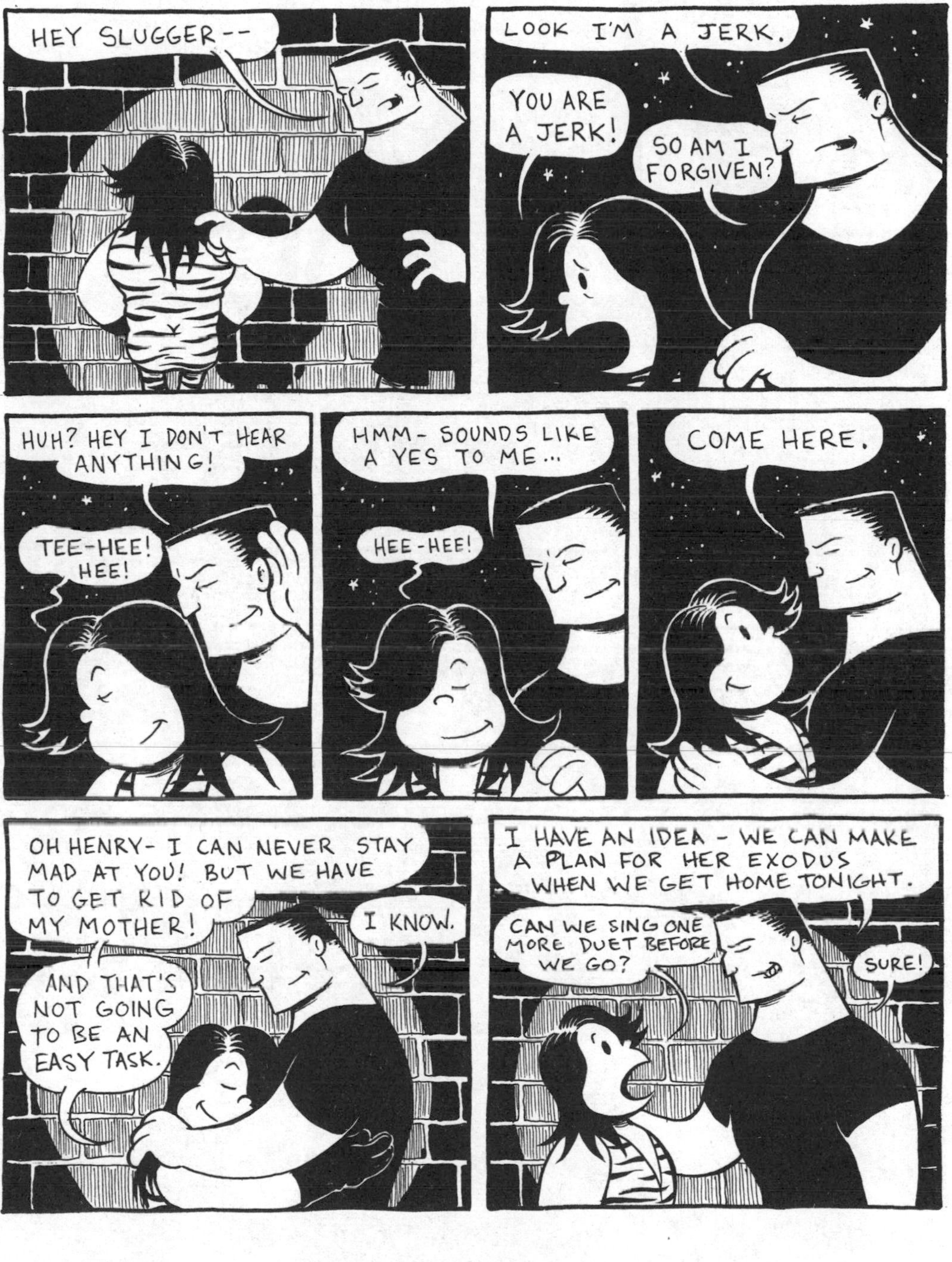

HEY SLUGGER--
LOOK I'M A JERK.
YOU ARE A JERK!
SO AM I FORGIVEN?
HUH? HEY I DON'T HEAR ANYTHING!
TEE-HEE! HEE!
HMM- SOUNDS LIKE A YES TO ME...
HEE-HEE!
COME HERE.
OH HENRY- I CAN NEVER STAY MAD AT YOU! BUT WE HAVE TO GET RID OF MY MOTHER!
I KNOW.
AND THAT'S NOT GOING TO BE AN EASY TASK.
I HAVE AN IDEA - WE CAN MAKE A PLAN FOR HER EXODUS WHEN WE GET HOME TONIGHT.
CAN WE SING ONE MORE DUET BEFORE WE GO?
SURE!

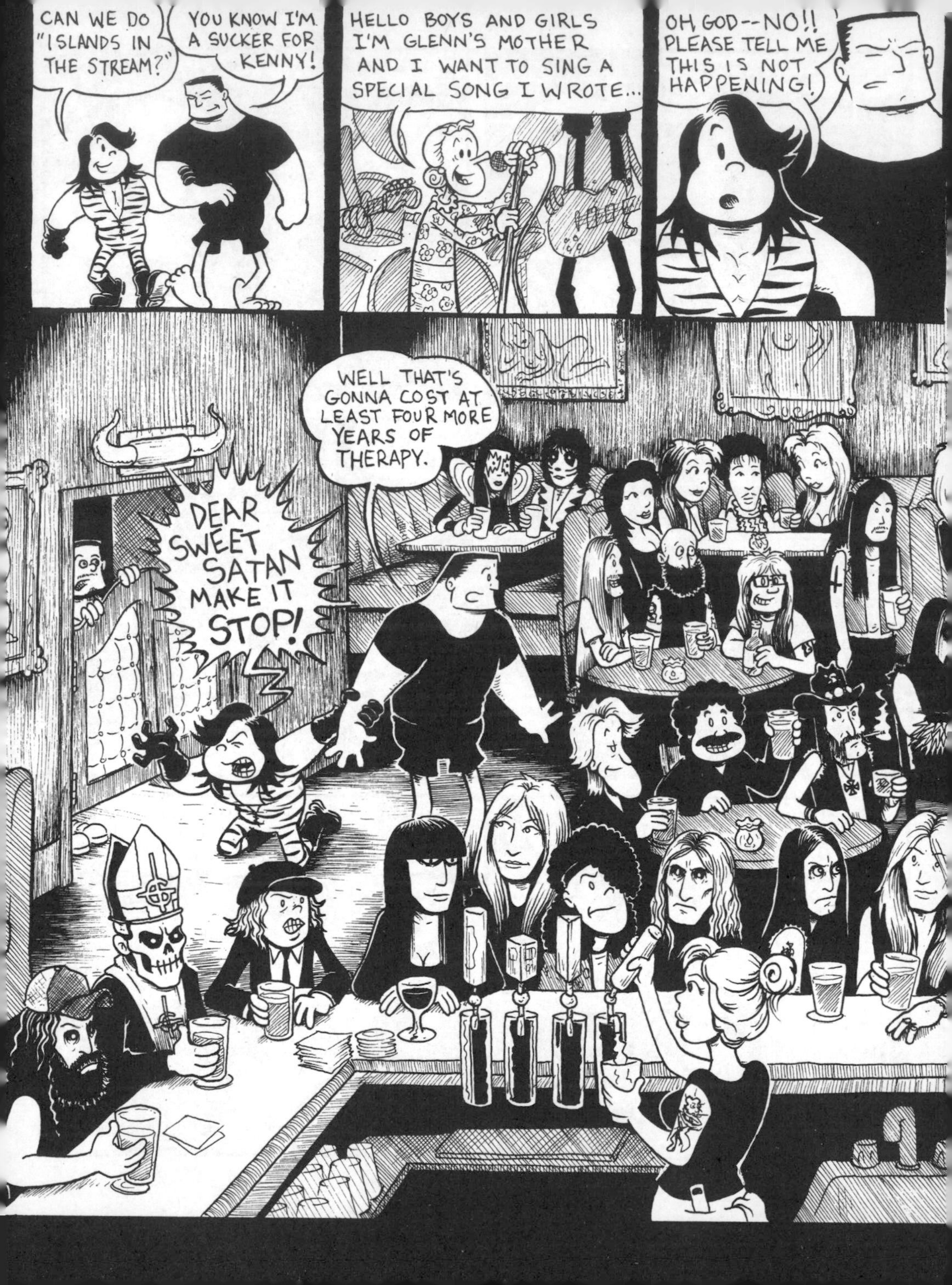
CAN WE DO "ISLANDS IN THE STREAM?"
YOU KNOW I'M A SUCKER FOR KENNY!
HELLO BOYS AND GIRLS I'M GLENN'S MOTHER AND I WANT TO SING A SPECIAL SONG I WROTE...
OH, GOD--NO!! PLEASE TELL ME THIS IS NOT HAPPENING!
WELL THAT'S GONNA COST AT LEAST FOUR MORE YEARS OF THERAPY.
DEAR SWEET SATAN MAKE IT STOP!

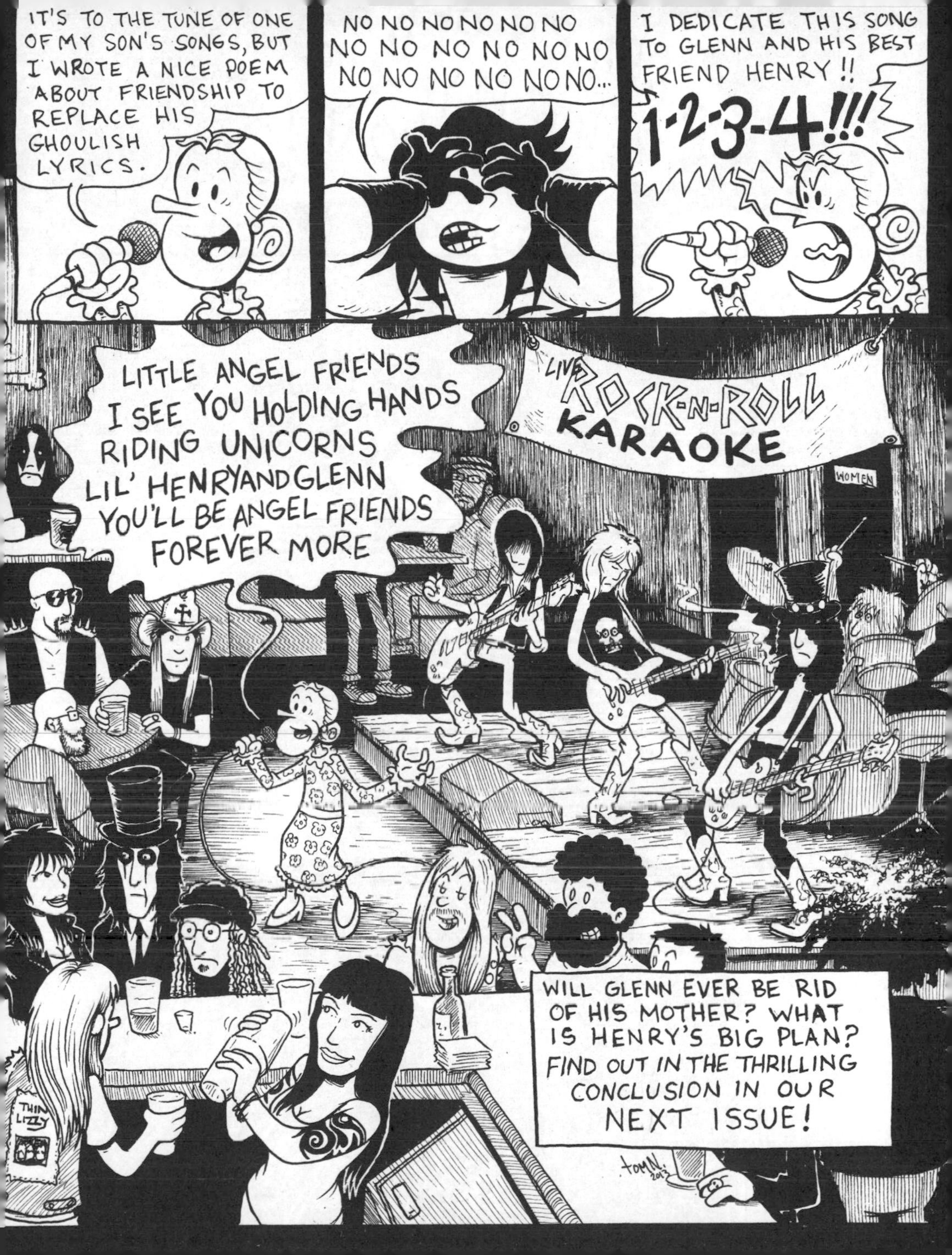

IT'S TO THE TUNE OF ONE OF MY SON'S SONGS, BUT I WROTE A NICE POEM ABOUT FRIENDSHIP TO REPLACE HIS GHOULISH LYRICS.
NO NO NO NO NO NO NO NO NO NO NO NO NO NO NO NO NO NO NO NO...
I DEDICATE THIS SONG TO GLENN AND HIS BEST FRIEND HENRY!!
1-2-3-4!!!
LITTLE ANGEL FRIENDS I SEE YOU HOLDING HANDS RIDING UNICORNS LIL' HENRY AND GLENN YOU'LL BE ANGEL FRIENDS FOREVER MORE
LIVE ROCK-N-ROLL KARAOKE
WOMEN
THIN LIZZY
WILL GLENN EVER BE RID OF HIS MOTHER? WHAT IS HENRY'S BIG PLAN? FIND OUT IN THE THRILLING CONCLUSION IN OUR NEXT ISSUE!
tom N. 2013

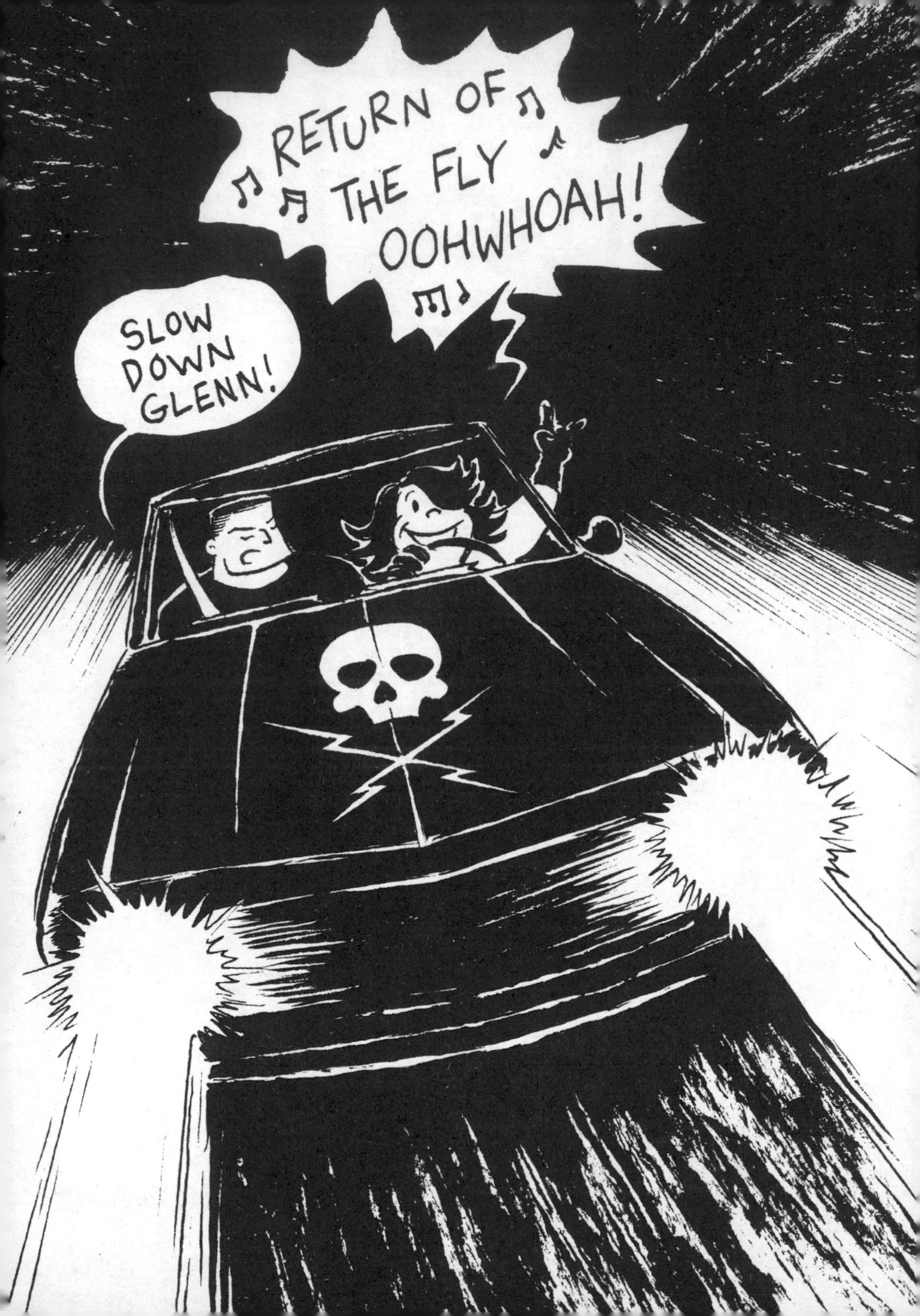
RETURN OF THE FLY OOHWHOAH!
SLOW DOWN GLENN!

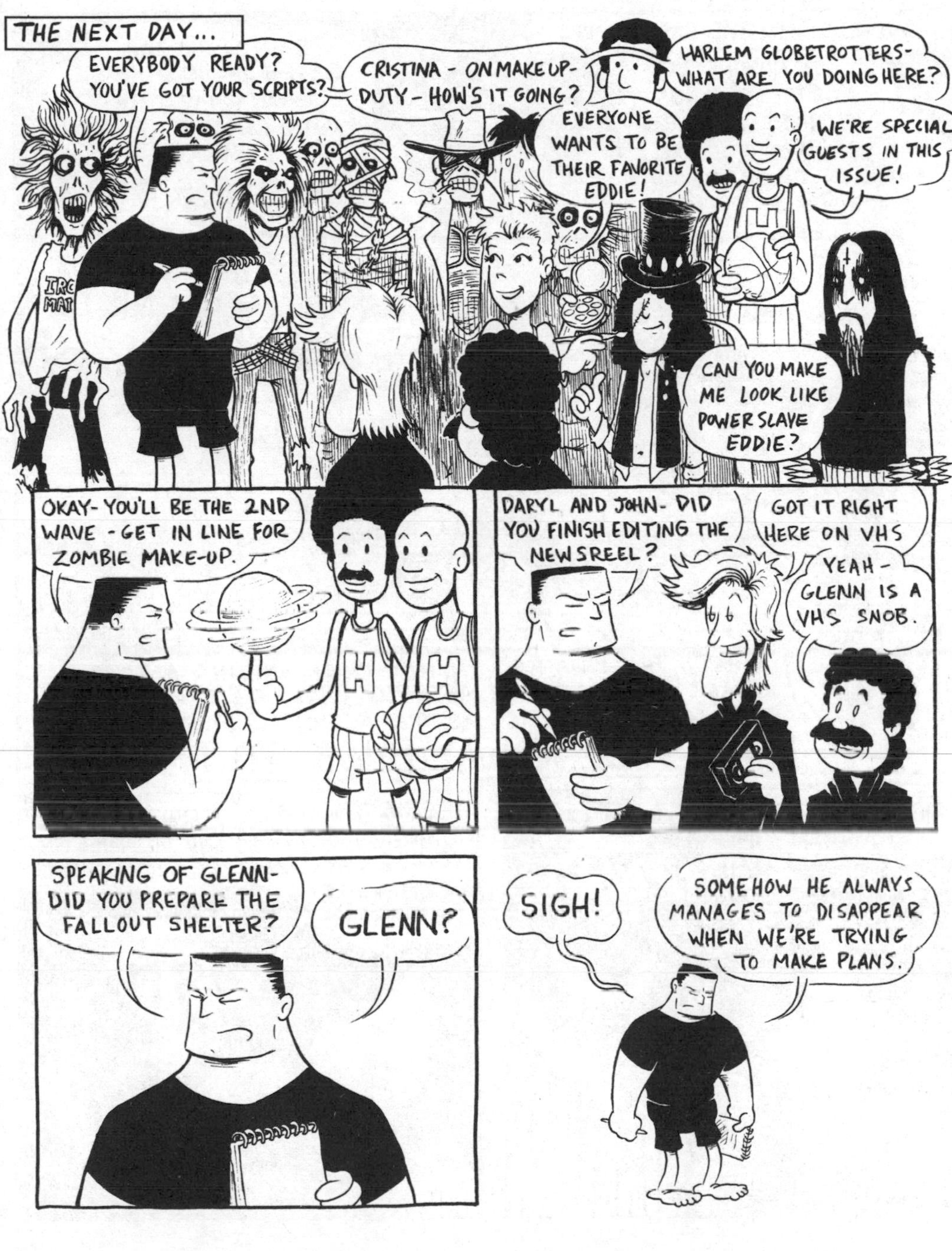
THE NEXT DAY...
EVERYBODY READY? YOU'VE GOT YOUR SCRIPTS?
CRISTINA - ON MAKE UP-DUTY - HOW'S IT GOING?
EVERYONE WANTS TO BE THEIR FAVORITE EDDIE!
HARLEM GLOBETROTTERS- WHAT ARE YOU DOING HERE?
WE'RE SPECIAL GUESTS IN THIS ISSUE!
CAN YOU MAKE ME LOOK LIKE POWER SLAVE EDDIE?
OKAY- YOU'LL BE THE 2ND WAVE - GET IN LINE FOR ZOMBIE MAKE-UP.
DARYL AND JOHN- DID YOU FINISH EDITING THE NEWSREEL?
GOT IT RIGHT HERE ON VHS
YEAH - GLENN IS A VHS SNOB.
SPEAKING OF GLENN- DID YOU PREPARE THE FALLOUT SHELTER?
GLENN?
SIGH!
SOMEHOW HE ALWAYS MANAGES TO DISAPPEAR WHEN WE'RE TRYING TO MAKE PLANS.

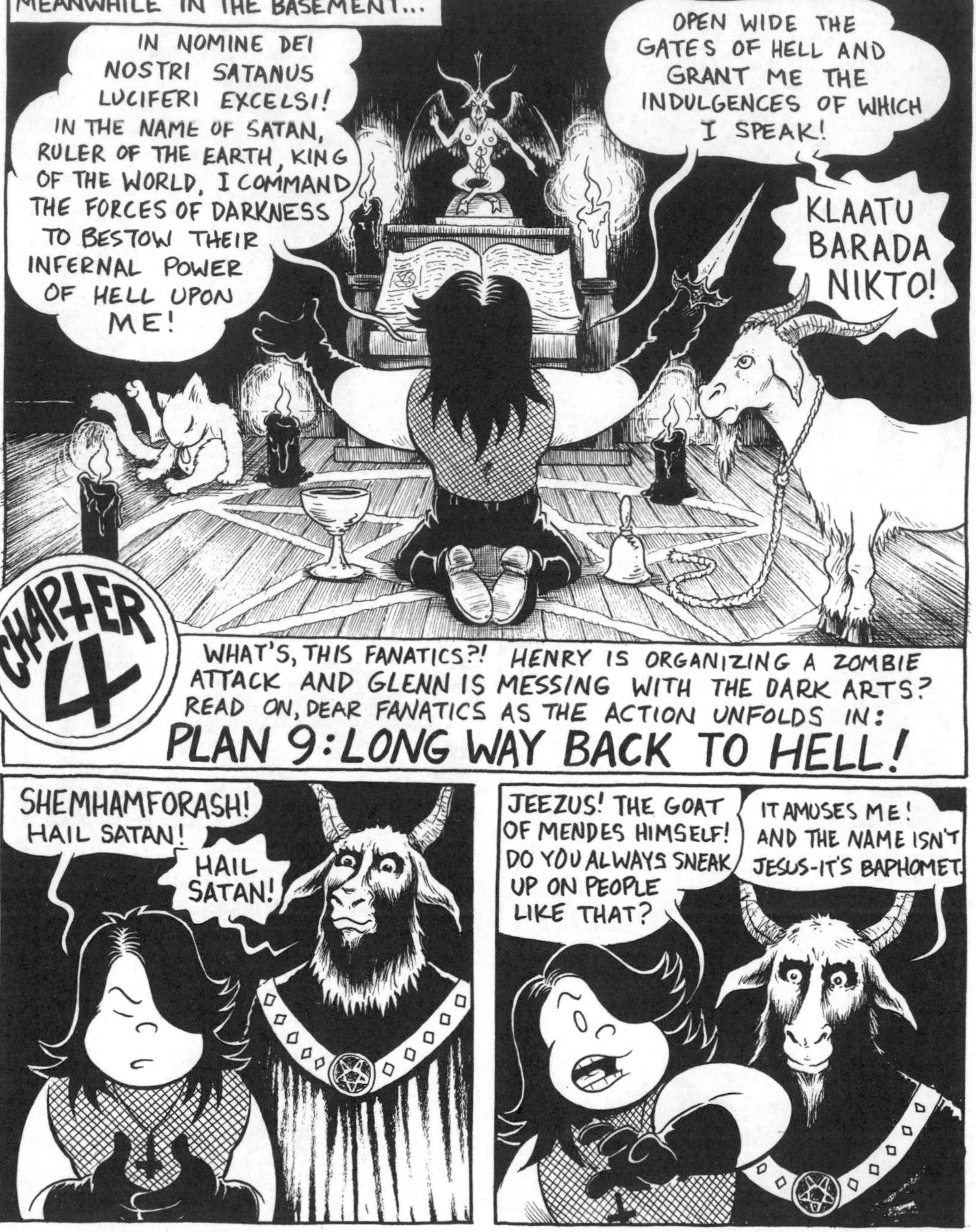
MEANWHILE IN THE BASEMENT...
IN NOMINE DEI NOSTRI SATANUS LUCIFERI EXCELSI! IN THE NAME OF SATAN, RULER OF THE EARTH, KING OF THE WORLD, I COMMAND THE FORCES OF DARKNESS TO BESTOW THEIR INFERNAL POWER OF HELL UPON ME!
OPEN WIDE THE GATES OF HELL AND GRANT ME THE INDULGENCES OF WHICH I SPEAK!
KLAATU BARADA NIKTO!
CHAPTER 4
WHAT'S, THIS FANATICS?! HENRY IS ORGANIZING A ZOMBIE ATTACK AND GLENN IS MESSING WITH THE DARK ARTS? READ ON, DEAR FANATICS AS THE ACTION UNFOLDS IN:
PLAN 9: LONG WAY BACK TO HELL!
SHEMHAMFORASH! HAIL SATAN!
HAIL SATAN!
JEEZUS! THE GOAT OF MENDES HIMSELF! DO YOU ALWAYS SNEAK UP ON PEOPLE LIKE THAT?
IT AMUSES ME! AND THE NAME ISN'T JESUS-IT'S BAPHOMET.

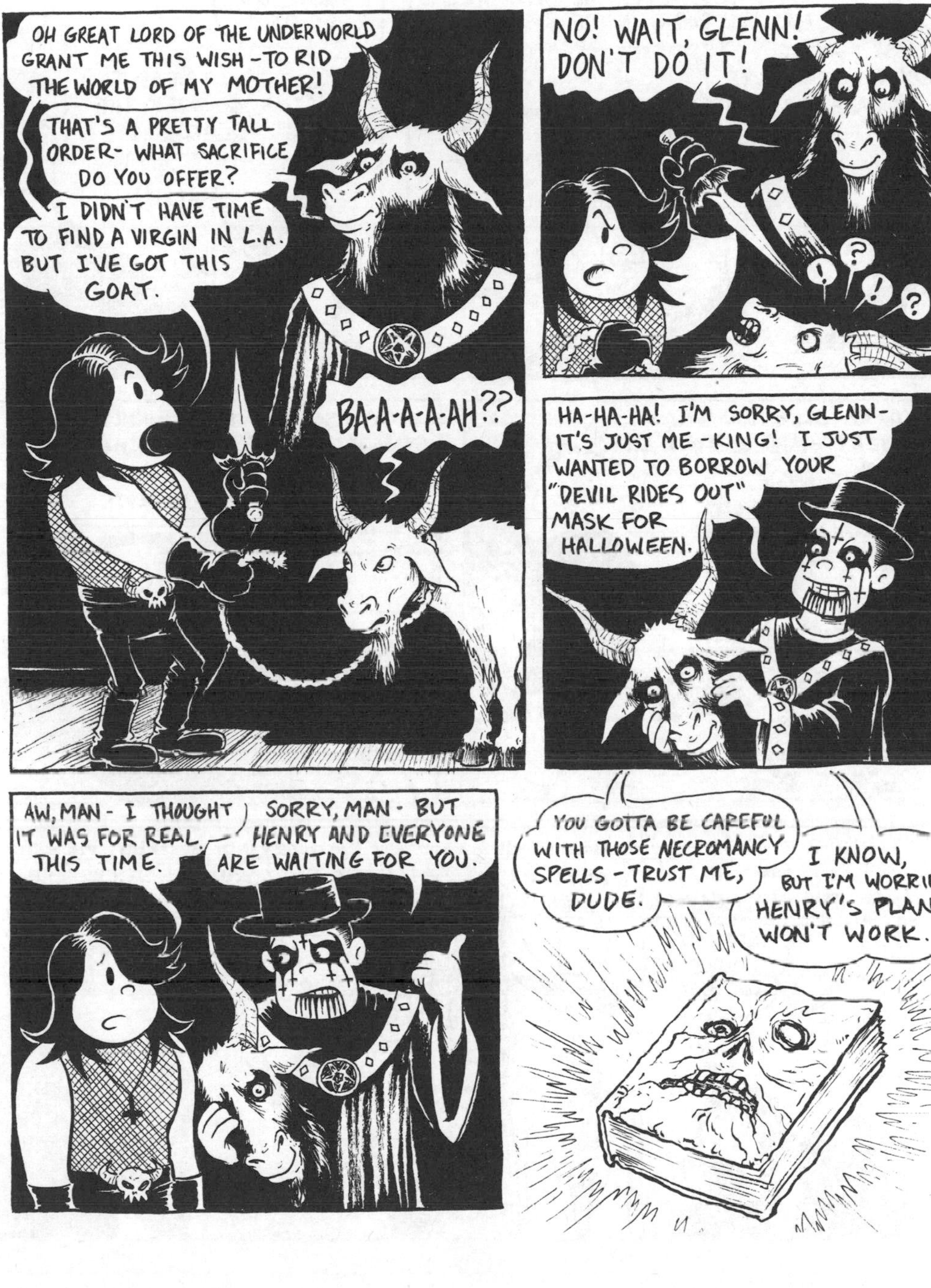

OH GREAT LORD OF THE UNDERWORLD GRANT ME THIS WISH - TO RID THE WORLD OF MY MOTHER!
THAT'S A PRETTY TALL ORDER- WHAT SACRIFICE DO YOU OFFER?
I DIDN'T HAVE TIME TO FIND A VIRGIN IN L.A. BUT I'VE GOT THIS GOAT.
BA-A-A-A-AH??
NO! WAIT, GLENN! DON'T DO IT!
! ? ! ?
HA-HA-HA! I'M SORRY, GLENN- IT'S JUST ME - KING! I JUST WANTED TO BORROW YOUR "DEVIL RIDES OUT" MASK FOR HALLOWEEN.
AW, MAN - I THOUGHT IT WAS FOR REAL THIS TIME.
SORRY, MAN - BUT HENRY AND EVERYONE ARE WAITING FOR YOU.
YOU GOTTA BE CAREFUL WITH THOSE NECROMANCY SPELLS - TRUST ME, DUDE.
I KNOW, BUT I'M WORRIED HENRY'S PLAN WON'T WORK.

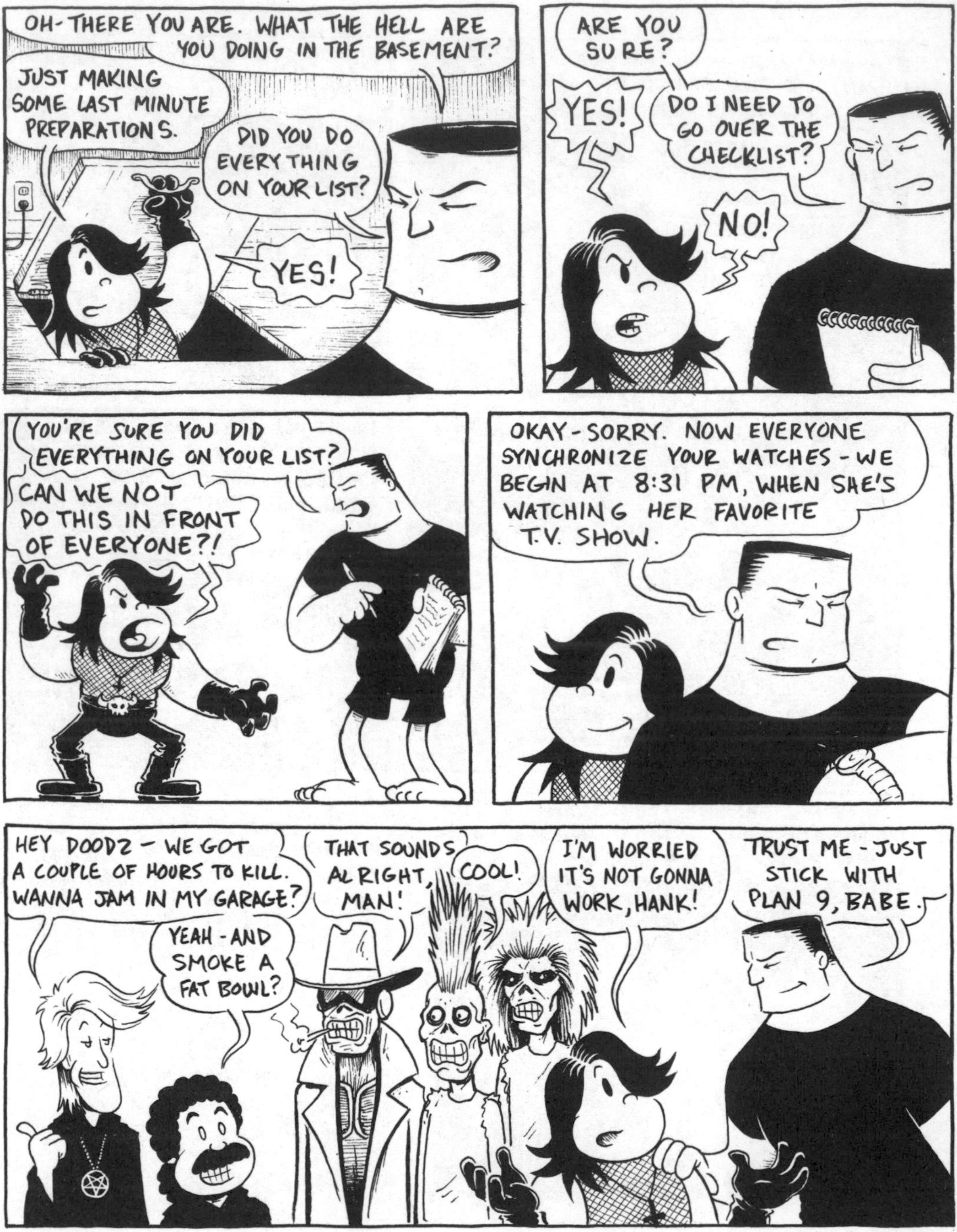

OH- THERE YOU ARE. WHAT THE HELL ARE YOU DOING IN THE BASEMENT?
JUST MAKING SOME LAST MINUTE PREPARATIONS.
DID YOU DO EVERYTHING ON YOUR LIST?
YES!
ARE YOU SURE?
YES!
DO I NEED TO GO OVER THE CHECKLIST?
NO!
YOU'RE SURE YOU DID EVERYTHING ON YOUR LIST?
CAN WE NOT DO THIS IN FRONT OF EVERYONE?!
OKAY - SORRY. NOW EVERYONE SYNCHRONIZE YOUR WATCHES - WE BEGIN AT 8:31 PM, WHEN SHE'S WATCHING HER FAVORITE T.V. SHOW.
HEY DOODZ - WE GOT A COUPLE OF HOURS TO KILL. WANNA JAM IN MY GARAGE?
YEAH - AND SMOKE A FAT BOWL?
THAT SOUNDS ALRIGHT, MAN!
COOL!
I'M WORRIED IT'S NOT GONNA WORK, HANK!
TRUST ME - JUST STICK WITH PLAN 9, BABE.

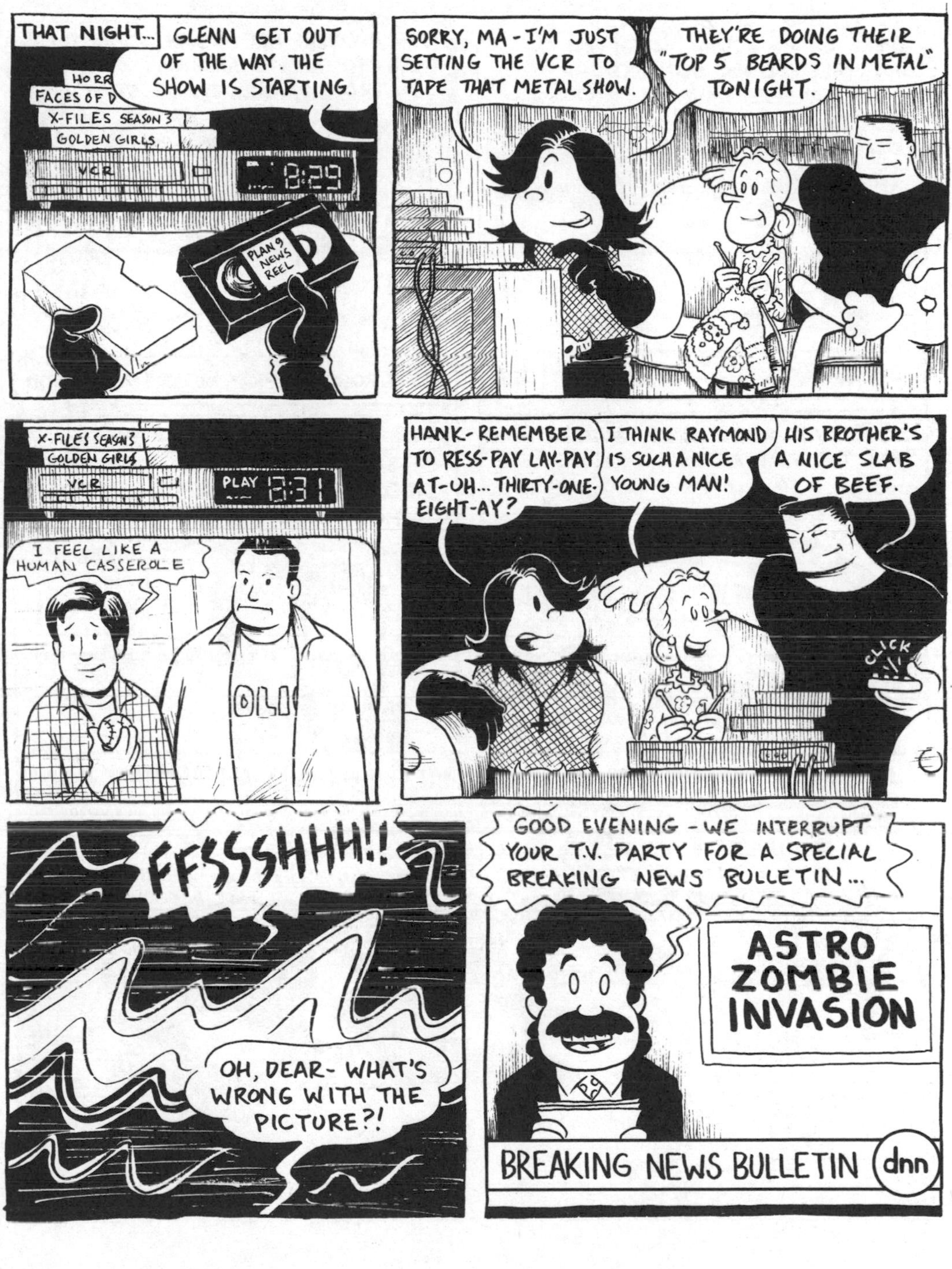
THAT NIGHT...
GLENN GET OUT OF THE WAY. THE SHOW IS STARTING.
HORR
FACES OF D
X-FILES SEASON 3
GOLDEN GIRLS
VCR
8:29
PLAN 9 NEWS REEL
SORRY, MA - I'M JUST SETTING THE VCR TO TAPE THAT METAL SHOW.
THEY'RE DOING THEIR "TOP 5 BEARDS IN METAL" TONIGHT.
X-FILES SEASON 3
GOLDEN GIRLS
VCR
PLAY 8:31
I FEEL LIKE A HUMAN CASSEROLE
HANK- REMEMBER TO RESS-PAY LAY-PAY AT-UH... THIRTY-ONE-EIGHT-AY?
I THINK RAYMOND IS SUCH A NICE YOUNG MAN!
HIS BROTHER'S A NICE SLAB OF BEEF.
CLICK
FFSSSHHH!!
OH, DEAR- WHAT'S WRONG WITH THE PICTURE?!
GOOD EVENING - WE INTERRUPT YOUR T.V. PARTY FOR A SPECIAL BREAKING NEWS BULLETIN...
ASTRO ZOMBIE INVASION
BREAKING NEWS BULLETIN
dnn

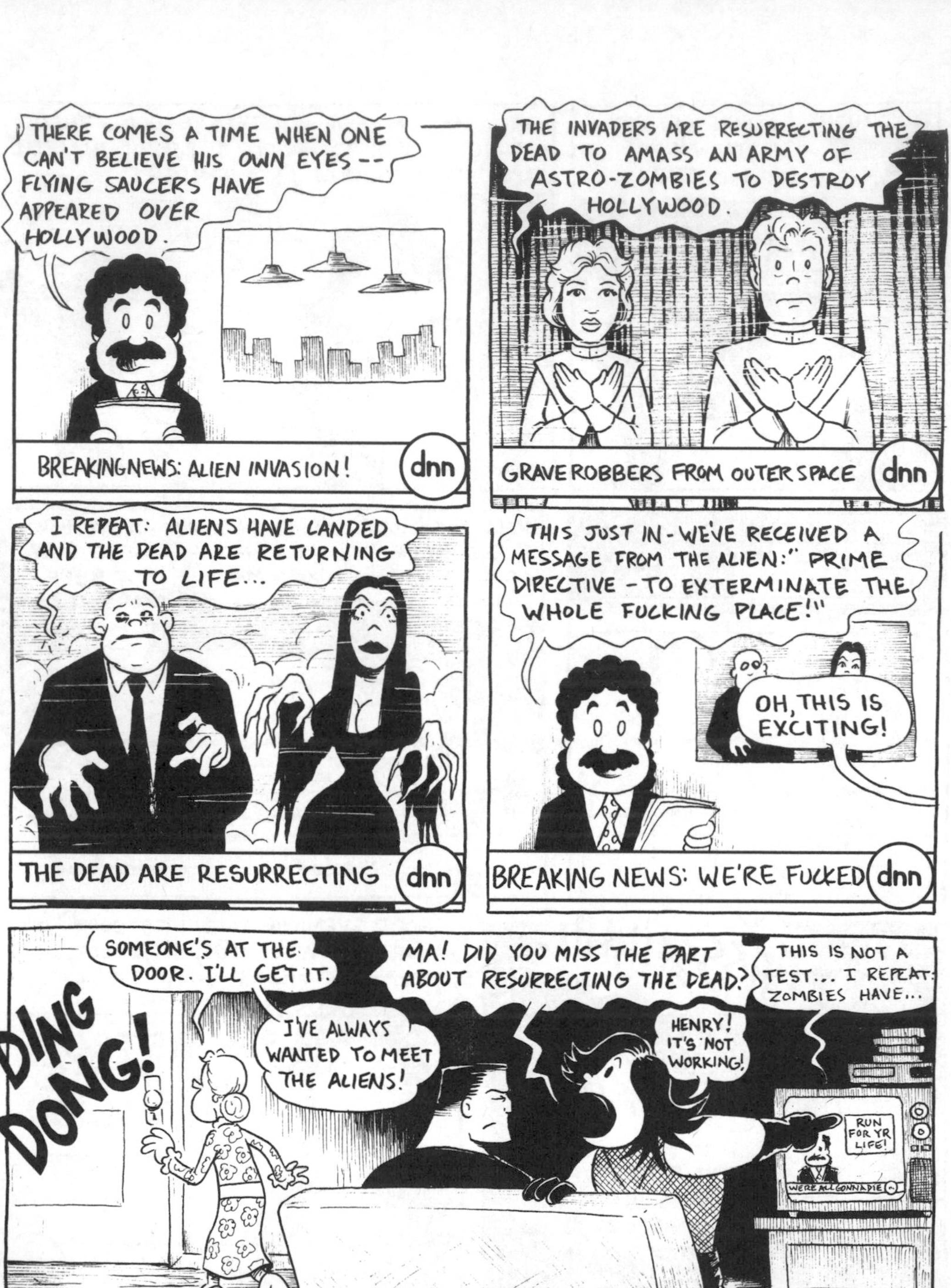
THERE COMES A TIME WHEN ONE CAN'T BELIEVE HIS OWN EYES -- FLYING SAUCERS HAVE APPEARED OVER HOLLYWOOD.
BREAKINGNEWS: ALIEN INVASION!
dnn
THE INVADERS ARE RESURRECTING THE DEAD TO AMASS AN ARMY OF ASTRO-ZOMBIES TO DESTROY HOLLYWOOD.
GRAVEROBBERS FROM OUTER SPACE
dnn
I REPEAT: ALIENS HAVE LANDED AND THE DEAD ARE RETURNING TO LIFE...
THE DEAD ARE RESURRECTING
dnn
THIS JUST IN - WE'VE RECEIVED A MESSAGE FROM THE ALIEN: "PRIME DIRECTIVE - TO EXTERMINATE THE WHOLE FUCKING PLACE!"
OH, THIS IS EXCITING!
BREAKING NEWS: WE'RE FUCKED
dnn
DING DONG!
SOMEONE'S AT THE DOOR. I'LL GET IT.
I'VE ALWAYS WANTED TO MEET THE ALIENS!
MA! DID YOU MISS THE PART ABOUT RESURRECTING THE DEAD?
HENRY! IT'S NOT WORKING!
THIS IS NOT A TEST... I REPEAT: ZOMBIES HAVE...
RUN FOR YR LIFE!
WE'RE ALL GONNA DIE

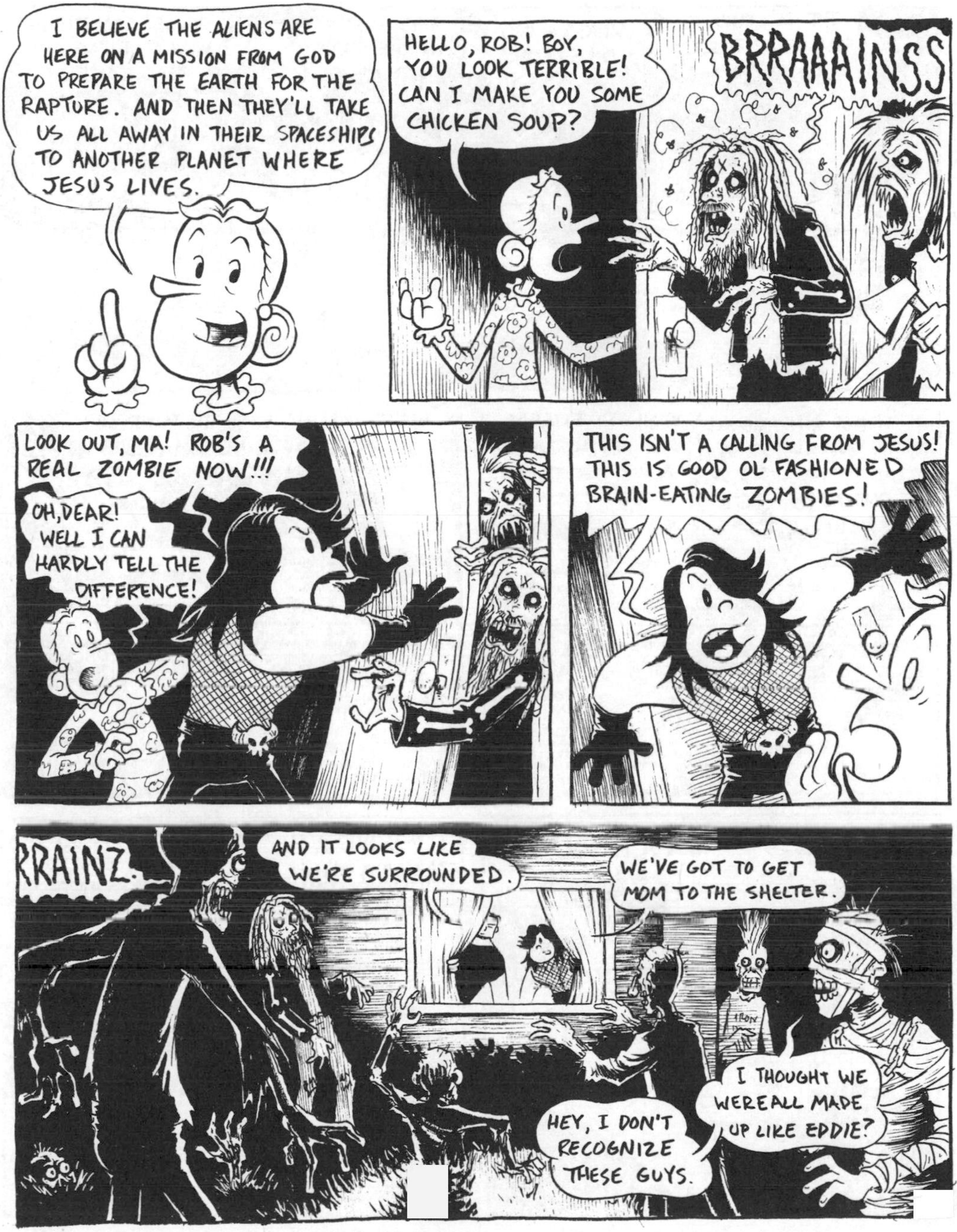
I BELIEVE THE ALIENS ARE HERE ON A MISSION FROM GOD TO PREPARE THE EARTH FOR THE RAPTURE. AND THEN THEY'LL TAKE US ALL AWAY IN THEIR SPACESHIPS TO ANOTHER PLANET WHERE JESUS LIVES.
HELLO, ROB! BOY, YOU LOOK TERRIBLE! CAN I MAKE YOU SOME CHICKEN SOUP?
BRRAAAINSS
LOOK OUT, MA! ROB'S A REAL ZOMBIE NOW!!!
OH, DEAR! WELL I CAN HARDLY TELL THE DIFFERENCE!
THIS ISN'T A CALLING FROM JESUS! THIS IS GOOD OL' FASHIONED BRAIN-EATING ZOMBIES!
RRAINZ.
AND IT LOOKS LIKE WE'RE SURROUNDED.
WE'VE GOT TO GET MOM TO THE SHELTER.
HEY, I DON'T RECOGNIZE THESE GUYS.
I THOUGHT WE WERE ALL MADE UP LIKE EDDIE?

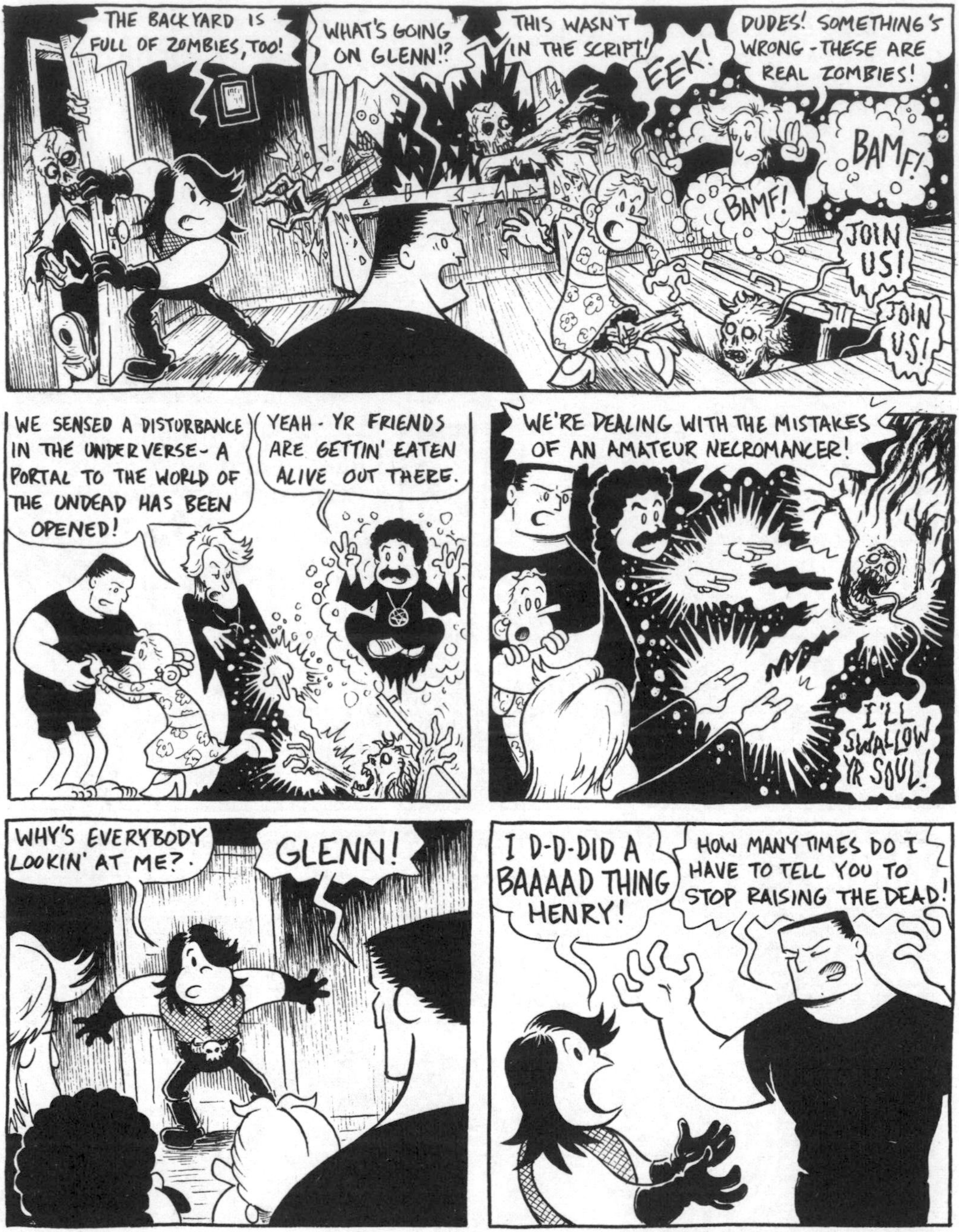
THE BACKYARD IS FULL OF ZOMBIES, TOO!
WHAT'S GOING ON GLENN!?
THIS WASN'T IN THE SCRIPT!
EEK!
DUDES! SOMETHING'S WRONG - THESE ARE REAL ZOMBIES!
BAMF!
BAMF!
JOIN US!
JOIN US!
WE SENSED A DISTURBANCE IN THE UNDERVERSE - A PORTAL TO THE WORLD OF THE UNDEAD HAS BEEN OPENED!
YEAH - YR FRIENDS ARE GETTIN' EATEN ALIVE OUT THERE.
WE'RE DEALING WITH THE MISTAKES OF AN AMATEUR NECROMANCER!
I'LL SWALLOW YR SOUL!
WHY'S EVERYBODY LOOKIN' AT ME?
GLENN!
I D-D-DID A BAAAAD THING HENRY!
HOW MANY TIMES DO I HAVE TO TELL YOU TO STOP RAISING THE DEAD!

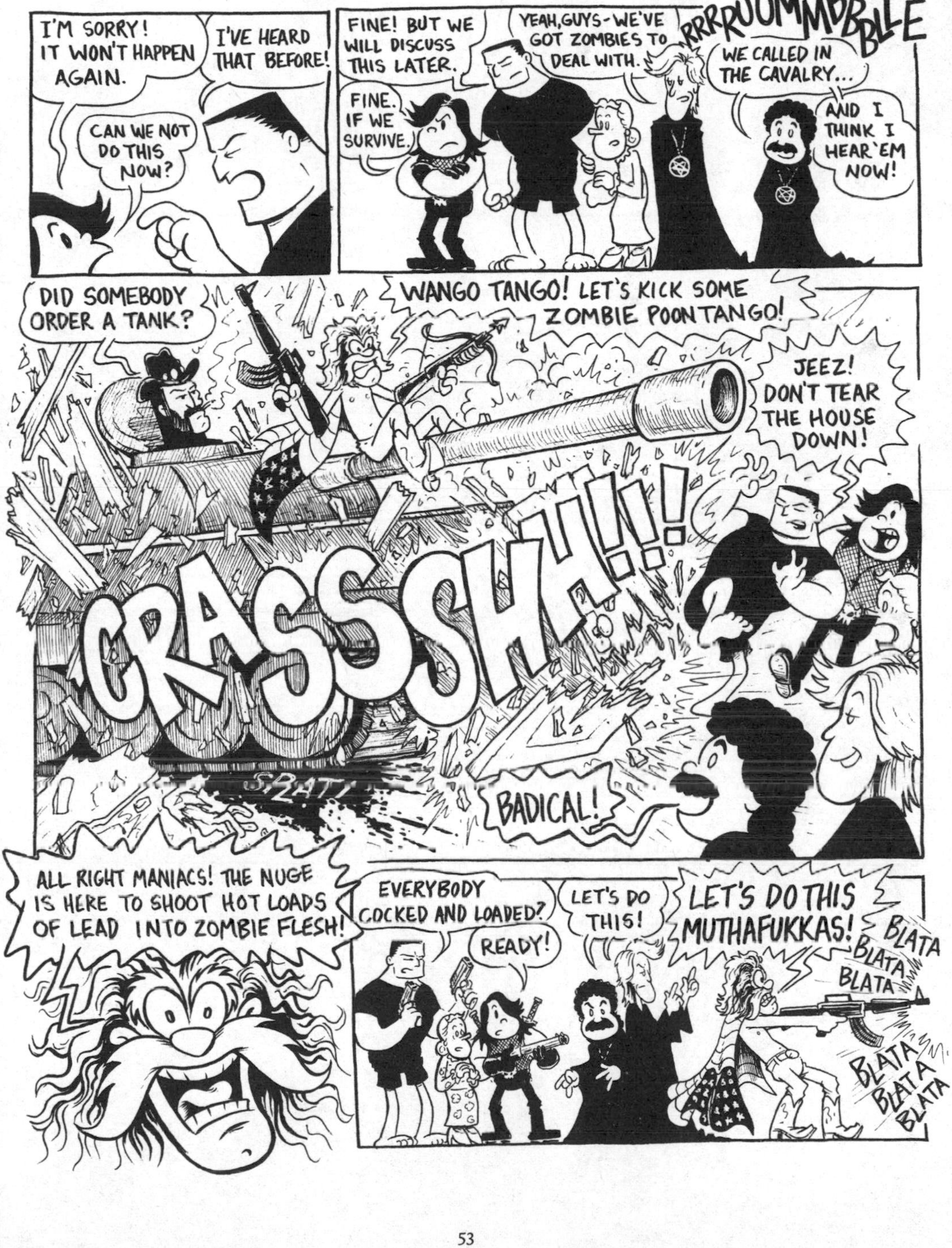

I'M SORRY! IT WON'T HAPPEN AGAIN.
I'VE HEARD THAT BEFORE!
CAN WE NOT DO THIS NOW?
FINE! BUT WE WILL DISCUSS THIS LATER.
FINE. IF WE SURVIVE.
YEAH, GUYS - WE'VE GOT ZOMBIES TO DEAL WITH.
RRRRUUMMBBBLLE
WE CALLED IN THE CAVALRY...
AND I THINK I HEAR 'EM NOW!
DID SOMEBODY ORDER A TANK?
WANGO TANGO! LET'S KICK SOME ZOMBIE POONTANGO!
JEEZ! DON'T TEAR THE HOUSE DOWN!
CRASSSHH!!!!
BADICAL!
ALL RIGHT MANIACS! THE NUGE IS HERE TO SHOOT HOT LOADS OF LEAD INTO ZOMBIE FLESH!
EVERYBODY COCKED AND LOADED?
READY!
LET'S DO THIS!
LET'S DO THIS MUTHAFUKKAS!
BLATA BLATA BLATA
BLATA BLATA BLATA

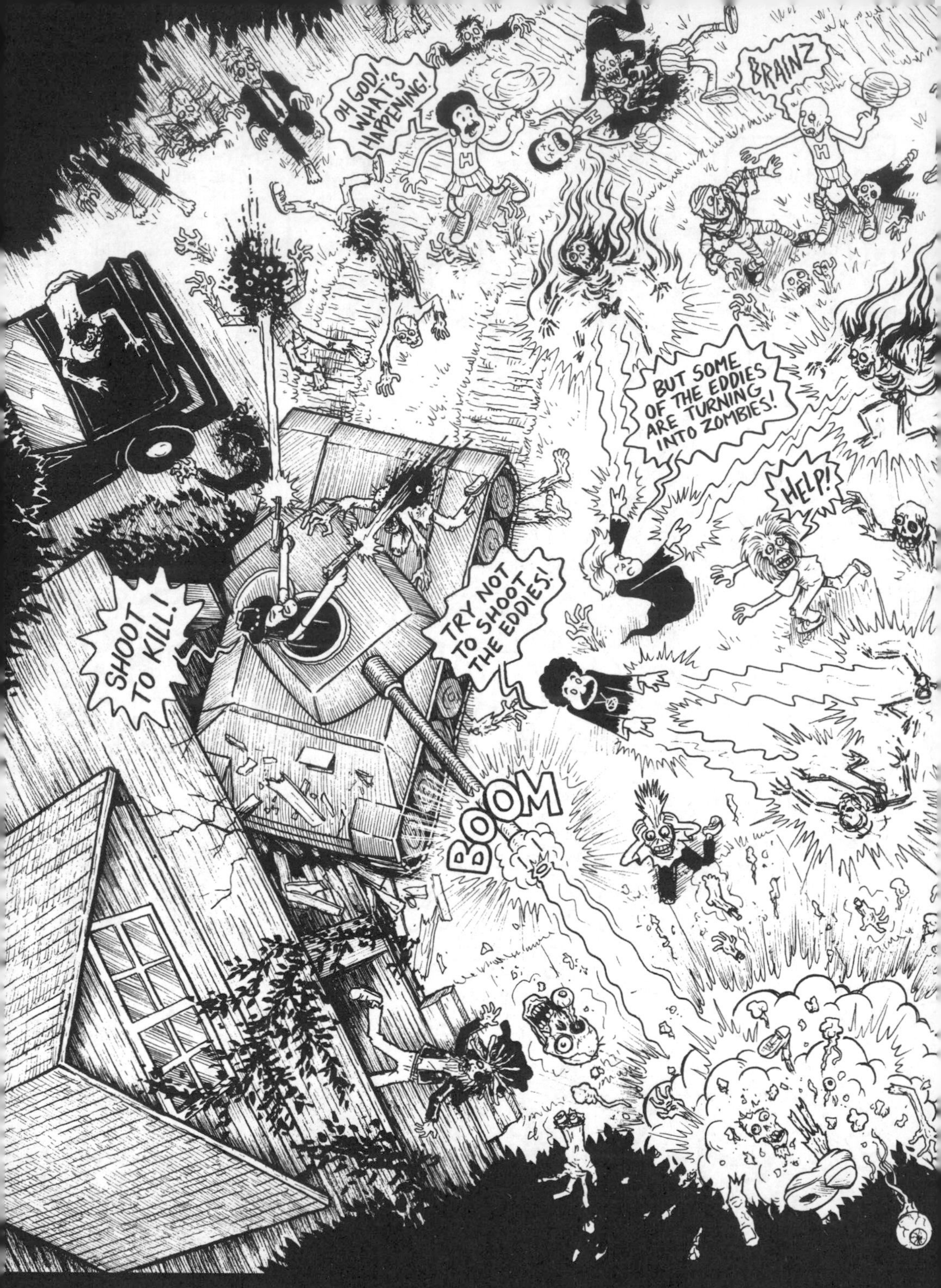
OH GOD! WHAT'S HAPPENING!
BRAINZ
BUT SOME OF THE EDDIES ARE TURNING INTO ZOMBIES!
HELP!
SHOOT TO KILL!
TRY NOT TO SHOOT THE EDDIES!
BOOM

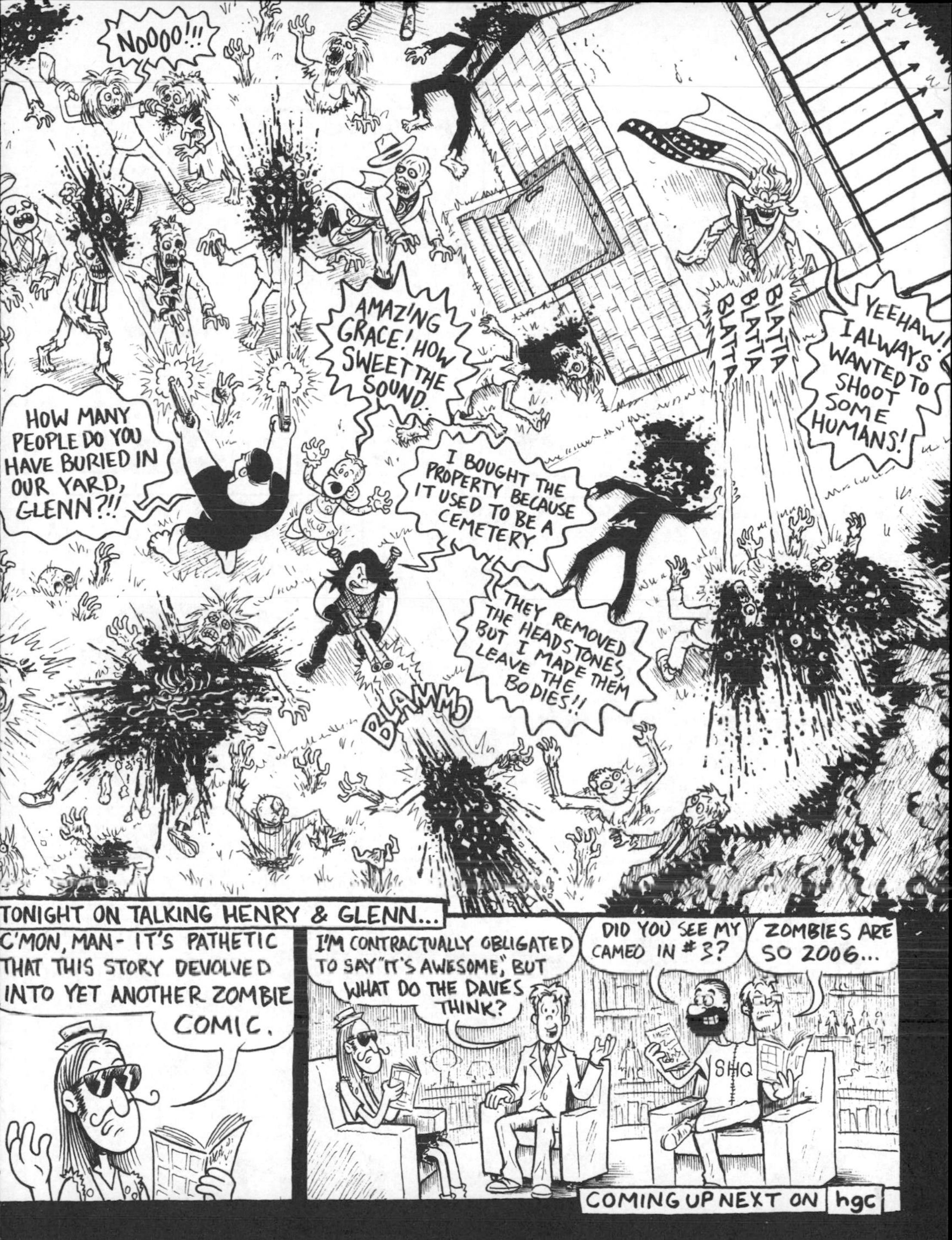
NOOOO!!!
AMAZING GRACE! HOW SWEET THE SOUND
BLATTA BLATTA BLATTA
YEEHAW! I ALWAYS WANTED TO SHOOT SOME HUMANS!
HOW MANY PEOPLE DO YOU HAVE BURIED IN OUR YARD, GLENN?!!
I BOUGHT THE PROPERTY BECAUSE IT USED TO BE A CEMETERY.
THEY REMOVED THE HEADSTONES, BUT I MADE THEM LEAVE THE BODIES!!
BLAMMO
TONIGHT ON TALKING HENRY & GLENN...
C'MON, MAN- IT'S PATHETIC THAT THIS STORY DEVOLVED INTO YET ANOTHER ZOMBIE COMIC.
I'M CONTRACTUALLY OBLIGATED TO SAY "IT'S AWESOME", BUT WHAT DO THE DAVES THINK?
DID YOU SEE MY CAMEO IN #3?
ZOMBIES ARE SO 2006...
SHQ
COMING UP NEXT ON hgc

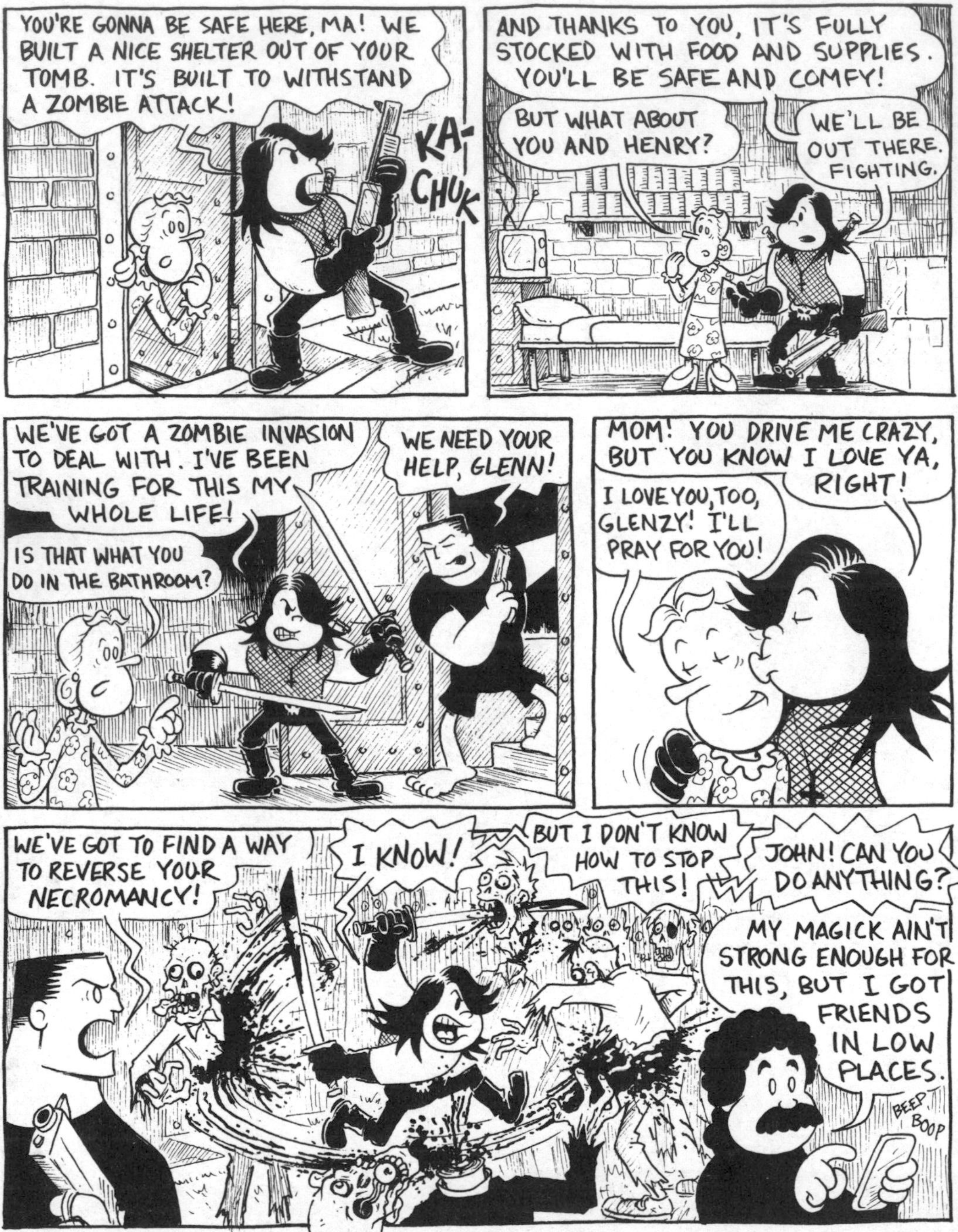
YOU'RE GONNA BE SAFE HERE, MA! WE BUILT A NICE SHELTER OUT OF YOUR TOMB. IT'S BUILT TO WITHSTAND A ZOMBIE ATTACK!
KA-CHUK
AND THANKS TO YOU, IT'S FULLY STOCKED WITH FOOD AND SUPPLIES. YOU'LL BE SAFE AND COMFY!
BUT WHAT ABOUT YOU AND HENRY?
WE'LL BE OUT THERE. FIGHTING.
WE'VE GOT A ZOMBIE INVASION TO DEAL WITH. I'VE BEEN TRAINING FOR THIS MY WHOLE LIFE!
WE NEED YOUR HELP, GLENN!
IS THAT WHAT YOU DO IN THE BATHROOM?
MOM! YOU DRIVE ME CRAZY, BUT YOU KNOW I LOVE YA, RIGHT!
I LOVE YOU, TOO, GLENZY! I'LL PRAY FOR YOU!
WE'VE GOT TO FIND A WAY TO REVERSE YOUR NECROMANCY!
I KNOW!
BUT I DON'T KNOW HOW TO STOP THIS!
JOHN! CAN YOU DO ANYTHING?
MY MAGICK AIN'T STRONG ENOUGH FOR THIS, BUT I GOT FRIENDS IN LOW PLACES.
BEEP BOOP

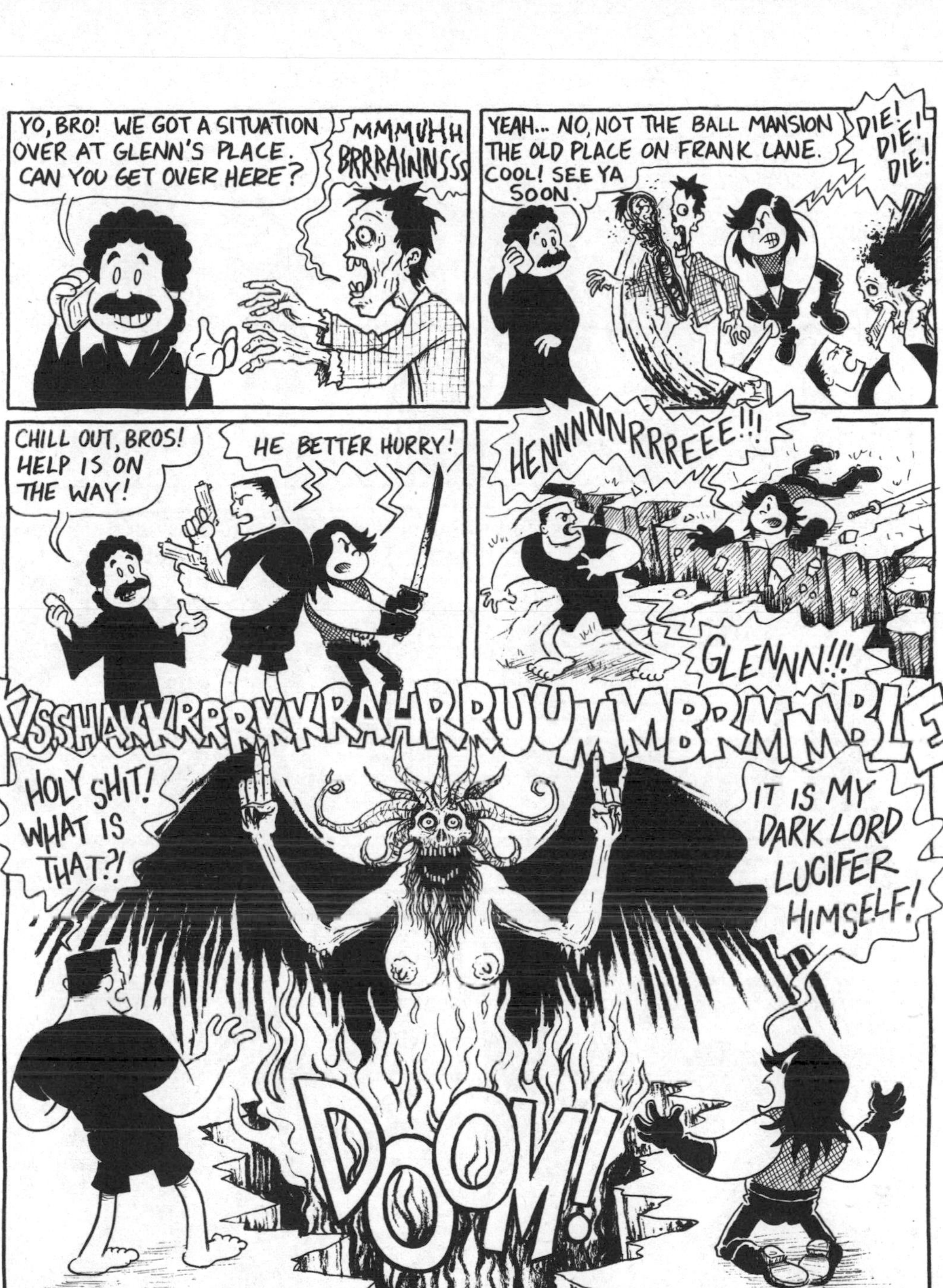

YO, BRO! WE GOT A SITUATION OVER AT GLENN'S PLACE. CAN YOU GET OVER HERE?
MMMUHH BRRRAINNSSS
YEAH... NO, NOT THE BALL MANSION THE OLD PLACE ON FRANK LANE. COOL! SEE YA SOON.
DIE! DIE! DIE!
CHILL OUT, BROS! HELP IS ON THE WAY!
HE BETTER HURRY!
HENNNNNRRREEE!!!
GLENNN!!!
KISSHAKKRRRKKRAHRRUUMMBRMMBLE
HOLY SHIT! WHAT IS THAT?!
IT IS MY DARK LORD LUCIFER HIMSELF!
DOOM!

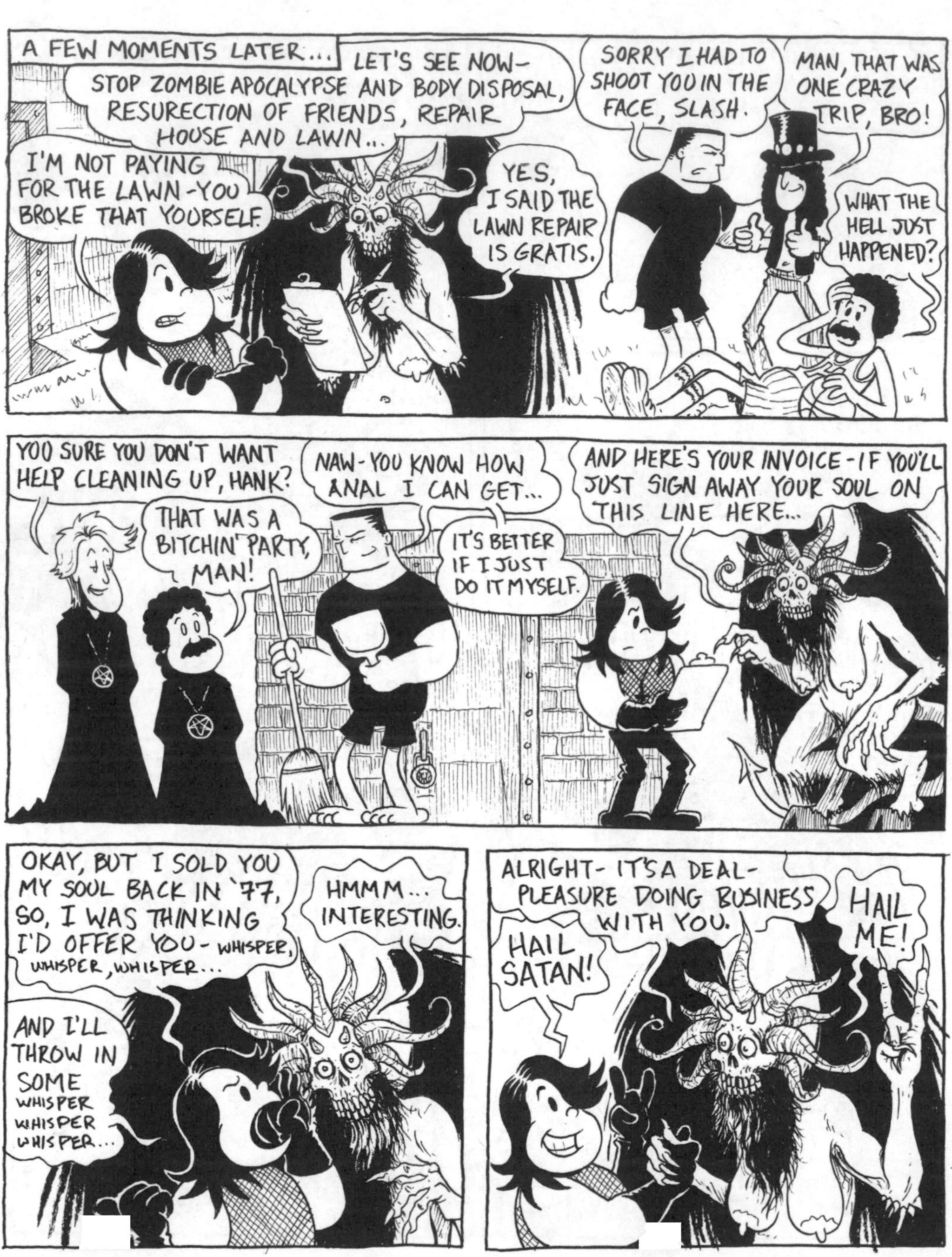

A FEW MOMENTS LATER...
LET'S SEE NOW- STOP ZOMBIE APOCALYPSE AND BODY DISPOSAL, RESURECTION OF FRIENDS, REPAIR HOUSE AND LAWN...
I'M NOT PAYING FOR THE LAWN-YOU BROKE THAT YOURSELF.
YES, I SAID THE LAWN REPAIR IS GRATIS.
SORRY I HAD TO SHOOT YOU IN THE FACE, SLASH.
MAN, THAT WAS ONE CRAZY TRIP, BRO!
WHAT THE HELL JUST HAPPENED?
YOU SURE YOU DON'T WANT HELP CLEANING UP, HANK?
THAT WAS A BITCHIN' PARTY, MAN!
NAW-YOU KNOW HOW ANAL I CAN GET...
IT'S BETTER IF I JUST DO IT MYSELF.
AND HERE'S YOUR INVOICE-IF YOU'LL JUST SIGN AWAY YOUR SOUL ON THIS LINE HERE...
OKAY, BUT I SOLD YOU MY SOUL BACK IN '77, SO, I WAS THINKING I'D OFFER YOU- WHISPER, WHISPER, WHISPER...
HMMM... INTERESTING.
AND I'LL THROW IN SOME WHISPER WHISPER WHISPER...
ALRIGHT- IT'S A DEAL- PLEASURE DOING BUSINESS WITH YOU.
HAIL SATAN!
HAIL ME!

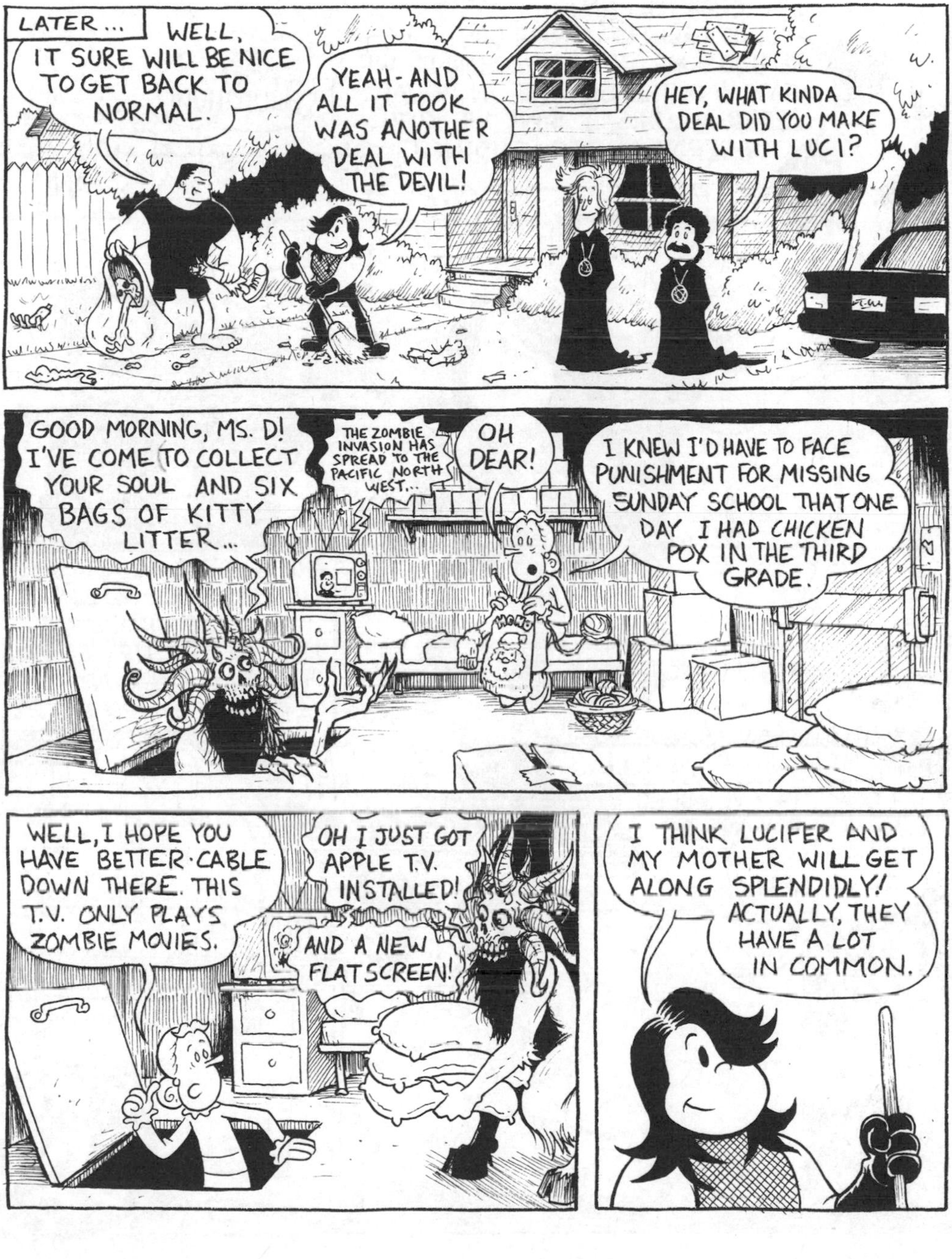
LATER...
WELL, IT SURE WILL BE NICE TO GET BACK TO NORMAL.
YEAH - AND ALL IT TOOK WAS ANOTHER DEAL WITH THE DEVIL!
HEY, WHAT KINDA DEAL DID YOU MAKE WITH LUCI?
GOOD MORNING, MS. D! I'VE COME TO COLLECT YOUR SOUL AND SIX BAGS OF KITTY LITTER...
THE ZOMBIE INVASION HAS SPREAD TO THE PACIFIC NORTH WEST...
OH DEAR!
I KNEW I'D HAVE TO FACE PUNISHMENT FOR MISSING SUNDAY SCHOOL THAT ONE DAY I HAD CHICKEN POX IN THE THIRD GRADE.
WELL, I HOPE YOU HAVE BETTER CABLE DOWN THERE. THIS T.V. ONLY PLAYS ZOMBIE MOVIES.
OH I JUST GOT APPLE T.V. INSTALLED!
AND A NEW FLATSCREEN!
I THINK LUCIFER AND MY MOTHER WILL GET ALONG SPLENDIDLY!
ACTUALLY, THEY HAVE A LOT IN COMMON.

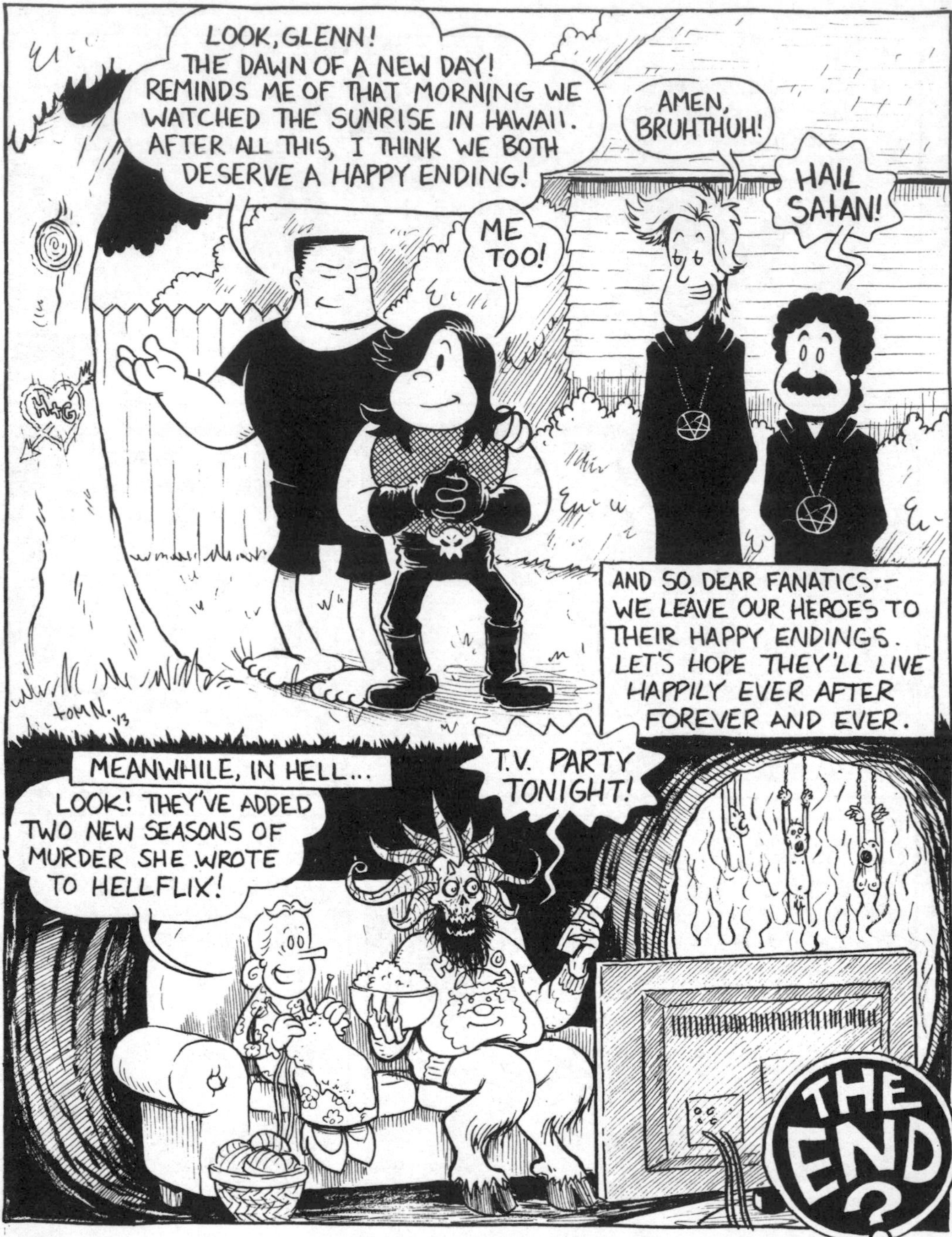
LOOK, GLENN! THE DAWN OF A NEW DAY! REMINDS ME OF THAT MORNING WE WATCHED THE SUNRISE IN HAWAII. AFTER ALL THIS, I THINK WE BOTH DESERVE A HAPPY ENDING!
ME TOO!
AMEN, BRUHTHUH!
HAIL SATAN!
H+G
tomN. '13
AND SO, DEAR FANATICS-- WE LEAVE OUR HEROES TO THEIR HAPPY ENDINGS. LET'S HOPE THEY'LL LIVE HAPPILY EVER AFTER FOREVER AND EVER.
MEANWHILE, IN HELL...
LOOK! THEY'VE ADDED TWO NEW SEASONS OF MURDER SHE WROTE TO HELLFLIX!
T.V. PARTY TONIGHT!
THE END ?

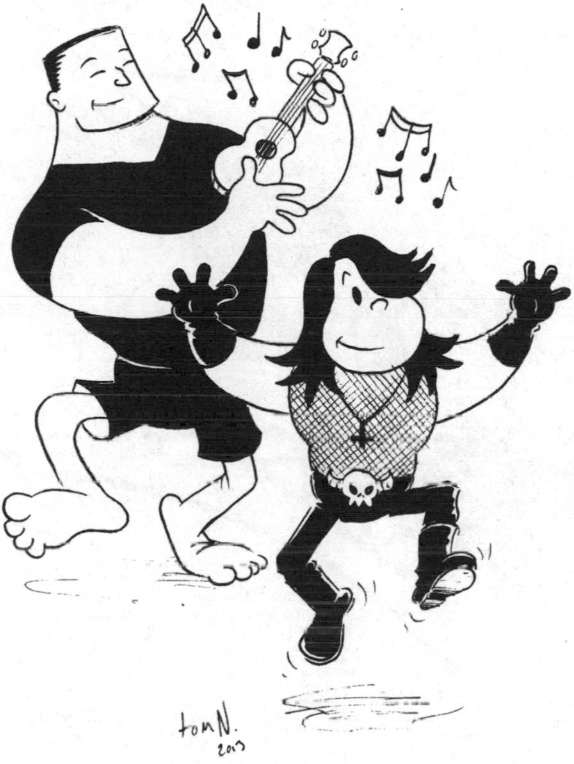
tomN.
2013

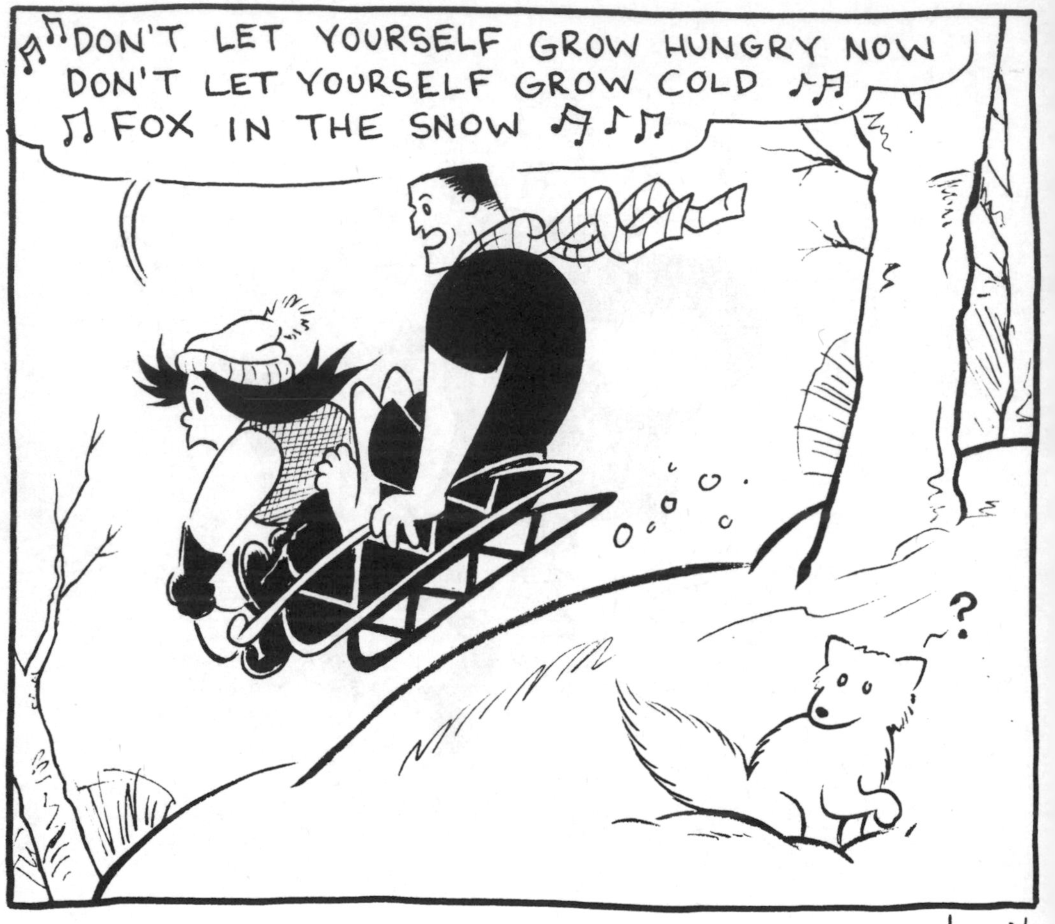
DON'T LET YOURSELF GROW HUNGRY NOW
DON'T LET YOURSELF GROW COLD
FOX IN THE SNOW
?
tom N. 2013

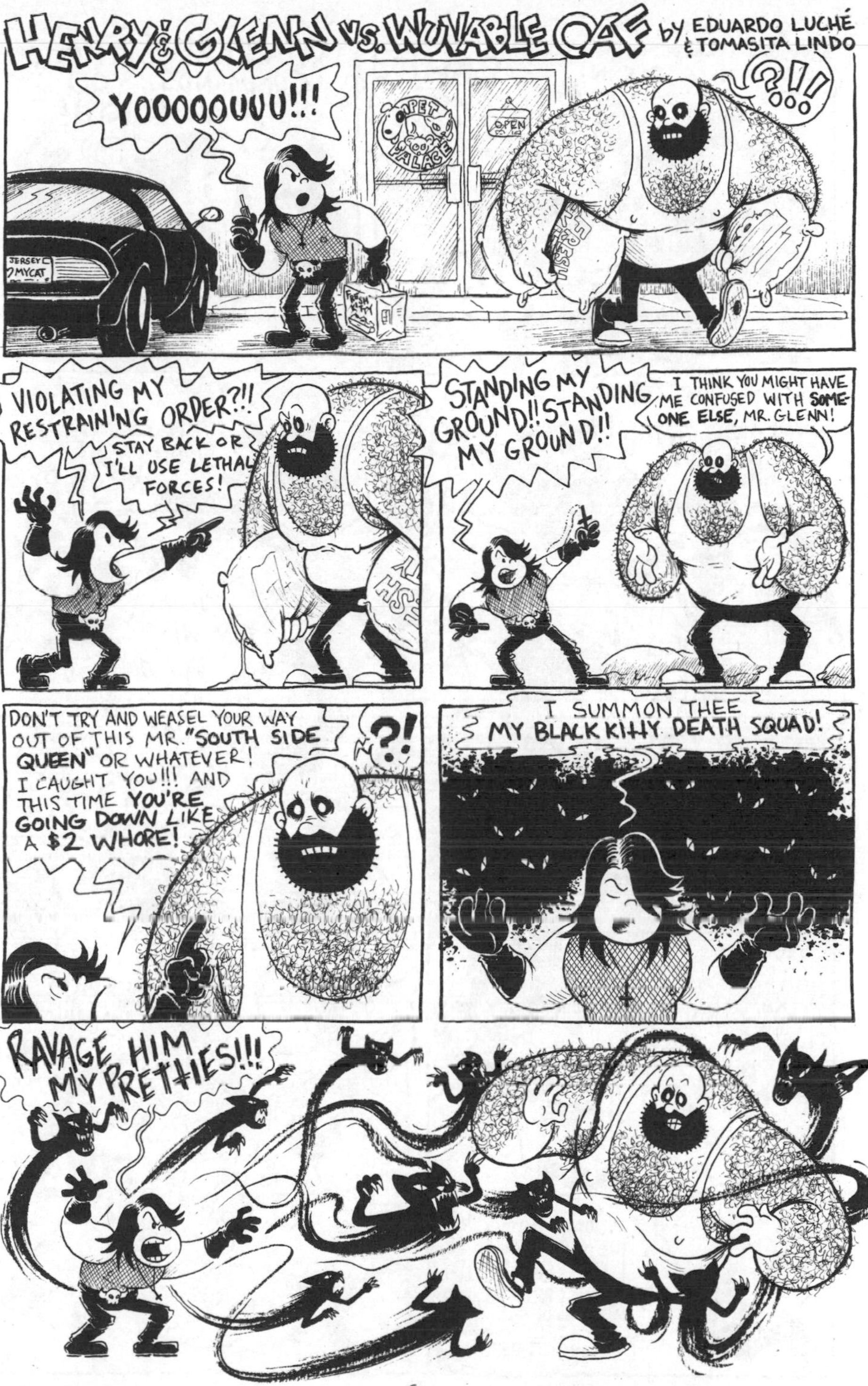
HENRY & GLENN vs. WUVABLE OAF by EDUARDO LUCHÉ & TOMASITA LINDO
YOOOOOUUU!!!
?!!
PET PALACE
OPEN
VIOLATING MY RESTRAINING ORDER?!!
STAY BACK OR I'LL USE LETHAL FORCES!
STANDING MY GROUND!! STANDING MY GROUND!!
I THINK YOU MIGHT HAVE ME CONFUSED WITH SOME-ONE ELSE, MR. GLENN!
DON'T TRY AND WEASEL YOUR WAY OUT OF THIS MR. "SOUTH SIDE QUEEN" OR WHATEVER! I CAUGHT YOU!!! AND THIS TIME YOU'RE GOING DOWN LIKE A $2 WHORE!
?!
I SUMMON THEE MY BLACK KITTY DEATH SQUAD!
RAVAGE HIM MY PRETTIES!!!

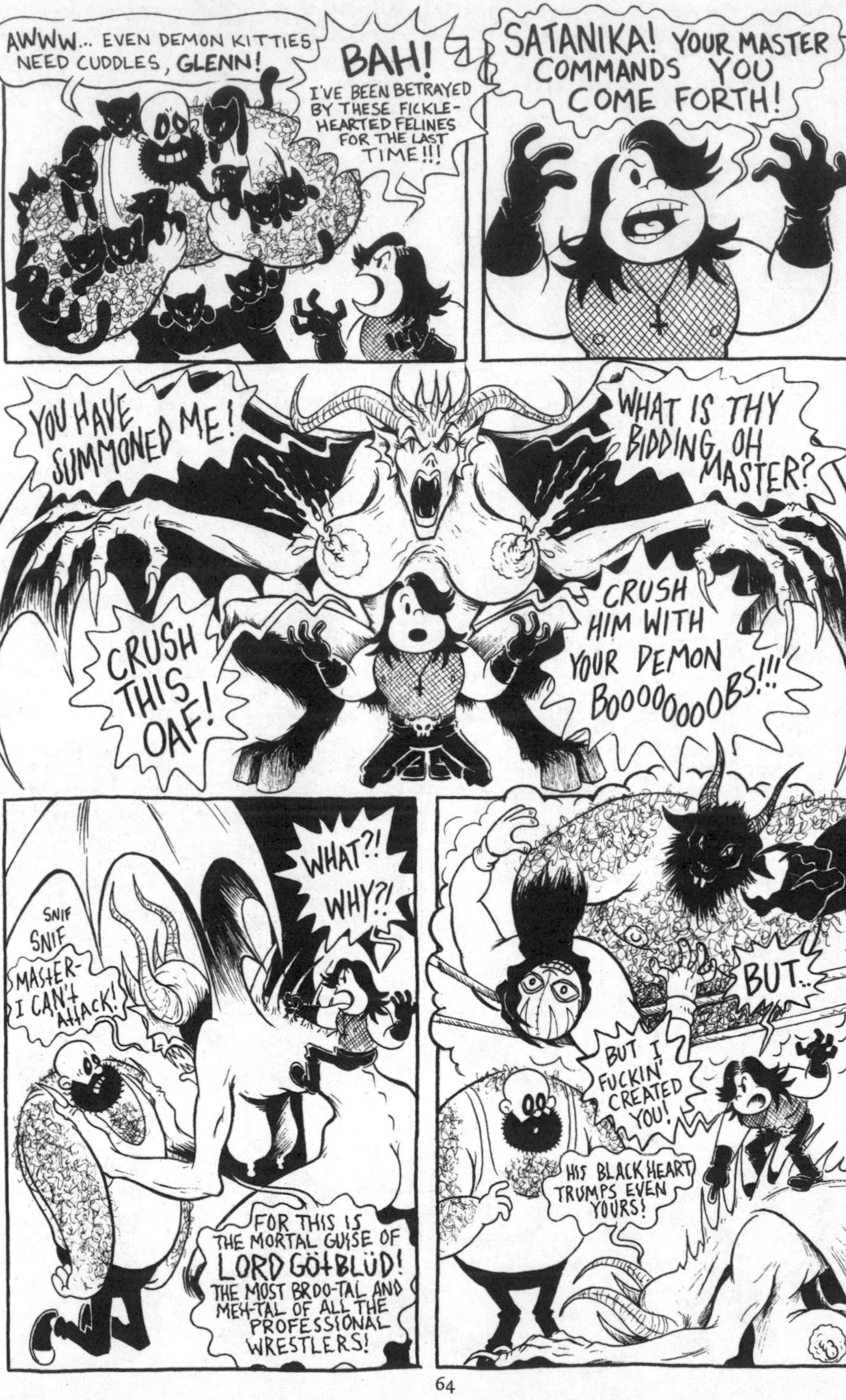
AWWW... EVEN DEMON KITTIES NEED CUDDLES, GLENN!
BAH! I'VE BEEN BETRAYED BY THESE FICKLE-HEARTED FELINES FOR THE LAST TIME!!!
SATANIKA! YOUR MASTER COMMANDS YOU COME FORTH!
YOU HAVE SUMMONED ME!
WHAT IS THY BIDDING OH MASTER?
CRUSH THIS OAF!
CRUSH HIM WITH YOUR DEMON BOOOOOOOOOBS!!!
WHAT?! WHY?!
SNIF SNIF
MASTER- I CAN'T ATTACK!
FOR THIS IS THE MORTAL GUISE OF LORD GÖTBLÜD! THE MOST BROO-TAL AND MEH-TAL OF ALL THE PROFESSIONAL WRESTLERS!
BUT...
BUT I FUCKIN' CREATED YOU!
HIS BLACK HEART TRUMPS EVEN YOURS!

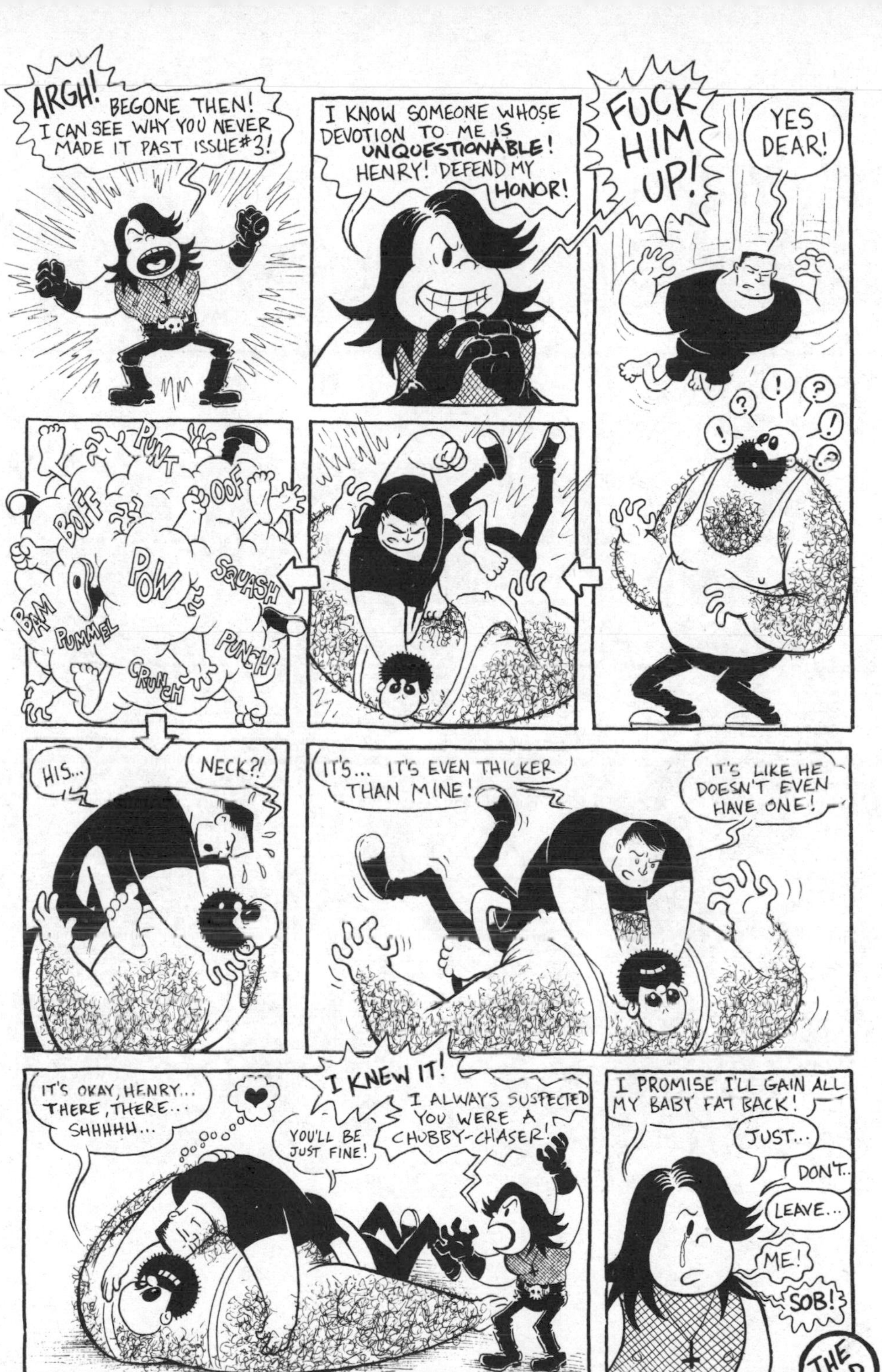

ARGH! BEGONE THEN! I CAN SEE WHY YOU NEVER MADE IT PAST ISSUE #3!
I KNOW SOMEONE WHOSE DEVOTION TO ME IS UNQUESTIONABLE! HENRY! DEFEND MY HONOR!
FUCK HIM UP!
YES DEAR!
?
!
?
!
?
PUNT
OOF
BOFF
POW
SQUASH
BAM
PUMMEL
PUNCH
CRUNCH
HIS...
NECK?!
IT'S... IT'S EVEN THICKER THAN MINE!
IT'S LIKE HE DOESN'T EVEN HAVE ONE!
IT'S OKAY, HENRY... THERE, THERE... SHHHHH...
I KNEW IT!
I ALWAYS SUSPECTED YOU WERE A CHUBBY-CHASER!
YOU'LL BE JUST FINE!
I PROMISE I'LL GAIN ALL MY BABY FAT BACK!
JUST...
DON'T...
LEAVE...
ME!
SOB!
THE END

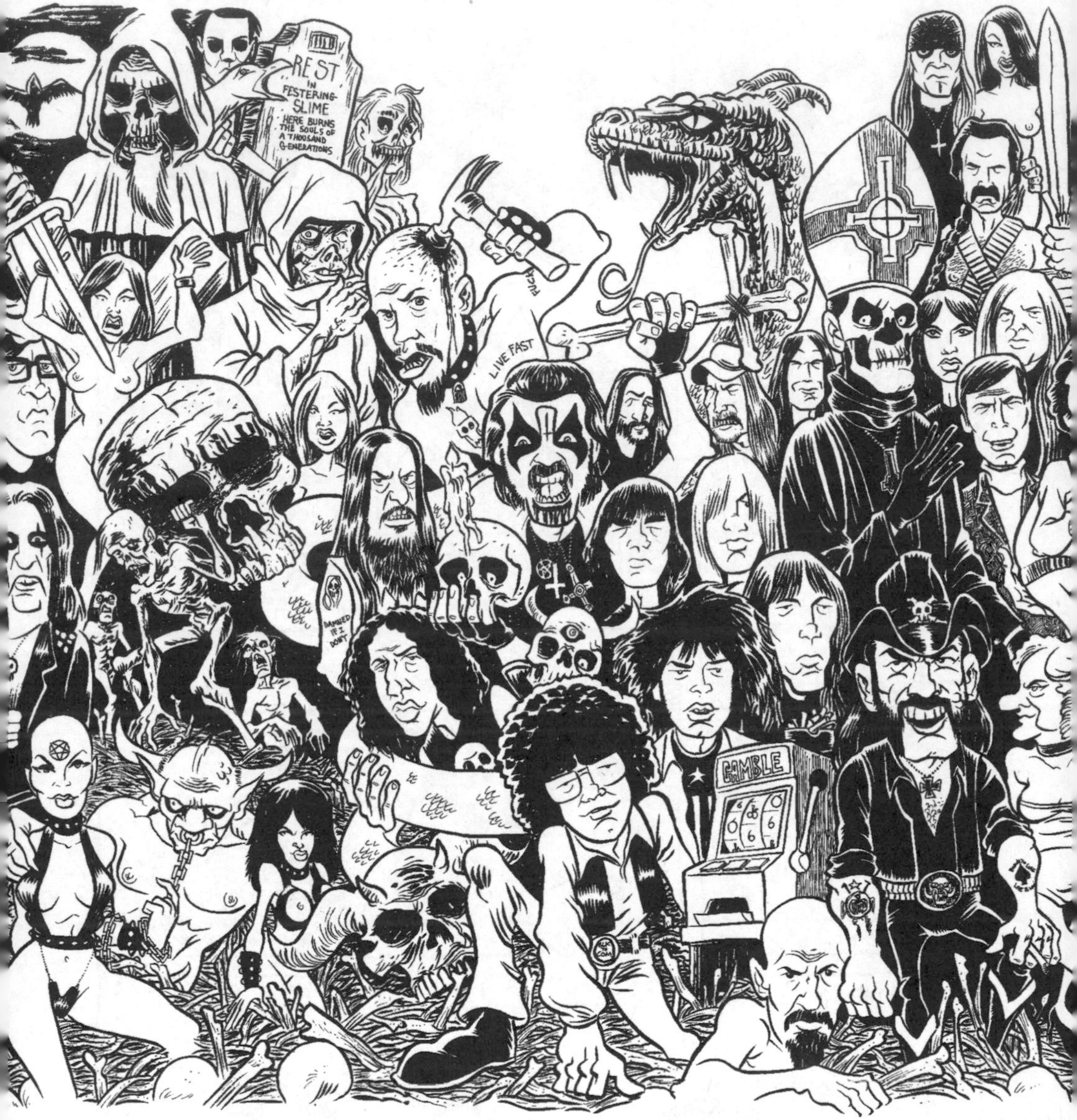
REST IN FESTERING SLIME
HERE BURNS THE SOULS OF A THOUSAND GENERATIONS
FUCK
LIVE FAST
DAMNED IF I DON'T
GAMBLE

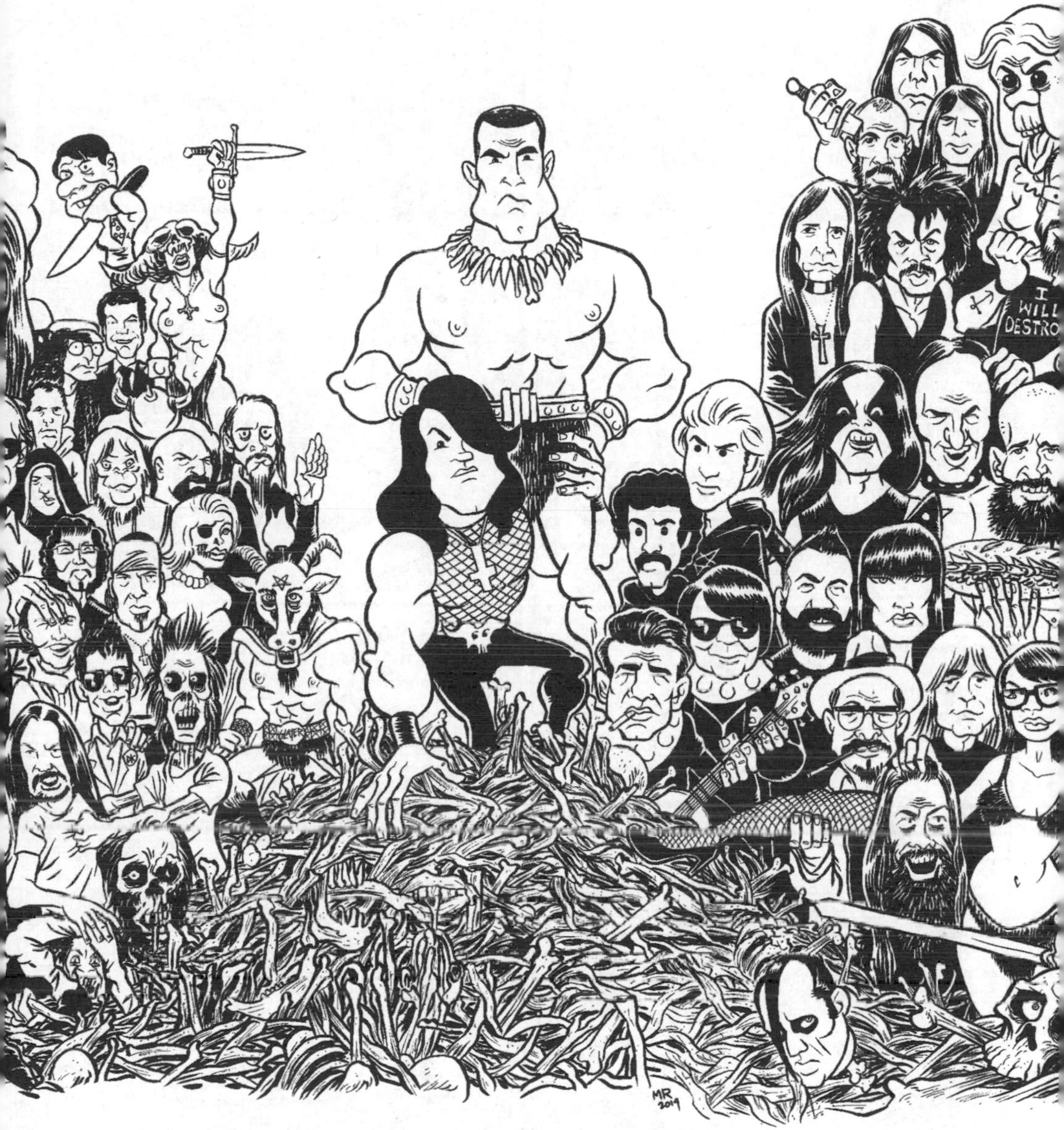
I
WILL
DESTRO
MR
2019

MARK RUDOLPH

"THE NEELY STRIP"
WRITTEN BY M. MOSELEY SMITH
DRAWN BY REUBEN STORGY
YAP?
HEY MIKE. DO YOU WANNA DO A COMIC FOR A HENRY N' GLENN BOOK? NEELY WUZ TALKIN' TO ME ABOUT IT AT SHORT RUN.
AW MAN
I DON'T KNOW..
I CAN'T STAND HENRY OR GLENN. THAT STUFF KINDA TAKES SOME ADMIRATION FOR THE GUYS TO DO RIGHT.
REUBEN, I THINK I'D PREFER TO JUST KEEP PRETENDING THEY DON'T EXIST.
C'MANN DUDE, YOU CAN PROBABLY COME UP WITH SOMETHING.
YEAH, BUT WHY WOULD I? THAT SOUNDS AS APPEALING TO ME AS WRITING A COMIC ABOUT TED NUGENT BOFFING DAVID LEE ROTH.
RASCALLY BOYS IN THE YARD
HAW HAW! HOLY SHIT! WRITE 'EM BOTH!
NAH BUDDY, FERGIT THAT. LET'S DO A STRIP ABOUT ROB HALFORD AND THE DUDE FROM METAL CHURCH TAKING A BATH TOGETHER.
BAD BOYS RUNNIN WILD

NO DUDE, I GOT IT! COMIC ABOUT TYPE-O NEGATIVE ERA PETER STEELE SEDUCING CARNIVORE ERA PETER STEELE!
HA HA HA! HO!!
TOM OF FINLANDIA MEETS THE ROD WARRIOR! HO! MAN, KROGER IS FREKKIN' OUT. GOD DAMN GRAY CAT IS PROBABLY OUT THERE.
NAUGHTY BOYS SO SEXUAL
EAT
GAMES
CROMIX
GOD-FUCKING-DAMMIT! IT'S HENRY AND GLENN IN THE FRONT YARD AGAIN! I GOTTA CALL YOU BACK DUDE!
TOLDJA DUMMY
GUYS, LEAVE! STOP DOING THIS IN FRONT OF MY HOUSE! PLEASE GO HOME!
GRUNT!
PANT!
SEARCH
WE'LL NEVER STOP, MIKE! WE'LL NEVER STOP!!
WHOOPEE!! WEEE!
DAMN IT ALL!
PLEASE TAKE ME TOO NAUGHTY BOYS
THE END

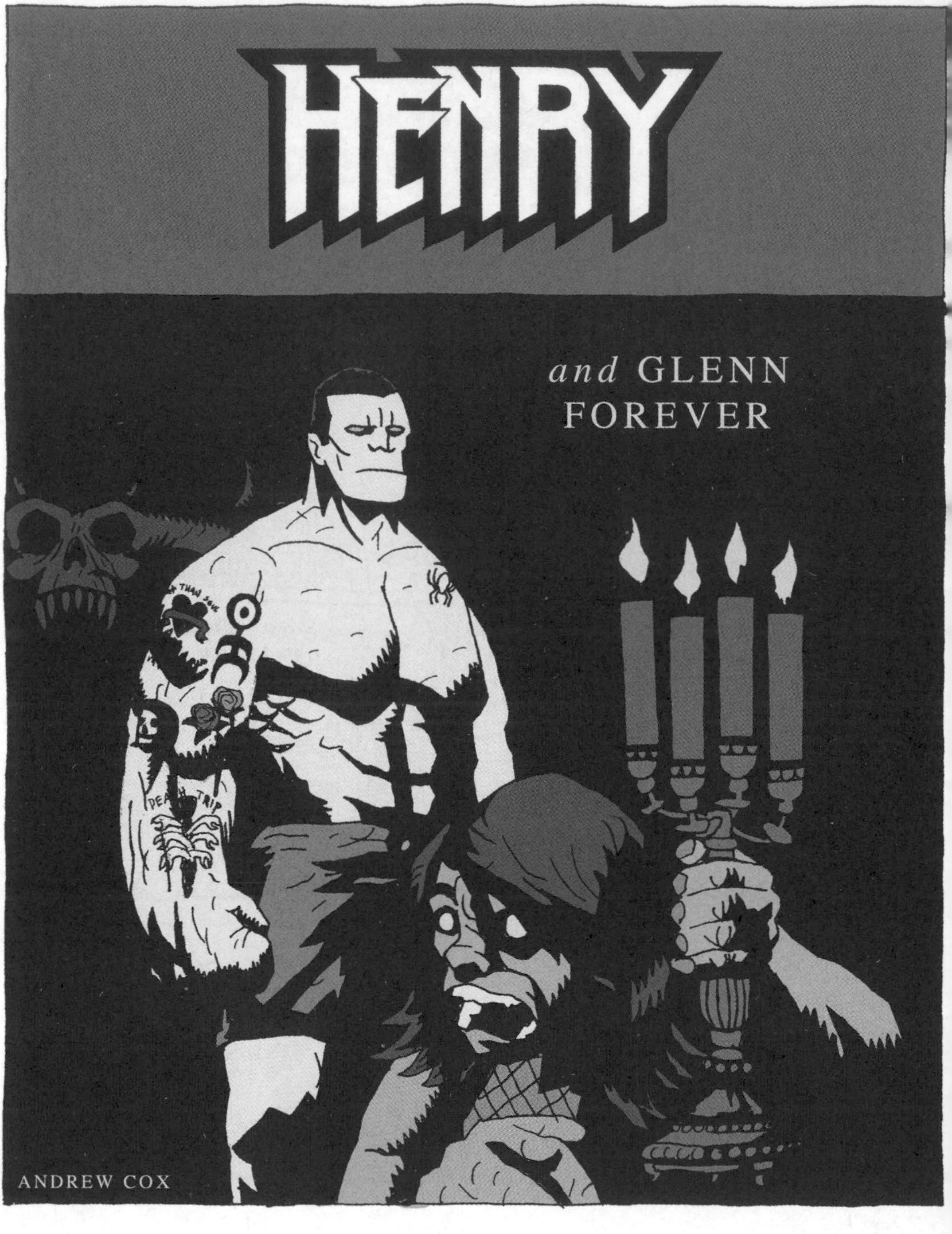
HENRY
and GLENN
FOREVER
ANDREW COX

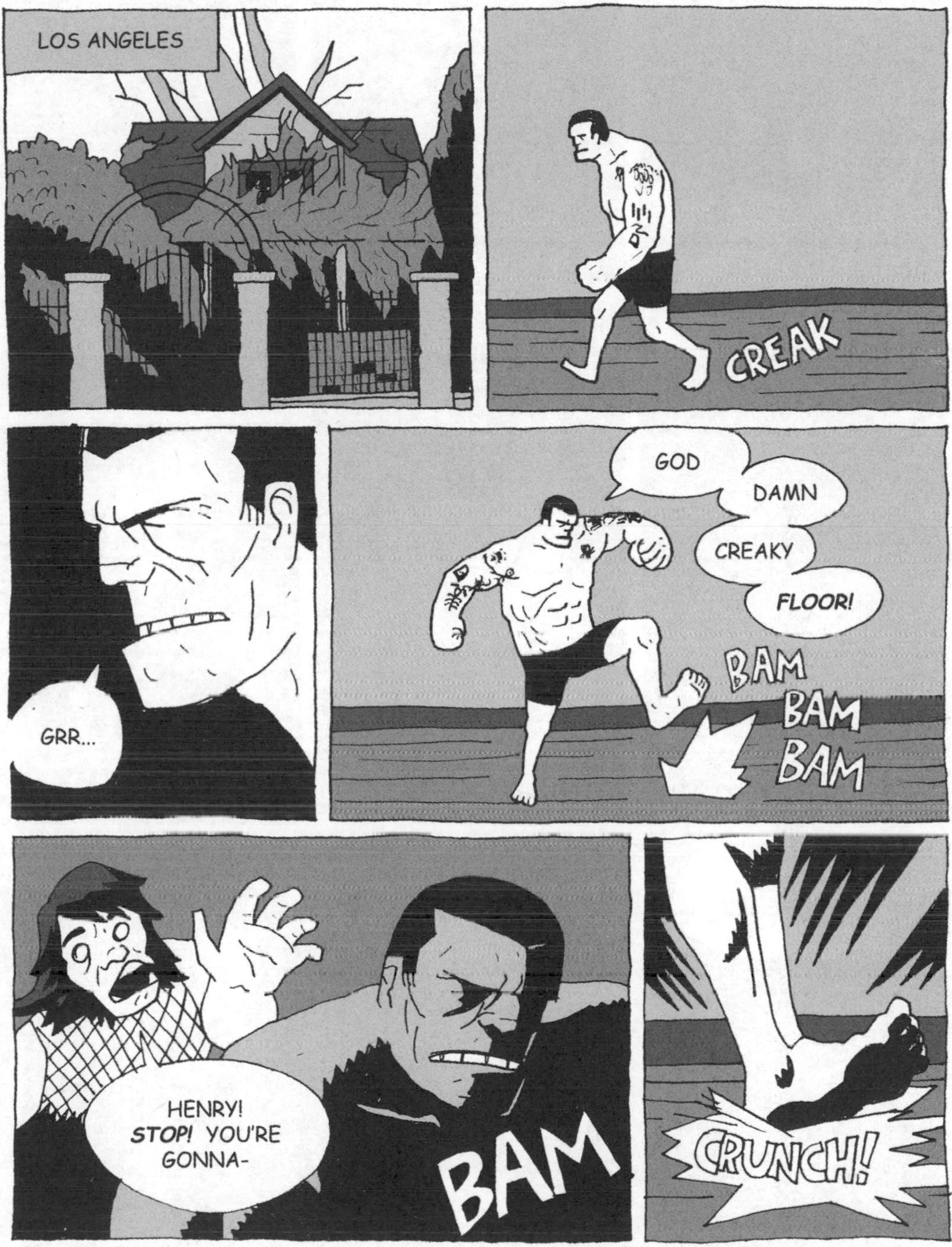
LOS ANGELES
CREAK
GRR...
GOD
DAMN
CREAKY
FLOOR!
BAM
BAM
BAM
HENRY! STOP! YOU'RE GONNA-
BAM
CRUNCH!

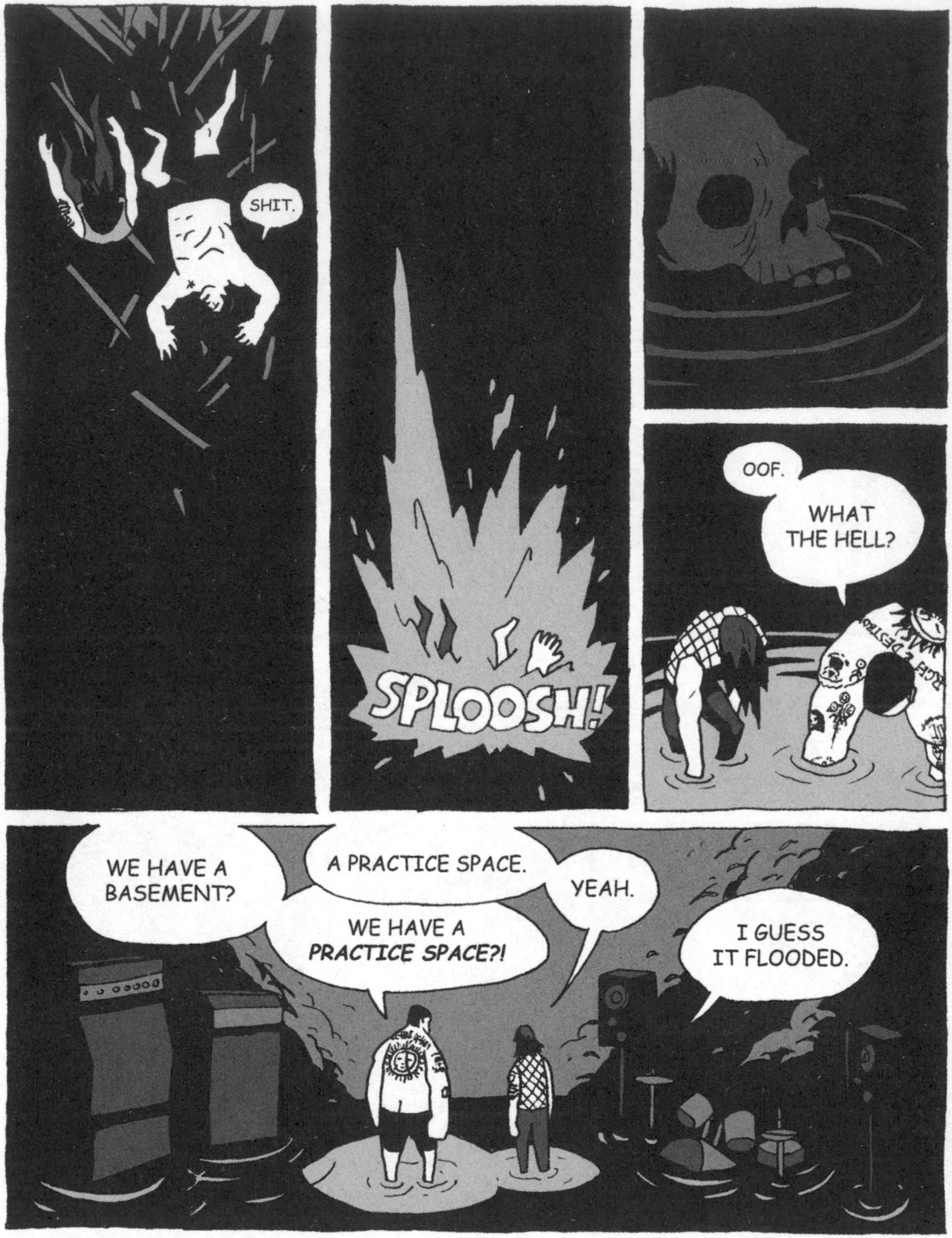
SHIT.
SPLOOSH!
OOF.
WHAT THE HELL?
WE HAVE A BASEMENT?
A PRACTICE SPACE.
WE HAVE A PRACTICE SPACE?!
YEAH.
I GUESS IT FLOODED.

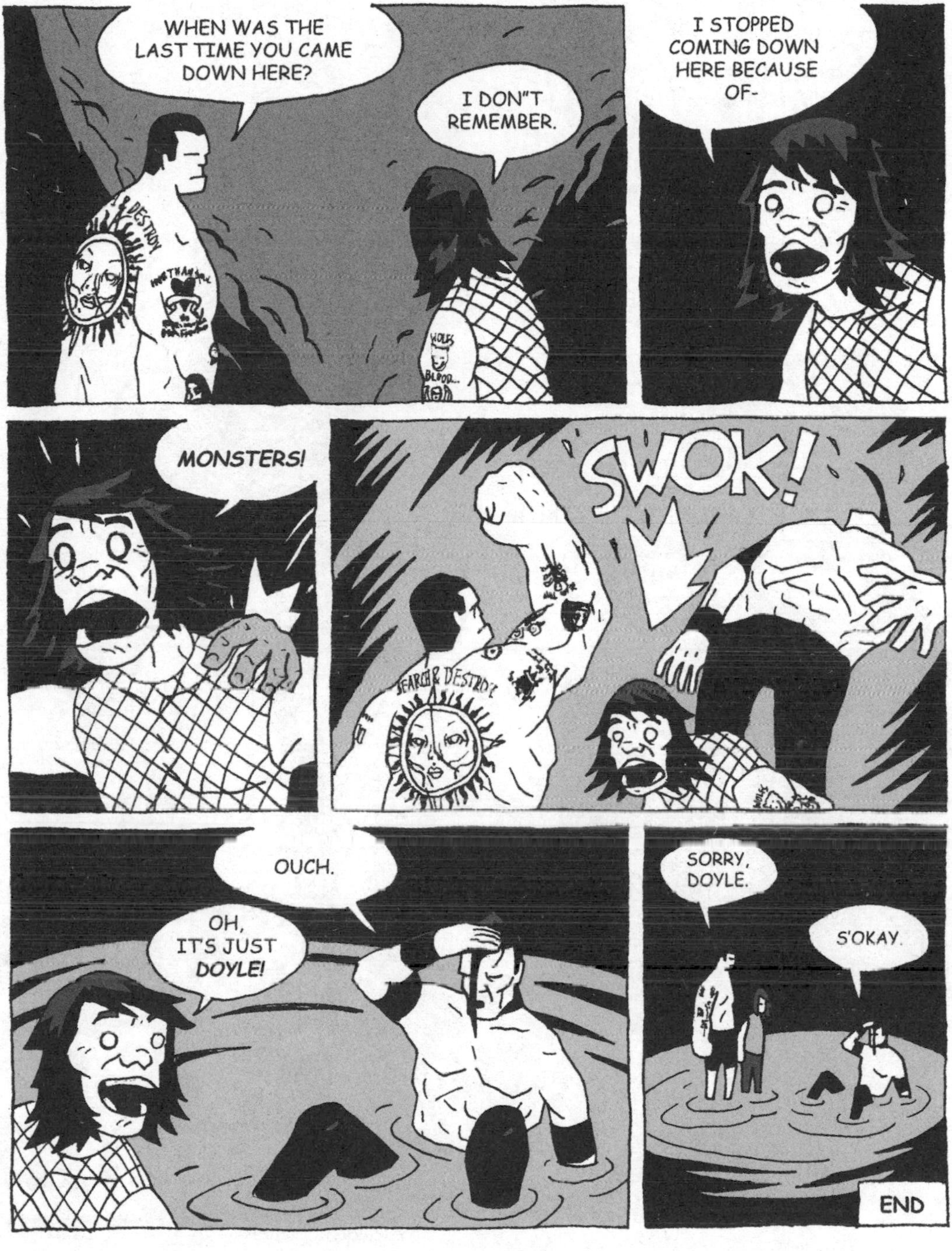
WHEN WAS THE LAST TIME YOU CAME DOWN HERE?
I DON"T REMEMBER.
I STOPPED COMING DOWN HERE BECAUSE OF-
MONSTERS!
SWOK!
OUCH.
OH, IT'S JUST DOYLE!
SORRY, DOYLE.
S'OKAY.
END

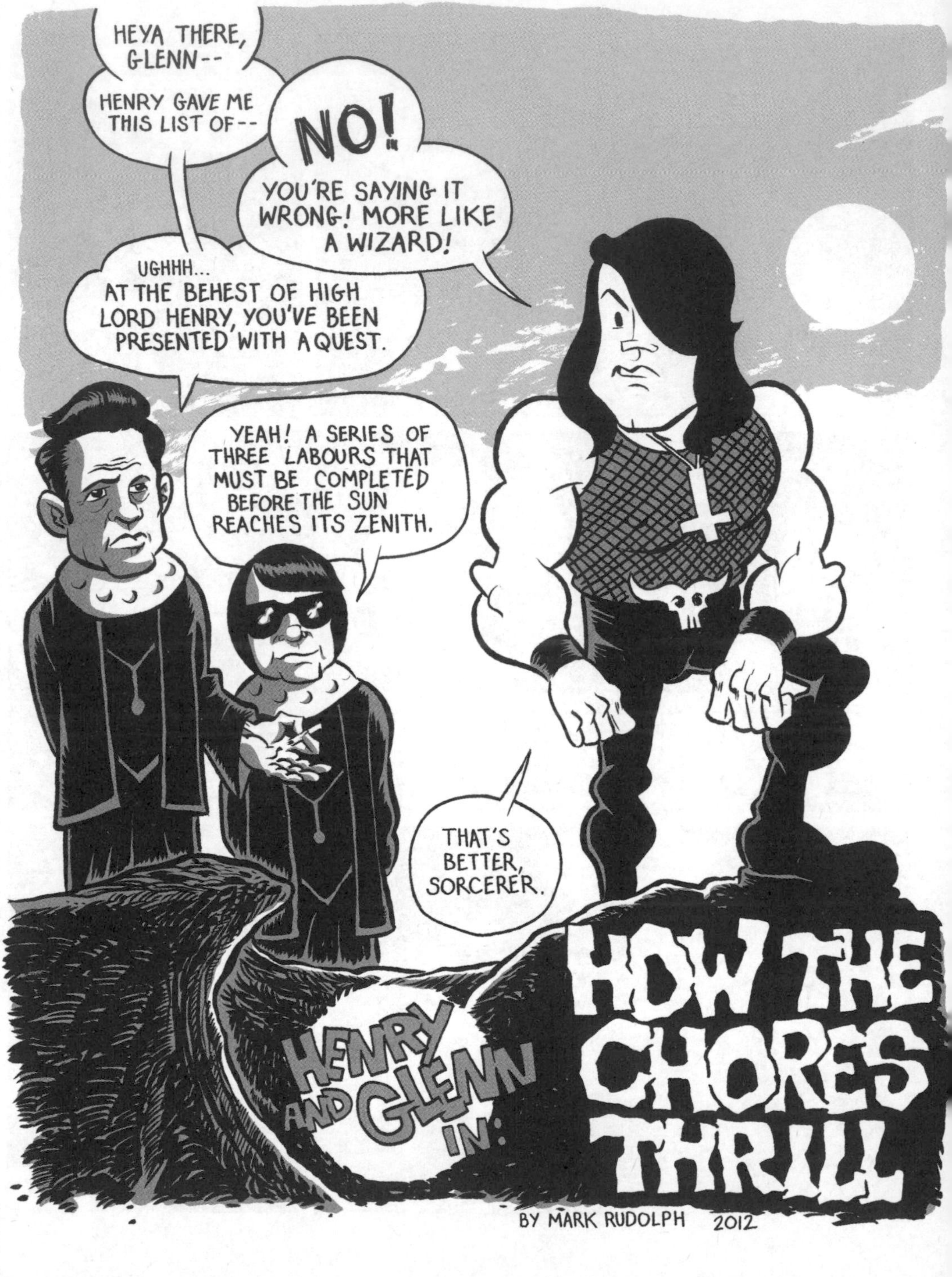
HEYA THERE, GLENN--
HENRY GAVE ME THIS LIST OF--
NO!
YOU'RE SAYING IT WRONG! MORE LIKE A WIZARD!
UGHHH... AT THE BEHEST OF HIGH LORD HENRY, YOU'VE BEEN PRESENTED WITH A QUEST.
YEAH! A SERIES OF THREE LABOURS THAT MUST BE COMPLETED BEFORE THE SUN REACHES ITS ZENITH.
THAT'S BETTER, SORCERER.
HENRY AND GLENN IN:
HOW THE CHORES THRILL
BY MARK RUDOLPH 2012

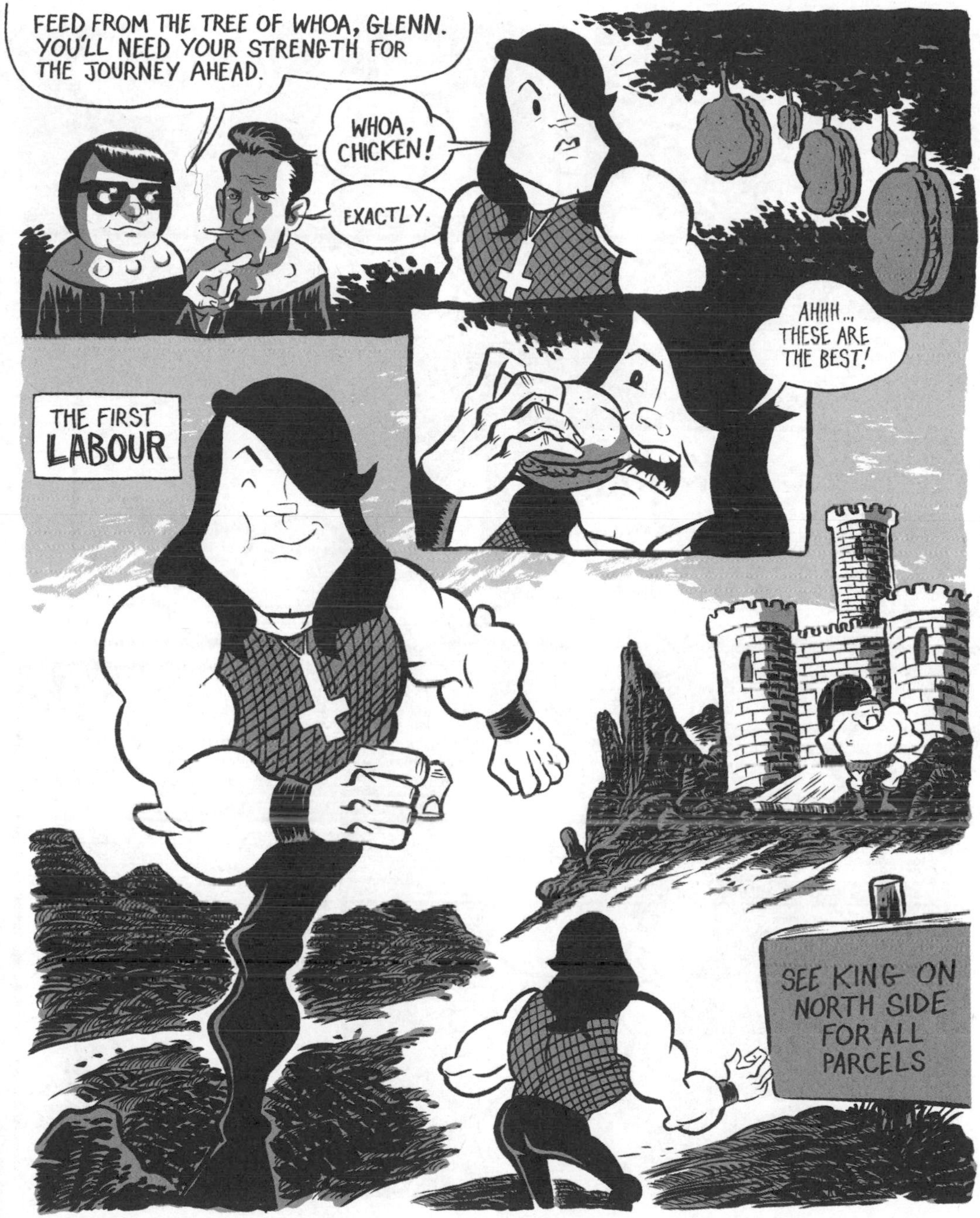
FEED FROM THE TREE OF WHOA, GLENN. YOU'LL NEED YOUR STRENGTH FOR THE JOURNEY AHEAD.
WHOA, CHICKEN!
EXACTLY.
AHHH... THESE ARE THE BEST!
THE FIRST LABOUR
SEE KING ON NORTH SIDE FOR ALL PARCELS

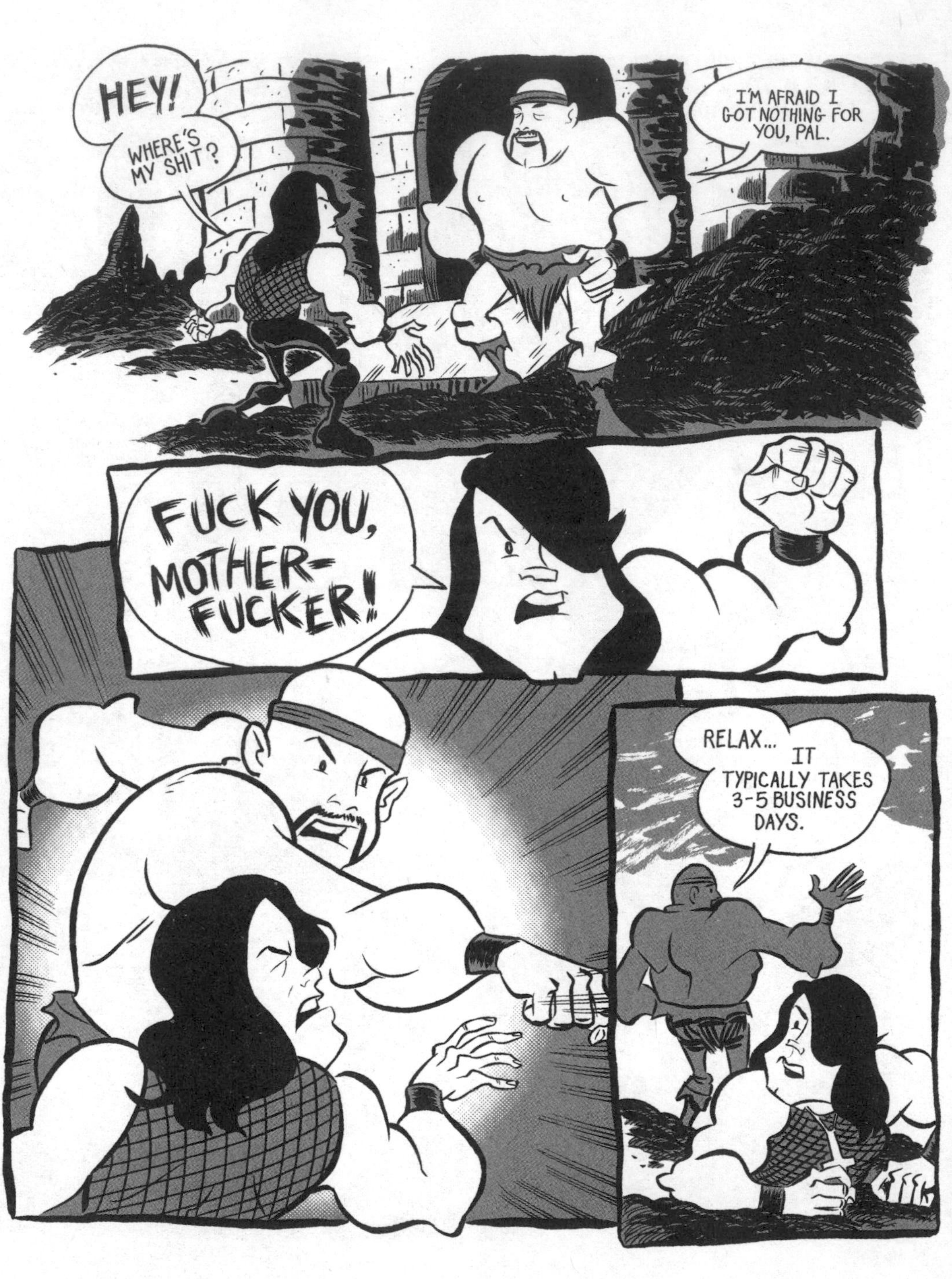
HEY!
WHERE'S MY SHIT?
I'M AFRAID I GOT NOTHING FOR YOU, PAL.
FUCK YOU, MOTHER-FUCKER!
RELAX... IT TYPICALLY TAKES 3-5 BUSINESS DAYS.

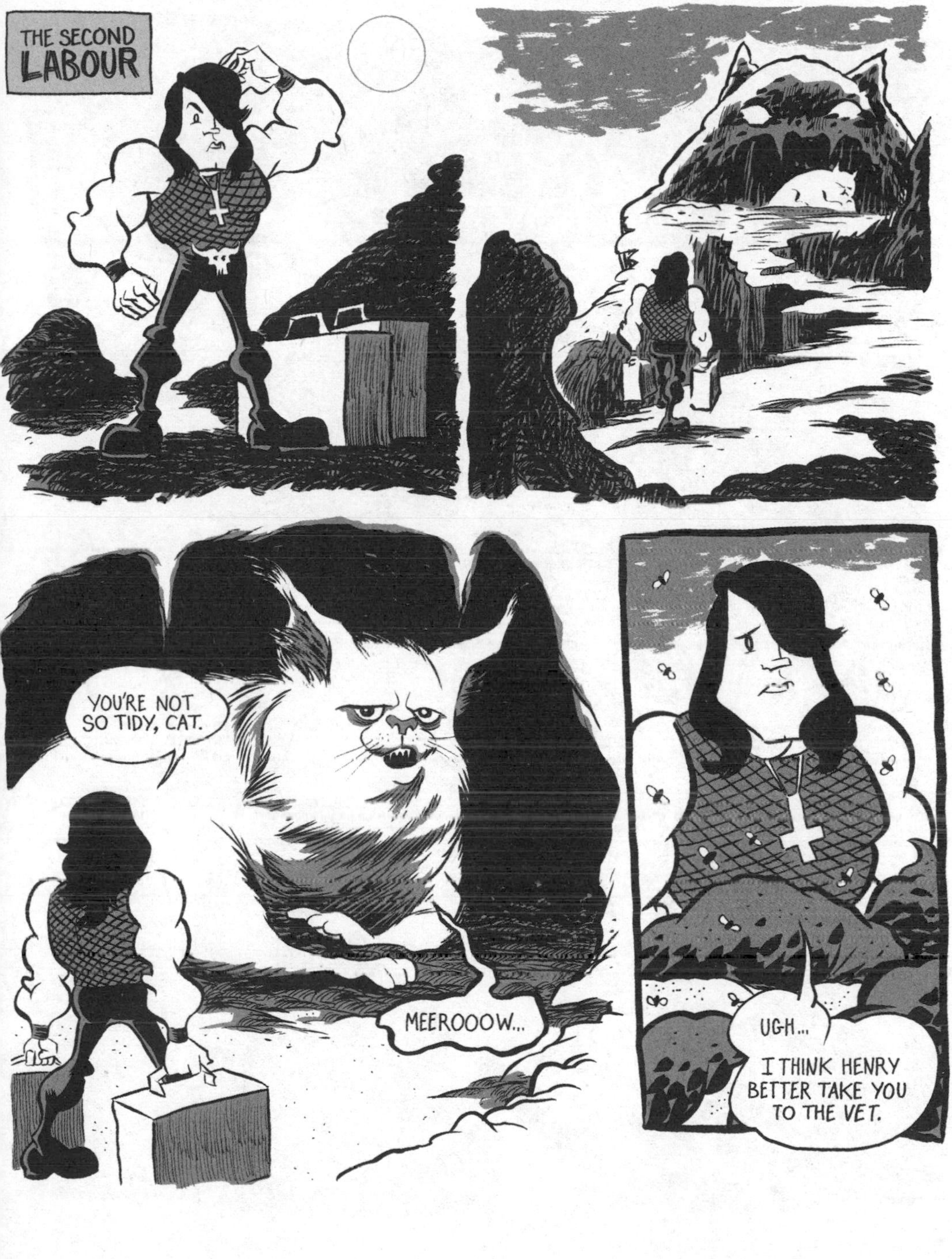
THE SECOND LABOUR
YOU'RE NOT SO TIDY, CAT.
MEEROOOW...
UGH...
I THINK HENRY BETTER TAKE YOU TO THE VET.

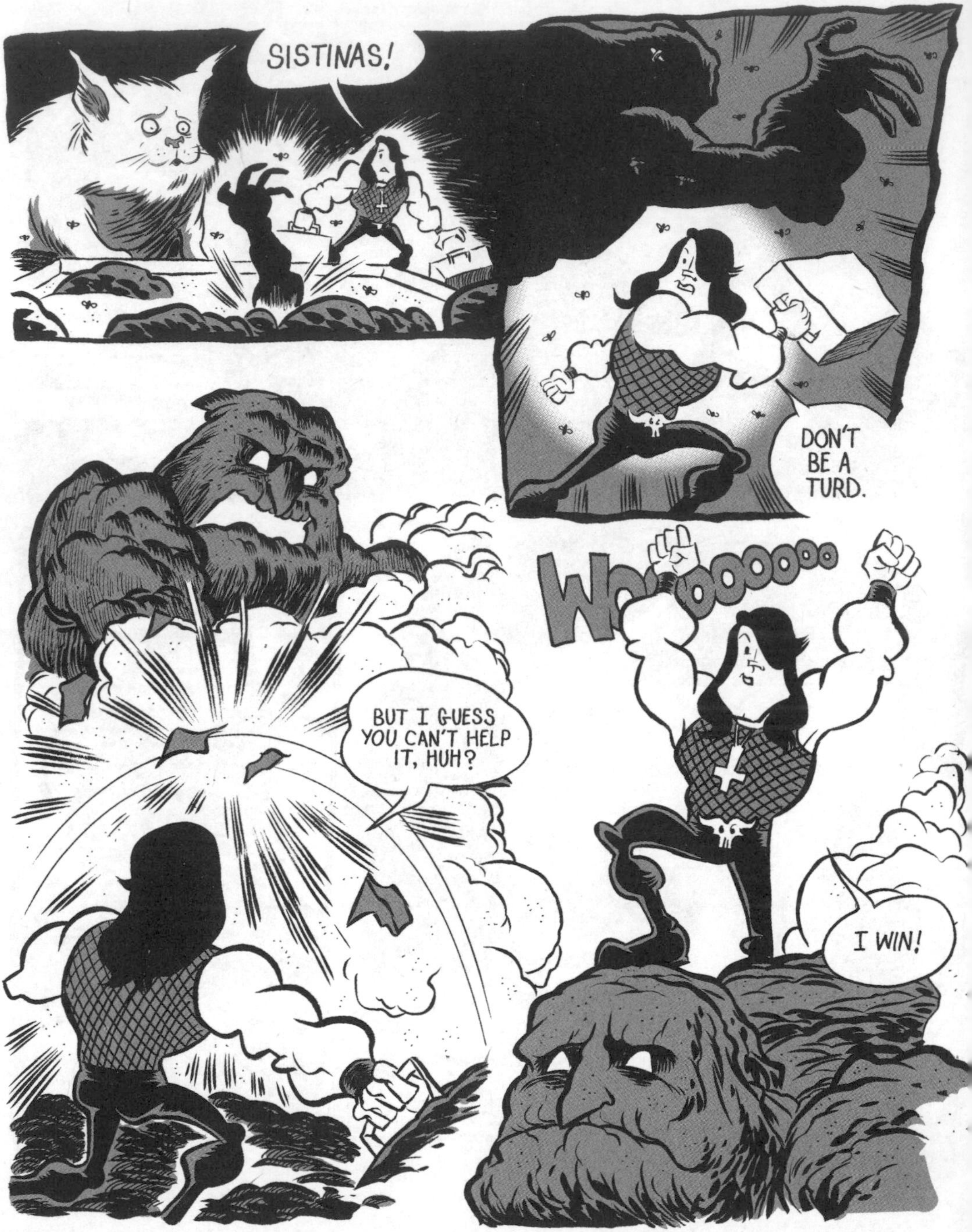
SISTINAS!
DON'T BE A TURD.
BUT I GUESS YOU CAN'T HELP IT, HUH?
WOOOOOOO
I WIN!

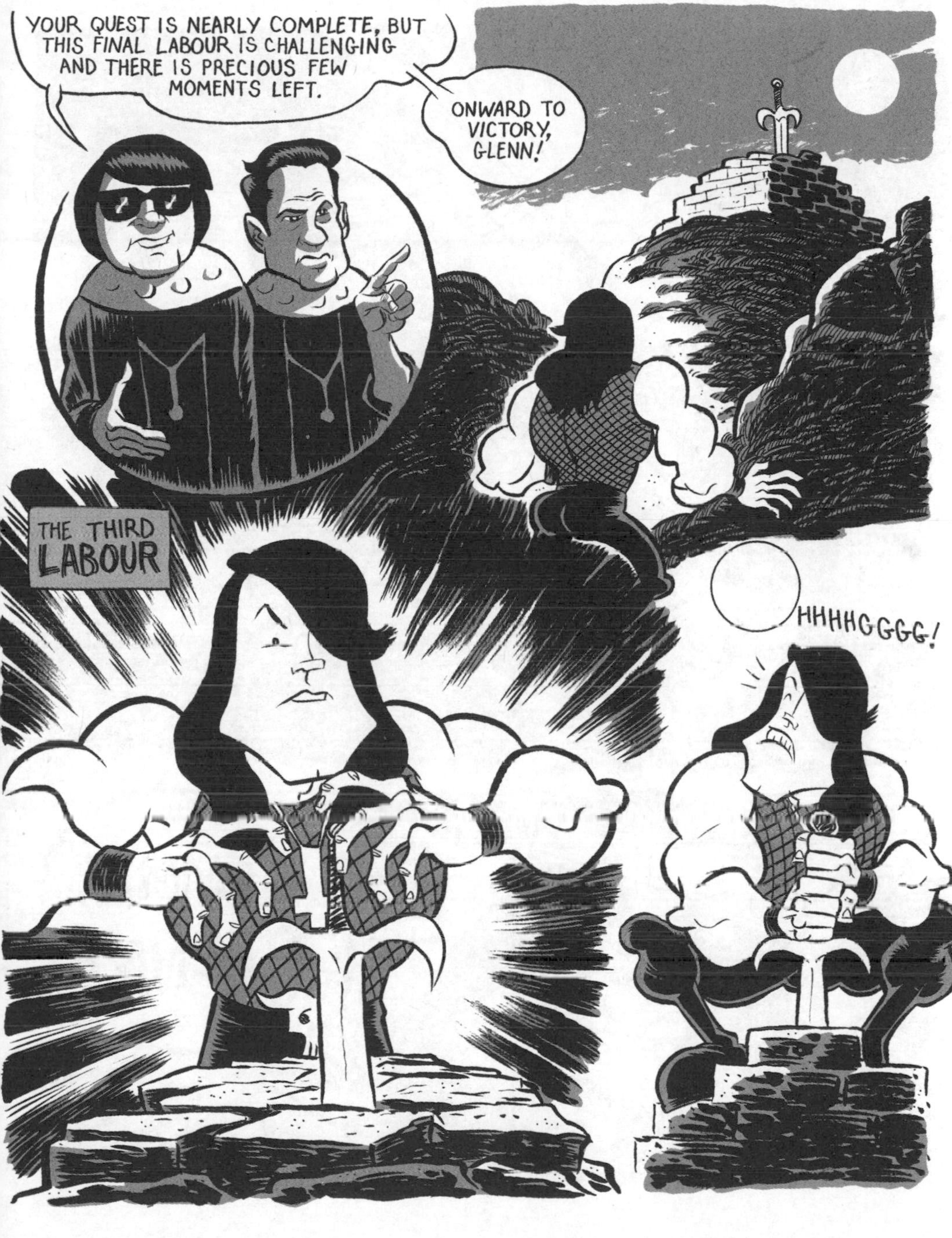
YOUR QUEST IS NEARLY COMPLETE, BUT THIS FINAL LABOUR IS CHALLENGING AND THERE IS PRECIOUS FEW MOMENTS LEFT.
ONWARD TO VICTORY, GLENN!
THE THIRD LABOUR
HHHHGGGG!

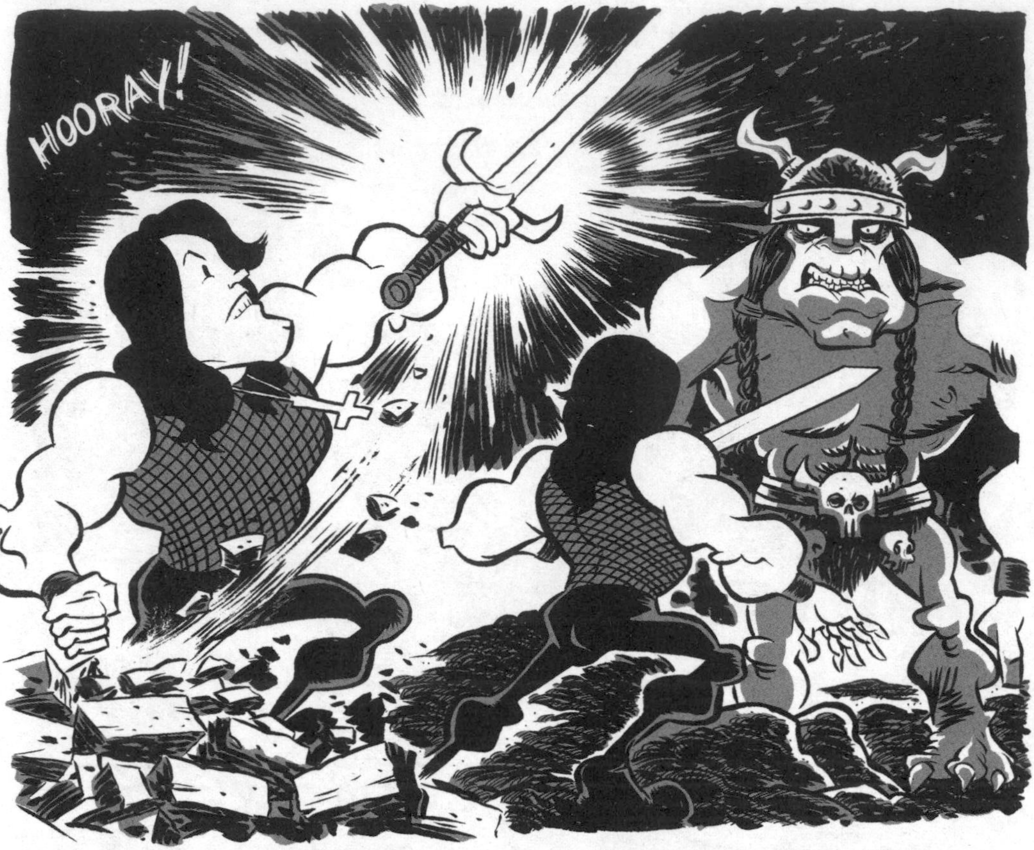
HOORAY!

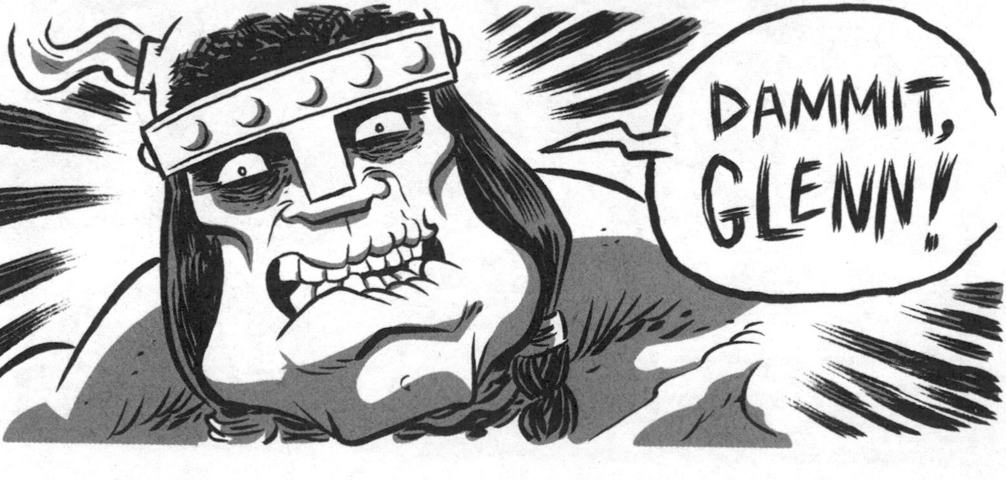
DAMMIT, GLENN!

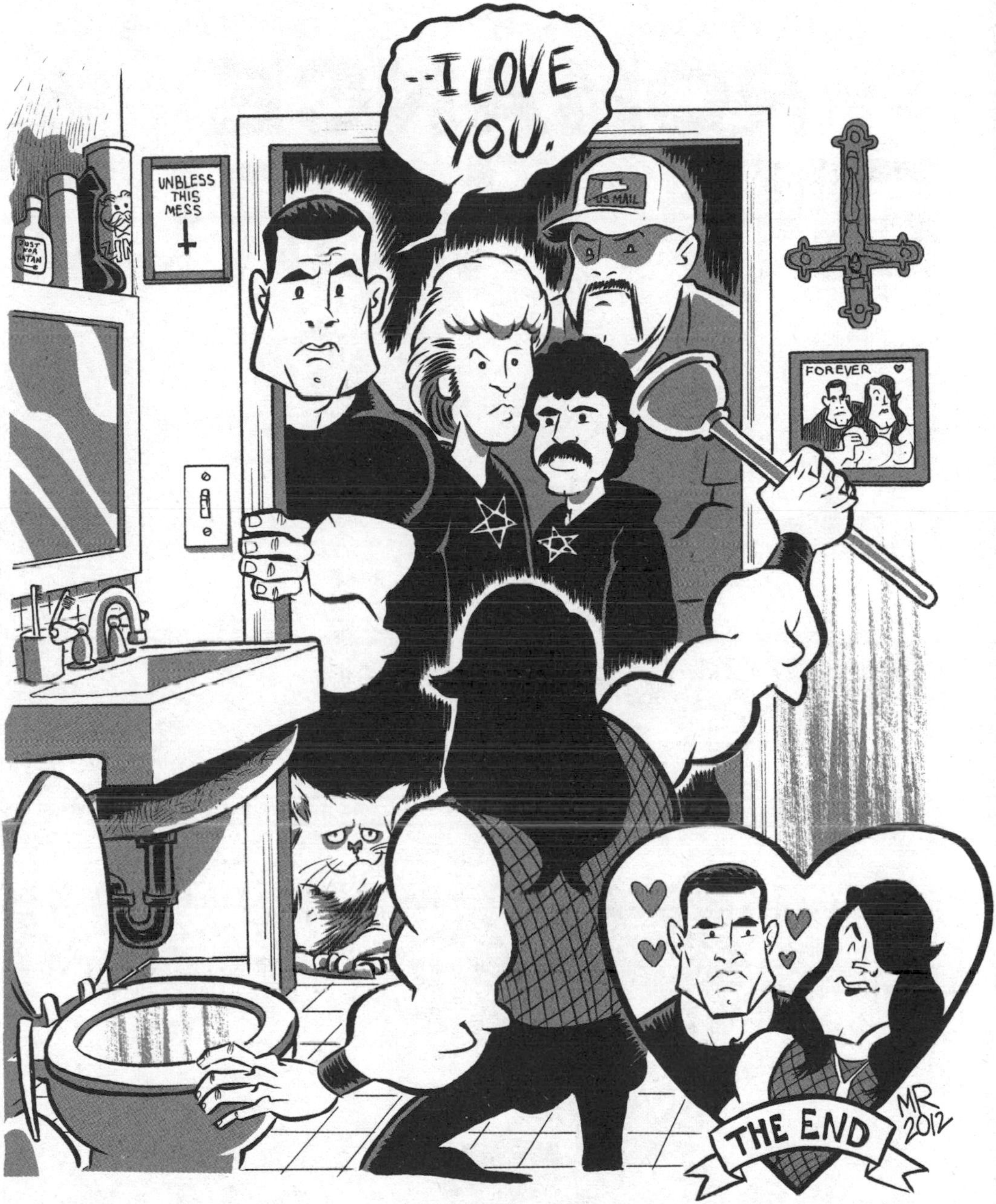
--I LOVE YOU.
UNBLESS THIS MESS
JUST FOR SATAN
US MAIL
FOREVER
THE END
MR 2012

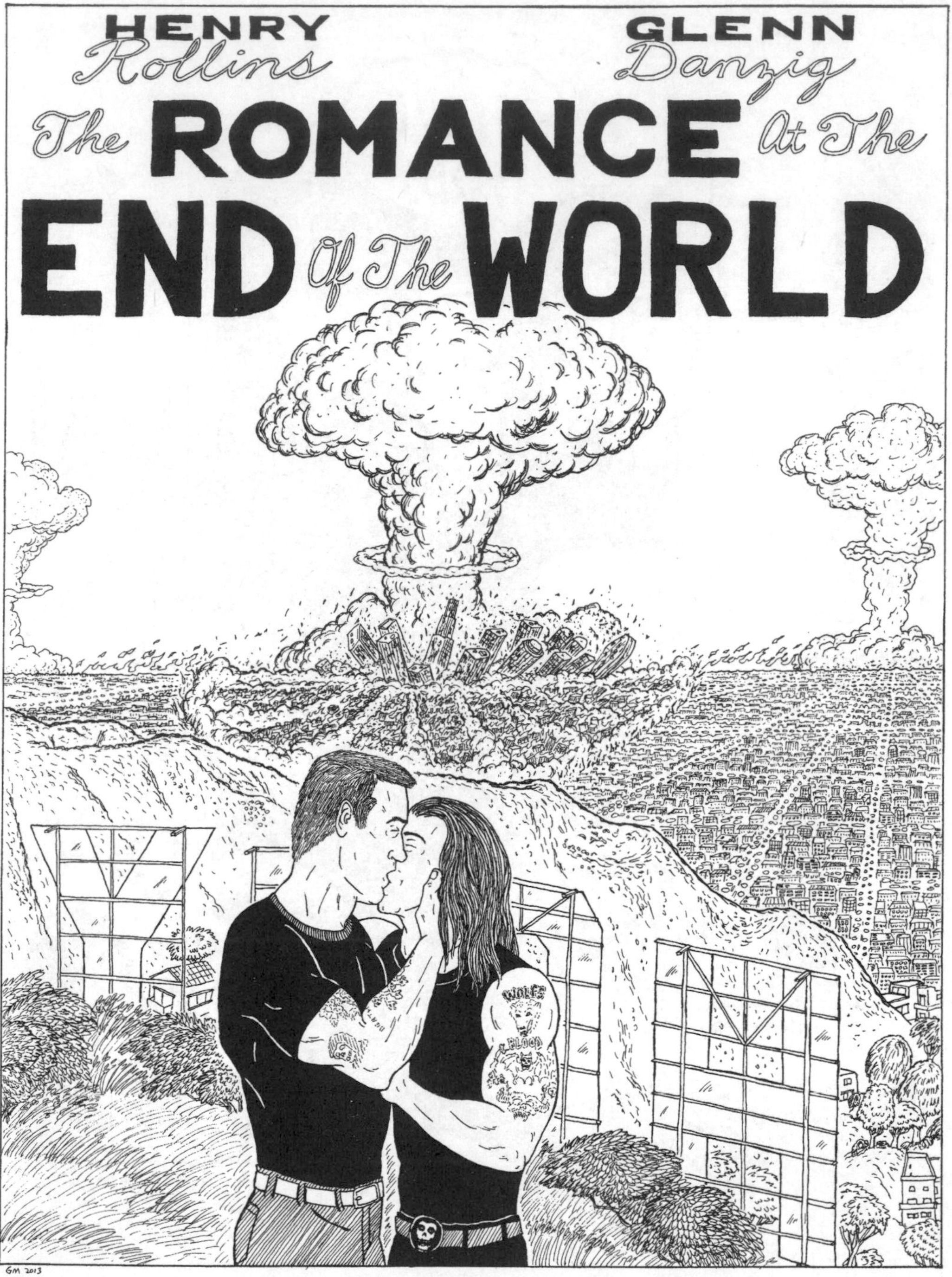
HENRY Rollins
GLENN Danzig
The ROMANCE At The
END Of The WORLD
WOLFS
BLOOD

GM 2013

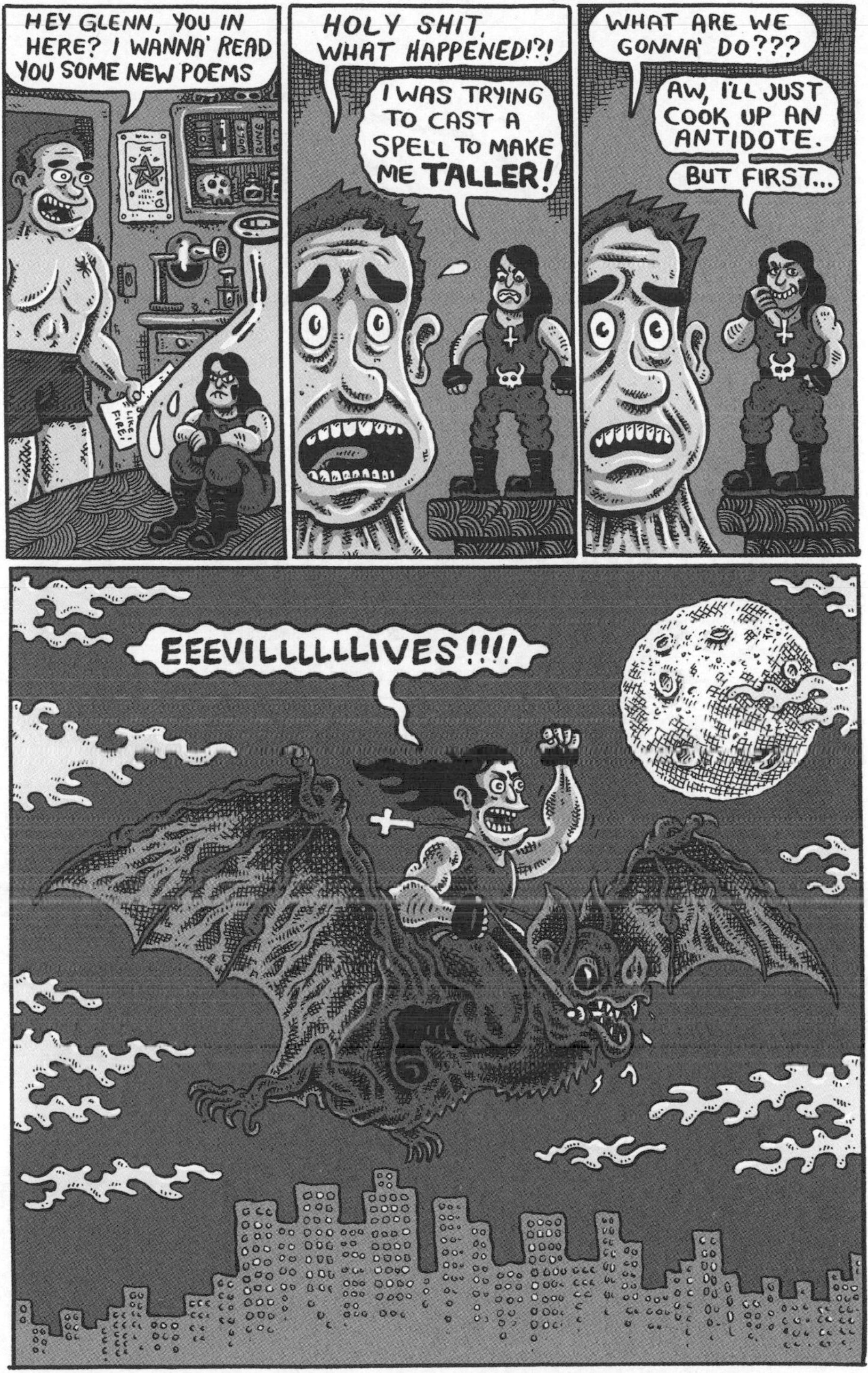
HEY GLENN, YOU IN HERE? I WANNA' READ YOU SOME NEW POEMS
LIKE FIRE!
HOLY SHIT, WHAT HAPPENED!?!
I WAS TRYING TO CAST A SPELL TO MAKE ME TALLER!
WHAT ARE WE GONNA' DO???
AW, I'LL JUST COOK UP AN ANTIDOTE.
BUT FIRST...
EEEVILLLLLLIVES!!!!

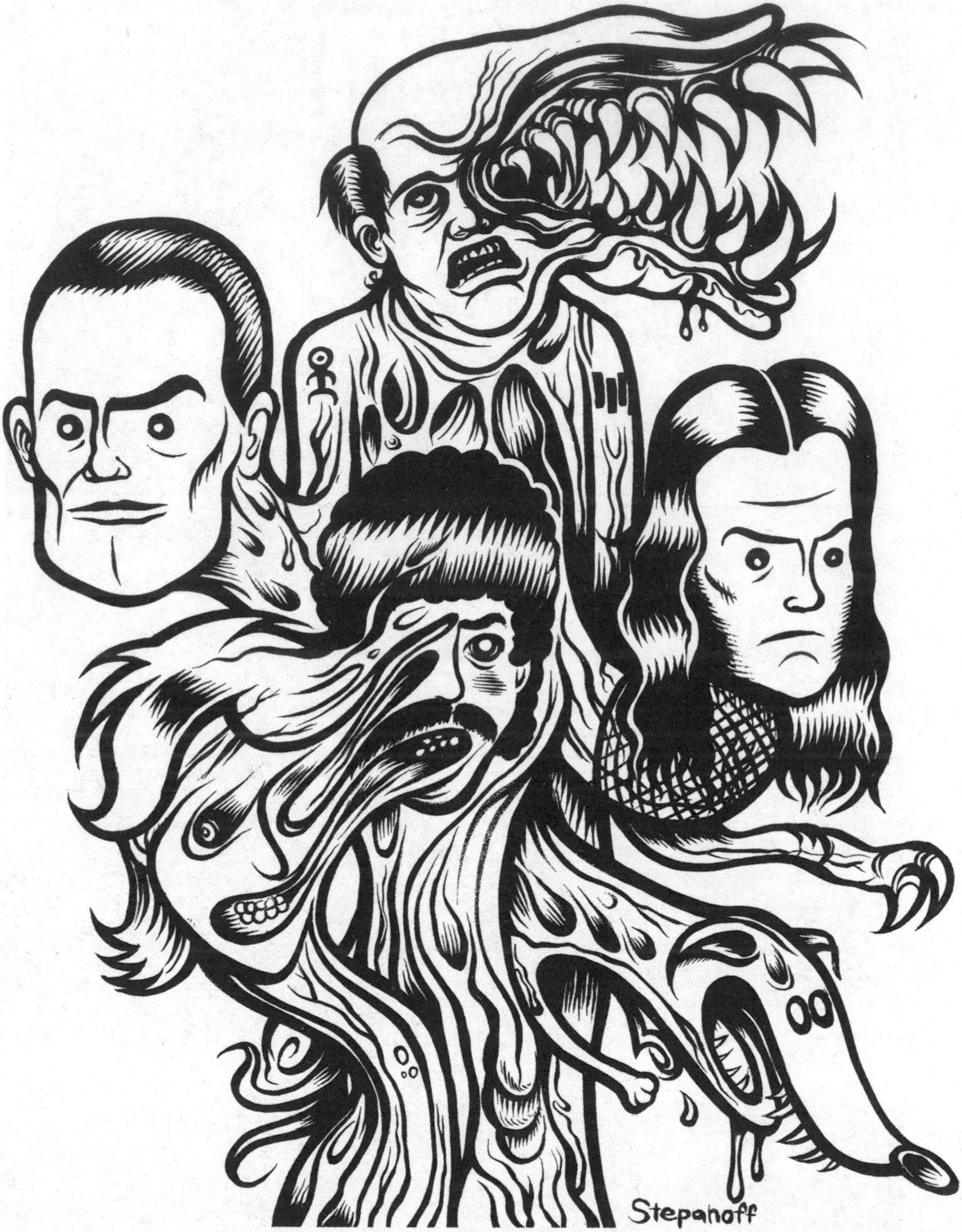
Stepanoff

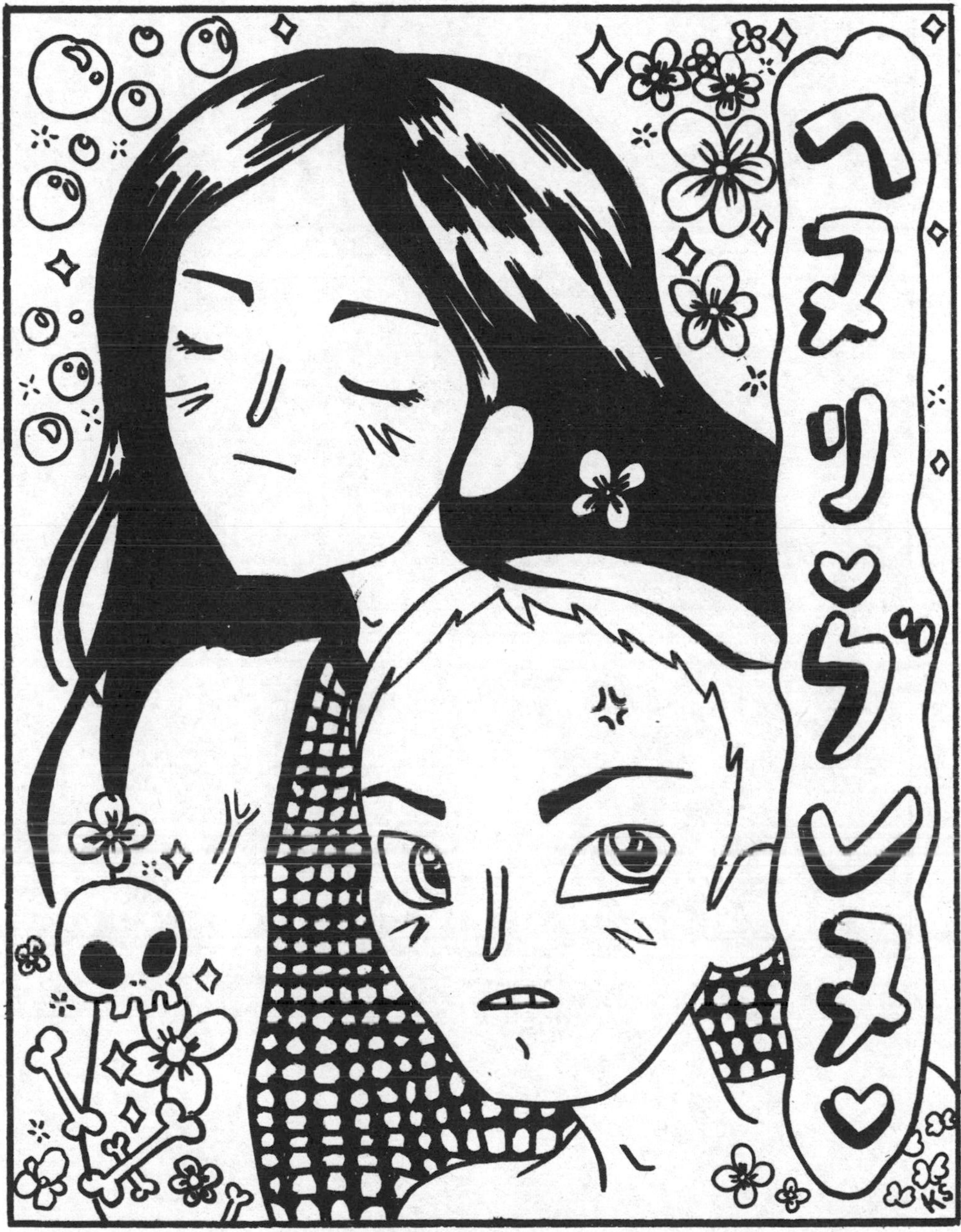

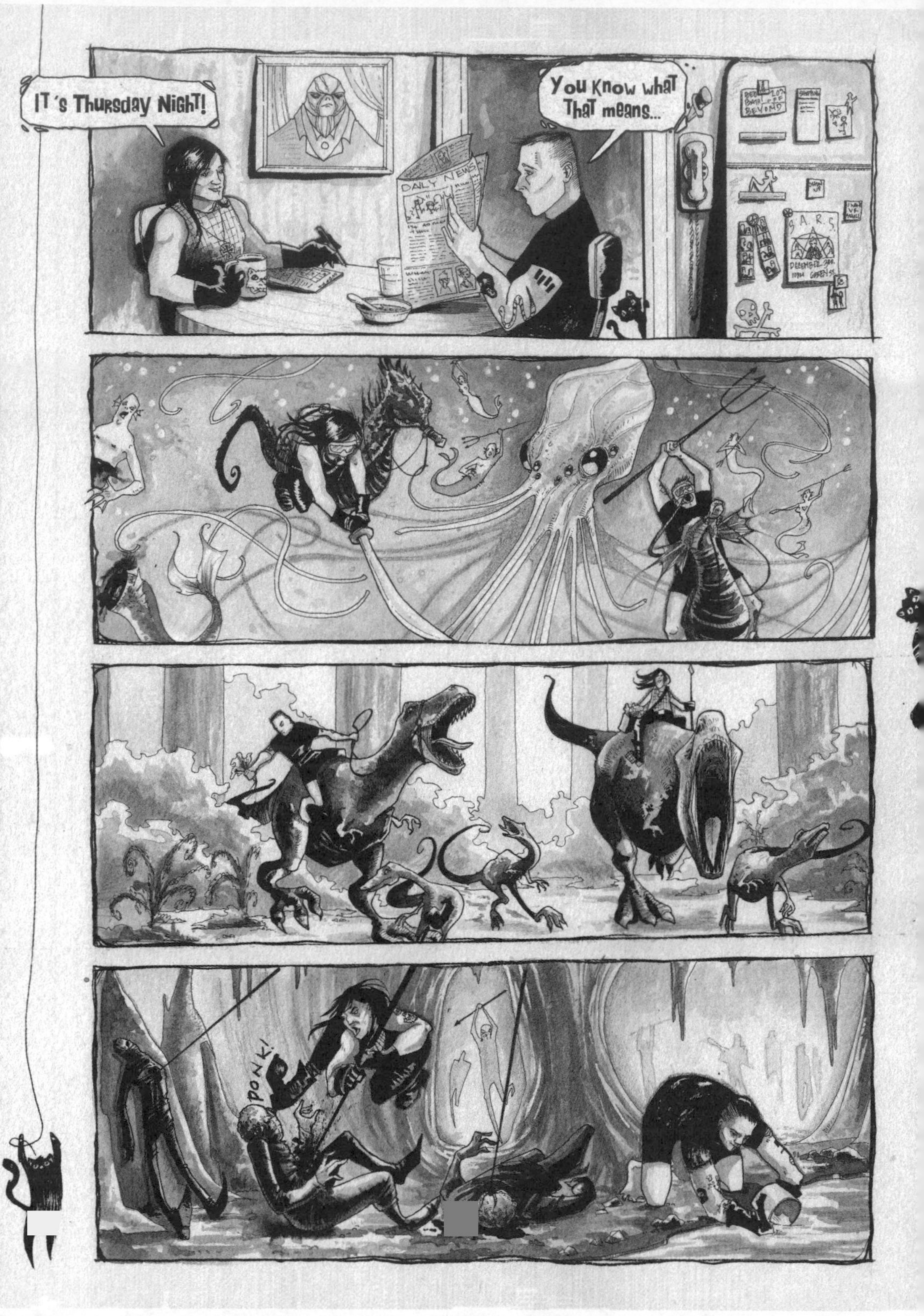

IT's Thursday NighT!
You Know what That means...
DAILY NEWS
PONK!

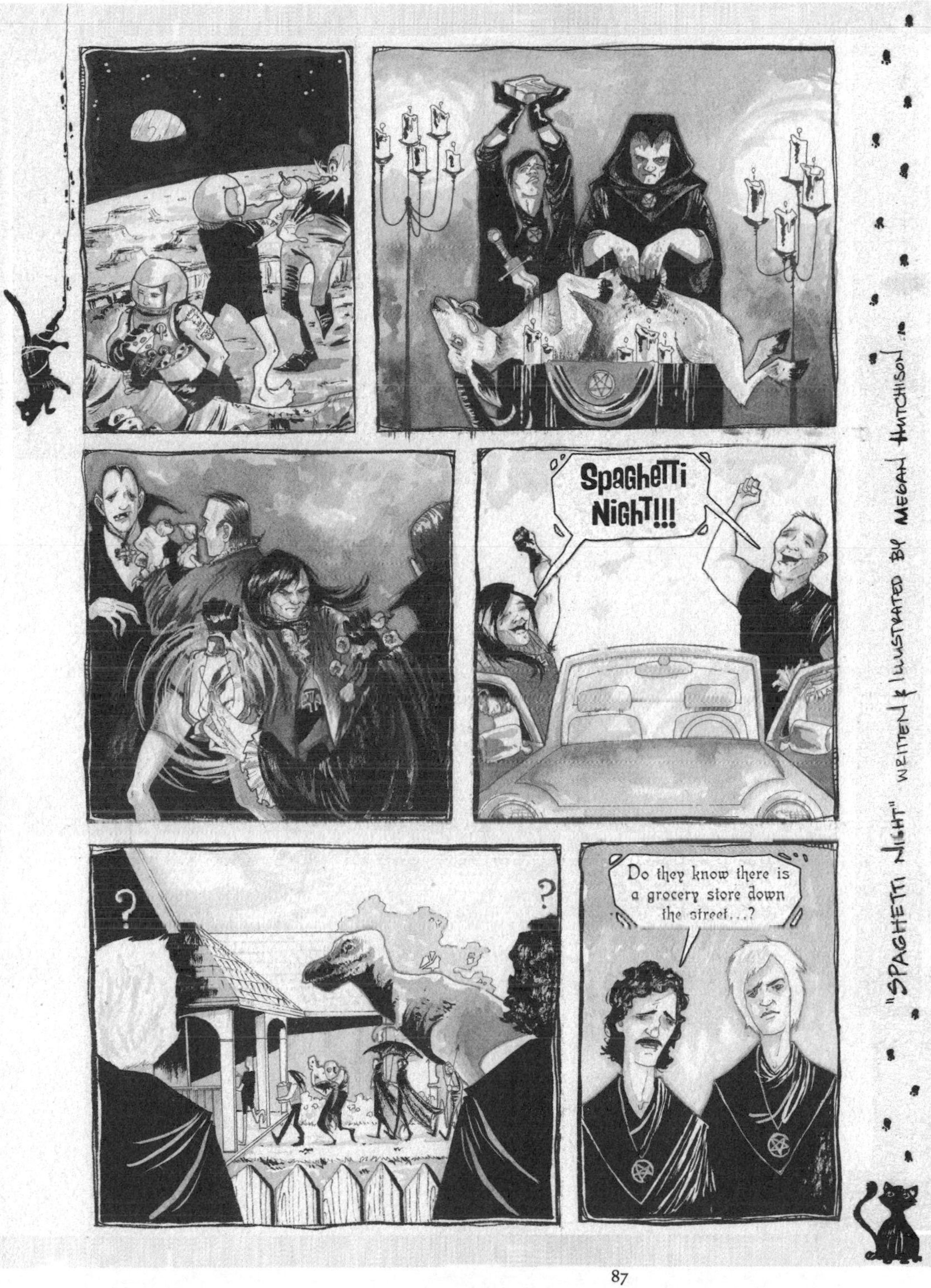
Spaghetti Night!!!
Do they know there is a grocery store down the street...?
"SPAGHETTI NIGHT" WRITTEN & ILLUSTRATED BY MEGAN HUTCHISON

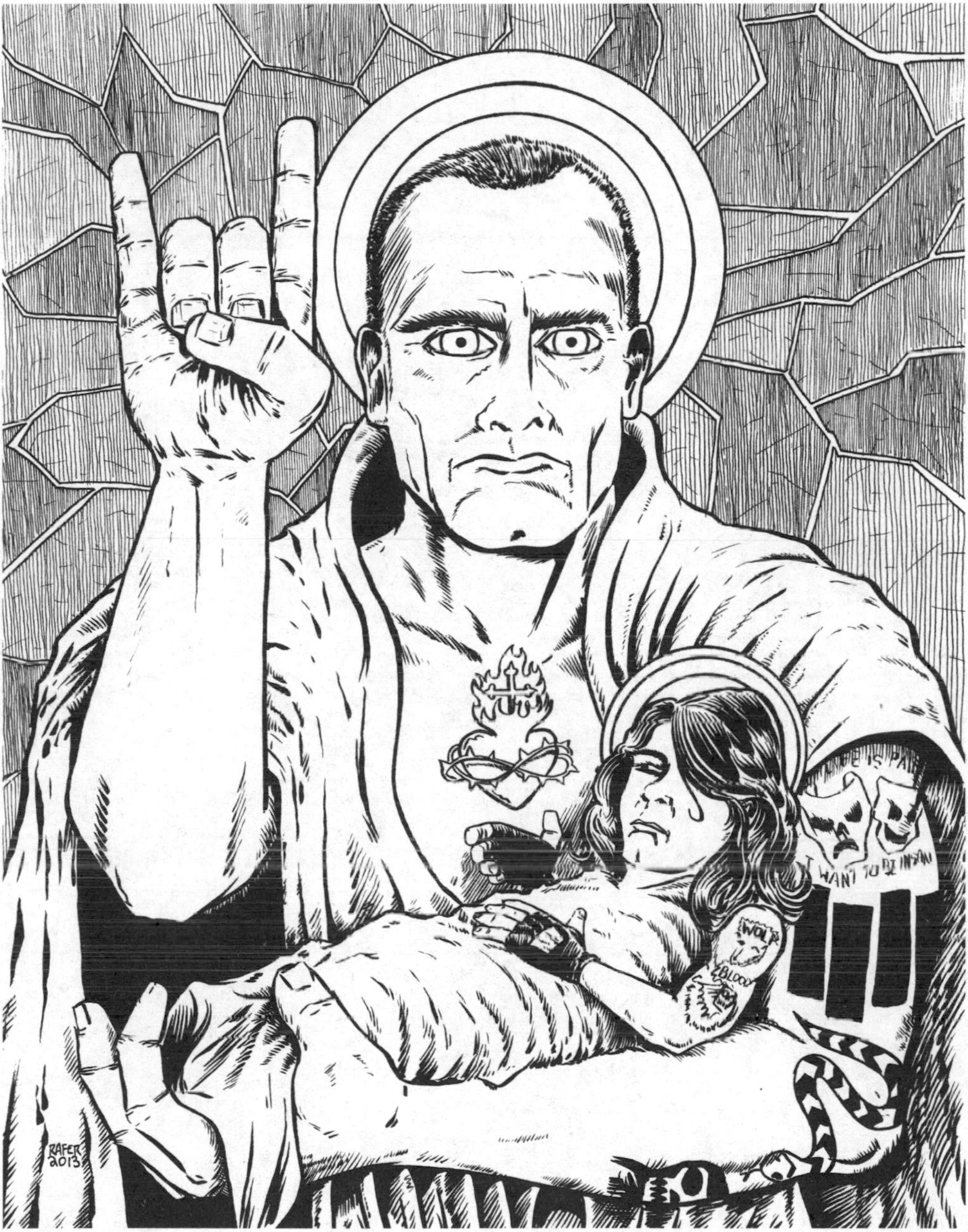
I WANT TO
BLOOD
RAFER 2013

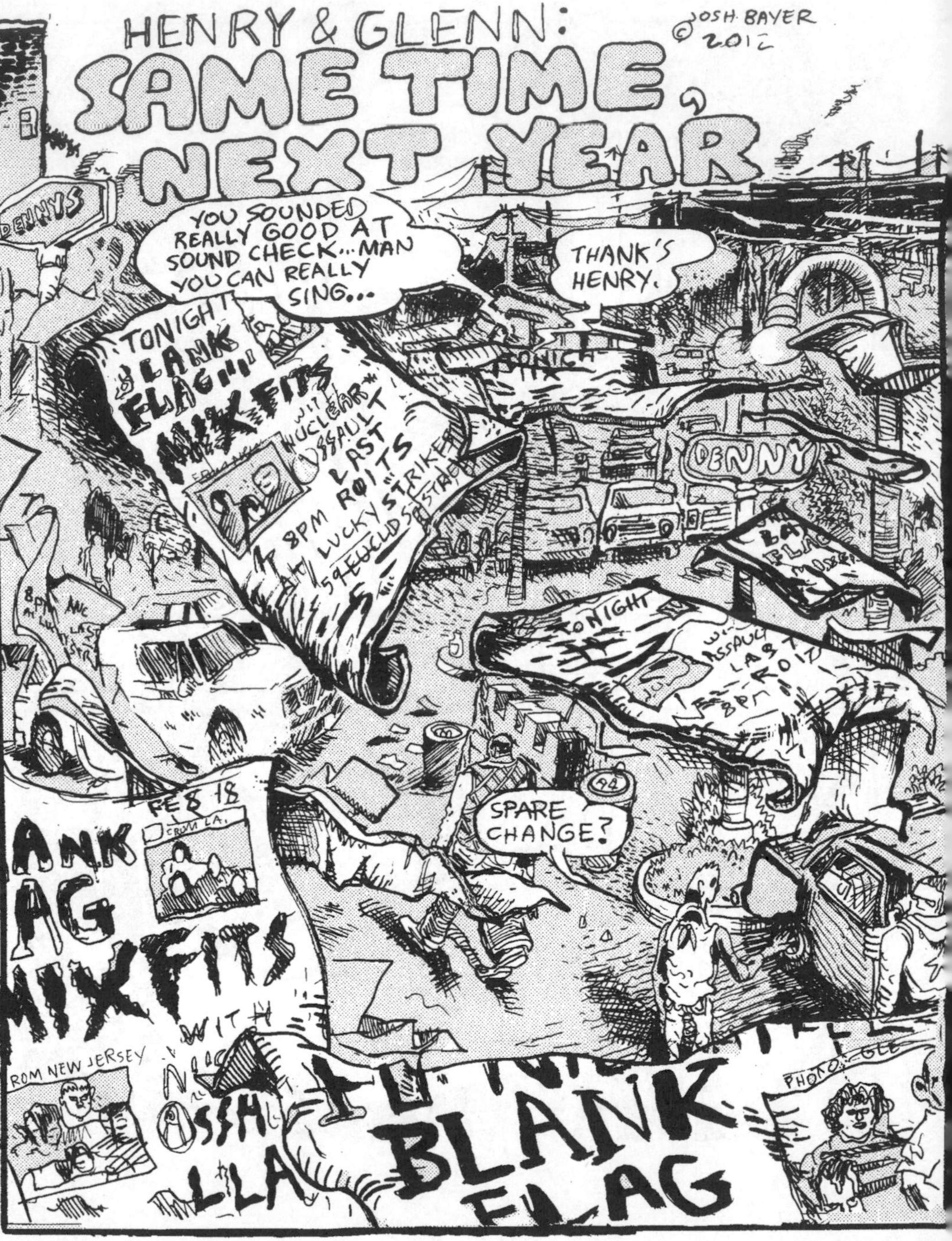
HENRY & GLENN:
SAME TIME, NEXT YEAR
© JOSH BAYER 2012
YOU SOUNDED REALLY GOOD AT SOUND CHECK... MAN YOU CAN REALLY SING...
THANK'S HENRY.
DENNYS
DENNY
TONIGHT
SPARE CHANGE?
ROM NEW JERSEY
BLANK FLAG

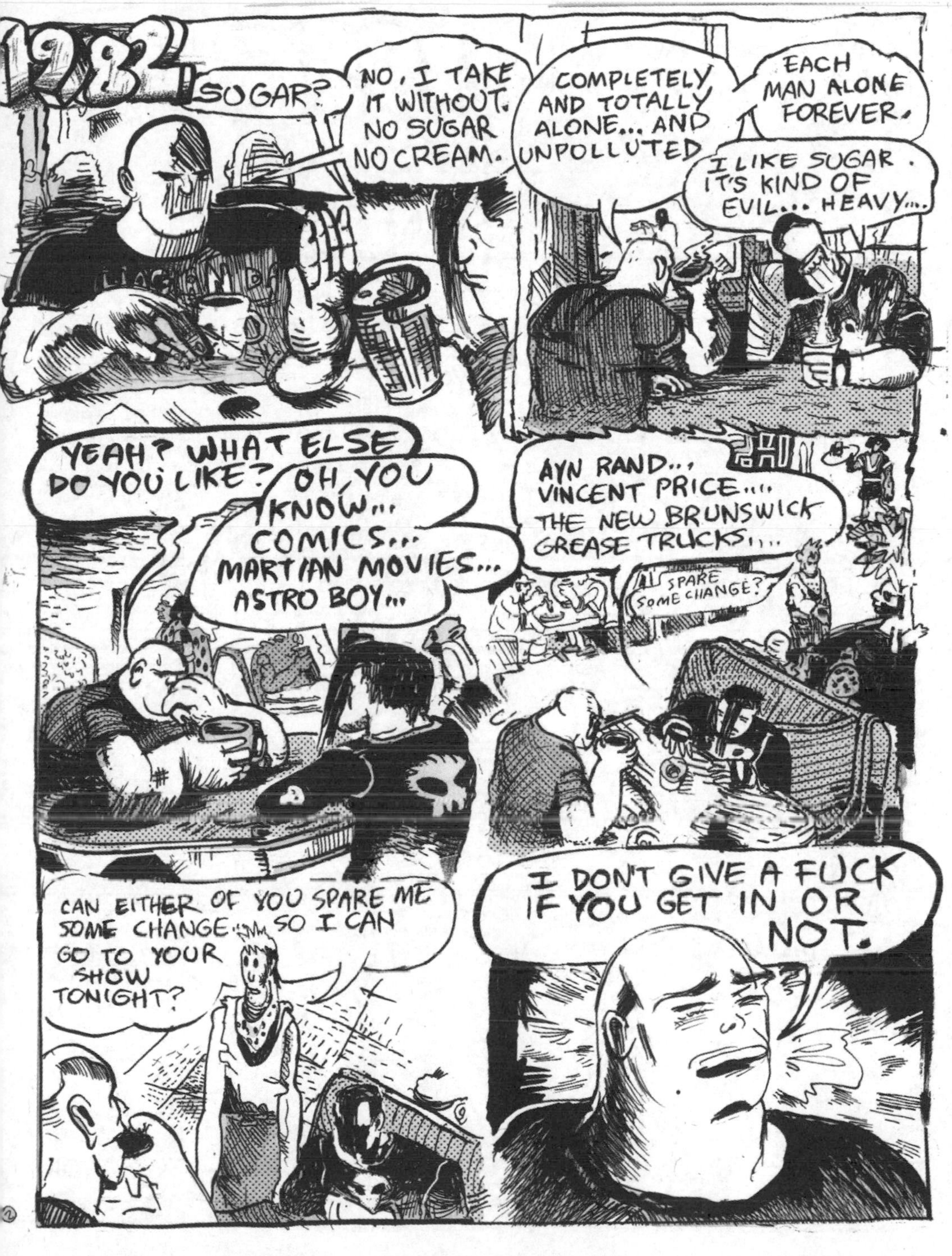
1982
SUGAR?
NO, I TAKE IT WITHOUT. NO SUGAR NO CREAM.
COMPLETELY AND TOTALLY ALONE... AND UNPOLLUTED
EACH MAN ALONE FOREVER.
I LIKE SUGAR. IT'S KIND OF EVIL... HEAVY....
YEAH? WHAT ELSE DO YOU LIKE?
OH, YOU KNOW... COMICS... MARTIAN MOVIES... ASTRO BOY...
AYN RAND..., VINCENT PRICE.... THE NEW BRUNSWICK GREASE TRUCKS,...
SPARE SOME CHANGE?
CAN EITHER OF YOU SPARE ME SOME CHANGE... SO I CAN GO TO YOUR SHOW TONIGHT?
I DON'T GIVE A FUCK IF YOU GET IN OR NOT.
2

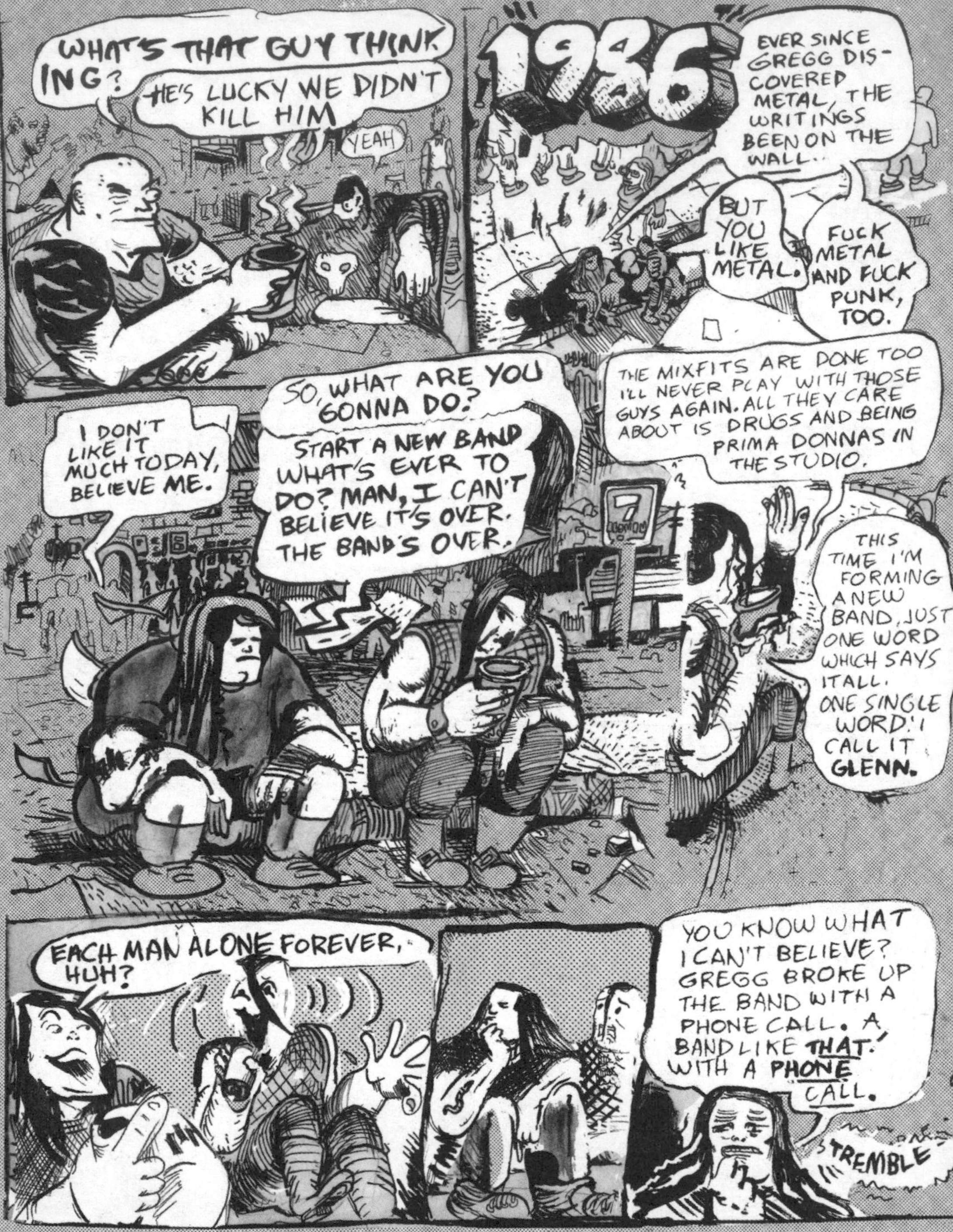
WHAT'S THAT GUY THINKING?
HE'S LUCKY WE DIDN'T KILL HIM
YEAH
1986
EVER SINCE GREGG DISCOVERED METAL, THE WRITINGS BEEN ON THE WALL..
BUT YOU LIKE METAL.
FUCK METAL AND FUCK PUNK, TOO.
I DON'T LIKE IT MUCH TODAY, BELIEVE ME.
SO, WHAT ARE YOU GONNA DO?
START A NEW BAND WHAT'S EVER TO DO? MAN, I CAN'T BELIEVE IT'S OVER. THE BAND'S OVER.
THE MIXFITS ARE DONE TOO I'LL NEVER PLAY WITH THOSE GUYS AGAIN. ALL THEY CARE ABOUT IS DRUGS AND BEING PRIMA DONNAS IN THE STUDIO.
THIS TIME I'M FORMING A NEW BAND, JUST ONE WORD WHICH SAYS IT ALL. ONE SINGLE WORD! I CALL IT GLENN.
EACH MAN ALONE FOREVER, HUH?
YOU KNOW WHAT I CAN'T BELIEVE? GREGG BROKE UP THE BAND WITH A PHONE CALL. A BAND LIKE THAT! WITH A PHONE CALL.
TREMBLE

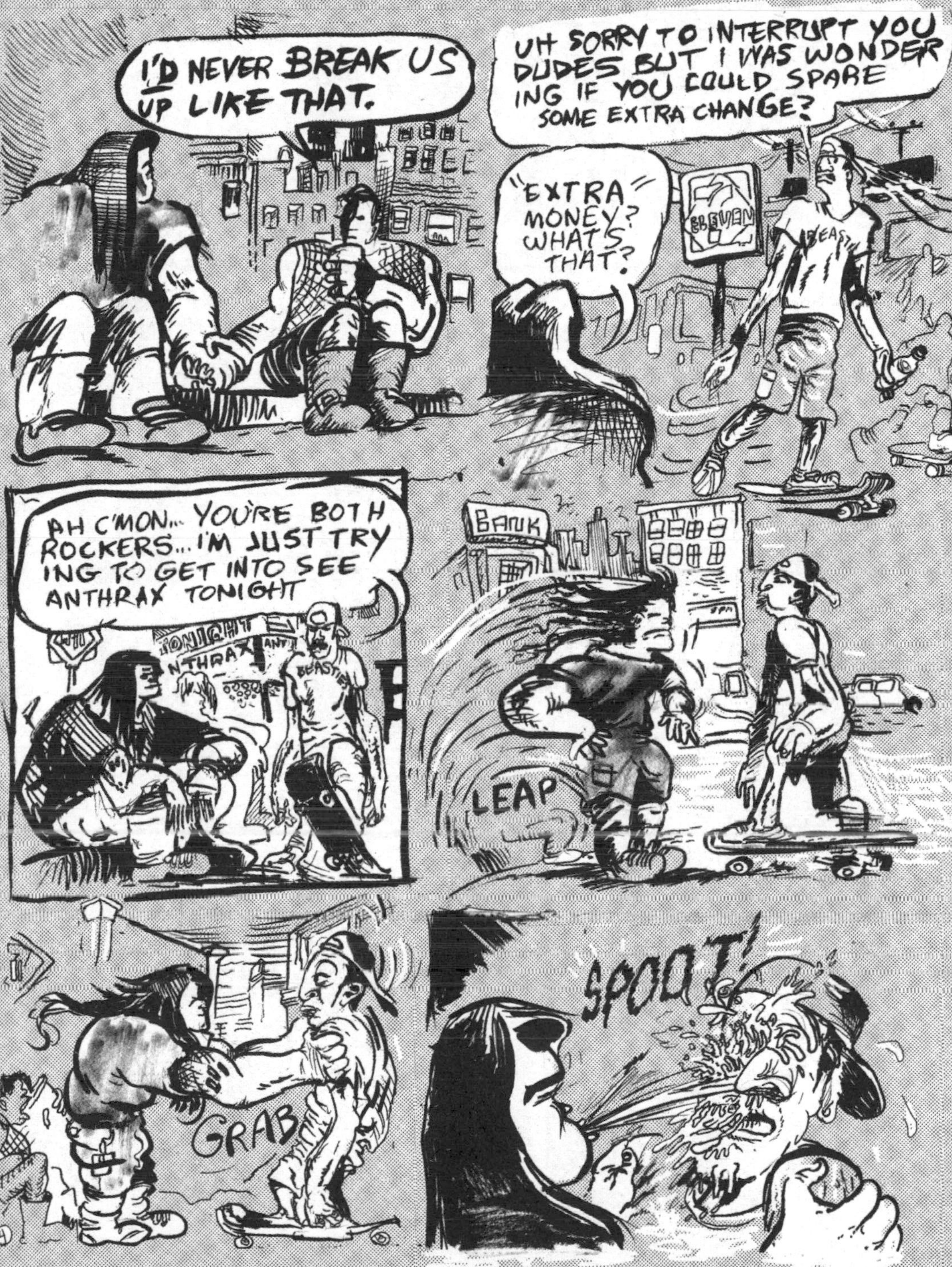
I'D NEVER BREAK US UP LIKE THAT.
UH SORRY TO INTERRUPT YOU DUDES BUT I WAS WONDER ING IF YOU COULD SPARE SOME EXTRA CHANGE?
"EXTRA MONEY? WHAT'S THAT?
ELEVEN
BEAST
AH C'MON... YOU'RE BOTH ROCKERS... I'M JUST TRY ING TO GET INTO SEE ANTHRAX TONIGHT
TONIGHT
NTHRAX
BEASTIE
BANK
LEAP
GRAB
SPOOT!

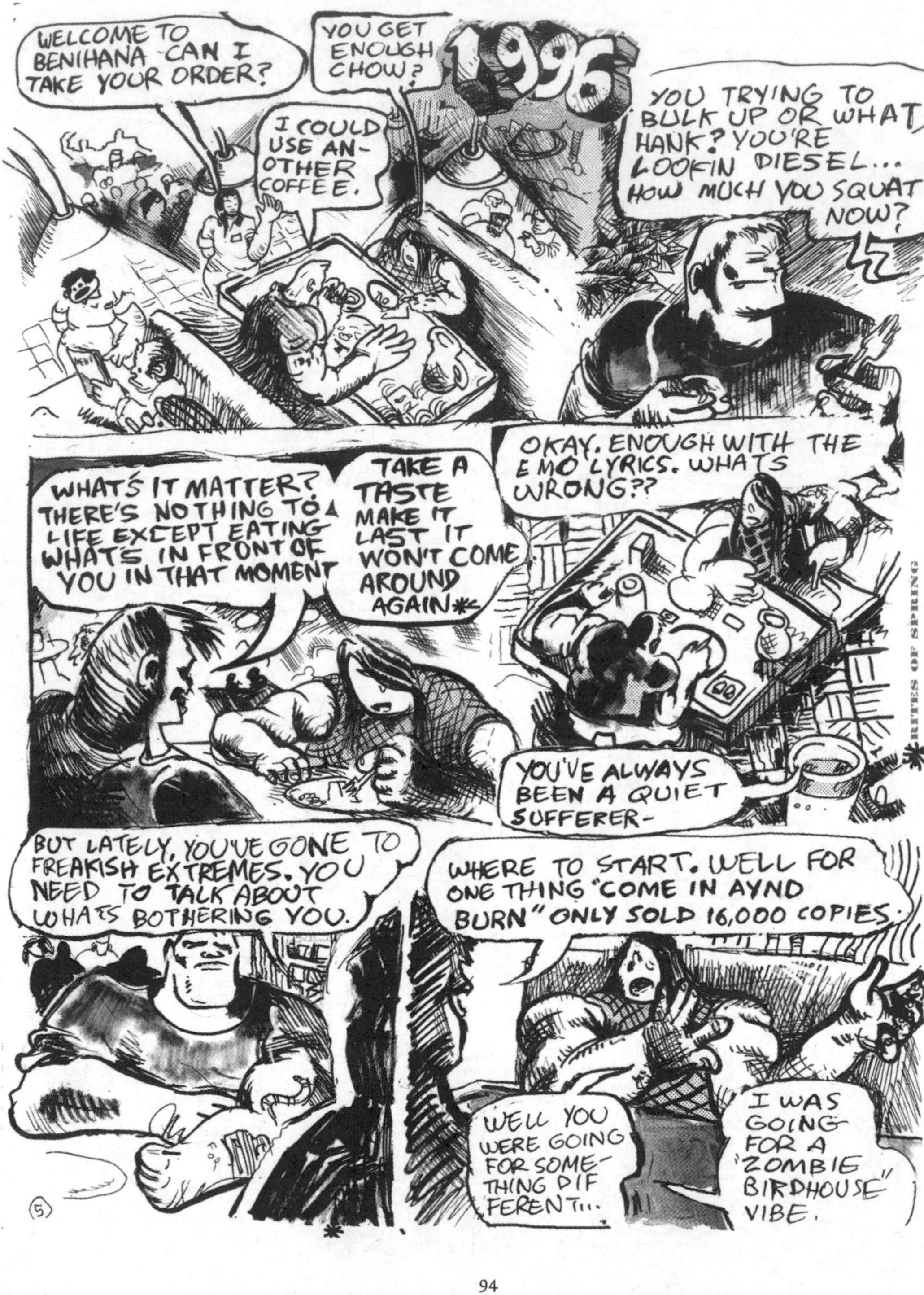
WELCOME TO BENIHANA CAN I TAKE YOUR ORDER?
YOU GET ENOUGH CHOW?
1996
I COULD USE AN-OTHER COFFEE.
YOU TRYING TO BULK UP OR WHAT, HANK? YOU'RE LOOKIN DIESEL... HOW MUCH YOU SQUAT NOW?
WHAT'S IT MATTER? THERE'S NOTHING TO A LIFE EXCEPT EATING WHAT'S IN FRONT OF YOU IN THAT MOMENT
TAKE A TASTE MAKE IT LAST IT WON'T COME AROUND AGAIN
OKAY. ENOUGH WITH THE EMO LYRICS. WHATS WRONG??
YOU'VE ALWAYS BEEN A QUIET SUFFERER-
BUT LATELY, YOU'VE GONE TO FREAKISH EXTREMES. YOU NEED TO TALK ABOUT WHATS BOTHERING YOU.
WHERE TO START. WELL FOR ONE THING "COME IN AYND BURN" ONLY SOLD 16,000 COPIES.
WELL YOU WERE GOING FOR SOME-THING DIF FERENT...
I WAS GOING FOR A "ZOMBIE BIRDHOUSE" VIBE.
5

RITES OF SPRING

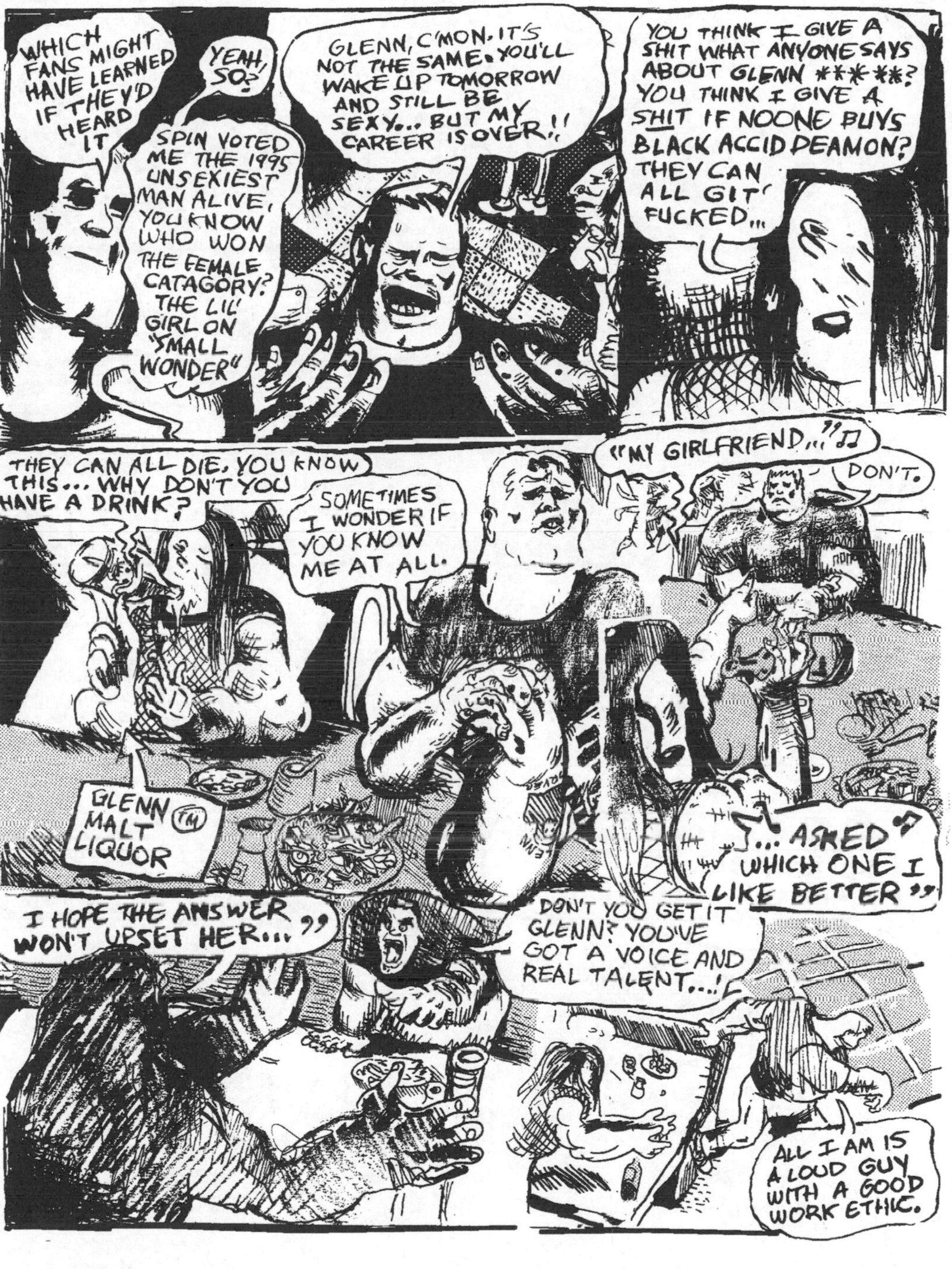

WHICH FANS MIGHT HAVE LEARNED IF THEY'D HEARD IT
YEAH, SO?
SPIN VOTED ME THE 1995 UNSEXIEST MAN ALIVE, YOU KNOW WHO WON THE FEMALE CATAGORY? THE LIL' GIRL ON "SMALL WONDER"
GLENN, C'MON. IT'S NOT THE SAME. YOU'LL WAKE UP TOMORROW AND STILL BE SEXY... BUT MY CAREER IS OVER!!
YOU THINK I GIVE A SHIT WHAT ANYONE SAYS ABOUT GLENN ****? YOU THINK I GIVE A SHIT IF NOONE BUYS BLACK ACCID DEAMON? THEY CAN ALL GIT' FUCKED...
THEY CAN ALL DIE, YOU KNOW THIS... WHY DON'T YOU HAVE A DRINK?
SOMETIMES I WONDER IF YOU KNOW ME AT ALL.
"MY GIRLFRIEND..."
DON'T.
GLENN MALT LIQUOR TM
"...ASKED WHICH ONE I LIKE BETTER"
I HOPE THE ANSWER WON'T UPSET HER..."
DON'T YOU GET IT GLENN? YOU'VE GOT A VOICE AND REAL TALENT...!
ALL I AM IS A LOUD GUY WITH A GOOD WORK ETHIC.

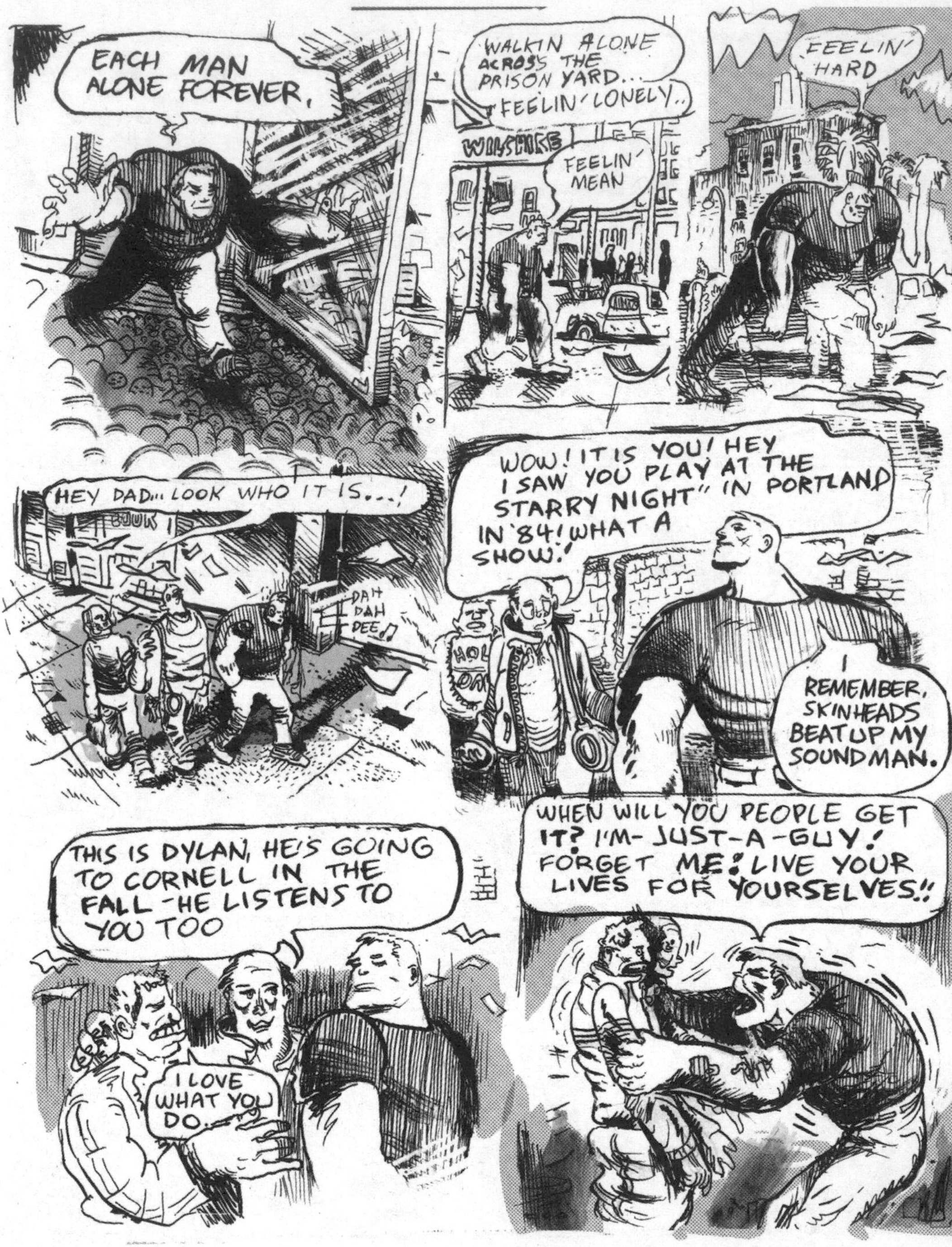
EACH MAN ALONE FOREVER.
WALKIN ALONE ACROSS THE PRISON YARD...
FEELIN' LONELY..
FEELIN' MEAN
FEELIN' HARD
HEY DAD... LOOK WHO IT IS...!
DAH DAH DEE♫
WOW! IT IS YOU! HEY I SAW YOU PLAY AT THE "STARRY NIGHT" IN PORTLAND IN '84! WHAT A SHOW!
I REMEMBER. SKINHEADS BEAT UP MY SOUNDMAN.
THIS IS DYLAN, HE'S GOING TO CORNELL IN THE FALL - HE LISTENS TO YOU TOO
I LOVE WHAT YOU DO.
WHEN WILL YOU PEOPLE GET IT? I'M-JUST-A-GUY! FORGET ME! LIVE YOUR LIVES FOR YOURSELVES!!

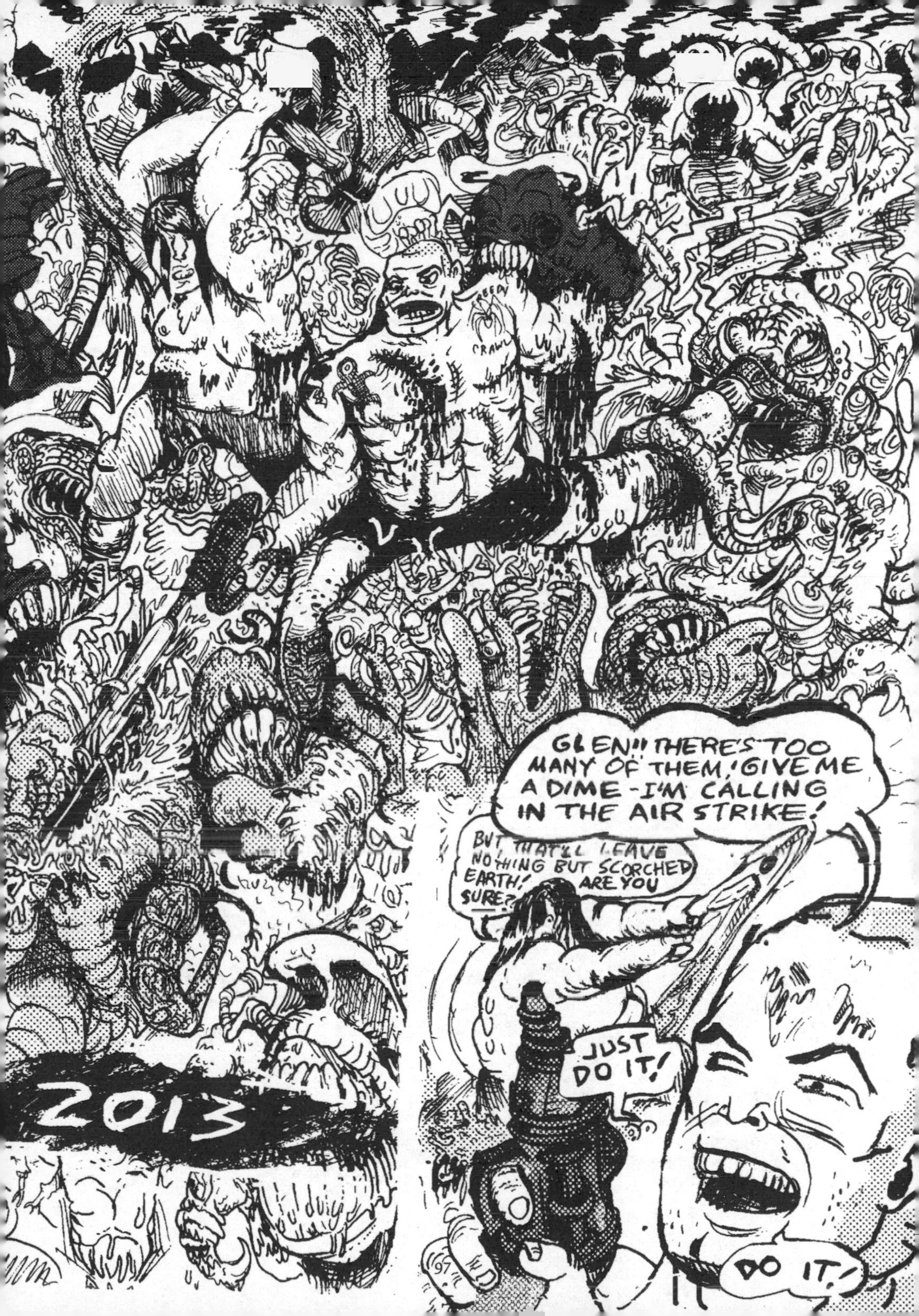
GLEN!! THERE'S TOO MANY OF THEM, GIVE ME A DIME - I'M CALLING IN THE AIR STRIKE!
BUT THAT'LL LEAVE NOTHING BUT SCORCHED EARTH! ARE YOU SURE?
JUST DO IT!
DO IT!
2013

HEY... IS THAT COFFEE I SMELL?
SOMETHING LIKE THAT
HOW'D YOU MAKE IT THIS TIME? YOU USE ASH AND CRUNCHED UP DXM TABLETS?
NAH-I FOUND IT... A CONTAINER OF SINGLE SERVING INSTANT AT THE 7-11. MIGHT BE THE LAST...
EVER.
SO. YOU WANT SOMETHING IN IT? SUGAR MAYBE?
...CREAM?
2038

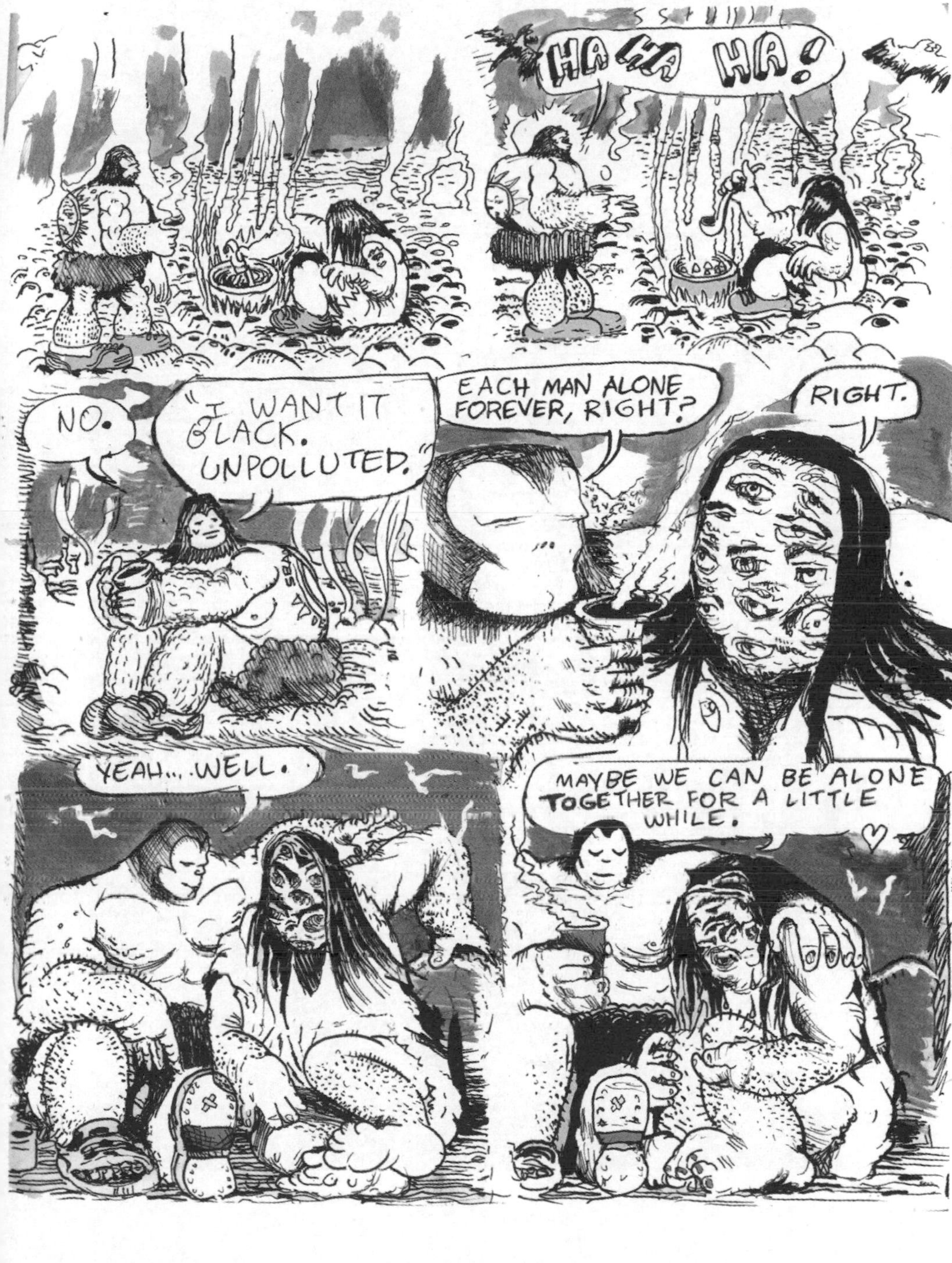
HA HA HA!
NO.
"I WANT IT BLACK. UNPOLLUTED."
EACH MAN ALONE FOREVER, RIGHT?
RIGHT.
YEAH... WELL.
MAYBE WE CAN BE ALONE TOGETHER FOR A LITTLE WHILE.

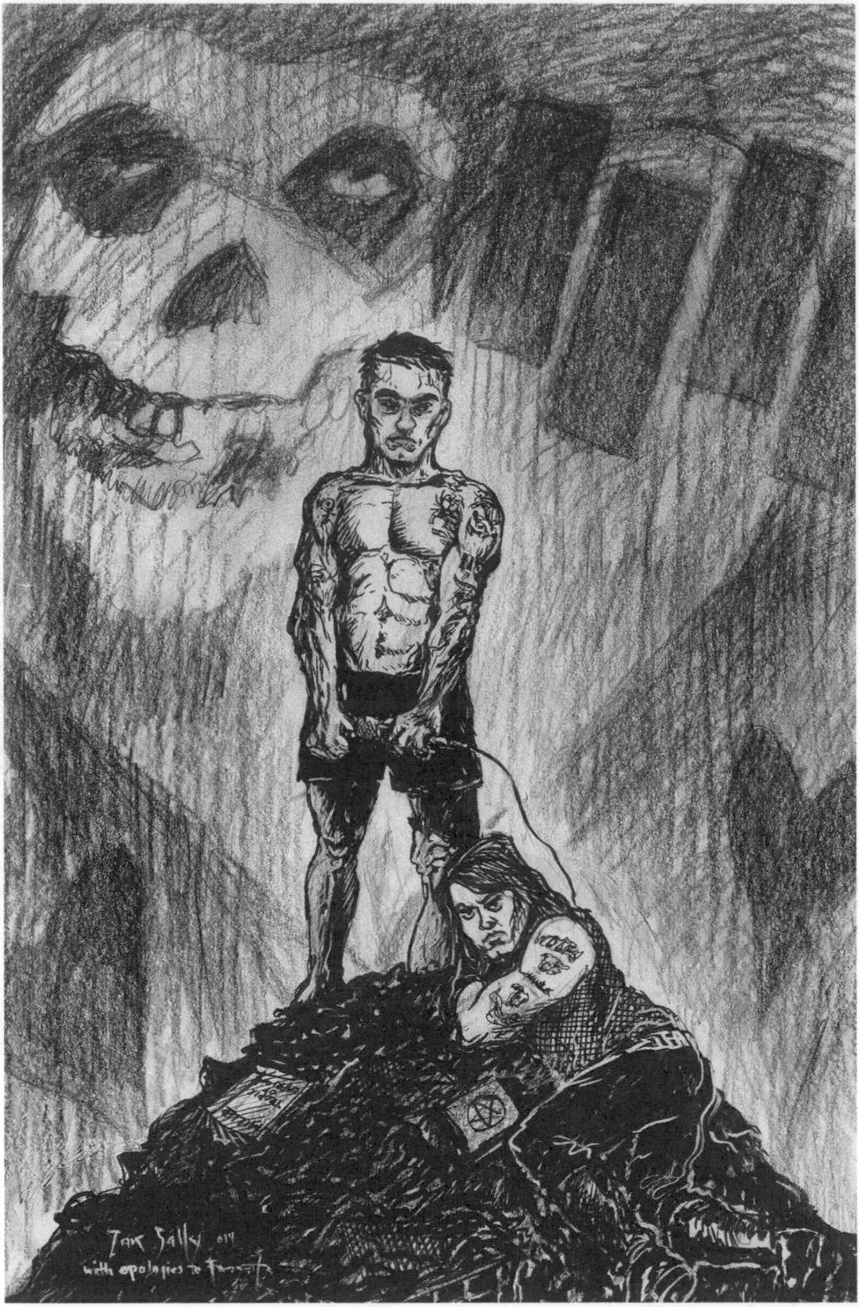

H: "WOULD YOU *PLEASE* GET A HANDLE ON THE LAUNDRY?" G: "I DID THE DISHES."

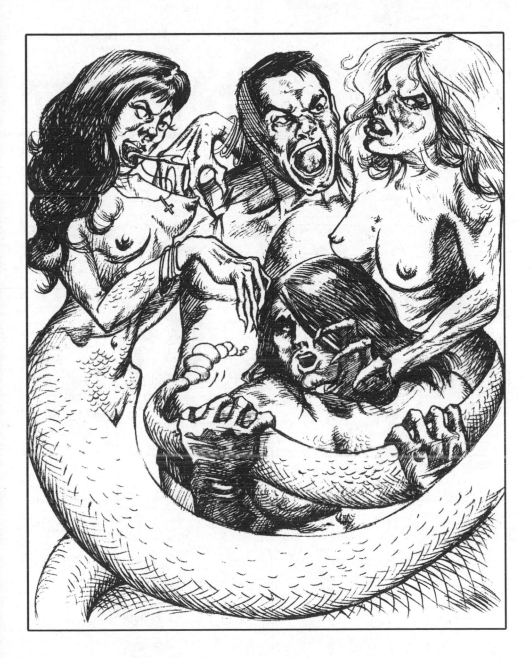

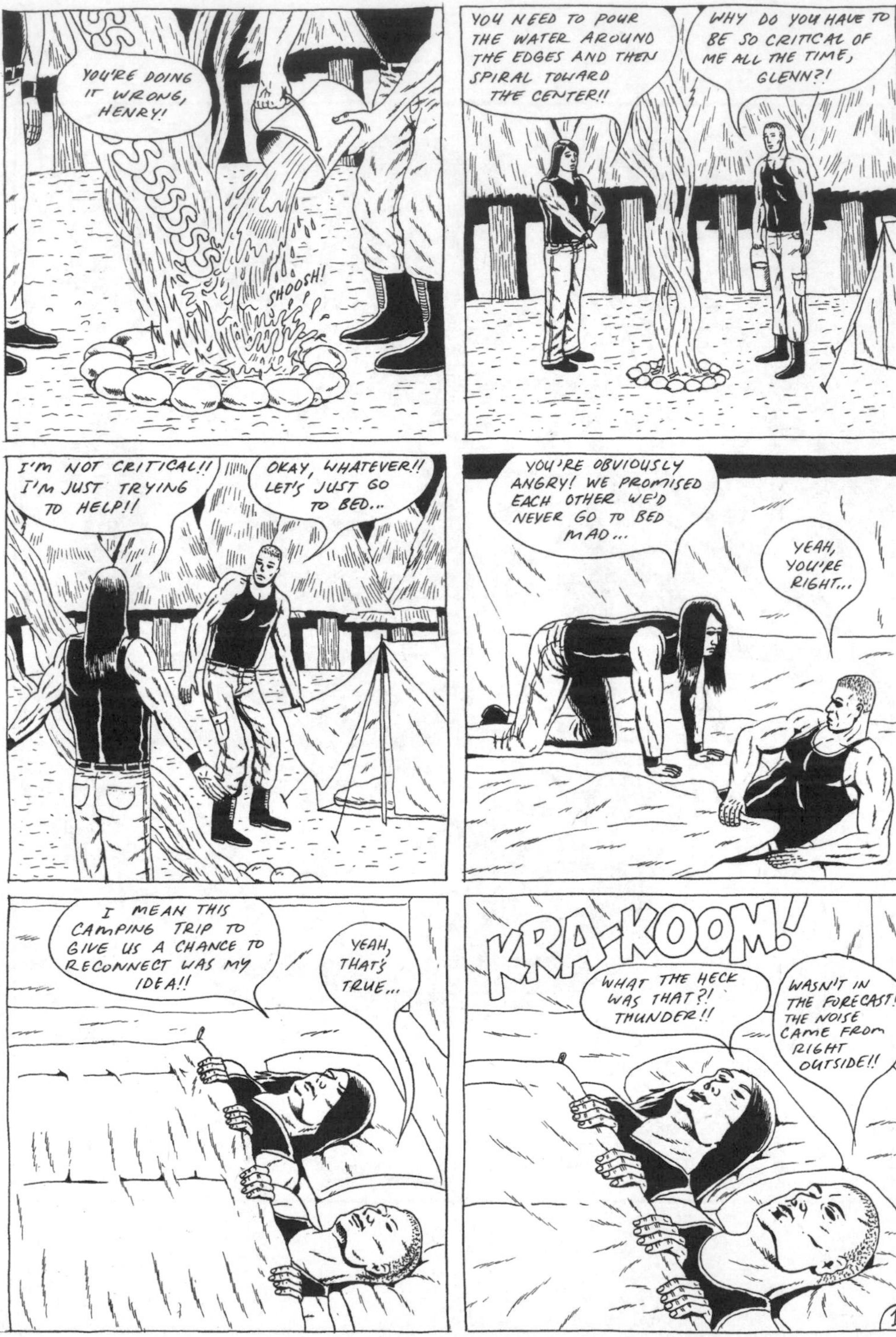
YOU'RE DOING IT WRONG, HENRY!
SSSSSSS
SHOOSH!
YOU NEED TO POUR THE WATER AROUND THE EDGES AND THEN SPIRAL TOWARD THE CENTER!!
WHY DO YOU HAVE TO BE SO CRITICAL OF ME ALL THE TIME, GLENN?!
I'M NOT CRITICAL!! I'M JUST TRYING TO HELP!!
OKAY, WHATEVER!! LET'S JUST GO TO BED...
YOU'RE OBVIOUSLY ANGRY! WE PROMISED EACH OTHER WE'D NEVER GO TO BED MAD...
YEAH, YOU'RE RIGHT...
I MEAN THIS CAMPING TRIP TO GIVE US A CHANCE TO RECONNECT WAS MY IDEA!!
YEAH, THAT'S TRUE...
KRA-KOOM!
WHAT THE HECK WAS THAT?! THUNDER!!
WASN'T IN THE FORECAST! THE NOISE CAME FROM RIGHT OUTSIDE!!
1

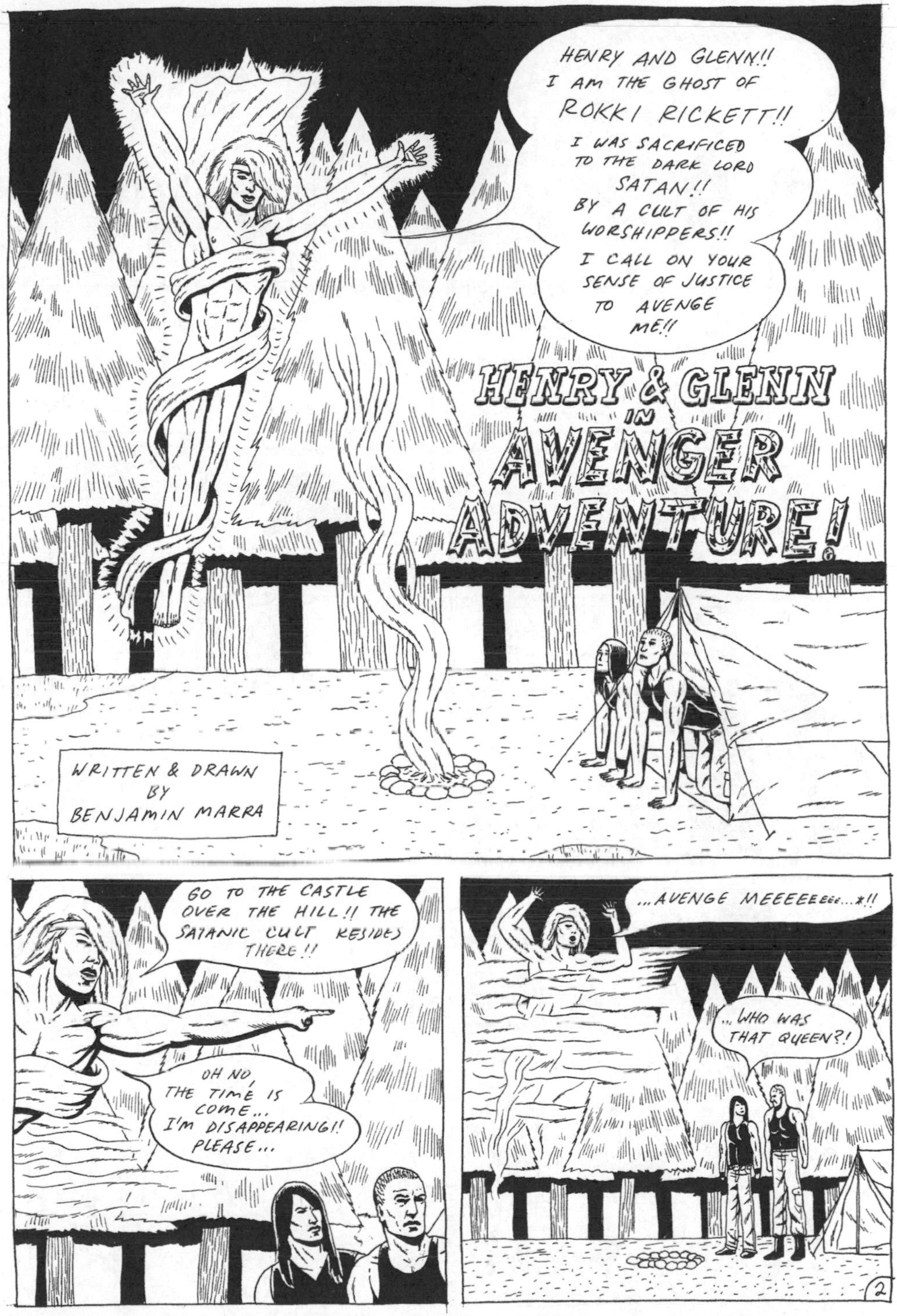
HENRY AND GLENN!! I AM THE GHOST OF ROKKI RICKETT!! I WAS SACRIFICED TO THE DARK LORD SATAN!! BY A CULT OF HIS WORSHIPPERS!! I CALL ON YOUR SENSE OF JUSTICE TO AVENGE ME!!
HENRY & GLENN IN AVENGER ADVENTURE!
WRITTEN & DRAWN BY BENJAMIN MARRA
GO TO THE CASTLE OVER THE HILL!! THE SATANIC CULT RESIDES THERE!!
OH NO, THE TIME IS COME... I'M DISAPPEARING!! PLEASE...
...AVENGE MEEEEEeee...*!!
...WHO WAS THAT QUEEN?!
2

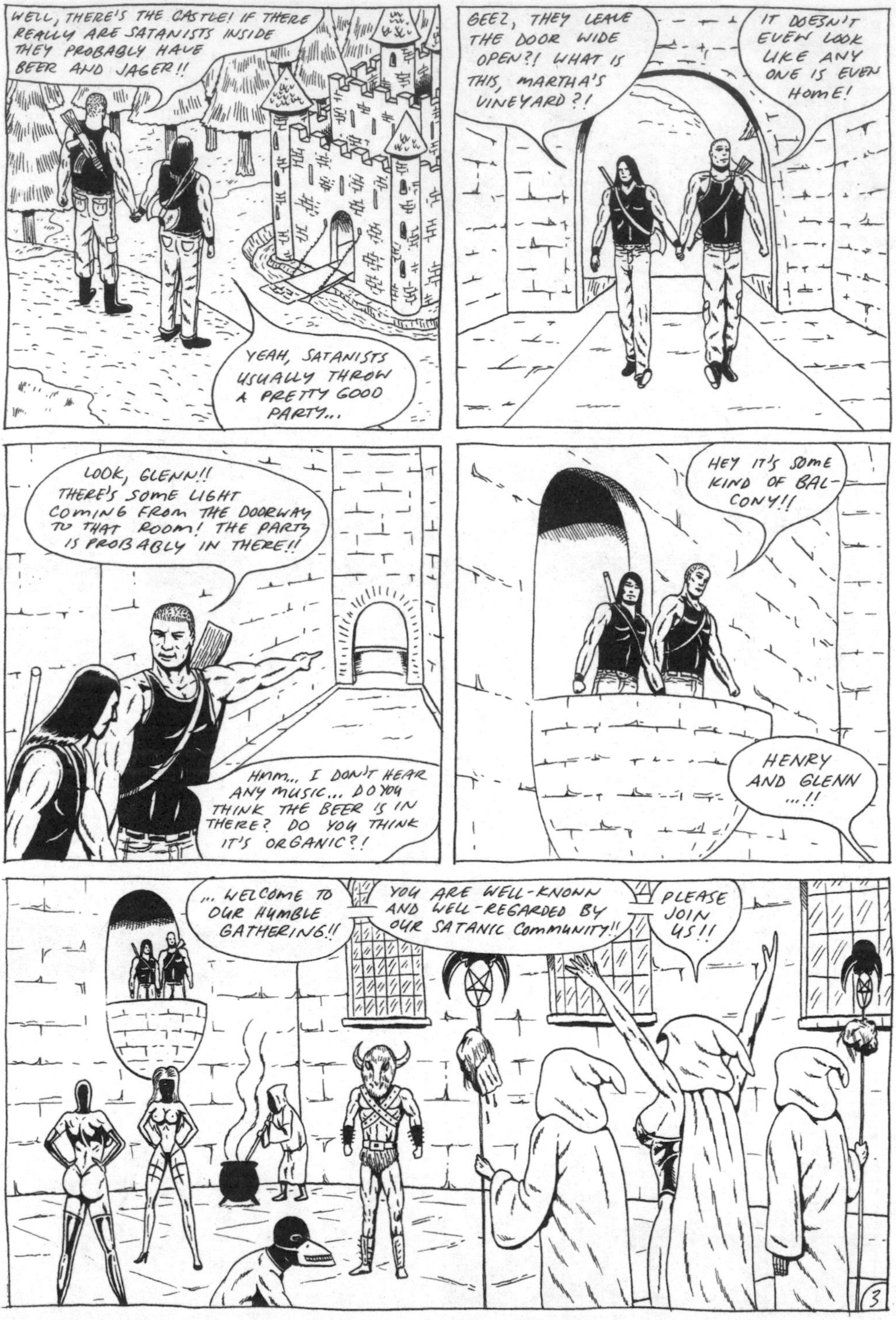
WELL, THERE'S THE CASTLE! IF THERE REALLY ARE SATANISTS INSIDE THEY PROBABLY HAVE BEER AND JAGER!!
YEAH, SATANISTS USUALLY THROW A PRETTY GOOD PARTY...
GEEZ, THEY LEAVE THE DOOR WIDE OPEN?! WHAT IS THIS, MARTHA'S VINEYARD?!
IT DOESN'T EVEN LOOK LIKE ANY ONE IS EVEN HOME!
LOOK, GLENN!! THERE'S SOME LIGHT COMING FROM THE DOORWAY TO THAT ROOM! THE PARTY IS PROBABLY IN THERE!!
HMM... I DON'T HEAR ANY MUSIC... DO YOU THINK THE BEER IS IN THERE? DO YOU THINK IT'S ORGANIC?!
HEY IT'S SOME KIND OF BAL-CONY!!
HENRY AND GLENN ...!!
... WELCOME TO OUR HUMBLE GATHERING!!
YOU ARE WELL-KNOWN AND WELL-REGARDED BY OUR SATANIC COMMUNITY!!
PLEASE JOIN US!!
3

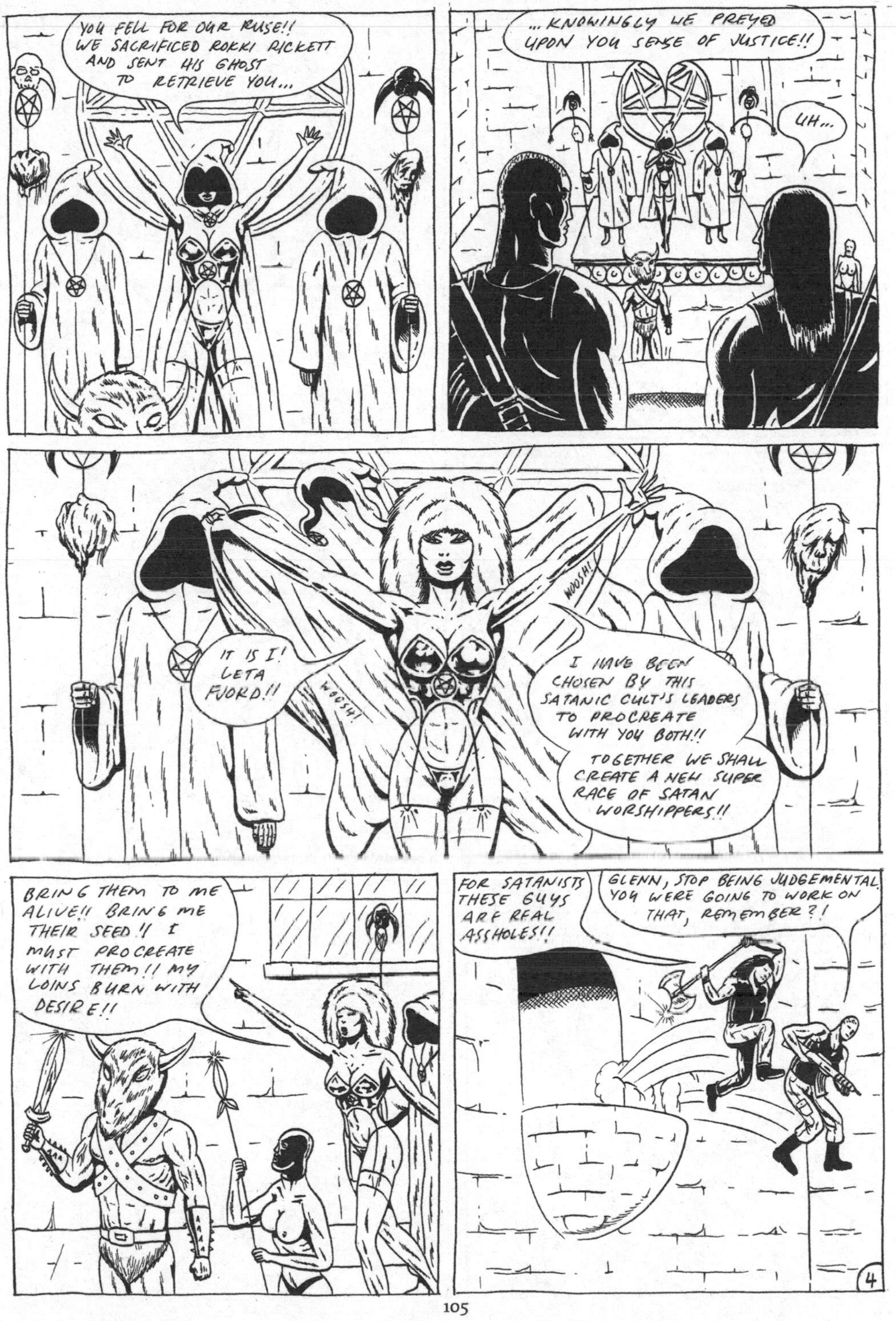
YOU FELL FOR OUR RUSE!! WE SACRIFICED ROKKI RICKETT AND SENT HIS GHOST TO RETRIEVE YOU...
...KNOWINGLY WE PREYED UPON YOU SENSE OF JUSTICE!!
UH...
WOOSH!
IT IS I! LETA FJORD!!
WOOSH!
I HAVE BEEN CHOSEN BY THIS SATANIC CULT'S LEADERS TO PROCREATE WITH YOU BOTH!!
TOGETHER WE SHALL CREATE A NEW SUPER RACE OF SATAN WORSHIPPERS!!
BRING THEM TO ME ALIVE!! BRING ME THEIR SEED!! I MUST PROCREATE WITH THEM!! MY LOINS BURN WITH DESIRE!!
FOR SATANISTS THESE GUYS ARE REAL ASSHOLES!!
GLENN, STOP BEING JUDGEMENTAL. YOU WERE GOING TO WORK ON THAT, REMEMBER?!
4

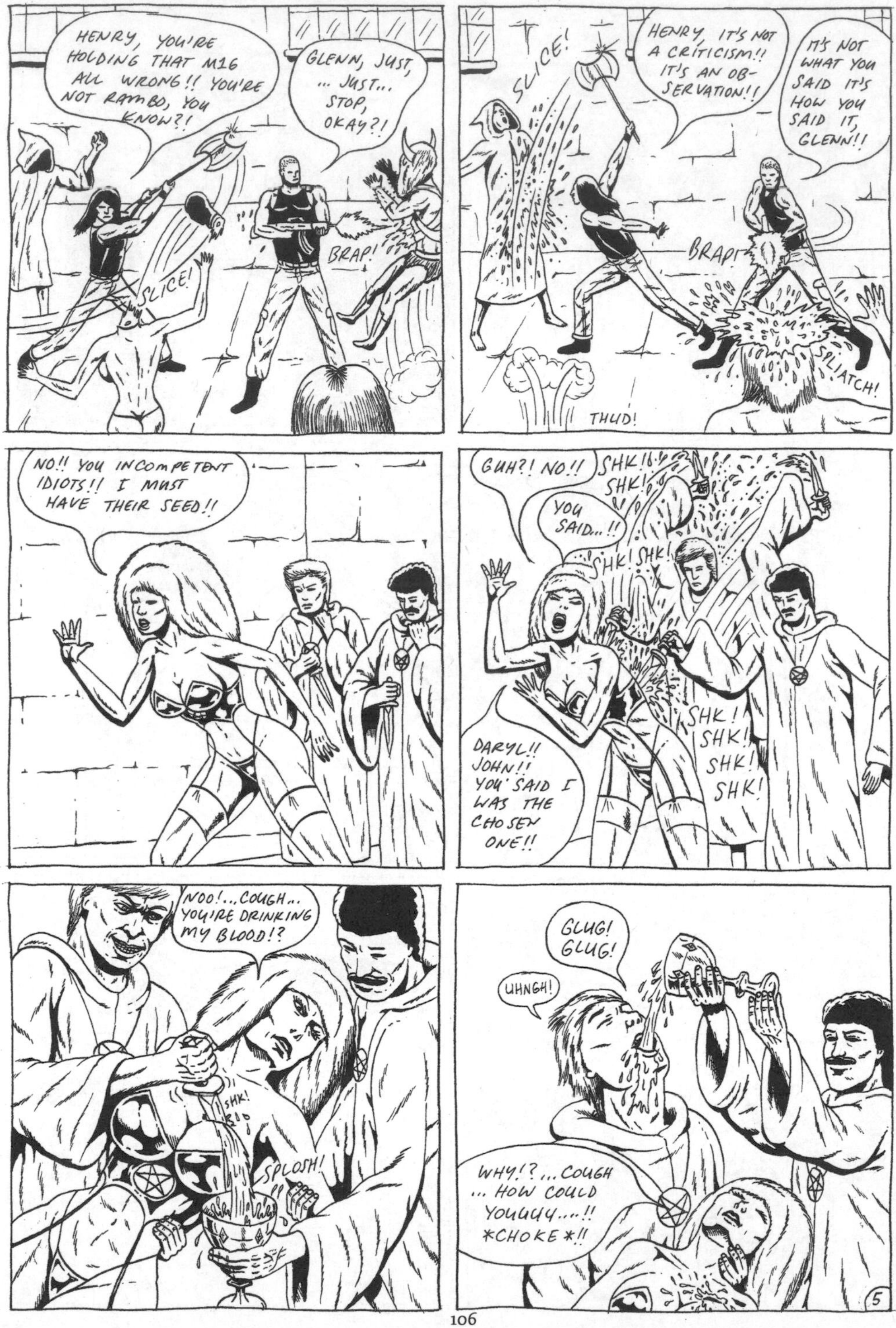
HENRY, YOU'RE HOLDING THAT M16 ALL WRONG!! YOU'RE NOT RAMBO, YOU KNOW?!
GLENN, JUST, ... JUST... STOP, OKAY?!
SLICE!
BRAP!
SLICE!
HENRY, IT'S NOT A CRITICISM!! IT'S AN OB-SERVATION!!
IT'S NOT WHAT YOU SAID IT'S HOW YOU SAID IT, GLENN!!
BRAP!
SPLATCH!
THUD!
NO!! YOU INCOMPETENT IDIOTS!! I MUST HAVE THEIR SEED!!
GUH?! NO!!
SHK! SHK!
YOU SAID...!!
SHK! SHK!
SHK! SHK! SHK! SHK!
DARYL!! JOHN!! YOU SAID I WAS THE CHOSEN ONE!!
NOO!... COUGH... YOU'RE DRINKING MY BLOOD!?
SHK!
SPLOSH!
GLUG! GLUG!
UHNGH!
WHY!?... COUGH ... HOW COULD YOUUUU....!! *CHOKE*!!
5

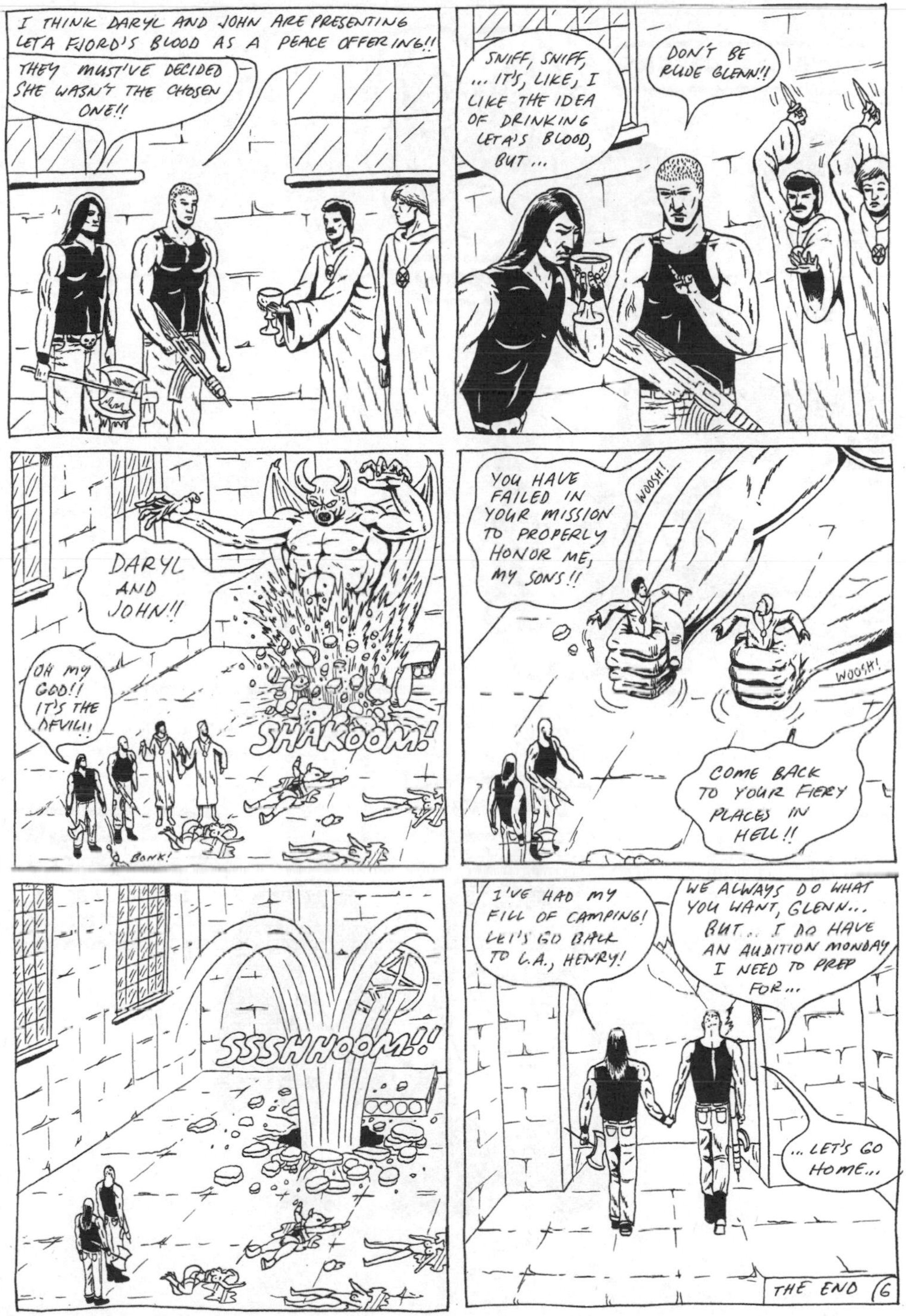

I THINK DARYL AND JOHN ARE PRESENTING LETA FJORD'S BLOOD AS A PEACE OFFERING!!
THEY MUST'VE DECIDED SHE WASN'T THE CHOSEN ONE!!
SNIFF, SNIFF, ... IT'S, LIKE, I LIKE THE IDEA OF DRINKING LETA'S BLOOD, BUT ...
DON'T BE RUDE GLENN!!
DARYL AND JOHN!!
OH MY GOD!! IT'S THE DEVIL!!
SHAKOOM!
BONK!
YOU HAVE FAILED IN YOUR MISSION TO PROPERLY HONOR ME, MY SONS!!
WOOSH!
WOOSH!
COME BACK TO YOUR FIERY PLACES IN HELL!!
SSSHHOOM!!
I'VE HAD MY FILL OF CAMPING! LET'S GO BACK TO L.A., HENRY!
WE ALWAYS DO WHAT YOU WANT, GLENN... BUT... I DO HAVE AN AUDITION MONDAY I NEED TO PREP FOR...
... LET'S GO HOME...
THE END
6

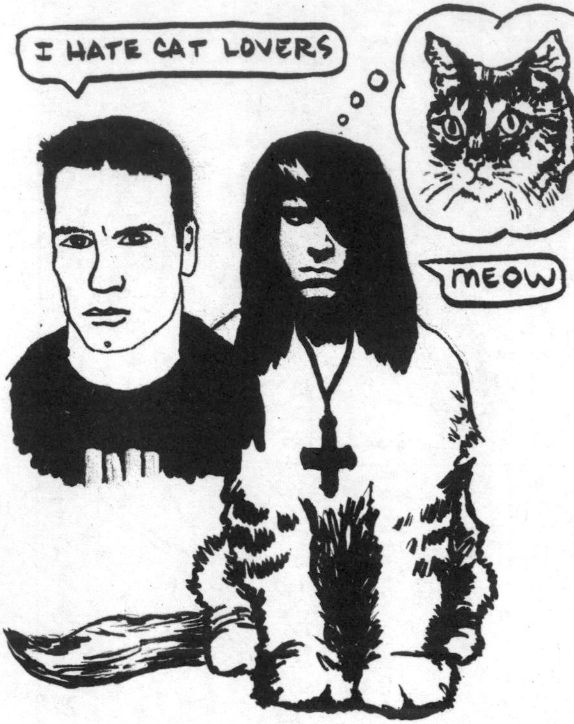
I HATE CAT LOVERS
MEOW

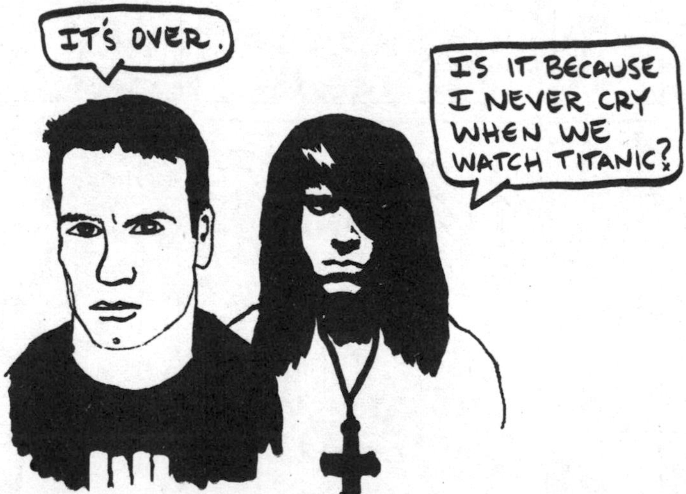
IT'S OVER.
IS IT BECAUSE I NEVER CRY WHEN WE WATCH TITANIC?

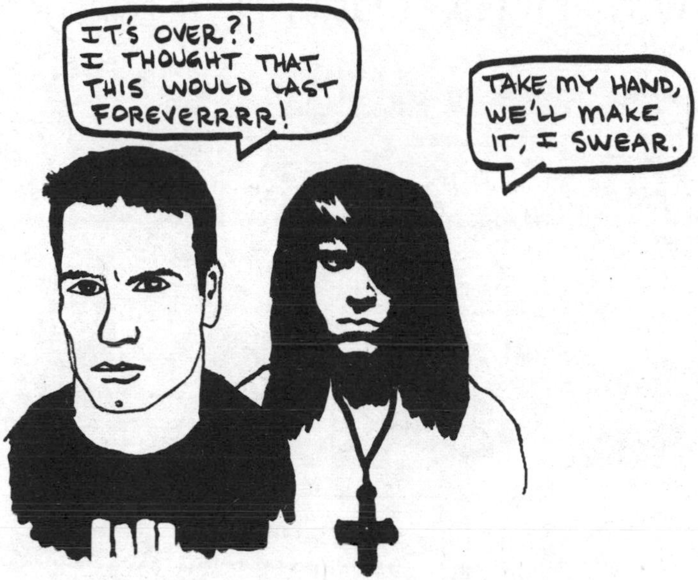
IT'S OVER?! I THOUGHT THAT THIS WOULD LAST FOREVERRRR!
TAKE MY HAND, WE'LL MAKE IT, I SWEAR.

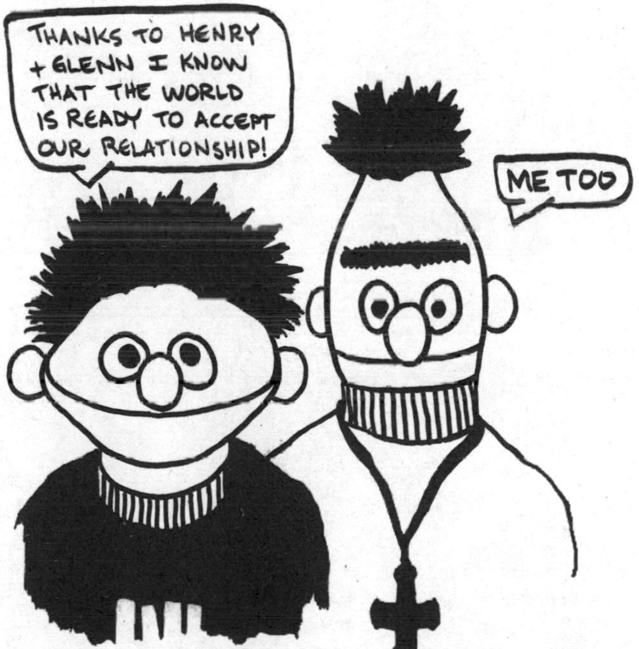
THANKS TO HENRY + GLENN I KNOW THAT THE WORLD IS READY TO ACCEPT OUR RELATIONSHIP!
ME TOO

D.I.Y. with HENRY & GLENN

by Gabby Gamboa

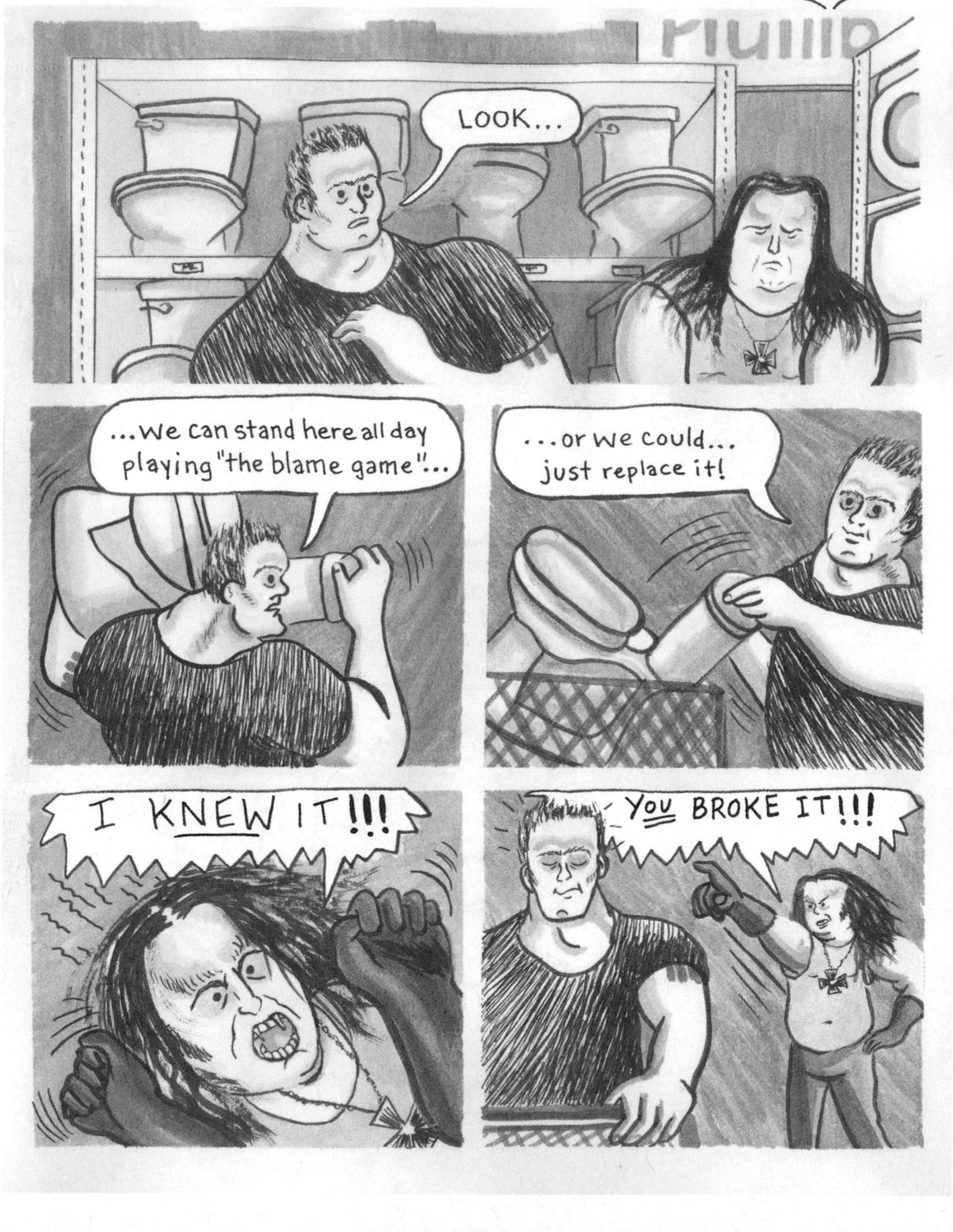
LOOK...
...we can stand here all day playing "the blame game"...
...or we could... just replace it!
I KNEW IT!!!
YOU BROKE IT!!!

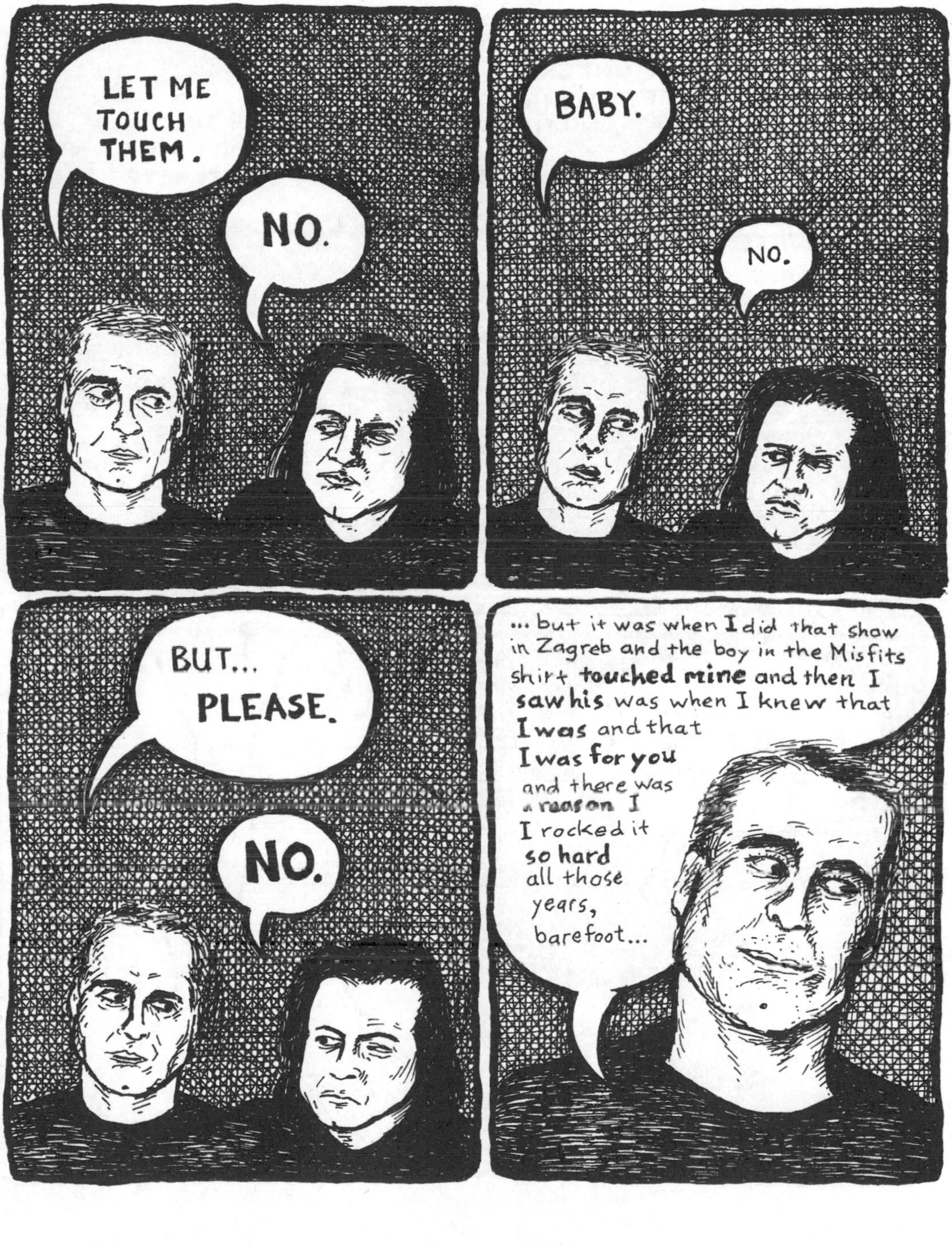
LET ME TOUCH THEM.
NO.
BABY.
NO.
BUT... PLEASE.
NO.
... but it was when I did that show in Zagreb and the boy in the Misfits shirt touched mine and then I saw his was when I knew that I was and that I was for you and there was a reason I I rocked it so hard all those years, barefoot...

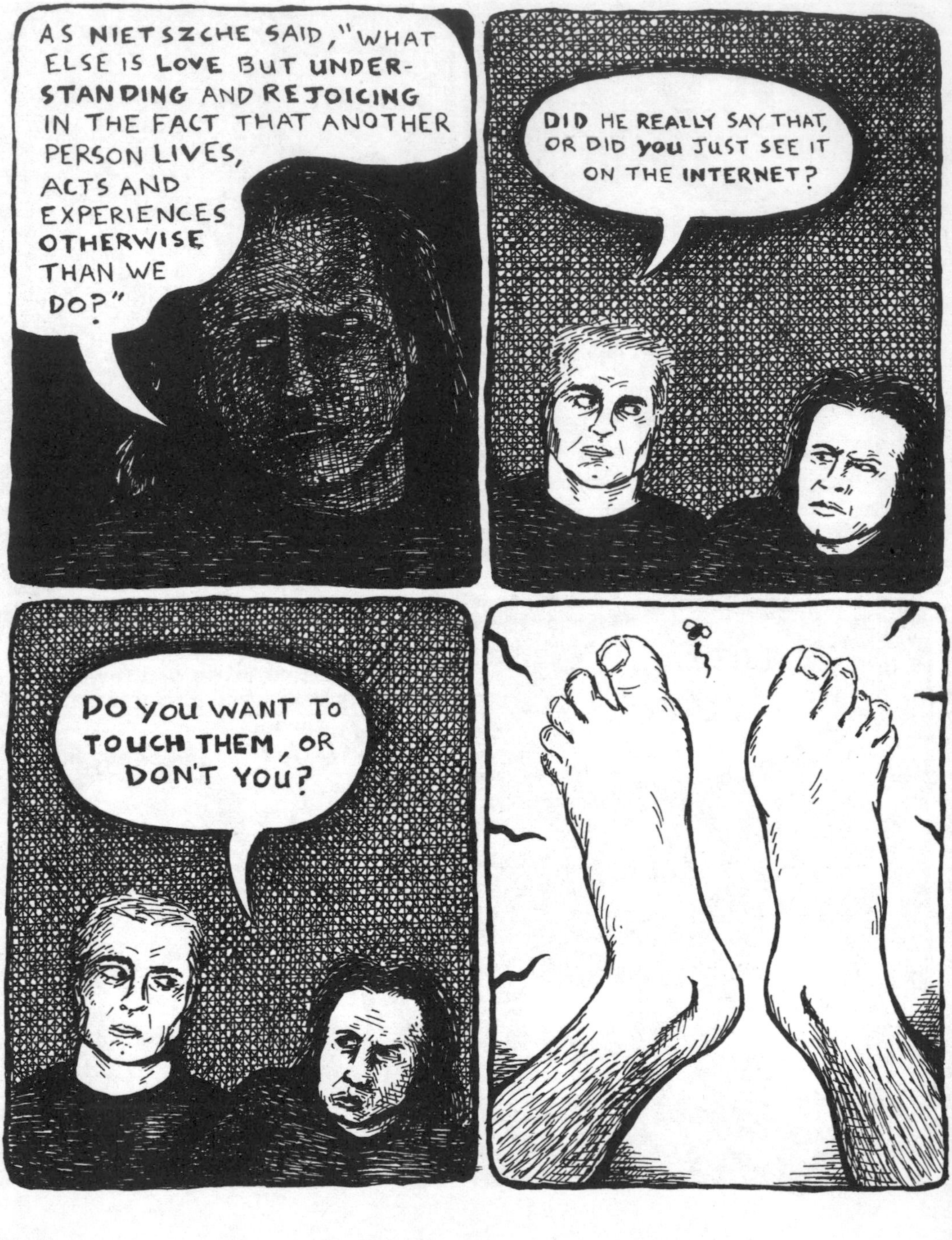
AS NIETSZCHE SAID, "WHAT ELSE IS LOVE BUT UNDER-STANDING AND REJOICING IN THE FACT THAT ANOTHER PERSON LIVES, ACTS AND EXPERIENCES OTHERWISE THAN WE DO?"
DID HE REALLY SAY THAT, OR DID YOU JUST SEE IT ON THE INTERNET?
DO YOU WANT TO TOUCH THEM, OR DON'T YOU?

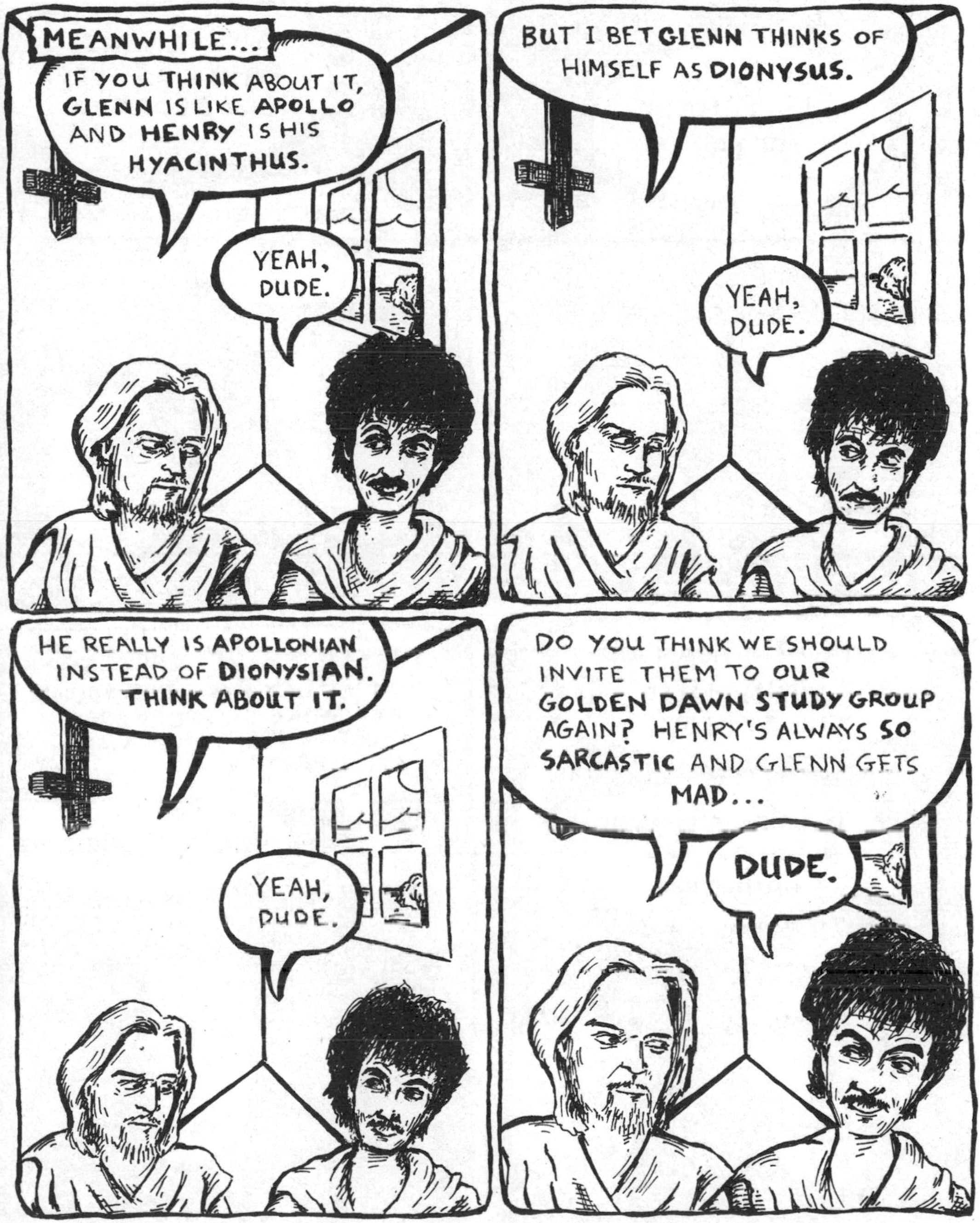
MEANWHILE...
IF YOU THINK ABOUT IT, GLENN IS LIKE APOLLO AND HENRY IS HIS HYACINTHUS.
YEAH, DUDE.
BUT I BET GLENN THINKS OF HIMSELF AS DIONYSUS.
YEAH, DUDE.
HE REALLY IS APOLLONIAN INSTEAD OF DIONYSIAN. THINK ABOUT IT.
YEAH, DUDE.
DO YOU THINK WE SHOULD INVITE THEM TO OUR GOLDEN DAWN STUDY GROUP AGAIN? HENRY'S ALWAYS SO SARCASTIC AND GLENN GETS MAD...
DUDE.

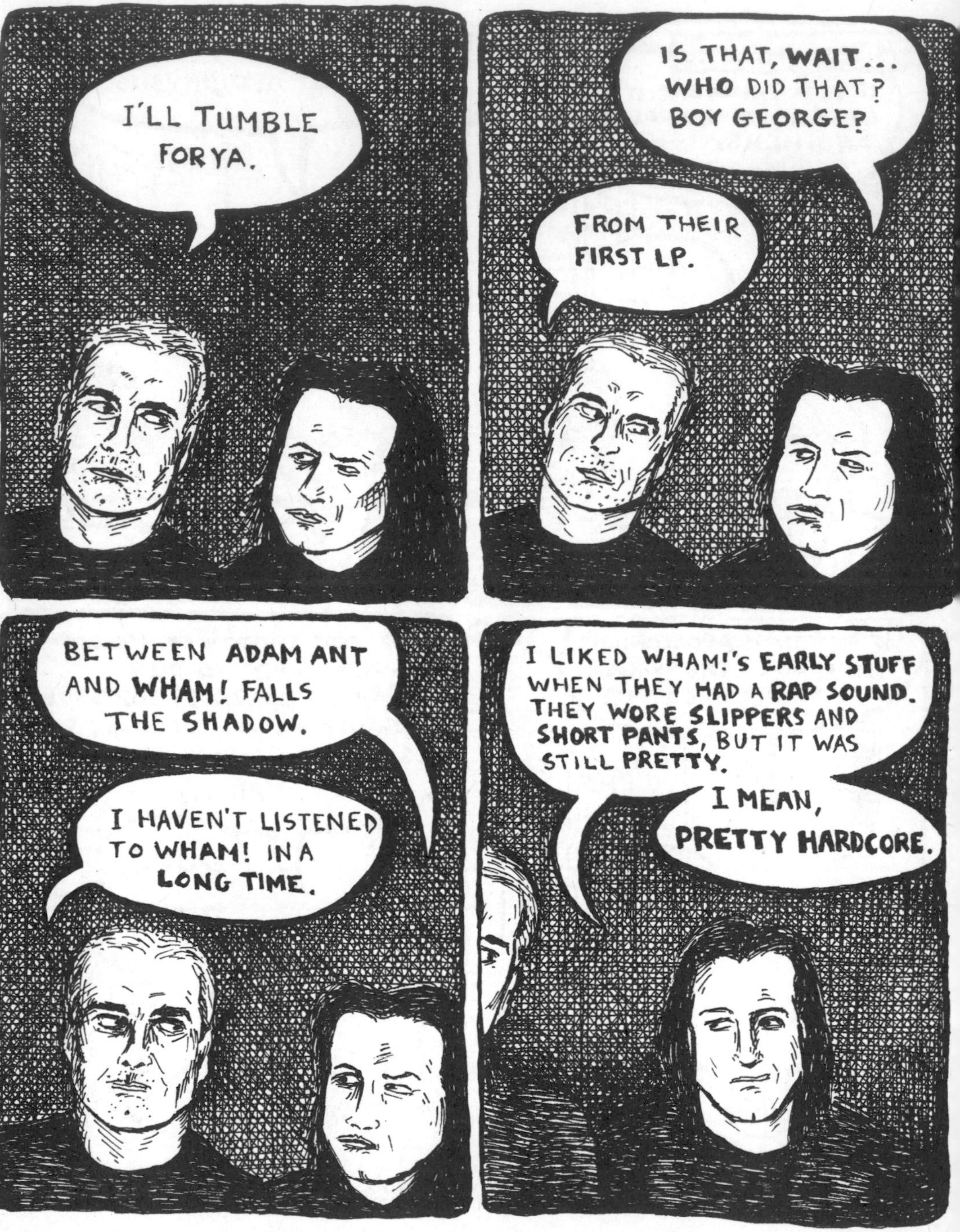
I'LL TUMBLE FOR YA.
IS THAT, WAIT... WHO DID THAT? BOY GEORGE?
FROM THEIR FIRST LP.
BETWEEN ADAM ANT AND WHAM! FALLS THE SHADOW.
I HAVEN'T LISTENED TO WHAM! IN A LONG TIME.
I LIKED WHAM!'s EARLY STUFF WHEN THEY HAD A RAP SOUND. THEY WORE SLIPPERS AND SHORT PANTS, BUT IT WAS STILL PRETTY.
I MEAN, PRETTY HARDCORE.

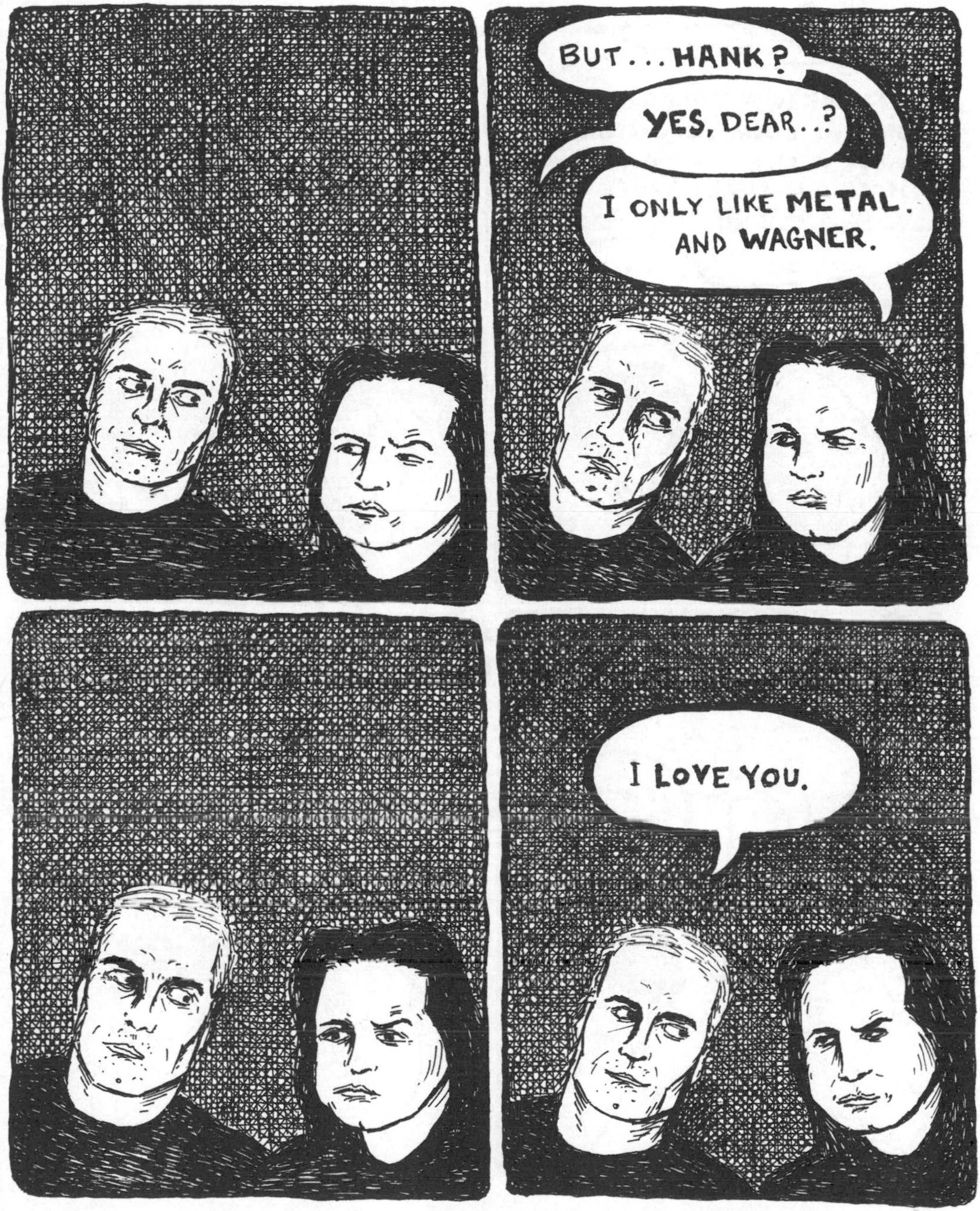
BUT . . . HANK?
YES, DEAR . . ?
I ONLY LIKE METAL. AND WAGNER.
I LOVE YOU.

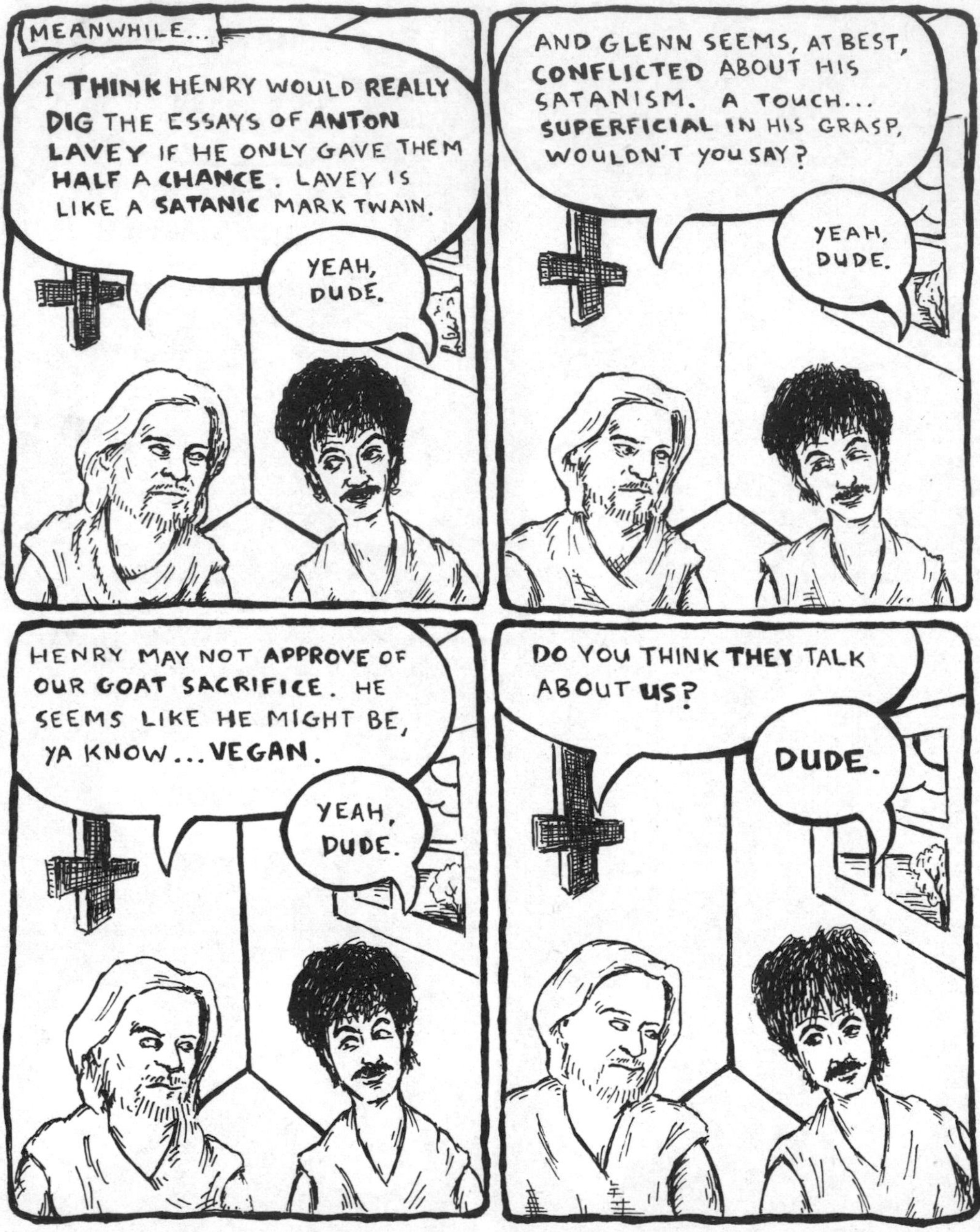
MEANWHILE...
I THINK HENRY WOULD REALLY DIG THE ESSAYS OF ANTON LAVEY IF HE ONLY GAVE THEM HALF A CHANCE. LAVEY IS LIKE A SATANIC MARK TWAIN.
YEAH, DUDE.
AND GLENN SEEMS, AT BEST, CONFLICTED ABOUT HIS SATANISM. A TOUCH... SUPERFICIAL IN HIS GRASP, WOULDN'T YOU SAY?
YEAH, DUDE.
HENRY MAY NOT APPROVE OF OUR GOAT SACRIFICE. HE SEEMS LIKE HE MIGHT BE, YA KNOW... VEGAN.
YEAH, DUDE.
DO YOU THINK THEY TALK ABOUT US?
DUDE.

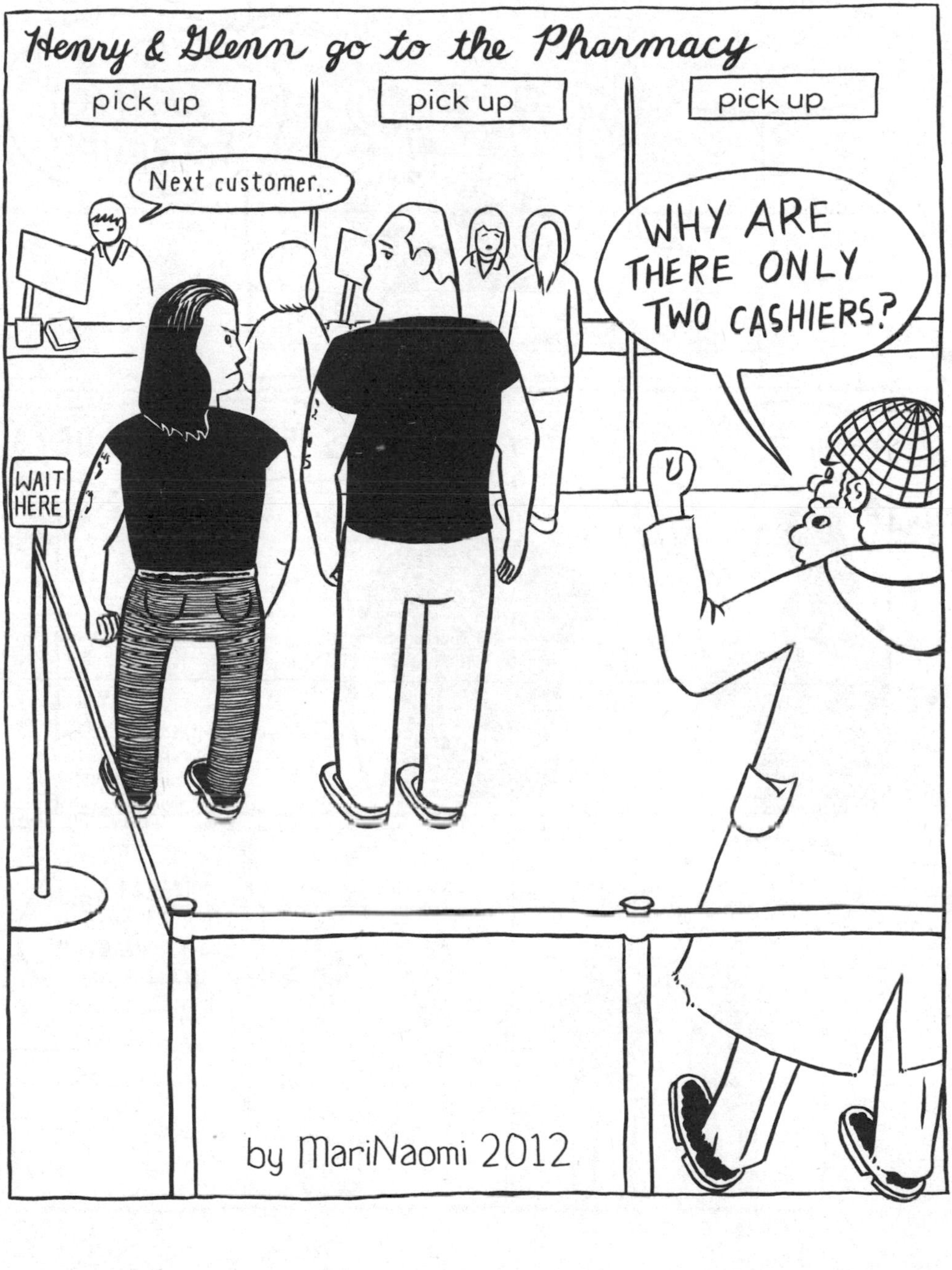
Henry & Glenn go to the Pharmacy
pick up
pick up
pick up
Next customer...
WHY ARE THERE ONLY TWO CASHIERS?
WAIT HERE
by MariNaomi 2012

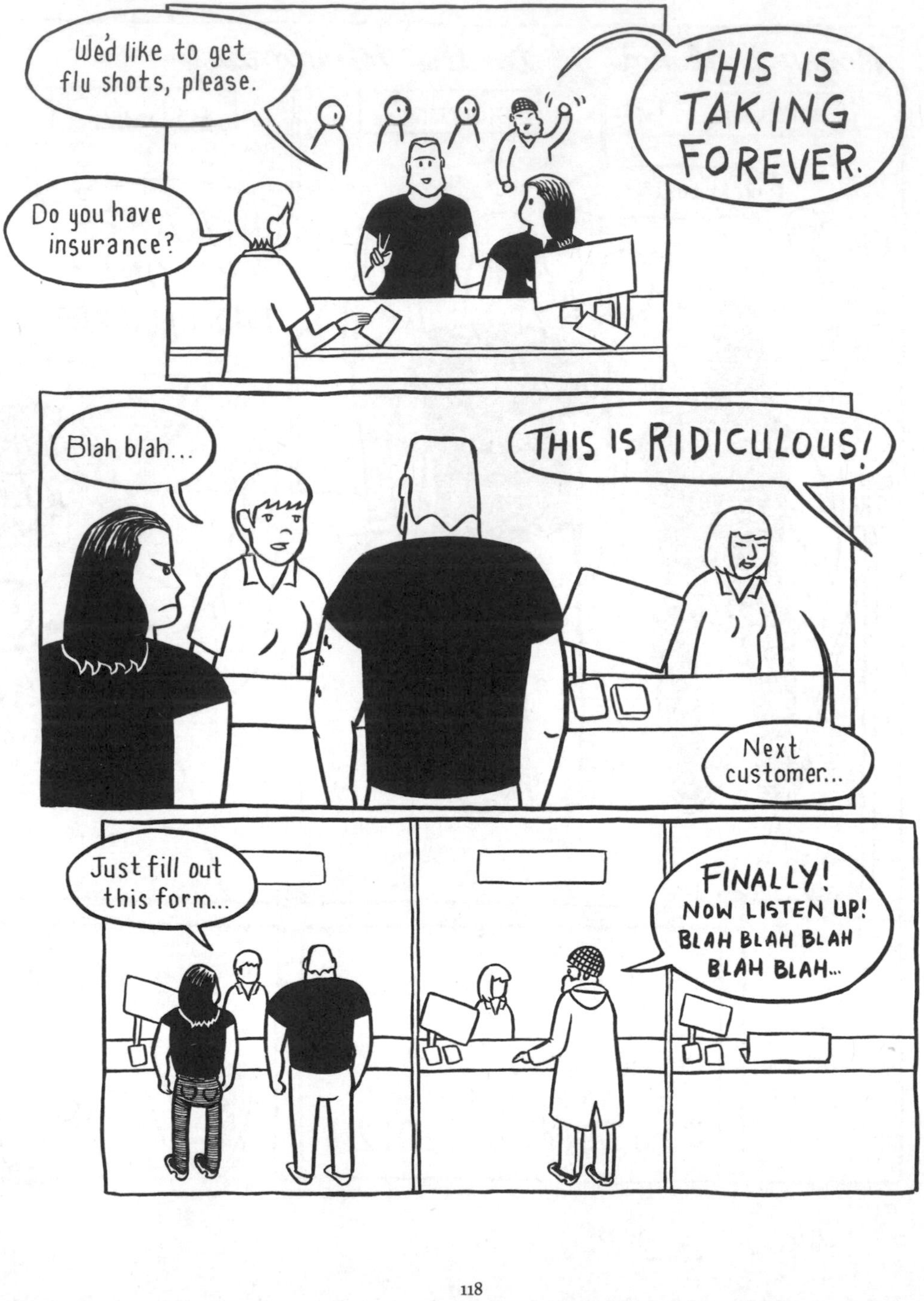
We'd like to get flu shots, please.
THIS IS TAKING FOREVER.
Do you have insurance?
Blah blah...
THIS IS RIDICULOUS!
Next customer...
Just fill out this form...
FINALLY! NOW LISTEN UP! BLAH BLAH BLAH BLAH BLAH...

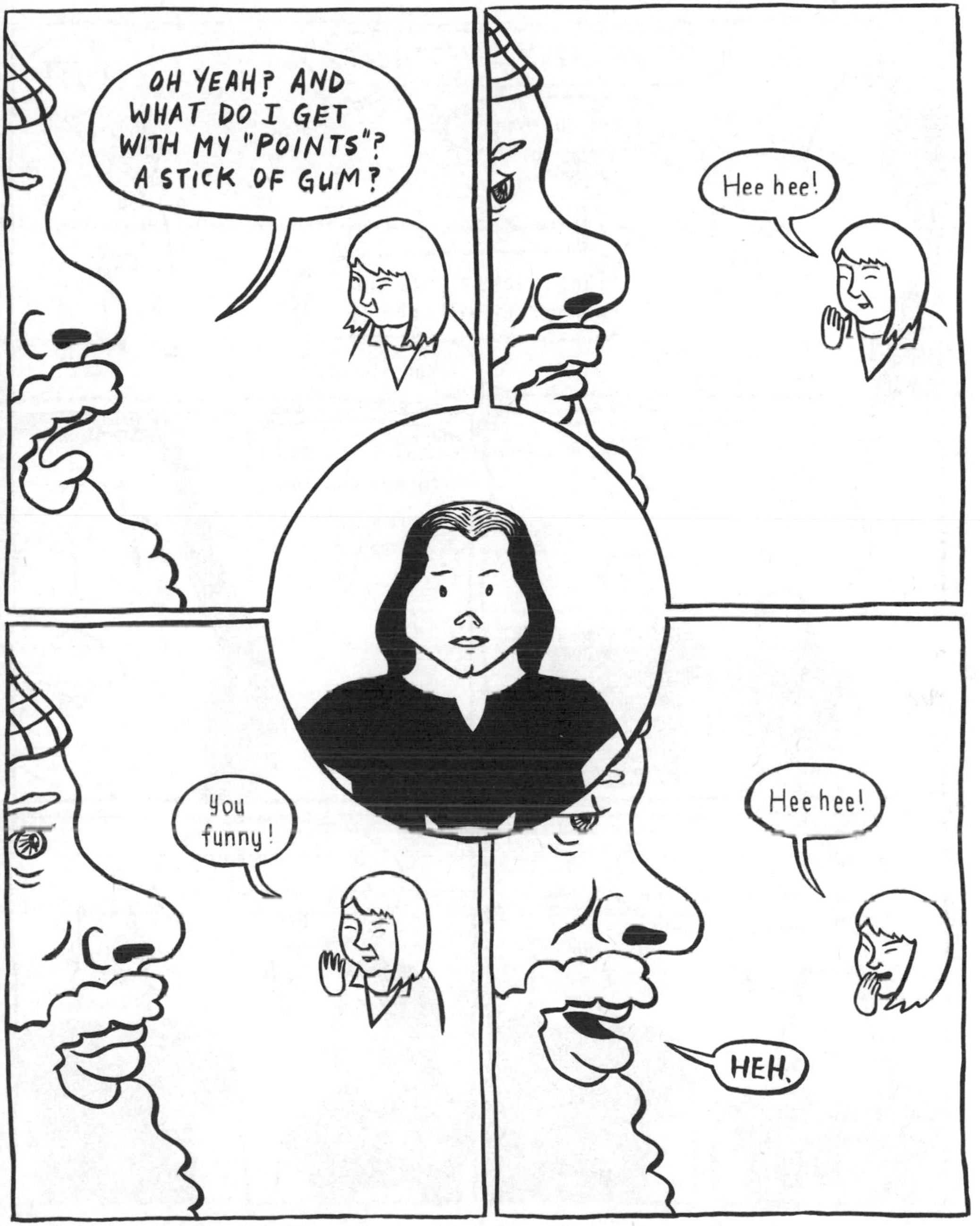
OH YEAH? AND WHAT DO I GET WITH MY "POINTS"? A STICK OF GUM?
Hee hee!
You funny!
Hee hee!
HEH.

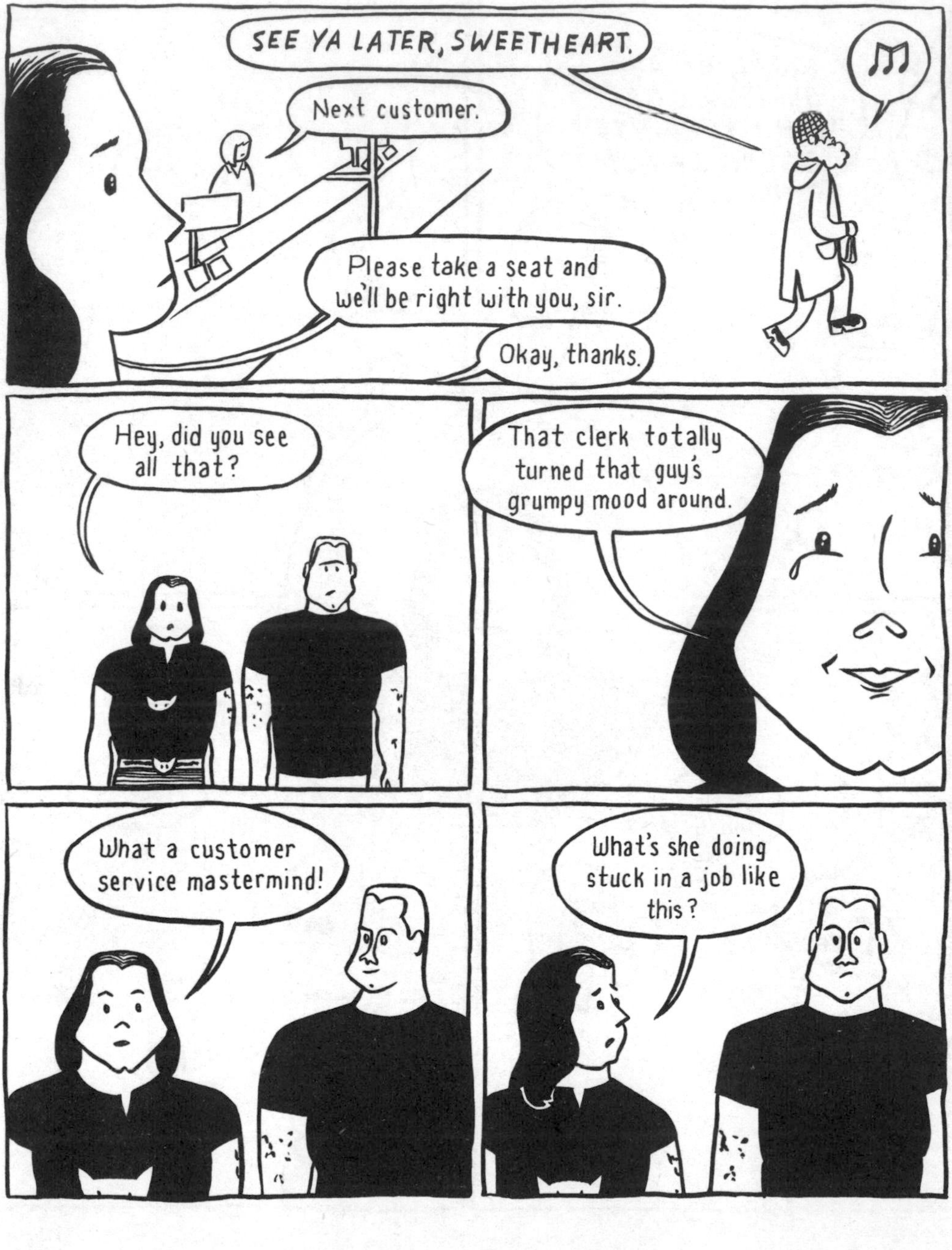
SEE YA LATER, SWEETHEART.
Next customer.
Please take a seat and we'll be right with you, sir.
Okay, thanks.
Hey, did you see all that?
That clerk totally turned that guy's grumpy mood around.
What a customer service mastermind!
What's she doing stuck in a job like this?

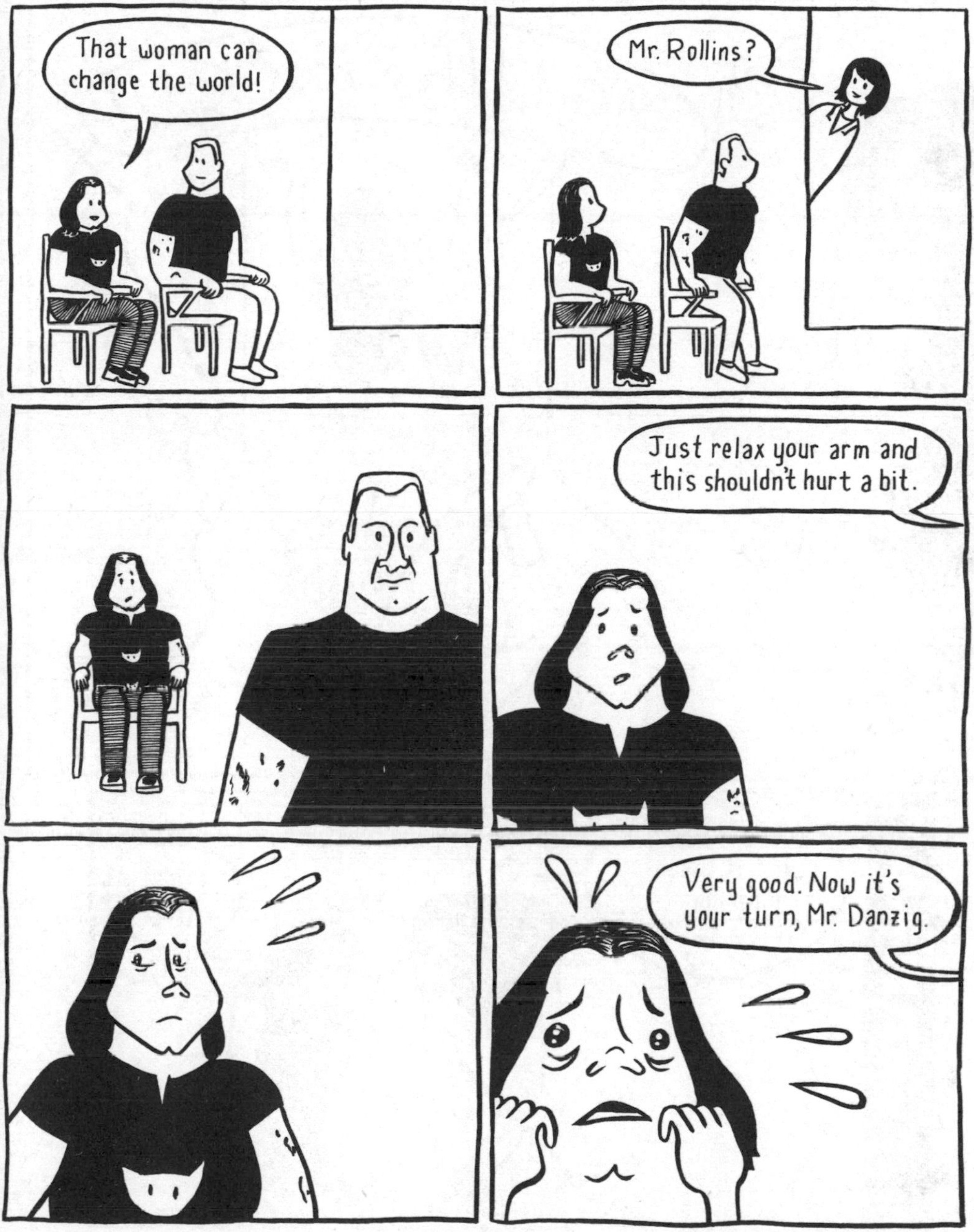
That woman can change the world!
Mr. Rollins?
Just relax your arm and this shouldn't hurt a bit.
Very good. Now it's your turn, Mr. Danzig.

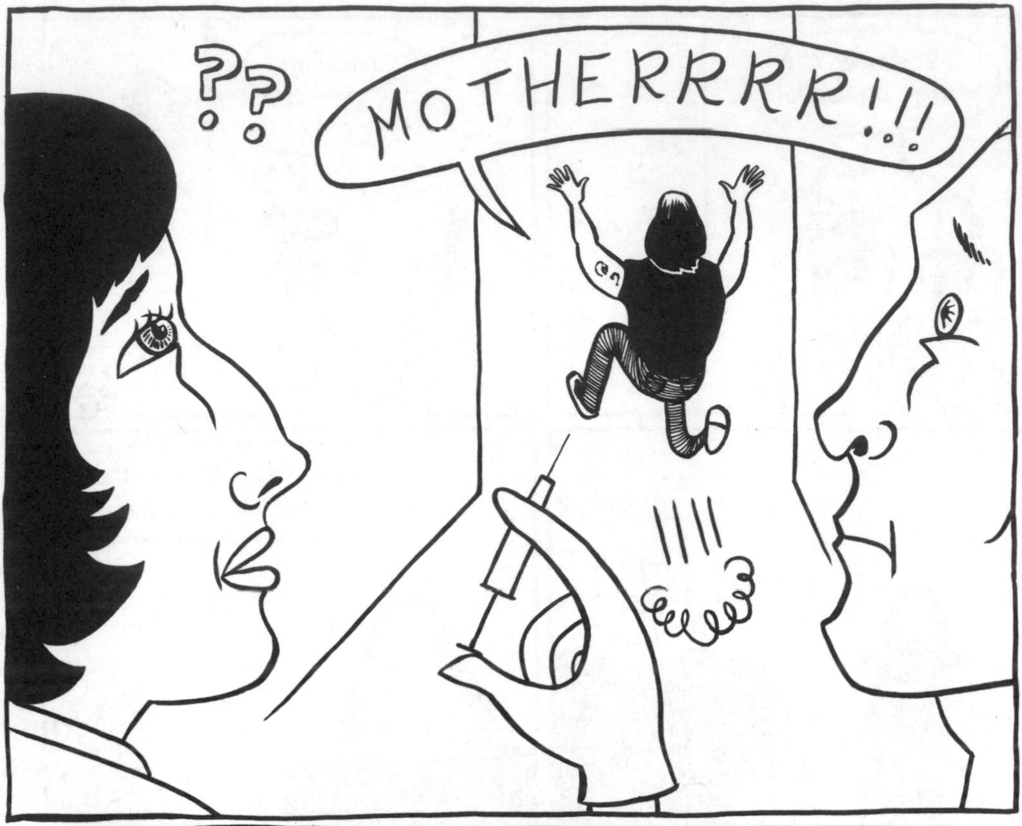
??
MOTHERRRRR!!!

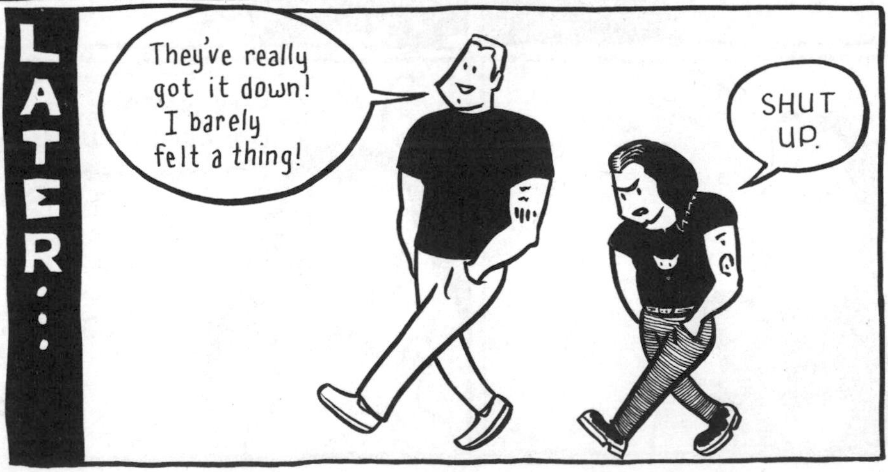
LATER...
They've really got it down! I barely felt a thing!
SHUT UP.

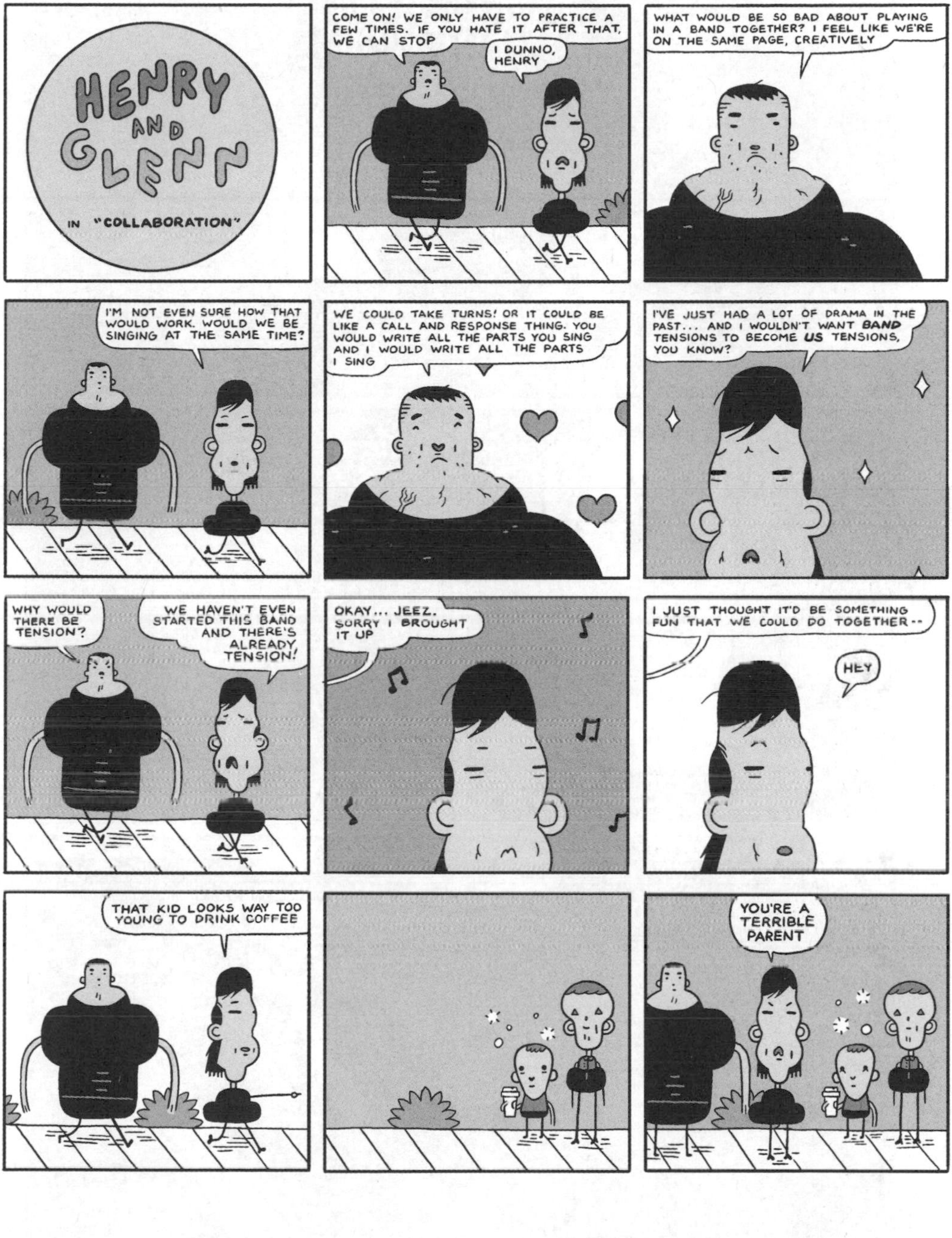
HENRY AND GLENN
IN "COLLABORATION"
COME ON! WE ONLY HAVE TO PRACTICE A FEW TIMES. IF YOU HATE IT AFTER THAT, WE CAN STOP
I DUNNO, HENRY
WHAT WOULD BE SO BAD ABOUT PLAYING IN A BAND TOGETHER? I FEEL LIKE WE'RE ON THE SAME PAGE, CREATIVELY
I'M NOT EVEN SURE HOW THAT WOULD WORK. WOULD WE BE SINGING AT THE SAME TIME?
WE COULD TAKE TURNS! OR IT COULD BE LIKE A CALL AND RESPONSE THING. YOU WOULD WRITE ALL THE PARTS YOU SING AND I WOULD WRITE ALL THE PARTS I SING
I'VE JUST HAD A LOT OF DRAMA IN THE PAST... AND I WOULDN'T WANT BAND TENSIONS TO BECOME US TENSIONS, YOU KNOW?
WHY WOULD THERE BE TENSION?
WE HAVEN'T EVEN STARTED THIS BAND AND THERE'S ALREADY TENSION!
OKAY... JEEZ. SORRY I BROUGHT IT UP
I JUST THOUGHT IT'D BE SOMETHING FUN THAT WE COULD DO TOGETHER--
HEY
THAT KID LOOKS WAY TOO YOUNG TO DRINK COFFEE
YOU'RE A TERRIBLE PARENT

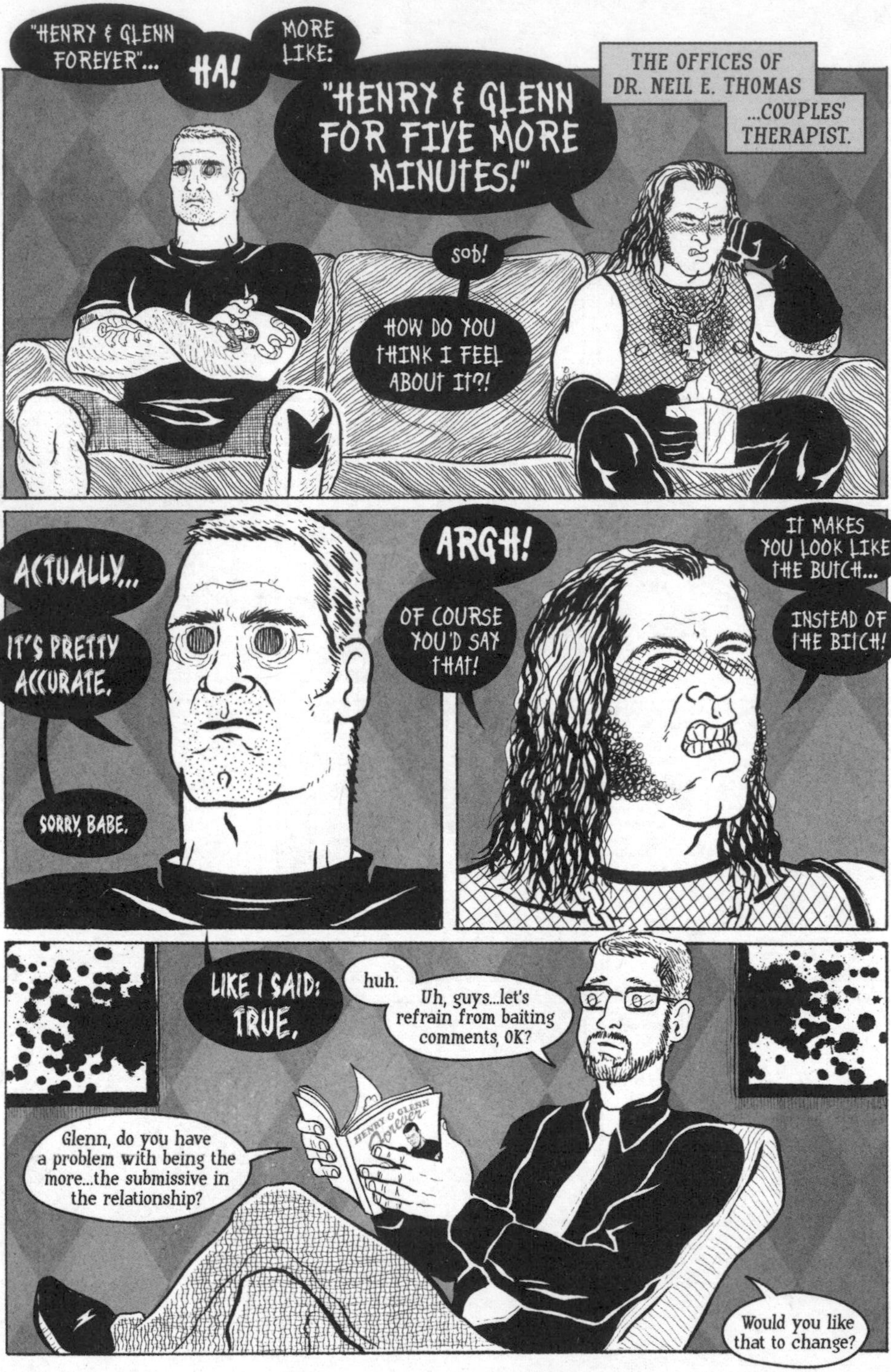
"HENRY & GLENN FOREVER"...
HA!
MORE LIKE:
"HENRY & GLENN FOR FIVE MORE MINUTES!"
THE OFFICES OF DR. NEIL E. THOMAS ...COUPLES' THERAPIST.
SOB!
HOW DO YOU THINK I FEEL ABOUT IT?!
ACTUALLY...
IT'S PRETTY ACCURATE.
SORRY, BABE.
ARGH!
OF COURSE YOU'D SAY THAT!
IT MAKES YOU LOOK LIKE THE BUTCH...
INSTEAD OF THE BITCH!
LIKE I SAID: TRUE.
huh.
Uh, guys...let's refrain from baiting comments, OK?
Glenn, do you have a problem with being the more...the submissive in the relationship?
Would you like that to change?
HENRY & GLENN Forever

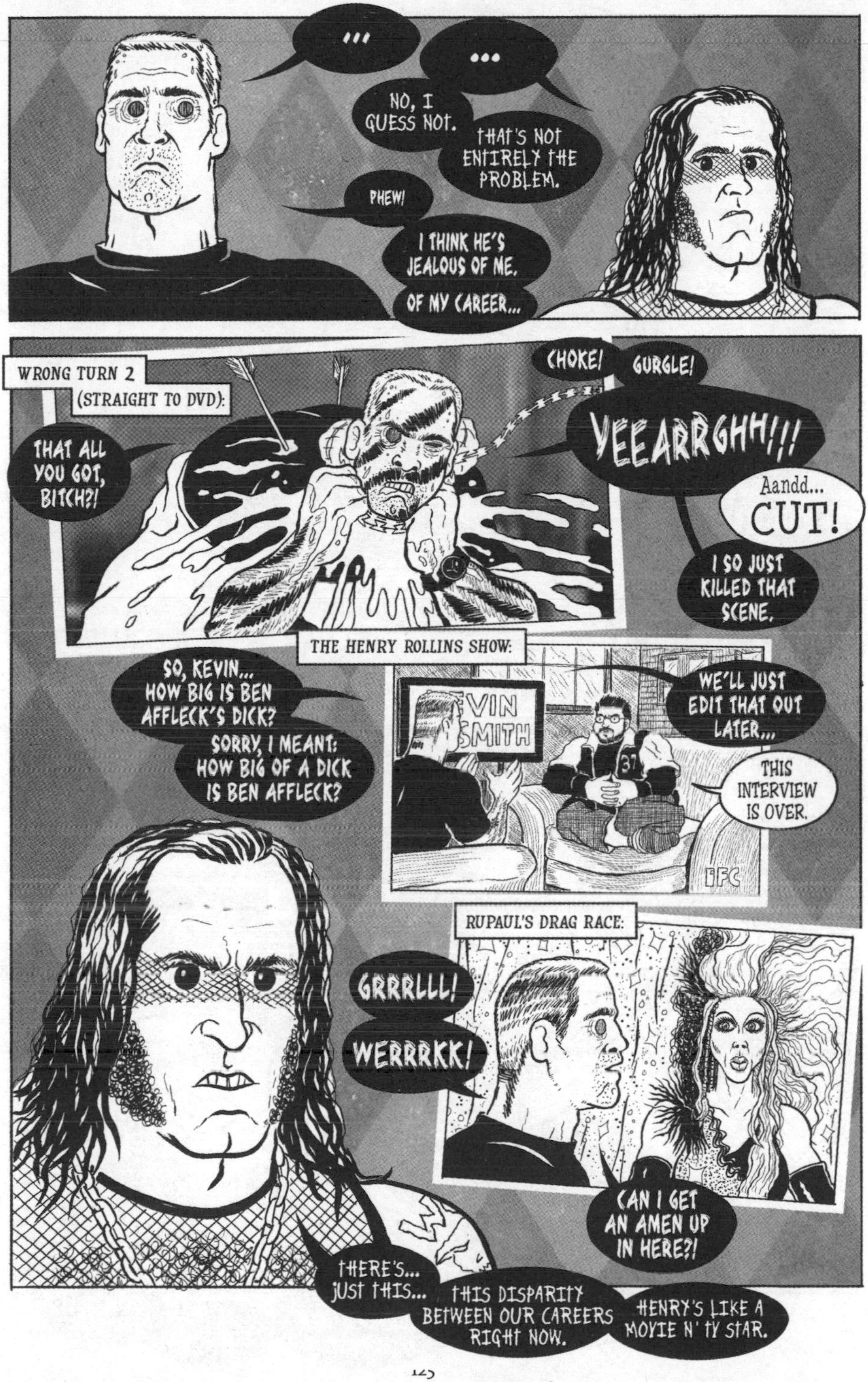
...
...
NO, I GUESS NOT.
THAT'S NOT ENTIRELY THE PROBLEM.
PHEW!
I THINK HE'S JEALOUS OF ME.
OF MY CAREER...
WRONG TURN 2 (STRAIGHT TO DVD):
CHOKE!
GURGLE!
THAT ALL YOU GOT, BITCH?!
YEEARRGHH!!!
Aandd... CUT!
I SO JUST KILLED THAT SCENE.
THE HENRY ROLLINS SHOW:
SO, KEVIN... HOW BIG IS BEN AFFLECK'S DICK?
SORRY, I MEANT: HOW BIG OF A DICK IS BEN AFFLECK?
EVIN SMITH
WE'LL JUST EDIT THAT OUT LATER...
THIS INTERVIEW IS OVER.
IFC
RUPAUL'S DRAG RACE:
GRRRLLL!
WERRRKK!
CAN I GET AN AMEN UP IN HERE?!
THERE'S... JUST THIS...
THIS DISPARITY BETWEEN OUR CAREERS RIGHT NOW.
HENRY'S LIKE A MOVIE N' TV STAR.

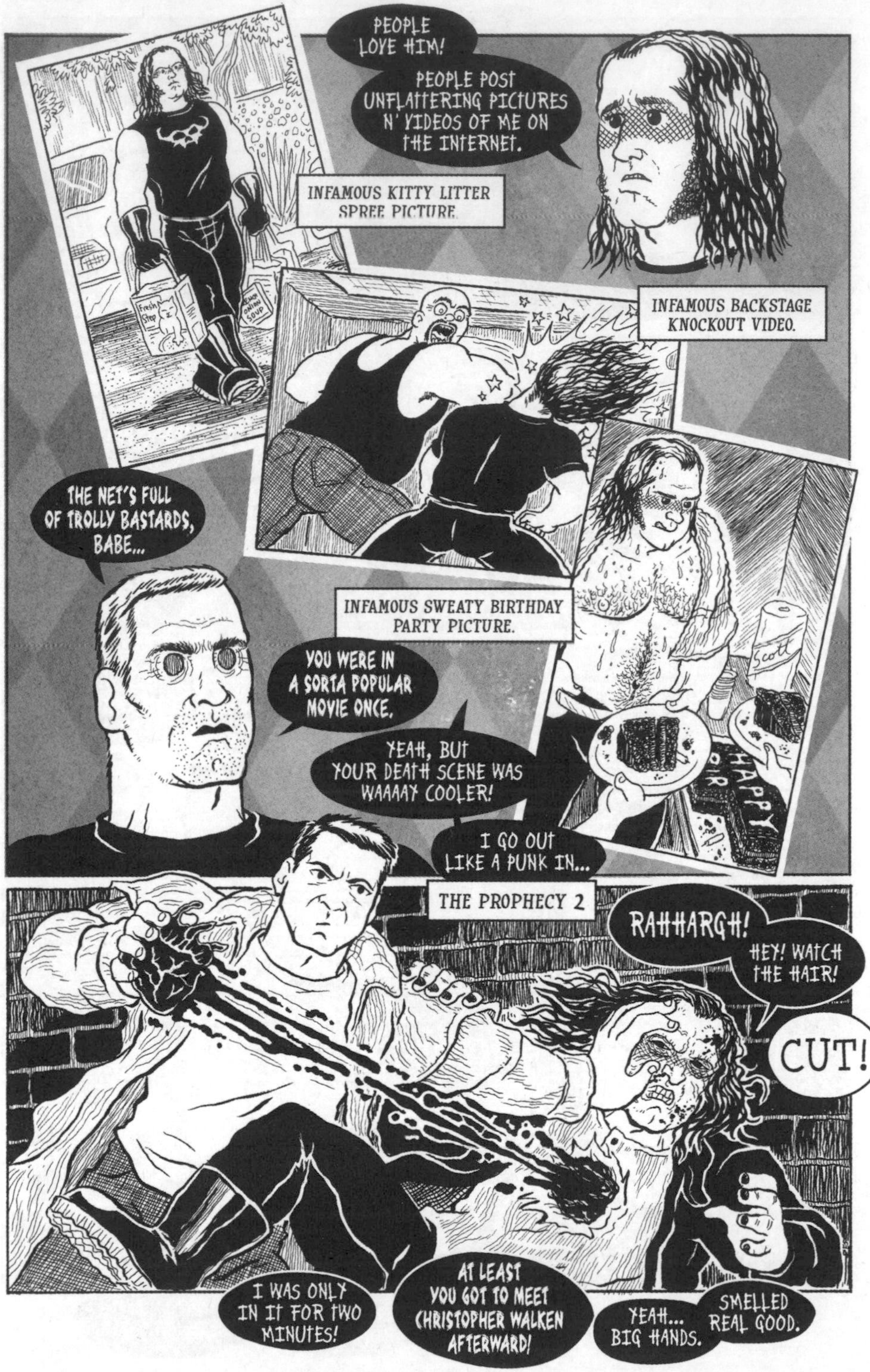
PEOPLE LOVE HIM!
PEOPLE POST UNFLATTERING PICTURES N' VIDEOS OF ME ON THE INTERNET.
INFAMOUS KITTY LITTER SPREE PICTURE.
Fresh Step
INFAMOUS BACKSTAGE KNOCKOUT VIDEO.
THE NET'S FULL OF TROLLY BASTARDS, BABE...
INFAMOUS SWEATY BIRTHDAY PARTY PICTURE.
Scott
YOU WERE IN A SORTA POPULAR MOVIE ONCE.
YEAH, BUT YOUR DEATH SCENE WAS WAAAAY COOLER!
HAPPY
I GO OUT LIKE A PUNK IN...
THE PROPHECY 2
RAHHARGH!
HEY! WATCH THE HAIR!
CUT!
I WAS ONLY IN IT FOR TWO MINUTES!
AT LEAST YOU GOT TO MEET CHRISTOPHER WALKEN AFTERWARD!
YEAH... BIG HANDS.
SMELLED REAL GOOD.

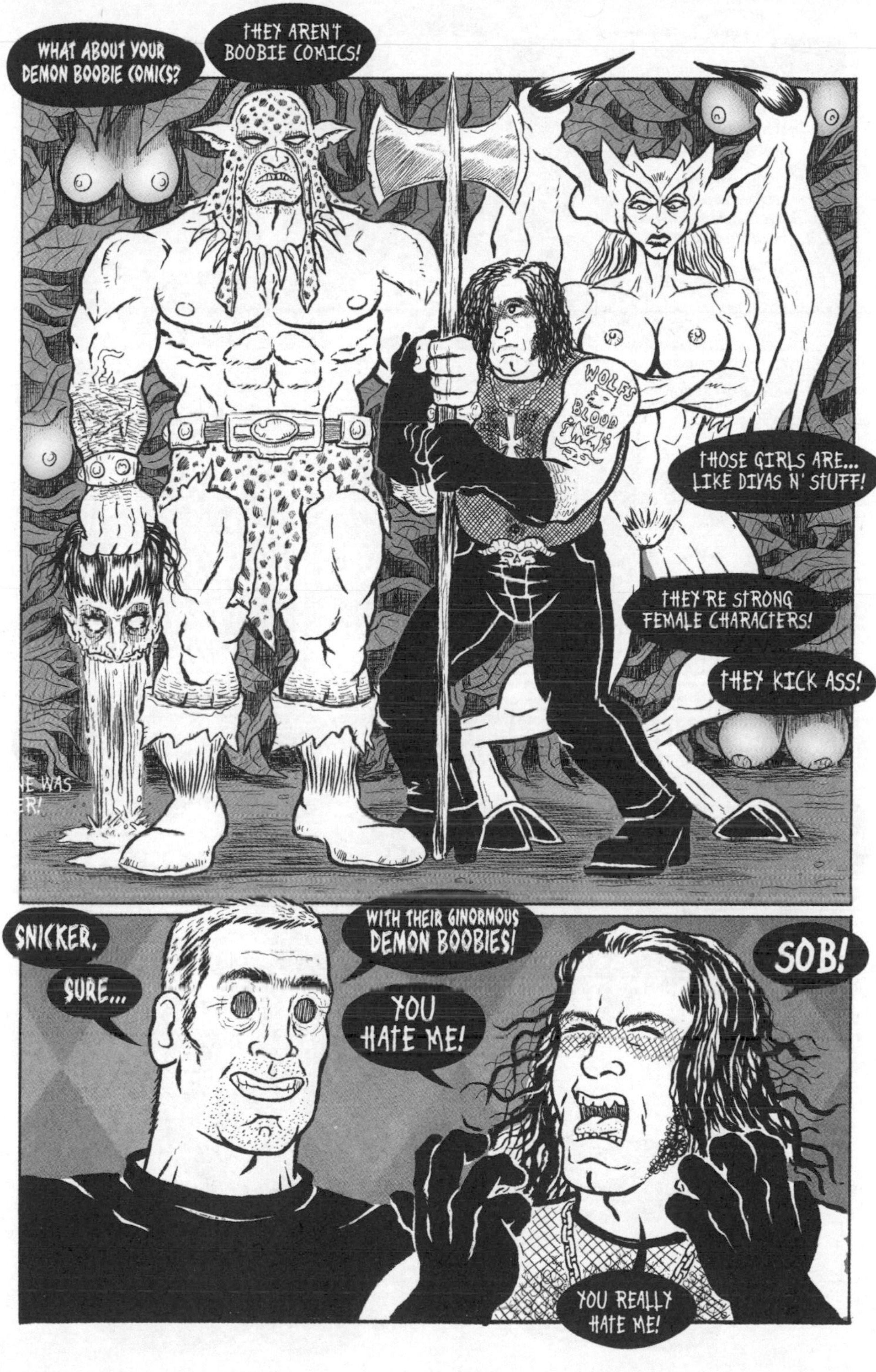
WHAT ABOUT YOUR DEMON BOOBIE COMICS?
THEY AREN'T BOOBIE COMICS!
THOSE GIRLS ARE... LIKE DIVAS N' STUFF!
THEY'RE STRONG FEMALE CHARACTERS!
THEY KICK ASS!
SNICKER.
SURE...
WITH THEIR GINORMOUS DEMON BOOBIES!
YOU HATE ME!
SOB!
YOU REALLY HATE ME!

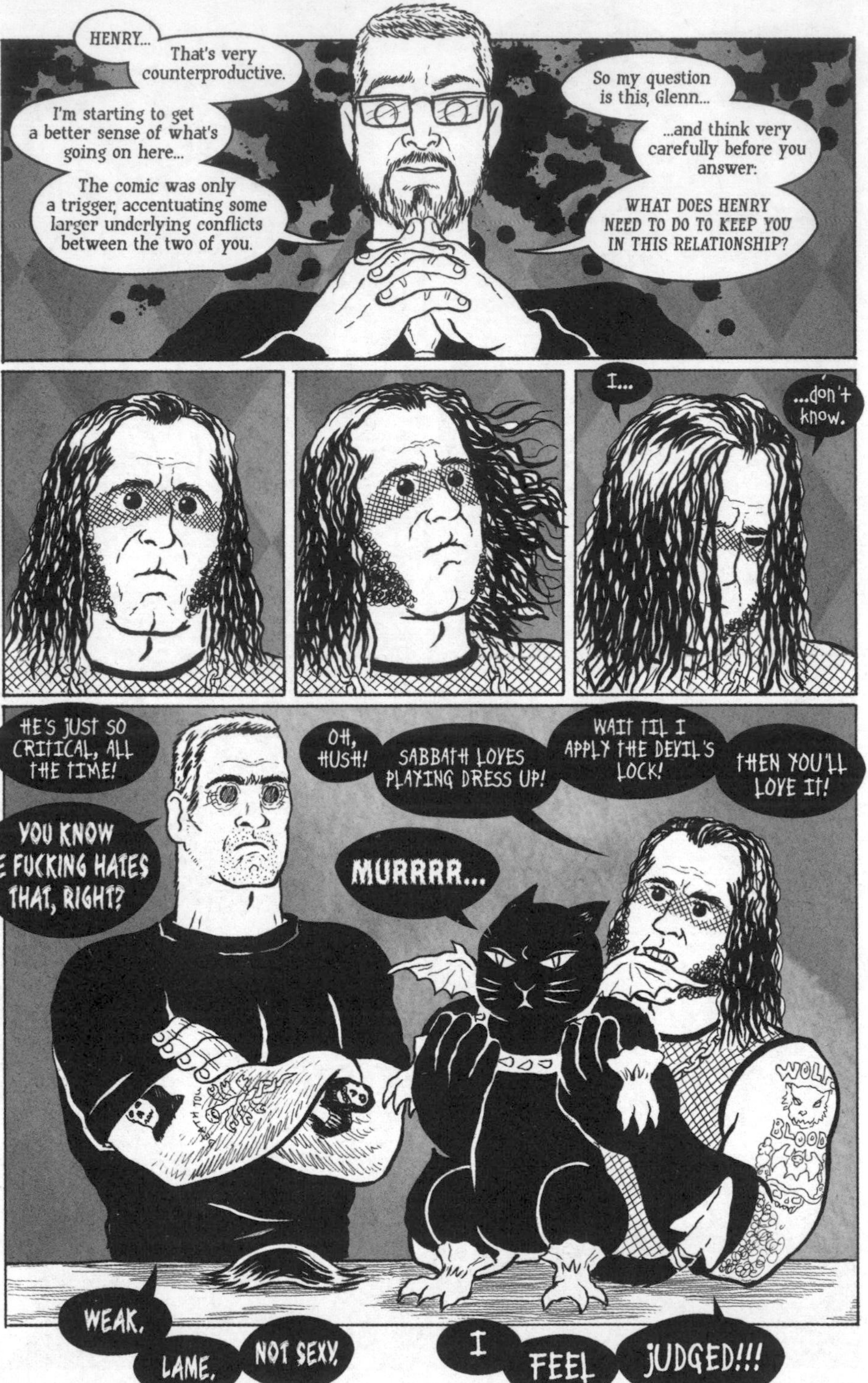
HENRY...
That's very counterproductive.
I'm starting to get a better sense of what's going on here...
The comic was only a trigger, accentuating some larger underlying conflicts between the two of you.
So my question is this, Glenn...
...and think very carefully before you answer:
WHAT DOES HENRY NEED TO DO TO KEEP YOU IN THIS RELATIONSHIP?
I...
...don't know.
HE'S JUST SO CRITICAL, ALL THE TIME!
OH, HUSH!
SABBATH LOVES PLAYING DRESS UP!
WAIT TIL I APPLY THE DEVIL'S LOCK!
THEN YOU'LL LOVE IT!
YOU KNOW HE FUCKING HATES THAT, RIGHT?
MURRRR...
WEAK.
LAME.
NOT SEXY.
I
FEEL
JUDGED!!!

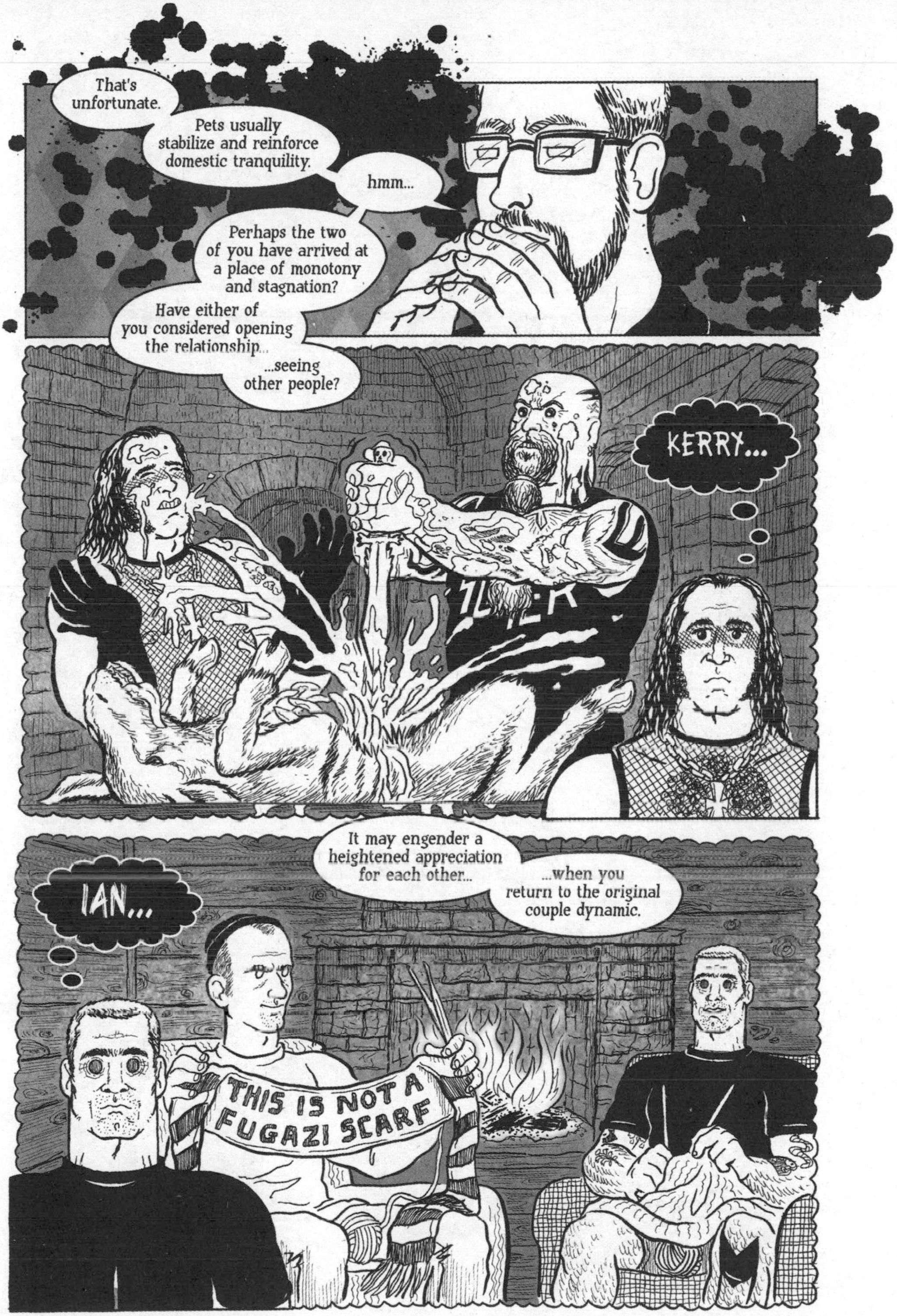

That's unfortunate.
Pets usually stabilize and reinforce domestic tranquility.
hmm...
Perhaps the two of you have arrived at a place of monotony and stagnation?
Have either of you considered opening the relationship...
...seeing other people?
KERRY...
It may engender a heightened appreciation for each other...
...when you return to the original couple dynamic.
IAN...
THIS IS NOT A FUGAZI SCARF

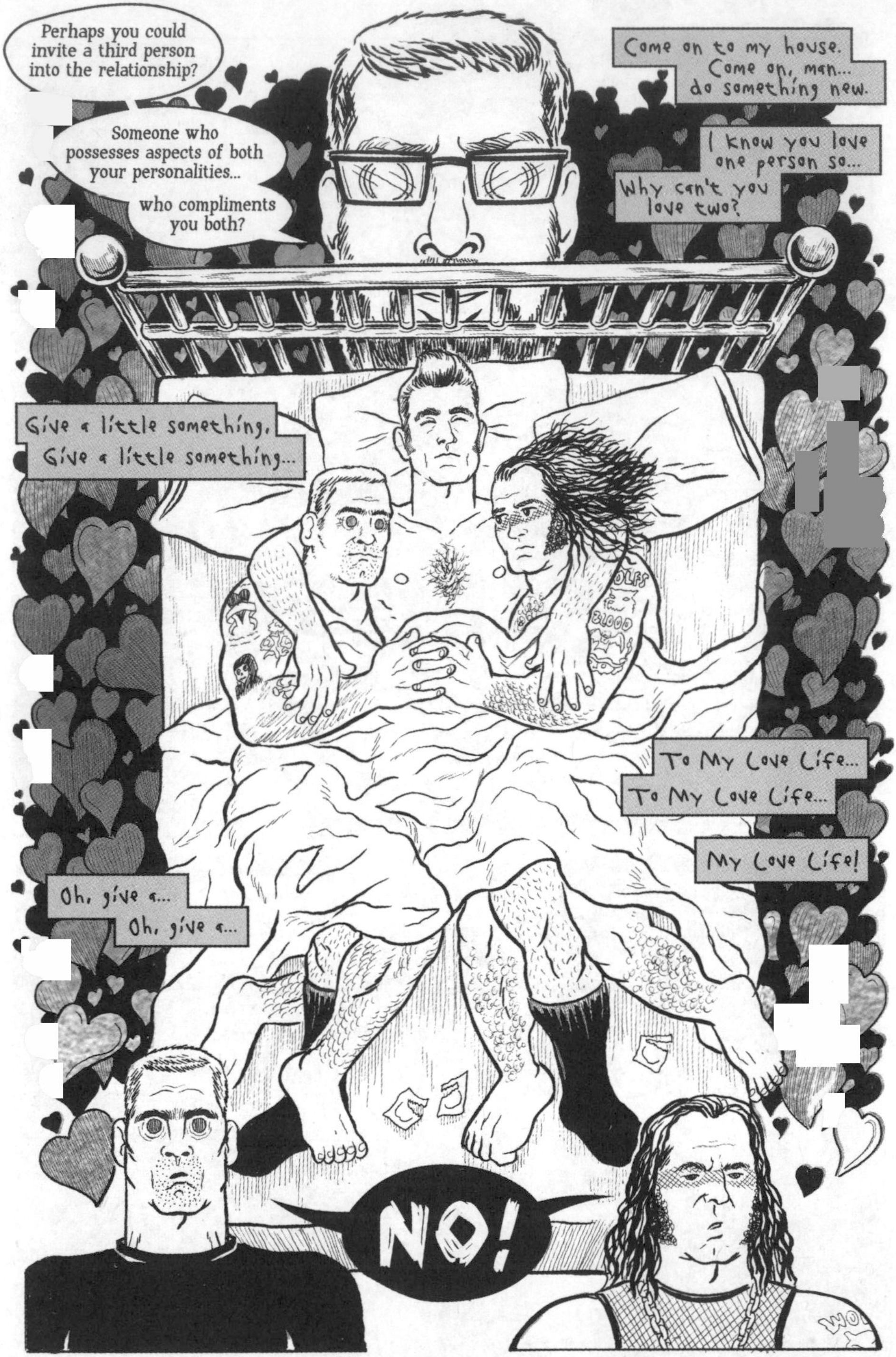

Perhaps you could invite a third person into the relationship?
Someone who possesses aspects of both your personalities...
who compliments you both?
Come on to my house. Come on, man... do something new.
I know you love one person so...
Why can't you love two?
Give a little something, Give a little something...
To My Love Life... To My Love Life...
My Love Life!
Oh, give a... Oh, give a...
NO!

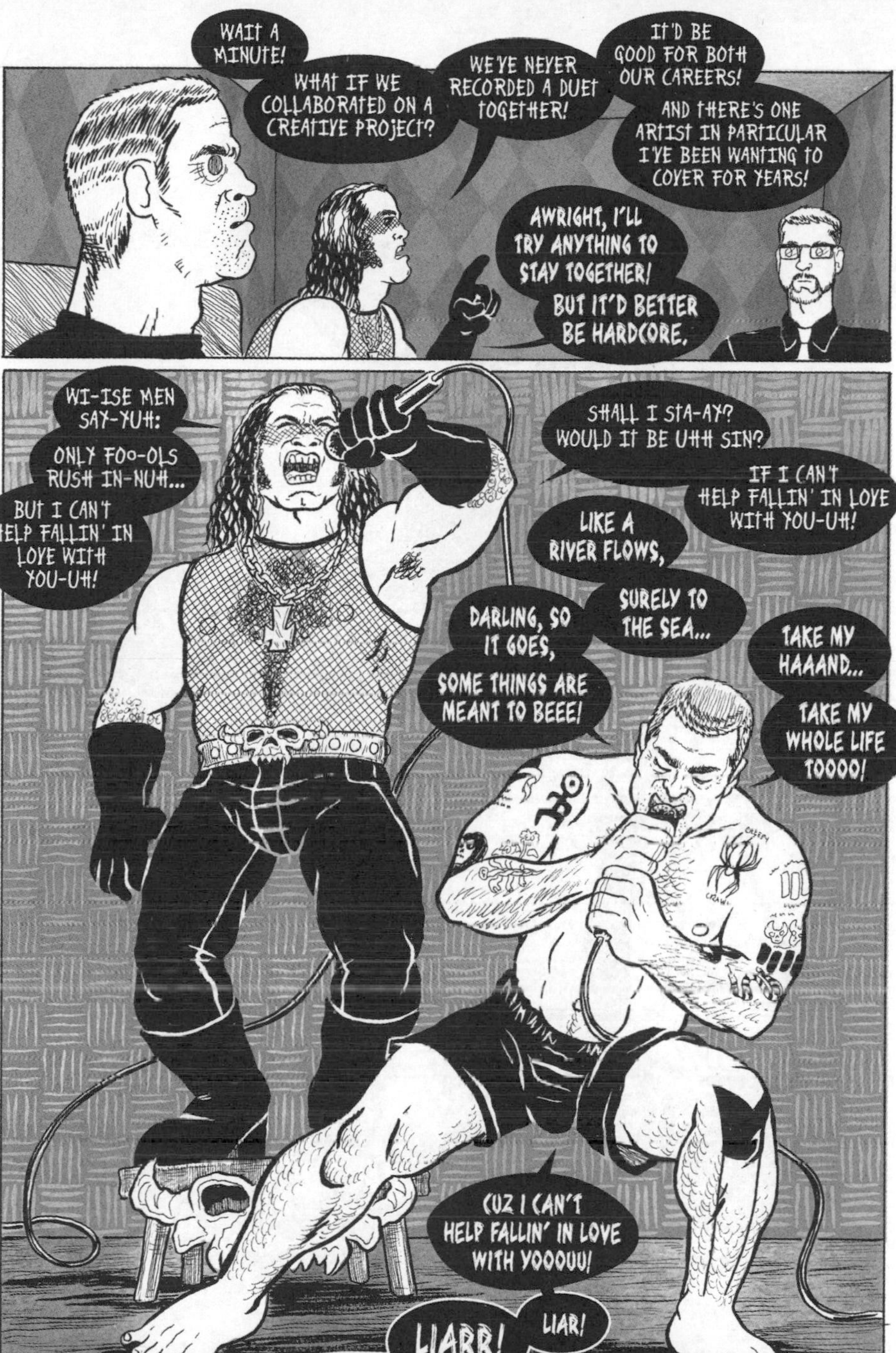

WAIT A MINUTE!
WHAT IF WE COLLABORATED ON A CREATIVE PROJECT?
WE'VE NEVER RECORDED A DUET TOGETHER!
IT'D BE GOOD FOR BOTH OUR CAREERS!
AND THERE'S ONE ARTIST IN PARTICULAR I'VE BEEN WANTING TO COVER FOR YEARS!
AWRIGHT, I'LL TRY ANYTHING TO STAY TOGETHER!
BUT IT'D BETTER BE HARDCORE.
WI-ISE MEN SAY-YUH:
ONLY FOO-OLS RUSH IN-NUH...
BUT I CAN'T HELP FALLIN' IN LOVE WITH YOU-UH!
SHALL I STA-AY? WOULD IT BE UHH SIN?
IF I CAN'T HELP FALLIN' IN LOVE WITH YOU-UH!
LIKE A RIVER FLOWS,
SURELY TO THE SEA...
DARLING, SO IT GOES,
SOME THINGS ARE MEANT TO BEEE!
TAKE MY HAAAND...
TAKE MY WHOLE LIFE TOOOO!
CUZ I CAN'T HELP FALLIN' IN LOVE WITH YOOOUU!
LIAR!
LIARR!
LIA-YUH!
HENRY! YOU'RE RUINING THIS!
SORRY, BABE!

WRITTEN & DRAWN
by ED LUCE

THE END

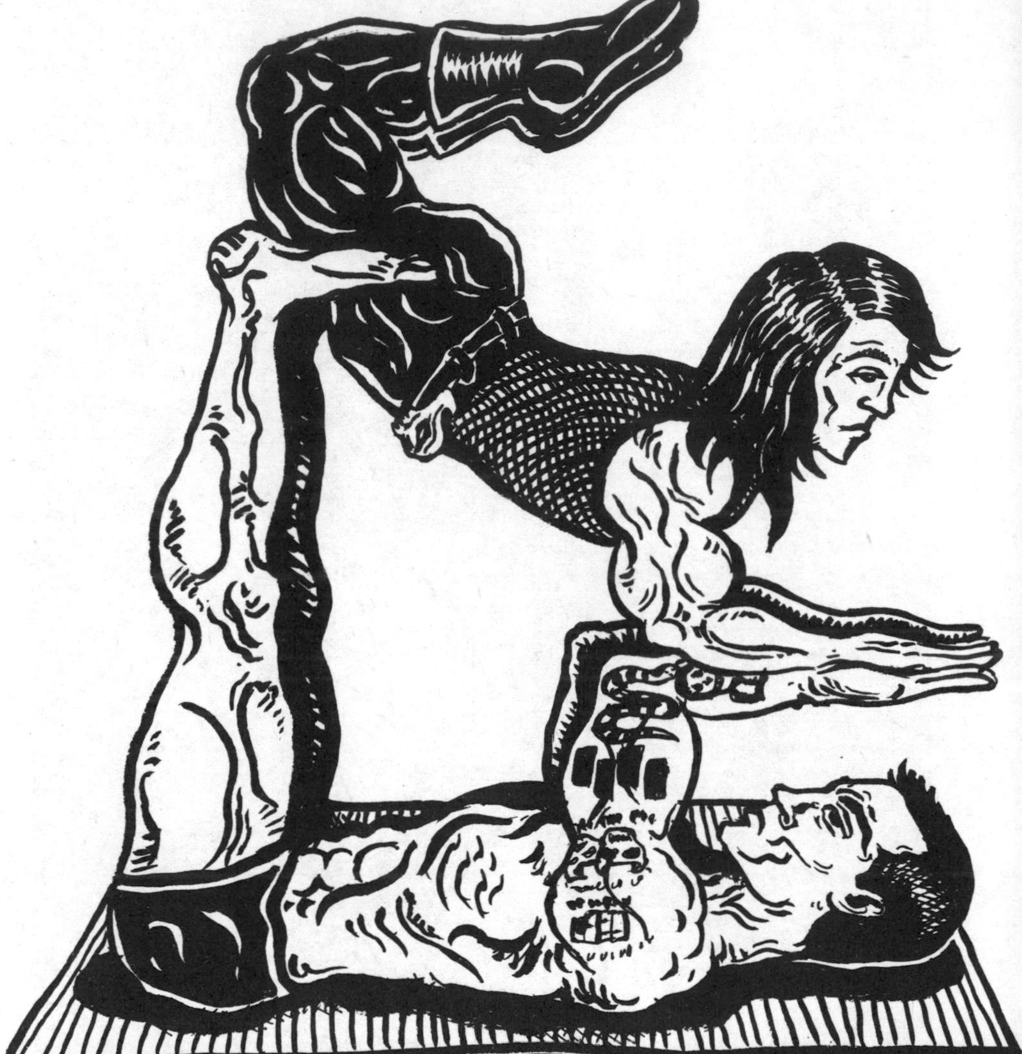
ALEX CHIU 2013

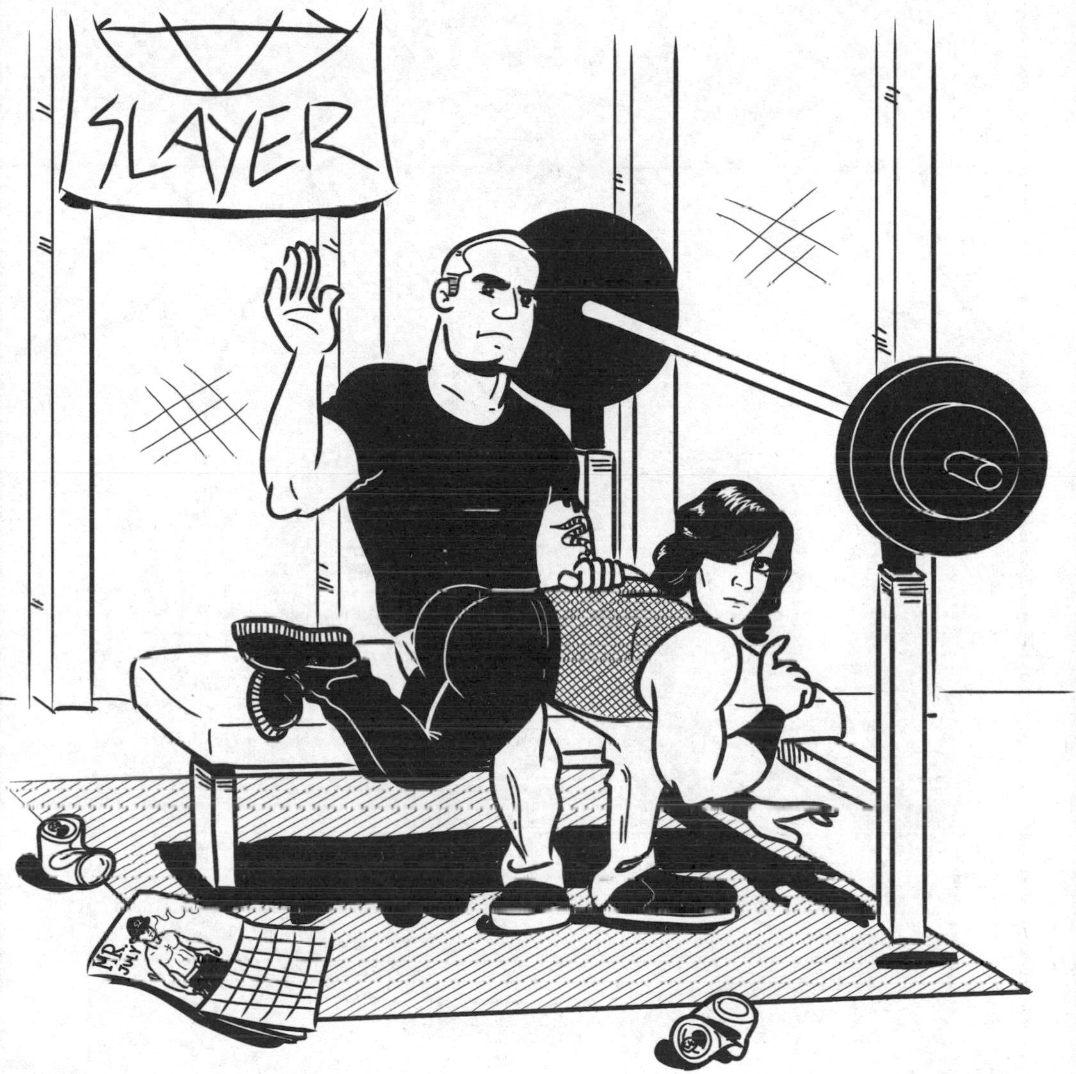
SLAYER
MR. JULY

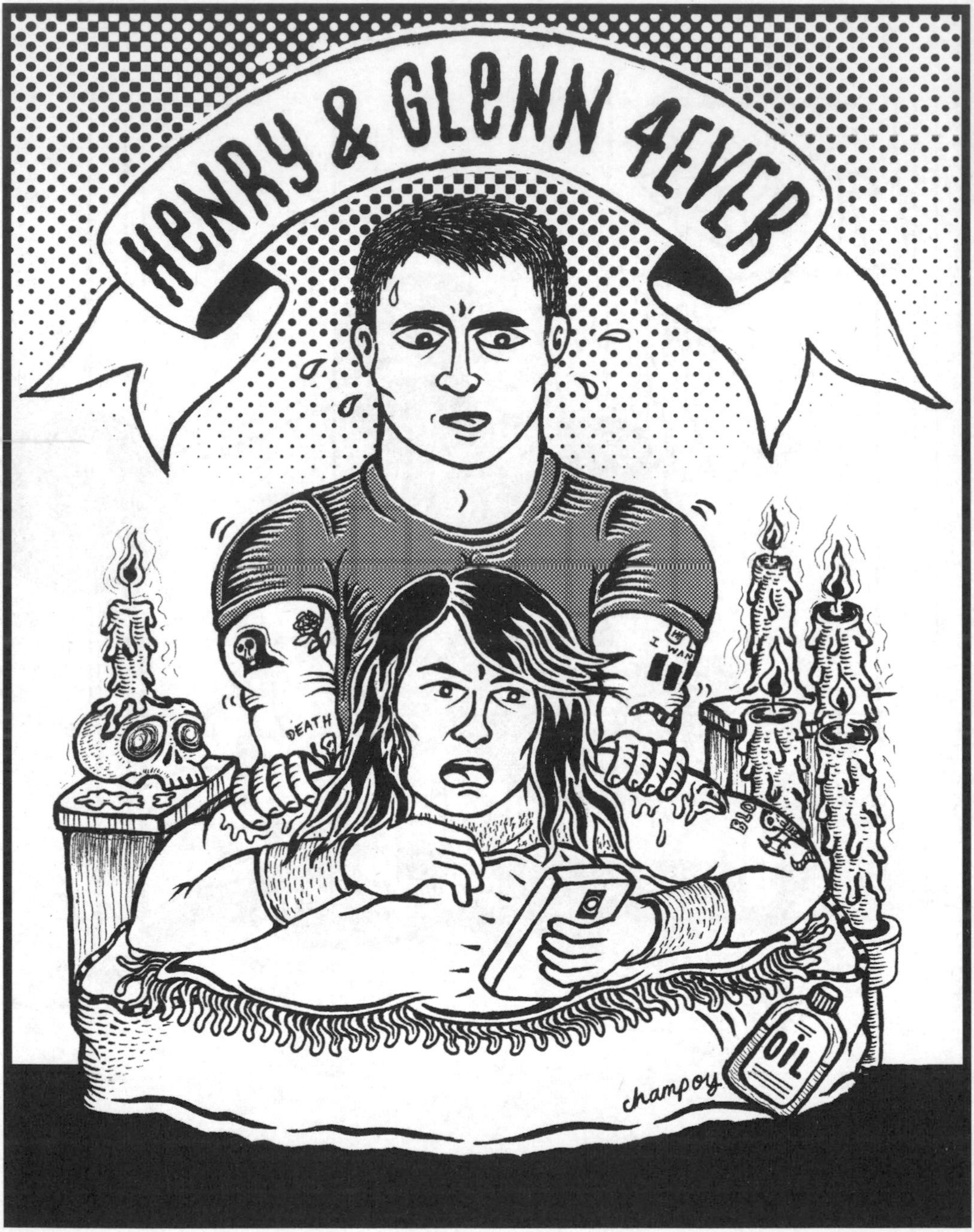
HENRY & GLENN 4EVER
DEATH
OIL
champoy

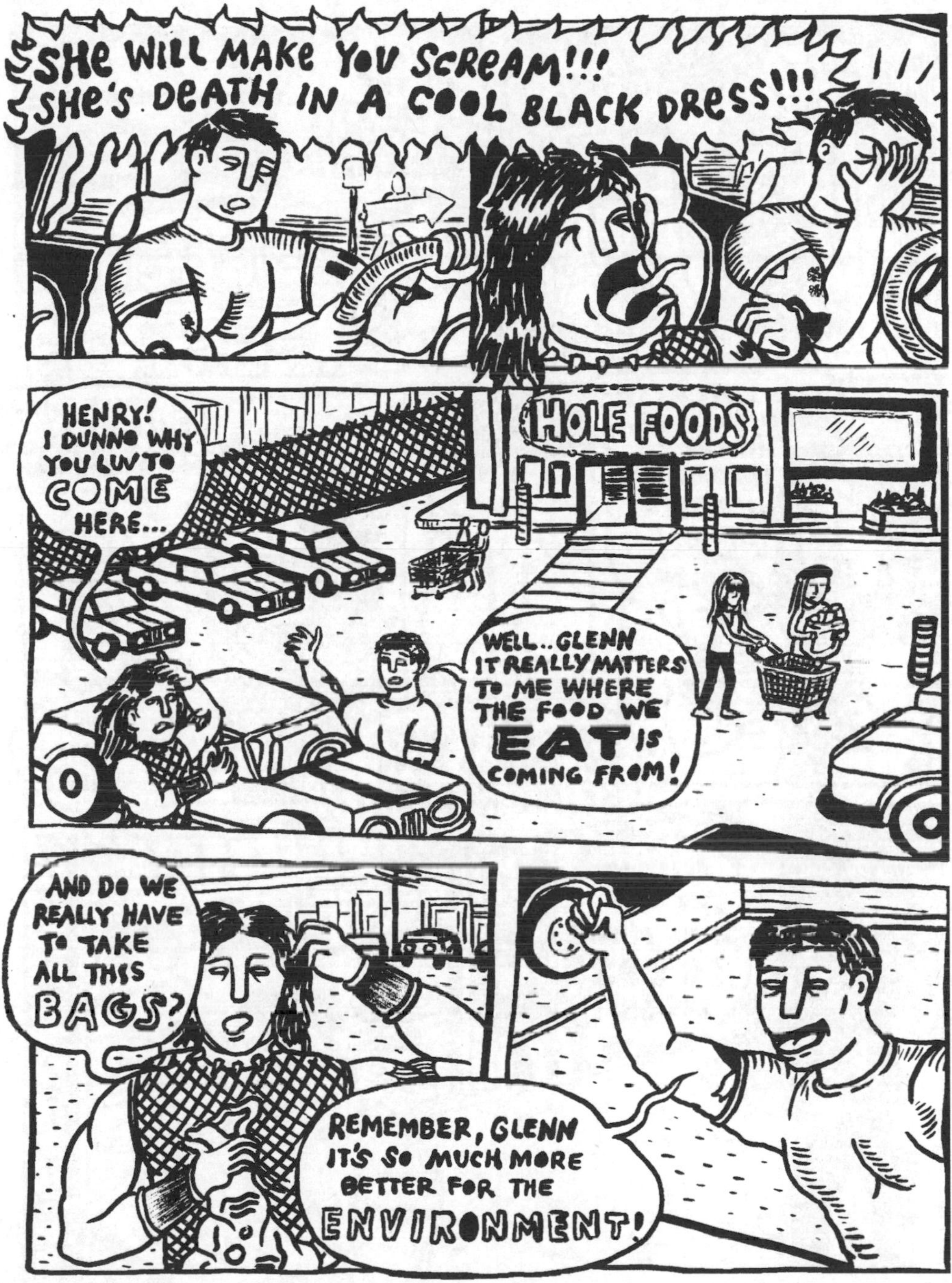
SHE WILL MAKE YOU SCREAM!!!
SHE'S DEATH IN A COOL BLACK DRESS!!!
HENRY! I DUNNO WHY YOU LUV TO COME HERE...
HOLE FOODS
WELL.. GLENN IT REALLY MATTERS TO ME WHERE THE FOOD WE EAT IS COMING FROM!
AND DO WE REALLY HAVE TO TAKE ALL THIS BAGS?
REMEMBER, GLENN IT'S SO MUCH MORE BETTER FOR THE ENVIRONMENT!

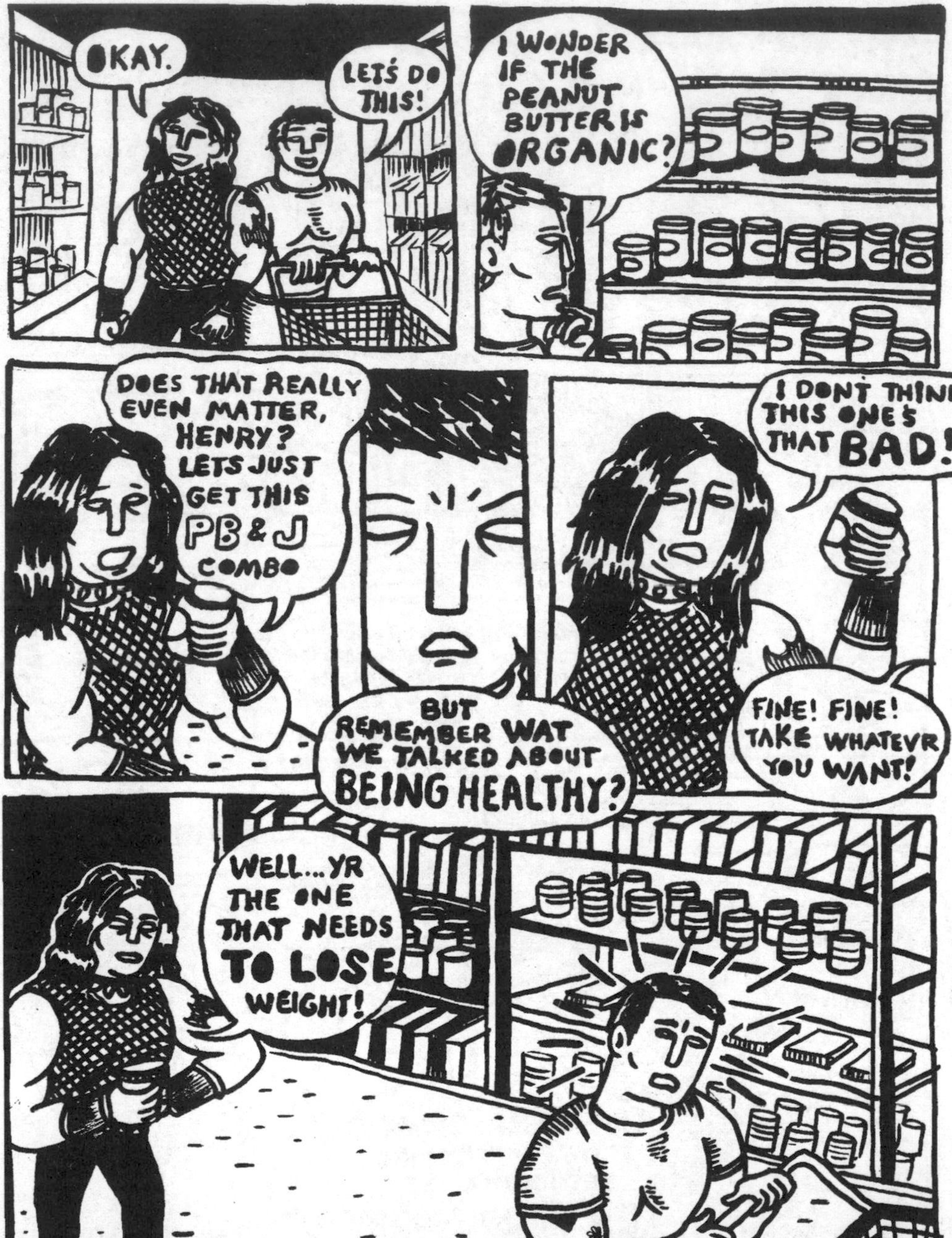
OKAY.
LET'S DO THIS!
I WONDER IF THE PEANUT BUTTER IS ORGANIC?
DOES THAT REALLY EVEN MATTER, HENRY? LETS JUST GET THIS PB & J COMBO
BUT REMEMBER WAT WE TALKED ABOUT BEING HEALTHY?
I DONT THINK THIS ONE'S THAT BAD!
FINE! FINE! TAKE WHATEVR YOU WANT!
WELL... YR THE ONE THAT NEEDS TO LOSE WEIGHT!

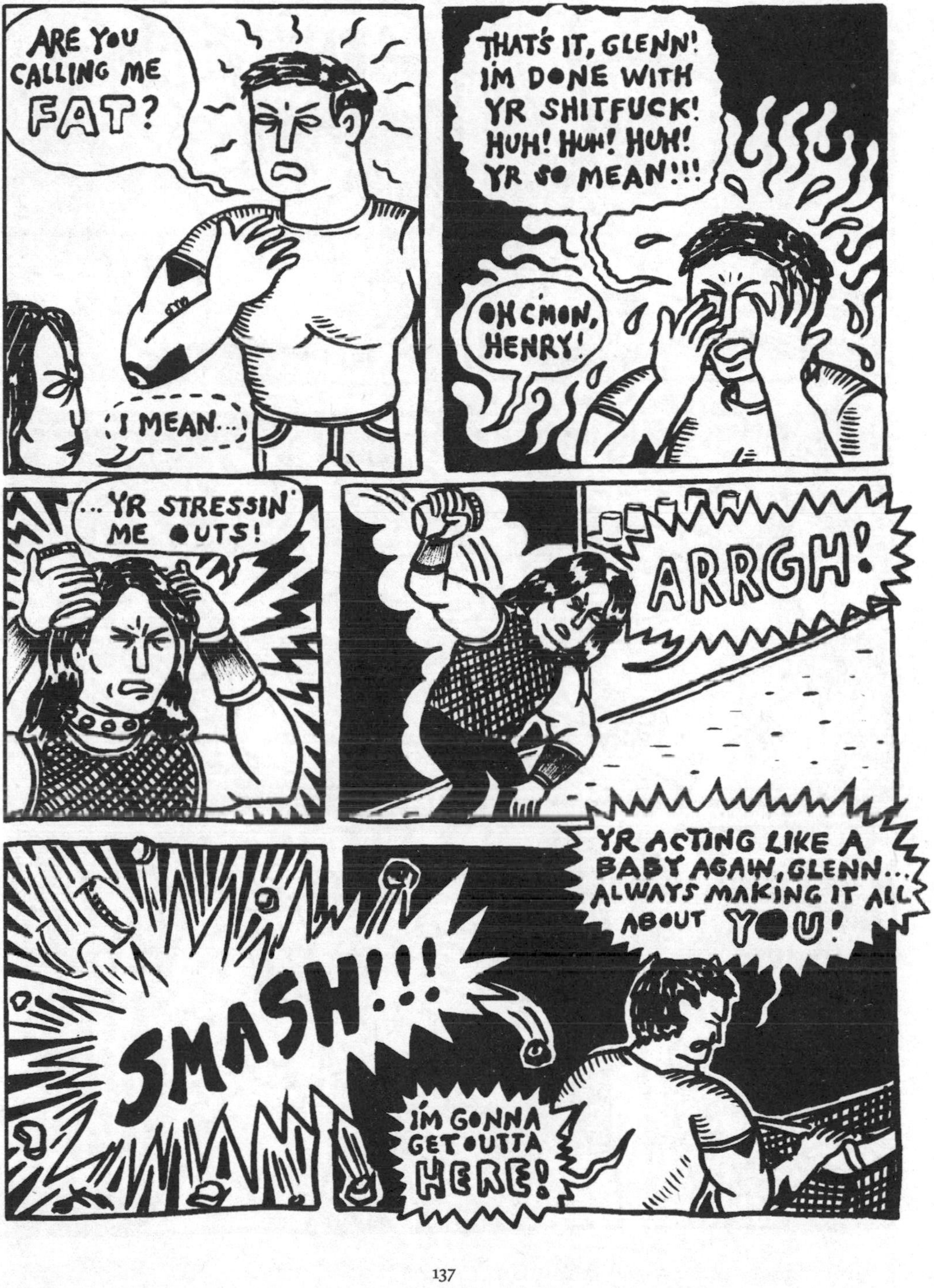
ARE YOU CALLING ME FAT?
I MEAN...
THAT'S IT, GLENN! I'M DONE WITH YR SHITFUCK! HUH! HUH! HUH! YR SO MEAN!!!
OH C'MON, HENRY!
...YR STRESSIN' ME OUTS!
ARRGH!
YR ACTING LIKE A BABY AGAIN, GLENN... ALWAYS MAKING IT ALL ABOUT YOU!
SMASH!!!
I'M GONNA GET OUTTA HERE!

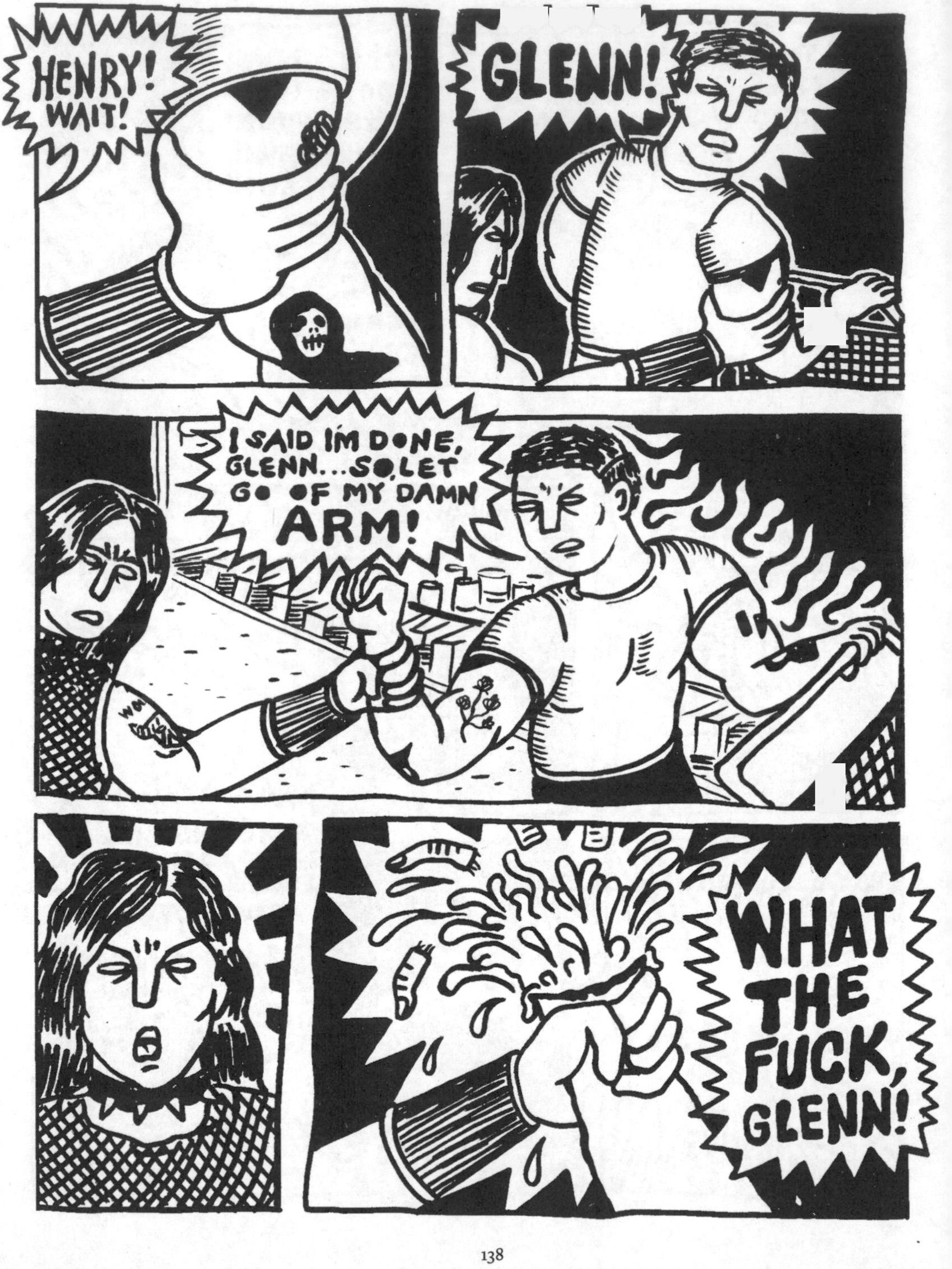
HENRY! WAIT!
GLENN!
I SAID IM DONE, GLENN... SO, LET GO OF MY DAMN ARM!
WHAT THE FUCK, GLENN!

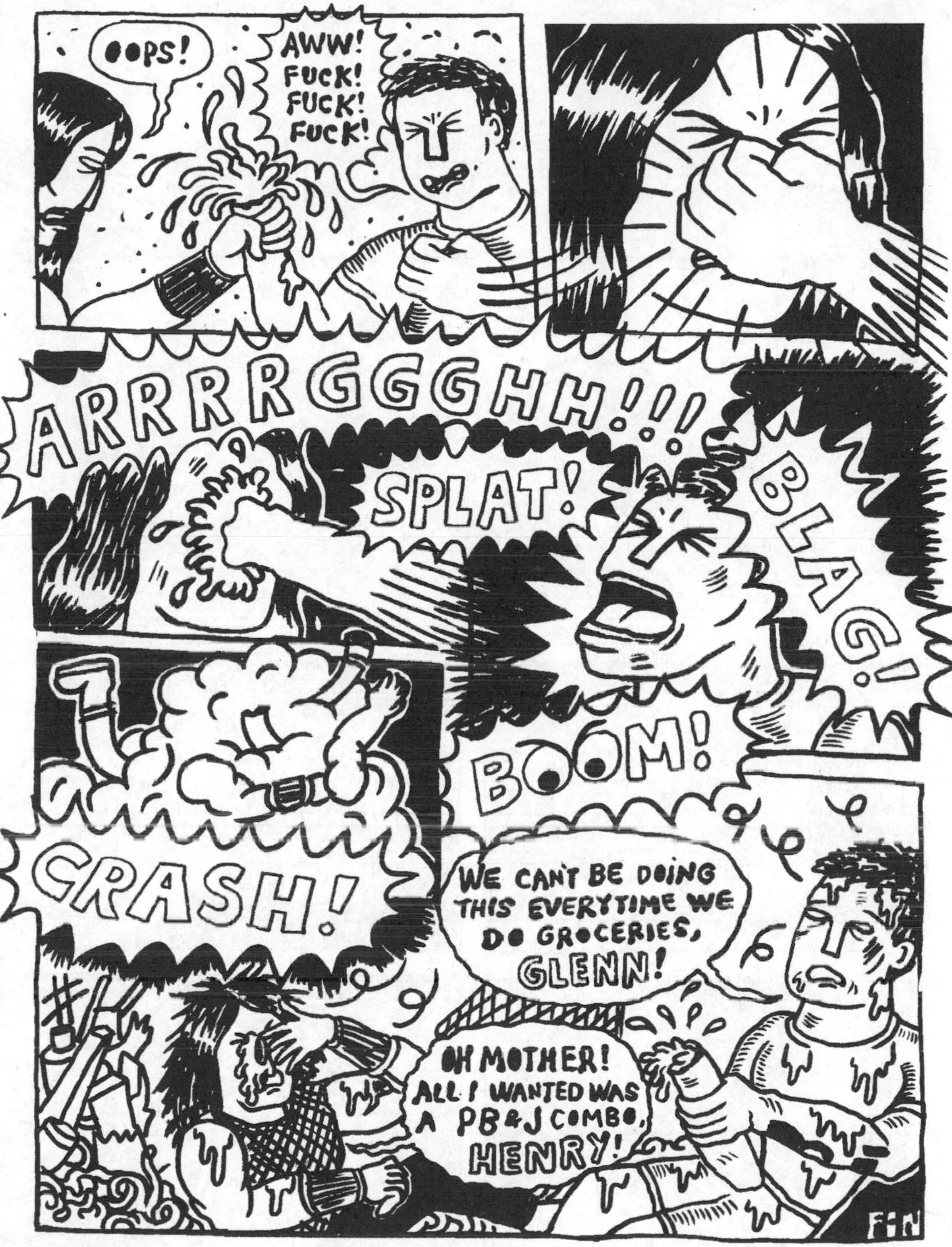
OOPS!
AWW! FUCK! FUCK! FUCK!
ARRRRGGGHH!!!
SPLAT!
BLAG!
BOOM!
CRASH!
WE CAN'T BE DOING THIS EVERYTIME WE DO GROCERIES, GLENN!
OH MOTHER! ALL I WANTED WAS A PB&J COMBO, HENRY!
FTN

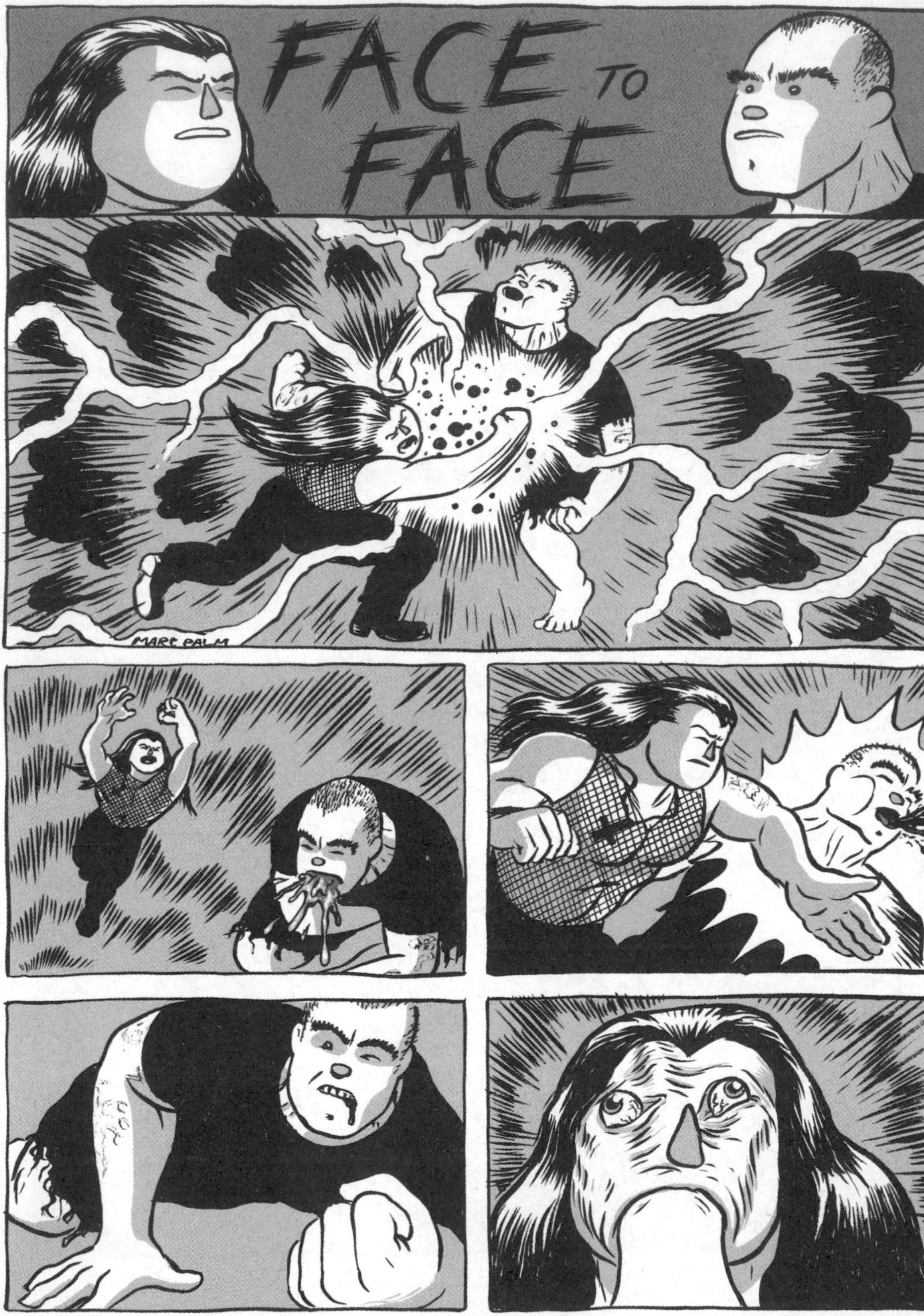
FACE TO FACE
MARC PALM

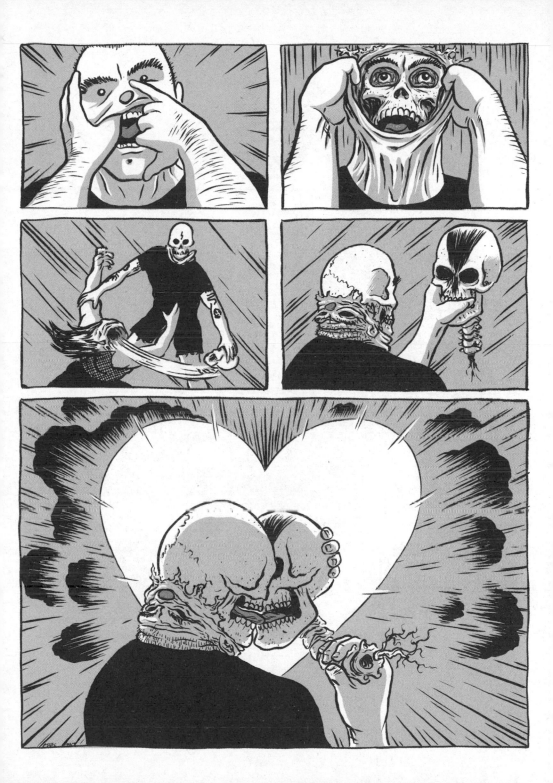

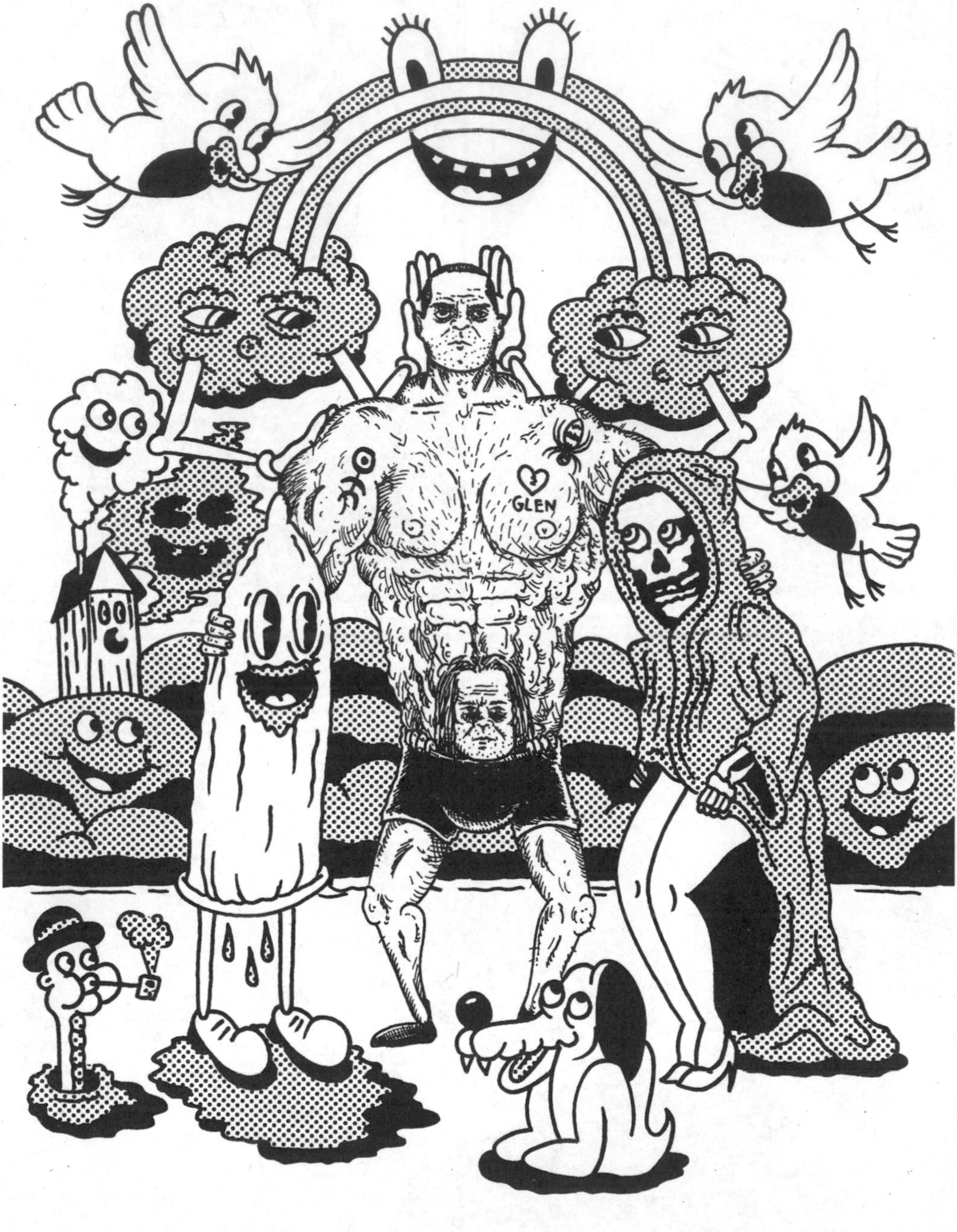
GLEN

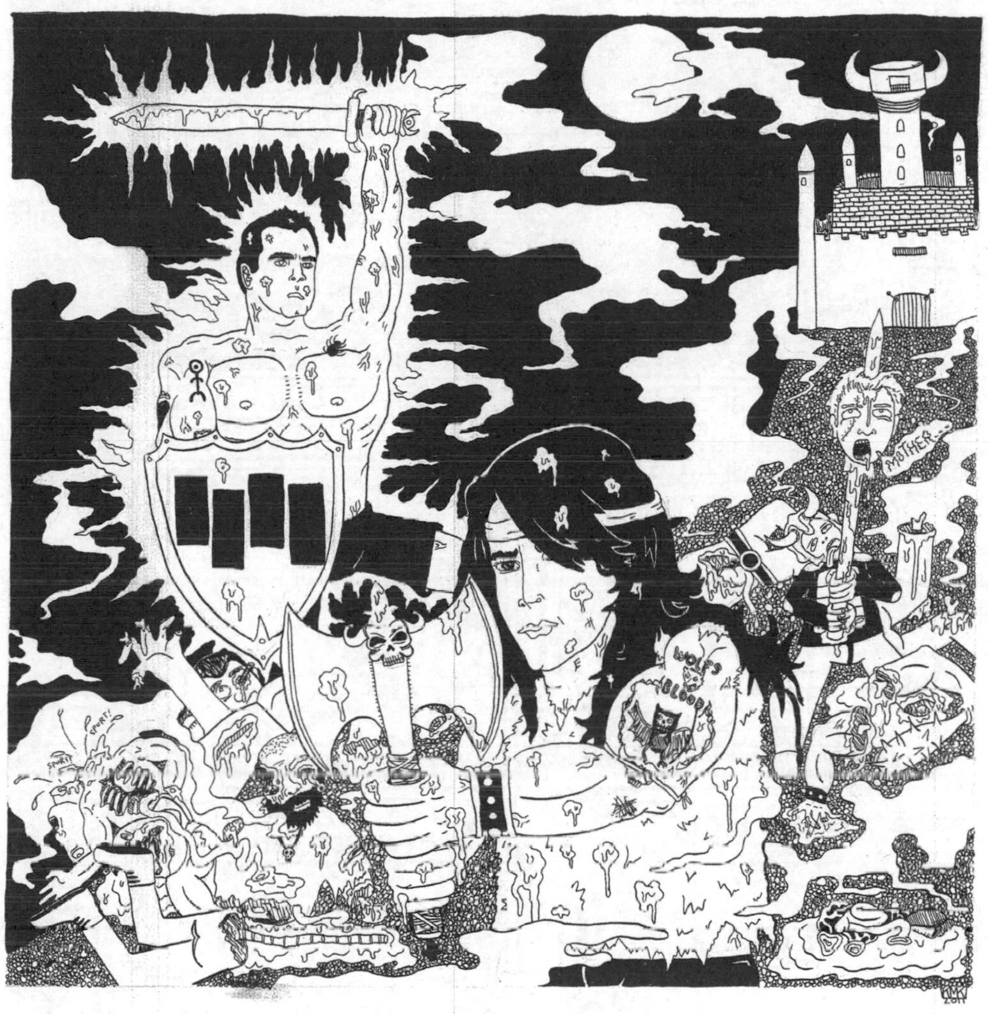
MOTHER
WOLF'S BLOOD
SPURT!
SPURT!
SPURT!

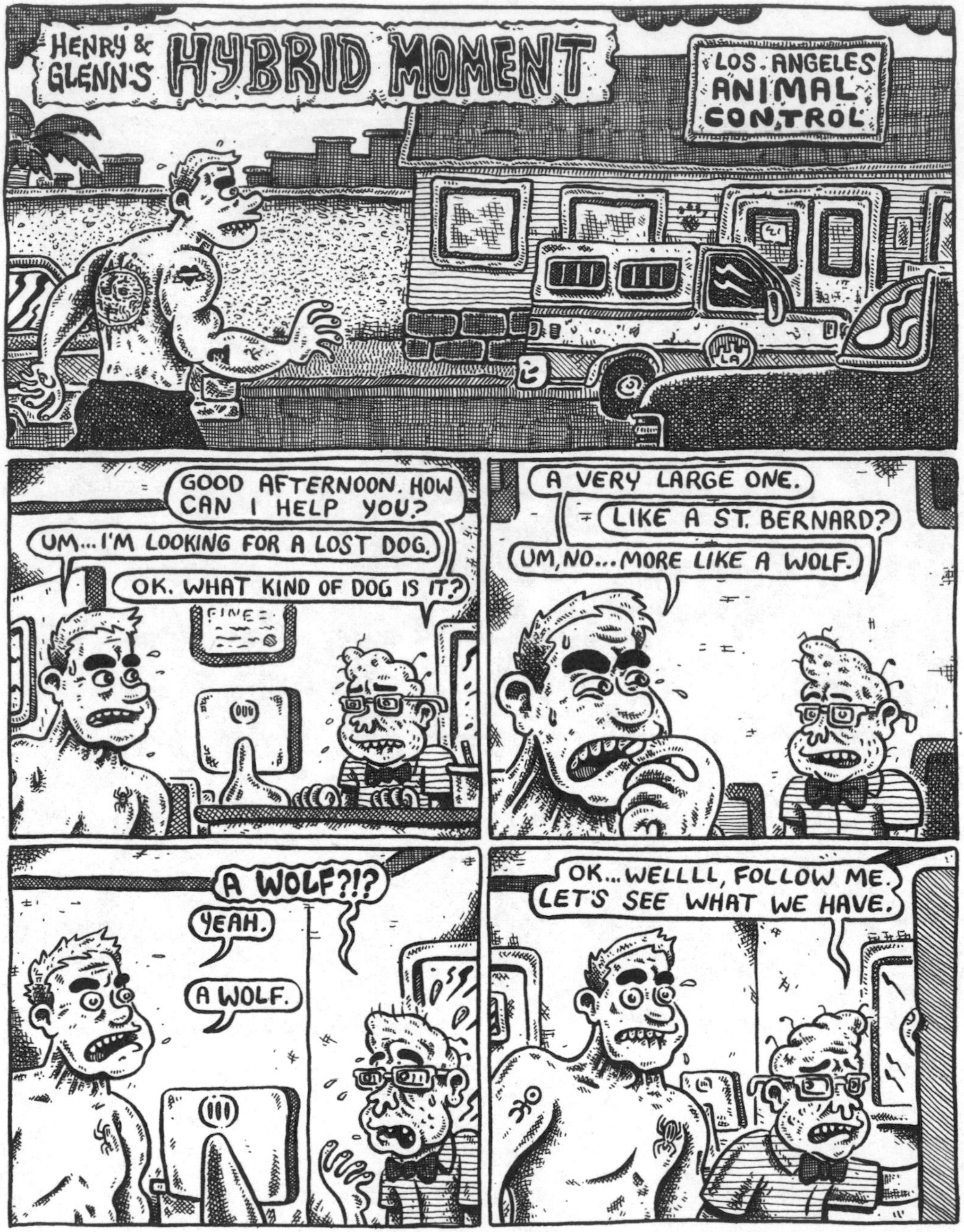
HENRY & GLENN'S HYBRID MOMENT
LOS ANGELES ANIMAL CONTROL
GOOD AFTERNOON. HOW CAN I HELP YOU?
UM... I'M LOOKING FOR A LOST DOG.
OK. WHAT KIND OF DOG IS IT?
FINE
A VERY LARGE ONE.
LIKE A ST. BERNARD?
UM, NO... MORE LIKE A WOLF.
A WOLF?!?
YEAH.
A WOLF.
OK... WELLLL, FOLLOW ME. LET'S SEE WHAT WE HAVE.

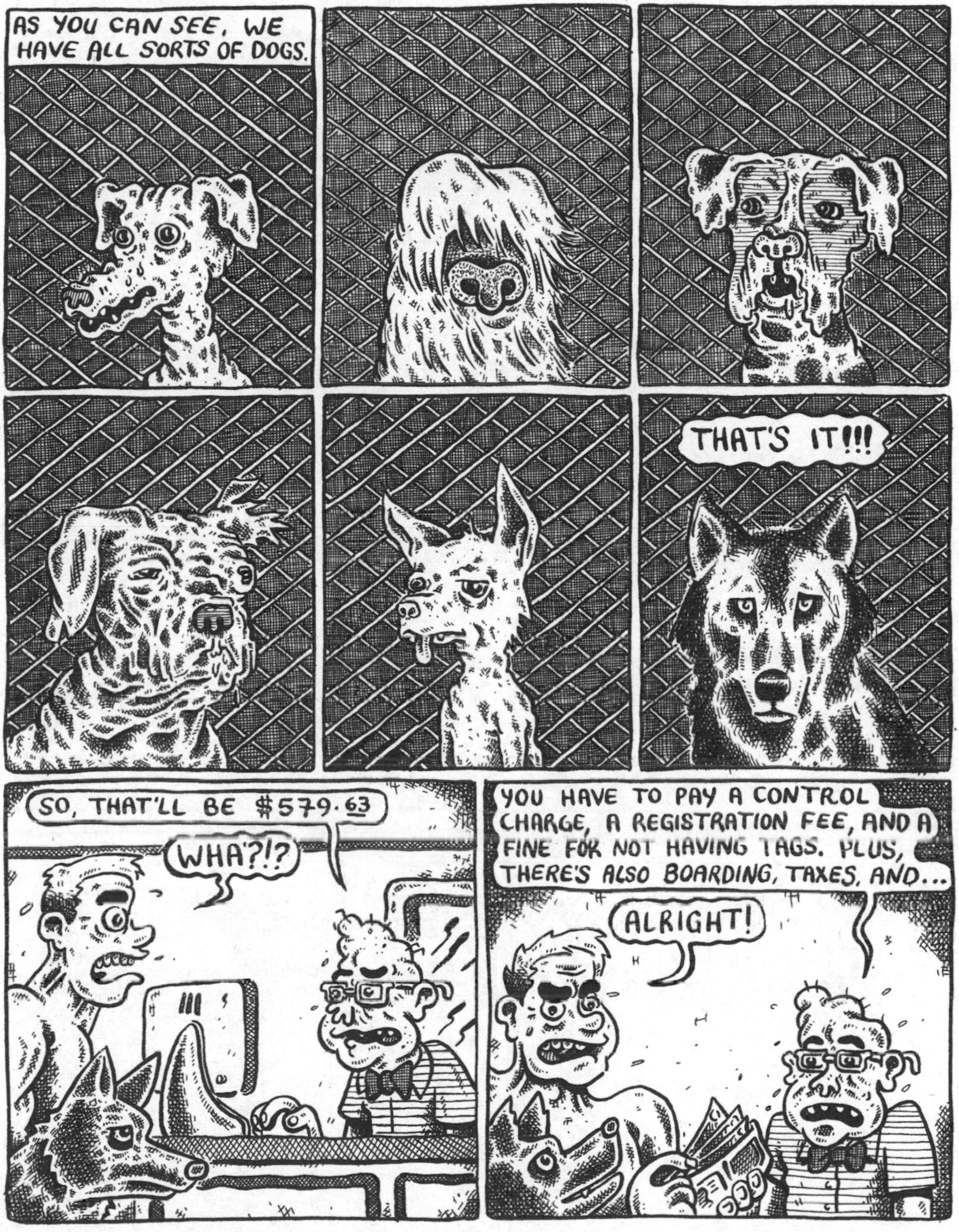
AS YOU CAN SEE, WE HAVE ALL SORTS OF DOGS.
THAT'S IT!!!
SO, THAT'LL BE $579.63
WHA'?!?
YOU HAVE TO PAY A CONTROL CHARGE, A REGISTRATION FEE, AND A FINE FOR NOT HAVING TAGS. PLUS, THERE'S ALSO BOARDING, TAXES, AND...
ALRIGHT!

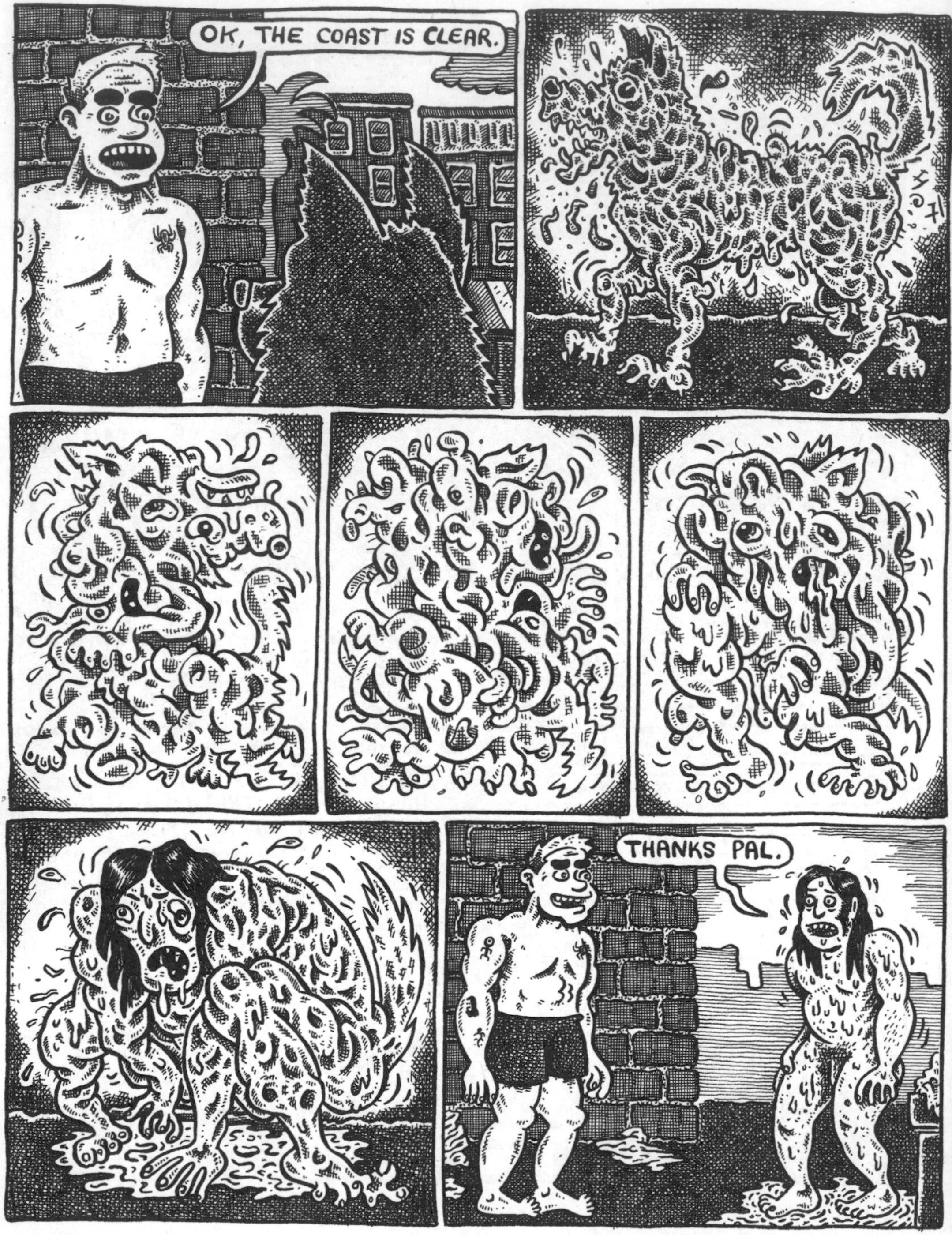
OK, THE COAST IS CLEAR.
THANKS PAL.

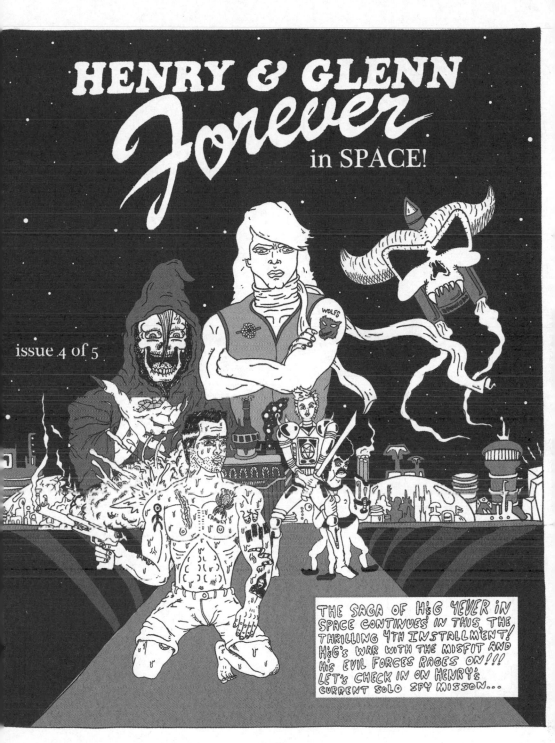

HENRY & GLENN *Forever* in SPACE!

issue 4 of 5

THE SAGA OF H&G 4EVER IN SPACE CONTINUES IN THIS, THE THRILLING 4TH INSTALLMENT! H&G'S WAR WITH THE MISFIT AND HIS EVIL FORCES RAGES ON!!! LET'S CHECK IN ON HENRY'S CURRENT SOLO SPY MISSON...

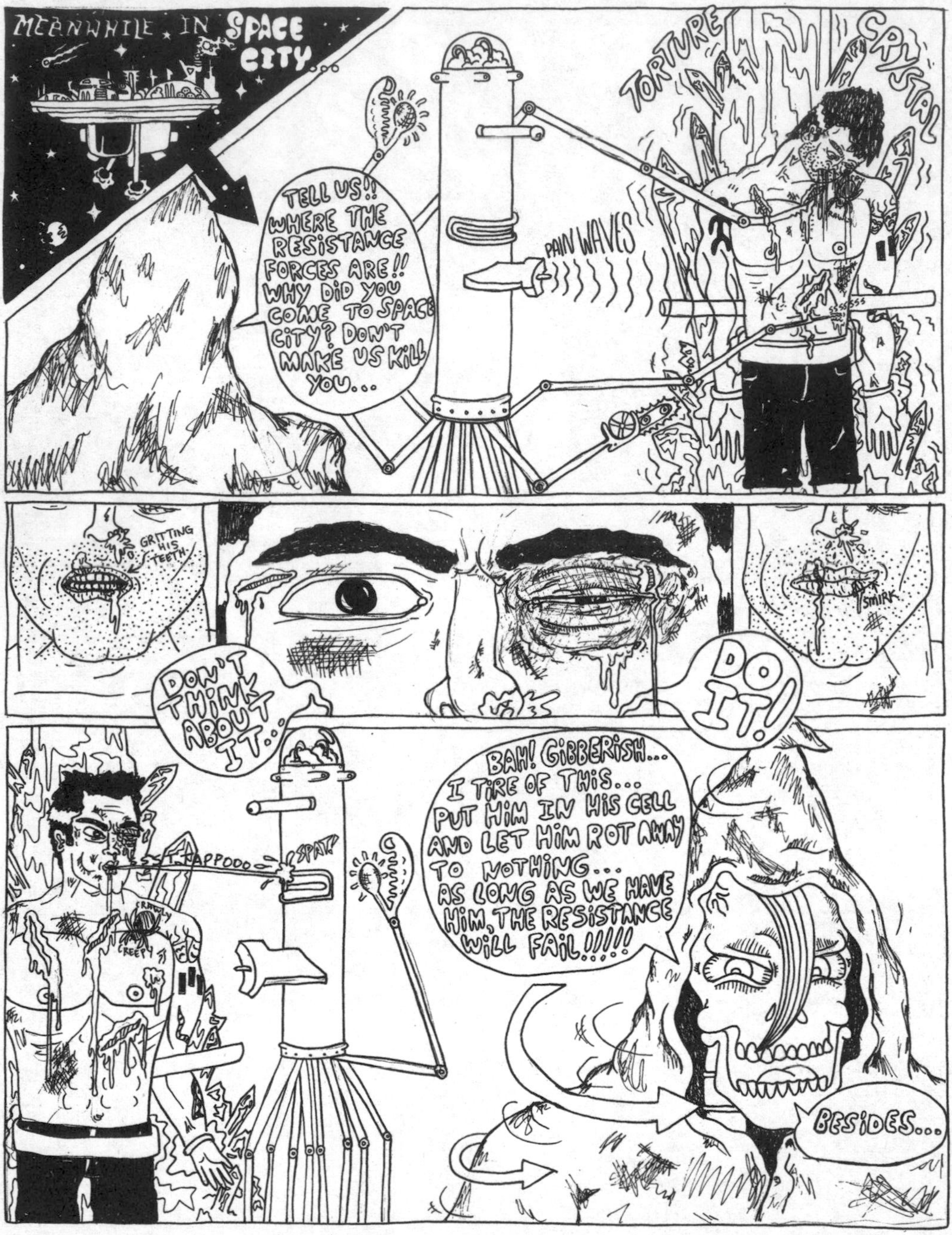
MEANWHILE IN SPACE CITY...
TORTURE CRYSTAL
TELL US!! WHERE THE RESISTANCE FORCES ARE!! WHY DID YOU COME TO SPACE CITY? DON'T MAKE US KILL YOU...
PAIN WAVES
GRITTING HIS TEETH
SMIRK
DON'T THINK ABOUT IT...
DO IT!
SPAT!
BAH! GIBBERISH... I TIRE OF THIS... PUT HIM IN HIS CELL AND LET HIM ROT AWAY TO NOTHING... AS LONG AS WE HAVE HIM, THE RESISTANCE WILL FAIL!!!!!
BESIDES...

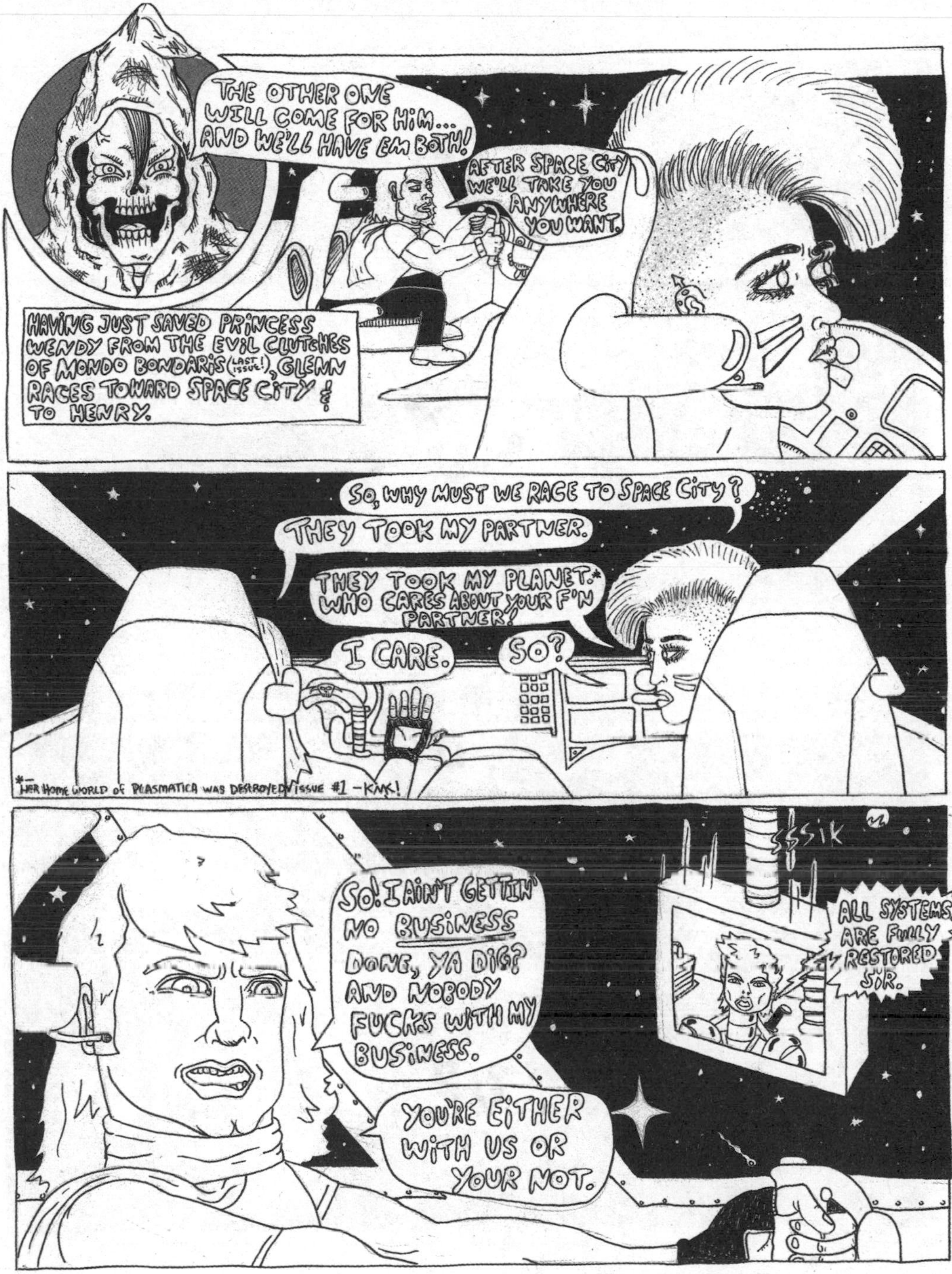

THE OTHER ONE WILL COME FOR HIM... AND WE'LL HAVE EM BOTH!
AFTER SPACE CITY WE'LL TAKE YOU ANYWHERE YOU WANT.
HAVING JUST SAVED PRINCESS WENDY FROM THE EVIL CLUTCHES OF MONDO BONDARIS (LAST ISSUE!), GLENN RACES TOWARD SPACE CITY & TO HENRY.
SO, WHY MUST WE RACE TO SPACE CITY?
THEY TOOK MY PARTNER.
THEY TOOK MY PLANET.* WHO CARES ABOUT YOUR F'N PARTNER!
I CARE.
SO?
*— HER HOME WORLD OF PLASMATICA WAS DESTROYED ISSUE #1 - KMK!
SSSIK
SO! I AIN'T GETTIN' NO BUSINESS DONE, YA DIG? AND NOBODY FUCKS WITH MY BUSINESS.
ALL SYSTEMS ARE FULLY RESTORED SIR.
YOU'RE EITHER WITH US OR YOUR NOT.

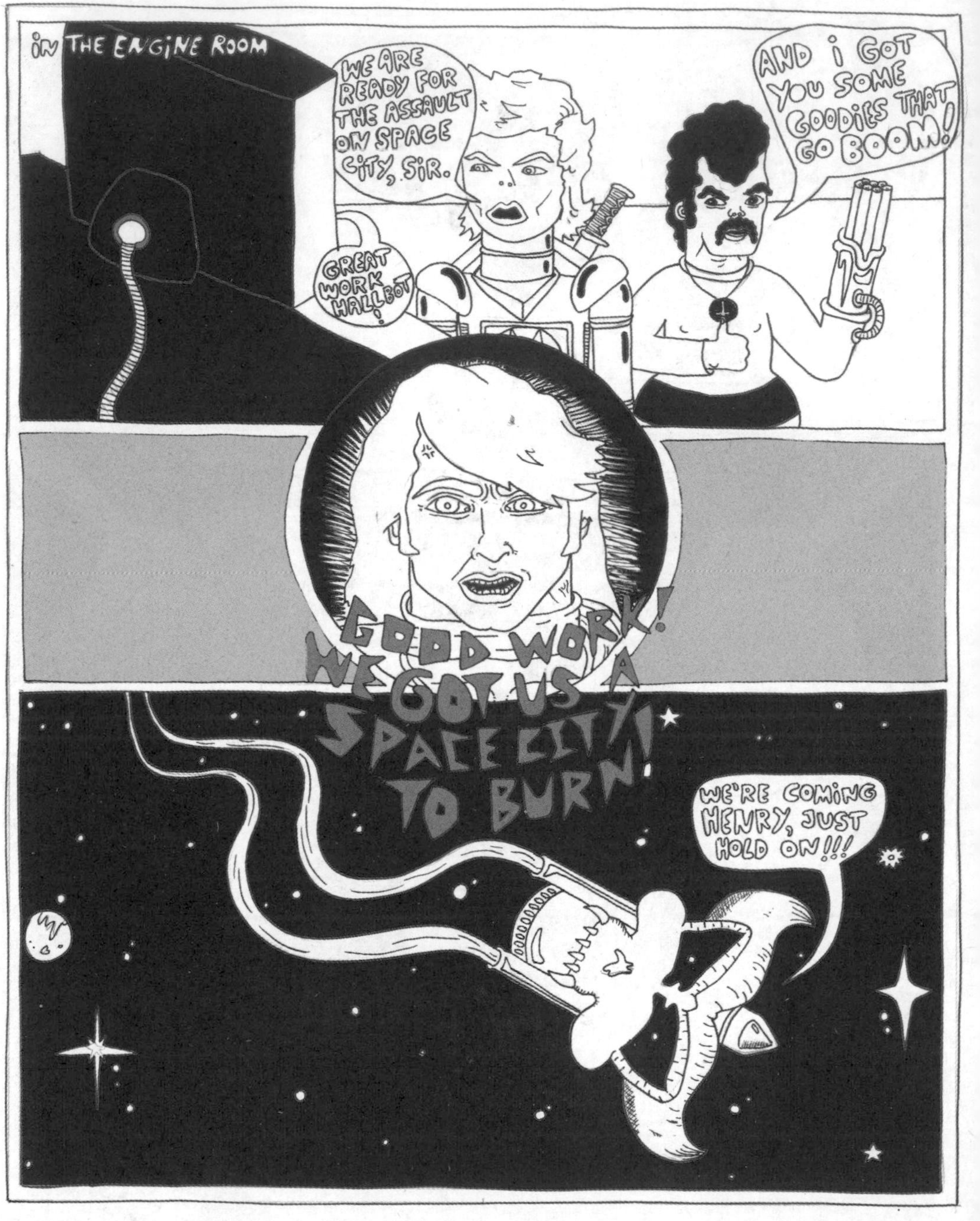
in THE ENGINE ROOM
WE ARE READY FOR THE ASSAULT ON SPACE CITY, SIR.
AND i GOT YOU SOME GOODIES THAT GO BOOM!
GREAT WORK HALLBOT!
GOOD WORK! WE GOT US A SPACE CITY TO BURN!
WE'RE COMING HENRY, JUST HOLD ON!!!

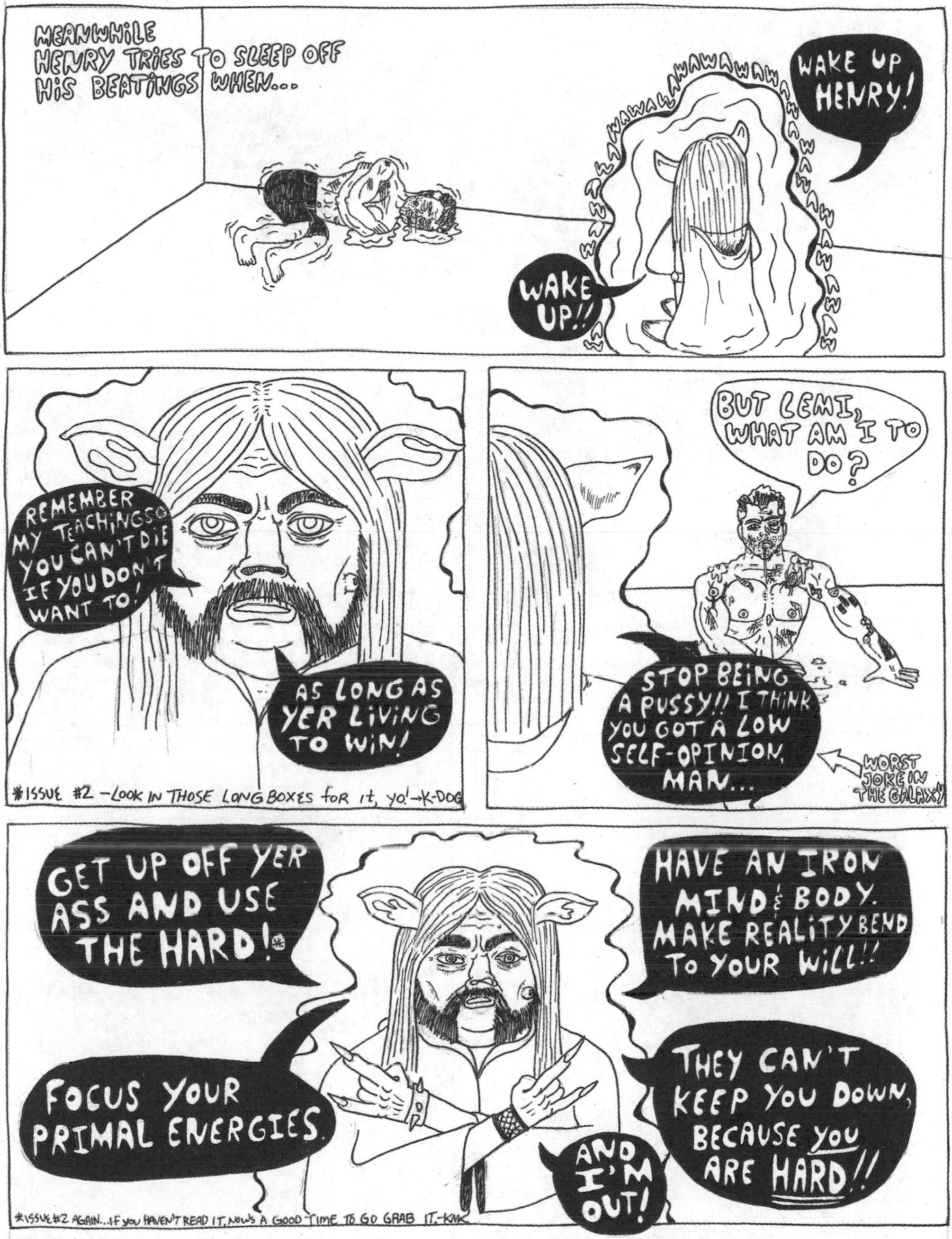

MEANWHILE HENRY TRIES TO SLEEP OFF HIS BEATINGS WHEN...
WAKE UP HENRY!
WAWAWAWAWAWAWAWAWAWAWAWAWAWAWAWAWAWAWAWAWA
WAKE UP!!
REMEMBER MY TEACHINGS* YOU CAN'T DIE IF YOU DON'T WANT TO!
AS LONG AS YER LIVING TO WIN!
*ISSUE #2 — LOOK IN THOSE LONG BOXES FOR IT, YO! →K-DOG
BUT LEMI, WHAT AM I TO DO?
STOP BEING A PUSSY!! I THINK YOU GOT A LOW SELF-OPINION, MAN...
WORST JOKE IN THE GALAXY
GET UP OFF YER ASS AND USE THE HARD!*
HAVE AN IRON MIND & BODY. MAKE REALITY BEND TO YOUR WILL!!
FOCUS YOUR PRIMAL ENERGIES.
THEY CAN'T KEEP YOU DOWN, BECAUSE YOU ARE HARD!!
AND I'M OUT!
*ISSUE #2 AGAIN... IF YOU HAVEN'T READ IT, NOW'S A GOOD TIME TO GO GRAB IT. -KMK

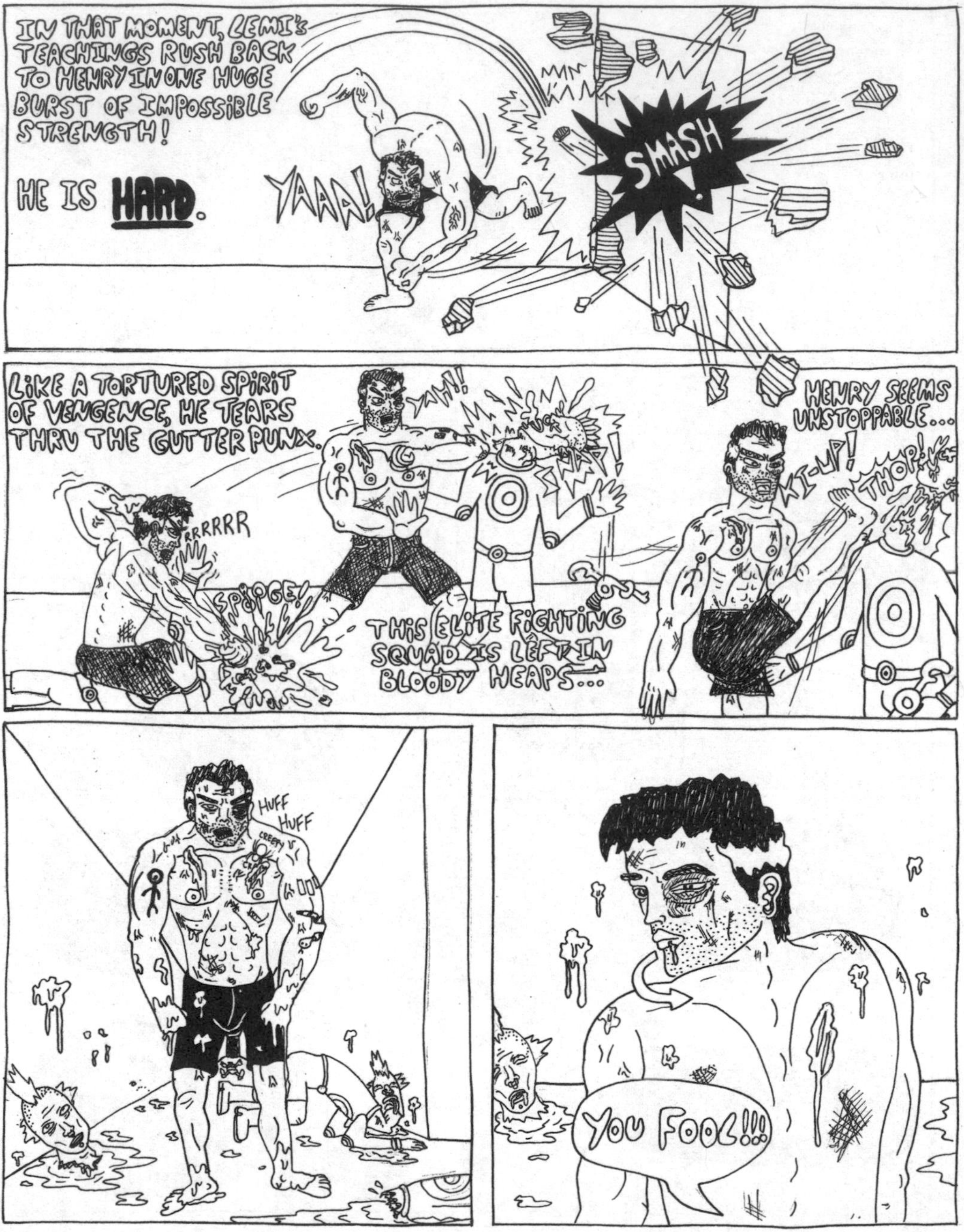

IN THAT MOMENT, LEMI's TEACHINGS RUSH BACK TO HENRY IN ONE HUGE BURST OF IMPOSSIBLE STRENGTH!
HE IS HARD.
YAAA!
SMASH
LIKE A TORTURED SPIRIT OF VENGENCE, HE TEARS THRU THE GUTTER PUNX.
YAH!
RRRRRR
SPLOOGE!
THIS ELITE FIGHTING SQUAD IS LEFT IN BLOODY HEAPS...
HENRY SEEMS UNSTOPPABLE...
THOP!
HUFF
HUFF
CREEPY
YOU FOOL!!!

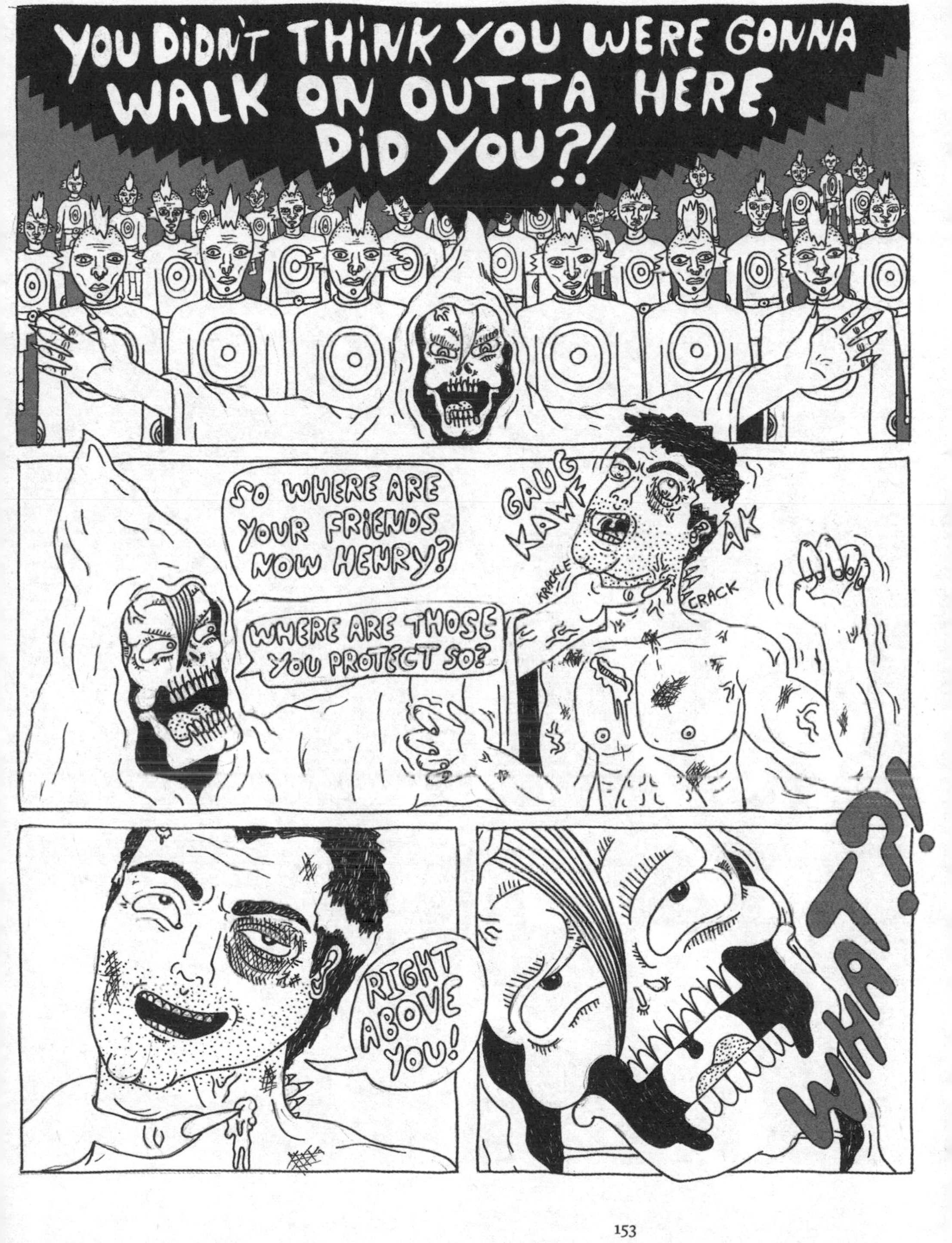
YOU DIDN'T THINK YOU WERE GONNA WALK ON OUTTA HERE, DID YOU?!
SO WHERE ARE YOUR FRIENDS NOW HENRY?
WHERE ARE THOSE YOU PROTECT SO?
GAUG
KAWF
AK
KRACKLE
CRACK
RIGHT ABOVE YOU!
WHAT?!

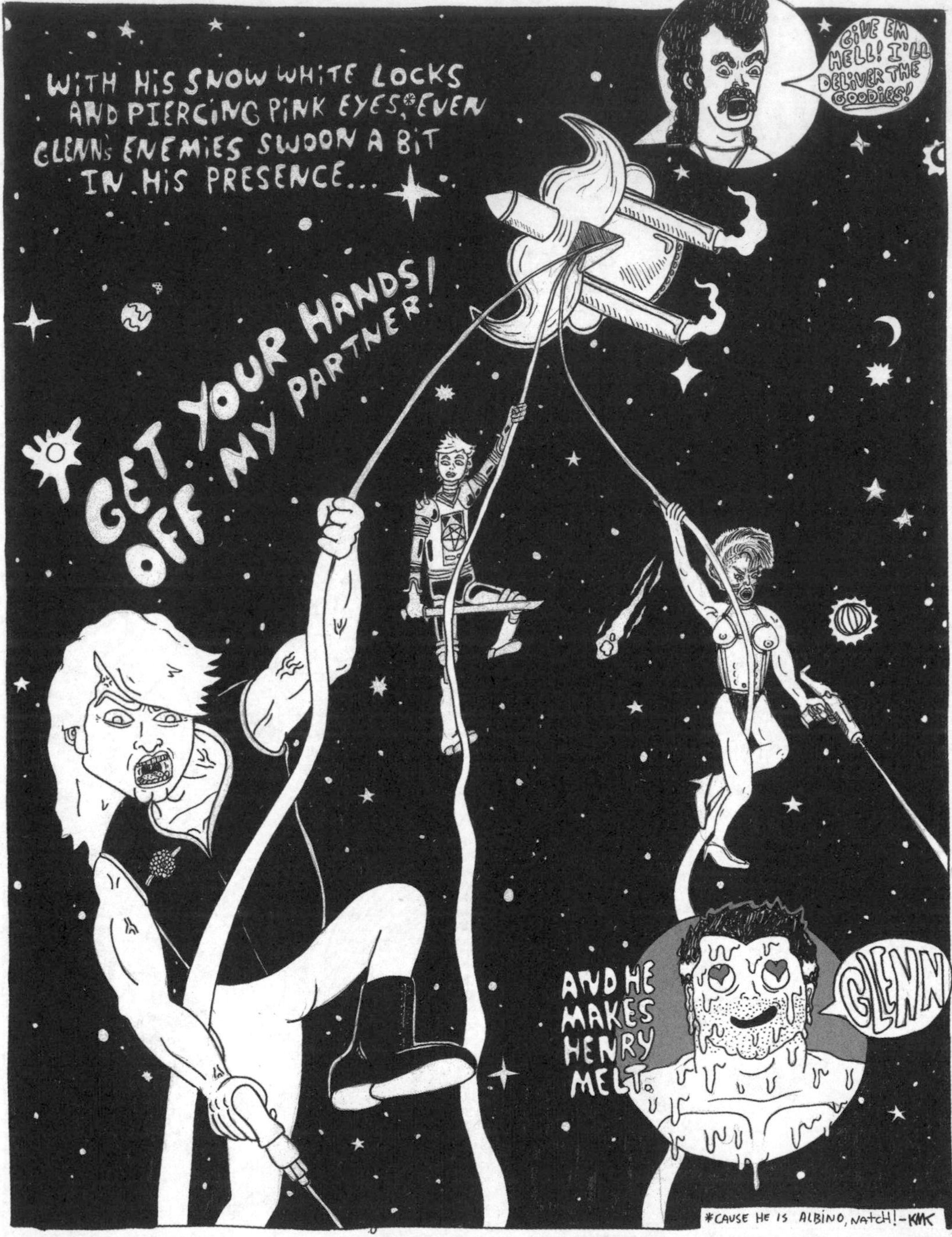
WITH HIS SNOW WHITE LOCKS AND PIERCING PINK EYES,* EVEN GLENN'S ENEMIES SWOON A BIT IN HIS PRESENCE...
GIVE EM HELL! I'LL DELIVER THE GOODIES!
GET YOUR HANDS OFF MY PARTNER!
AND HE MAKES HENRY MELT.
GLENN
*CAUSE HE IS ALBINO, NATCH! -KMK

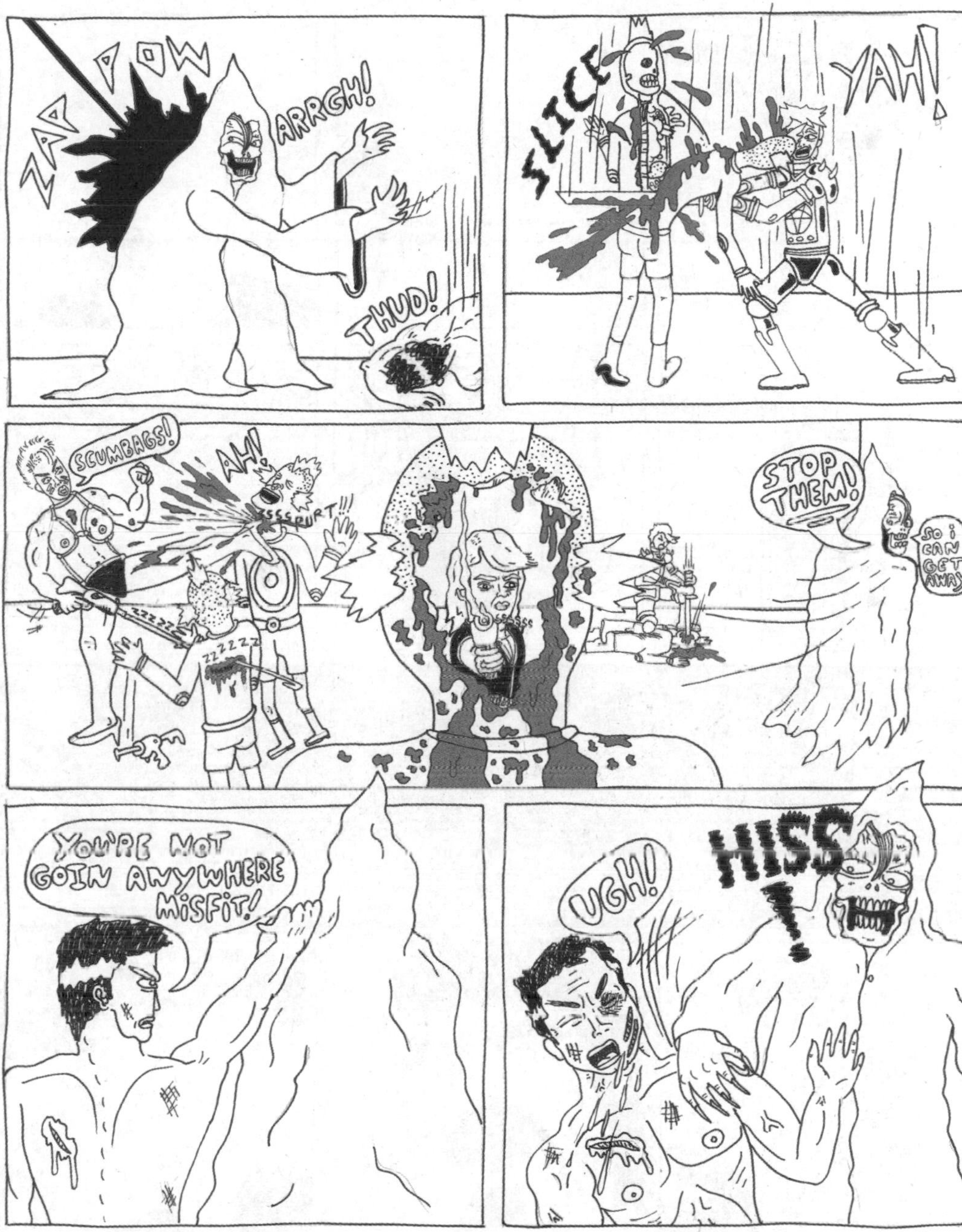
ZAP
POW
ARRGH!
THUD!
SLICE
YAH!
SCUMBAGS!
AH!
ZSSSPURT!!!
STOP THEM!
SO I CAN GET AWAY.
YOU'RE NOT GOIN ANYWHERE MISFIT!
UGH!
HISS!

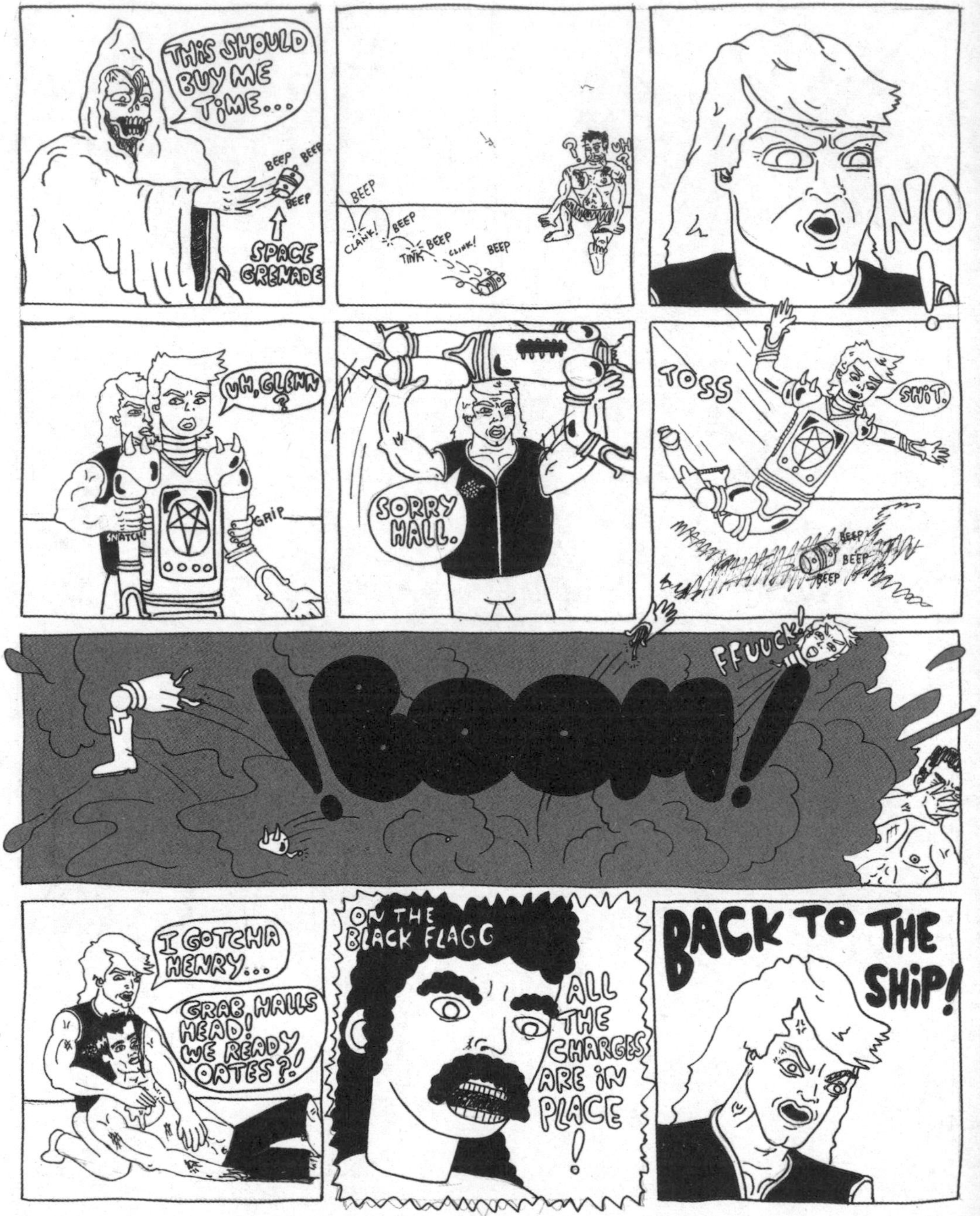
THIS SHOULD BUY ME TIME...
BEEP BEEP
BEEP
SPACE GRENADE
BEEP
CLANK!
BEEP
TINK BEEP
CLINK! BEEP
?
UH ?
NO !
UH, GLENN ?
SNATCH!
GRIP
SORRY HALL.
TOSS
SHIT.
BEEP
BEEP
BEEP
FFUUCK!
!BOOM!
I GOTCHA HENRY...
GRAB HALLS HEAD! WE READY OATES ?!
ON THE BLACK FLAGG
ALL THE CHARGES ARE IN PLACE !
BACK TO THE SHIP!

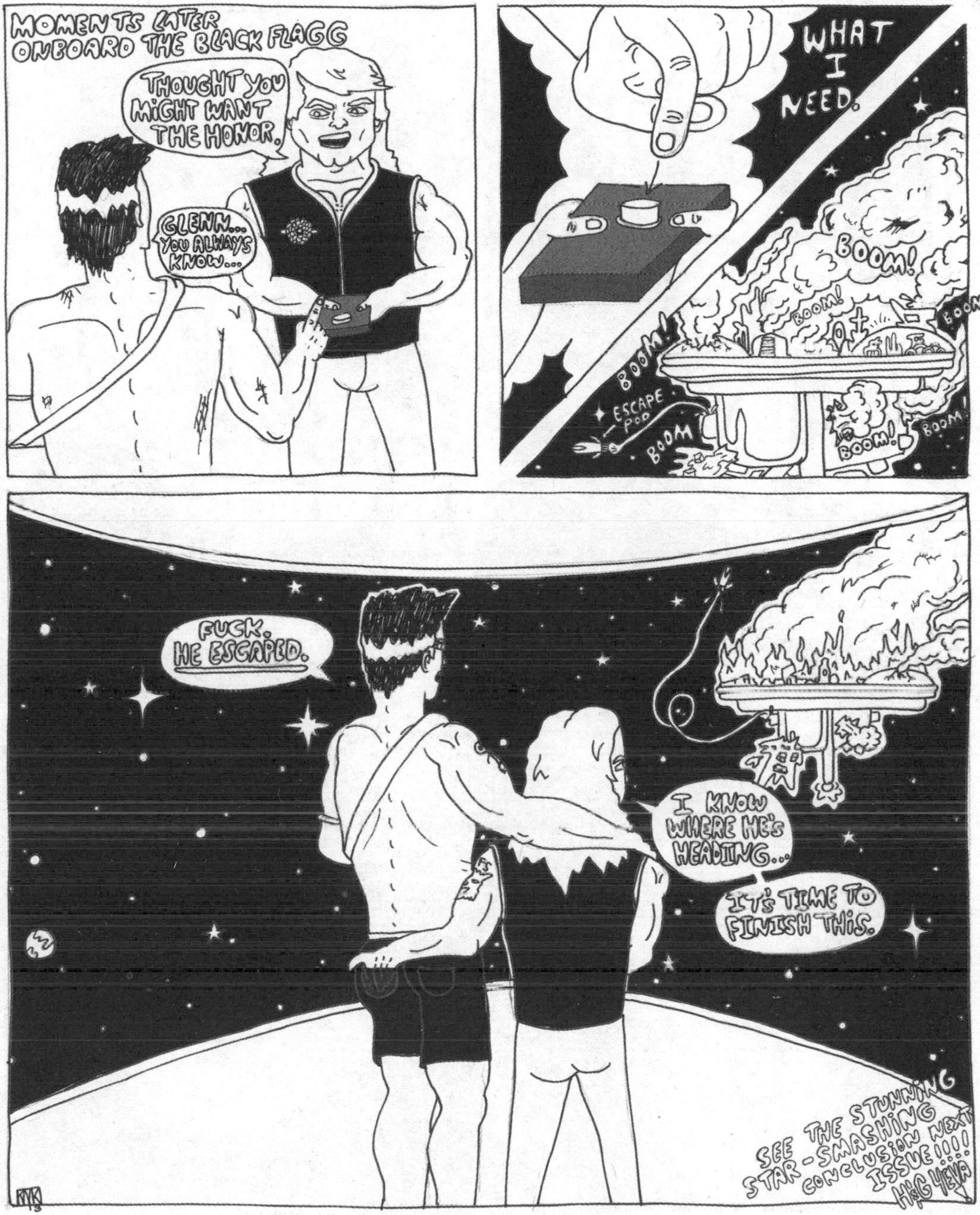
MOMENTS LATER ONBOARD THE BLACK FLAGG
THOUGHT YOU MIGHT WANT THE HONOR.
GLENN... YOU ALWAYS KNOW...
WHAT I NEED.
BOOM!
BOOM!
BOOM!
BOOM!
ESCAPE POD
BOOM
BOOM!
BOOM!
FUCK. HE ESCAPED.
I KNOW WHERE HE'S HEADING...
IT'S TIME TO FINISH THIS.
SEE THE STUNNING STAR-SMASHING CONCLUSION NEXT ISSUE!!!!

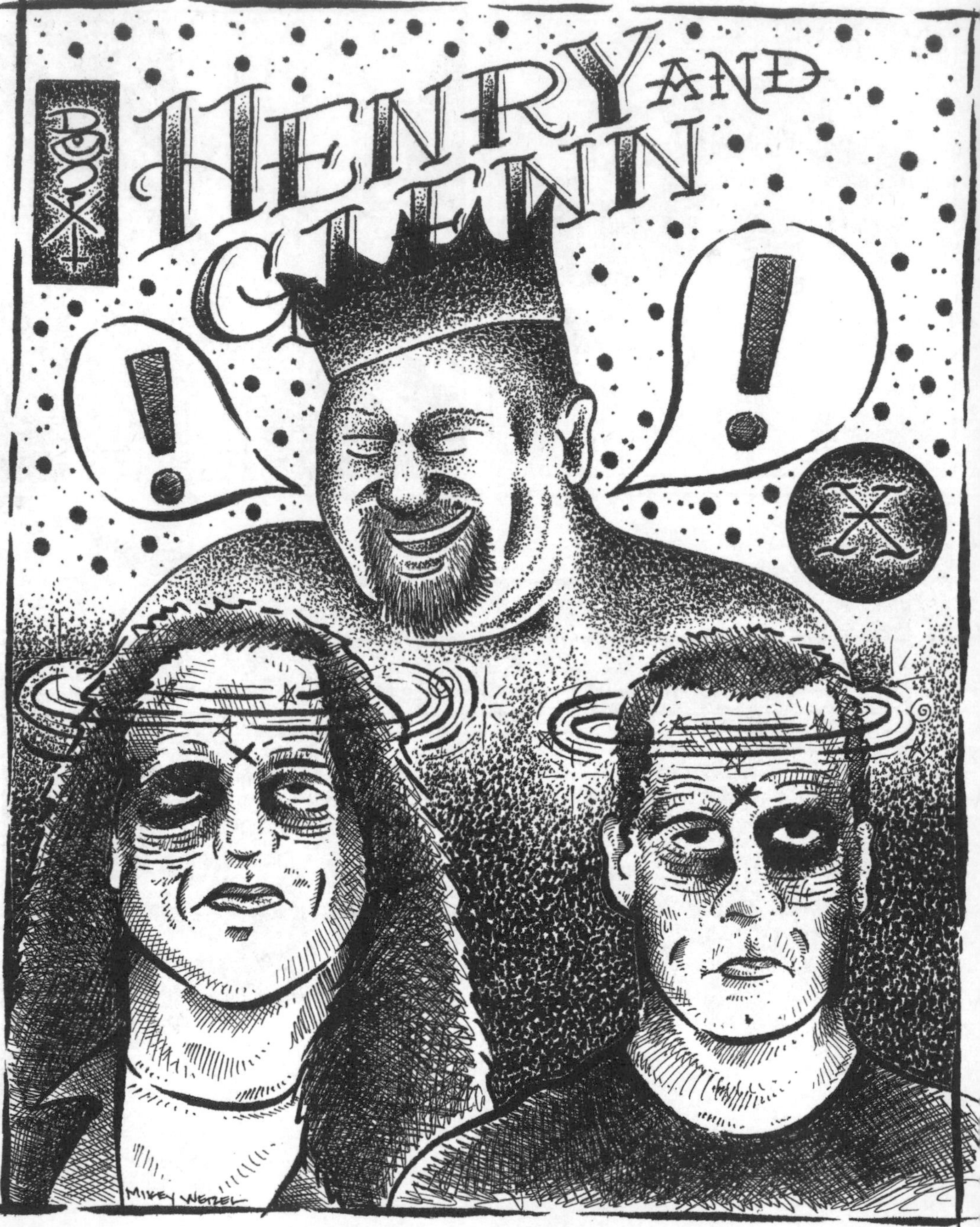
HENRY AND
!
!
X

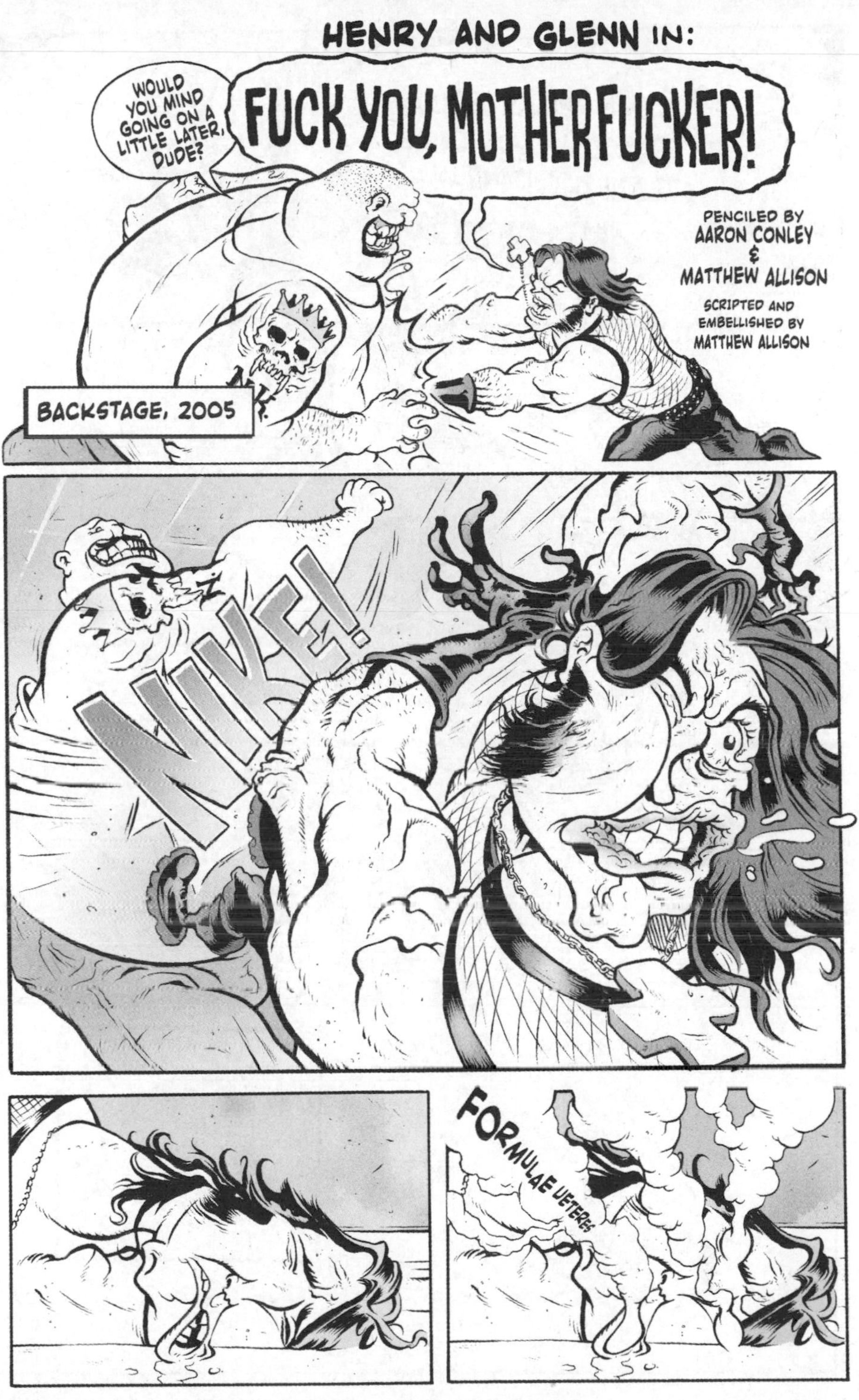
HENRY AND GLENN IN:
WOULD YOU MIND GOING ON A LITTLE LATER, DUDE?
FUCK YOU, MOTHERFUCKER!
PENCILED BY AARON CONLEY & MATTHEW ALLISON
SCRIPTED AND EMBELLISHED BY MATTHEW ALLISON
BACKSTAGE, 2005
NIKE!
FORMULAE UETERES

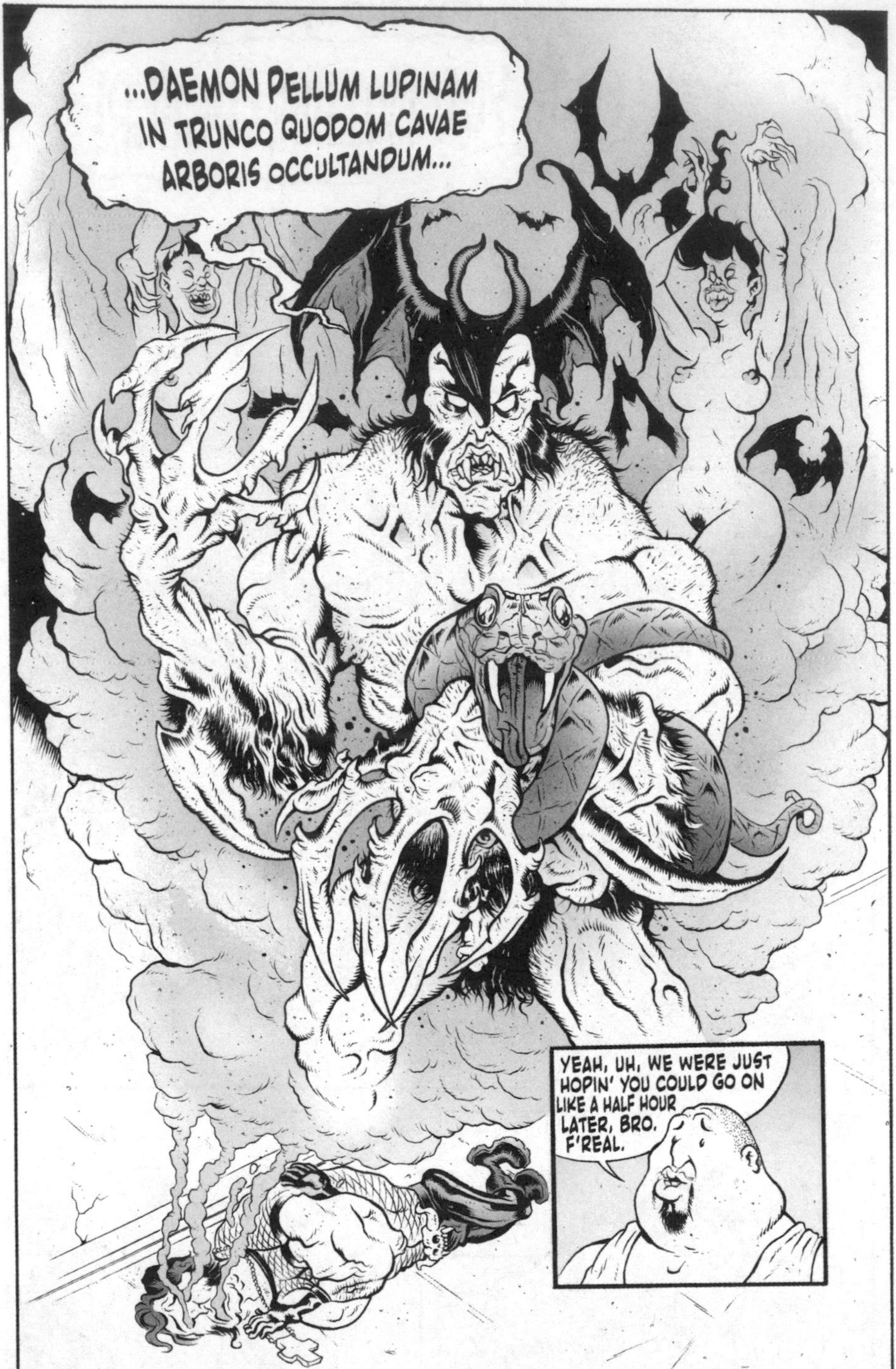
...DAEMON PELLUM LUPINAM IN TRUNCO QUODOM CAVAE ARBORIS OCCULTANDUM...
YEAH, UH, WE WERE JUST HOPIN' YOU COULD GO ON LIKE A HALF HOUR LATER, BRO. F'REAL.

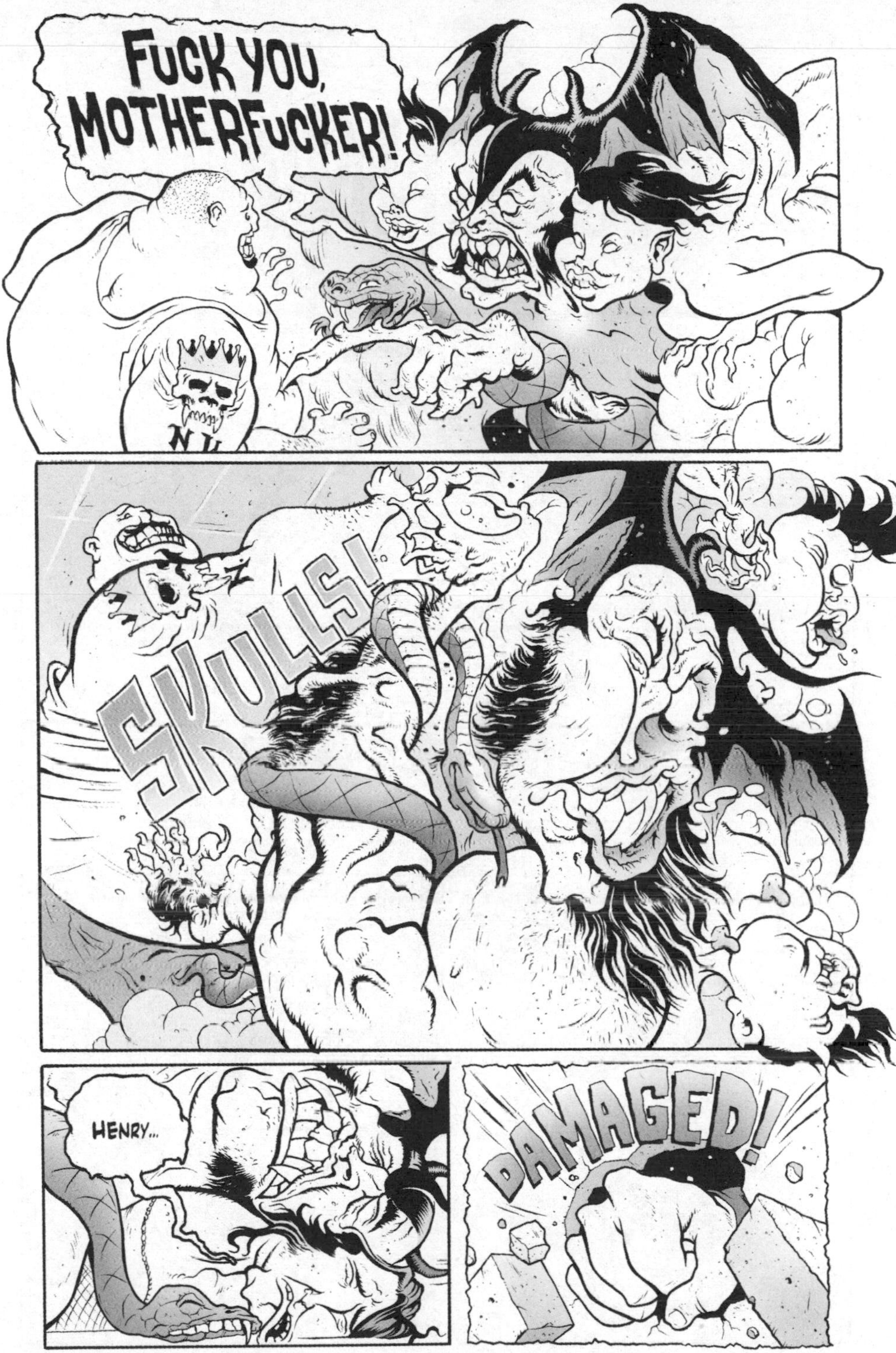
FUCK YOU, MOTHERFUCKER!
SKULLS!
HENRY...
DAMAGED!

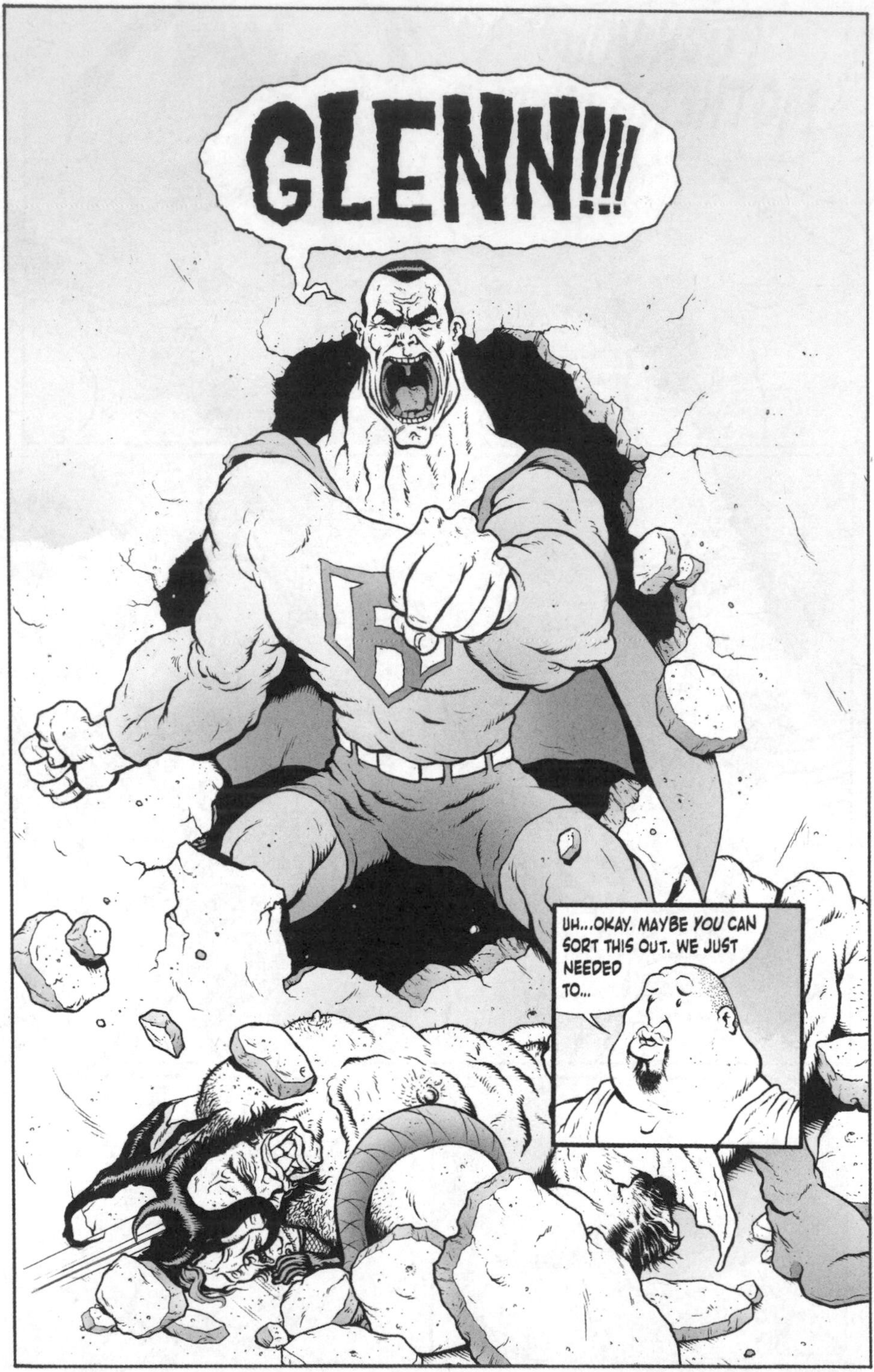
GLENN!!!
UH...OKAY. MAYBE YOU CAN SORT THIS OUT. WE JUST NEEDED TO...

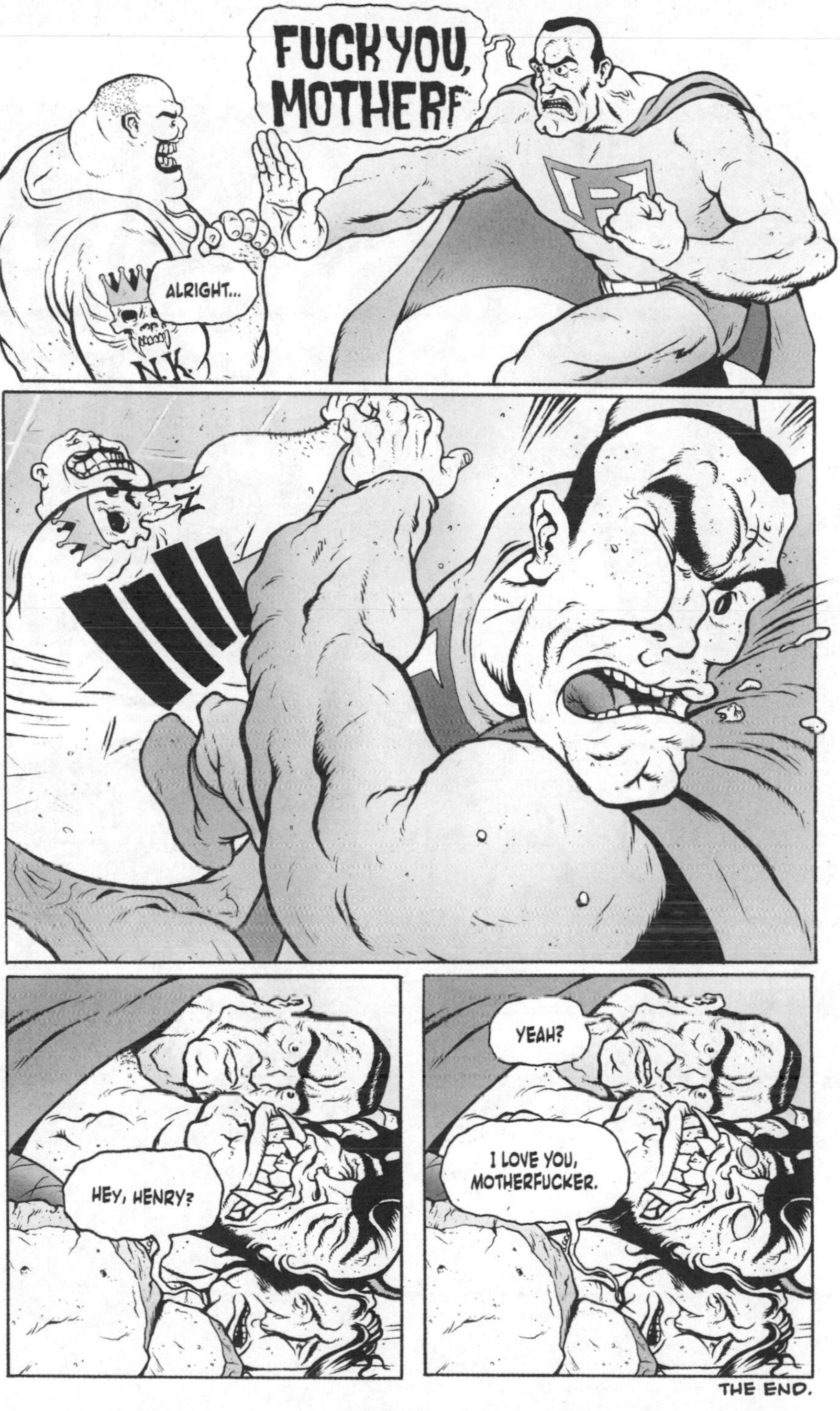
FUCK YOU, MOTHERF
ALRIGHT...
N.K.
HEY, HENRY?
YEAH?
I LOVE YOU, MOTHERFUCKER.

THE END.

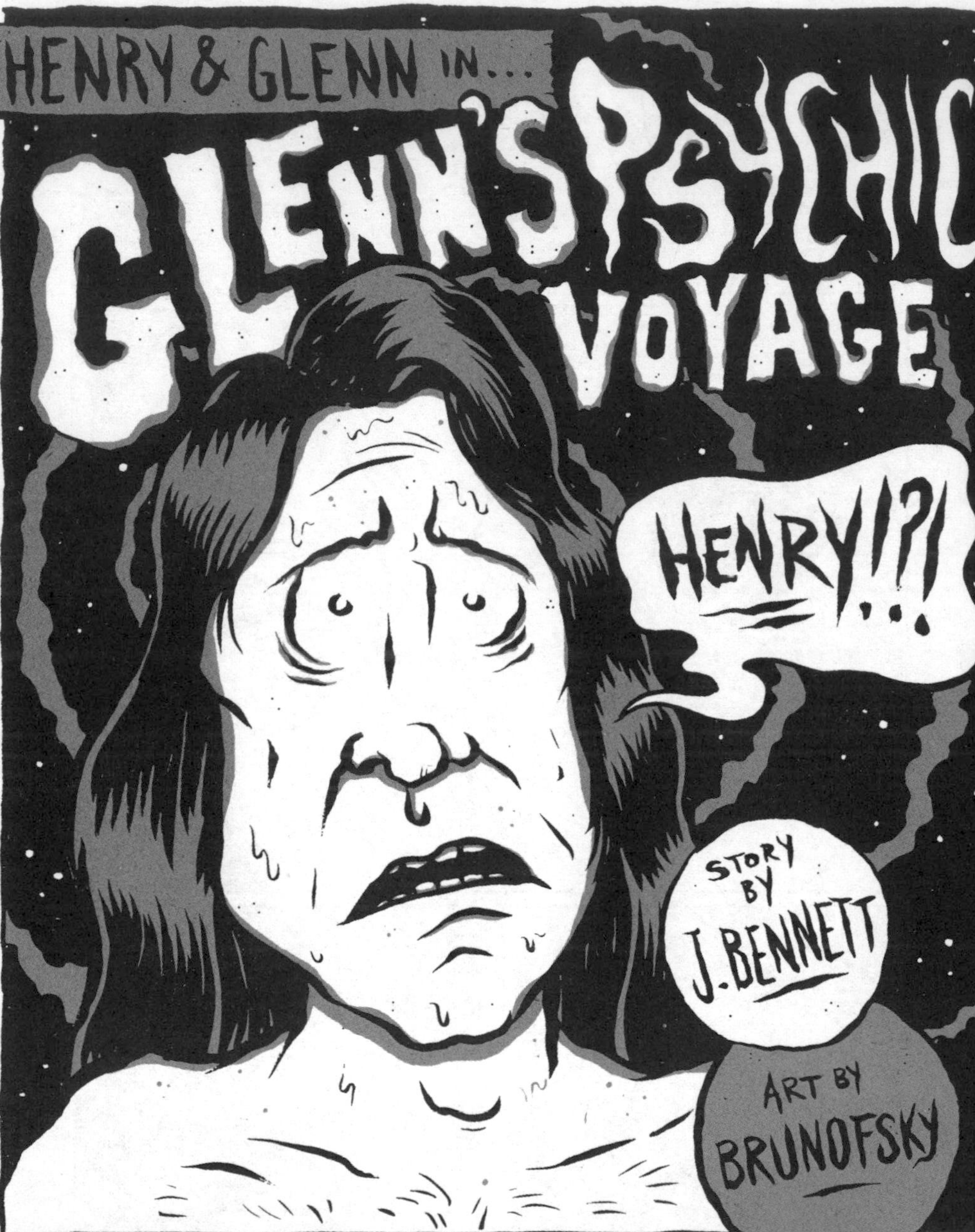
HENRY & GLENN IN...
GLENN'S PSYCHIC VOYAGE
HENRY!?!...!
STORY BY J. BENNETT
ART BY BRUNOFSKY

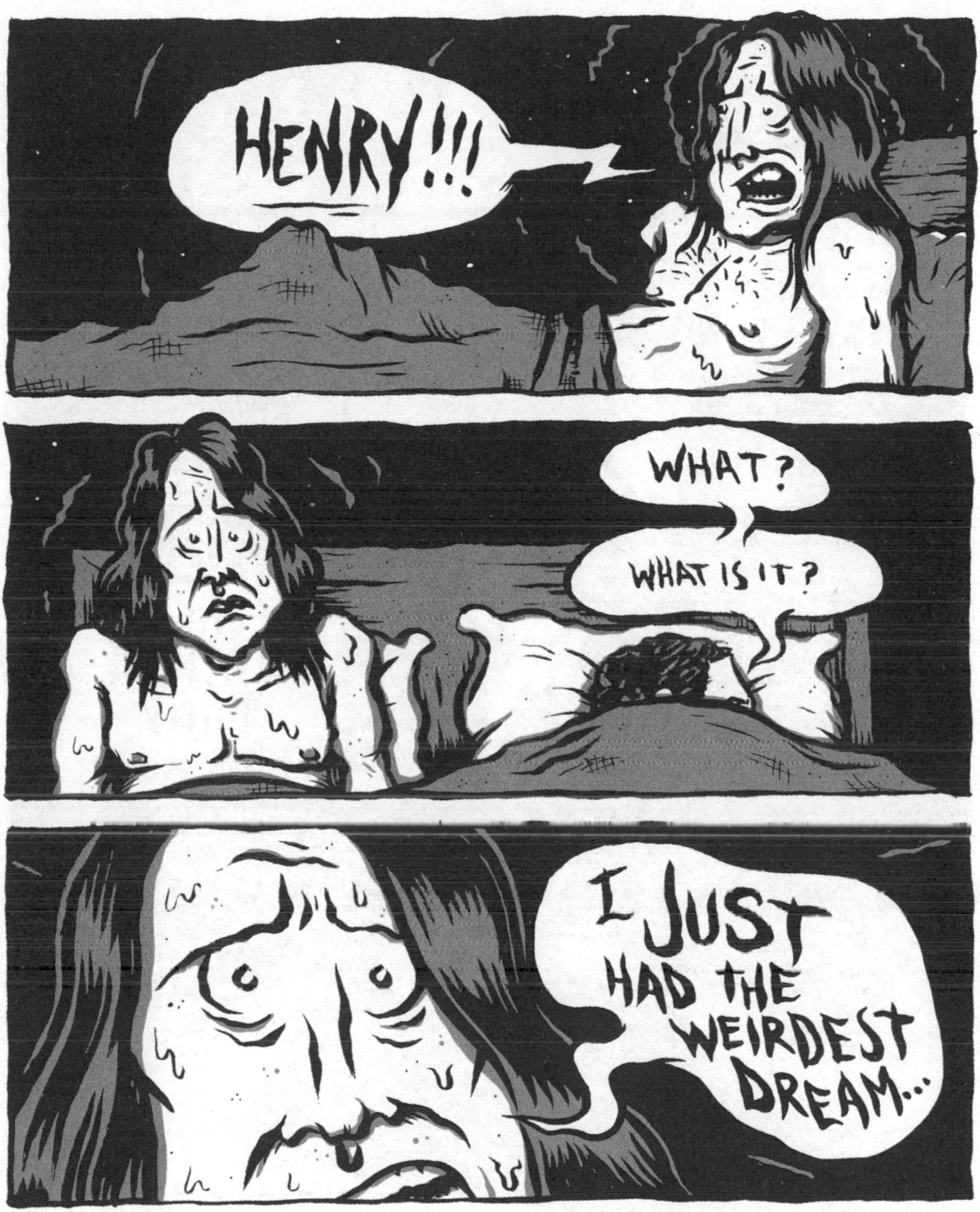
HENRY!!!
WHAT?
WHAT IS IT?
I JUST HAD THE WEIRDEST DREAM...

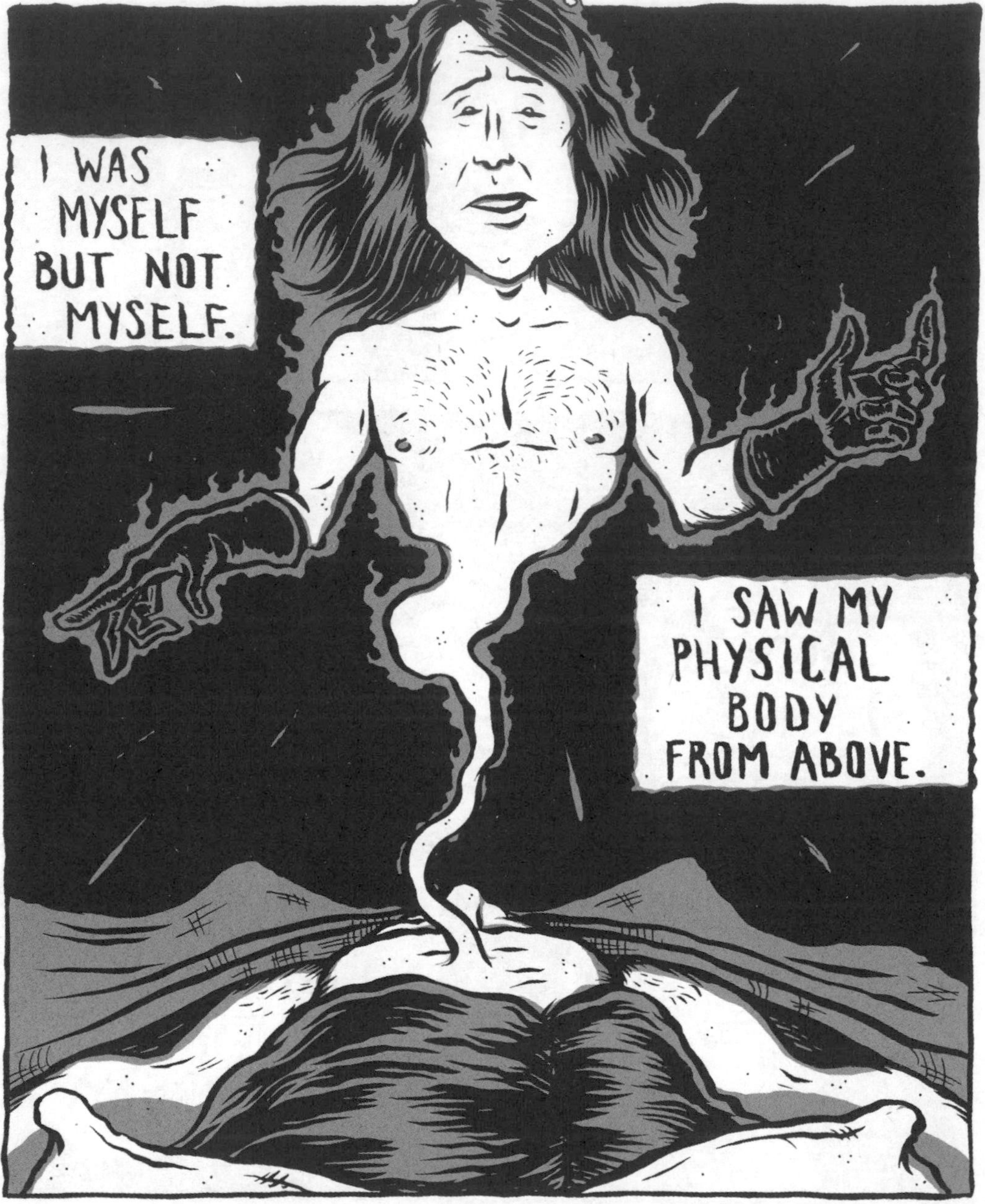
I WAS MYSELF BUT NOT MYSELF.
I SAW MY PHYSICAL BODY FROM ABOVE.

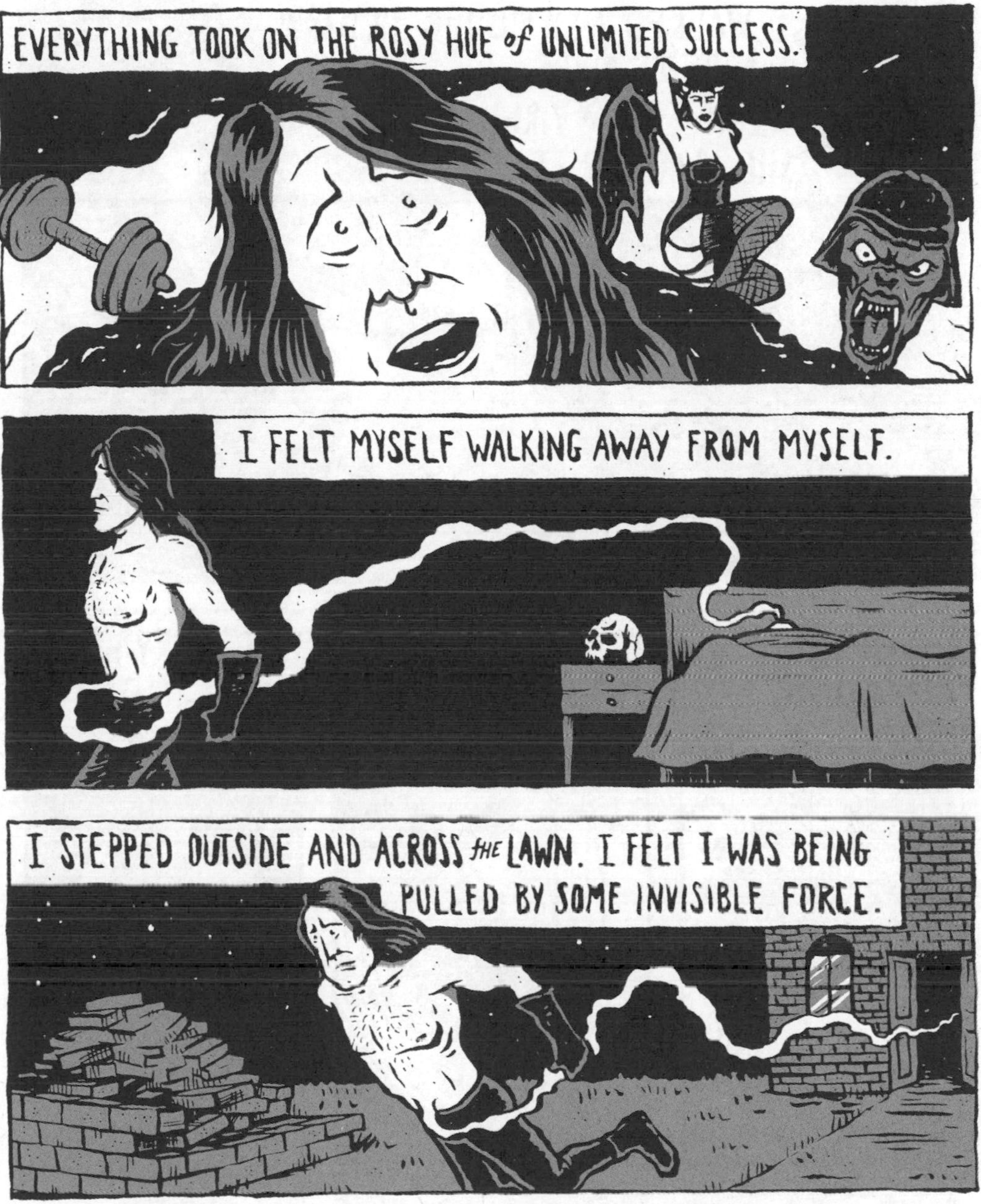

EVERYTHING TOOK ON THE ROSY HUE of UNLIMITED SUCCESS.
I FELT MYSELF WALKING AWAY FROM MYSELF.
I STEPPED OUTSIDE AND ACROSS THE LAWN. I FELT I WAS BEING PULLED BY SOME INVISIBLE FORCE.

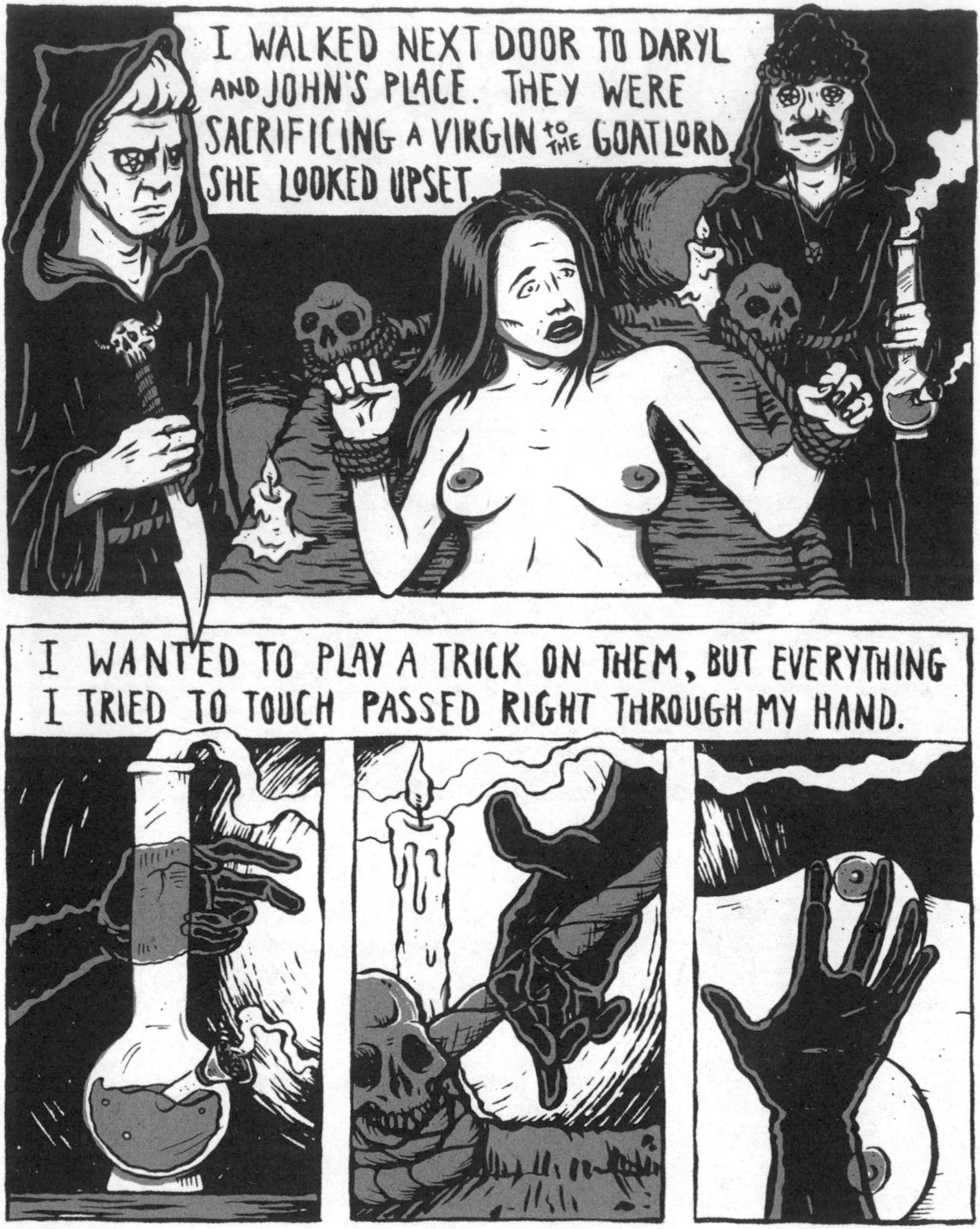
I WALKED NEXT DOOR TO DARYL AND JOHN'S PLACE. THEY WERE SACRIFICING A VIRGIN TO THE GOATLORD SHE LOOKED UPSET.
I WANTED TO PLAY A TRICK ON THEM, BUT EVERYTHING I TRIED TO TOUCH PASSED RIGHT THROUGH MY HAND.

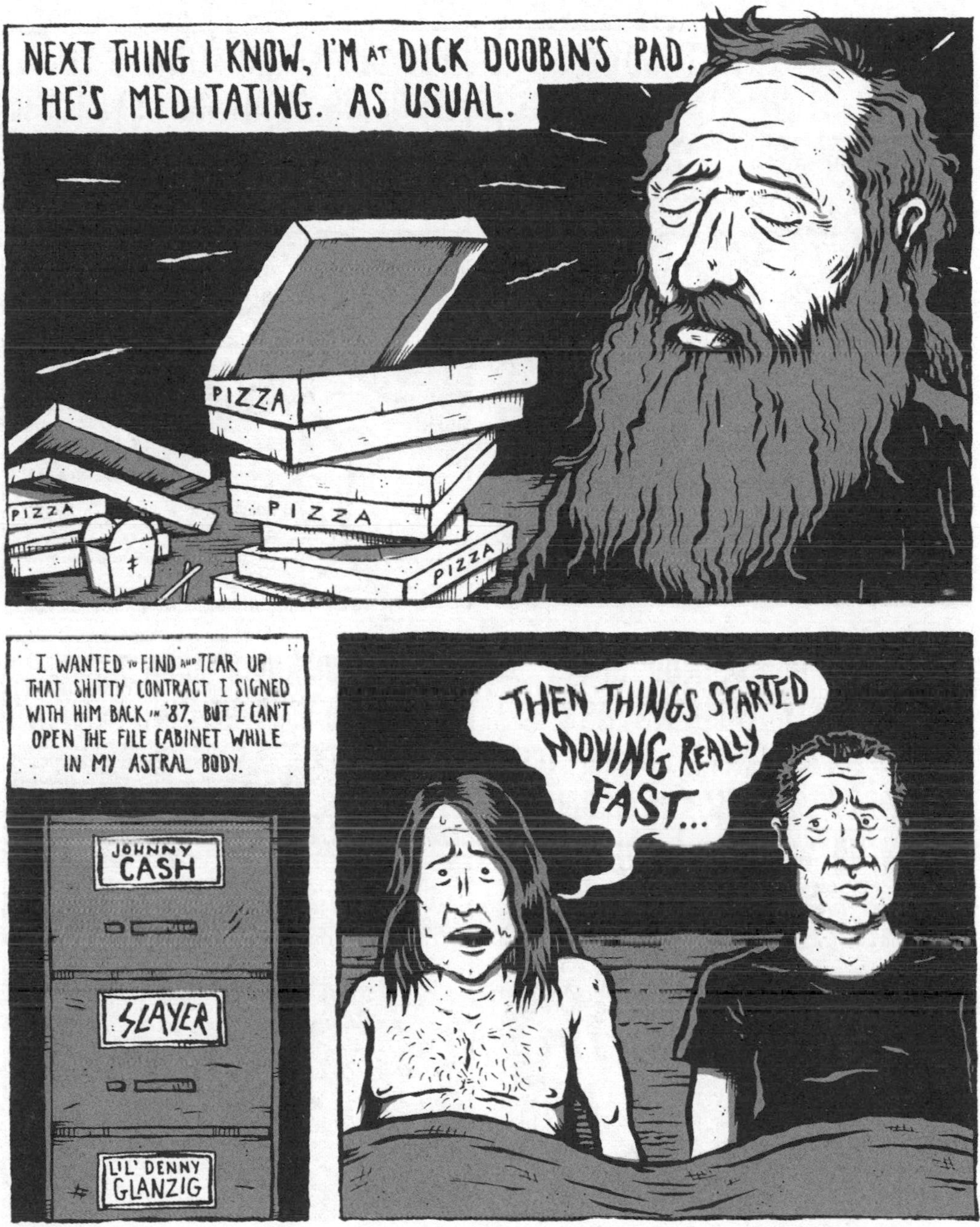
NEXT THING I KNOW, I'M AT DICK DOOBIN'S PAD. HE'S MEDITATING. AS USUAL.
PIZZA
PIZZA
PIZZA
PIZZA
I WANTED TO FIND AND TEAR UP THAT SHITTY CONTRACT I SIGNED WITH HIM BACK IN '87, BUT I CAN'T OPEN THE FILE CABINET WHILE IN MY ASTRAL BODY.
JOHNNY CASH
SLAYER
LIL' DENNY GLANZIG
THEN THINGS STARTED MOVING REALLY FAST...

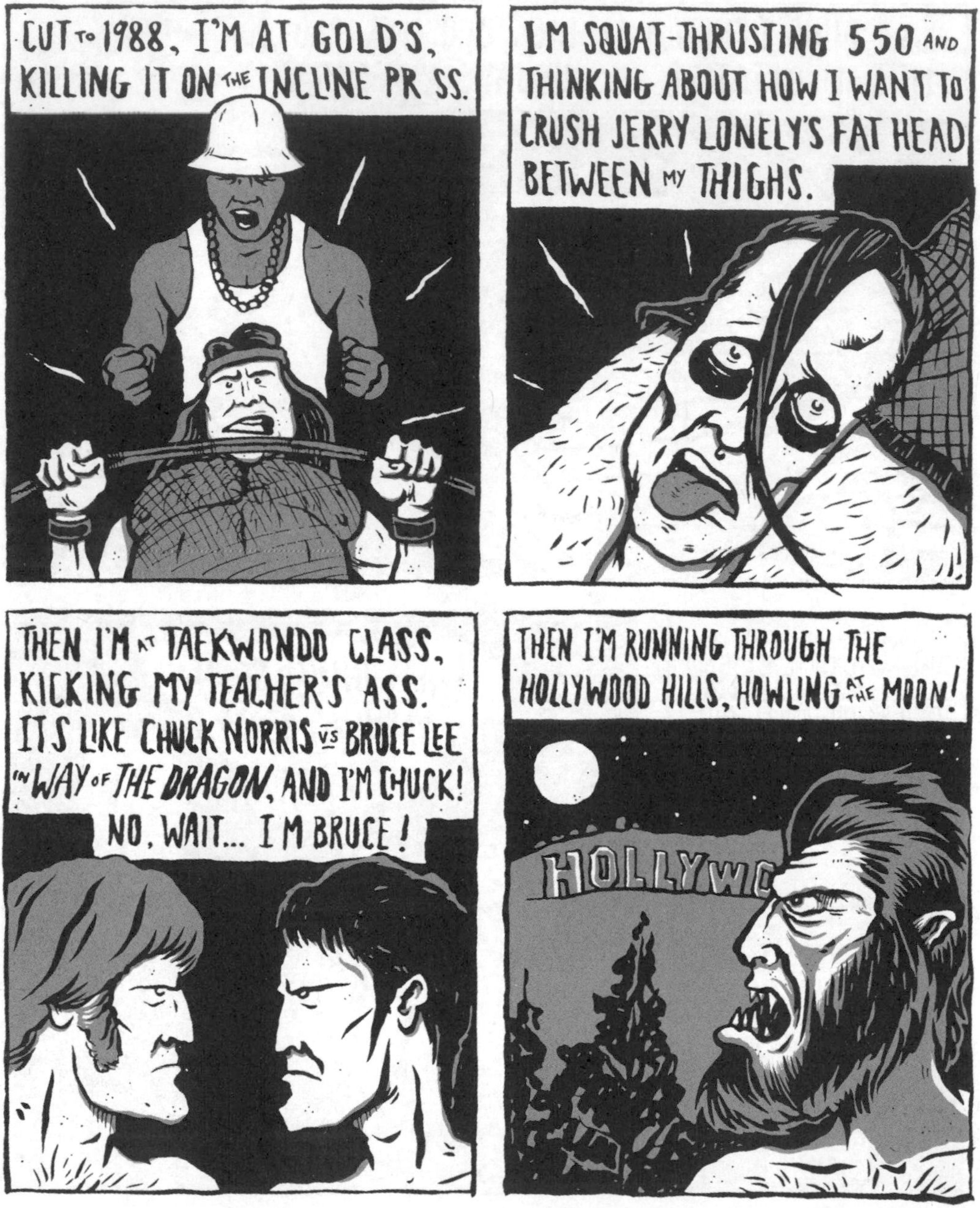
CUT TO 1988, I'M AT GOLD'S, KILLING IT ON THE INCLINE PR SS.
I M SQUAT-THRUSTING 550 AND THINKING ABOUT HOW I WANT TO CRUSH JERRY LONELY'S FAT HEAD BETWEEN MY THIGHS.
THEN I'M AT TAEKWONDO CLASS, KICKING MY TEACHER'S ASS. IT S LIKE CHUCK NORRIS VS BRUCE LEE IN WAY OF THE DRAGON, AND I'M CHUCK!
NO, WAIT... I M BRUCE!
THEN I'M RUNNING THROUGH THE HOLLYWOOD HILLS, HOWLING AT THE MOON!
HOLLYWO

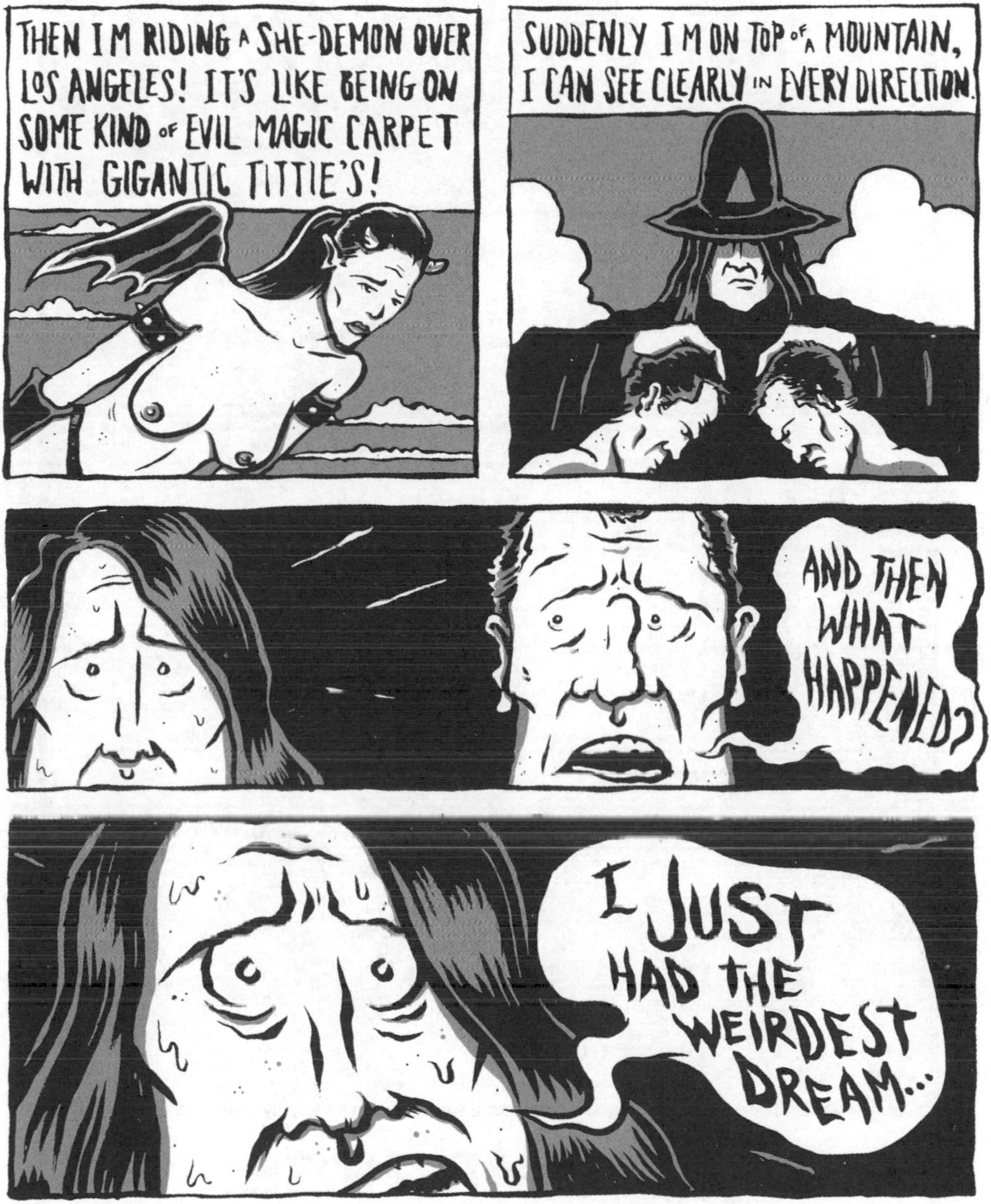
THEN I M RIDING A SHE-DEMON OVER LOS ANGELES! IT'S LIKE BEING ON SOME KIND OF EVIL MAGIC CARPET WITH GIGANTIC TITTIE'S!
SUDDENLY I M ON TOP OF A MOUNTAIN, I CAN SEE CLEARLY IN EVERY DIRECTION.
AND THEN WHAT HAPPENED?
I JUST HAD THE WEIRDEST DREAM...

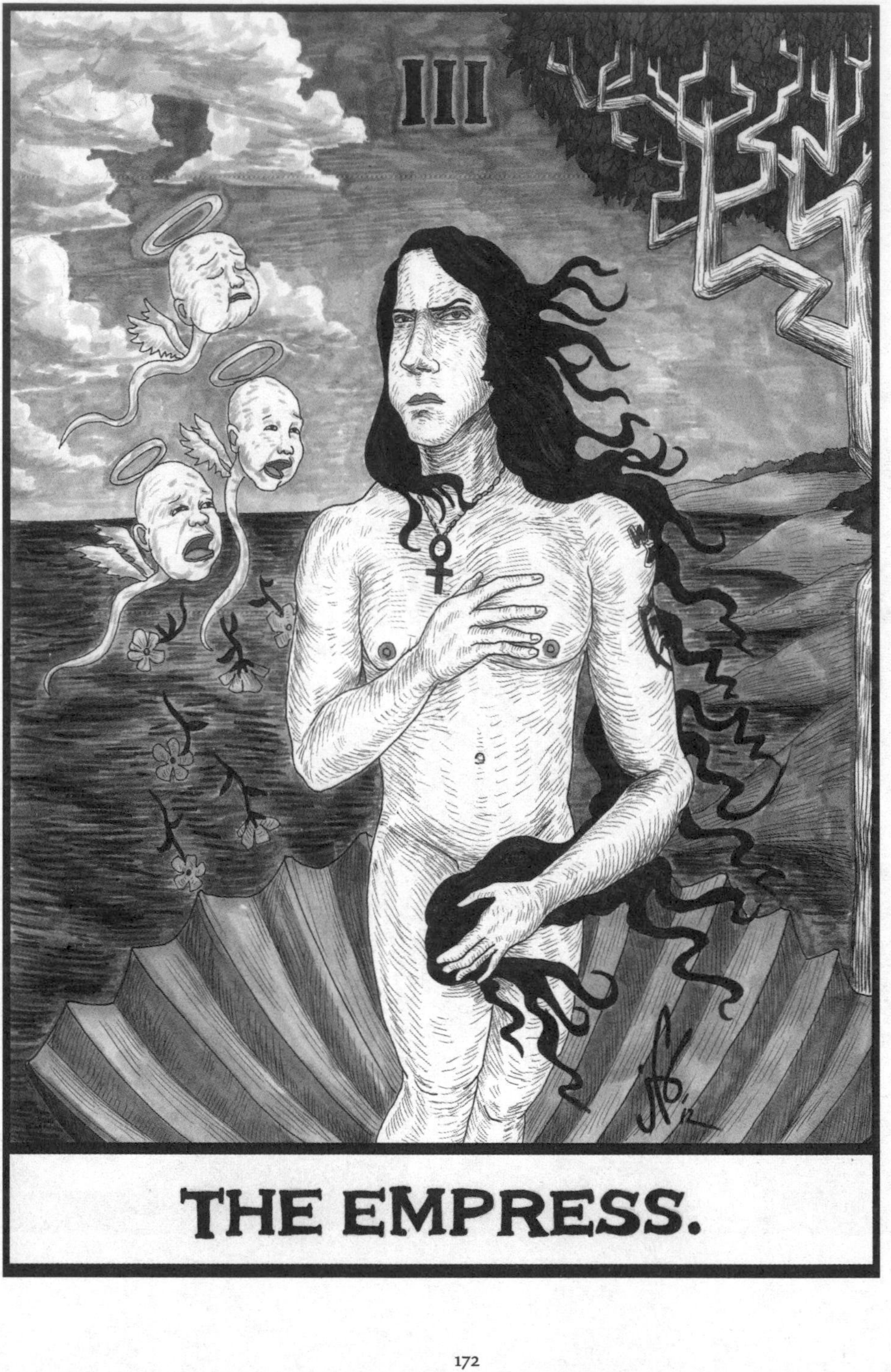
III
THE EMPRESS.

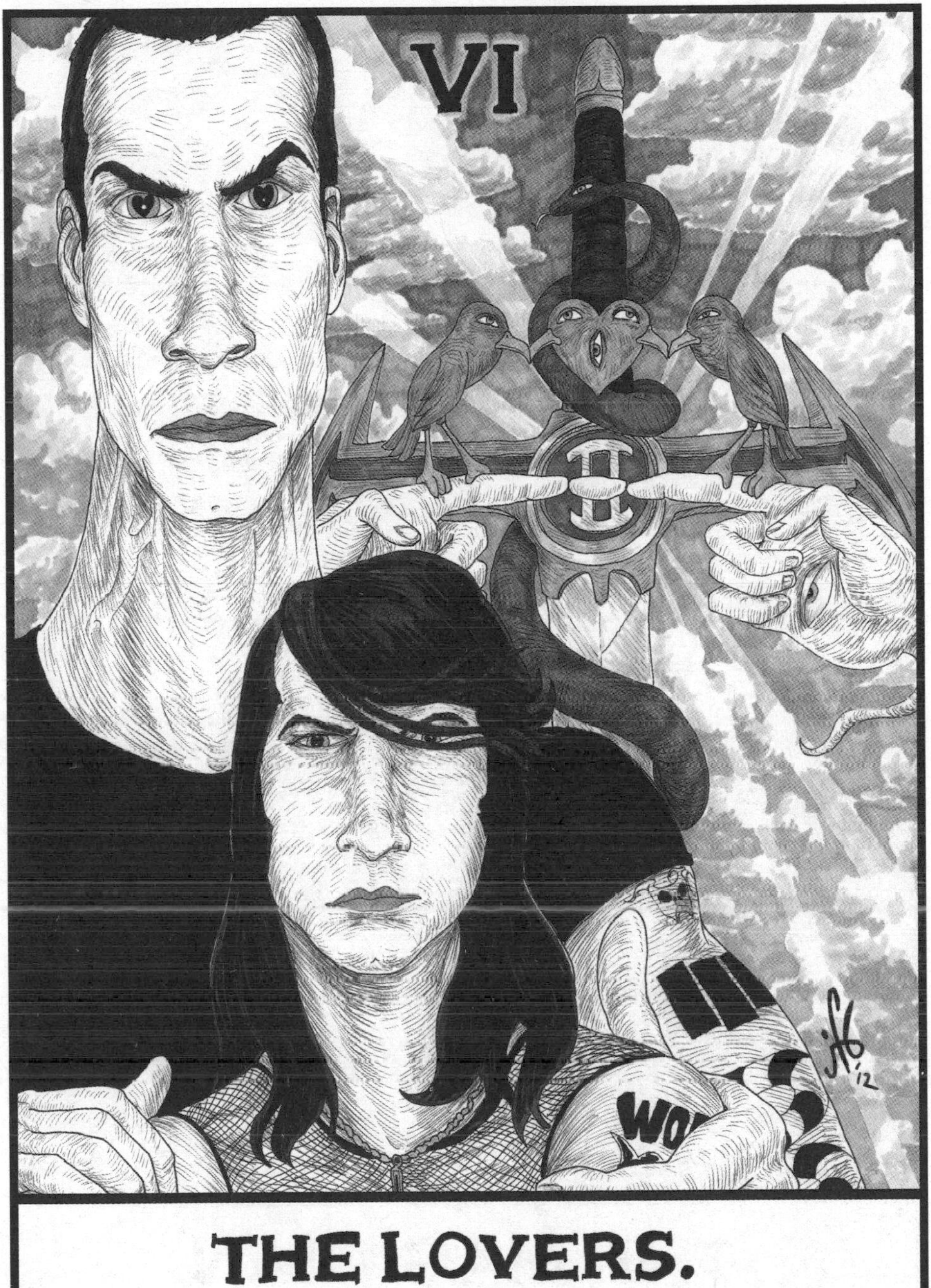
VI
WO
THE LOVERS.

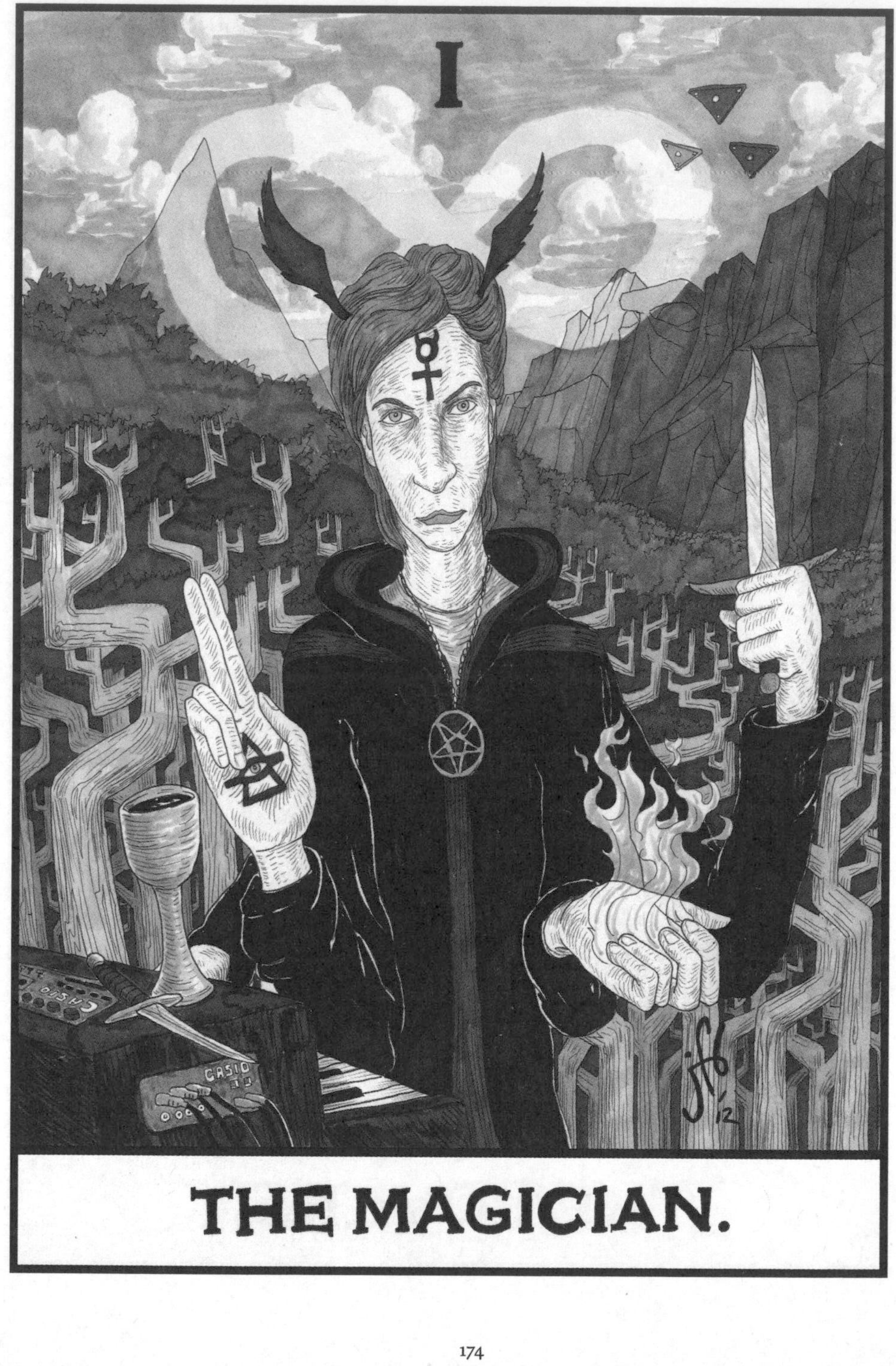
I
CASIO
CASIO
THE MAGICIAN.

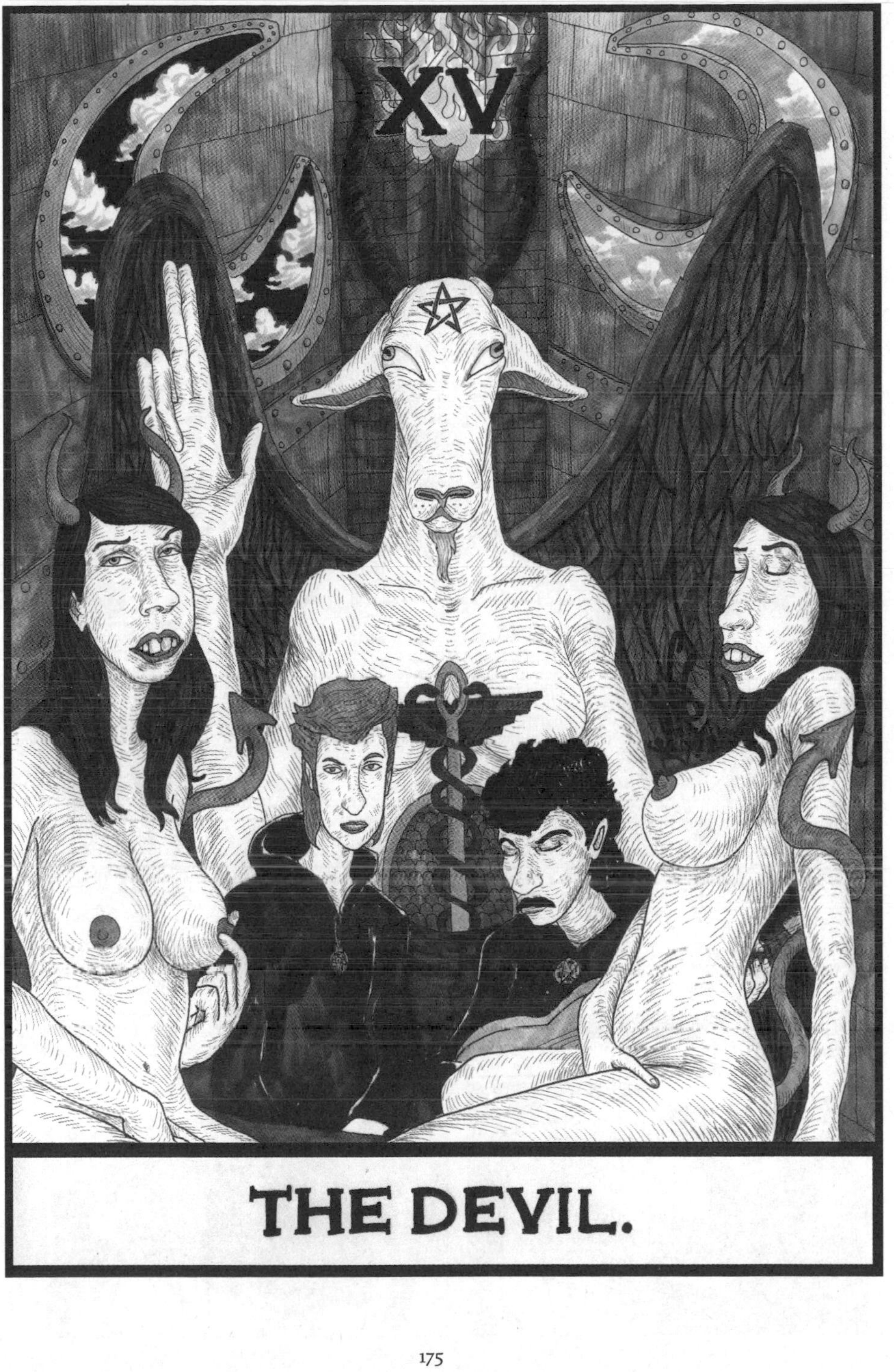
XV
THE DEVIL.

HENRY & GLENN IN *RECORD STORE DAY*

BY GEOFF VASILE

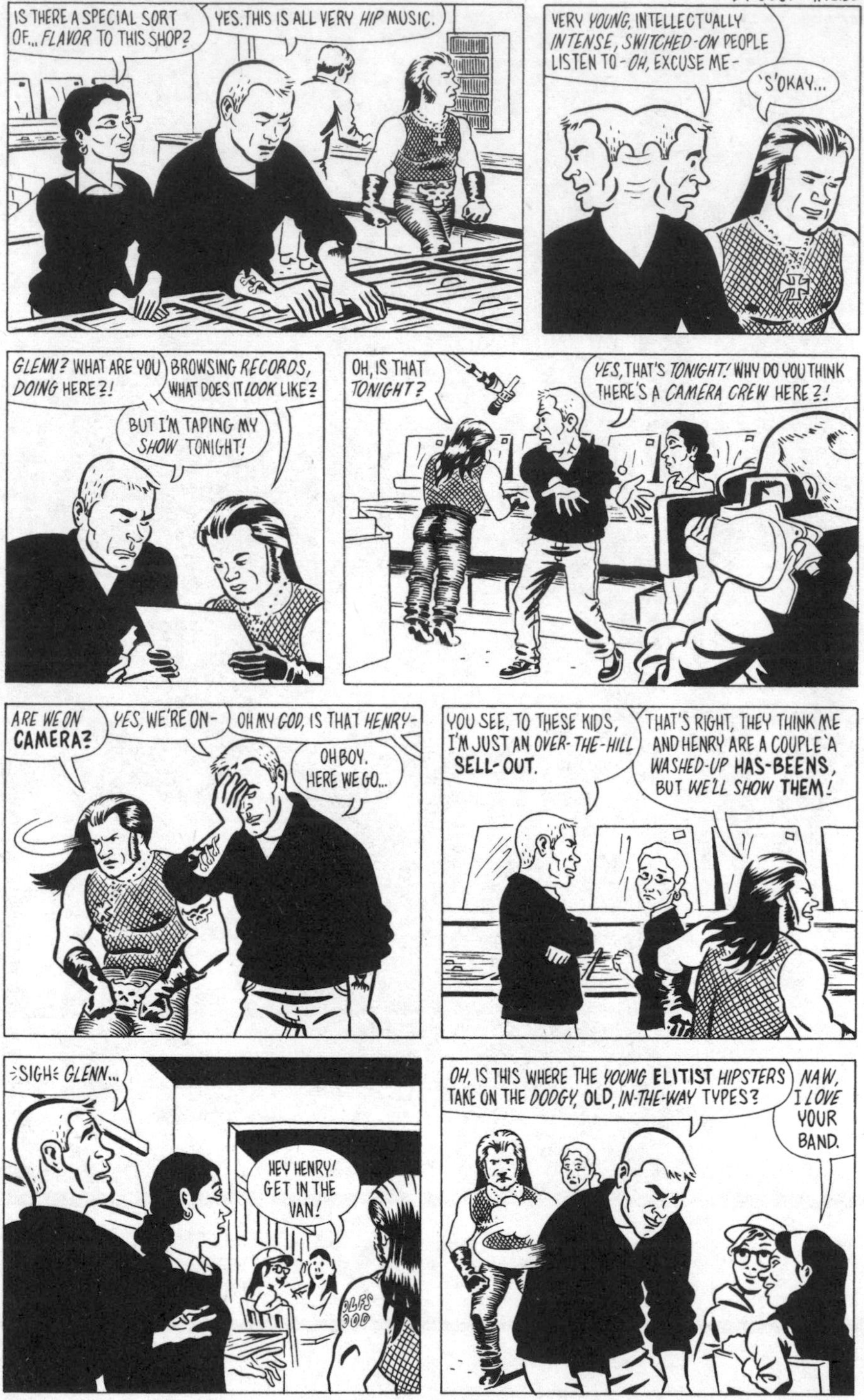
IS THERE A SPECIAL SORT OF... FLAVOR TO THIS SHOP?
YES. THIS IS ALL VERY HIP MUSIC.
VERY YOUNG, INTELLECTUALLY INTENSE, SWITCHED-ON PEOPLE LISTEN TO - OH, EXCUSE ME-
'S'OKAY...
GLENN? WHAT ARE YOU DOING HERE?!
BROWSING RECORDS, WHAT DOES IT LOOK LIKE?
BUT I'M TAPING MY SHOW TONIGHT!
OH, IS THAT TONIGHT?
YES, THAT'S TONIGHT! WHY DO YOU THINK THERE'S A CAMERA CREW HERE?!
ARE WE ON CAMERA?
YES, WE'RE ON-
OH MY GOD, IS THAT HENRY-
OH BOY. HERE WE GO...
YOU SEE, TO THESE KIDS, I'M JUST AN OVER-THE-HILL SELL-OUT.
THAT'S RIGHT, THEY THINK ME AND HENRY ARE A COUPLE 'A WASHED-UP HAS-BEENS, BUT WE'LL SHOW THEM!
SIGH GLENN...
HEY HENRY! GET IN THE VAN!
OH, IS THIS WHERE THE YOUNG ELITIST HIPSTERS TAKE ON THE DODGY, OLD, IN-THE-WAY TYPES?
NAW, I LOVE YOUR BAND.

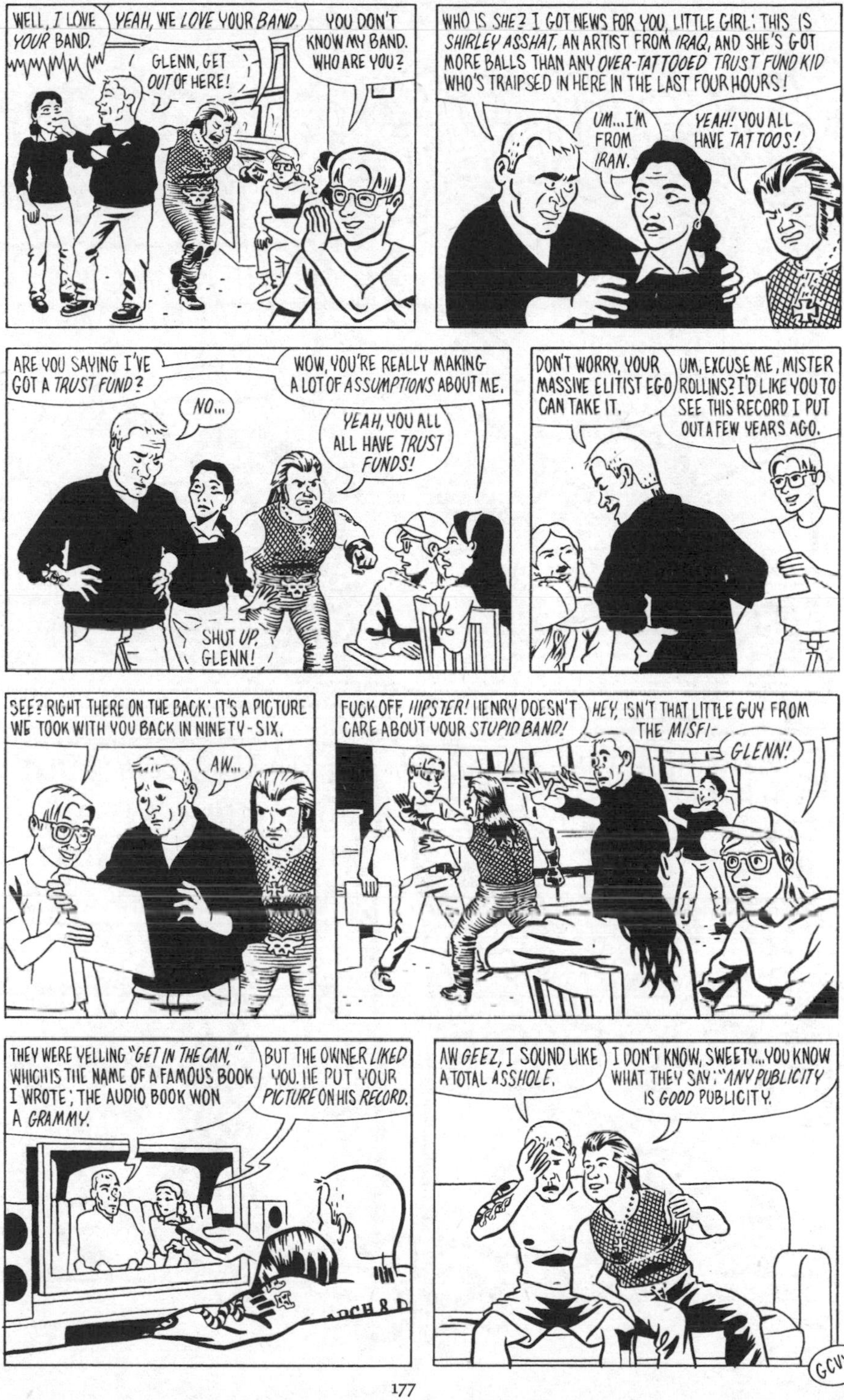
WELL, I LOVE YOUR BAND.
YEAH, WE LOVE YOUR BAND.
YOU DON'T KNOW MY BAND. WHO ARE YOU?
GLENN, GET OUT OF HERE!
WHO IS SHE? I GOT NEWS FOR YOU, LITTLE GIRL: THIS IS SHIRLEY ASSHAT, AN ARTIST FROM IRAQ, AND SHE'S GOT MORE BALLS THAN ANY OVER-TATTOOED TRUST FUND KID WHO'S TRAIPSED IN HERE IN THE LAST FOUR HOURS!
UM...I'M FROM IRAN.
YEAH! YOU ALL HAVE TATTOOS!
ARE YOU SAYING I'VE GOT A TRUST FUND?
WOW, YOU'RE REALLY MAKING A LOT OF ASSUMPTIONS ABOUT ME.
NO...
YEAH, YOU ALL ALL HAVE TRUST FUNDS!
SHUT UP, GLENN!
DON'T WORRY, YOUR MASSIVE ELITIST EGO CAN TAKE IT.
UM, EXCUSE ME, MISTER ROLLINS? I'D LIKE YOU TO SEE THIS RECORD I PUT OUT A FEW YEARS AGO.
SEE? RIGHT THERE ON THE BACK: IT'S A PICTURE WE TOOK WITH YOU BACK IN NINETY-SIX.
AW...
FUCK OFF, HIPSTER! HENRY DOESN'T CARE ABOUT YOUR STUPID BAND!
HEY, ISN'T THAT LITTLE GUY FROM THE MISFI-
GLENN!
THEY WERE YELLING "GET IN THE CAN," WHICH IS THE NAME OF A FAMOUS BOOK I WROTE; THE AUDIO BOOK WON A GRAMMY.
BUT THE OWNER LIKED YOU. HE PUT YOUR PICTURE ON HIS RECORD.
AW GEEZ, I SOUND LIKE A TOTAL ASSHOLE.
I DON'T KNOW, SWEETY... YOU KNOW WHAT THEY SAY: "ANY PUBLICITY IS GOOD PUBLICITY.
GCV'14

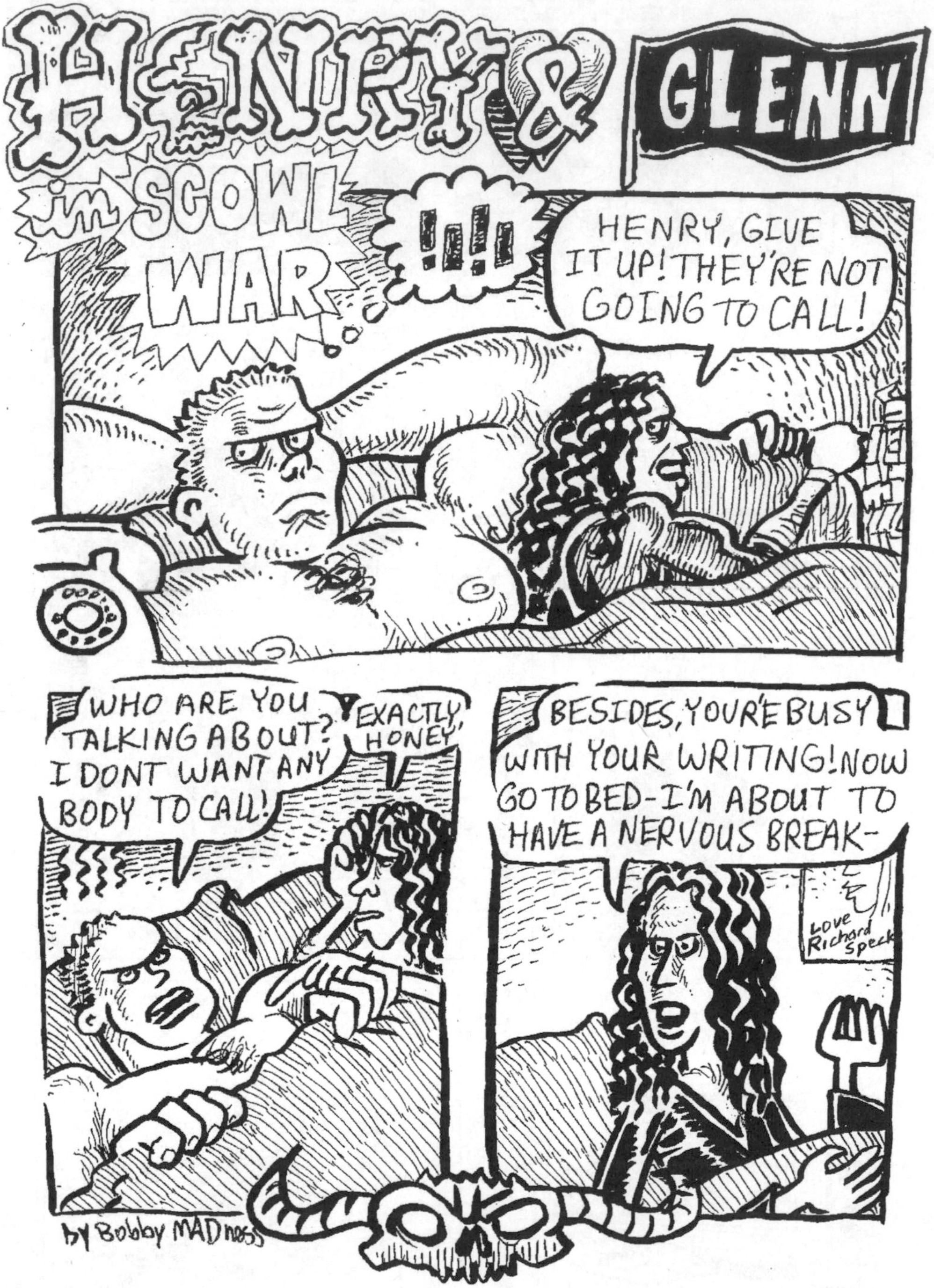
HENRY & GLENN
in SCOWL WAR
!!!!
HENRY, GIVE IT UP! THEY'RE NOT GOING TO CALL!
WHO ARE YOU TALKING ABOUT? I DONT WANT ANY BODY TO CALL!
EXACTLY, HONEY
BESIDES, YOUR'E BUSY WITH YOUR WRITING! NOW GO TO BED - I'M ABOUT TO HAVE A NERVOUS BREAK-
Love Richard Speck
by Bobby MADness

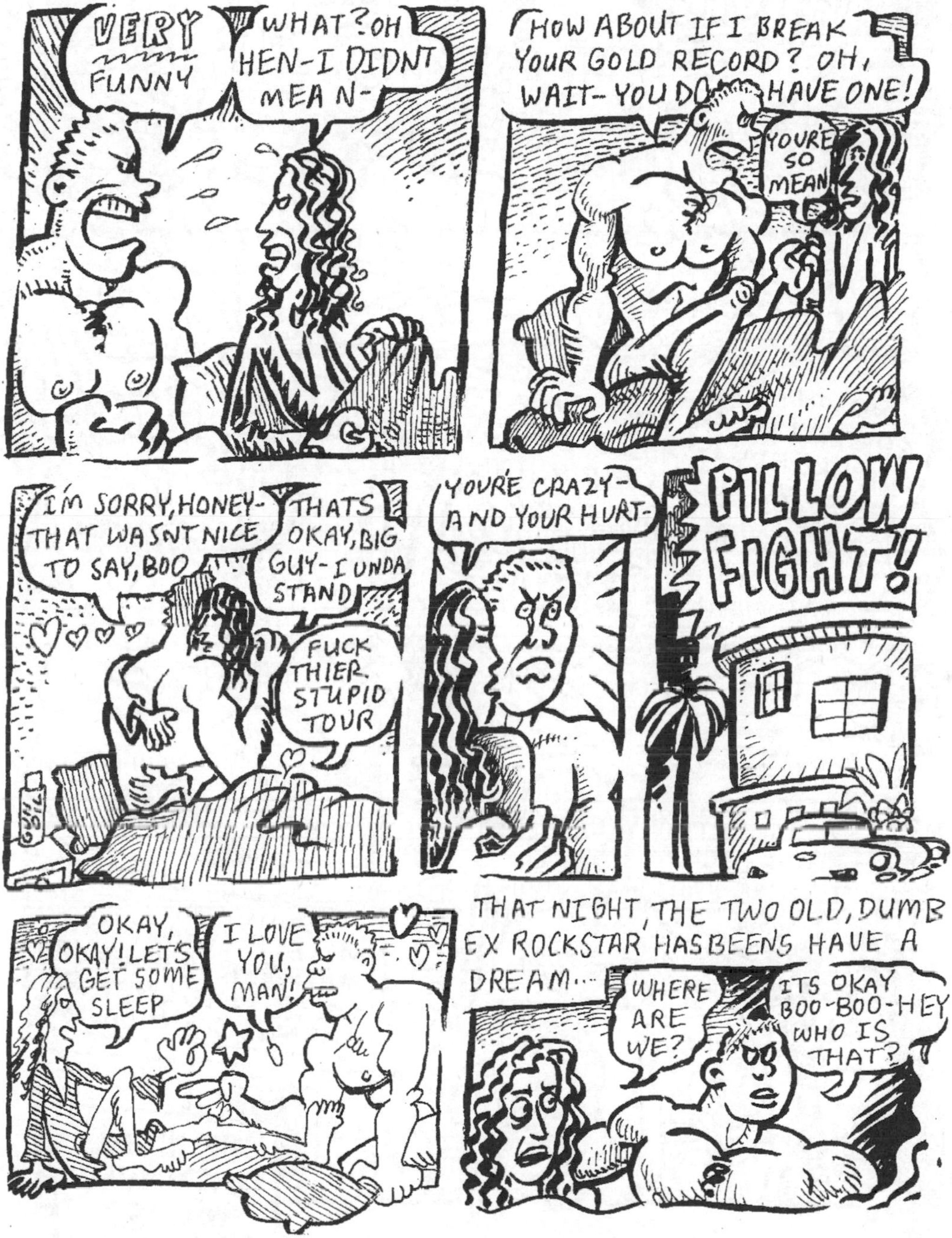
VERY FUNNY
WHAT? OH HEN-I DIDNT MEAN-
HOW ABOUT IF I BREAK YOUR GOLD RECORD? OH, WAIT- YOU D HAVE ONE!
YOU'RE SO MEAN
I'M SORRY, HONEY- THAT WASNT NICE TO SAY, BOO
THATS OKAY, BIG GUY- I UNDA STAND
FUCK THIER STUPID TOUR
YOU'RE CRAZY- AND YOUR HURT-
PILLOW FIGHT!
OKAY, OKAY! LET'S GET SOME SLEEP
I LOVE YOU, MAN!
THAT NIGHT, THE TWO OLD, DUMB EX ROCKSTAR HASBEENS HAVE A DREAM...
WHERE ARE WE?
ITS OKAY BOO-BOO-HEY WHO IS THAT?

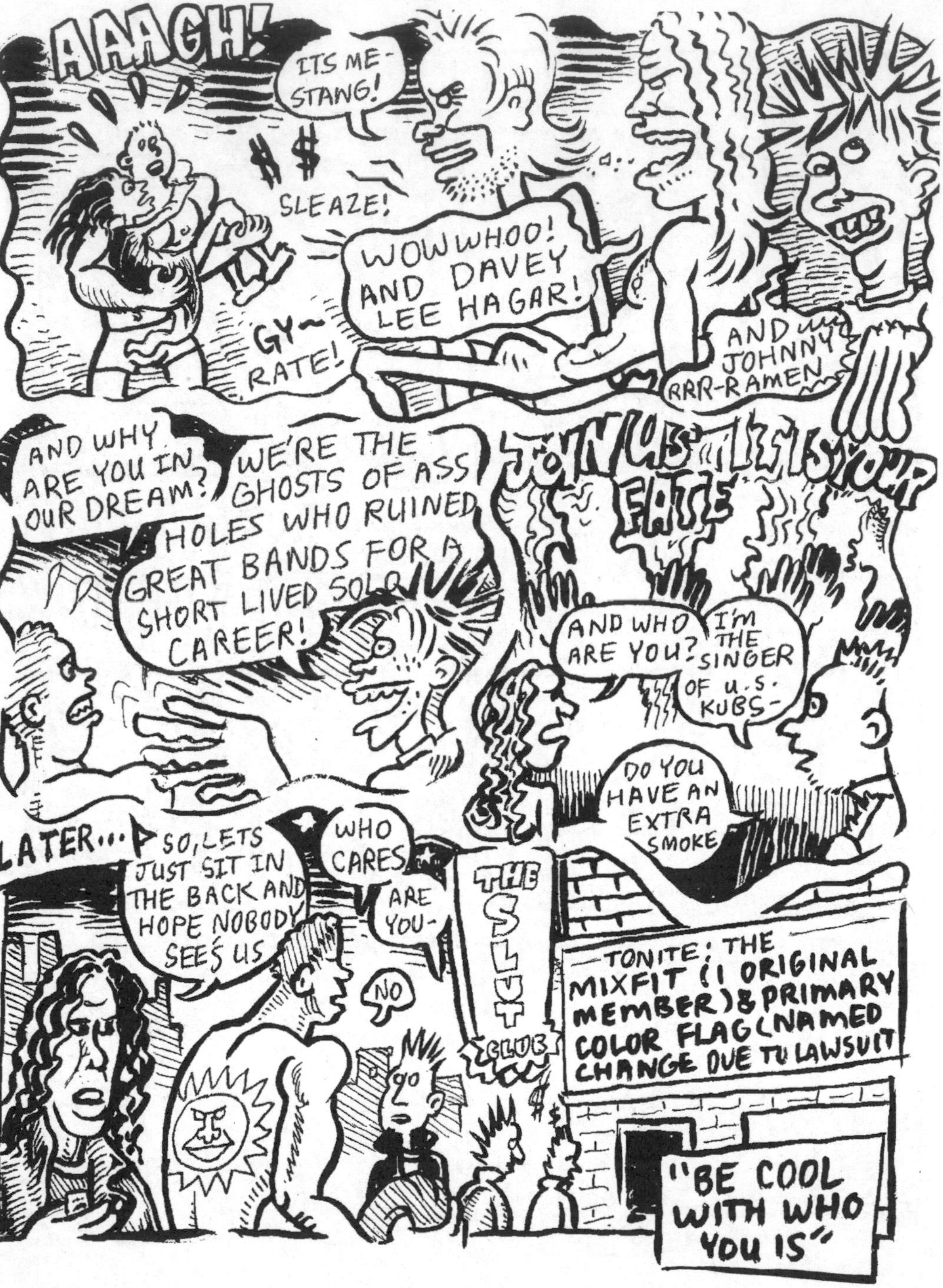
AAACH!
ITS ME-
STANG!
$ $
SLEAZE!
WOW WHOO!
AND DAVEY
LEE HAGAR!
GY-
RATE!
AND
JOHNNY
RRR-RAMEN
AND WHY
ARE YOU IN
OUR DREAM?
WE'RE THE
GHOSTS OF ASS
HOLES WHO RUINED
GREAT BANDS FOR A
SHORT LIVED SOLO
CAREER!
JOIN US! THIS IS YOUR FATE
AND WHO
ARE YOU?
I'M
THE
SINGER
OF U.S.
KUBS-
DO YOU
HAVE AN
EXTRA
SMOKE
LATER...
SO, LETS
JUST SIT IN
THE BACK AND
HOPE NOBODY
SEE'S US
WHO
CARES
ARE
YOU-
NO
THE SLUT! CLUB
TONITE: THE
MIXFIT (1 ORIGINAL
MEMBER) & PRIMARY
COLOR FLAG (NAMED
CHANGE DUE TO LAWSUIT
"BE COOL
WITH WHO
YOU IS"

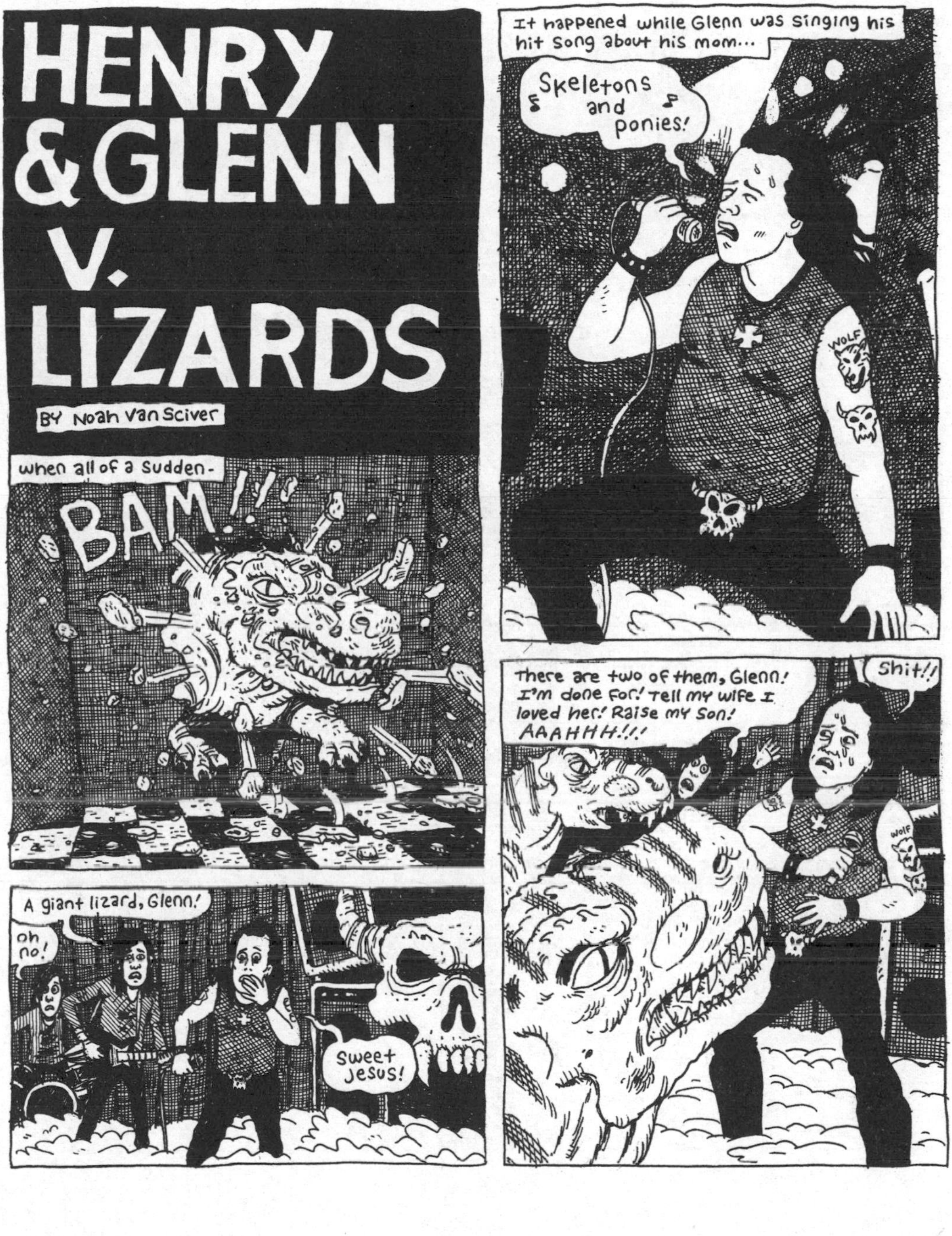
HENRY & GLENN v. LIZARDS
BY Noah Van Sciver
It happened while Glenn was singing his hit song about his mom...
Skeletons and ponies!
WOLF
when all of a sudden-
BAM!!
A giant lizard, Glenn!
oh no!
Sweet Jesus!
There are two of them, Glenn! I'm done for! Tell my wife I loved her! Raise my son! AAAHHH!!!
Shit!!
WOLF

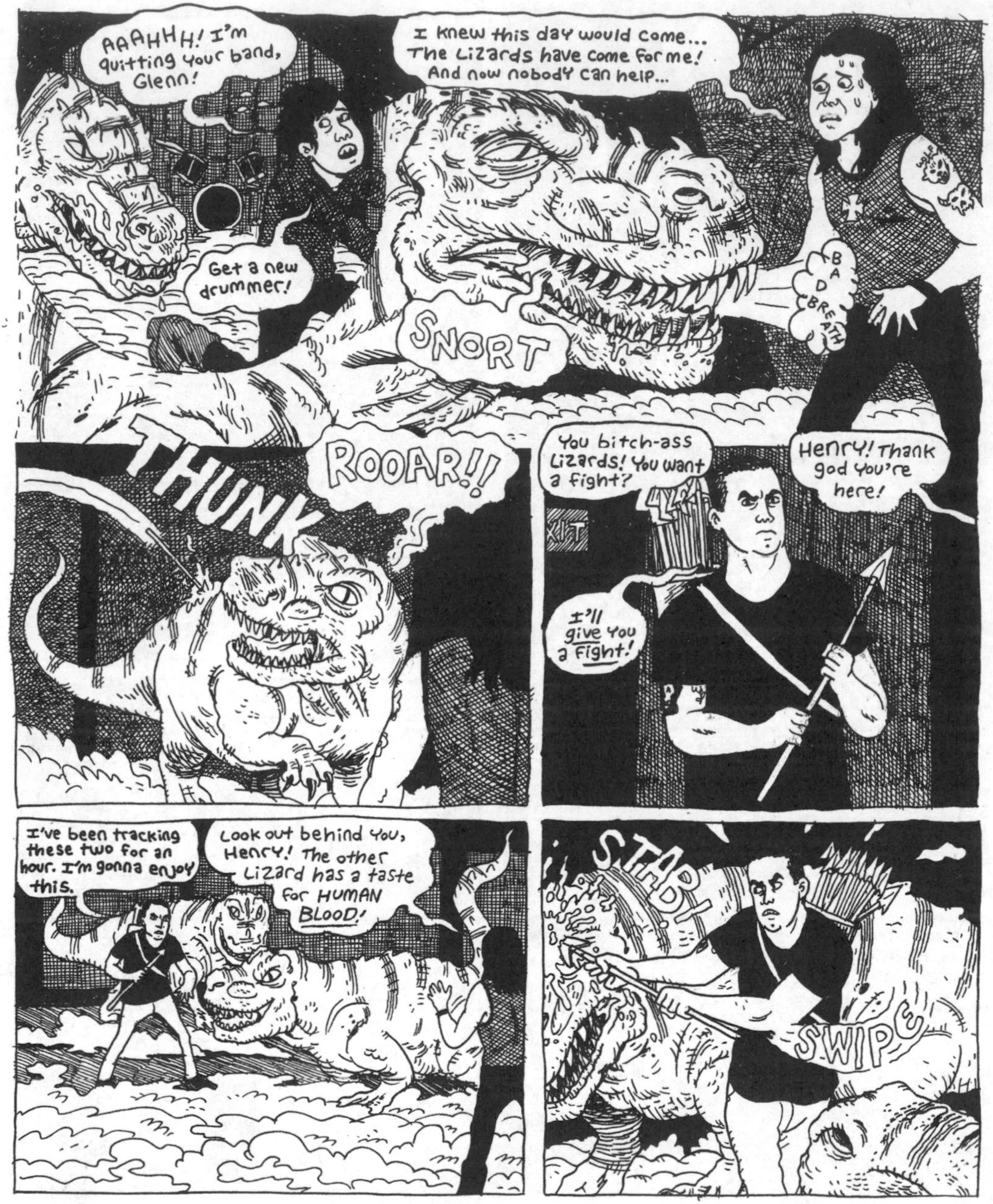
AAAHHH! I'm quitting your band, Glenn!
Get a new drummer!
I knew this day would come... The Lizards have come for me! And now nobody can help...
SNORT
BAD BREATH
THUNK
ROOAR!!
You bitch-ass Lizards! You want a fight?
Henry! Thank god you're here!
I'll give you a fight!
I've been tracking these two for an hour. I'm gonna enjoy this.
Look out behind you, Henry! The other Lizard has a taste for HUMAN BLOOD!
STAB!
SWIPE

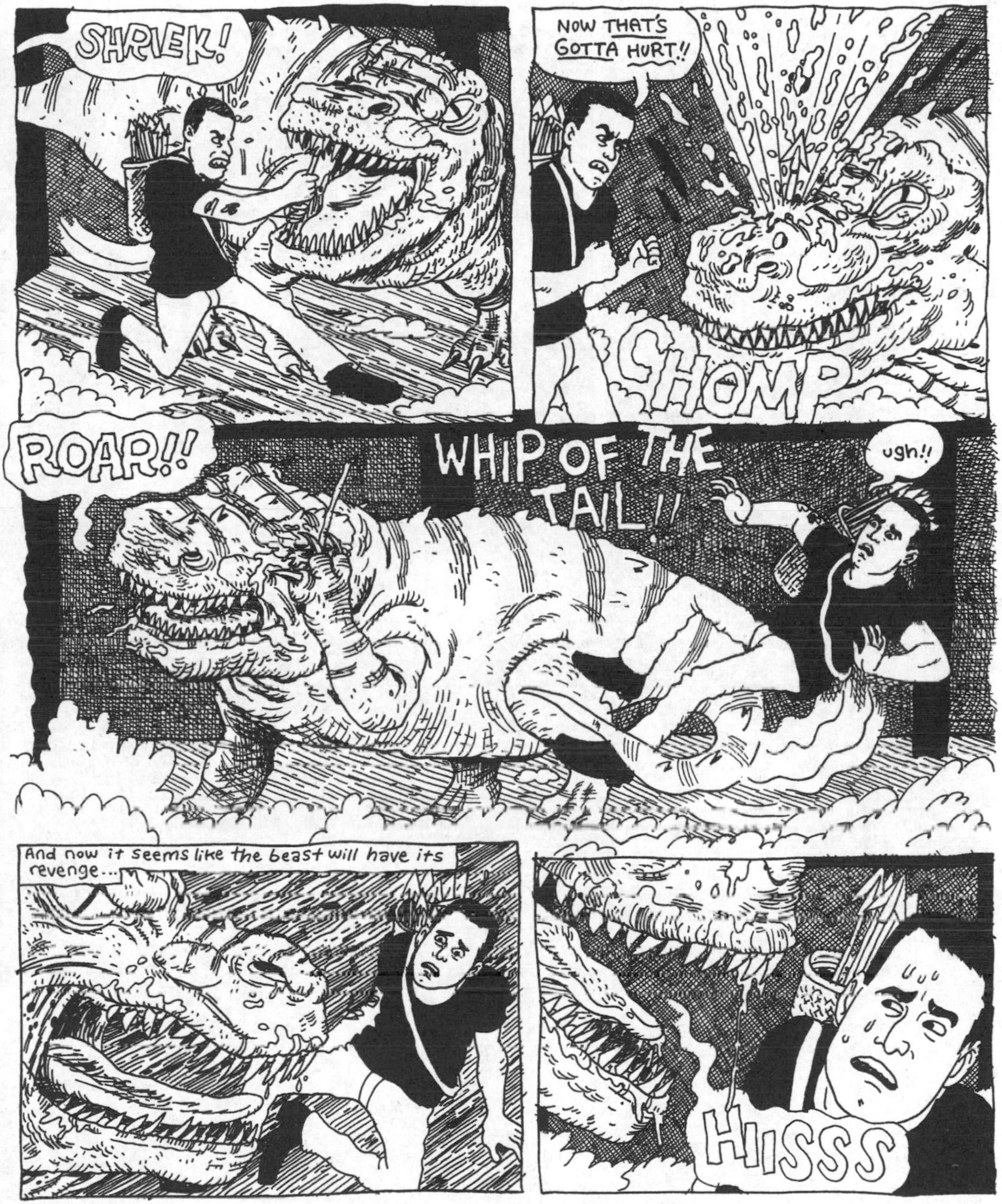
SHRIEK!
NOW THAT'S GOTTA HURT!!
CHOMP
ROAR!!
WHIP OF THE TAIL!!
ugh!!
And now it seems like the beast will have its revenge...
HIISSS

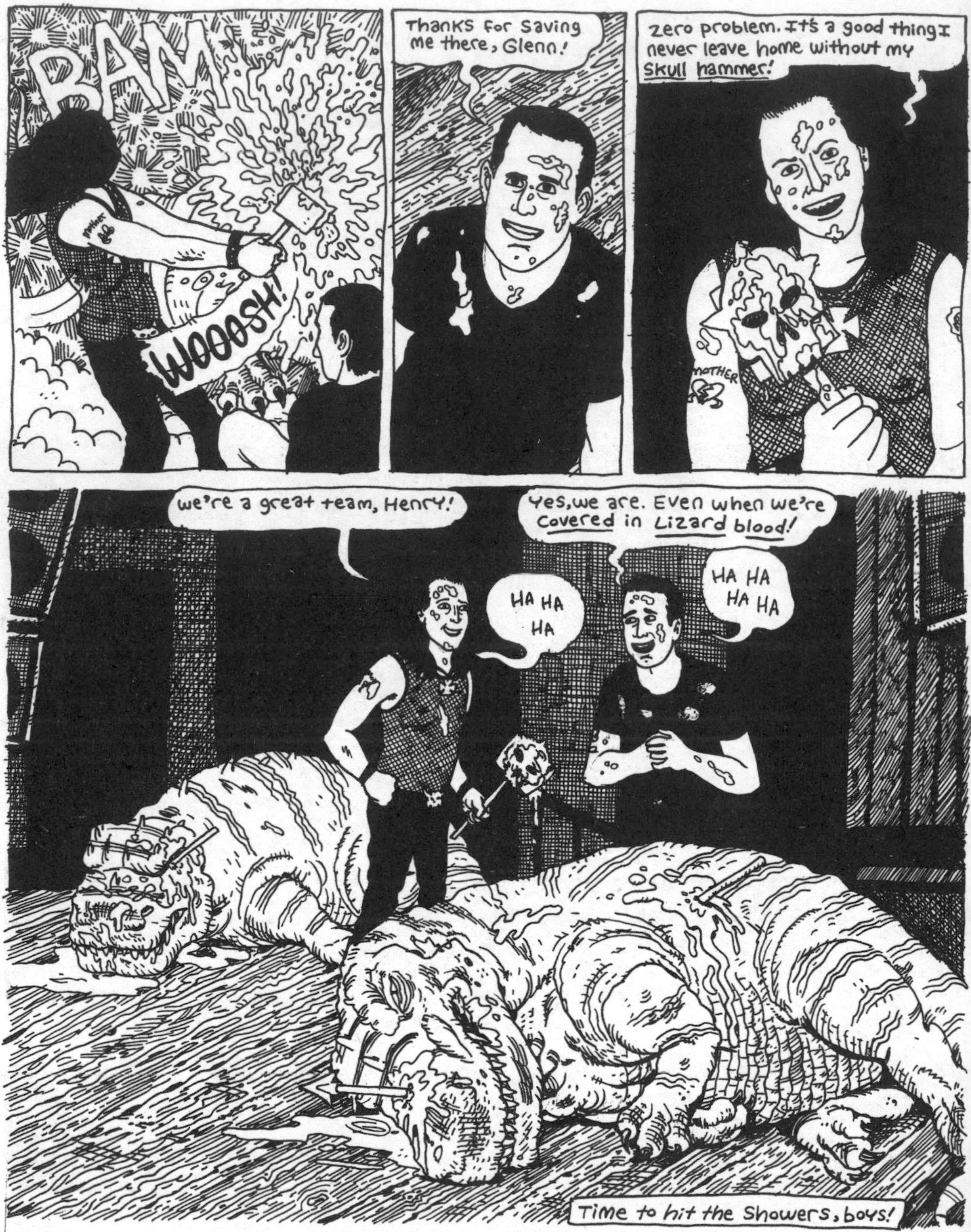
BAM!
WOOOSH!
Thanks for saving me there, Glenn!
zero problem. It's a good thing I never leave home without my skull hammer!
MOTHER
we're a great team, Henry!
Yes, we are. Even when we're covered in Lizard blood!
HA HA HA
HA HA HA HA
Time to hit the showers, boys!

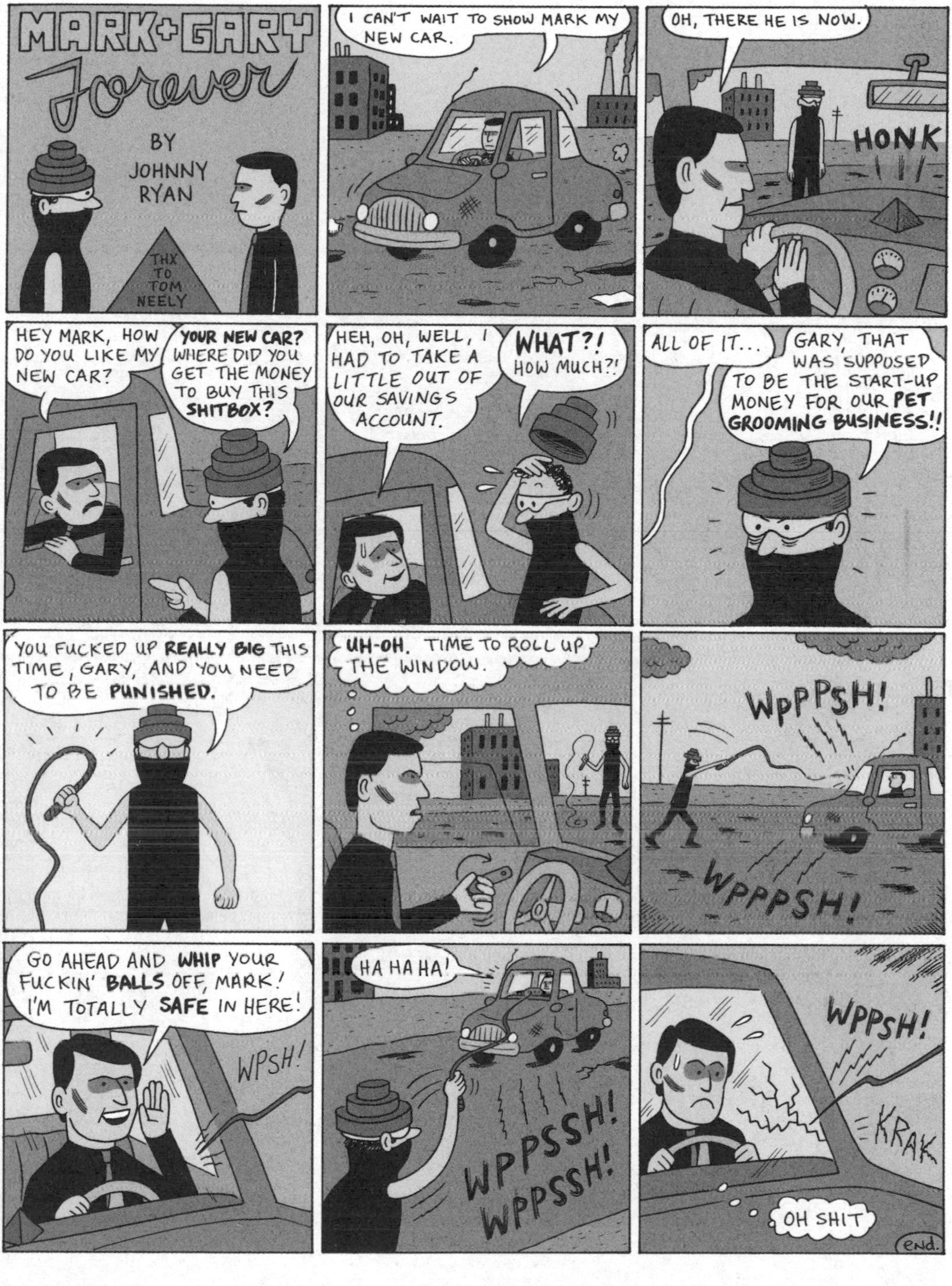
MARK+GARY
Forever
BY JOHNNY RYAN
THX TO TOM NEELY
I CAN'T WAIT TO SHOW MARK MY NEW CAR.
OH, THERE HE IS NOW.
HONK
HEY MARK, HOW DO YOU LIKE MY NEW CAR?
YOUR NEW CAR? WHERE DID YOU GET THE MONEY TO BUY THIS SHITBOX?
HEH, OH, WELL, I HAD TO TAKE A LITTLE OUT OF OUR SAVINGS ACCOUNT.
WHAT?! HOW MUCH?!
ALL OF IT...
GARY, THAT WAS SUPPOSED TO BE THE START-UP MONEY FOR OUR PET GROOMING BUSINESS!!
YOU FUCKED UP REALLY BIG THIS TIME, GARY, AND YOU NEED TO BE PUNISHED.
UH-OH. TIME TO ROLL UP THE WINDOW.
WPPPSH!
WPPPSH!
GO AHEAD AND WHIP YOUR FUCKIN' BALLS OFF, MARK! I'M TOTALLY SAFE IN HERE!
WPSH!
HA HA HA!
WPPSSH!
WPPSSH!
WPPSH!
KRAK
OH SHIT
end.

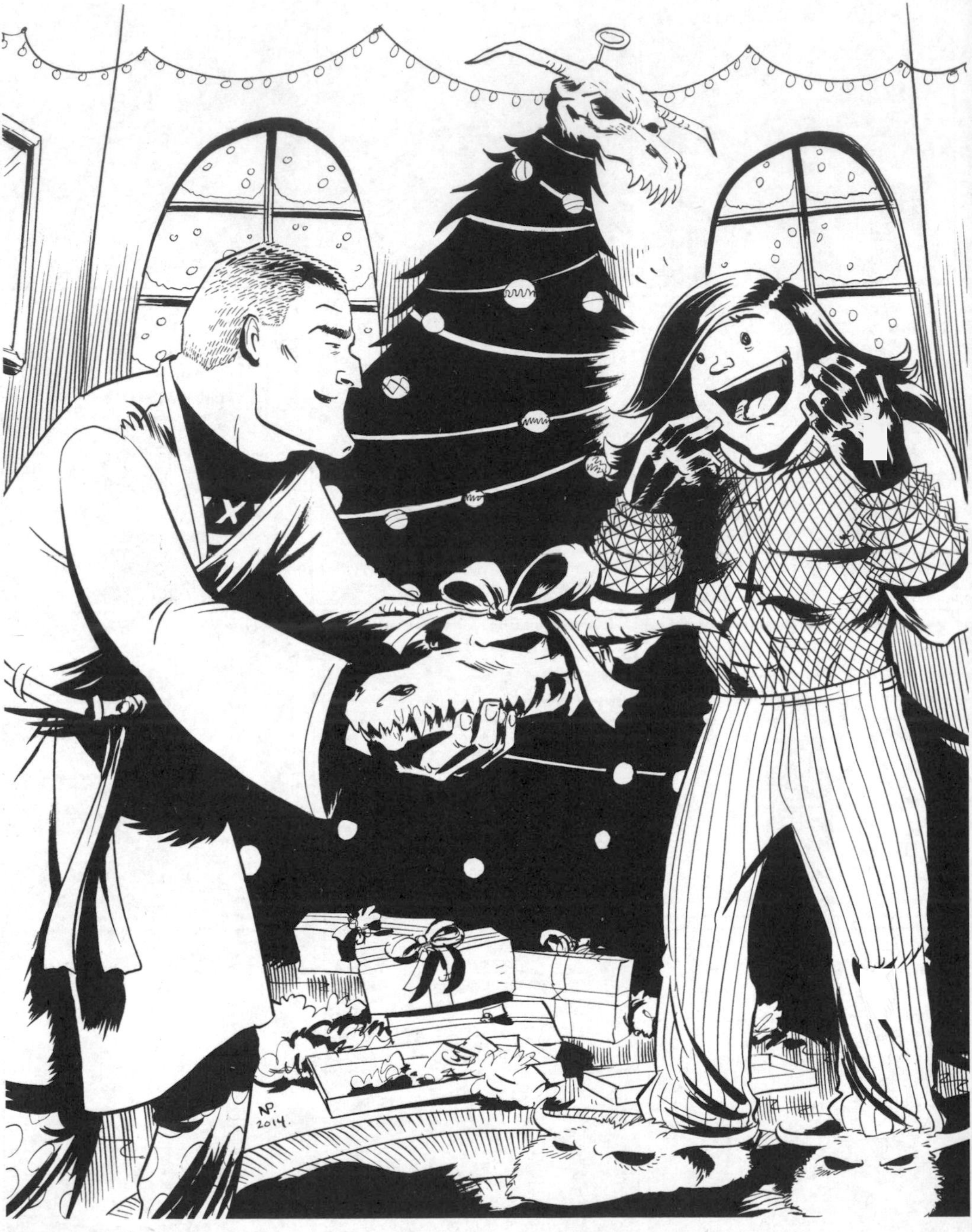
NP.
2014.

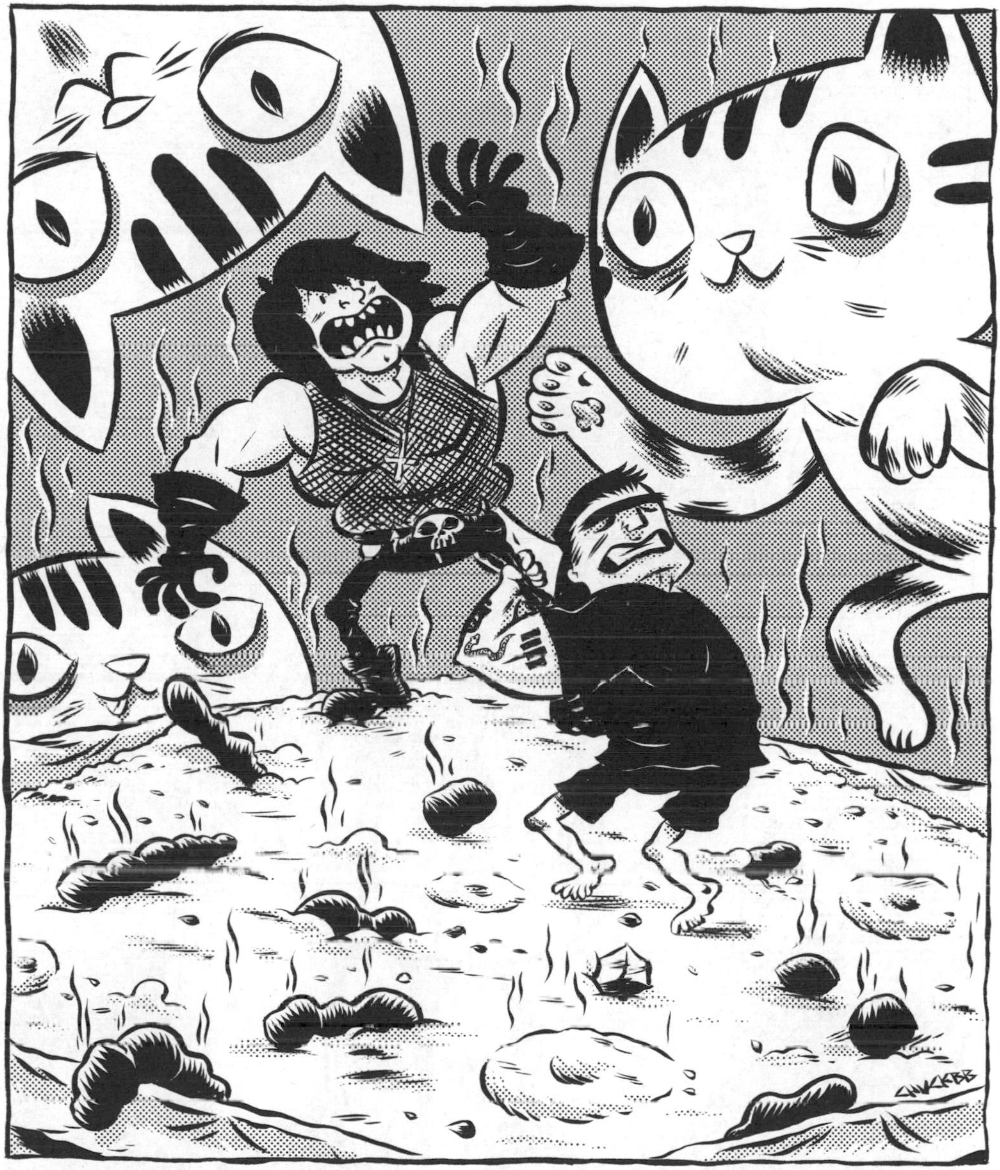

With certain doom impending, Glenn found some comfort in the familiar scent of Fresh Step.

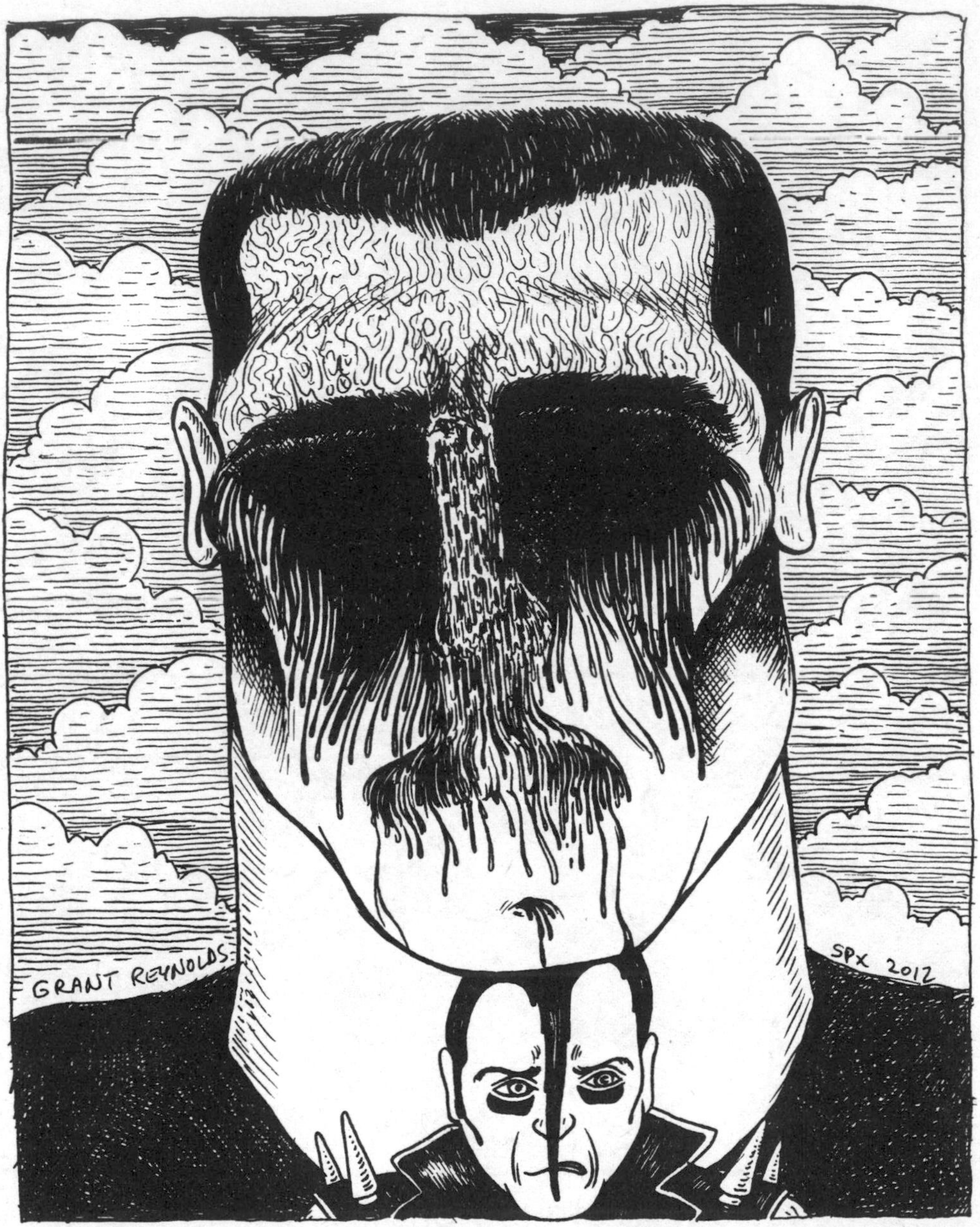
GRANT REYNOLDS
SPX 2012

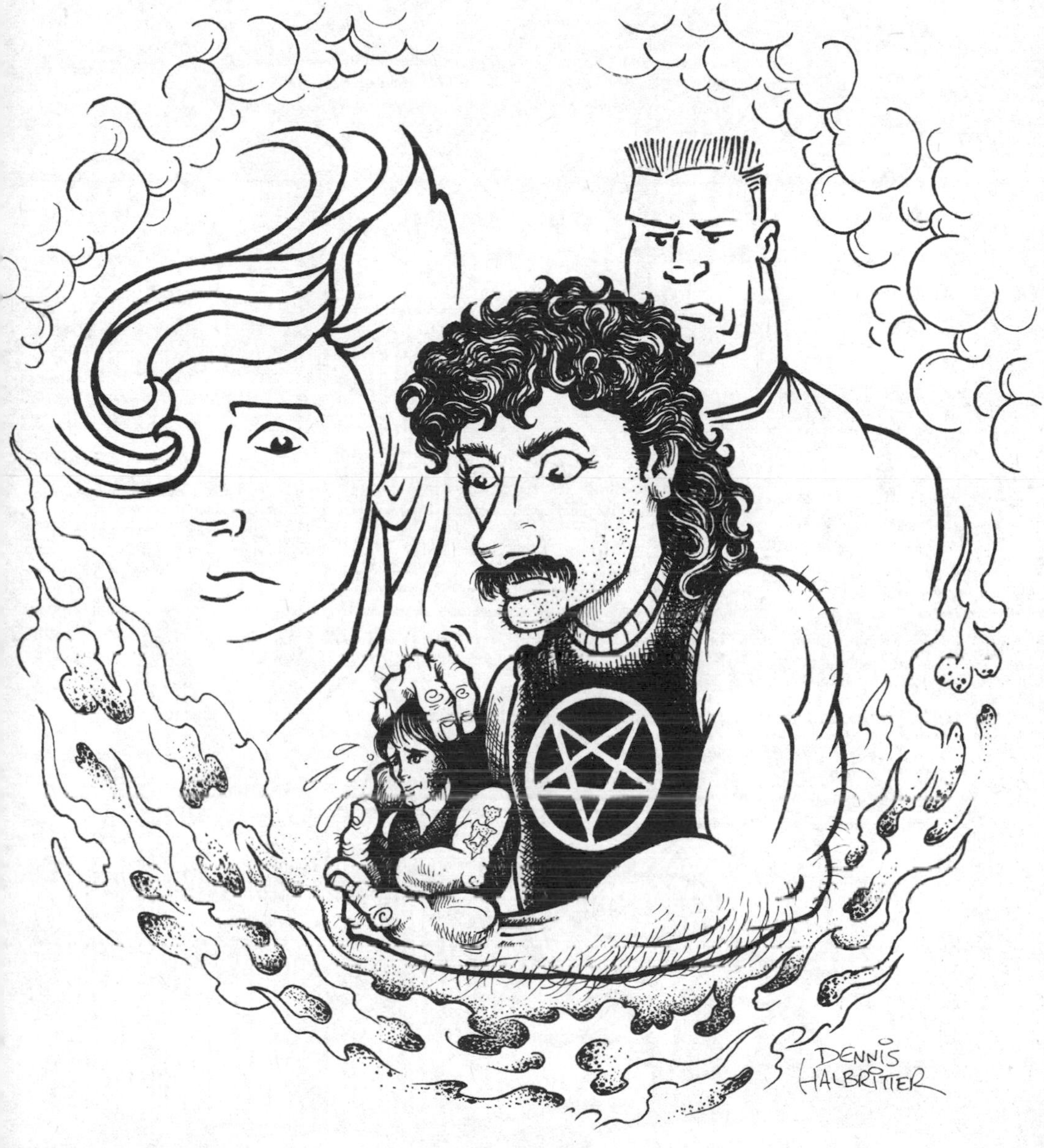
DENNIS HALBRITTER

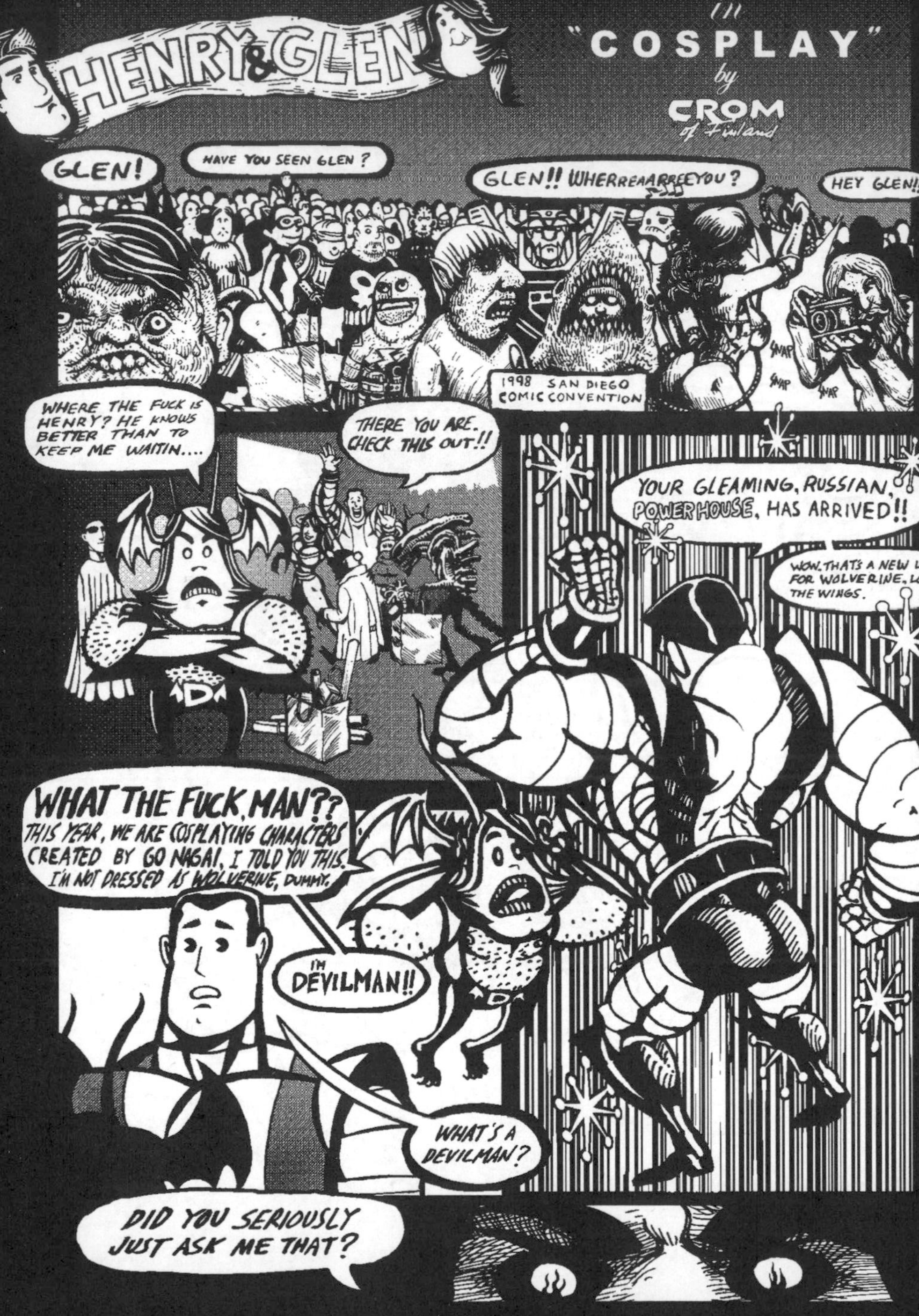
HENRY & GLEN
in
"COSPLAY"
by
CROM
of Finland
GLEN!
HAVE YOU SEEN GLEN ?
GLEN!! WHERREAARREEYOU ?
HEY GLEN!!
SNAP
SNAP
SNAP
1998 SAN DIEGO COMIC CONVENTION
WHERE THE FUCK IS HENRY? HE KNOWS BETTER THAN TO KEEP ME WAITIN....
THERE YOU ARE. CHECK THIS OUT!!
YOUR GLEAMING, RUSSIAN, POWERHOUSE, HAS ARRIVED!!
WOW. THAT'S A NEW LOOK FOR WOLVERINE. LOVE THE WINGS.
WHAT THE FUCK, MAN?? THIS YEAR, WE ARE COSPLAYING CHARACTERS CREATED BY GO NAGAI, I TOLD YOU THIS. I'M NOT DRESSED AS WOLVERINE, DUMMY.
I'M DEVILMAN!!
WHAT'S A DEVILMAN?
DID YOU SERIOUSLY JUST ASK ME THAT?

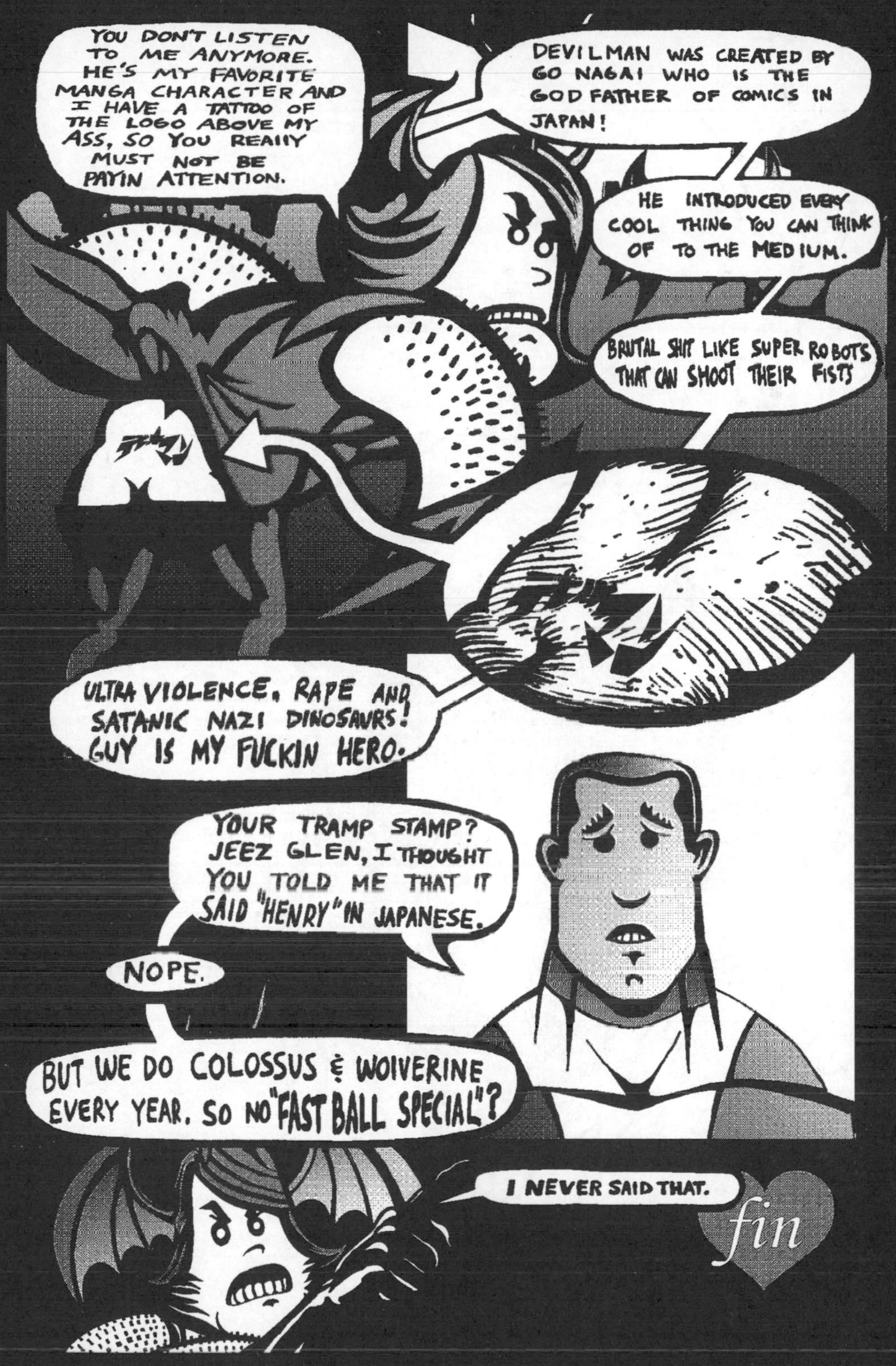
YOU DON'T LISTEN TO ME ANYMORE. HE'S MY FAVORITE MANGA CHARACTER AND I HAVE A TATTOO OF THE LOGO ABOVE MY ASS, SO YOU REALLY MUST NOT BE PAYIN ATTENTION.
DEVILMAN WAS CREATED BY GO NAGAI WHO IS THE GODFATHER OF COMICS IN JAPAN!
HE INTRODUCED EVERY COOL THING YOU CAN THINK OF TO THE MEDIUM.
BRUTAL SHIT LIKE SUPER ROBOTS THAT CAN SHOOT THEIR FISTS
ULTRA VIOLENCE, RAPE AND SATANIC NAZI DINOSAURS! GUY IS MY FUCKIN HERO.
YOUR TRAMP STAMP? JEEZ GLEN, I THOUGHT YOU TOLD ME THAT IT SAID "HENRY" IN JAPANESE.
NOPE.
BUT WE DO COLOSSUS & WOLVERINE EVERY YEAR. SO NO "FAST BALL SPECIAL"?
I NEVER SAID THAT.
fin

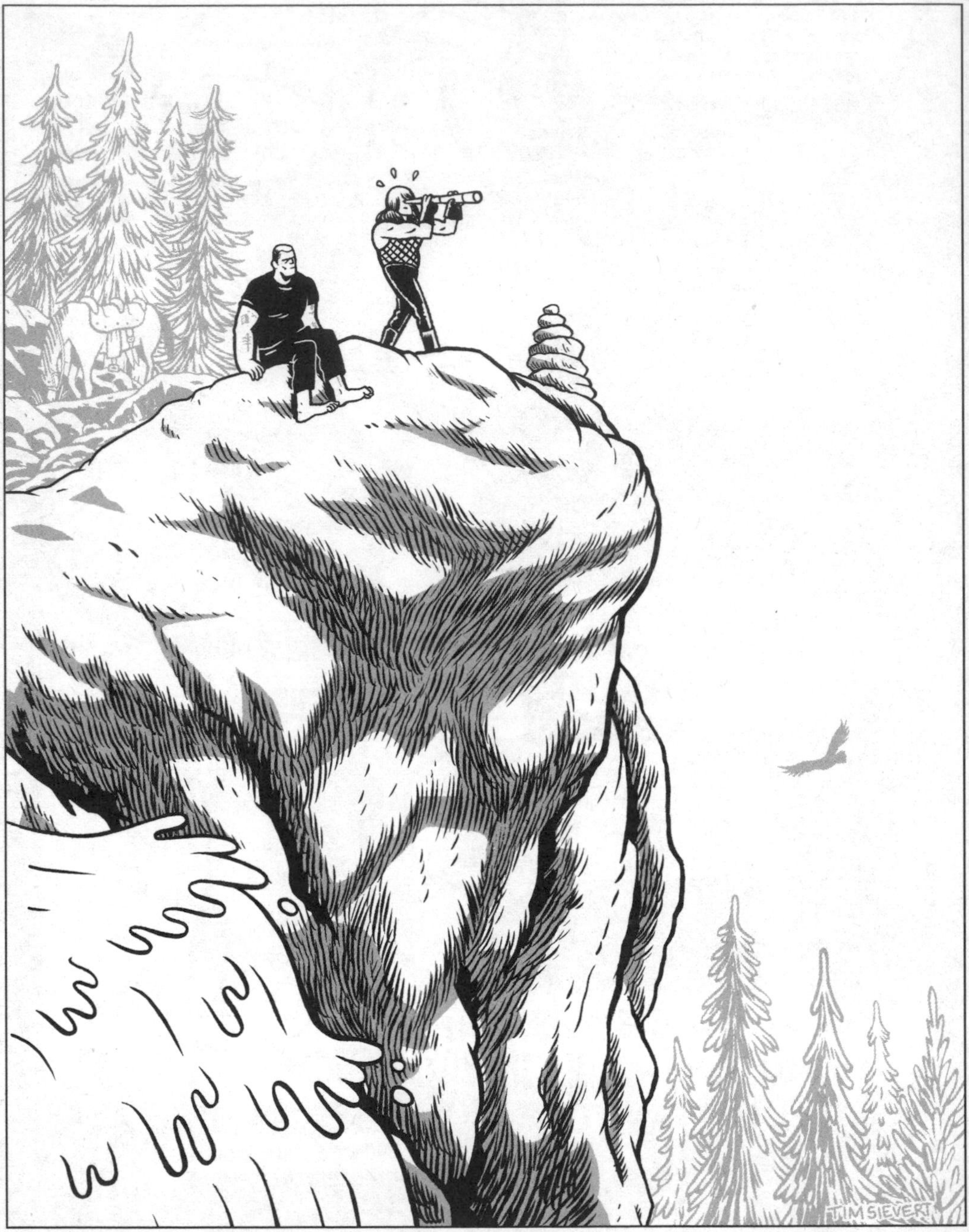
TIM SIEVERT

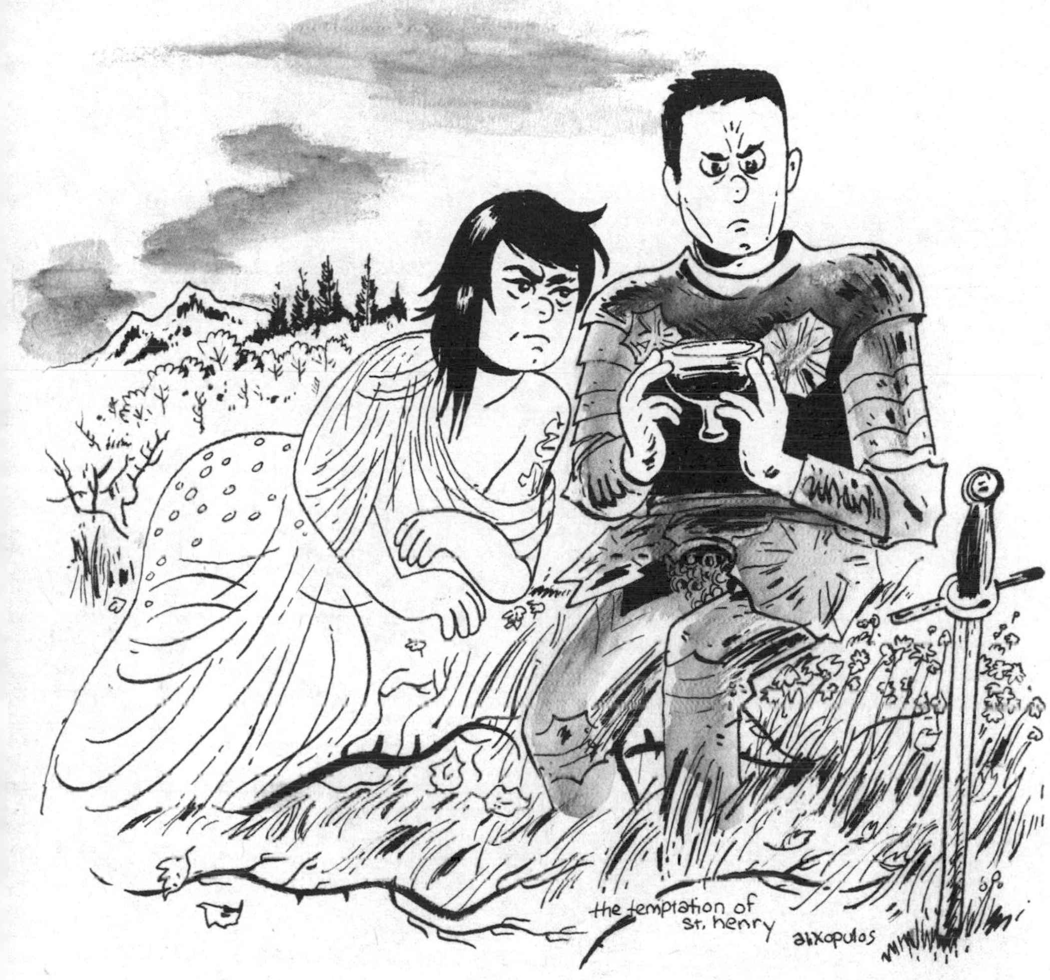
the temptation of st. henry
alixopulos

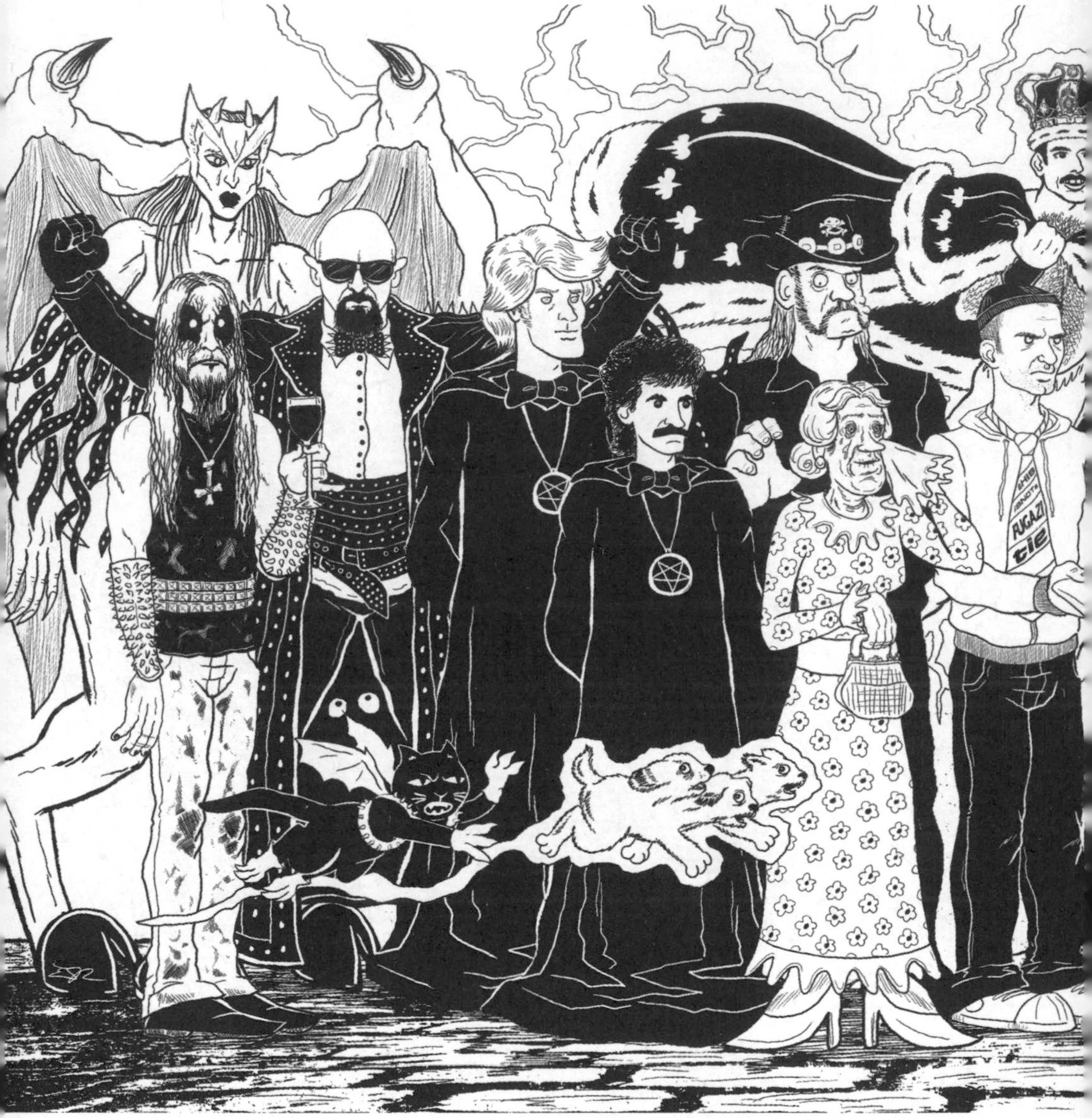
FUGAZI
tie

ED LUCE

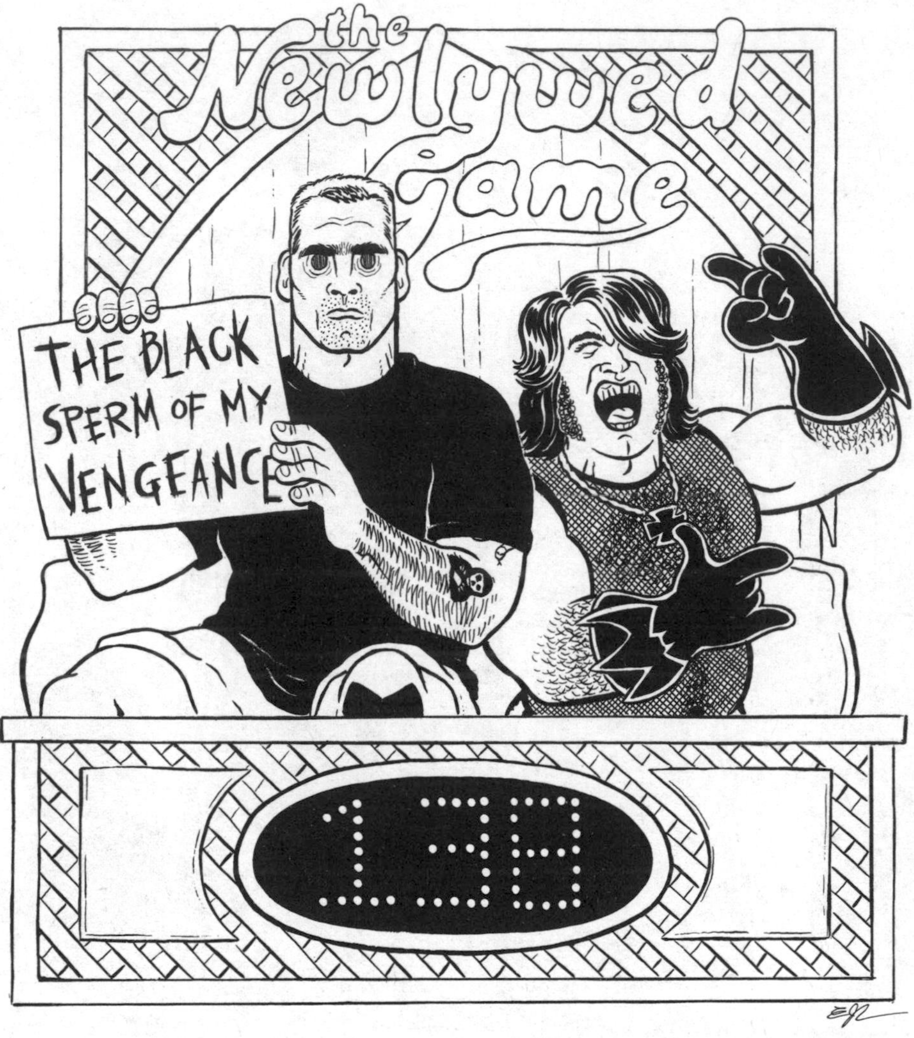
the Newlywed Game
THE BLACK SPERM OF MY VENGEANCE
132

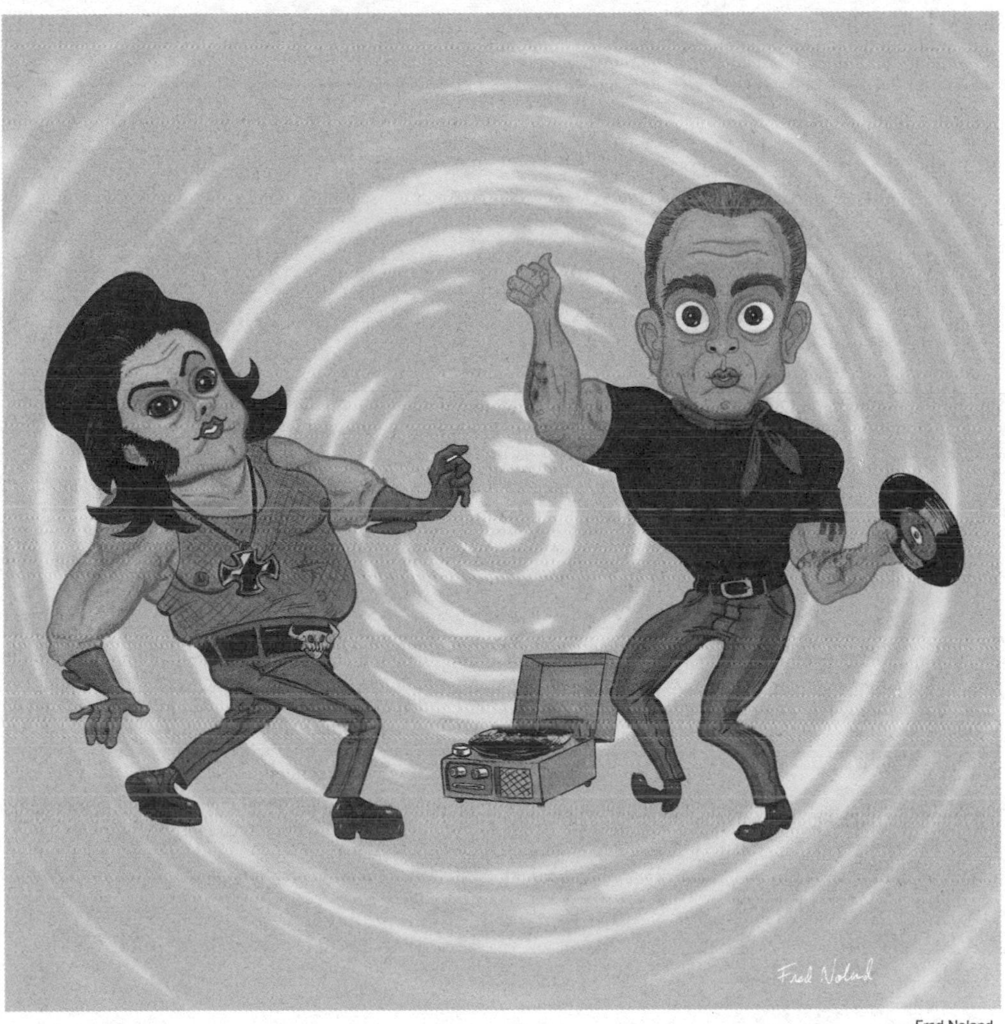
Fred Noland

Fred Noland

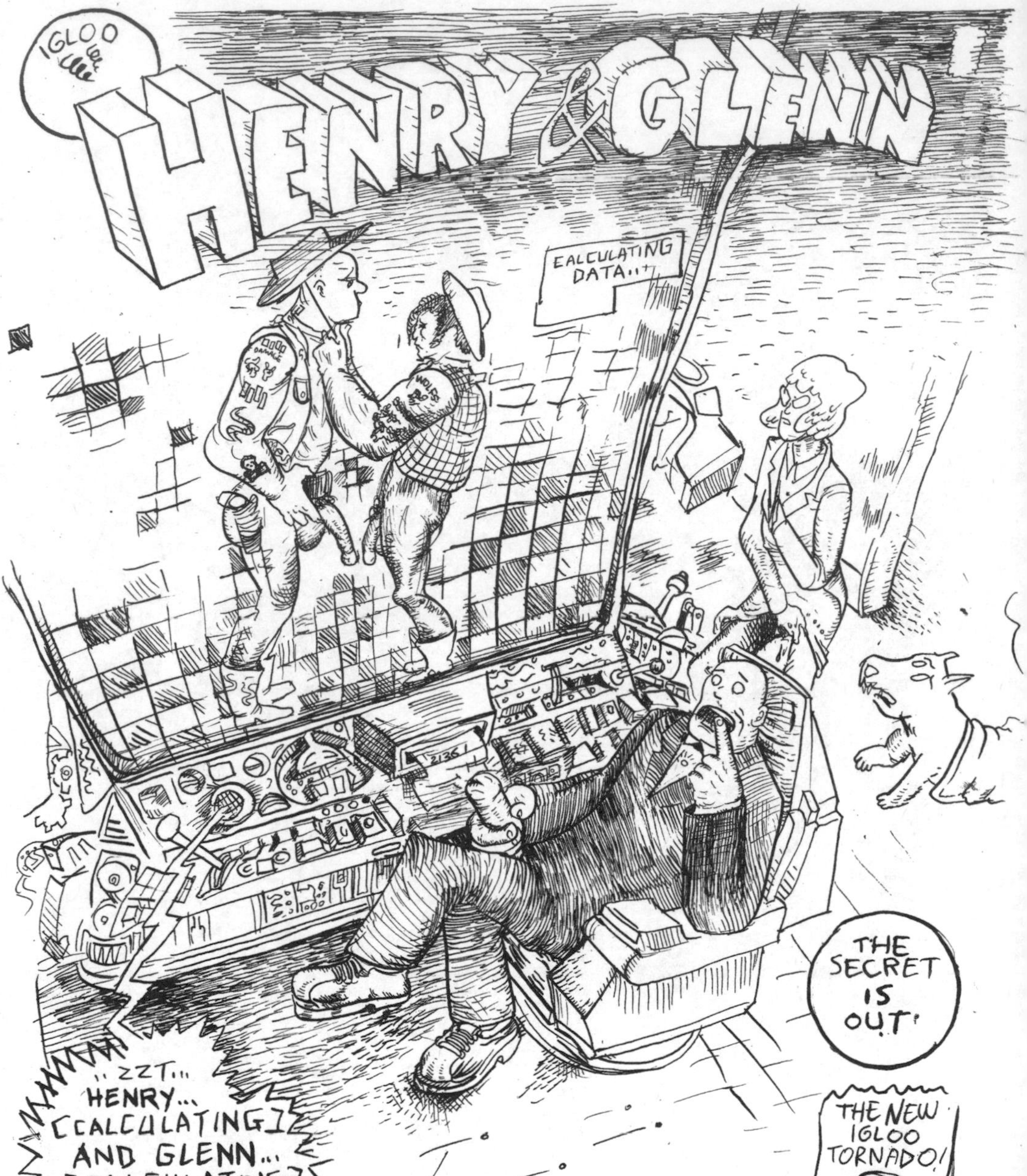
IGLOO
HENRY & GLENN!
CALCULATING DATA...
2136
THE SECRET IS OUT!
.. ZZT... HENRY... [CALCULATING] AND GLENN... [CALCULATING] ARE...
JOSH BAYER 2013
JOSH BAYER, 2013 AFTER JOHN BYRNE'S SUPERMAN #2, 1987
THE NEW IGLOO TORNADO!
THERE'S NO STOPPIN' US NOW!

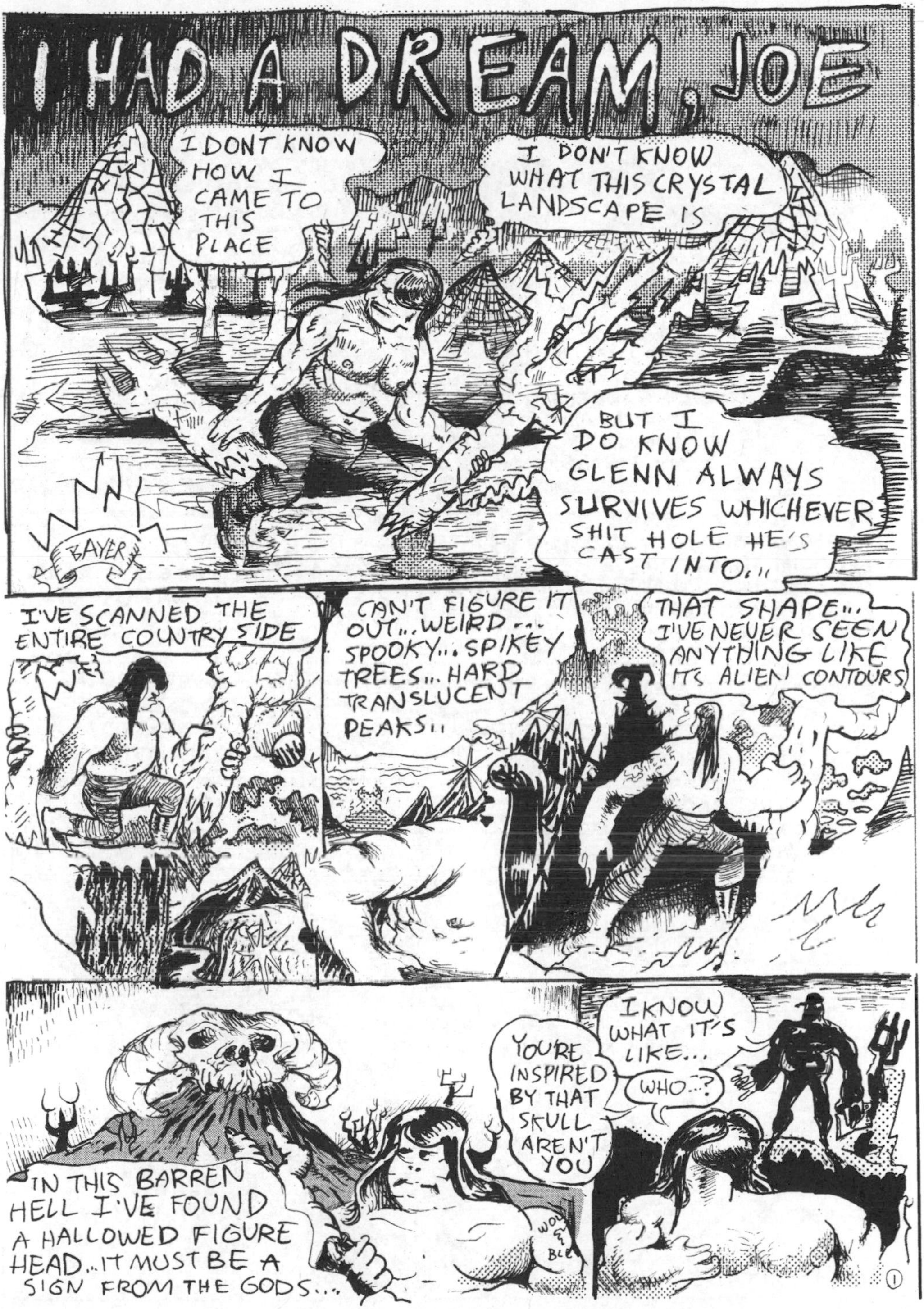
I HAD A DREAM, JOE
I DONT KNOW HOW I CAME TO THIS PLACE
I DON'T KNOW WHAT THIS CRYSTAL LANDSCAPE IS
BUT I DO KNOW GLENN ALWAYS SURVIVES WHICHEVER SHIT HOLE HE'S CAST INTO...
BAYER
I'VE SCANNED THE ENTIRE COUNTRY SIDE
CAN'T FIGURE IT OUT... WEIRD... SPOOKY... SPIKEY TREES... HARD TRANSLUCENT PEAKS..
THAT SHAPE... I'VE NEVER SEEN ANYTHING LIKE ITS ALIEN CONTOURS
IN THIS BARREN HELL I'VE FOUND A HALLOWED FIGURE HEAD.. IT MUST BE A SIGN FROM THE GODS...
YOU'RE INSPIRED BY THAT SKULL AREN'T YOU
I KNOW WHAT IT'S LIKE...
WHO...?
1

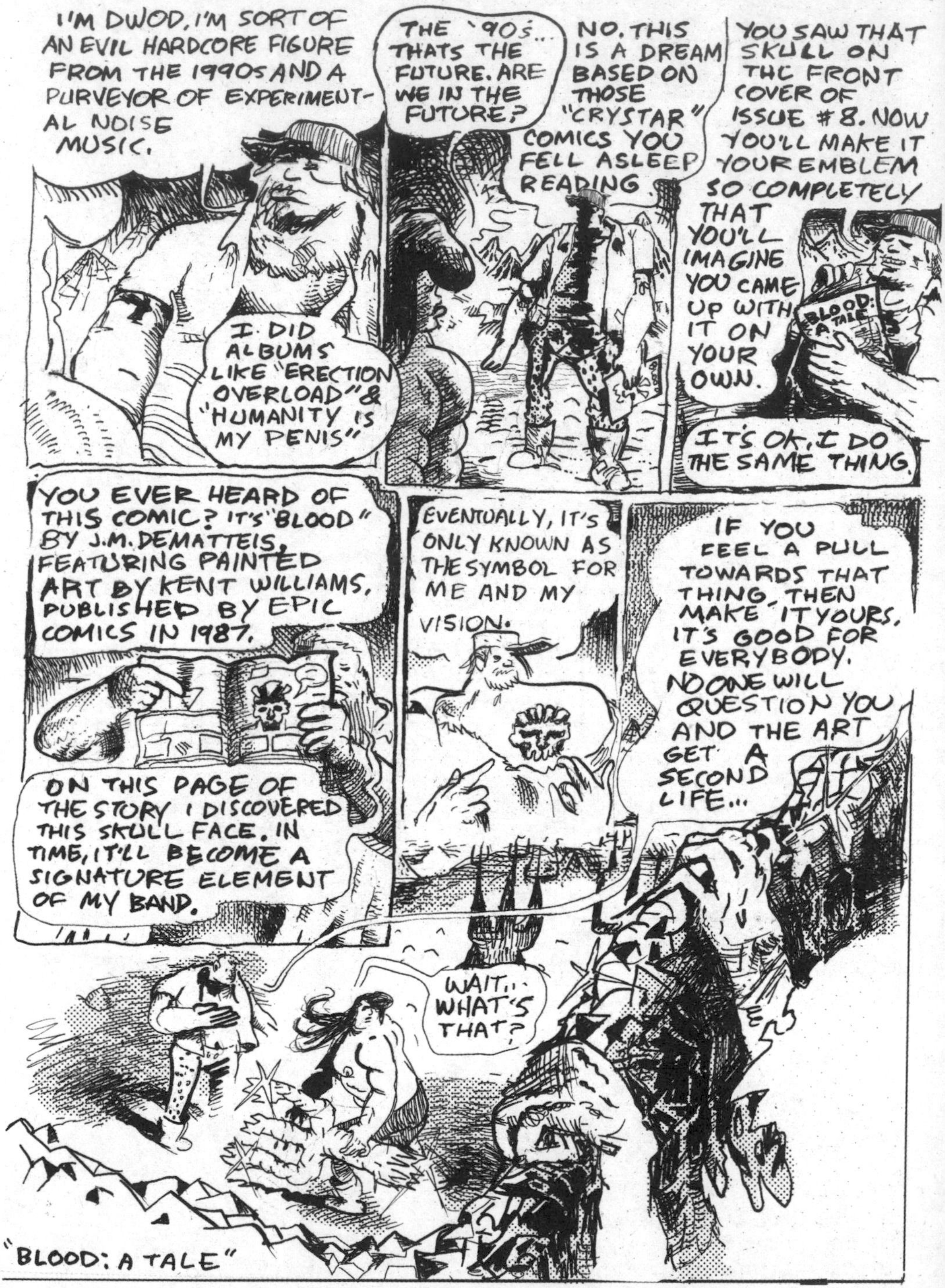
I'M DWOD, I'M SORT OF AN EVIL HARDCORE FIGURE FROM THE 1990S AND A PURVEYOR OF EXPERIMENTAL NOISE MUSIC.
I DID ALBUMS LIKE "ERECTION OVERLOAD" & "HUMANITY IS MY PENIS"
THE '90S... THATS THE FUTURE. ARE WE IN THE FUTURE?
NO. THIS IS A DREAM BASED ON THOSE "CRYSTAR" COMICS YOU FELL ASLEEP READING.
YOU SAW THAT SKULL ON THE FRONT COVER OF ISSUE #8. NOW YOU'LL MAKE IT YOUR EMBLEM SO COMPLETELY THAT YOU'LL IMAGINE YOU CAME UP WITH IT ON YOUR OWN.
BLOOD: A TALE
IT'S OK, I DO THE SAME THING.
YOU EVER HEARD OF THIS COMIC? IT'S "BLOOD" BY J.M. DEMATTEIS, FEATURING PAINTED ART BY KENT WILLIAMS, PUBLISHED BY EPIC COMICS IN 1987.
ON THIS PAGE OF THE STORY I DISCOVERED THIS SKULL FACE. IN TIME, IT'LL BECOME A SIGNATURE ELEMENT OF MY BAND.
EVENTUALLY, IT'S ONLY KNOWN AS THE SYMBOL FOR ME AND MY VISION.
IF YOU FEEL A PULL TOWARDS THAT THING, THEN MAKE IT YOURS. IT'S GOOD FOR EVERYBODY. NO ONE WILL QUESTION YOU AND THE ART GET A SECOND LIFE...
WAIT... WHAT'S THAT?
"BLOOD: A TALE"

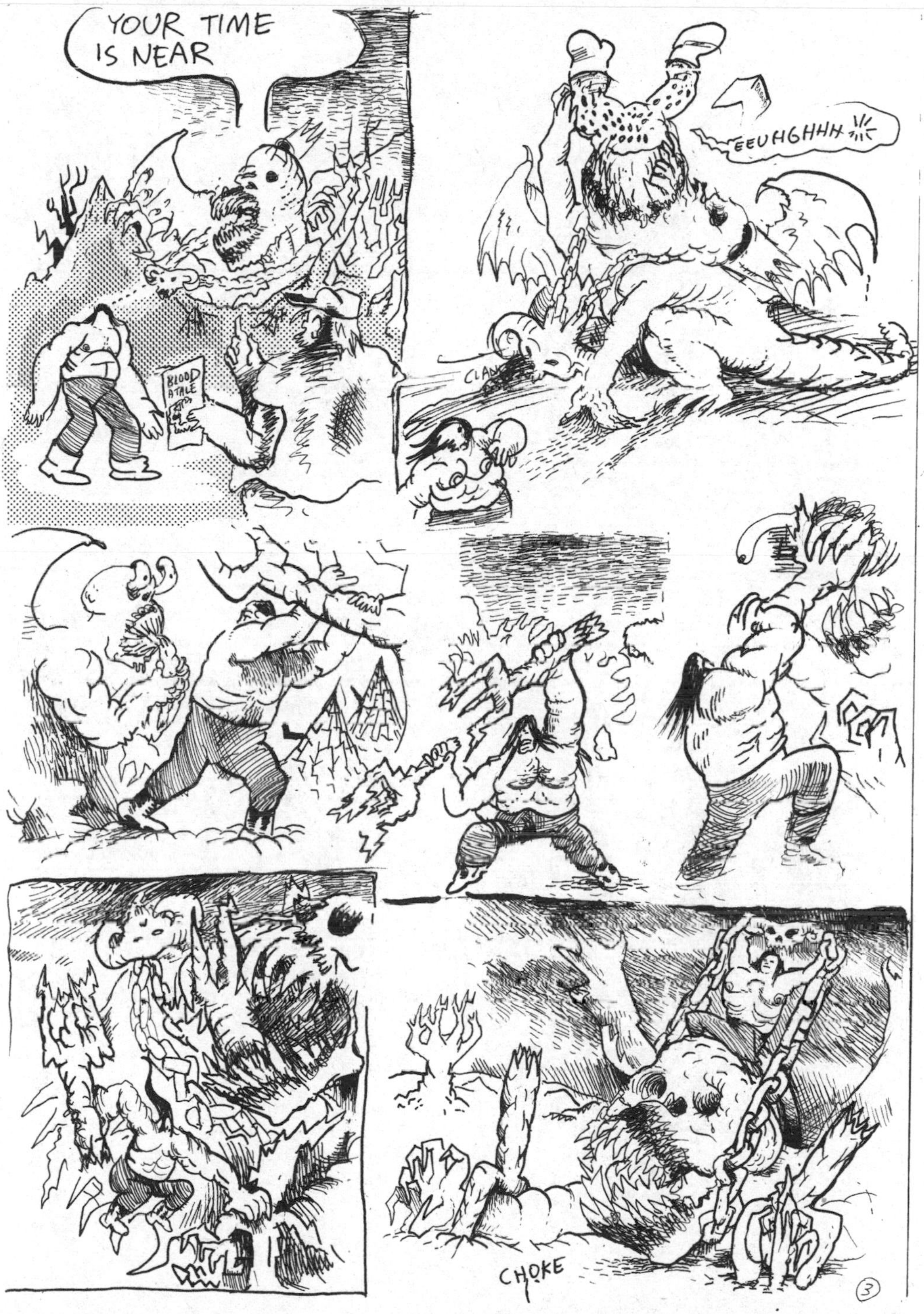
YOUR TIME IS NEAR
BLOOD A TALE
EEUHGHHH
CLANK
CHOKE
3

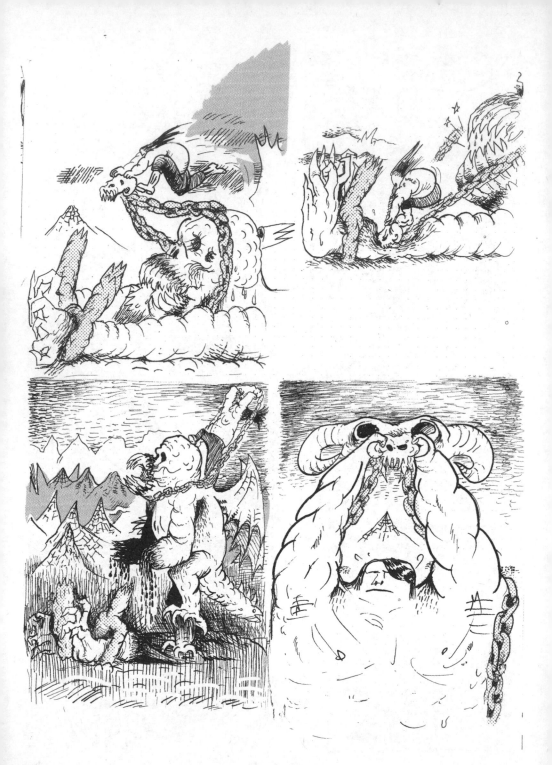

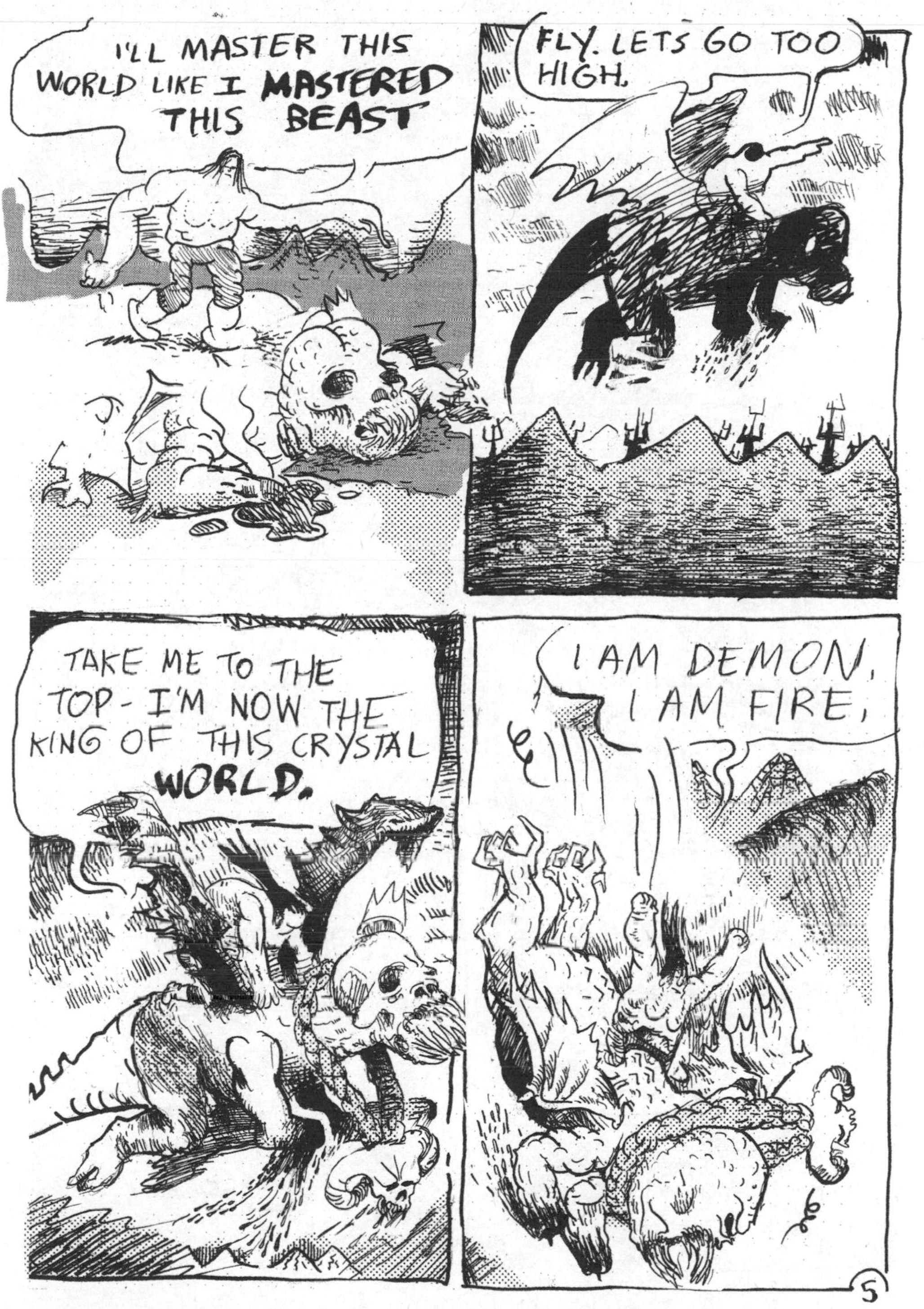
I'LL MASTER THIS WORLD LIKE I MASTERED THIS BEAST
FLY. LETS GO TOO HIGH.
TAKE ME TO THE TOP - I'M NOW THE KING OF THIS CRYSTAL WORLD.
I AM DEMON, I AM FIRE,

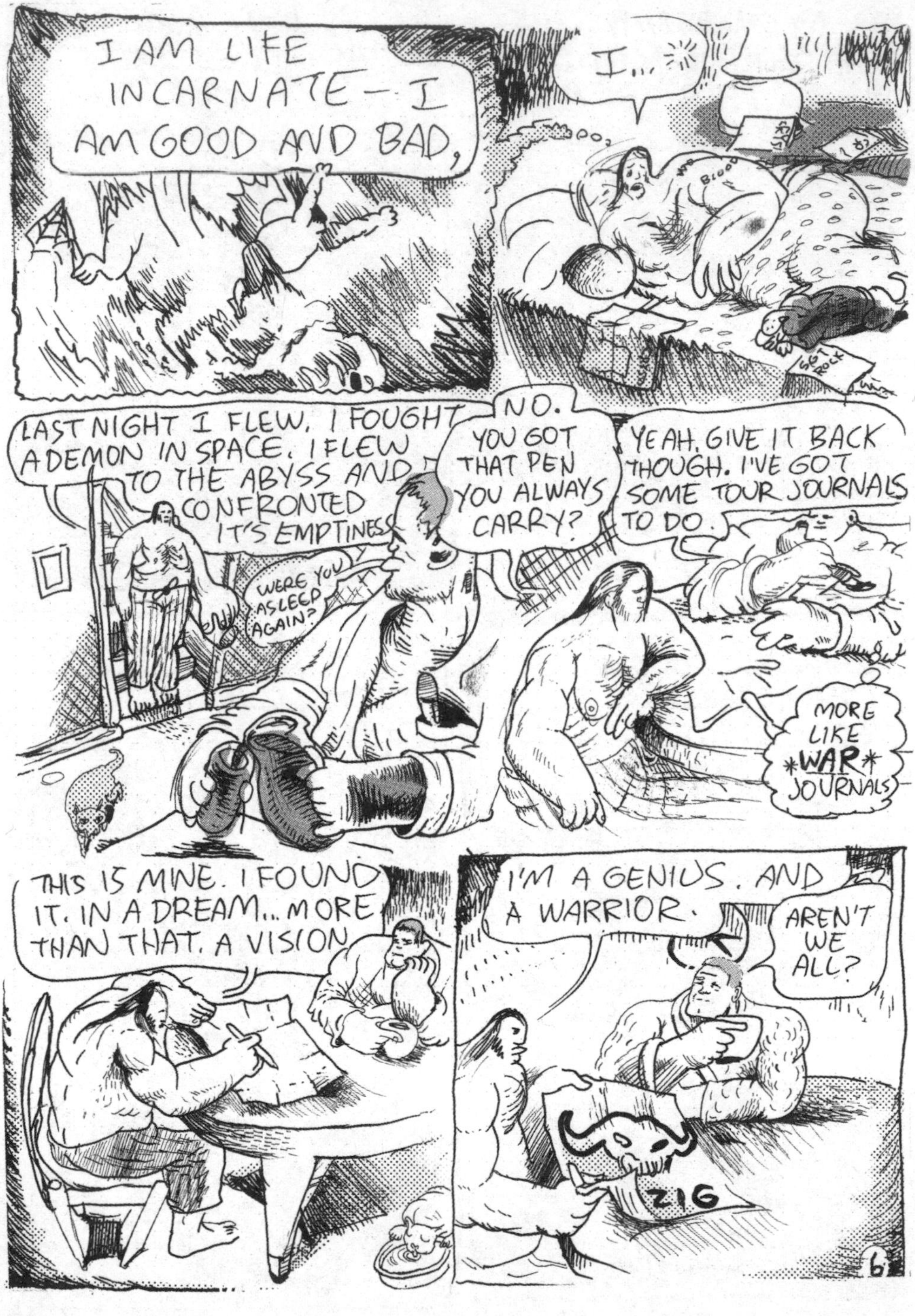
I AM LIFE INCARNATE — I AM GOOD AND BAD,
I...
LAST NIGHT I FLEW, I FOUGHT A DEMON IN SPACE. I FLEW TO THE ABYSS AND CONFRONTED IT'S EMPTINESS
WERE YOU ASLEEP AGAIN?
NO. YOU GOT THAT PEN YOU ALWAYS CARRY?
YEAH, GIVE IT BACK THOUGH. I'VE GOT SOME TOUR JOURNALS TO DO.
MORE LIKE *WAR* JOURNALS
THIS IS MINE. I FOUND IT. IN A DREAM... MORE THAN THAT. A VISION
I'M A GENIUS. AND A WARRIOR.
AREN'T WE ALL?
ZIG
6

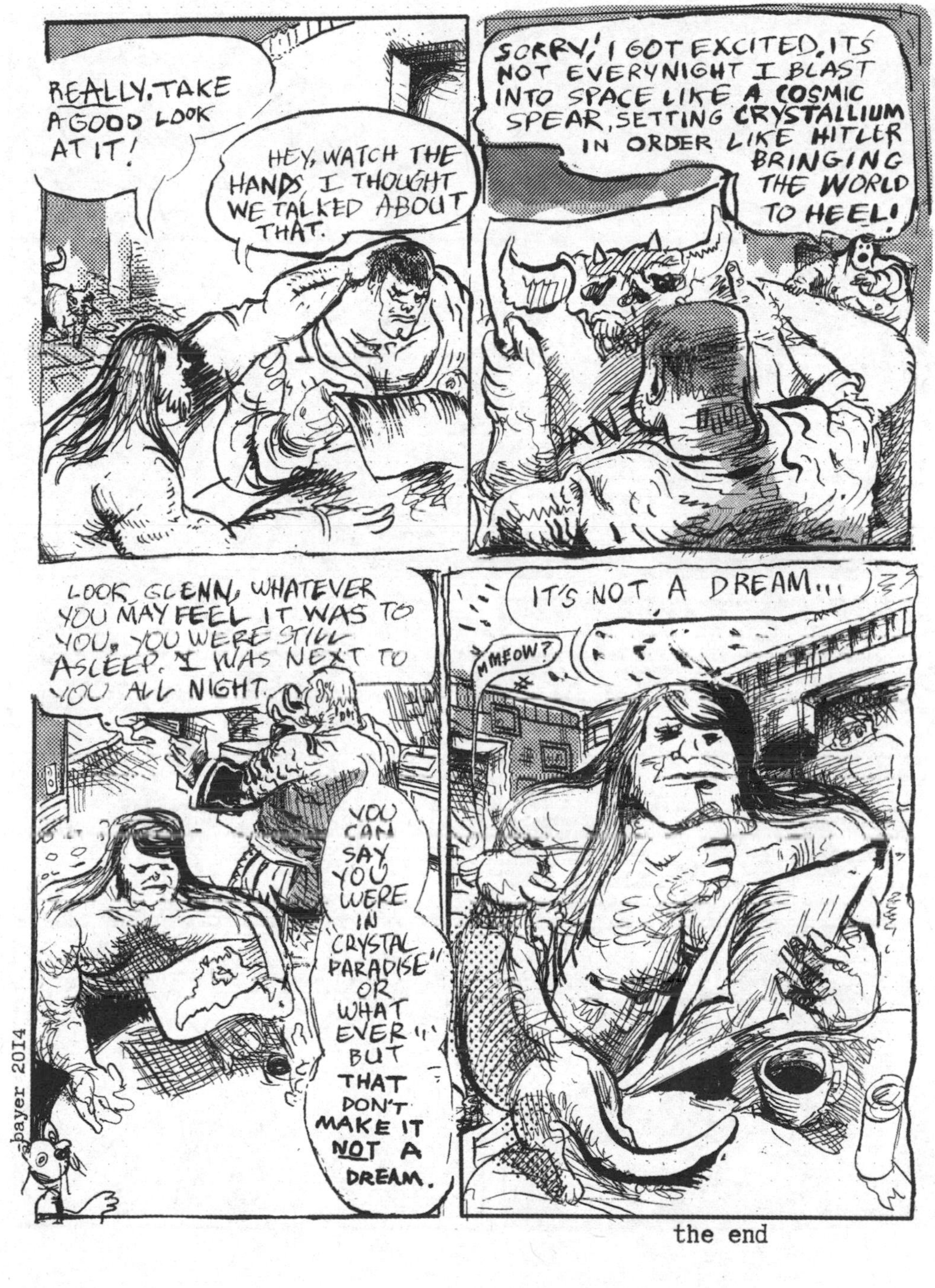
REALLY. TAKE A GOOD LOOK AT IT!
HEY, WATCH THE HANDS, I THOUGHT WE TALKED ABOUT THAT.
SORRY, I GOT EXCITED. IT'S NOT EVERYNIGHT I BLAST INTO SPACE LIKE A COSMIC SPEAR, SETTING CRYSTALLIUM IN ORDER LIKE HITLER BRINGING THE WORLD TO HEEL!
LOOK GLENN, WHATEVER YOU MAY FEEL IT WAS TO YOU, YOU WERE STILL ASLEEP. I WAS NEXT TO YOU ALL NIGHT.
YOU CAN SAY YOU WERE IN "CRYSTAL PARADISE" OR WHAT EVER" BUT THAT DON'T MAKE IT NOT A DREAM.
MMEOW?
IT'S NOT A DREAM...
bayer 2014

the end

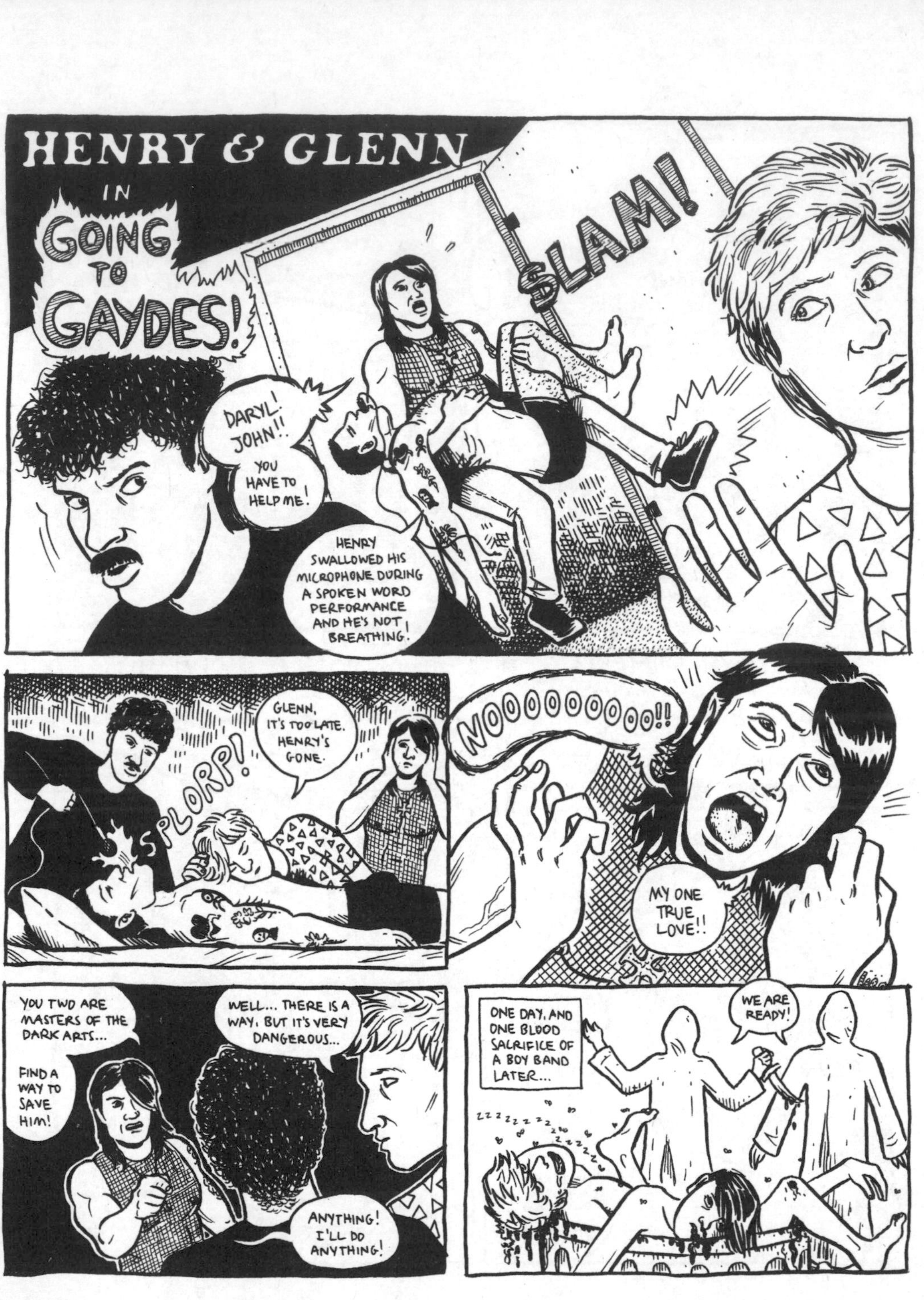
HENRY & GLENN
IN
GOING TO GAYDES!
SLAM!
DARYL! JOHN!!
YOU HAVE TO HELP ME!
HENRY SWALLOWED HIS MICROPHONE DURING A SPOKEN WORD PERFORMANCE AND HE'S NOT BREATHING!
SPLORP!
GLENN, IT'S TOO LATE. HENRY'S GONE.
NOOOOOOOOOO!!
MY ONE TRUE LOVE!!
YOU TWO ARE MASTERS OF THE DARK ARTS...
FIND A WAY TO SAVE HIM!
WELL... THERE IS A WAY, BUT IT'S VERY DANGEROUS...
ANYTHING! I'LL DO ANYTHING!
ONE DAY, AND ONE BLOOD SACRIFICE OF A BOY BAND LATER...
WE ARE READY!

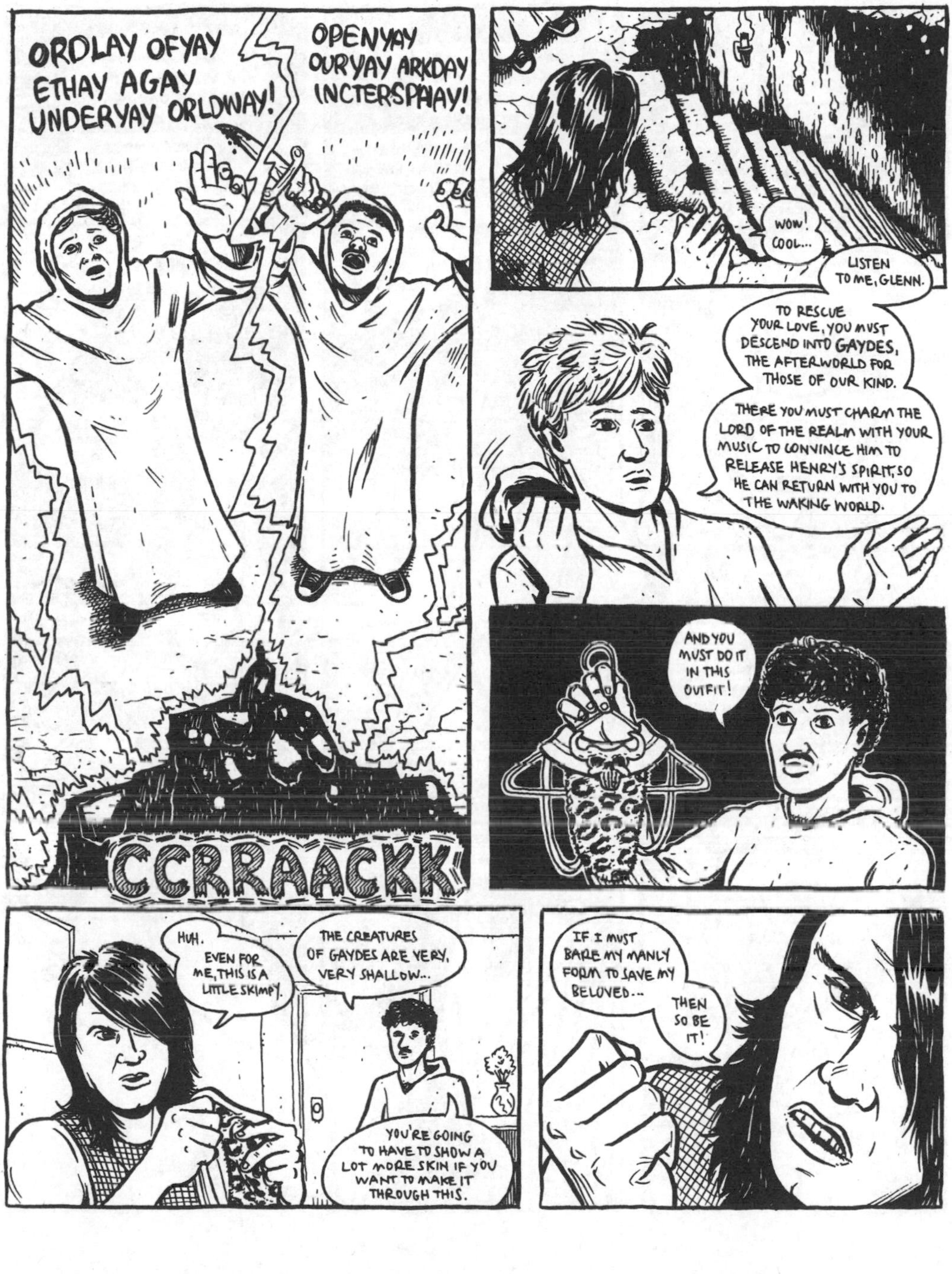
ORDLAY OFYAY ETHAY AGAY UNDERYAY ORLDWAY!
OPENYAY OURYAY ARKDAY INCTERSPHAY!
CCRRAACKK
WOW! COOL...
LISTEN TO ME, GLENN.
TO RESCUE YOUR LOVE, YOU MUST DESCEND INTO GAYDES, THE AFTERWORLD FOR THOSE OF OUR KIND.
THERE YOU MUST CHARM THE LORD OF THE REALM WITH YOUR MUSIC TO CONVINCE HIM TO RELEASE HENRY'S SPIRIT, SO HE CAN RETURN WITH YOU TO THE WAKING WORLD.
AND YOU MUST DO IT IN THIS OUTFIT!
HUH. EVEN FOR ME, THIS IS A LITTLE SKIMPY.
THE CREATURES OF GAYDES ARE VERY, VERY SHALLOW...
YOU'RE GOING TO HAVE TO SHOW A LOT MORE SKIN IF YOU WANT TO MAKE IT THROUGH THIS.
IF I MUST BARE MY MANLY FORM TO SAVE MY BELOVED...
THEN SO BE IT!

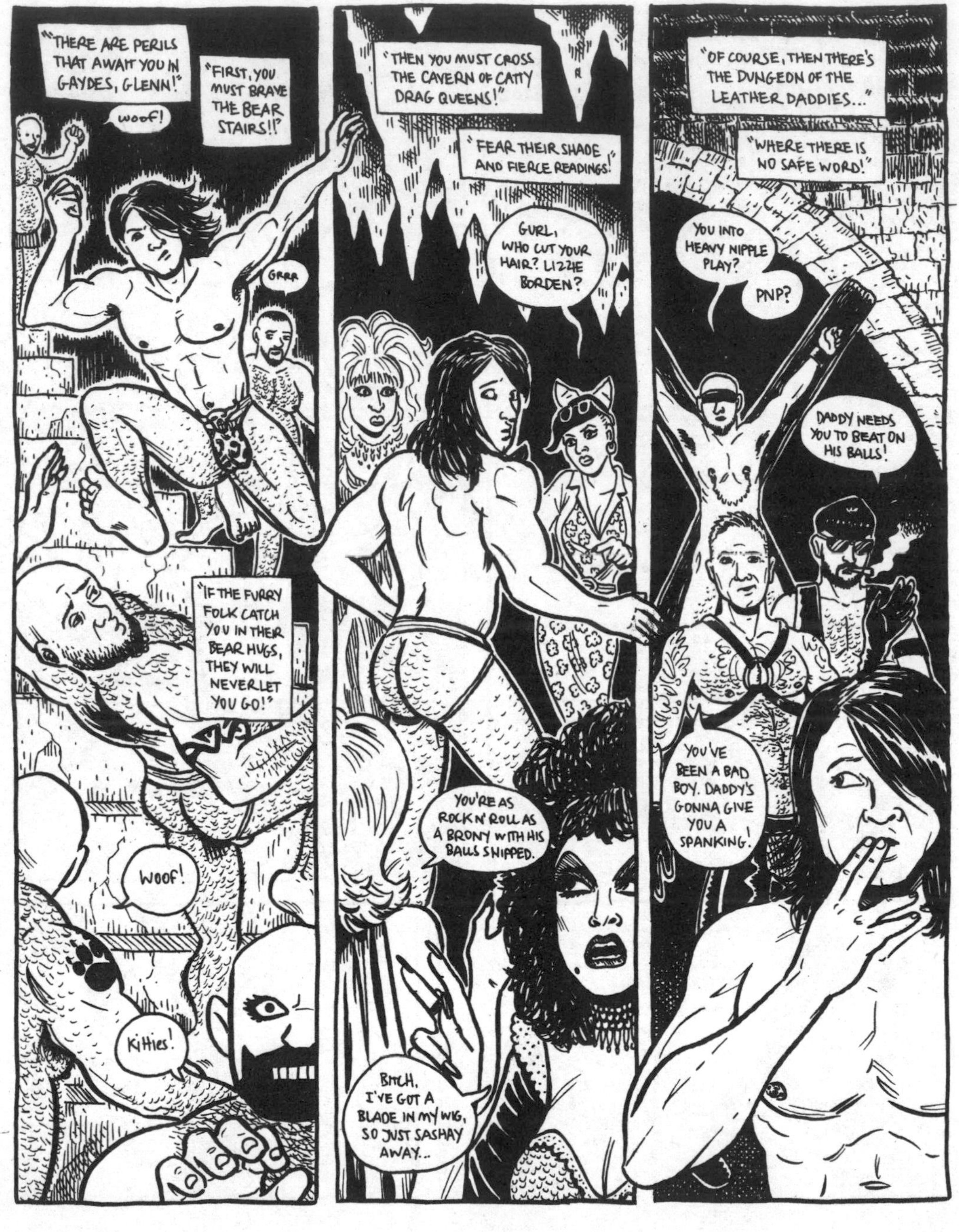
"THERE ARE PERILS THAT AWAIT YOU IN GAYDES, GLENN!"
"FIRST, YOU MUST BRAVE THE BEAR STAIRS!!"
WOOF!
GRRR
"IF THE FURRY FOLK CATCH YOU IN THEIR BEAR HUGS, THEY WILL NEVER LET YOU GO!"
WOOF!
KITTIES!
"THEN YOU MUST CROSS THE CAVERN OF CATTY DRAG QUEENS!"
"FEAR THEIR SHADE AND FIERCE READINGS!"
GURL, WHO CUT YOUR HAIR? LIZZIE BORDEN?
YOU'RE AS ROCK N' ROLL AS A BRONY WITH HIS BALLS SNIPPED.
BITCH, I'VE GOT A BLADE IN MY WIG, SO JUST SASHAY AWAY...
"OF COURSE, THEN THERE'S THE DUNGEON OF THE LEATHER DADDIES..."
"WHERE THERE IS NO SAFE WORD!"
YOU INTO HEAVY NIPPLE PLAY?
PNP?
DADDY NEEDS YOU TO BEAT ON HIS BALLS!
YOU'VE BEEN A BAD BOY. DADDY'S GONNA GIVE YOU A SPANKING!

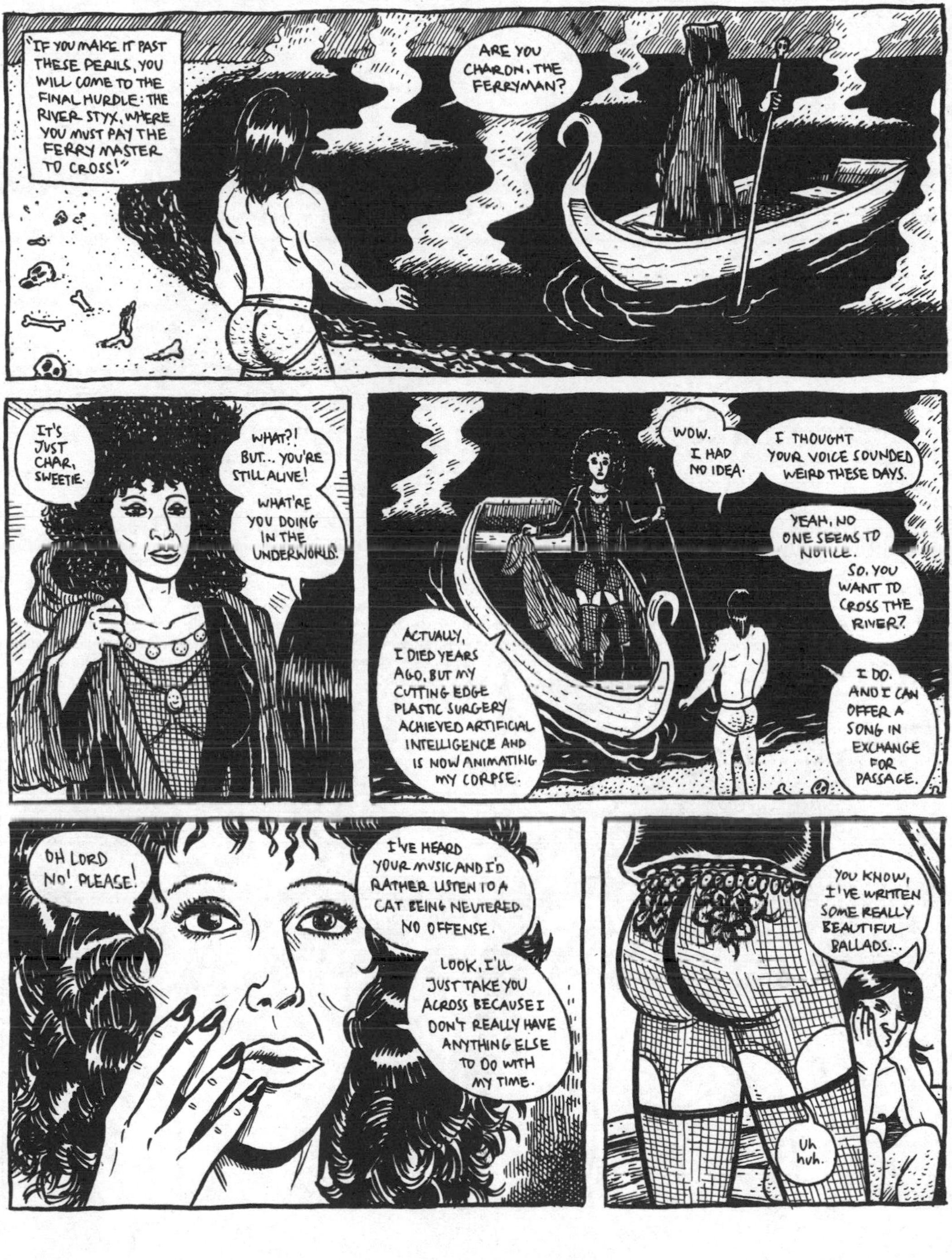
"IF YOU MAKE IT PAST THESE PERILS, YOU WILL COME TO THE FINAL HURDLE: THE RIVER STYX, WHERE YOU MUST PAY THE FERRY MASTER TO CROSS!"
ARE YOU CHARON, THE FERRYMAN?
IT'S JUST CHAR, SWEETIE.
WHAT?! BUT... YOU'RE STILL ALIVE!
WHAT'RE YOU DOING IN THE UNDERWORLD?
ACTUALLY, I DIED YEARS AGO, BUT MY CUTTING EDGE PLASTIC SURGERY ACHIEVED ARTIFICIAL INTELLIGENCE AND IS NOW ANIMATING MY CORPSE.
WOW. I HAD NO IDEA.
I THOUGHT YOUR VOICE SOUNDED WEIRD THESE DAYS.
YEAH, NO ONE SEEMS TO NOTICE.
SO, YOU WANT TO CROSS THE RIVER?
I DO. AND I CAN OFFER A SONG IN EXCHANGE FOR PASSAGE.
OH LORD NO! PLEASE!
I'VE HEARD YOUR MUSIC AND I'D RATHER LISTEN TO A CAT BEING NEUTERED. NO OFFENSE.
LOOK, I'LL JUST TAKE YOU ACROSS BECAUSE I DON'T REALLY HAVE ANYTHING ELSE TO DO WITH MY TIME.
YOU KNOW, I'VE WRITTEN SOME REALLY BEAUTIFUL BALLADS...
Uh huh.

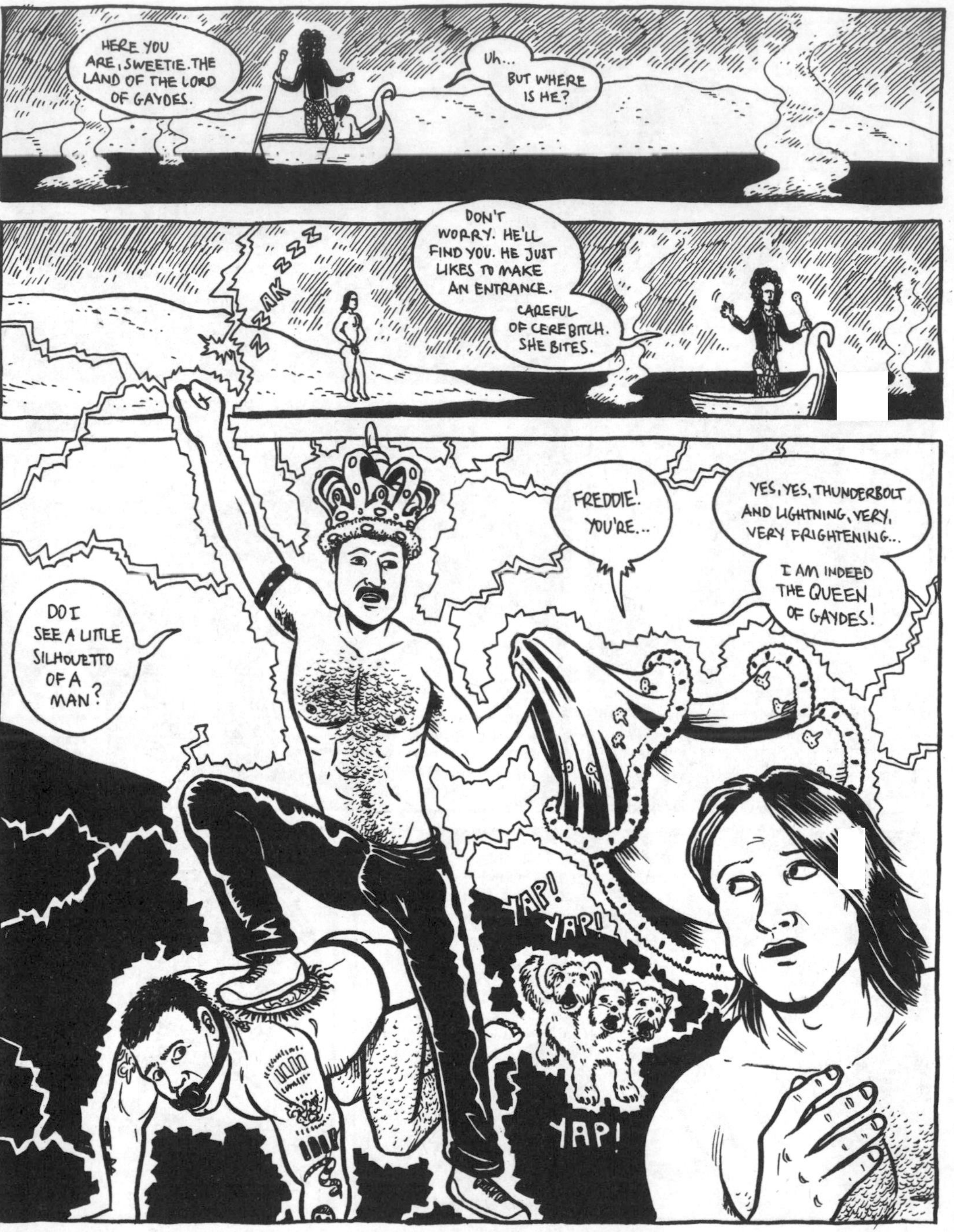
HERE YOU ARE, SWEETIE. THE LAND OF THE LORD OF GAYDES.
Uh... BUT WHERE IS HE?
ZZZAK
DON'T WORRY. HE'LL FIND YOU. HE JUST LIKES TO MAKE AN ENTRANCE.
CAREFUL OF CEREBITCH. SHE BITES.
DO I SEE A LITTLE SILHOUETTO OF A MAN?
FREDDIE! YOU'RE...
YES, YES, THUNDERBOLT AND LIGHTNING, VERY, VERY FRIGHTENING...
I AM INDEED THE QUEEN OF GAYDES!
YAP!
YAP!
YAP!

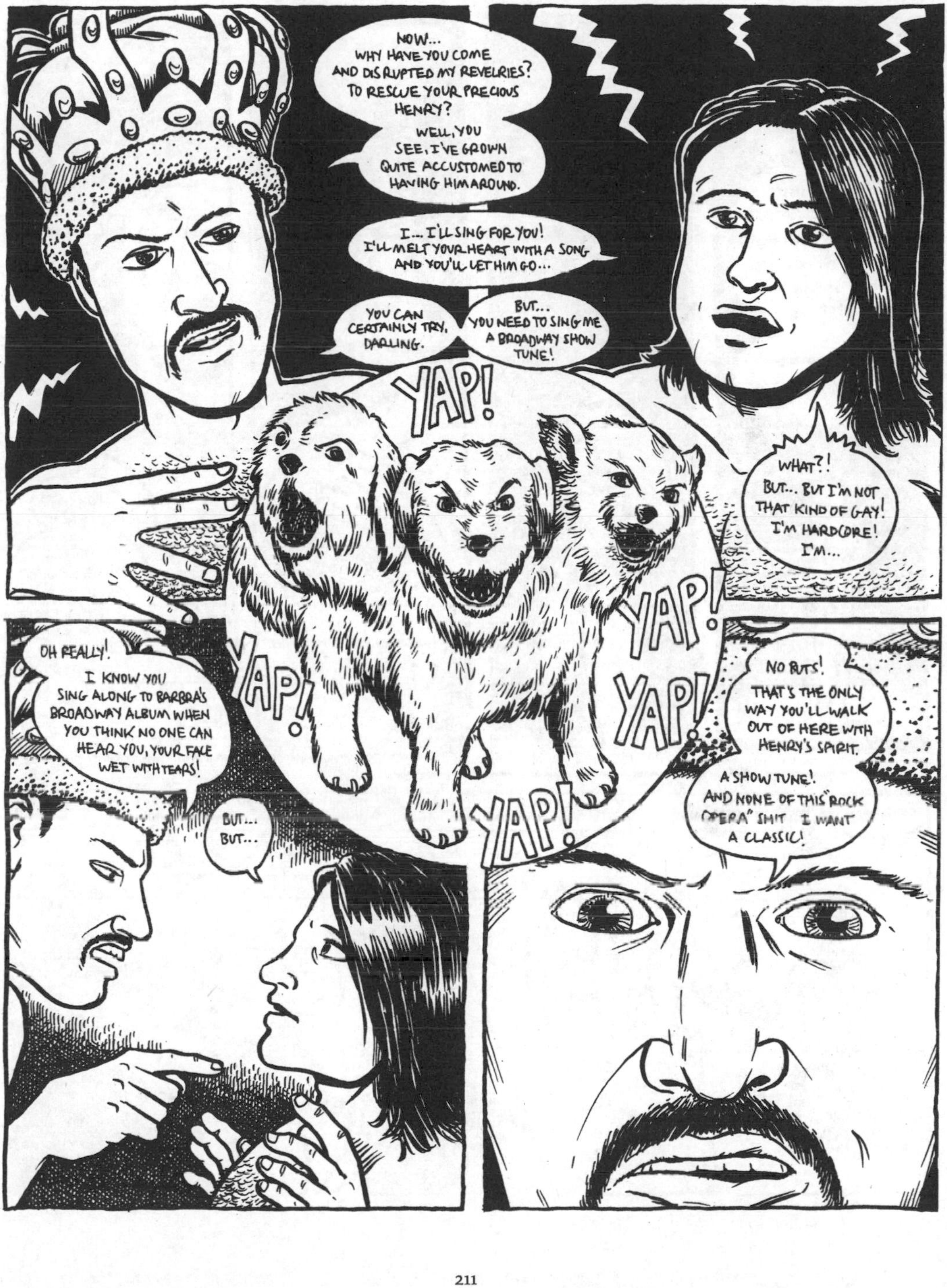
NOW... WHY HAVE YOU COME AND DISRUPTED MY REVELRIES? TO RESCUE YOUR PRECIOUS HENRY?
WELL, YOU SEE, I'VE GROWN QUITE ACCUSTOMED TO HAVING HIM AROUND.
I... I'LL SING FOR YOU! I'LL MELT YOUR HEART WITH A SONG AND YOU'LL LET HIM GO...
YOU CAN CERTAINLY TRY, DARLING.
BUT... YOU NEED TO SING ME A BROADWAY SHOW TUNE!
YAP!
WHAT?! BUT... BUT I'M NOT THAT KIND OF GAY! I'M HARDCORE! I'M...
YAP!
YAP!
YAP!
YAP!
OH REALLY! I KNOW YOU SING ALONG TO BARBRA'S BROADWAY ALBUM WHEN YOU THINK NO ONE CAN HEAR YOU, YOUR FACE WET WITH TEARS!
BUT... BUT...
NO BUTS! THAT'S THE ONLY WAY YOU'LL WALK OUT OF HERE WITH HENRY'S SPIRIT.
A SHOW TUNE! AND NONE OF THIS "ROCK OPERA" SHIT. I WANT A CLASSIC!

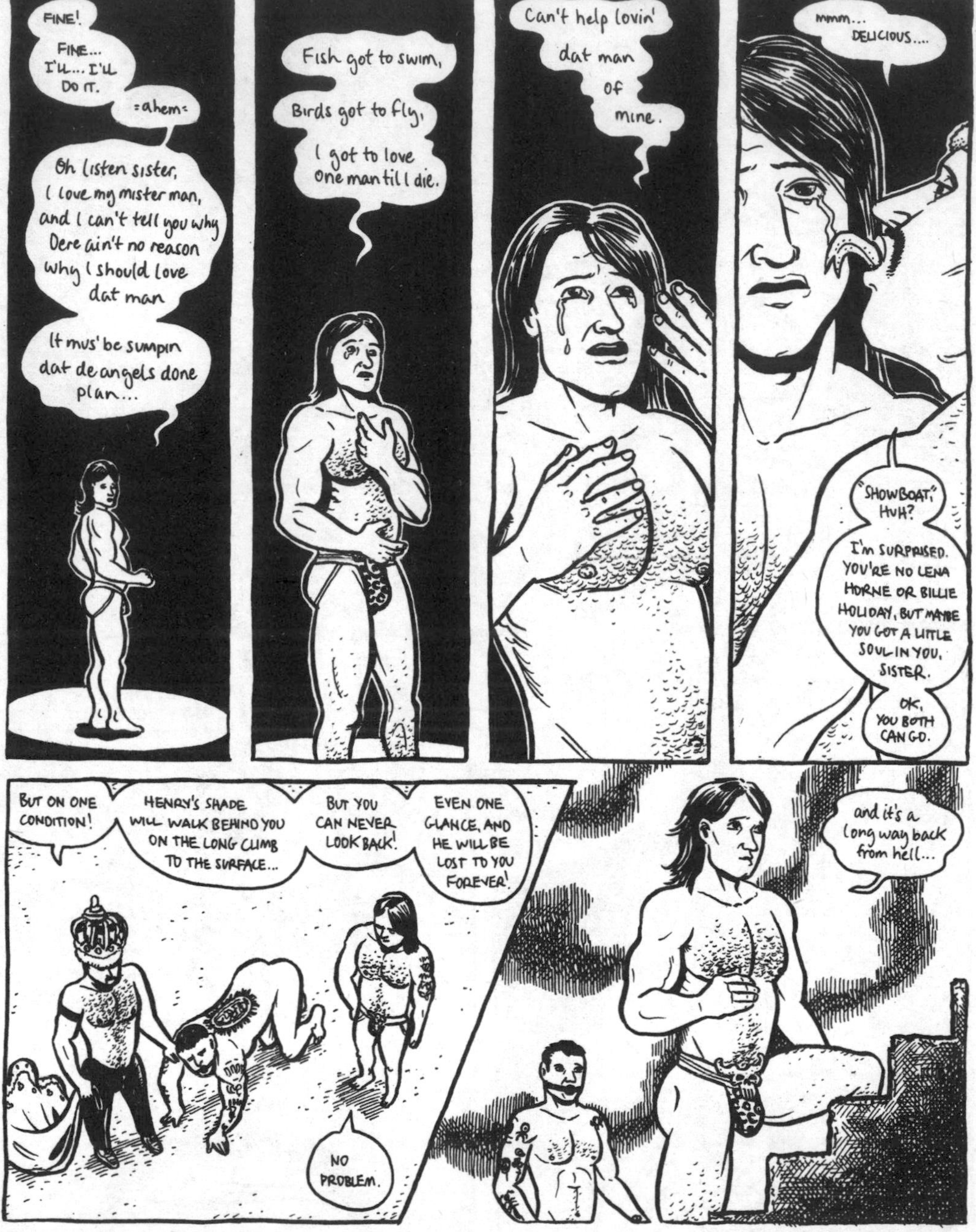
FINE!
FINE... I'LL... I'LL DO IT.
=ahem=
Oh listen sister, I love my mister man, and I can't tell you why
Dere ain't no reason why I should love dat man
It mus' be sumpin dat de angels done plan...
Fish got to swim,
Birds got to fly,
I got to love one man till I die.
Can't help lovin' dat man of mine.
mmm... DELICIOUS....
"SHOWBOAT," HUH?
I'M SURPRISED. YOU'RE NO LENA HORNE OR BILLIE HOLIDAY, BUT MAYBE YOU GOT A LITTLE SOUL IN YOU, SISTER.
OK, YOU BOTH CAN GO.
BUT ON ONE CONDITION!
HENRY'S SHADE WILL WALK BEHIND YOU ON THE LONG CLIMB TO THE SURFACE...
BUT YOU CAN NEVER LOOK BACK!
EVEN ONE GLANCE, AND HE WILL BE LOST TO YOU FOREVER!
NO PROBLEM.
and it's a long way back from hell...

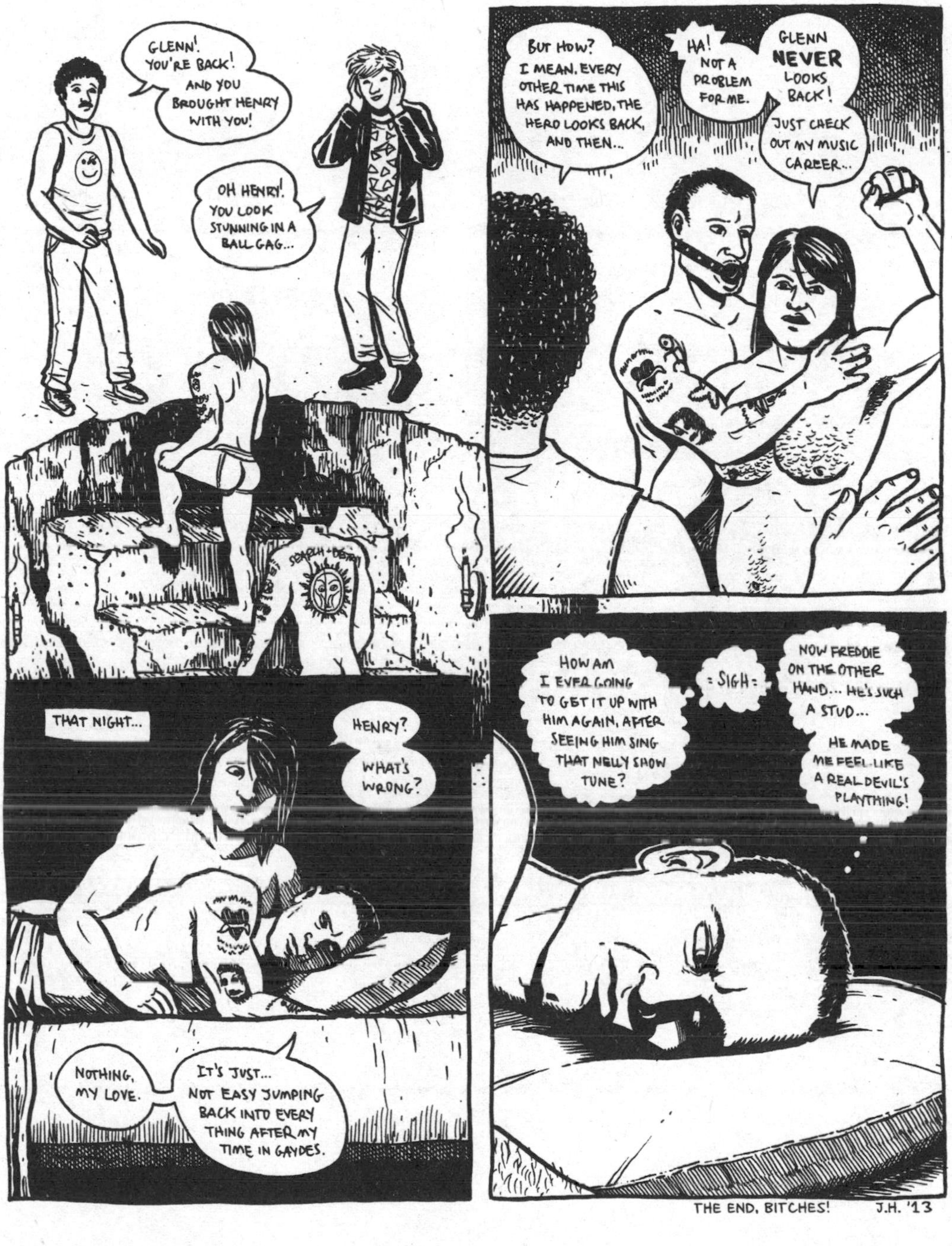
GLENN! YOU'RE BACK! AND YOU BROUGHT HENRY WITH YOU!
OH HENRY! YOU LOOK STUNNING IN A BALL GAG...
BUT HOW? I MEAN, EVERY OTHER TIME THIS HAS HAPPENED, THE HERO LOOKS BACK, AND THEN...
HA! NOT A PROBLEM FOR ME.
GLENN NEVER LOOKS BACK!
JUST CHECK OUT MY MUSIC CAREER...
THAT NIGHT...
HENRY?
WHAT'S WRONG?
NOTHING, MY LOVE.
IT'S JUST... NOT EASY JUMPING BACK INTO EVERY THING AFTER MY TIME IN GAYDES.
HOW AM I EVER GOING TO GET IT UP WITH HIM AGAIN, AFTER SEEING HIM SING THAT NELLY SHOW TUNE?
: SIGH :
NOW FREDDIE ON THE OTHER HAND... HE'S SUCH A STUD...
HE MADE ME FEEL LIKE A REAL DEVIL'S PLAYTHING!

THE END, BITCHES! J.H. '13

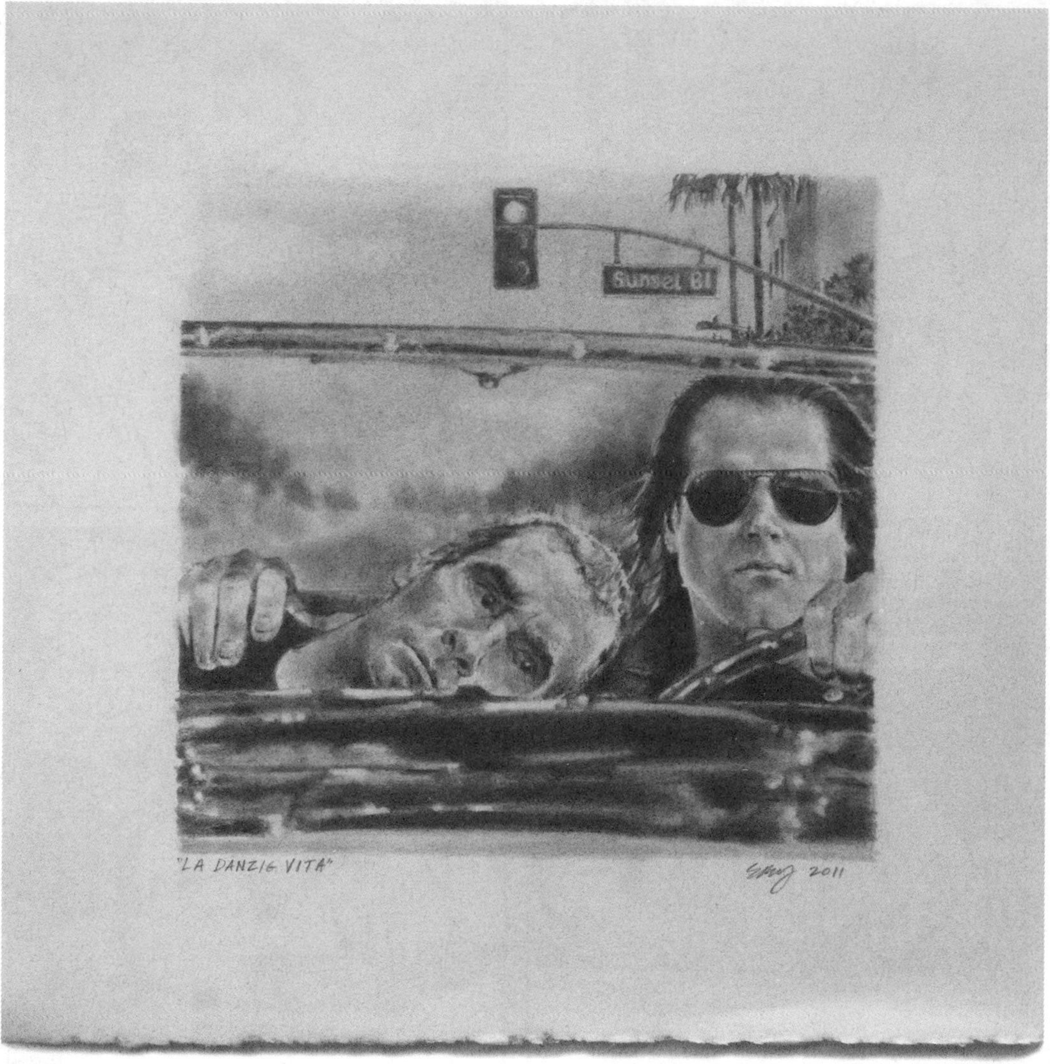
"LA DANZIG VITA"
2011

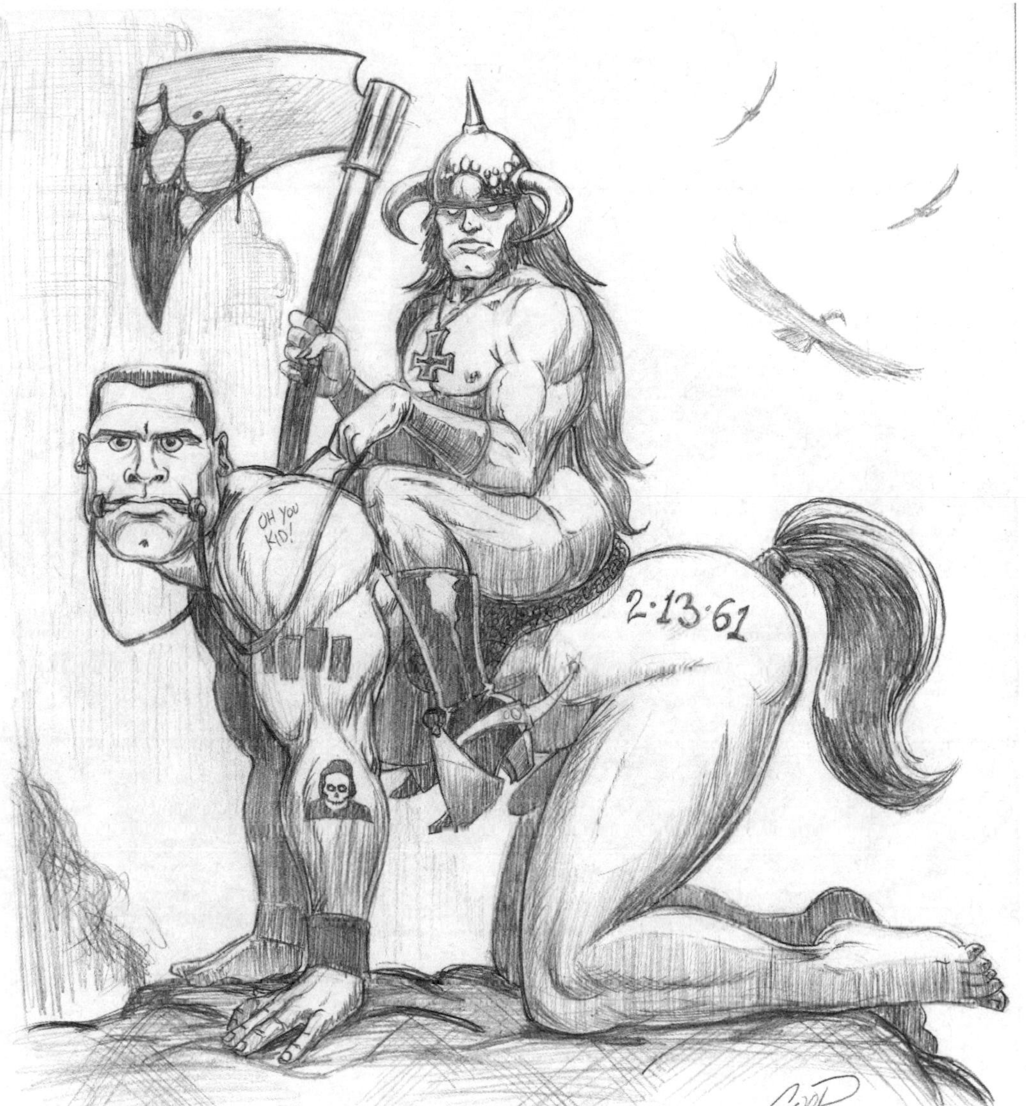
OH YOU KID!
2·13·61
COOP

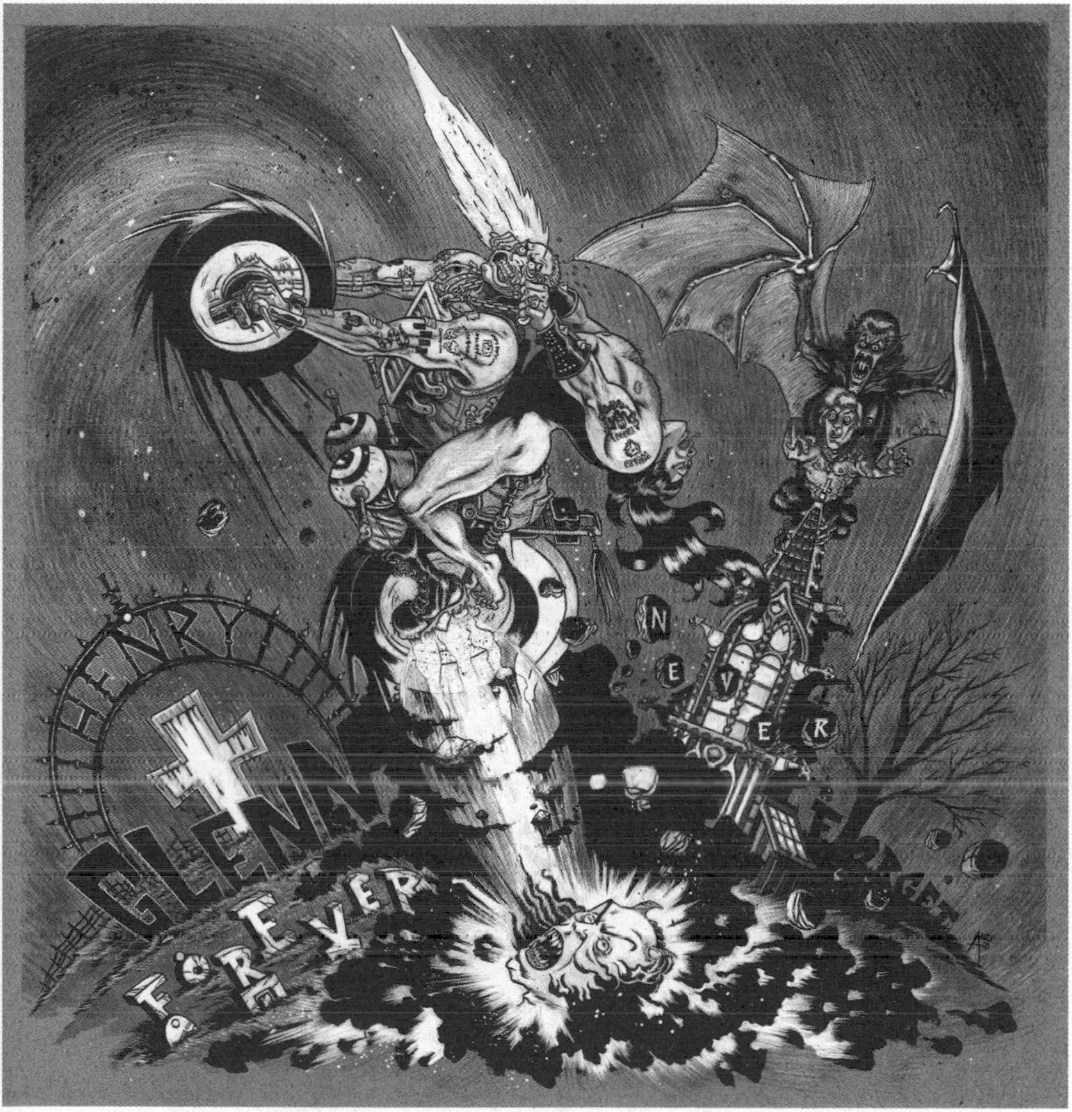
HENRY
GLENN
FOREVER
NEVER

Andy Belanger

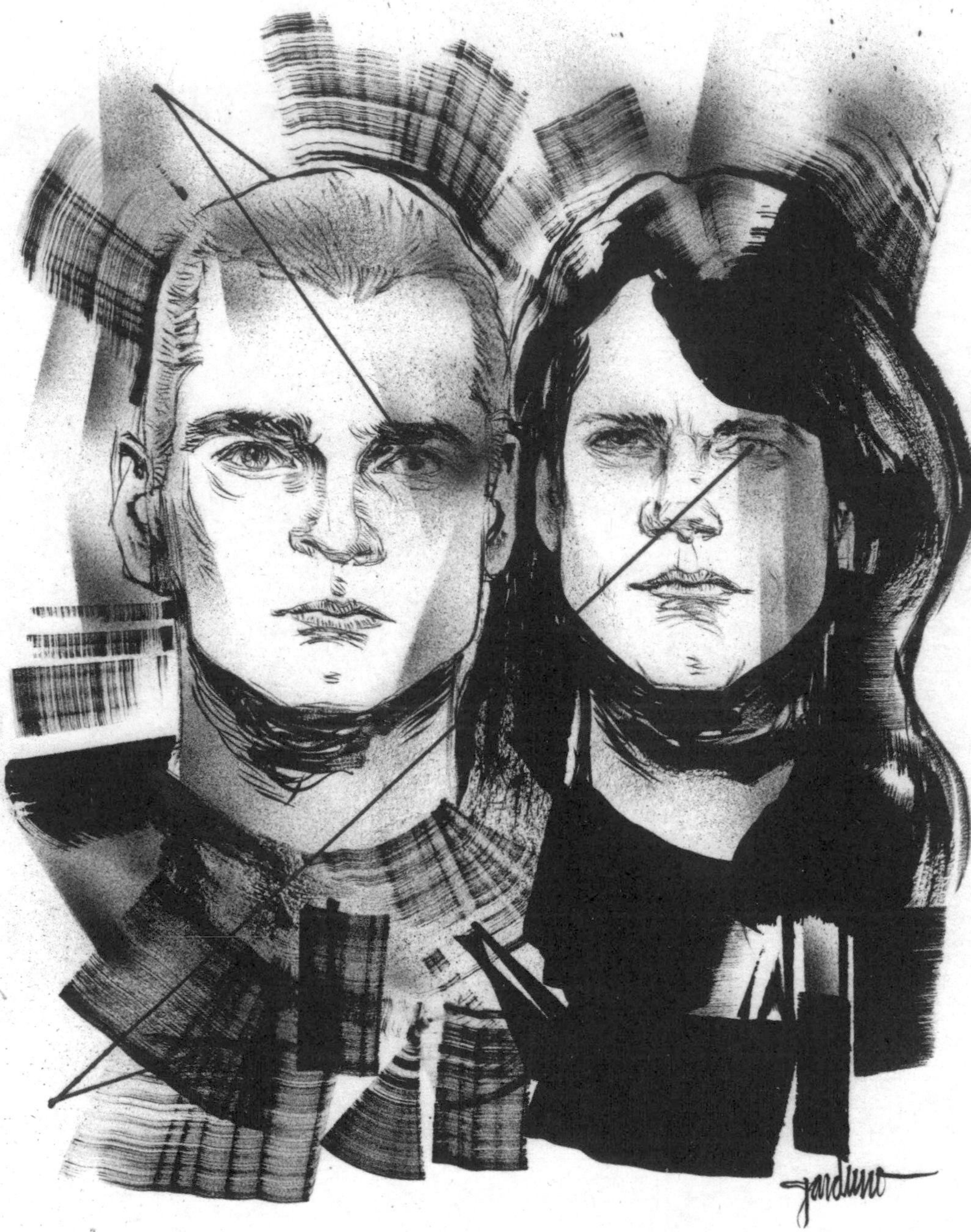

The Secret History of Henry & Glenn Comics

by Nick Green

In World War II America, able-bodied men joined the armed forces, their wives went to work in torpedo factories and wide-eyed children thrilled to the ten cent adventures of the ultimate defenders of truth and justice, pulp heroes like Superman, Batman, and Captain Marvel. And, of course, Henry & Glenn: The characters' humble origins were spotlighted in 1939's *American Comics #1*, where the 98-pound flat-footed 4H weaklings were approached by Uncle Sam to join an experimental training program for the U.S. Army. After receiving injections of irradiated super serum, Henry grew into a lantern-jawed strongman and Glenn became a barrel-chested fighter. These sensitive souls would be bullied no more; from that point on, they vowed to kick sand in the face of America's enemies.

HENRY AND GLENN
FIGHT FOR
AMERICA
NO. 13
10¢
MARCH

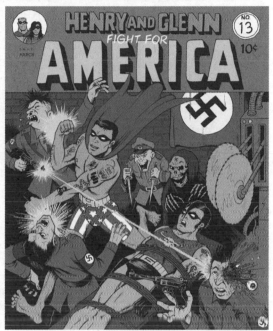

Henry & Glenn's contributions to America's wartime efforts cannot be understated. As U.S. forces entered the European theatre of operations, Henry & Glenn were on the frontlines, smashing fascism and upholding the American way. The now-iconic cover of *American Comics #27* features Henry bending Benito Mussolini and Emperor Tojo into a human pretzel, while Glenn punches Adolf Hitler so hard that the dictator flies out of his jackboots and lands on the Moon (although, in a surprise twist, Hitler boards a rocket back to Earth and lives to fight another day). Kids everywhere were captivated by the four-color chronicles of Henry & Glenn, but as Allied forces beat back the Axis threat, victory gardens went fallow and interest in hyper-realistic depictions of war waned.

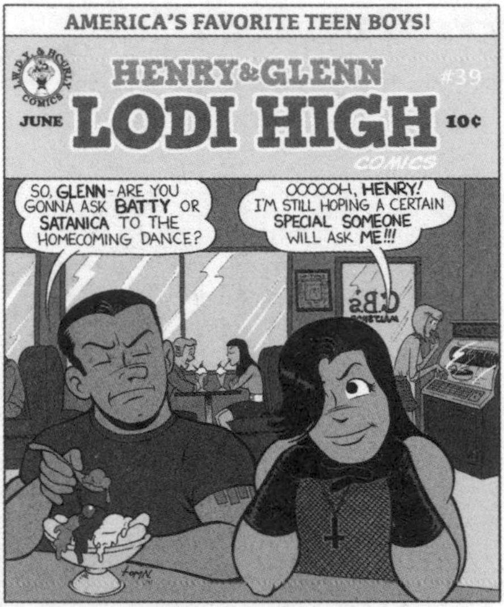
AMERICA'S FAVORITE TEEN BOYS!
HENRY&GLENN
#39
JUNE
LODI HIGH
10¢
COMICS
SO, GLENN - ARE YOU GONNA ASK BATTY OR SATANICA TO THE HOMECOMING DANCE?
OOOOOH, HENRY! I'M STILL HOPING A CERTAIN SPECIAL SOMEONE WILL ASK ME!!!

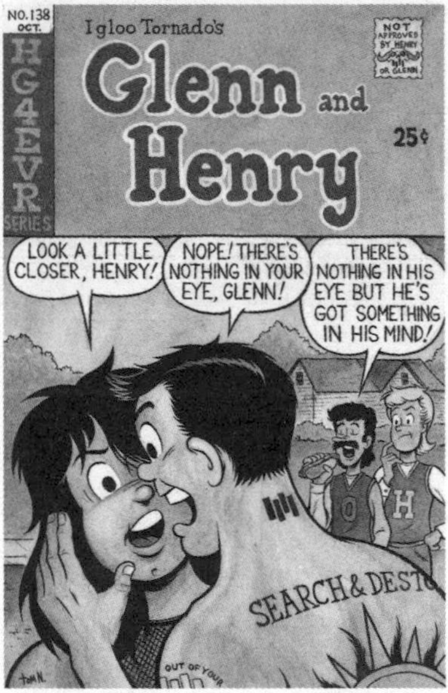
NO. 138 OCT.
Igloo Tornado's
NOT APPROVED BY HENRY OR GLENN
Glenn and Henry
25¢
HG4EVR SERIES
LOOK A LITTLE CLOSER, HENRY!
NOPE! THERE'S NOTHING IN YOUR EYE, GLENN!
THERE'S NOTHING IN HIS EYE BUT HE'S GOT SOMETHING IN HIS MIND!
SEARCH&DEST

In an effort to reflect an appetite for more wholesome entertainment, comics imprint Hourly recast Henry & Glenn as a pair of fresh-faced teenagers. The first issue of the new series (1950's *Henry & Glenn at Lodi High #1*) followed the pair painting posters for a pep rally and hanging out with their best friends, a hirsute jock named Bear and the cool greaser Leather Daddy-O. Subsequent issues depicted Henry & Glenn eating hamburgers at the malt shop, helping old ladies across the street and rescuing cats from trees. The content was undoubtedly wholesome, though the series began to draw fire from moral crusader Dr. Frederick Wertham, who railed against Henry & Glenn's close-knit relationship as "a wish dream of two homosexuals living together."

The success of *Henry & Glenn at Lodi High* enabled Hourly to expand its line with romance titles, Westerns, and most notably, the horror anthology series *Horror Hotel*, "hosted" by a pair of creepy cultists named "Daryl" and "John." Dr. Wertham responded by lambasting Hourly's entire line, particularly a lurid 1952 story from *Horror Hotel* called *"Twist of Cain,"* where Daryl and John command their followers to worship Satan and plunge knives deep into their brothers' hearts. After a wave of negative publicity following the release of Dr. Wertham's *Seduction of the Innocent* in 1954, Hourly was forced to file for bankruptcy and sell off its entire line to creditors.

Flash forward ten years later: An irascible huckster named Tom Neely takes over his father's publishing empire and decides to channel the public's renewed fascination with superheroes by branching out into comics. Neely assembles a Murderer's Row of veteran artists for the fledgling enterprise and dubs the frigid bullpen the "Igloo Tornado." Joining Neely is Gulpin' Gin Stevens, who originally created Henry & Glenn and illustrated some of the pair's greatest Nazi-fighting adventures in American Comics; Leapin' Levon Jihanian, a publicity-shy dreamer known for his angular lines and flair for the macabre; Sensational Scot Nobles, a superb draftsman who had honed his craft on romance and genre books a decade earlier.

For the company's flagship title, the Igloo Tornado bullpen decides to re-launch Henry & Glenn and restore the iconic everymen as larger-than-life superheroes. In *Henry & Glenn Adventures #1*, Henry & Glenn are thawed from a block of ice in the Arctic Circle and re-turned to America, where they struggle to adjust to the new realities of a very different society. With the Axis powers in shambles and the House Un-American Activities Committee on the wane, Henry & Glenn team up to strike fear in the hearts of petty criminals everywhere. The new series was a smashing success, and soon, all four Igloo Tornado members were working in tandem to meet the public's demand.

"A Murderer's Row of veteran artists"
The early years of the Igloo Tornado
Clockwise from top left:
Tom Neely, Gin Stevens
Scot Nobles, Levon Jihanian

The offical crest of the Igloo Tornado

By the fourth issue of the new series, Igloo Tornado caved to public demand for an updated origin story by depicting Henry declining an invitation to a family dinner in order to cash in on his newfound abilities as a masked Luchador, before returning home to find his parents slaughtered. As the series continued, the Igloo Tornado team toyed with notions of time and space, and took Henry & Glenn on fantastical adventures below the Earth's surface, in outer space and into alternate dimensions. A three-part epic (issues #48-50) introducing the irritating and litigious devourer of ideas Ginnlactus and his herald Robo remains a favorite amongst comics scholars for its use of dramatic splash pages and is considered to be the pinnacle of the entire Henry & Glenn Adventures run.

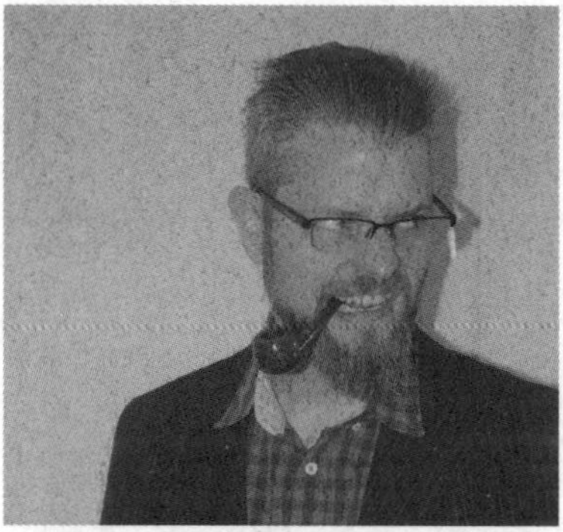

Tensions rose between the Igloo Tornado as Neely became increasingly paranoid and greedy.

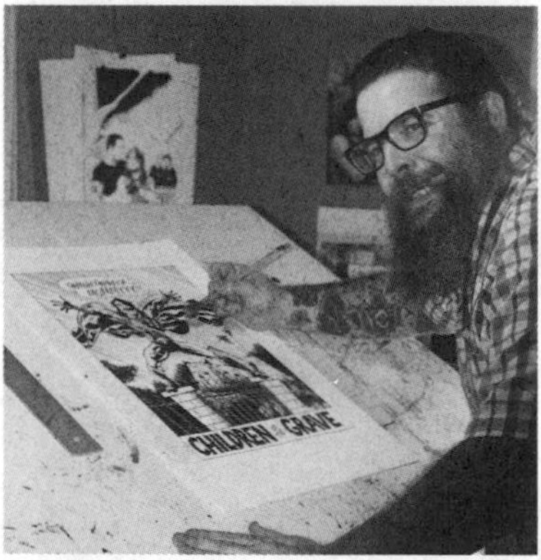
CHILDREN GRAVE

At the height of his career, it was said Gulpin' Gin Stevens could draw as many as 10 pages of comics per day.

But the honeymoon period was short-lived. In fanzine interviews from that era, Neely began to assume credit for the creation of these characters and constantly belittled the work of his collaborators, thumbing his nose at the bizarre objectivist tone of Ayn Rand devotee Jihanian's work and Stevens' seeming preference for fantastical tales about gods and monsters. Jihanian responded by destroying his own original art pages and quitting the industry entirely. "The art is what is important," sniffed Jihanian in his final interview with *The Comics Chronicle* in 1972. "Not the artist. Like the 'artist' minus the 'ist.' It rhymes with 'fart.' The A-R-T." Meanwhile, Stevens moved to a rival publisher and eventually spearheaded a lawsuit against Igloo Tornado for creator's rights. Nobles, a consummate company man, begrudgingly took on an increased workload in an effort to continue flooding the market with Henry & Glenn product.

As the popular media of the 1970s reveled in social realism, the illustrated adventures of Henry & Glenn followed with the times and the pair became vigilantes for hire. In a seminal issue of *Henry/ Glenn: Hard-Travelling Heroes*, Glenn discovers that one of his closest associates is a junkie; the cover of #76 depicts Glenn's ward Doyle with a needle in his arm and was one of the first single issues of a series to be published without the approval of the Comics Code Authority. During the same era, Igloo Tornado caught lightning in a bottle once again with the oversized newsstand black and white publication The Savage Steel of Henry and Glenn, a bare-chested barbarian saga that outsold special interest magazines Ball Club and Just Men by a wide margin.

Interest in Henry & Glenn waned somewhat in the 1980s, as Igloo Tornado shamelessly milked trends by transforming Glenn into a jeet kune do master and Henry as his Zen sensei. During the indie comics explosion, the market was suddenly flooded with blatant anthropomorphic rip-offs, including turtles, rabbits, and hamsters. Sales flagged throughout the decade, until Igloo Tornado buried the hatchet with former company linchpin Gin Stevens, who revived Henry & Glenn as cybernetic warriors in the cubic zirconium-encrusted *Xtreme H&G Force#1*. The issue was an instant hit with collectors, who hoarded millions of copies from specialty shops with the promise of paying for their children's college educations.

Unfortunately, when Stevens took four months to deliver the artwork for the following issue and submitted a series of inexplicable sideways layouts, Neely fired Stevens and replaced him with Nobles, who decided to draw every character in the series with Asian features. Within months, both Stevens and Nobles had each formed their own company and erased Igloo Tornado's stranglehold on the direct market. Neely successfully recruited a group of younger artists with no sense of anatomy and an inability to draw feet, and the Henry & Glenn brand was diluted by an endless array of excruciating gimmicks like holograms, skull-shaped covers, and leather-bound "bondage" editions.

In particular, the yearlong *"Death of Henry & Glenn"* storyline met with controversey, when the editors made the crass marketing ploy to put the fate or our heroes in the hands of the comic audience. A toll free number was printed at the end of issue #11 asking fans to vote on who would die: Henry or Glenn? When issue #12 hit the stands, Glenn's fate was sealed. Riots broke out in comic shops across the country as nerds clashed over the results. Now known as "Black Wednesday," it is still considered one of the bloodiest days in comic fandom. At the tail end of the decade, a now bitter and alcoholic Neely was forced to sell off the entire line to Microcosm publisher Joe Biel, who had made his first million in the disposal of literal garbage, and was looking to build a "punk rock" empire (and purchase more yachts).

In early 2014—the 75th anniversary of Henry & Glenn's fabulous introduction—a near-mint copy of *American Comics #1* sold at public auction for $666,666. Interest in rare issues from the early run has soared amongst Henry & Glenn collectors, but the series speaks as much to novice readers as it does to the die-hards with neck beards that still live in their mommies and daddies' basements. The artistry and writing informing the pair's ongoing saga remains intricate and accomplished, and the sense of discovery that accompanies cracking the spine of a Henry & Glenn comic and drawing in the "macho" smell of the fresh pages is as potent as ever. These comics are meant to be treasured, displayed as proudly as Henry's weightlifting equipment or Glenn's voluminous book collection, not encased in mylar sheaths—as the dynamic duo can attest, it's a shame to keep anything you love in a closet.

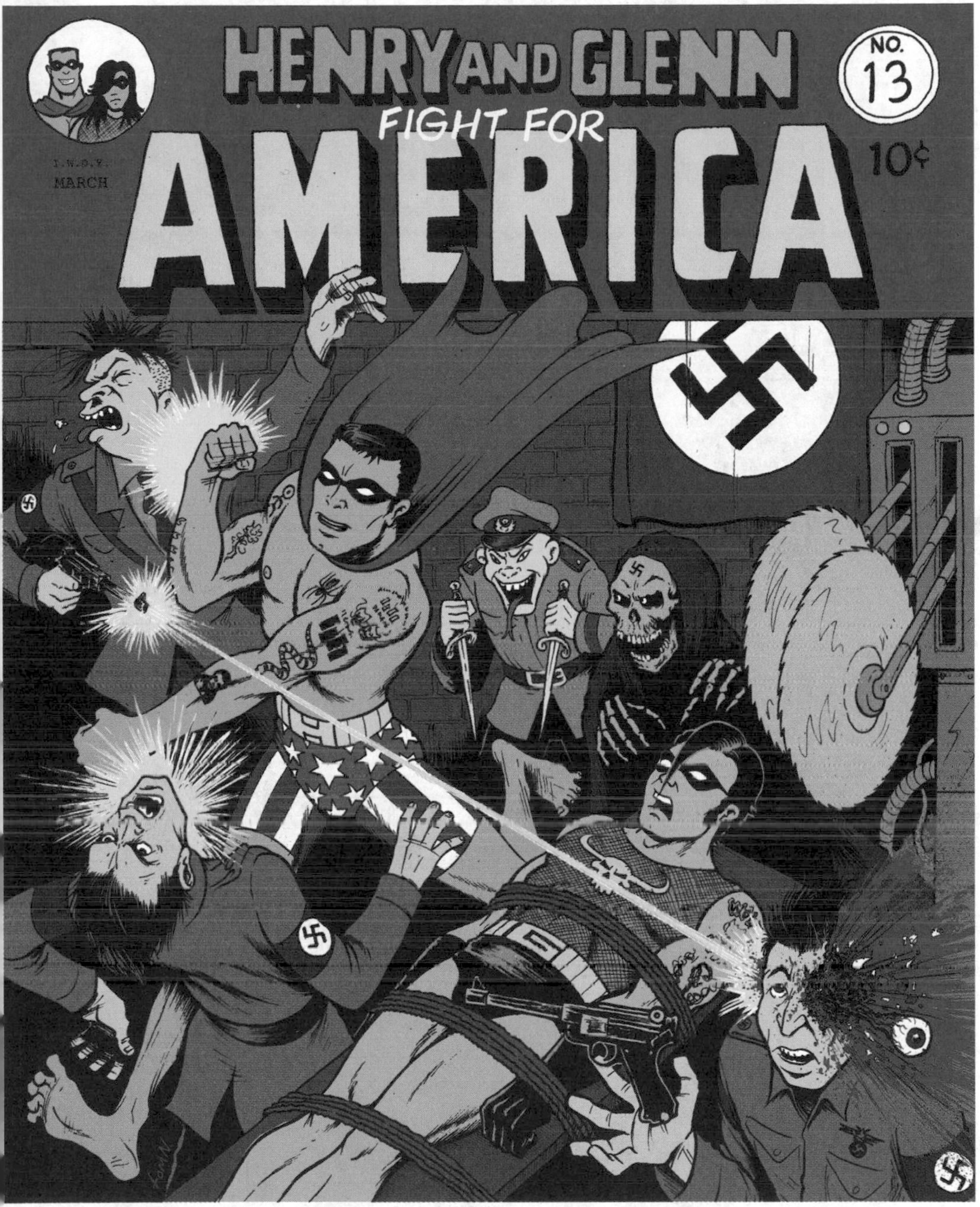
HENRY AND GLENN
NO. 13
FIGHT FOR
AMERICA
10¢
MARCH

Tom Neely

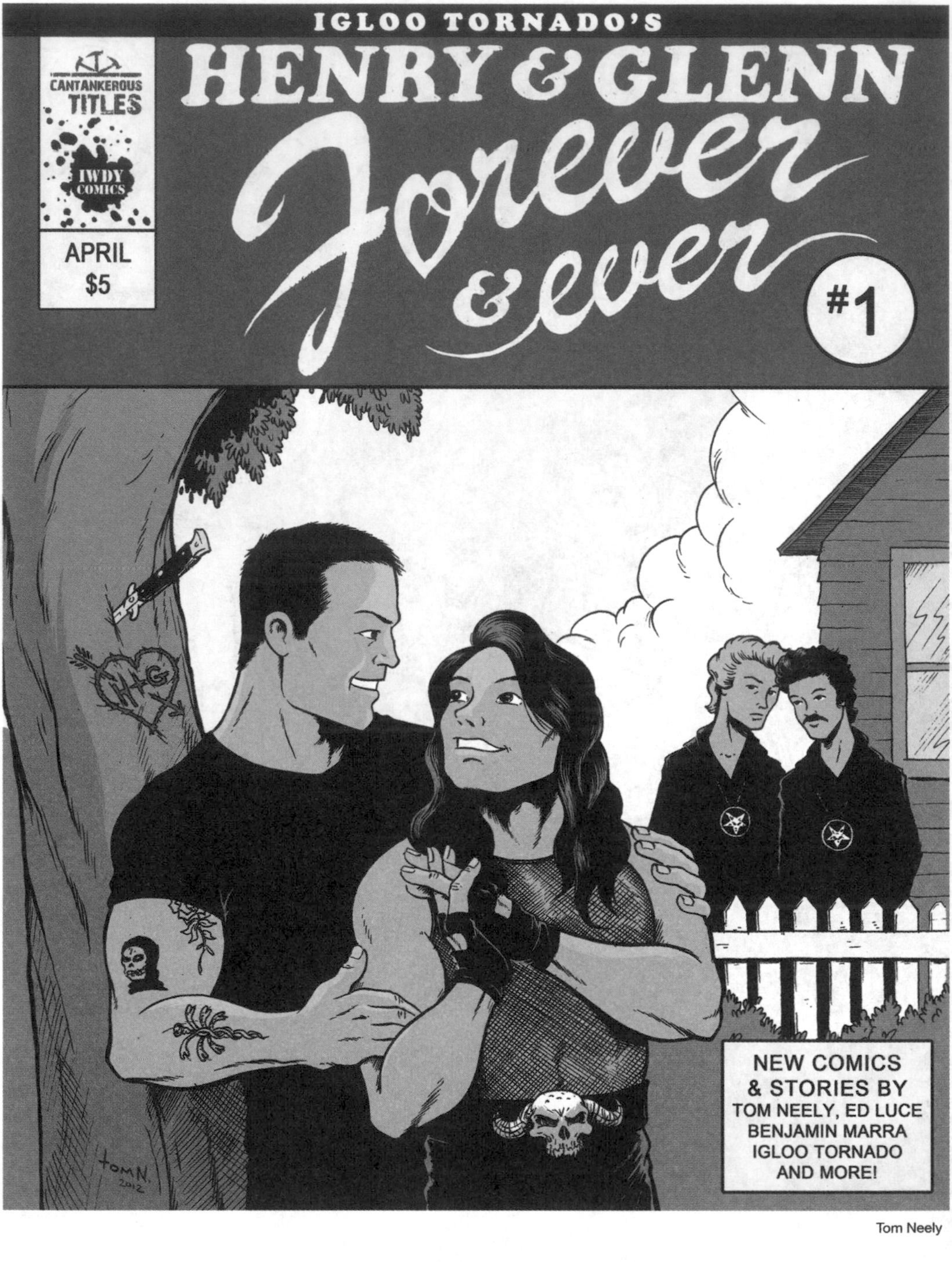

IGLOO TORNADO'S
HENRY & GLENN
Forever & ever
#1
CANTANKEROUS TITLES
IWDY COMICS
APRIL
$5
NEW COMICS
& STORIES BY
TOM NEELY, ED LUCE
BENJAMIN MARRA
IGLOO TORNADO
AND MORE!
TOM N.
2012

Tom Neely

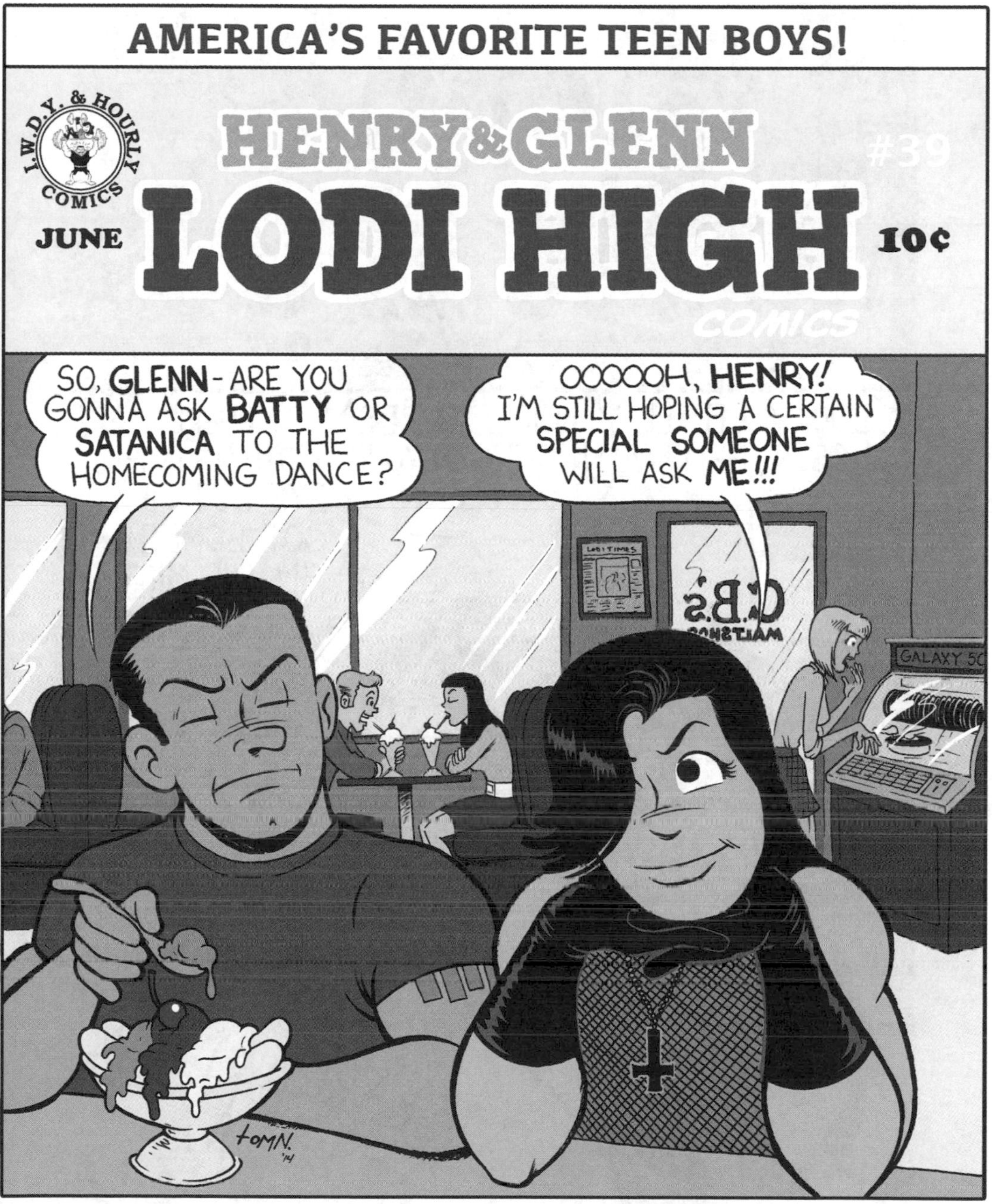
AMERICA'S FAVORITE TEEN BOYS!
I.W.D.Y. & HOURLY COMICS
HENRY & GLENN
#39
JUNE
LODI HIGH
10¢
COMICS
SO, GLENN - ARE YOU GONNA ASK BATTY OR SATANICA TO THE HOMECOMING DANCE?
OOOOOH, HENRY! I'M STILL HOPING A CERTAIN SPECIAL SOMEONE WILL ASK ME!!!
LODI TIMES
GALAXY 50
TOM N. '14

Tom Neely

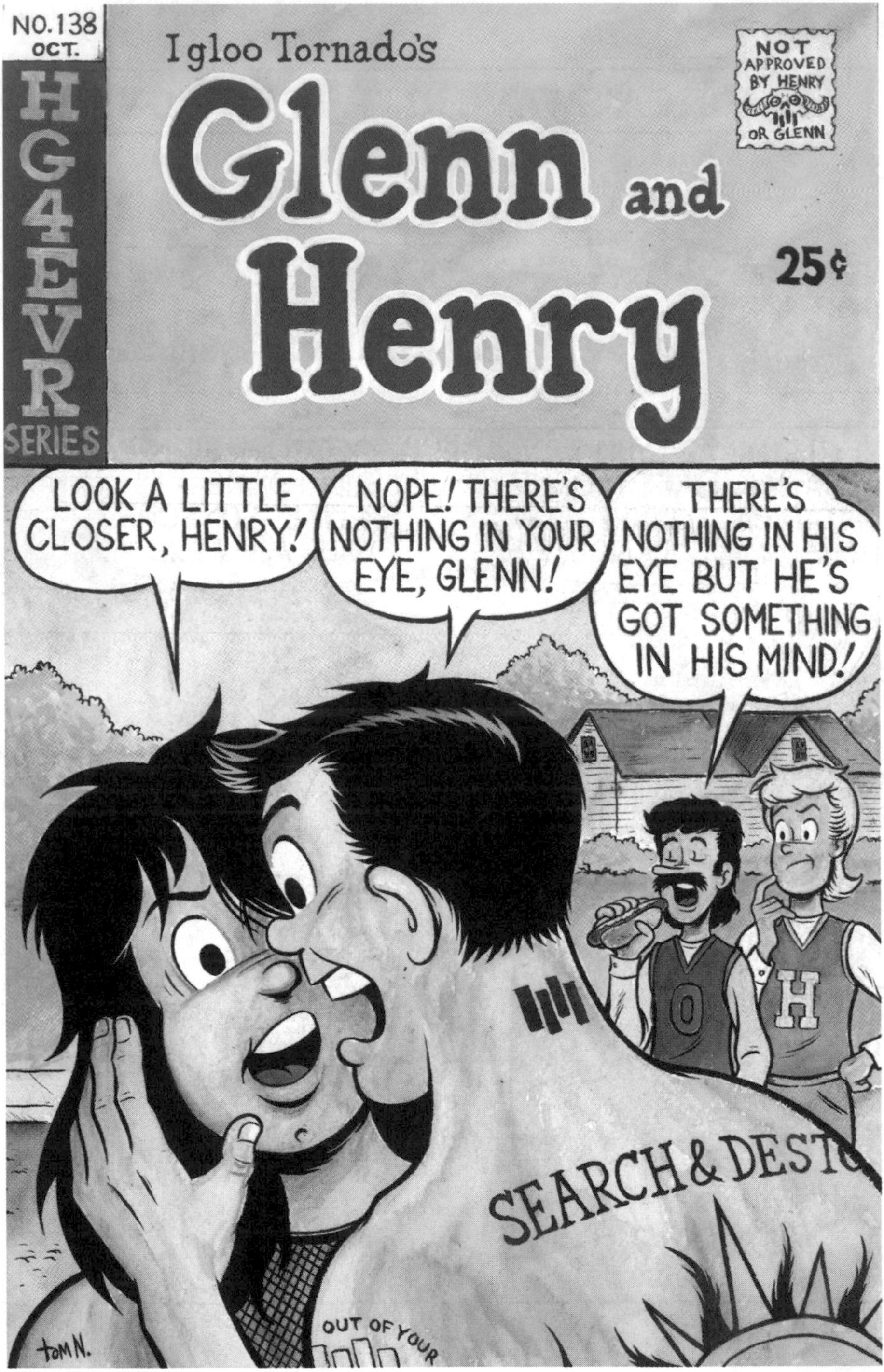
NO.138
OCT.
HG4EVR
SERIES
Igloo Tornado's
Glenn and Henry
NOT APPROVED BY HENRY OR GLENN
25¢
LOOK A LITTLE CLOSER, HENRY!
NOPE! THERE'S NOTHING IN YOUR EYE, GLENN!
THERE'S NOTHING IN HIS EYE BUT HE'S GOT SOMETHING IN HIS MIND!
SEARCH & DEST
OUT OF YOUR
tom N.
Tom Neely

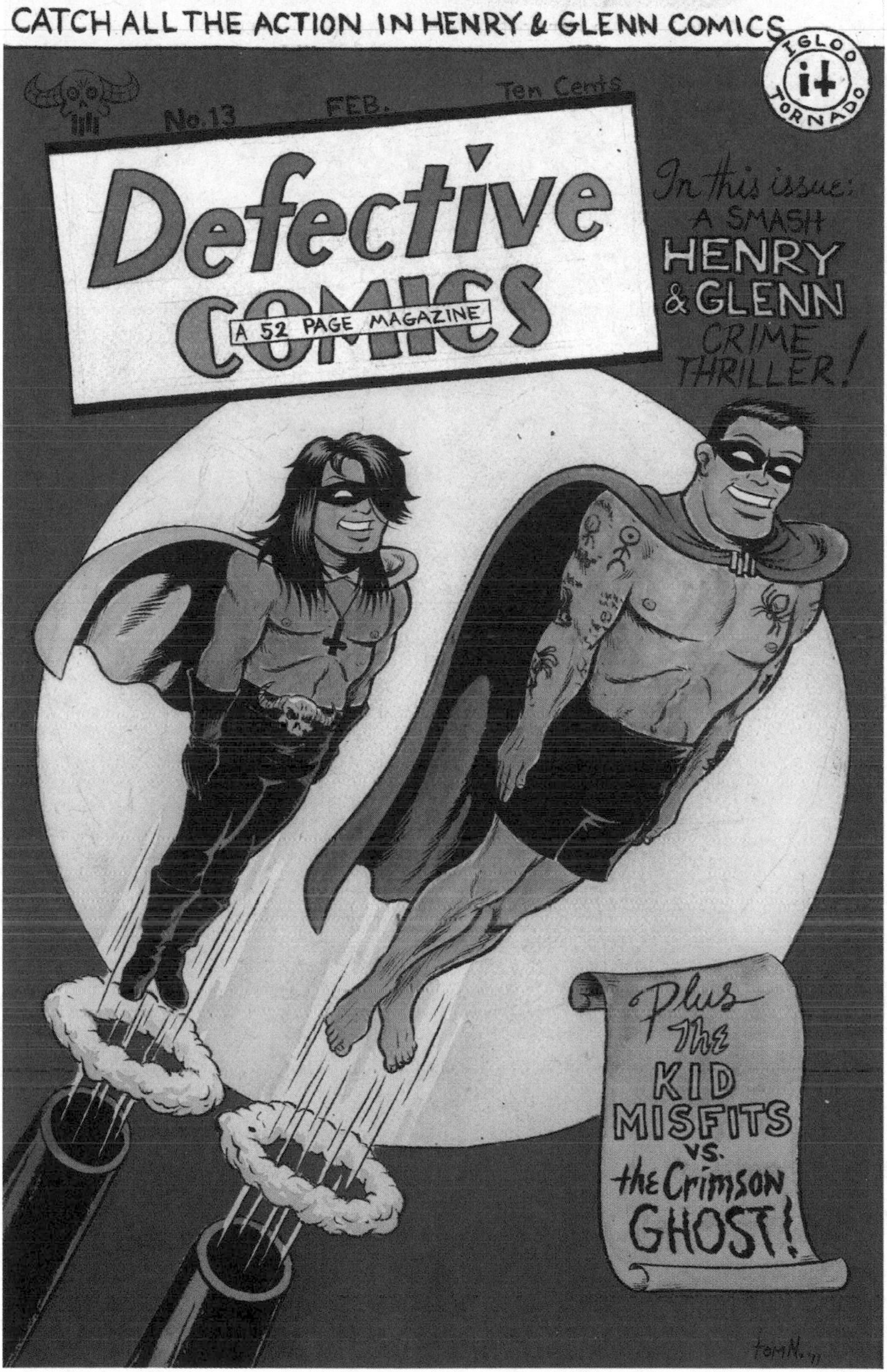

CATCH ALL THE ACTION IN HENRY & GLENN COMICS
IGLOO it TORNADO
No. 13
FEB.
Ten Cents
Defective COMICS
A 52 PAGE MAGAZINE
In this issue: A SMASH HENRY & GLENN CRIME THRILLER!
Plus The KID MISFITS vs. the Crimson GHOST!
tomN.

Tom Neely

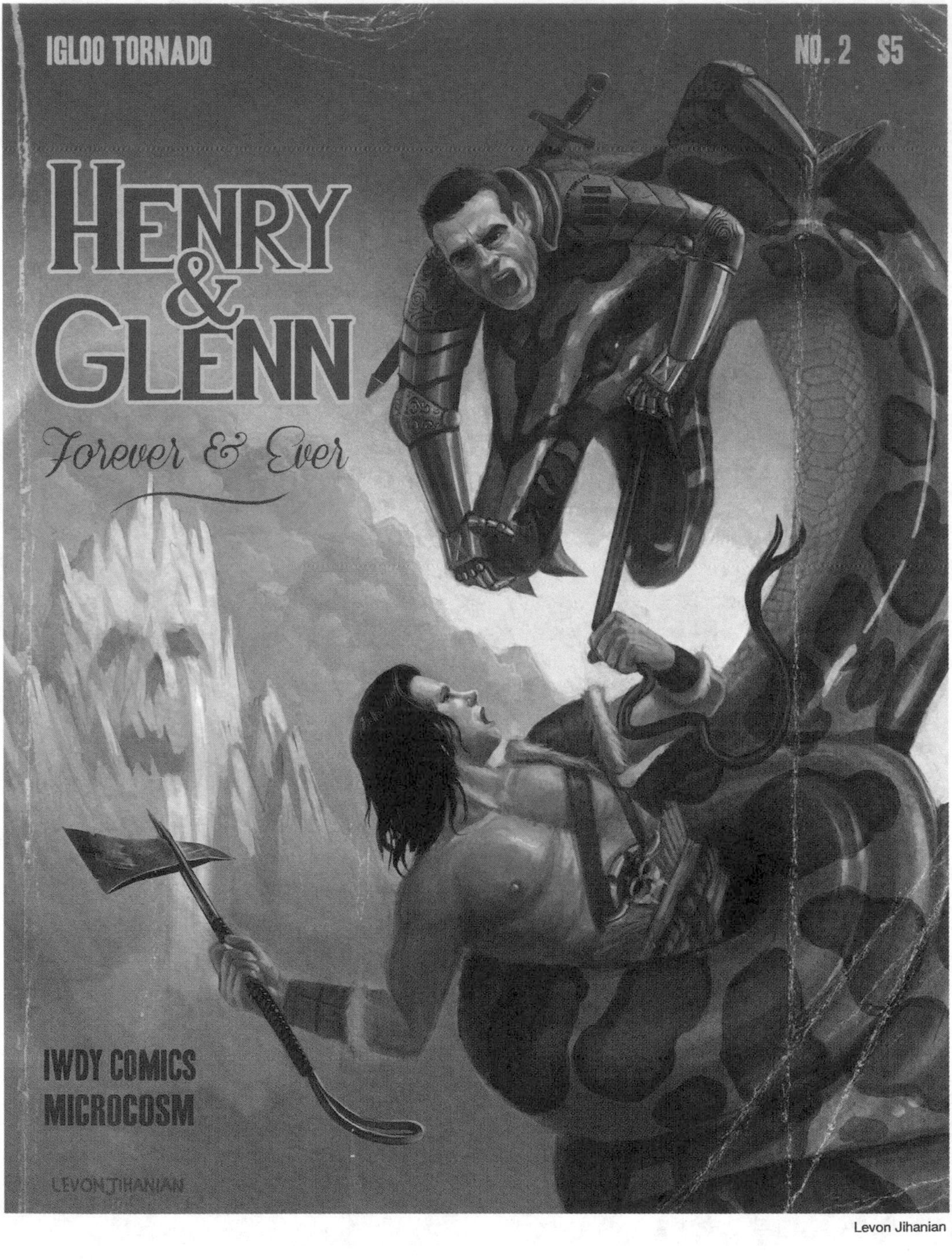
IGLOO TORNADO
NO. 2 $5
HENRY & GLENN
Forever & Ever
IWDY COMICS
MICROCOSM
LEVON JIHANIAN

Levon Jihanian

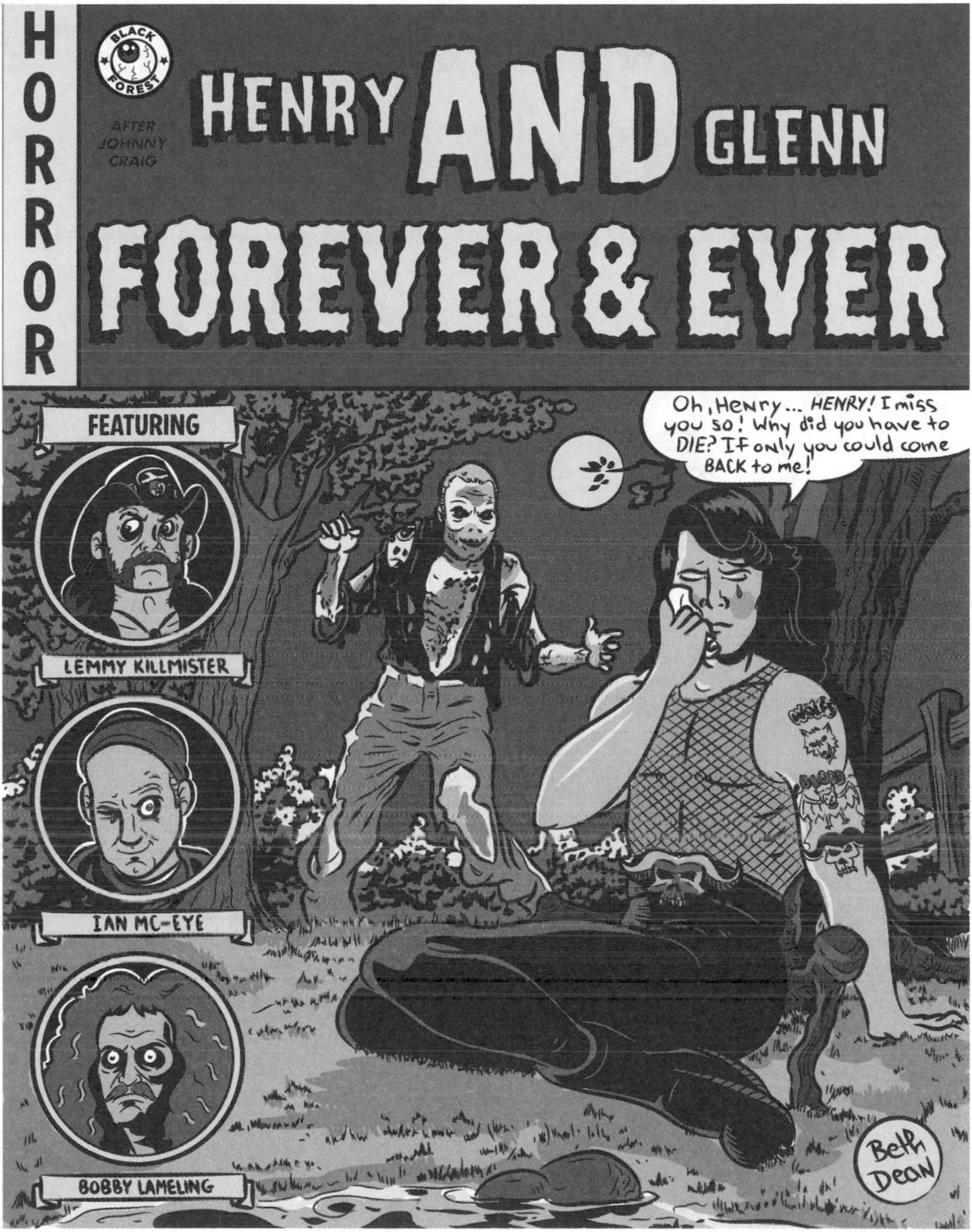
HORROR
BLACK FOREST
AFTER JOHNNY CRAIG
HENRY AND GLENN
FOREVER & EVER
FEATURING
LEMMY KILLMISTER
IAN MC-EYE
BOBBY LAMELING
Oh, Henry... HENRY! I miss you so! Why did you have to DIE? If only you could come BACK to me!
Beth Dean

Beth Dean

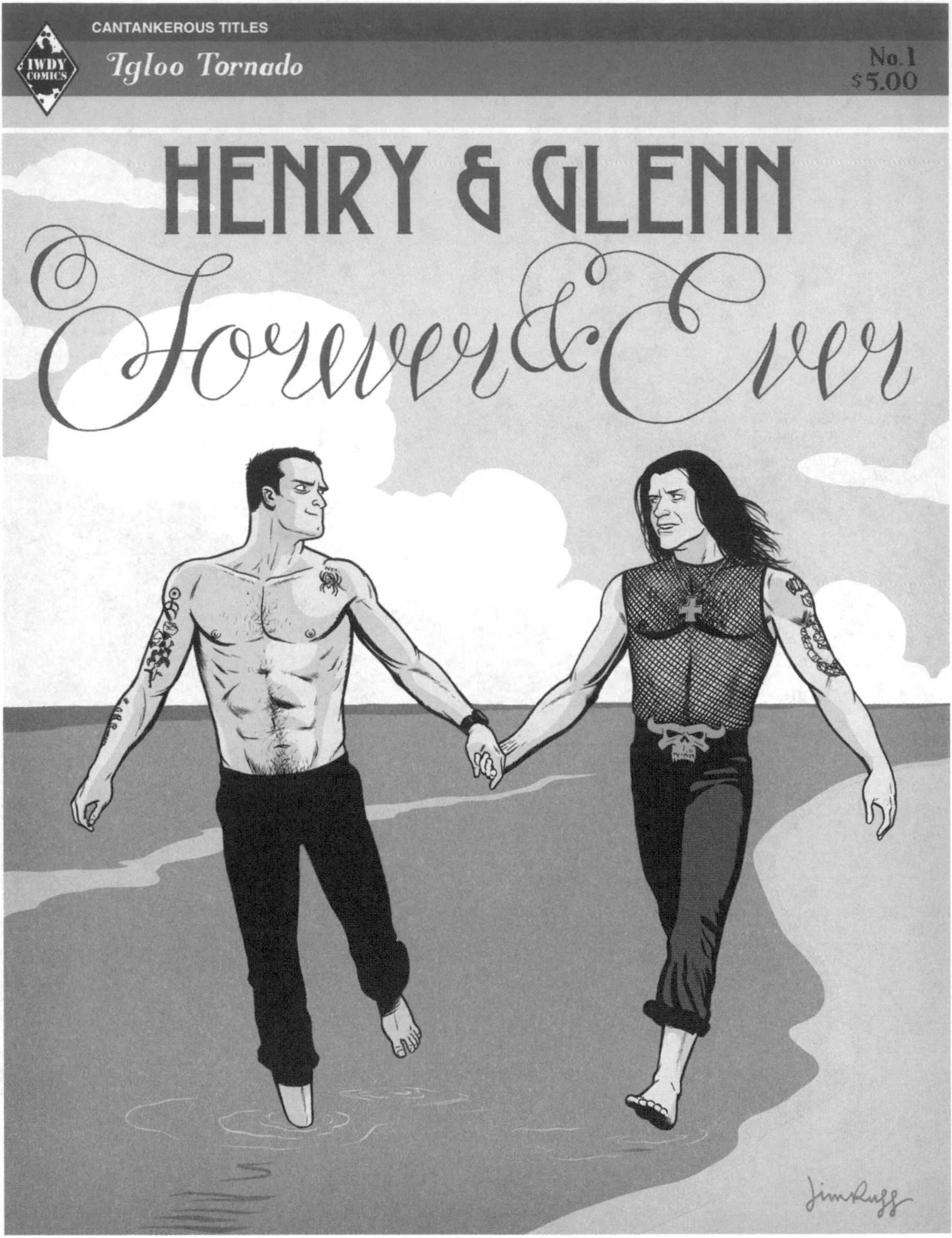
CANTANKEROUS TITLES
IWDY COMICS
Igloo Tornado
No. 1
$5.00
HENRY & GLENN
Forever & Ever
Jim Rugg

Jim Rugg

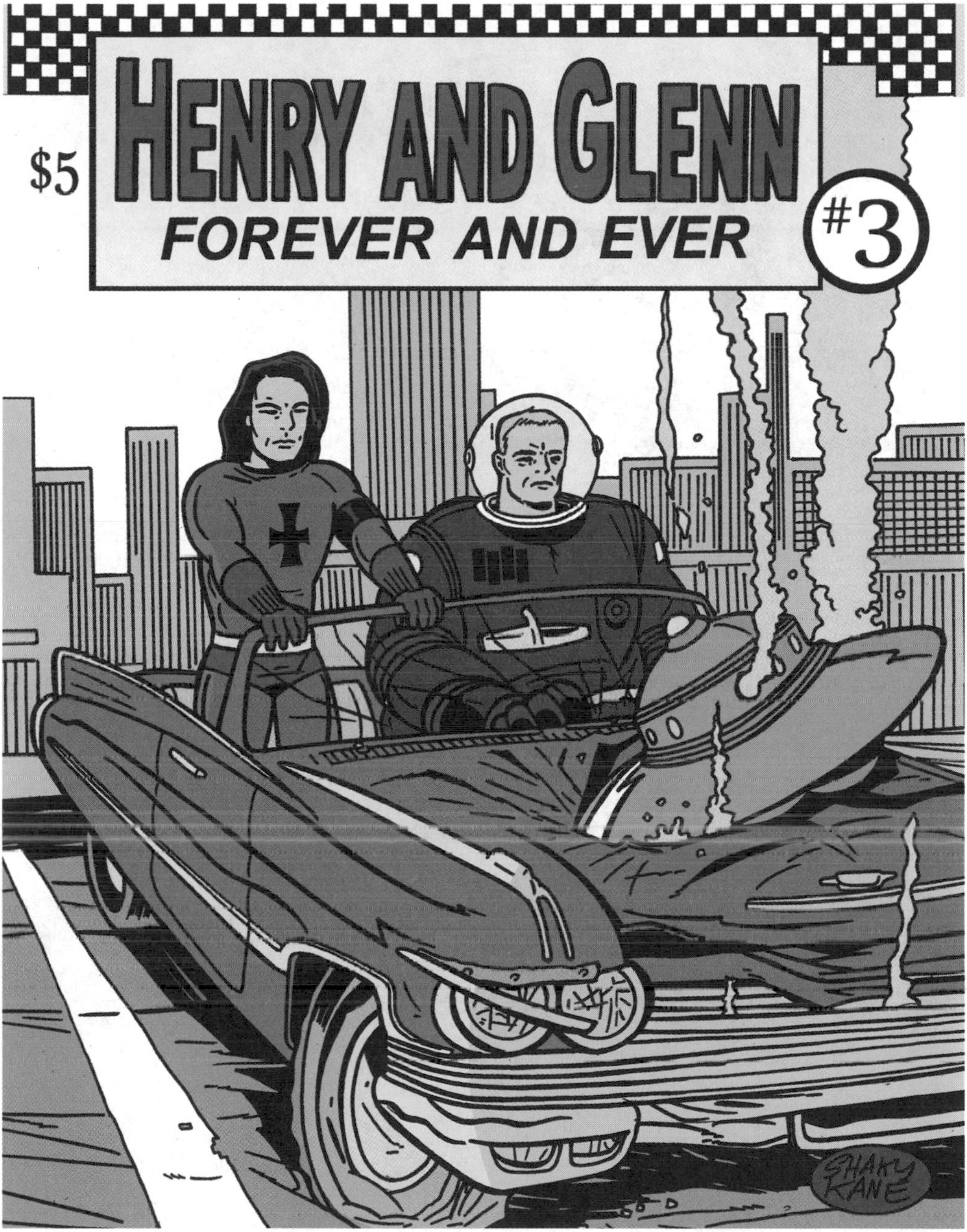
$5
HENRY AND GLENN
FOREVER AND EVER
#3
SHAKY KANE
Shaky Kane

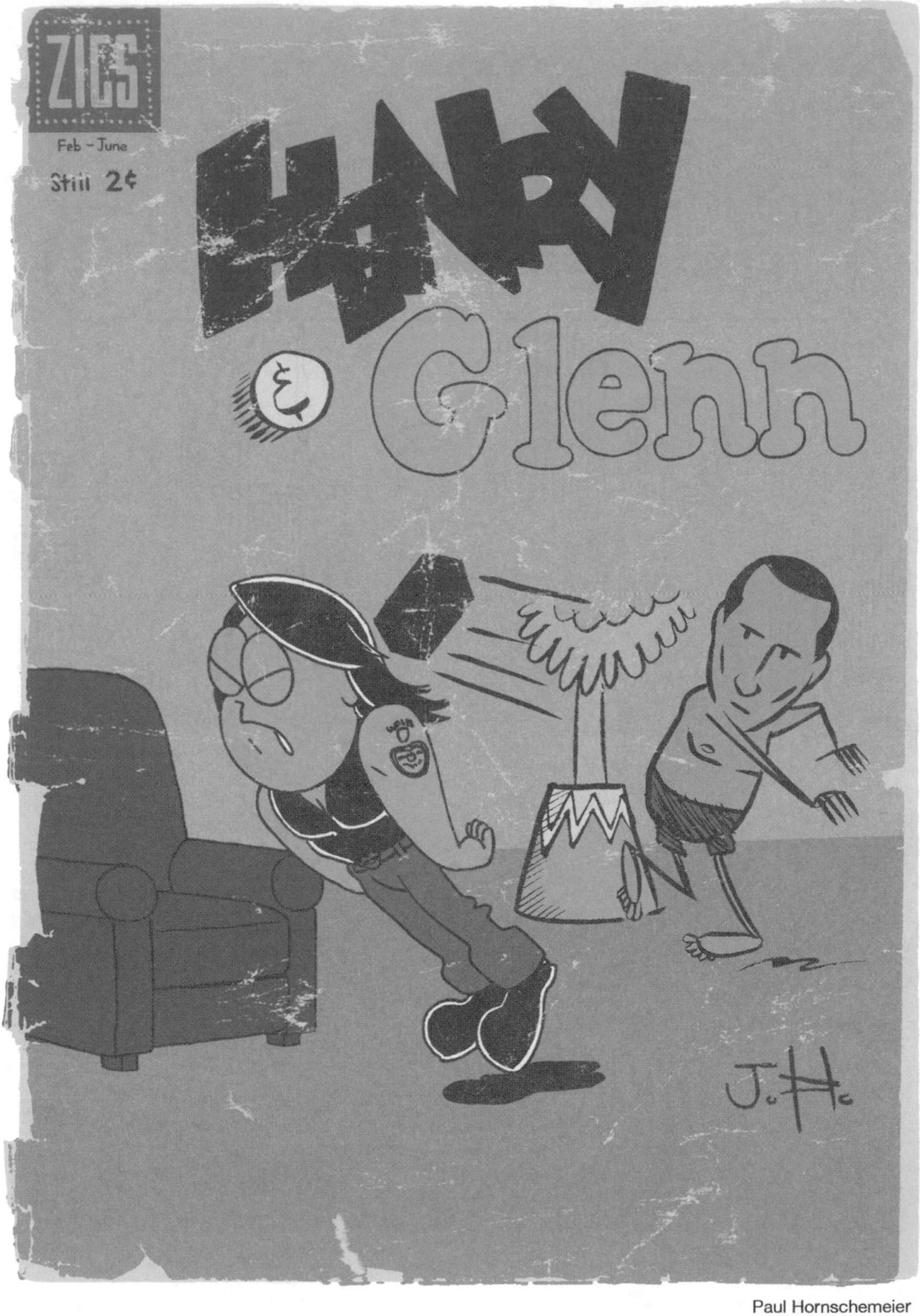

ZICS
Feb - June
Still 2¢
HENRY
&
Glenn
J. H.

Paul Hornschemeier

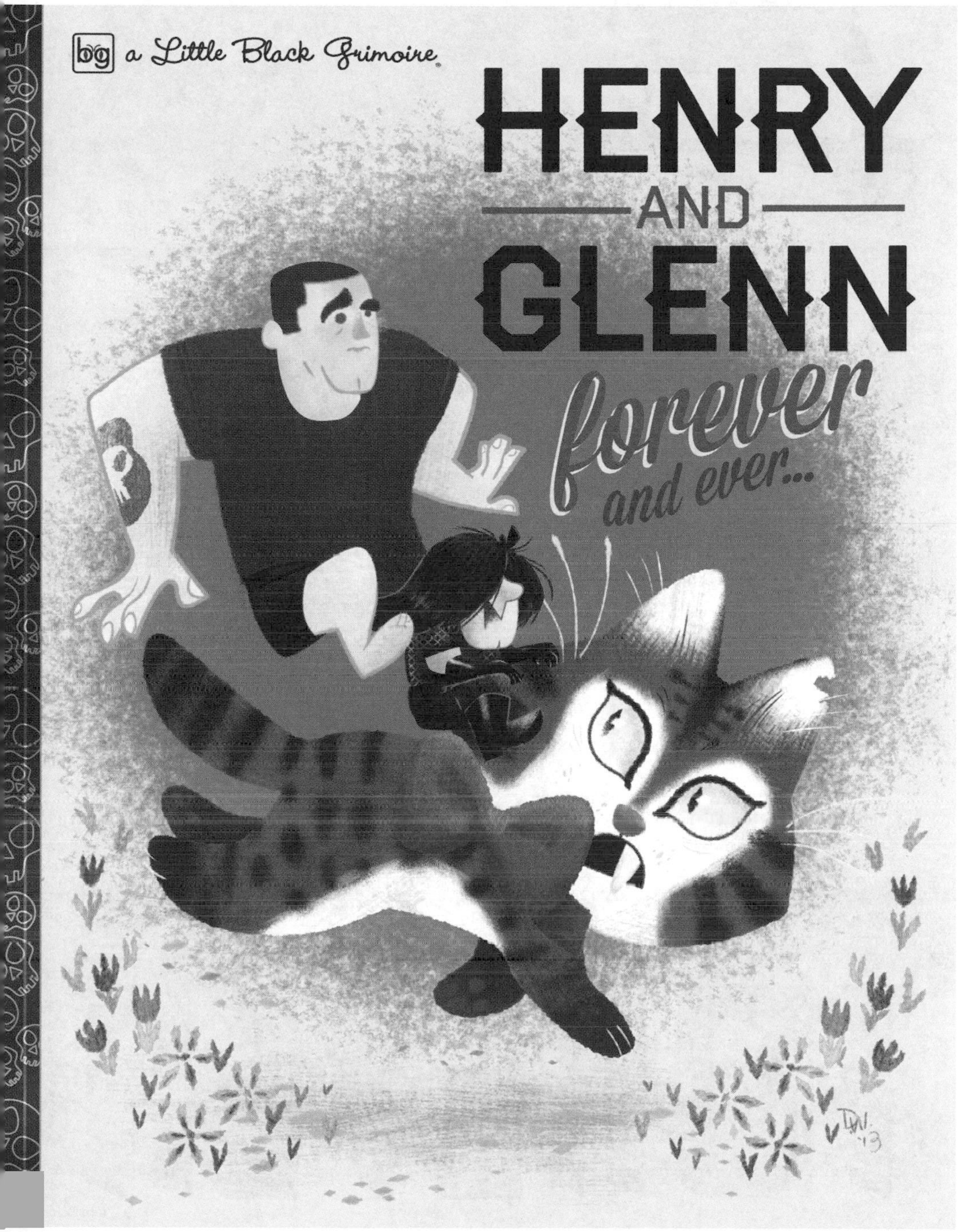
a Little Black Grimoire
HENRY
AND
GLENN
forever
and ever...
D.W. '13

Dalton Webb

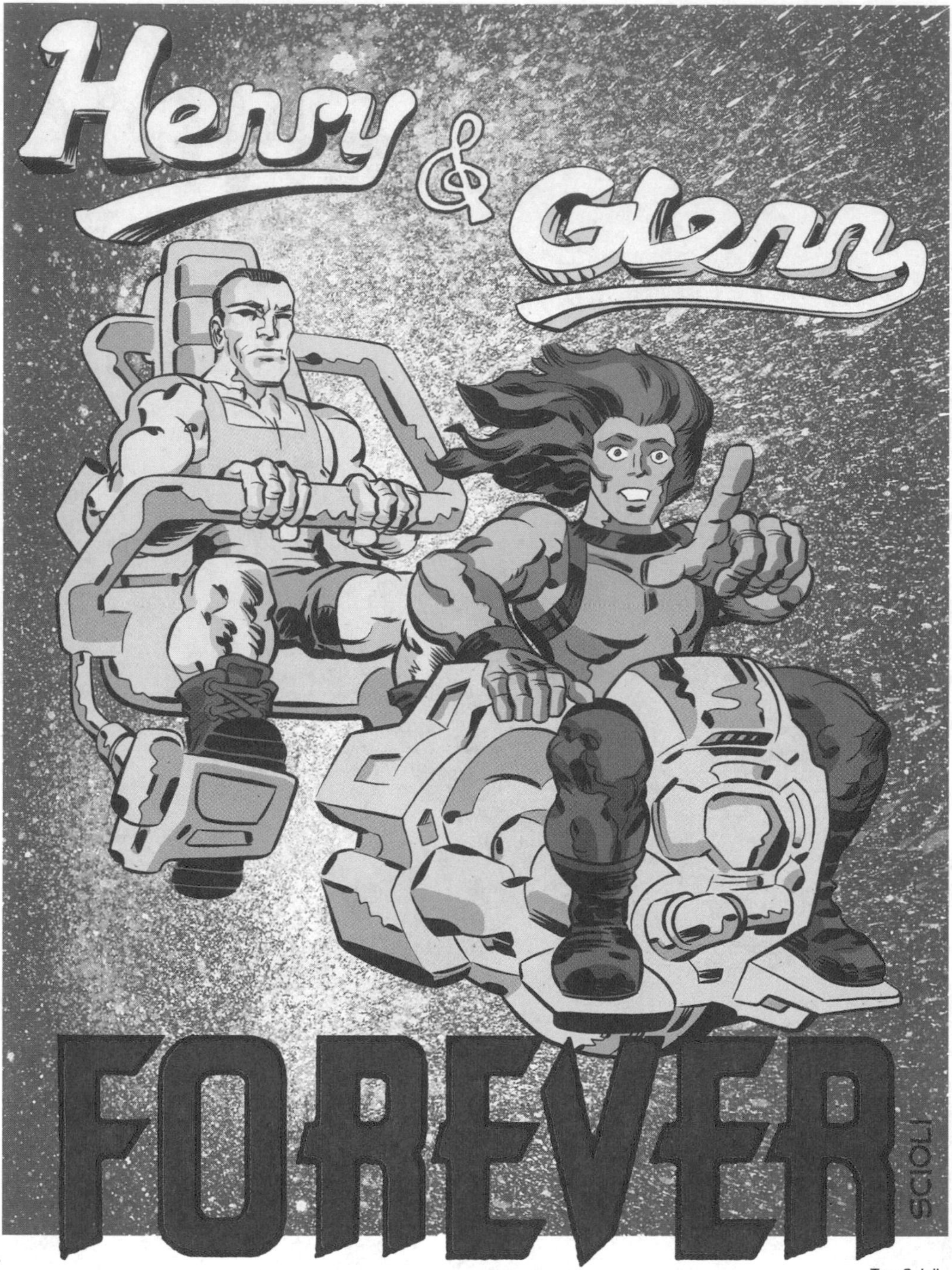
Henry & Glenn
FOREVER
SCIOLI

Tom Scioli

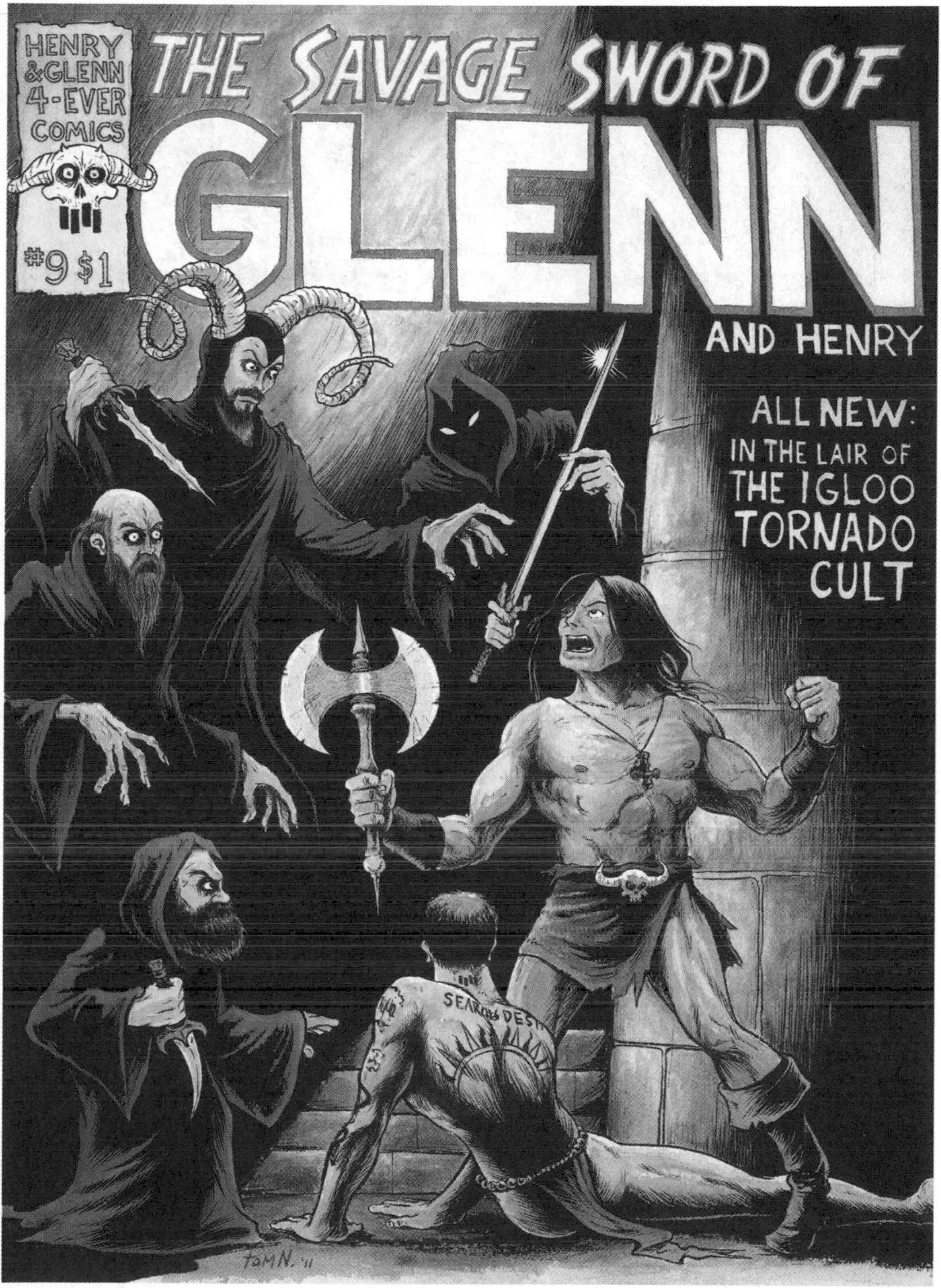
HENRY &GLENN 4-EVER COMICS
#9 $1
THE SAVAGE SWORD OF
GLENN
AND HENRY
ALL NEW:
IN THE LAIR OF
THE IGLOO
TORNADO
CULT
TOM N. '11

Tom Neely

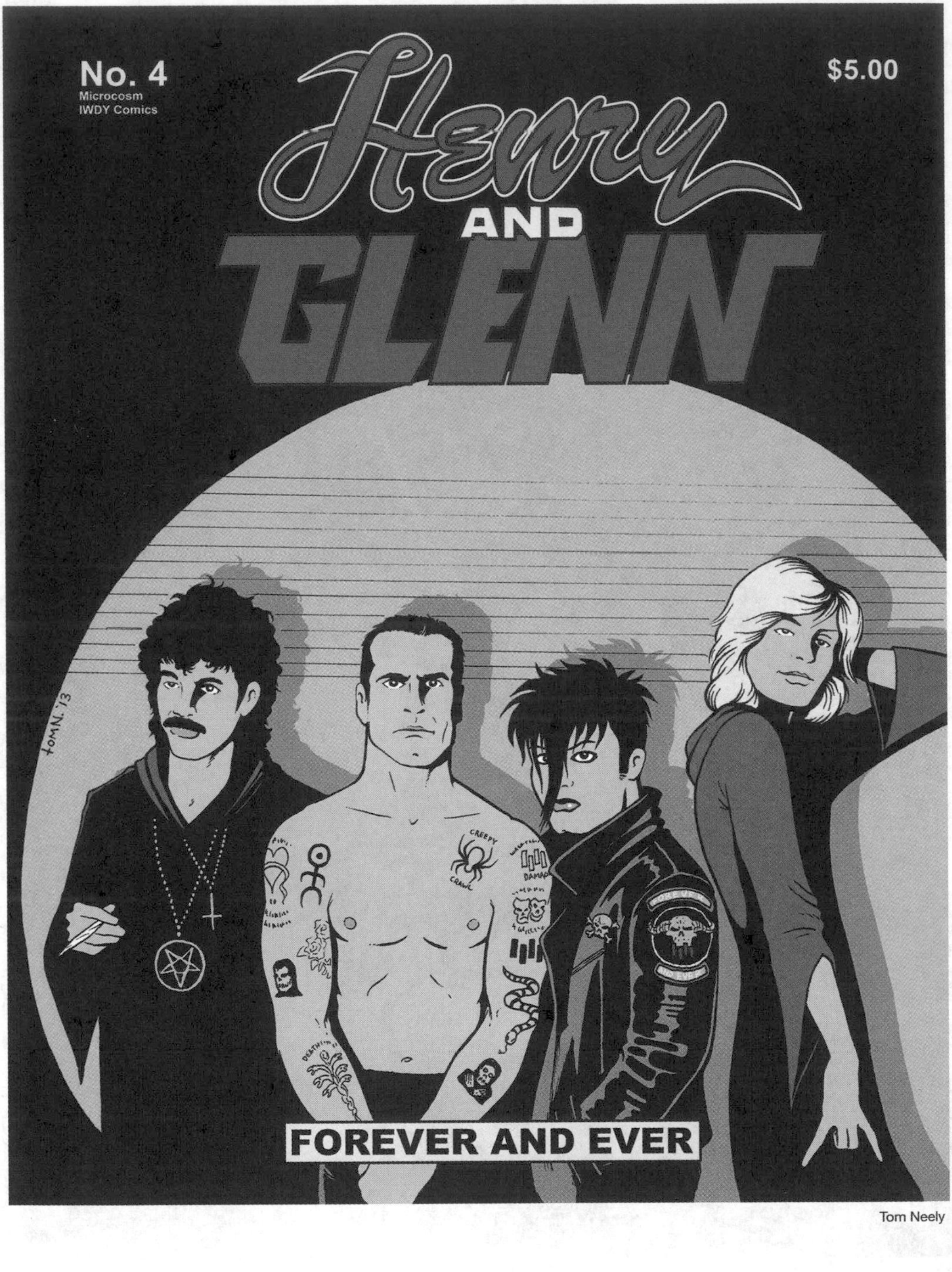
No. 4
Microcosm
IWDY Comics
Henry
AND
GLENN
$5.00
FOREVER AND EVER
Tom Neely

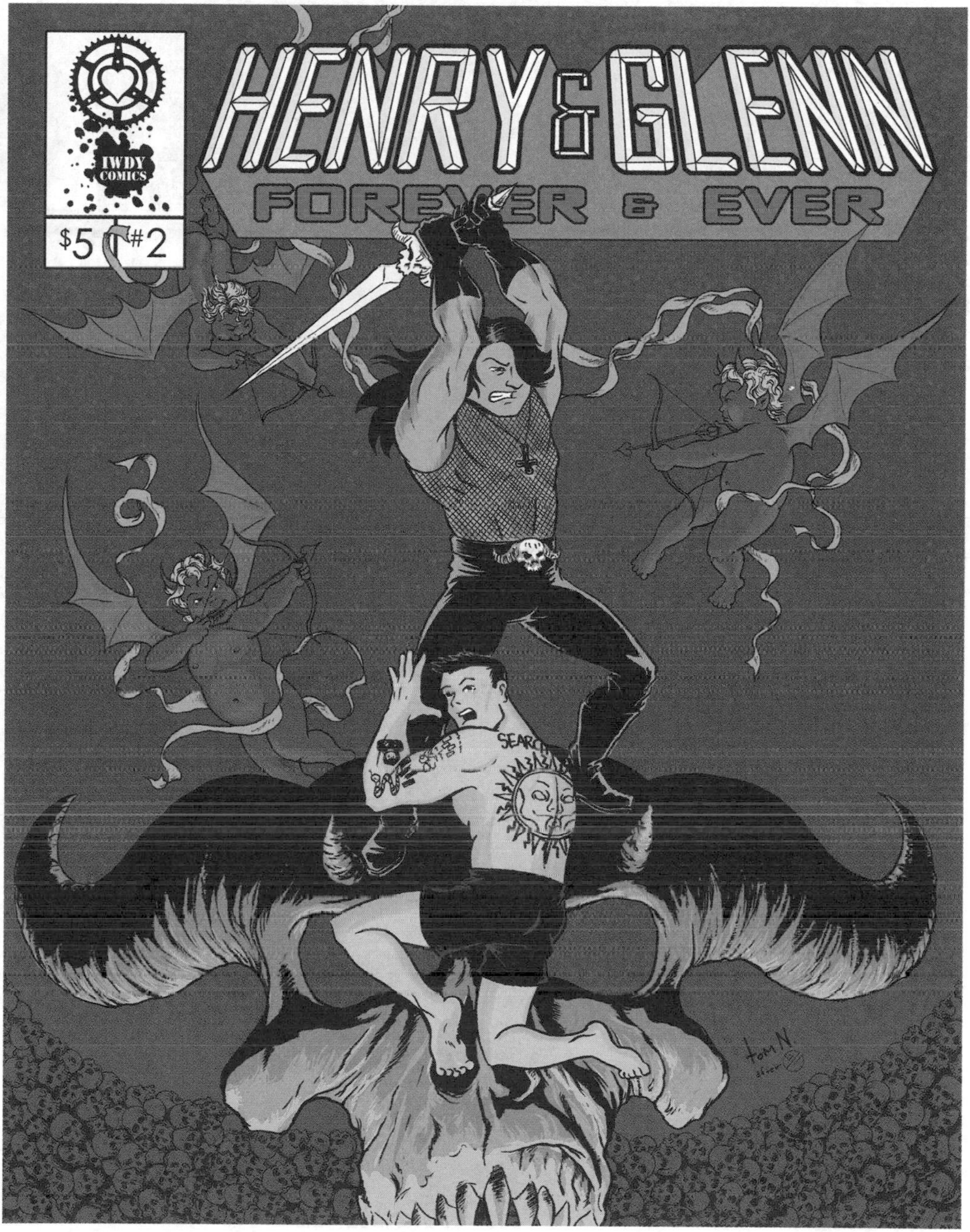

IWDY COMICS
$5 #2
HENRY & GLENN
FOREVER & EVER
SEARCH

Tom Neely

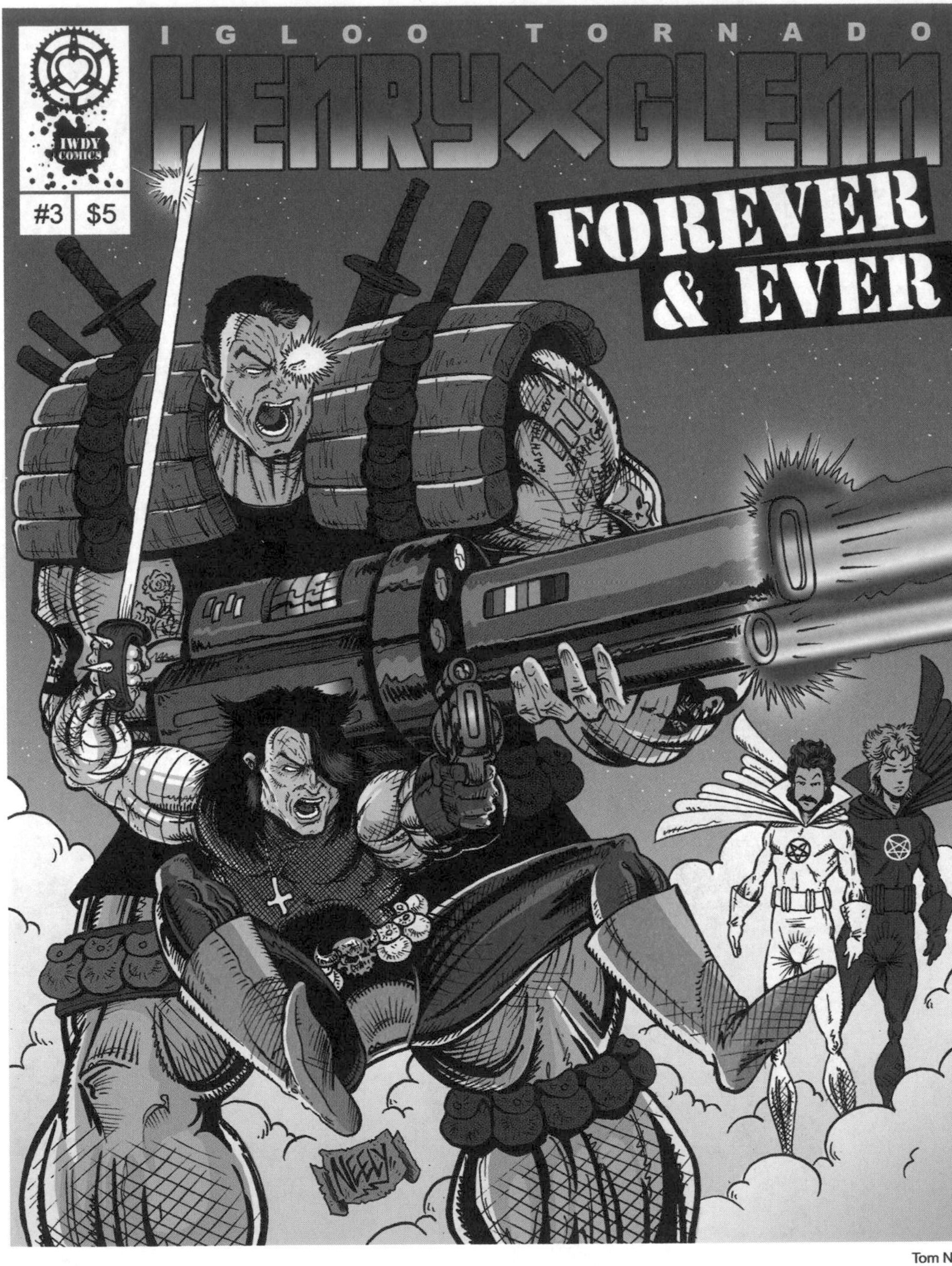
IGLOO TORNADO
HENRY × GLENN
IWDY COMICS
#3 $5
FOREVER & EVER
NEELY

Tom Neely

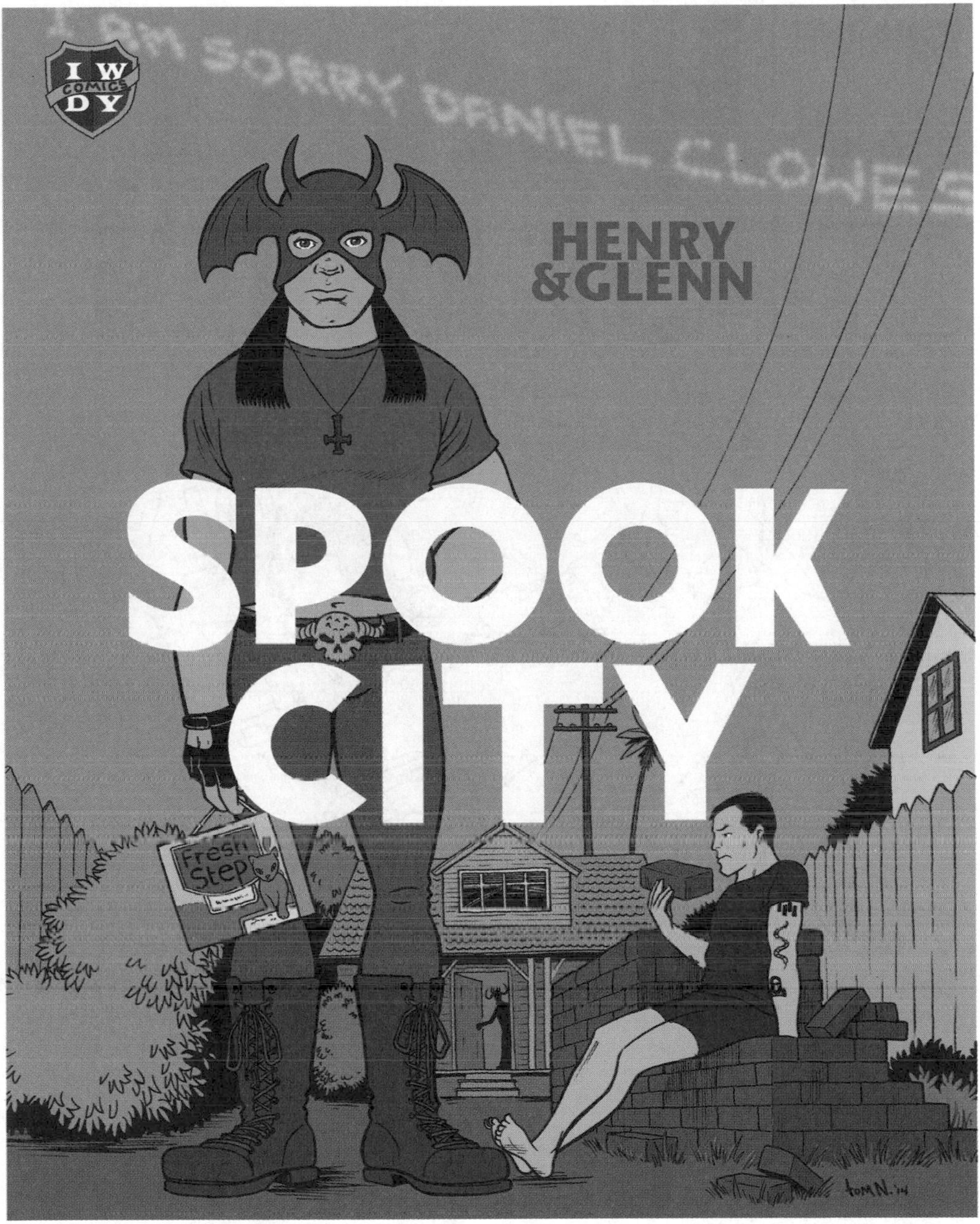
I W COMICS D Y
I AM SORRY DANIEL CLOWES
HENRY &GLENN
SPOOK CITY
Fresh Step
tomN. '14

Tom Neely

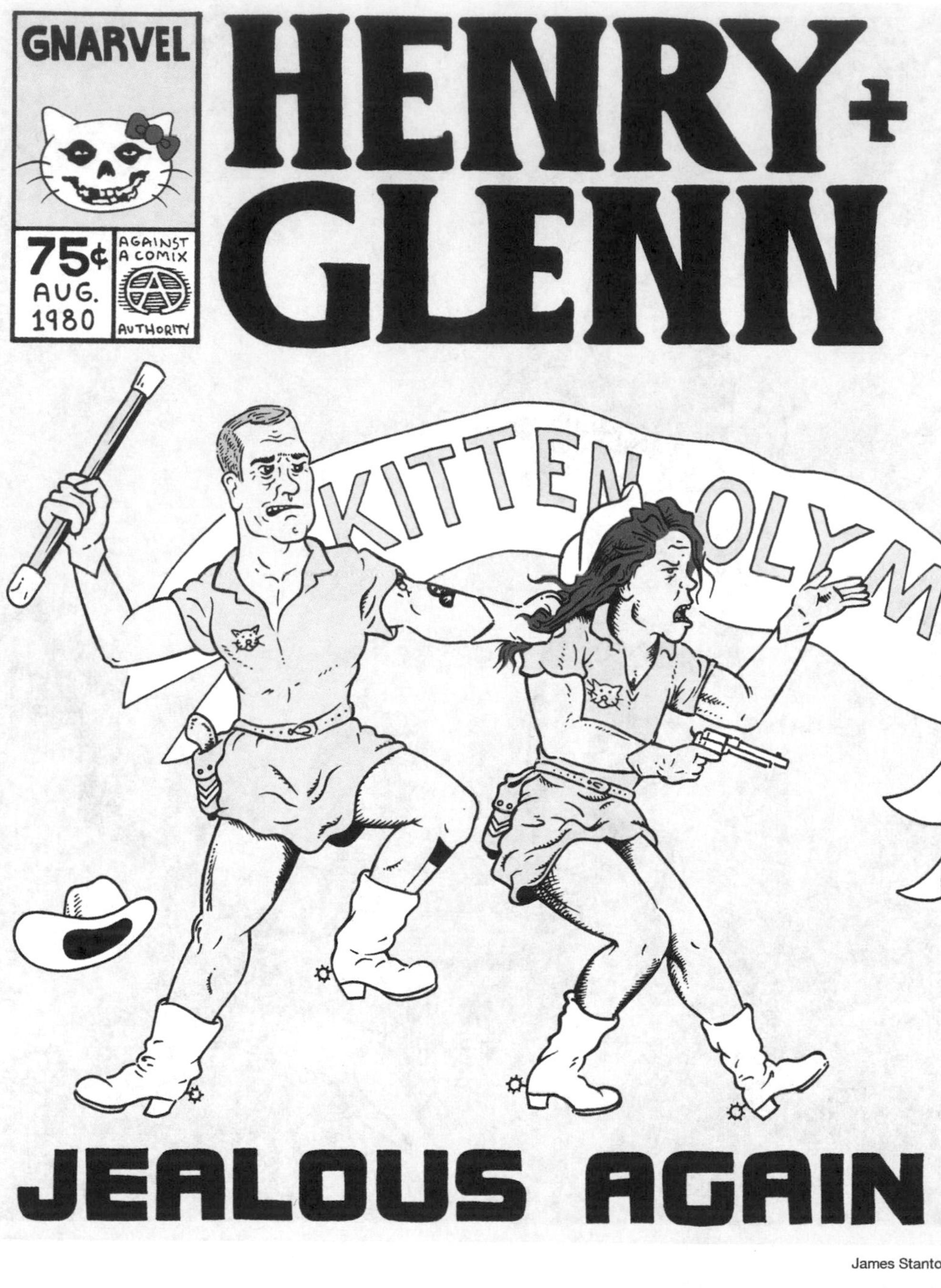
GNARVEL
HENRY + GLENN
75¢
AUG.
1980
AGAINST
A COMIX
AUTHORITY
KITTEN OLYM
JEALOUS AGAIN

James Stanton

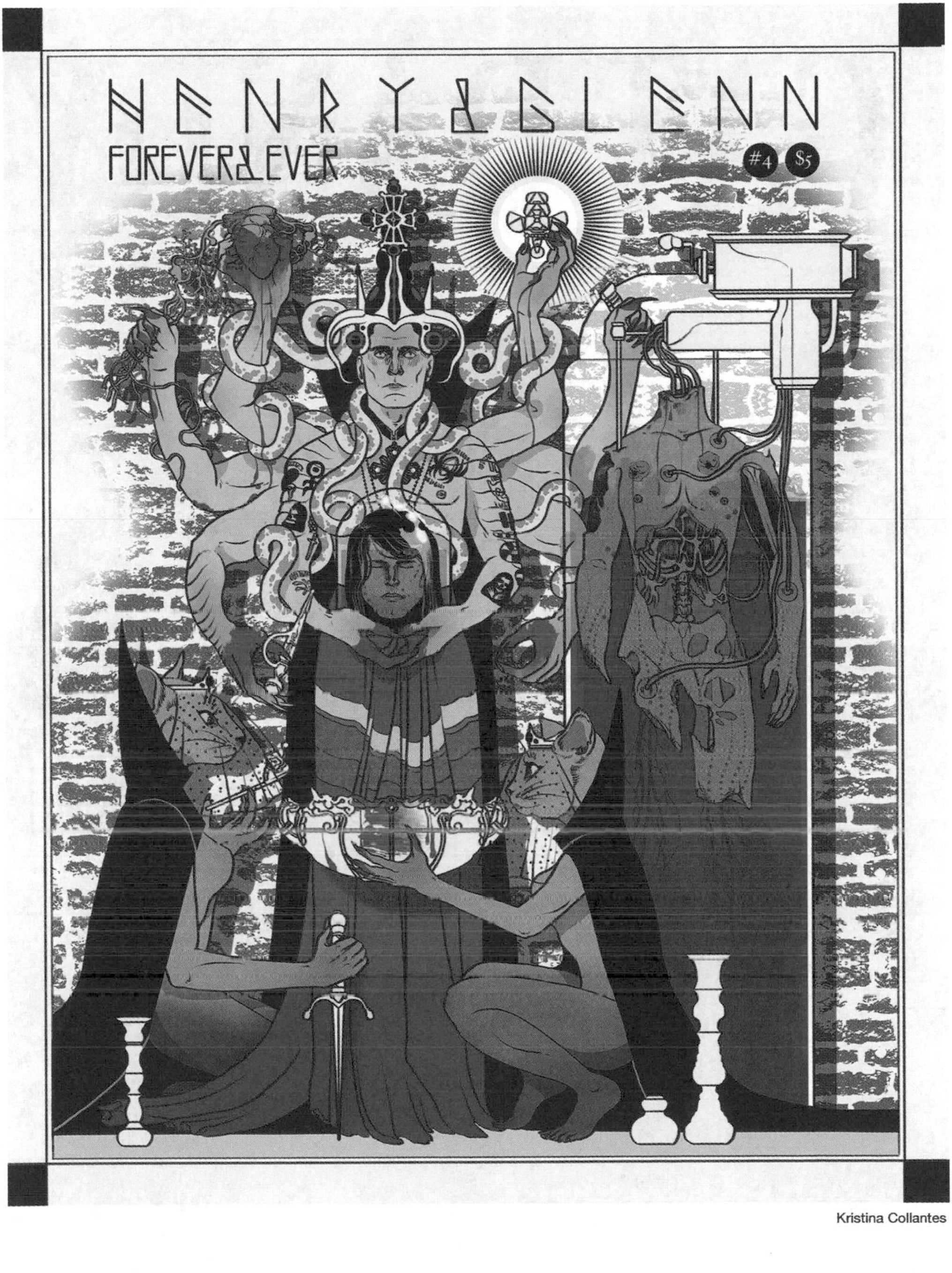
HENRY & GLENN
FOREVER & EVER
#4
$5

Kristina Collantes

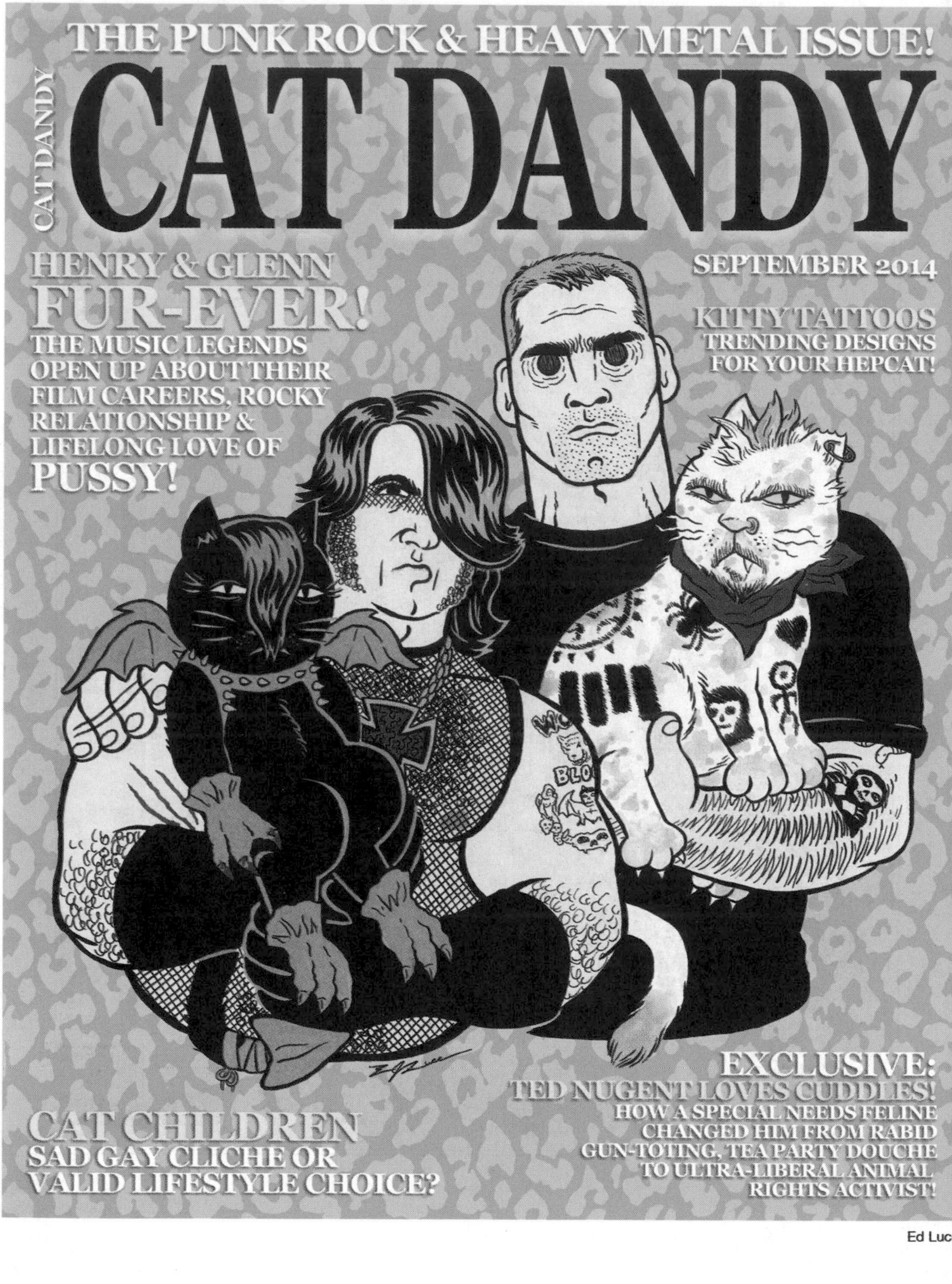
THE PUNK ROCK & HEAVY METAL ISSUE!
CAT DANDY
CAT DANDY
SEPTEMBER 2014
HENRY & GLENN
FUR-EVER!
THE MUSIC LEGENDS OPEN UP ABOUT THEIR FILM CAREERS, ROCKY RELATIONSHIP & LIFELONG LOVE OF
PUSSY!
KITTY TATTOOS
TRENDING DESIGNS FOR YOUR HEPCAT!
EXCLUSIVE:
TED NUGENT LOVES CUDDLES!
HOW A SPECIAL NEEDS FELINE CHANGED HIM FROM RABID GUN-TOTING, TEA PARTY DOUCHE TO ULTRA-LIBERAL ANIMAL RIGHTS ACTIVIST!
CAT CHILDREN
SAD GAY CLICHE OR VALID LIFESTYLE CHOICE?

Ed Luce

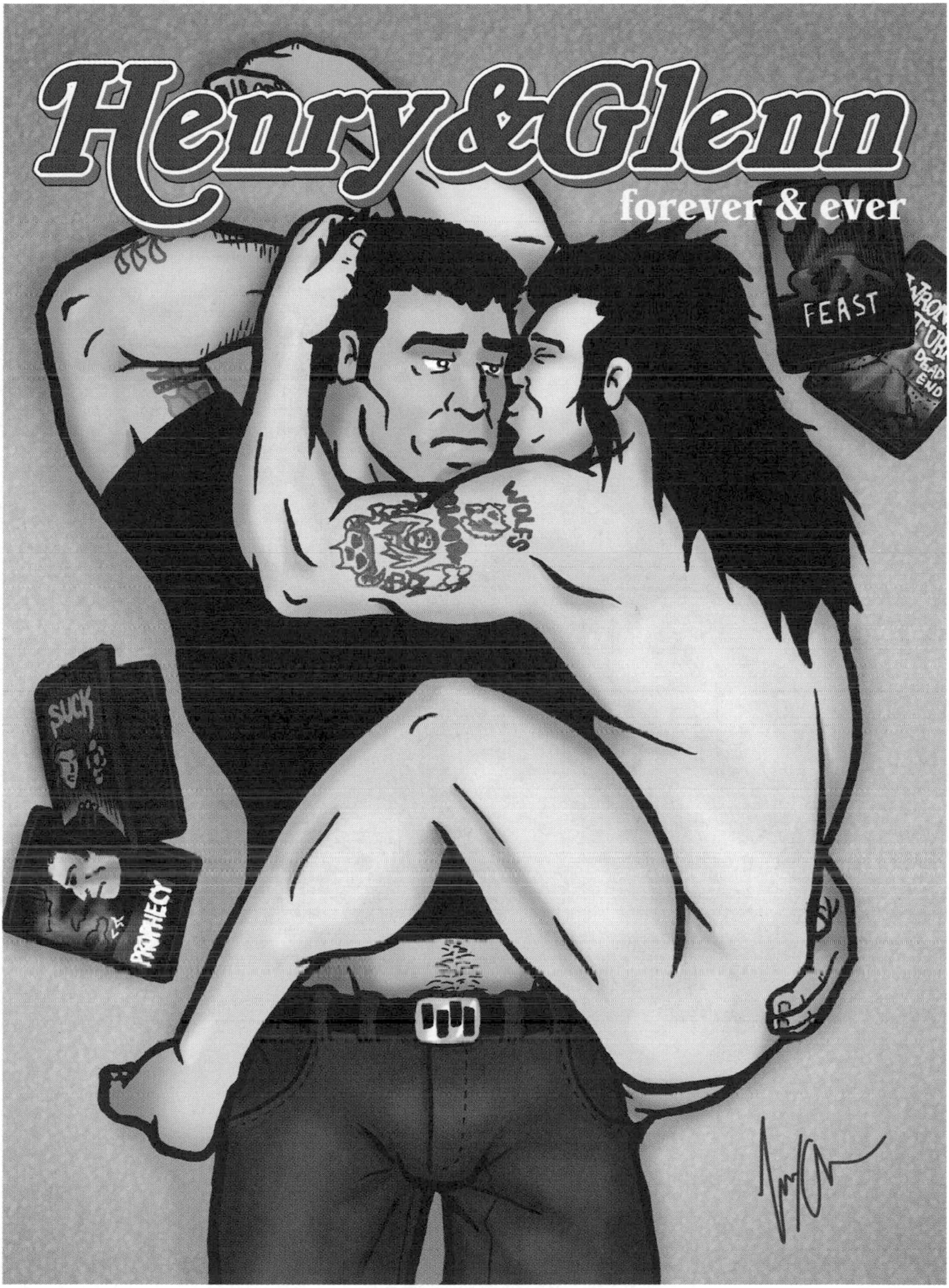
Henry&Glenn
forever & ever
FEAST
DEAD END
SUCK
PROPHECY
WOLFS

Jeremy Owen

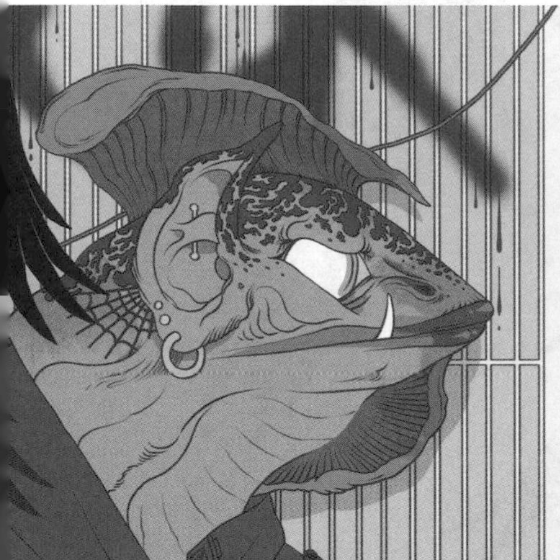

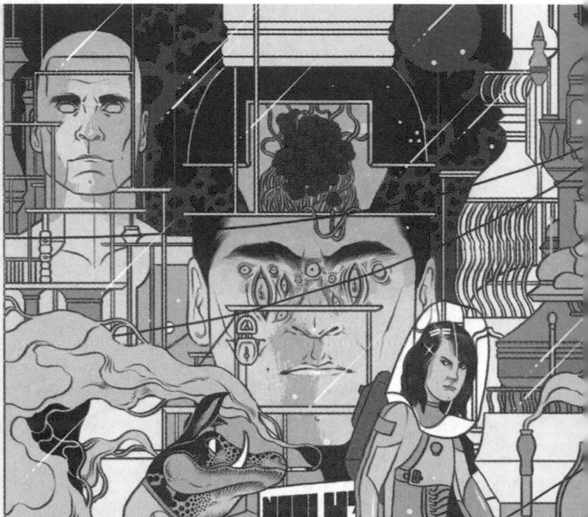

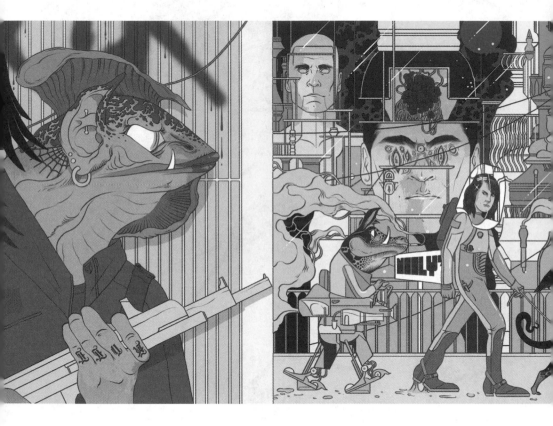

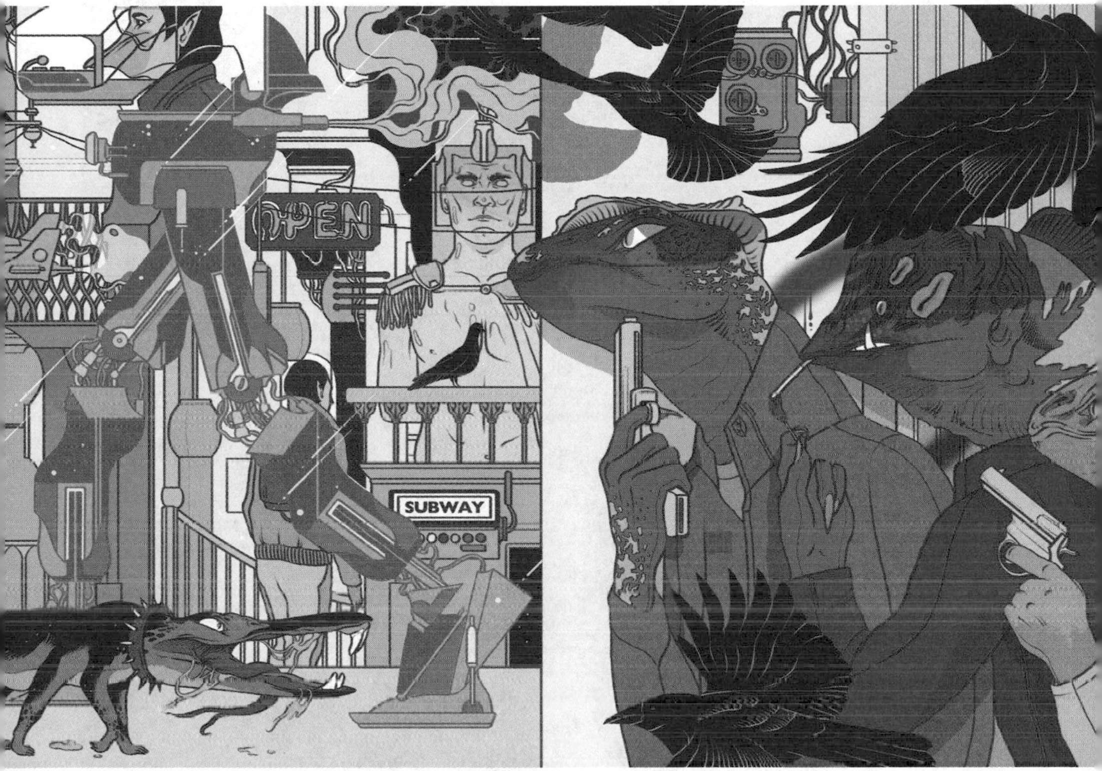
OPEN
SUBWAY

KRISTINA COLLANTES

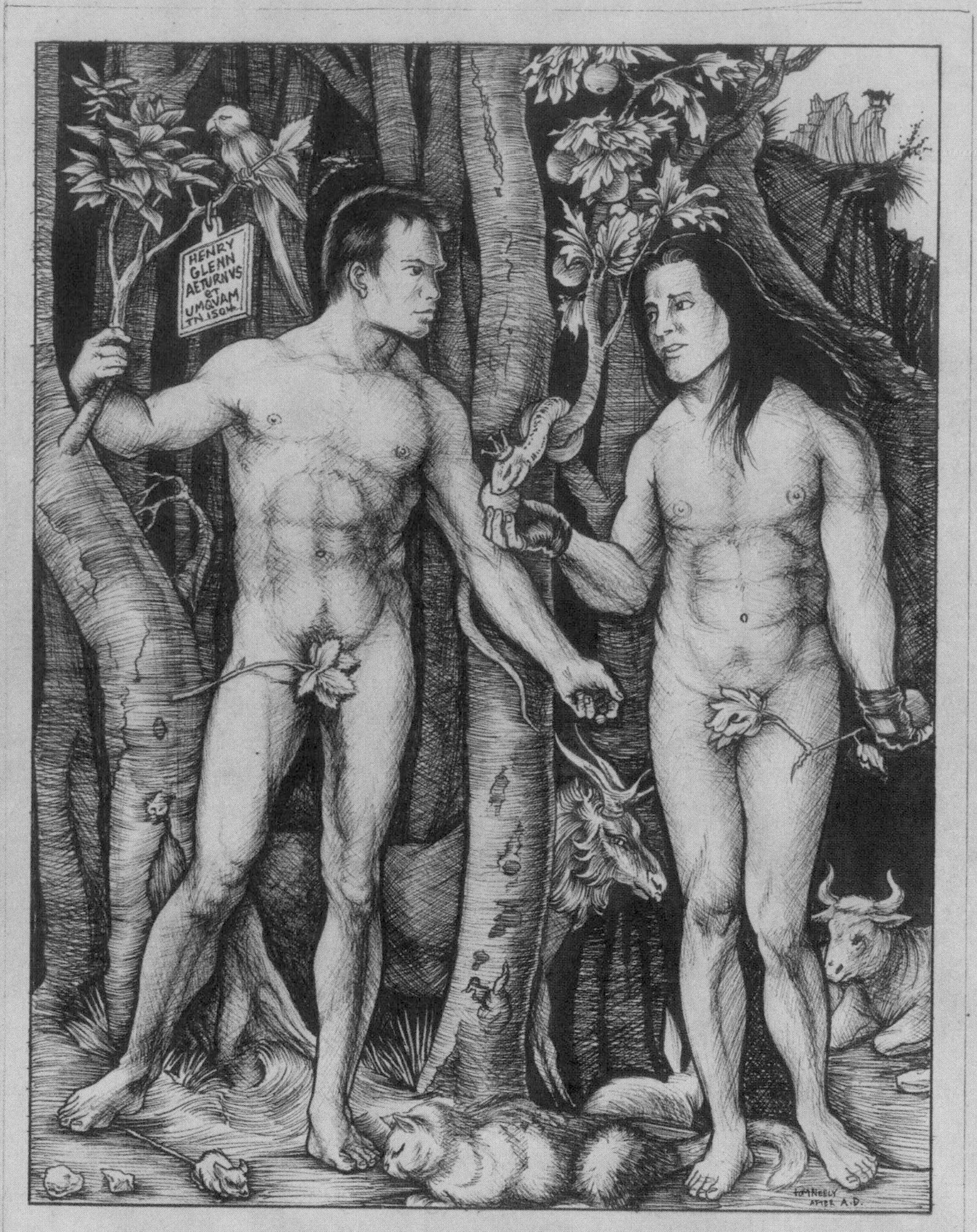
HENRY
GLENN
AETURNVS
et
UMQVAM
TN 1504

In the beginning, there was Henry and Glenn...

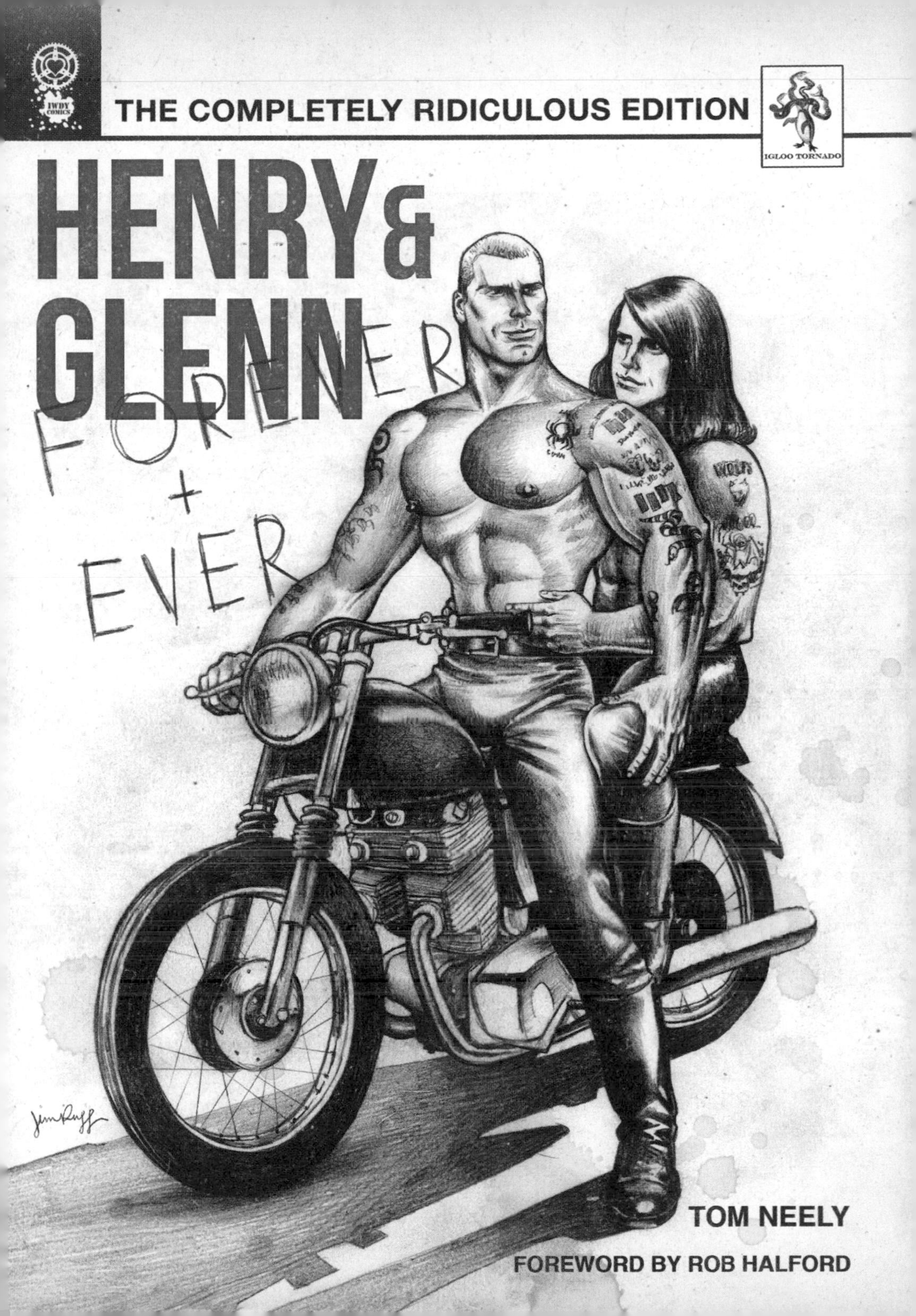
IWDY COMICS
THE COMPLETELY RIDICULOUS EDITION
IGLOO TORNADO
HENRY &
GLENN
FOREVER
+
EVER
TOM NEELY
FOREWORD BY ROB HALFORD

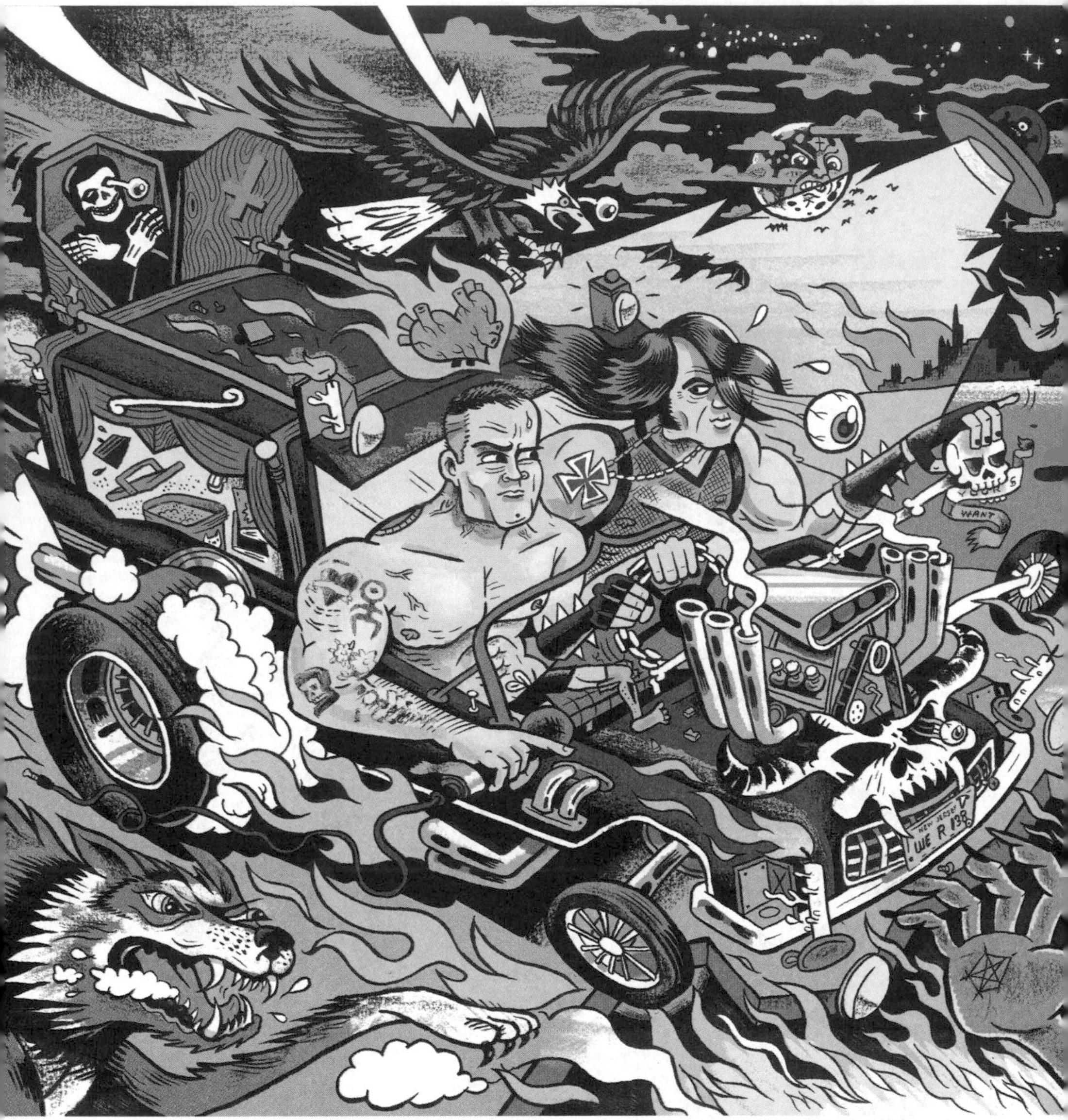
YOUR'S
WANT
NEW JERSEY
WE R 138

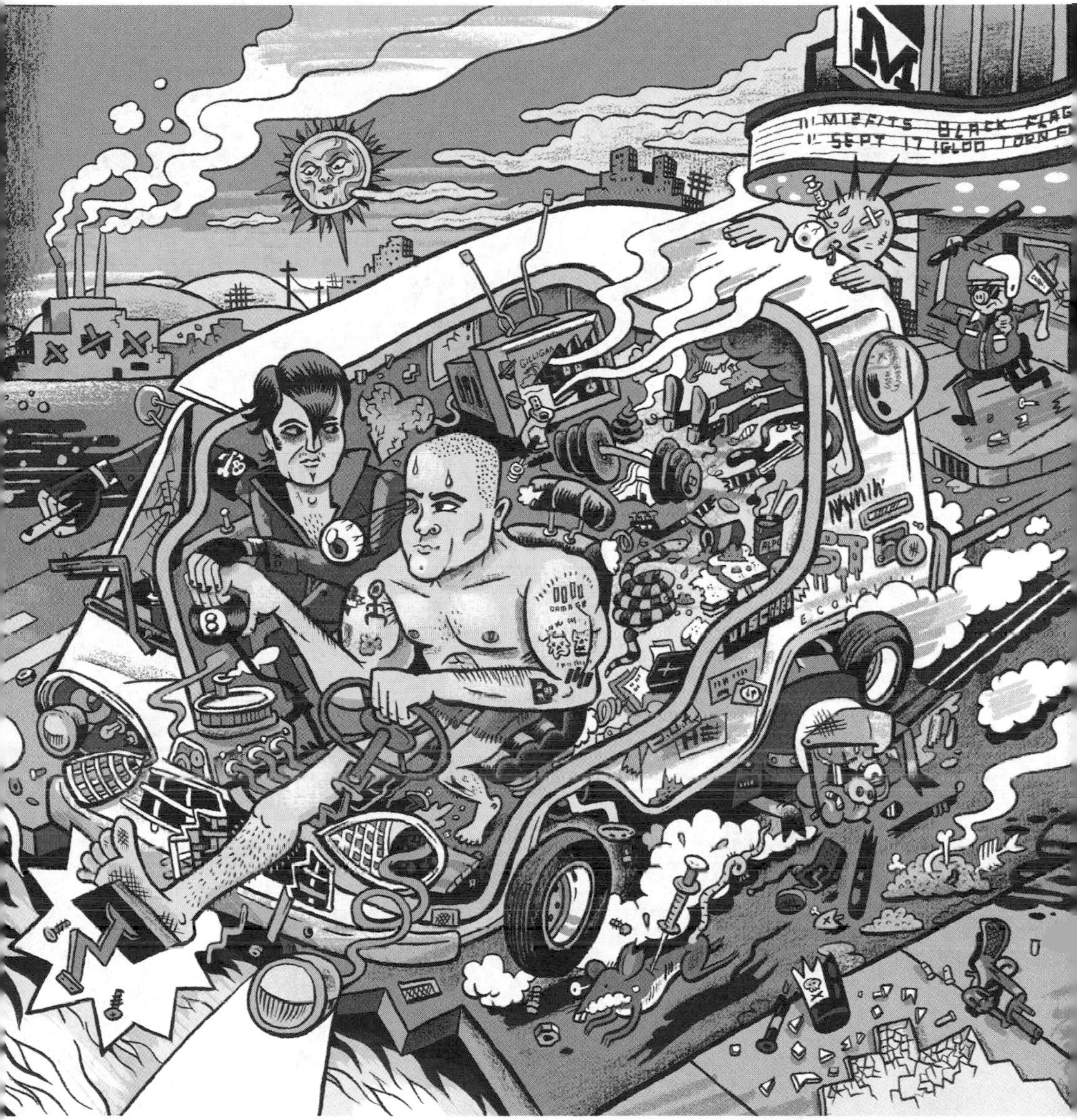
MISFITS BLACK FLAG
SEPT 17 IGLOO
GILLIGAN
DAMAGE

DAN ZETTWOCH

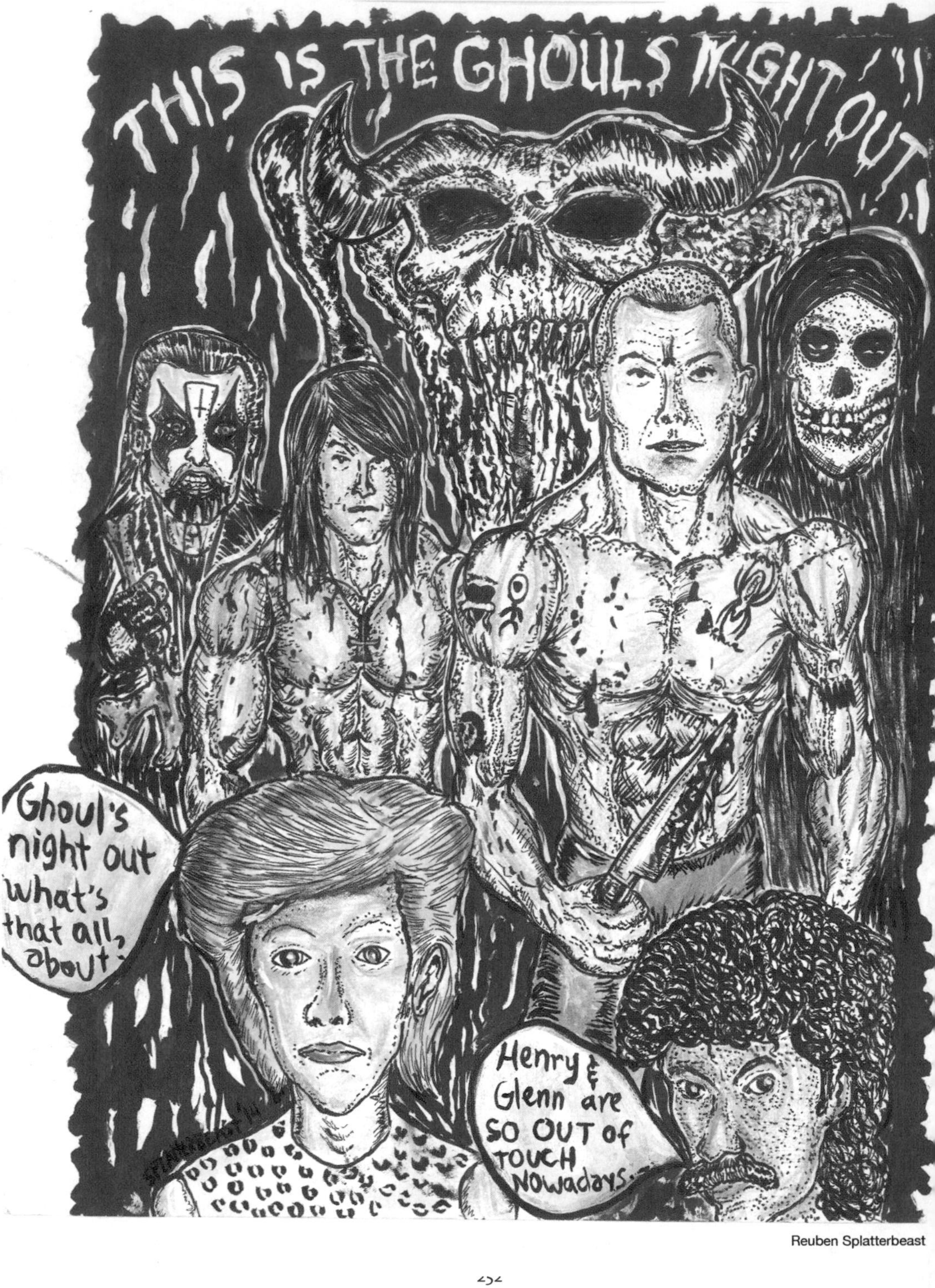
THIS IS THE GHOULS NIGHT OUT!!
Ghoul's night out what's that all about?
Henry & Glenn are SO OUT of TOUCH Nowadays.

Reuben Splatterbeast

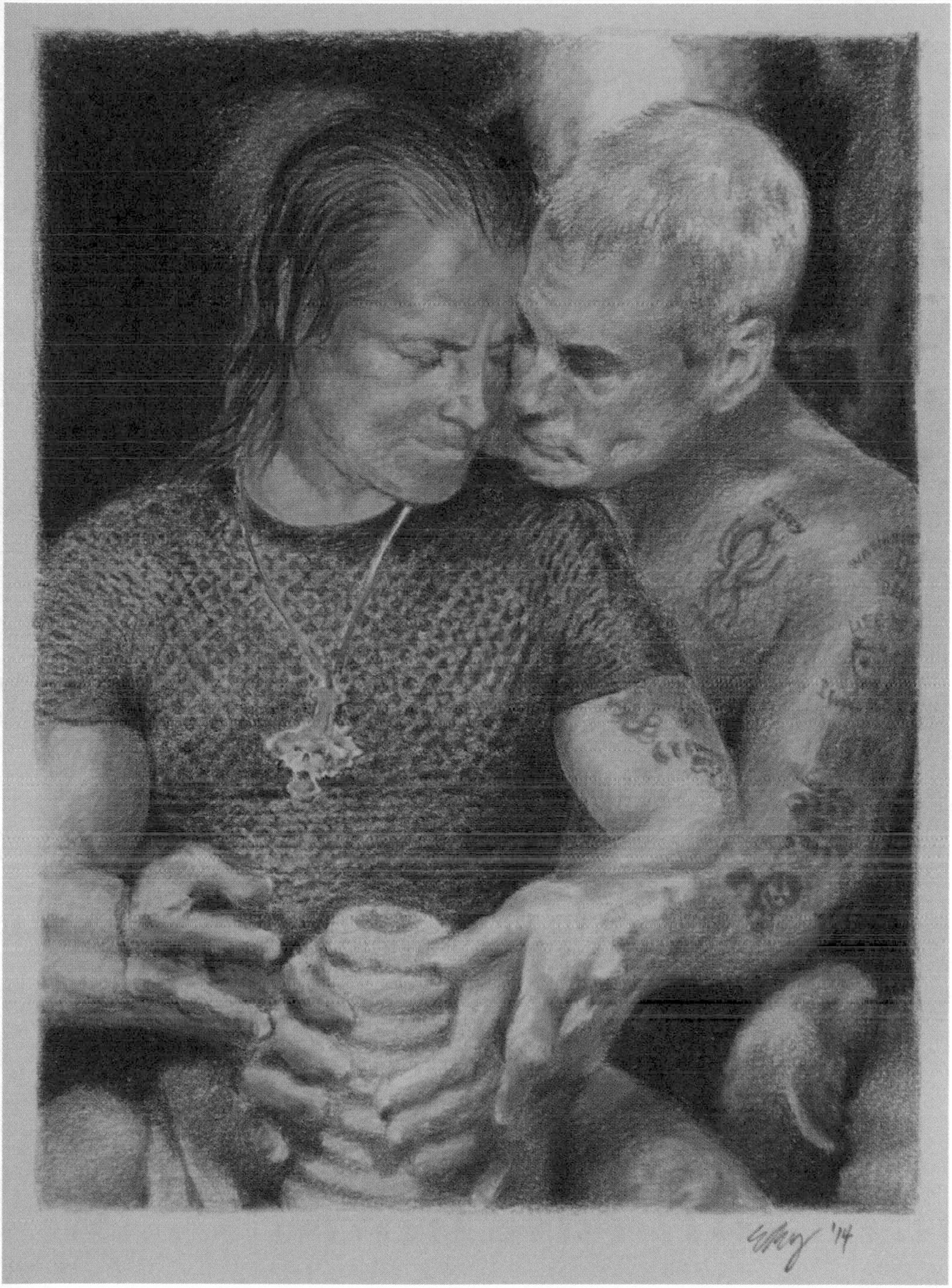

Eric Yahnker

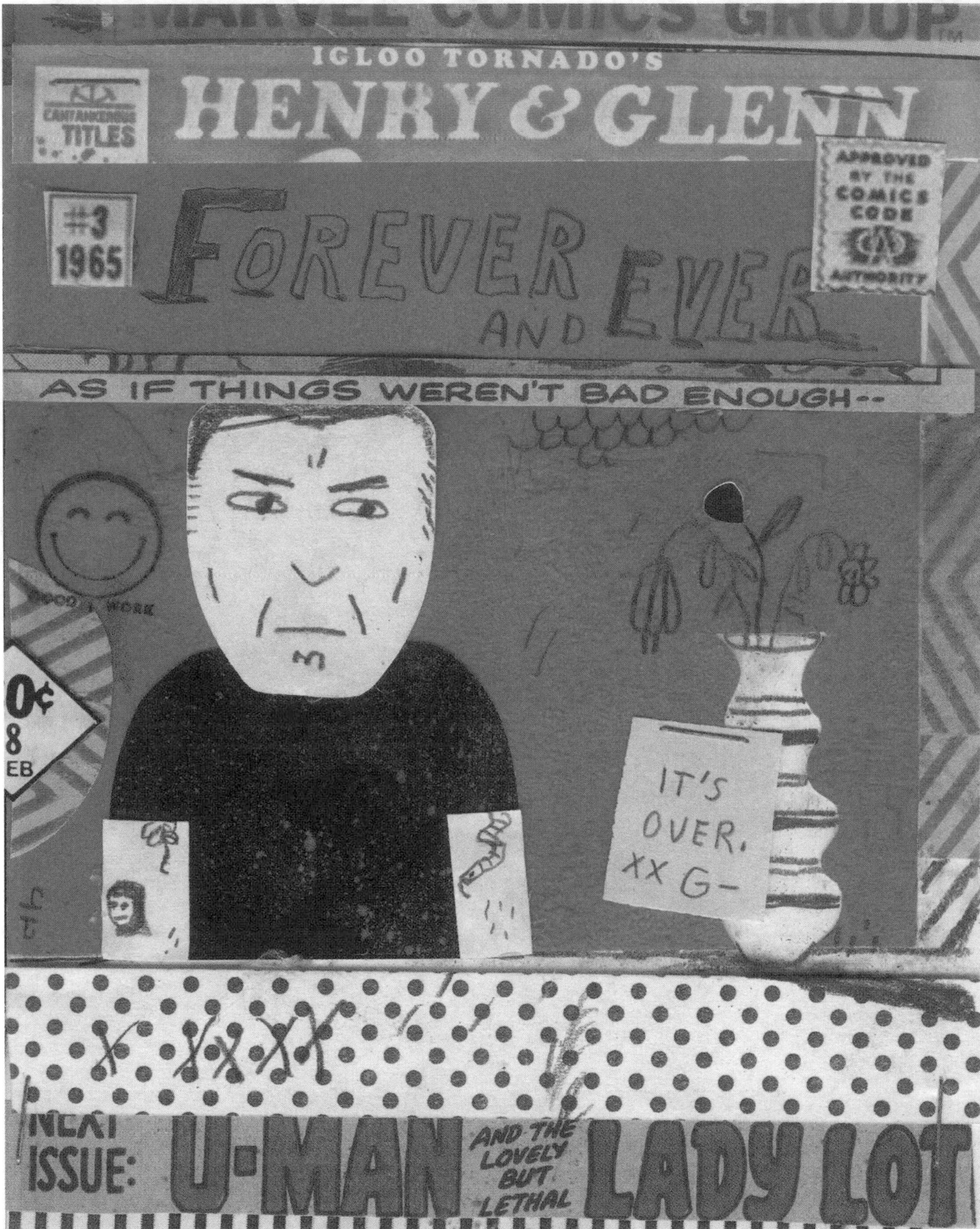

IGLOO TORNADO'S
HENRY & GLENN
APPROVED BY THE COMICS CODE AUTHORITY
#3
1965
FOREVER AND EVER
AS IF THINGS WEREN'T BAD ENOUGH--
IT'S OVER. XX G-
ISSUE:
U-MAN
AND THE LOVELY BUT LETHAL
LADY LOT

Mark Todd

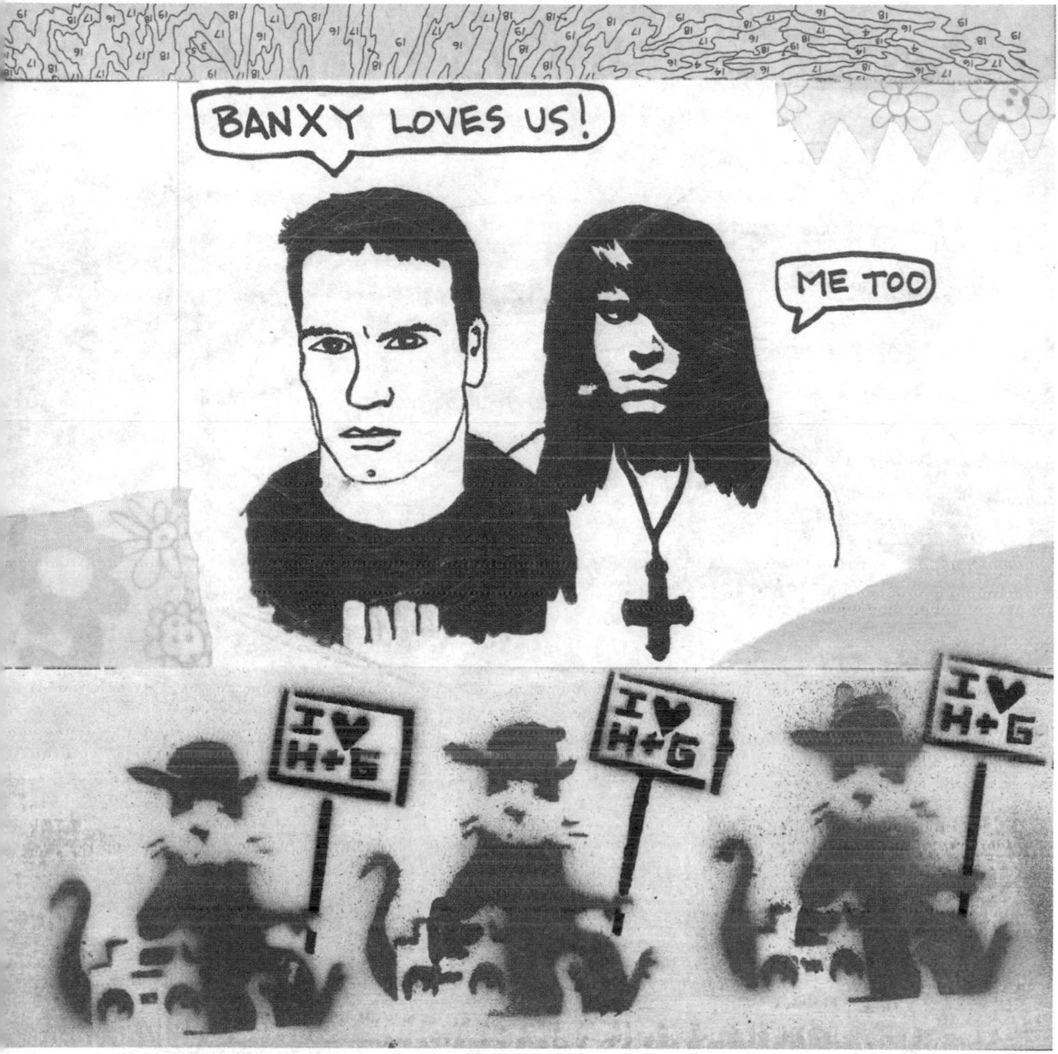
BANXY LOVES US!
ME TOO
I ♥ H+G
I ♥ H+G
I ♥ H+G

Scot Nobles

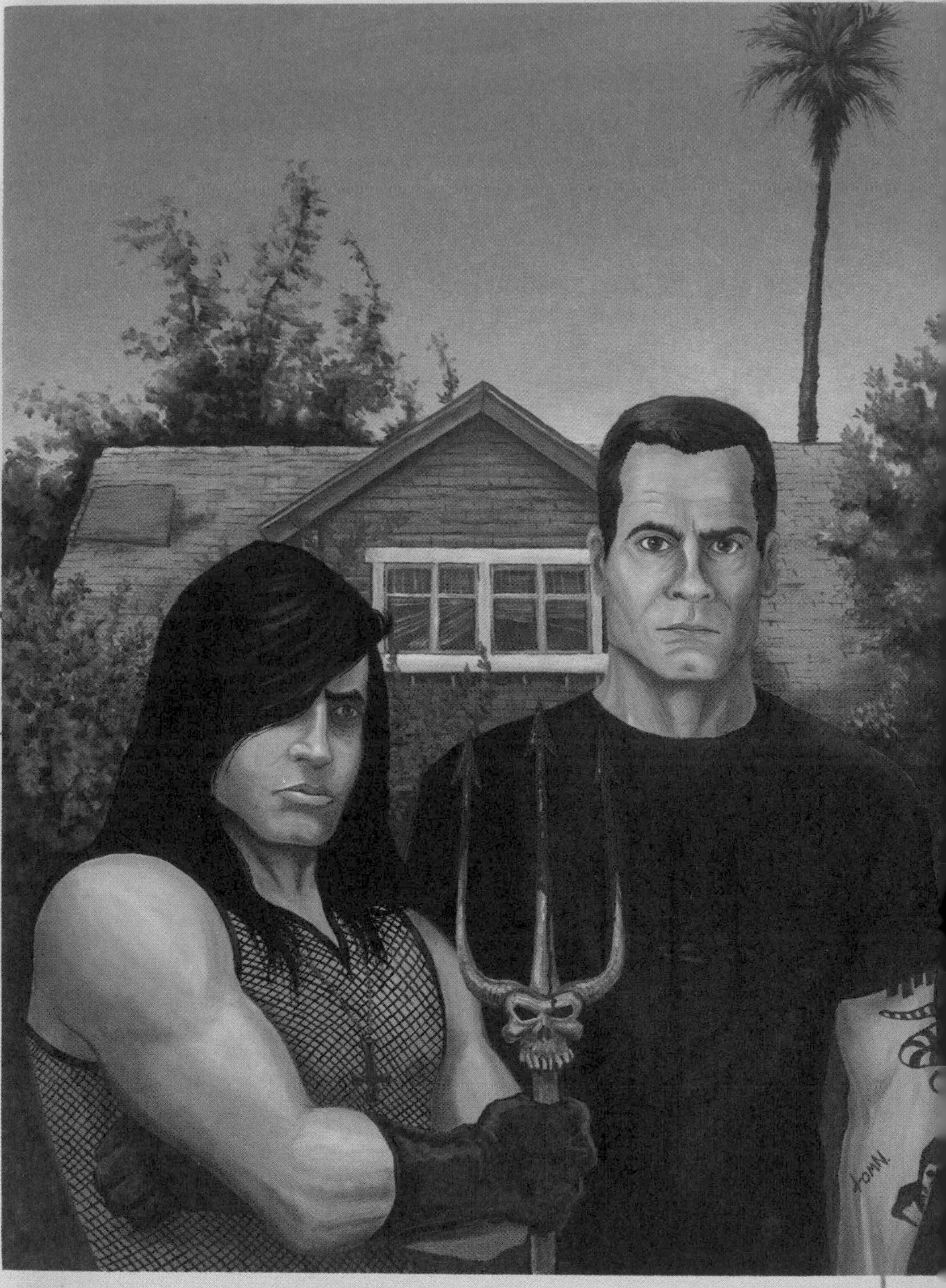

TOM NEELY

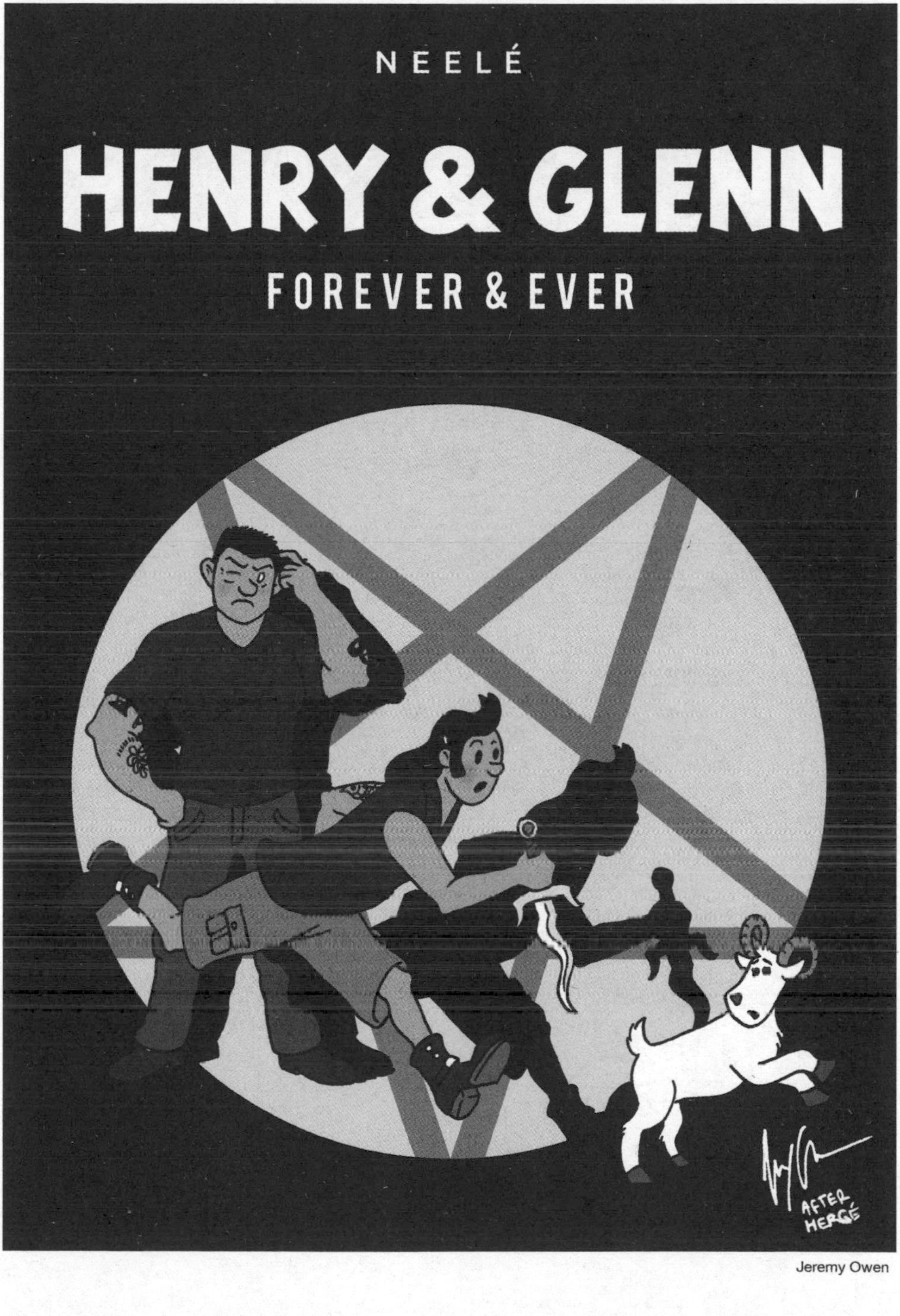
NEELÉ
HENRY & GLENN
FOREVER & EVER
AFTER HERGÉ

Jeremy Owen

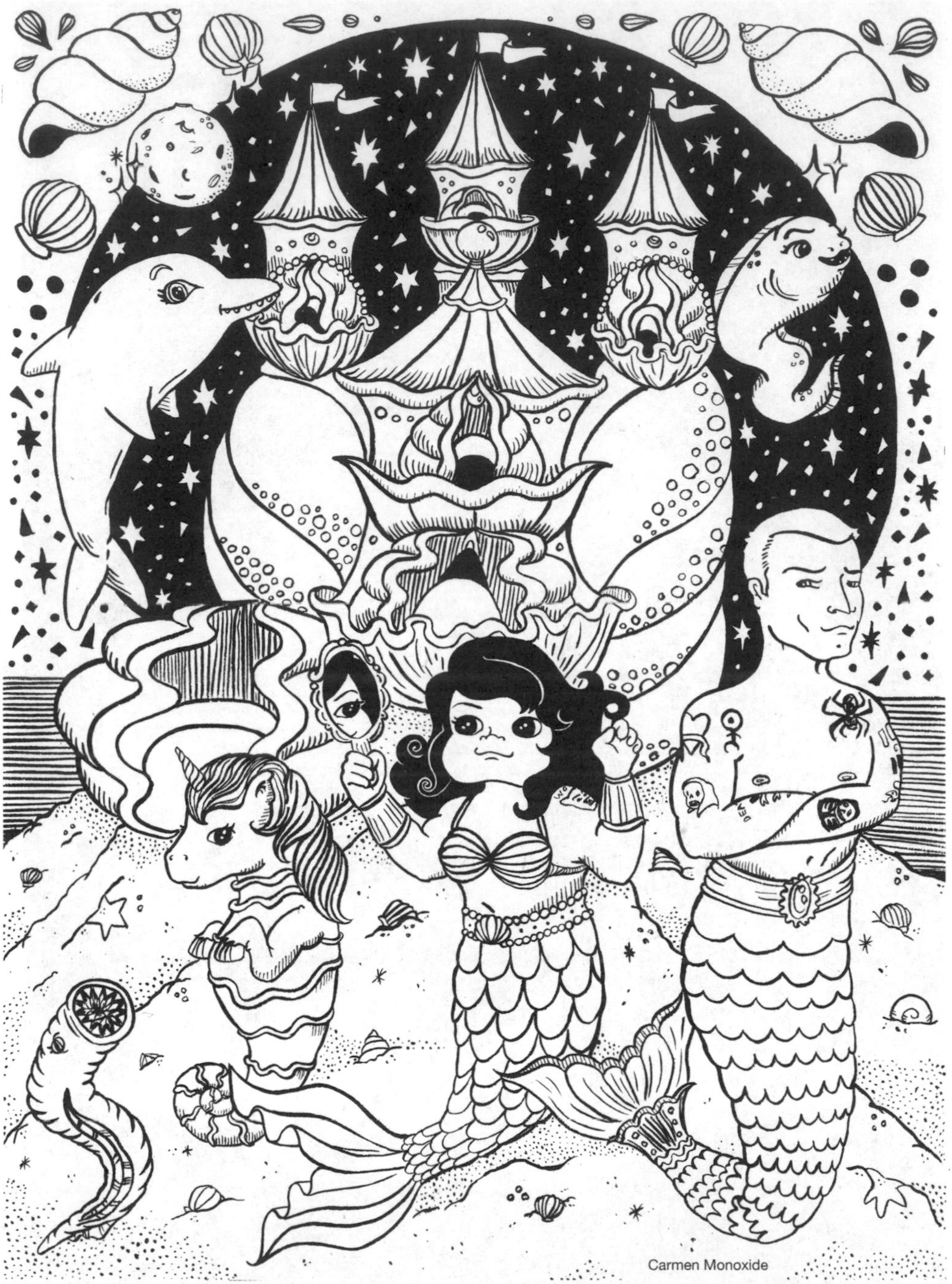
Carmen Monoxide

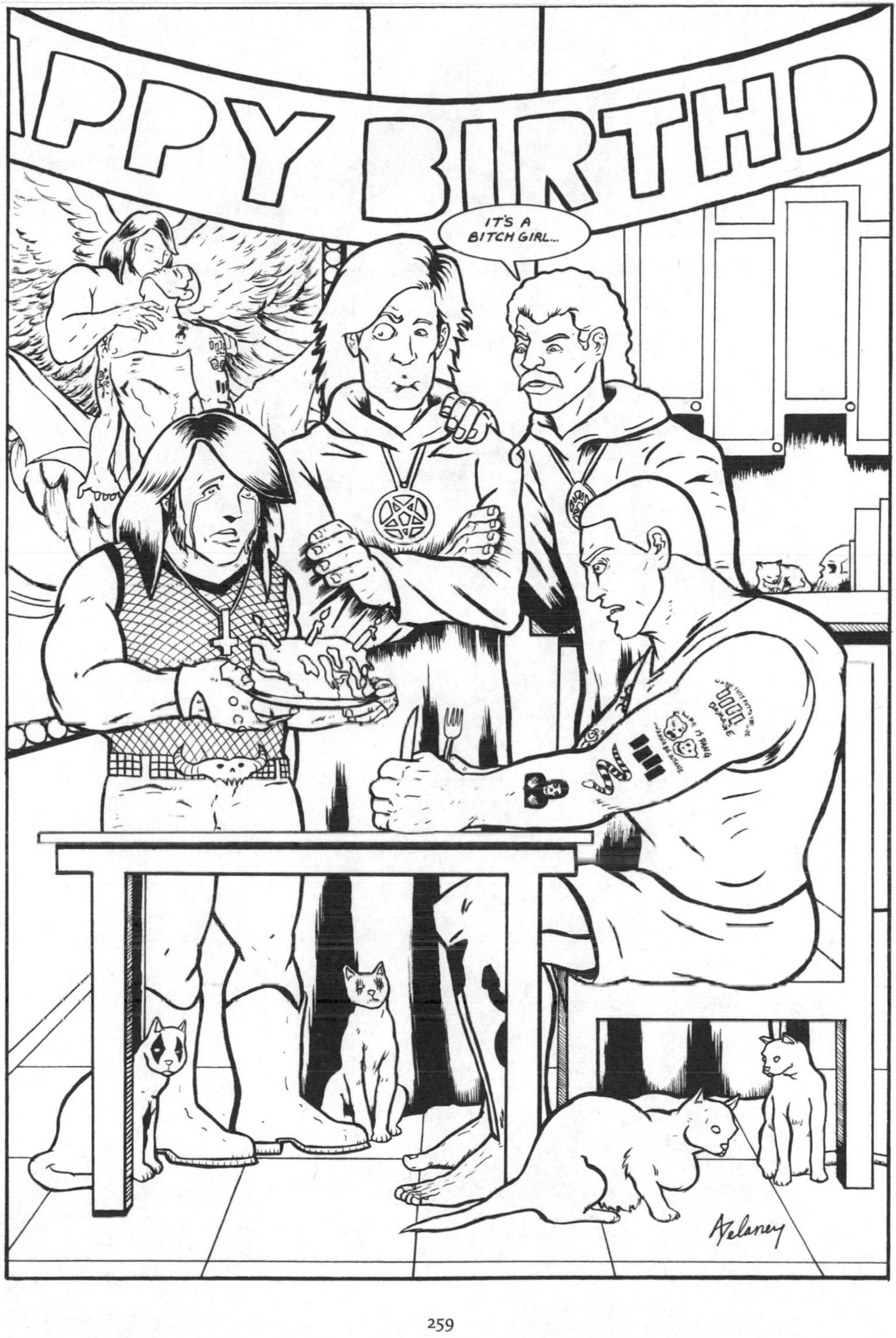
PPY BIRTHD
IT'S A BITCH GIRL...

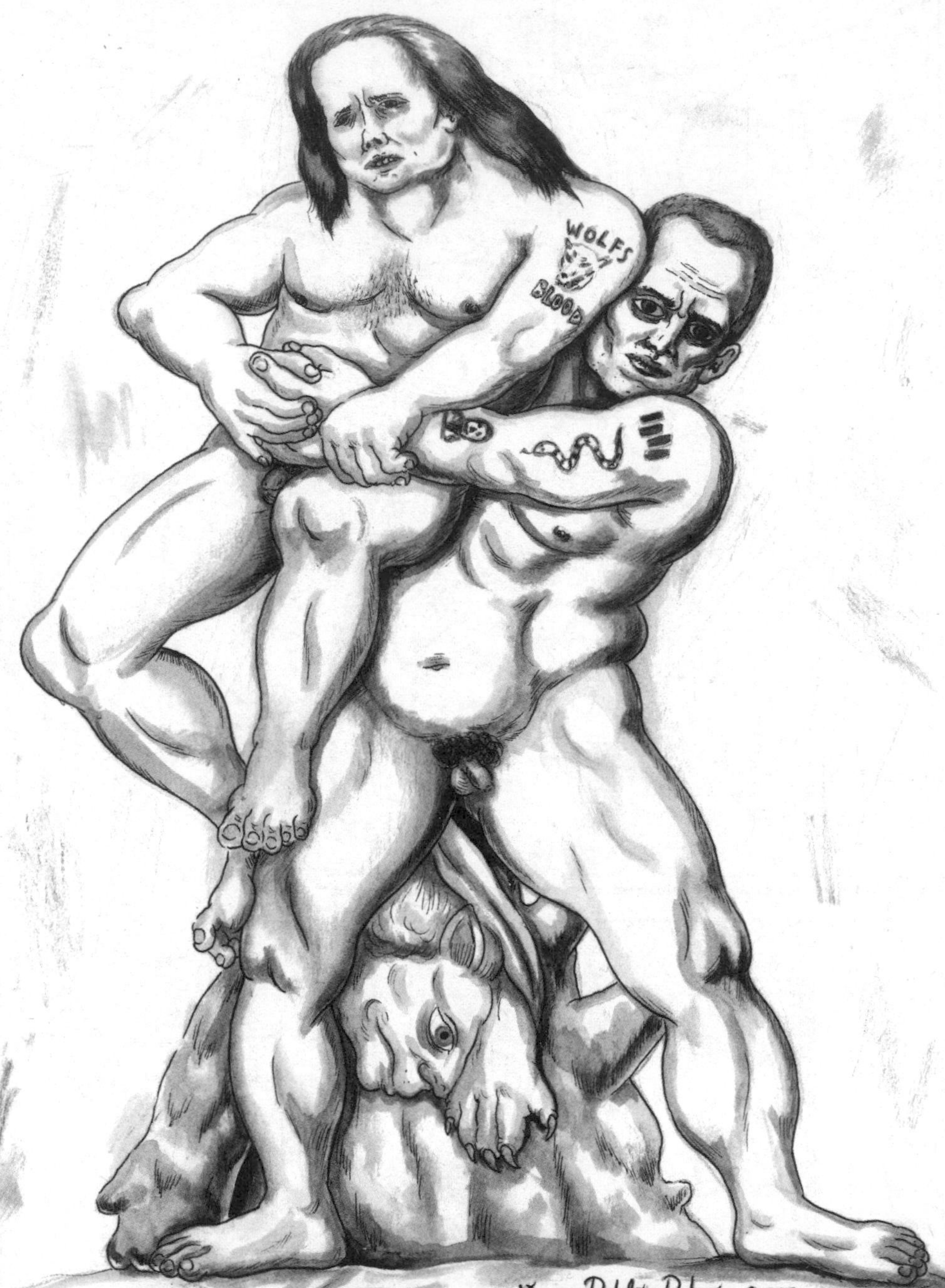
WOLFS
BLOOD
Don Pablo Pedro 2017

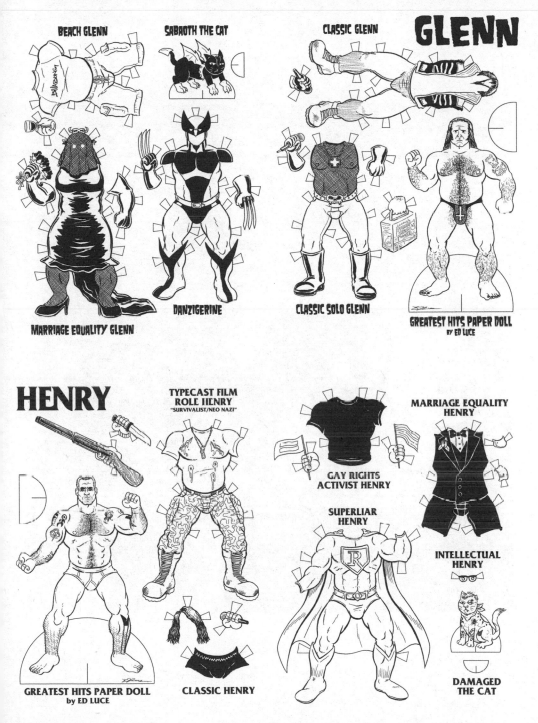

BEACH GLENN

SABAOTH THE CAT

CLASSIC GLENN

GLENN

MARRIAGE EQUALITY GLENN

DANZIGERINE

CLASSIC SOLO GLENN

GREATEST HITS PAPER DOLL
by ED LUCE

HENRY

TYPECAST FILM
ROLE HENRY
"SURVIVALIST/NEO NAZI"

MARRIAGE EQUALITY
HENRY

GAY RIGHTS
ACTIVIST HENRY

SUPERLIAR
HENRY

INTELLECTUAL
HENRY

GREATEST HITS PAPER DOLL
by ED LUCE

CLASSIC HENRY

DAMAGED
THE CAT

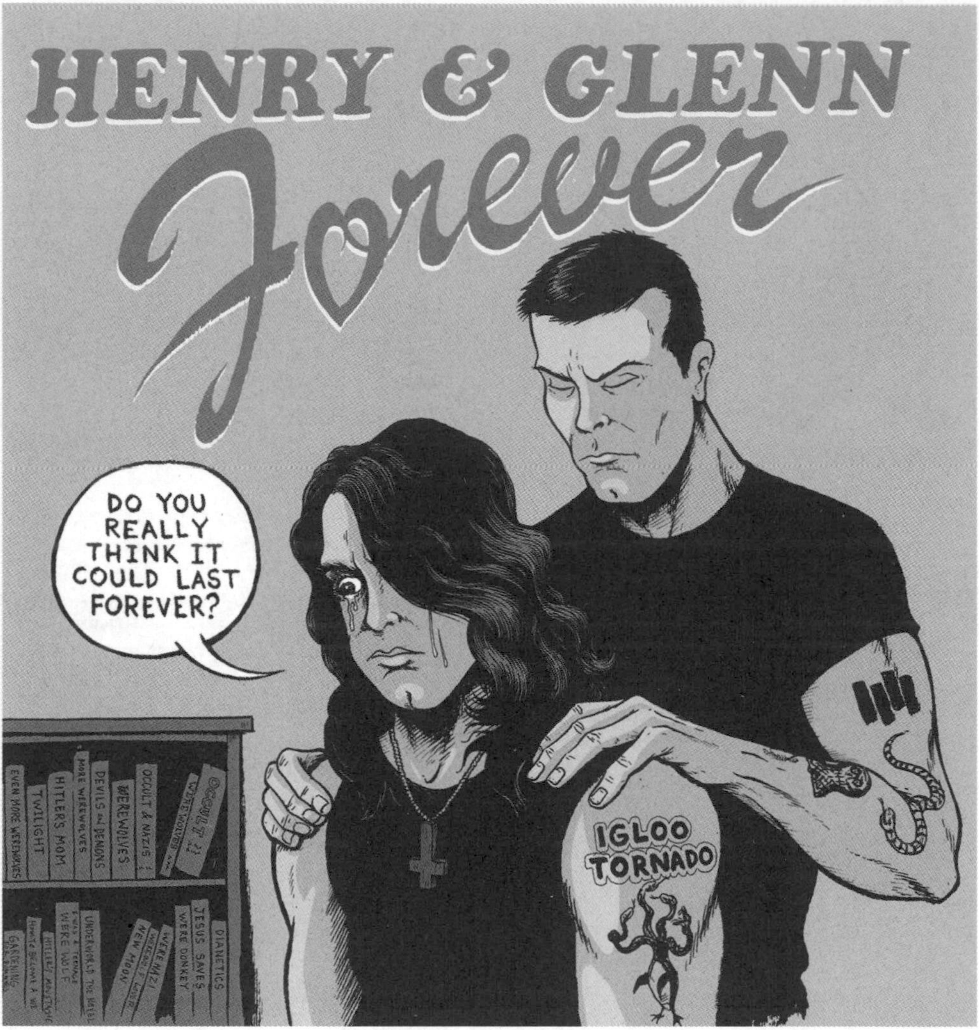
HENRY & GLENN
Forever
DO YOU REALLY THINK IT COULD LAST FOREVER?
TWILIGHT
HITLER'S MOM
MORE WEREWOLVES
DEVILS and DEMONS
WEREWOLVES
OCCULT & NAZIS
DIANETICS
JESUS SAVES
WERE DONKEY
WERE NAZI
NEW MOON
WERE WOLF
IGLOO
TORNADO

WHAT A LONG STRANGE TRIP...

People often ask me about the ACTUAL story of how this all happened...

One night while my "Art Fraternity , " The Igloo Tornado , and I were having some beers and doodling on napkins and sketchbooks together at our favorite bar Bigfoot Lodge, Gin Stevens joked: "We should do something like Tom Of Finland art, but with Henry Rollins and Glenn Danzig..." and I drunkenly exclaimed: "Yes! We are going to do this!"

And this stoopid book you hold in your hands was born!

One of the first things I drew was the "I've got something to say..." bathtub-abortion gag and we all laughed at the horror. The artist formerly known as Dino-Fucker complained that he didn't know anything about the real Henry and Glenn, so he drew them as Cyclops and Wolverine asking: "Does my butt look fat?" Scot Nobles randomly whipped out a portrait of Hall & Oates, to which I responded: "You know there were rumors that they were secret Satan worshippers? We should make them the Satanic next door neighbors..."And we all laughed into the night as we started doodling dumb drawings of them together. By the end of the night it had morphed from it's "Tom of Finland" origins into something else entirely. It seemed like the dumbest idea we ever had! So naturally it turned into a cult-hit among music nerds and punk/metal fans all over the world, selling over 100,000 books and launching my career sideways to new successes while causing my childhood heroes Henry Rollins and Glenn Danzig to not only know my name... but kinda hate me?!!

It's been a long, strange trip, but I am very grateful for all of it. What began as bar-napkin doodles between four friends, turned into a cult-phenomenon, and it all began with the following pages of crude, dumb jokes about two of our favorite punk, musclehead icons.

In a world full of trolls and snarky hate, I hope you see this was all done with the dumb/best of intentions... I love and respect both the real Henry and Glenn with deep regard, but as Sonic Youth once taught us: "Kill yr idols," and as Bongo once learned about love: "A bear likes to say it with a slap."

The following pages are all of the original Henry & Glenn gag drawings and bar-napkin doodles by The Igloo Tornado: Gin Stevens, Tom Neely, Scot Nobles and the artist formerly known as Dino-fucker. Enjoy!

- Tom Neely, 2017

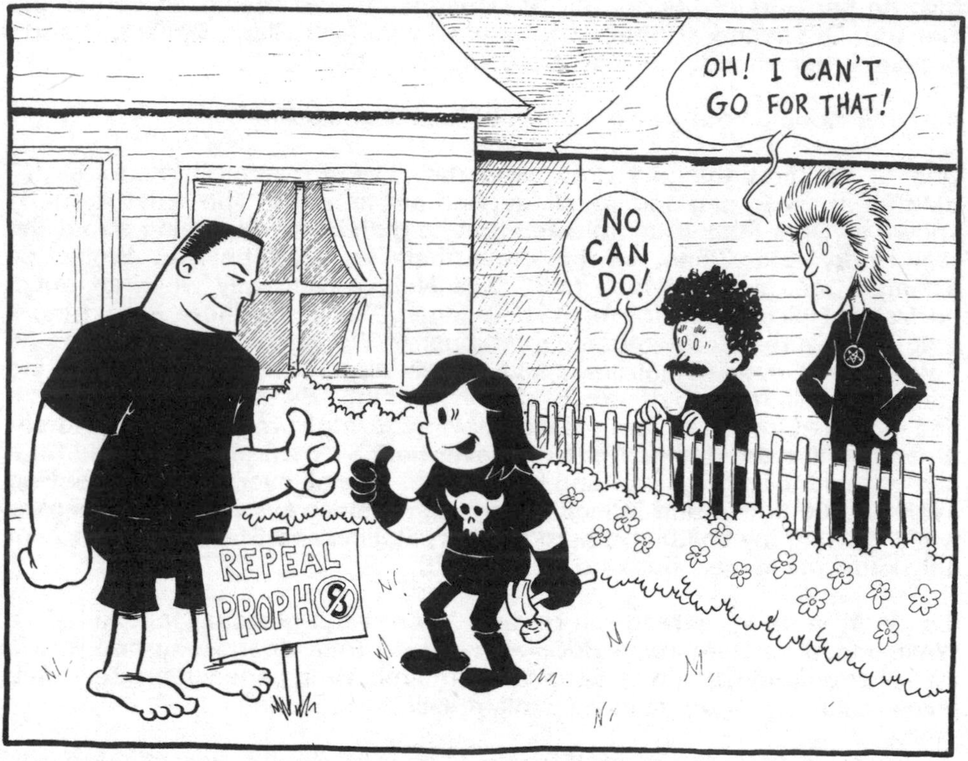
NO CAN DO!
OH! I CAN'T GO FOR THAT!
REPEAL PROP H

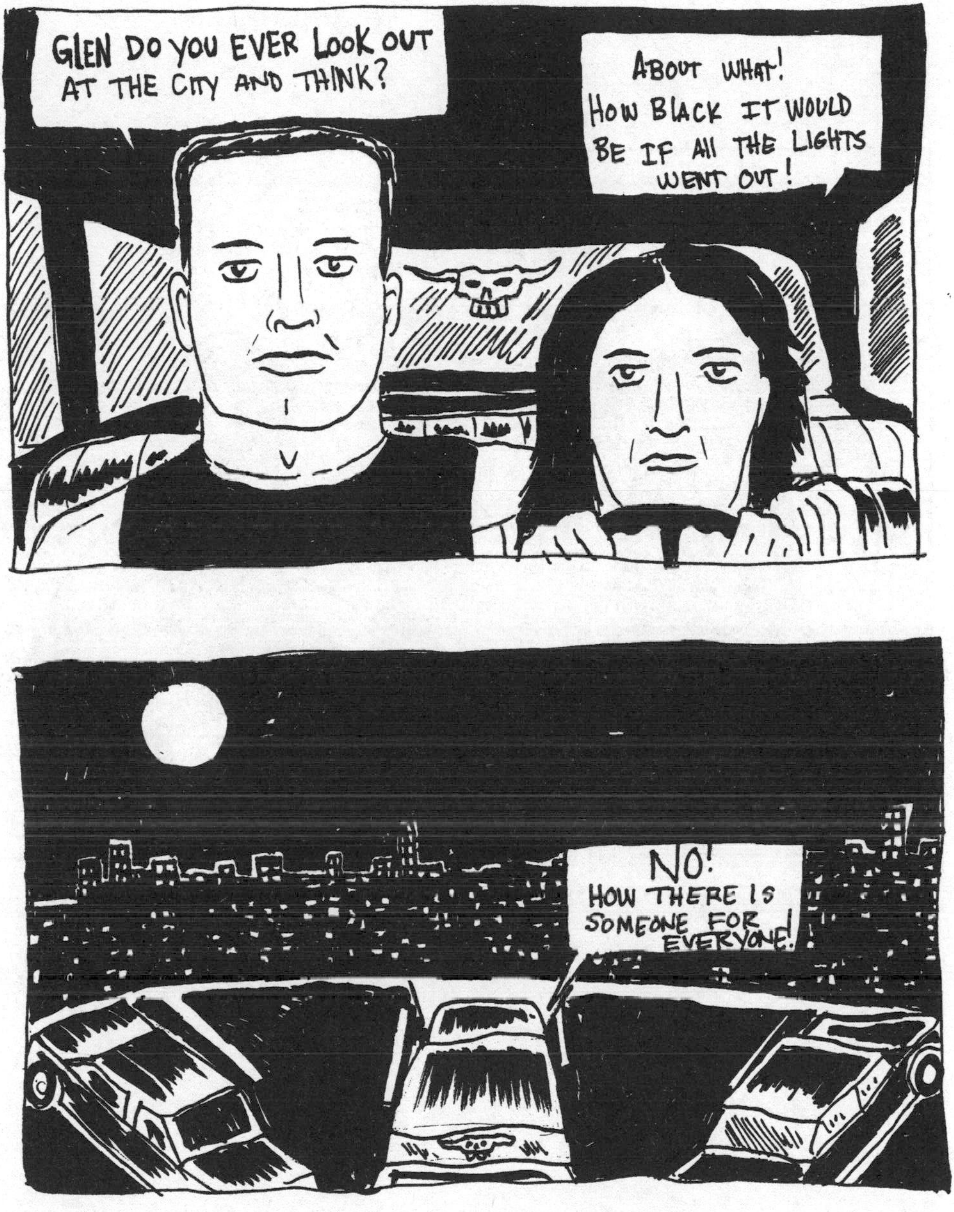
GLEN DO YOU EVER LOOK OUT AT THE CITY AND THINK?
ABOUT WHAT! HOW BLACK IT WOULD BE IF ALL THE LIGHTS WENT OUT!
NO! HOW THERE IS SOMEONE FOR EVERYONE!

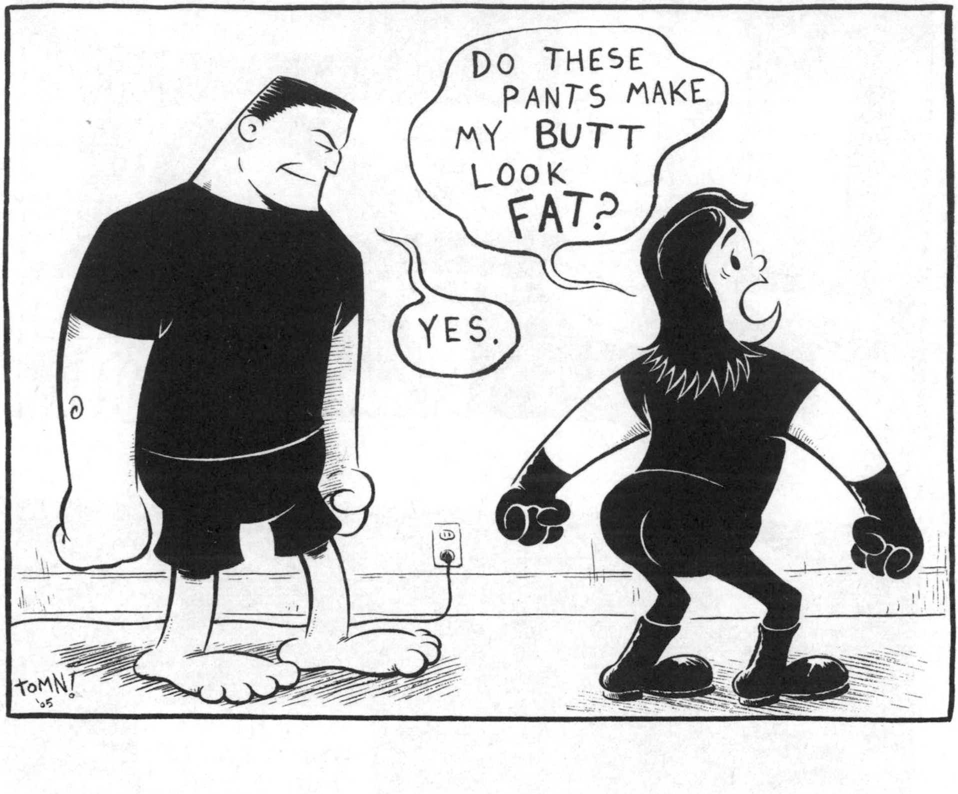
DO THESE PANTS MAKE MY BUTT LOOK FAT?
YES.
TOMN! '05

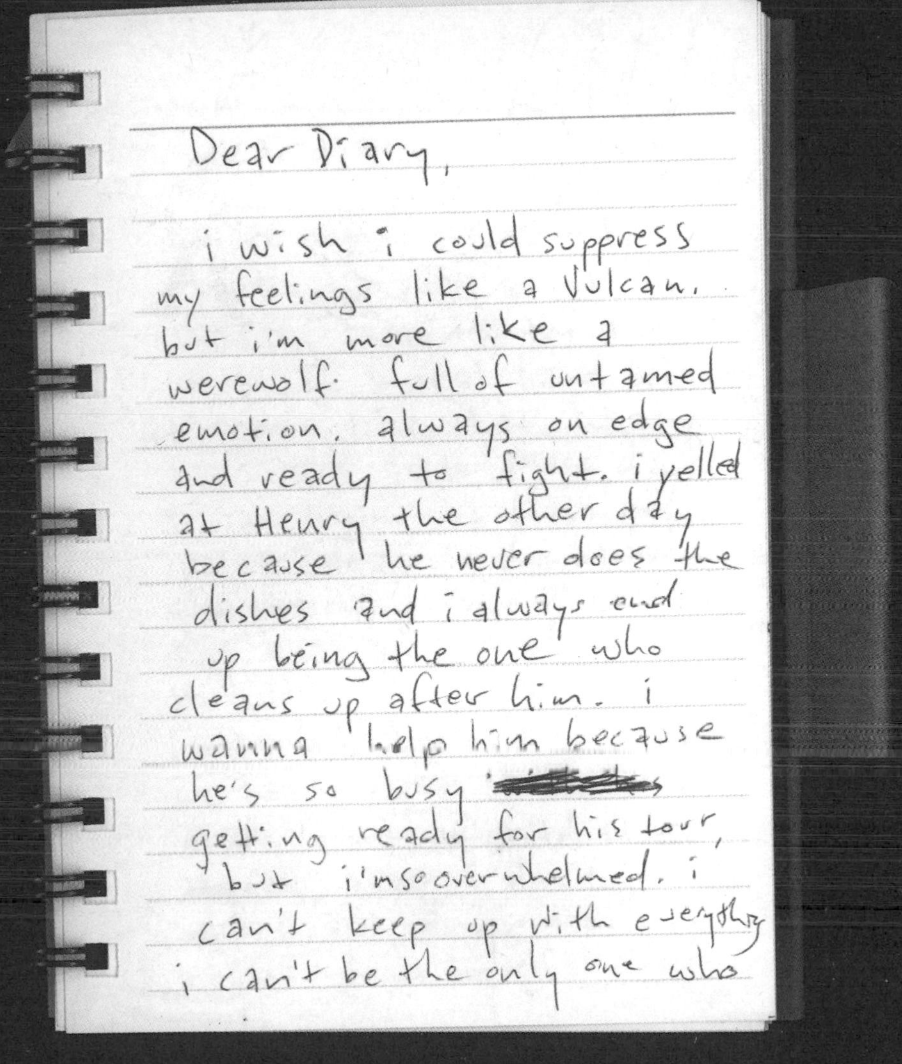
Dear Diary,
i wish i could suppress
my feelings like a Vulcan.
but i'm more like a
werewolf. full of untamed
emotion, always on edge
and ready to fight. i yelled
at Henry the other day
because he never does the
dishes and i always end
up being the one who
cleans up after him. i
wanna help him because
he's so busy
getting ready for his tour,
but i'm so overwhelmed. i
can't keep up with everything
i can't be the only one who

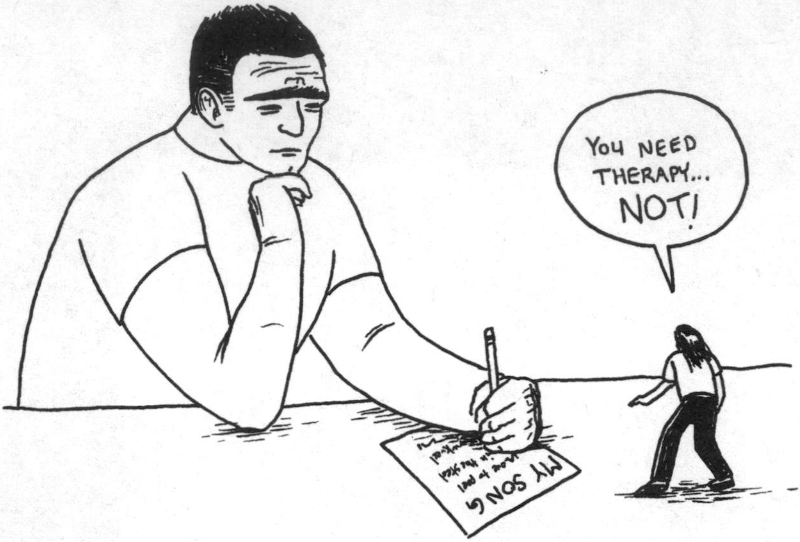
You NEED THERAPY... NOT!
MY SONG

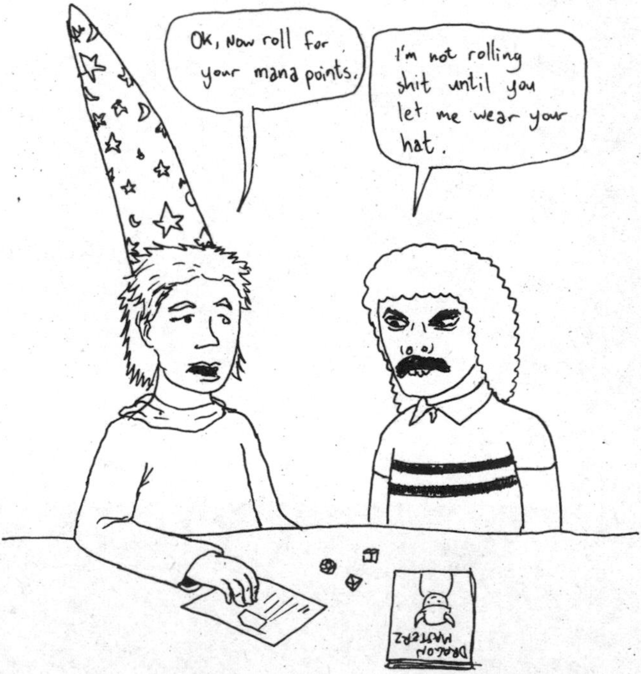
Ok, Now roll for your mana points.
I'm not rolling shit until you let me wear your hat.
DRAGON MASTERZ

11-08-08

Dear Henry,

I've been reading Glenn's diary again... I should spend some more time with him. Why am I writing to myself in the third person? I hate myself sometimes...

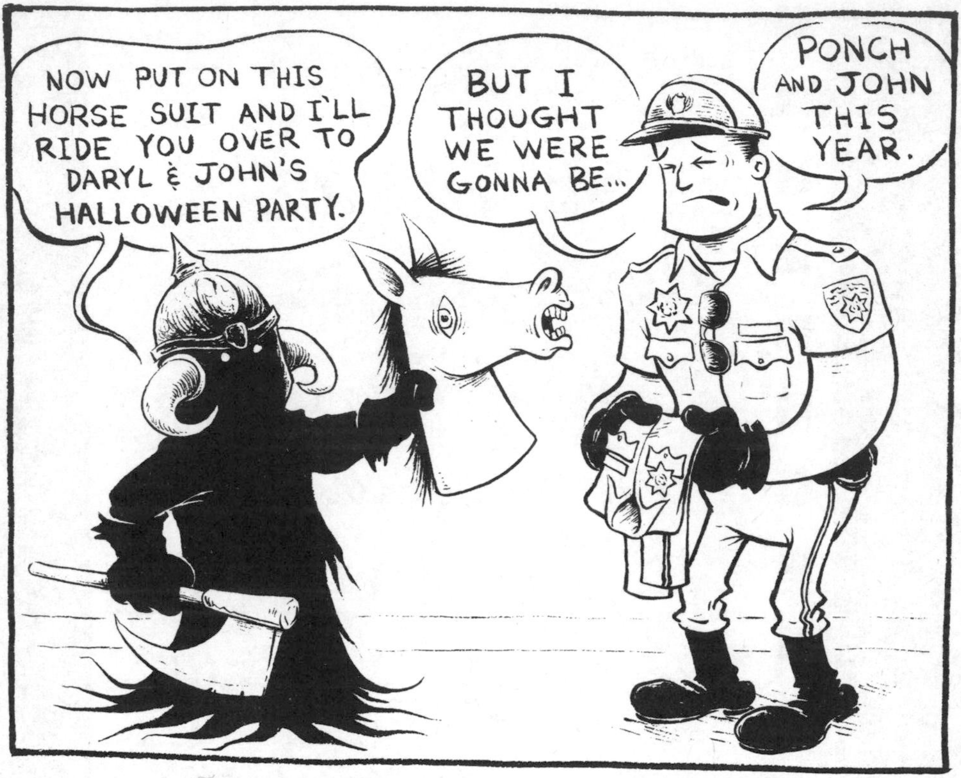
NOW PUT ON THIS HORSE SUIT AND I'LL RIDE YOU OVER TO DARYL & JOHN'S HALLOWEEN PARTY.
BUT I THOUGHT WE WERE GONNA BE...
PONCH AND JOHN THIS YEAR.

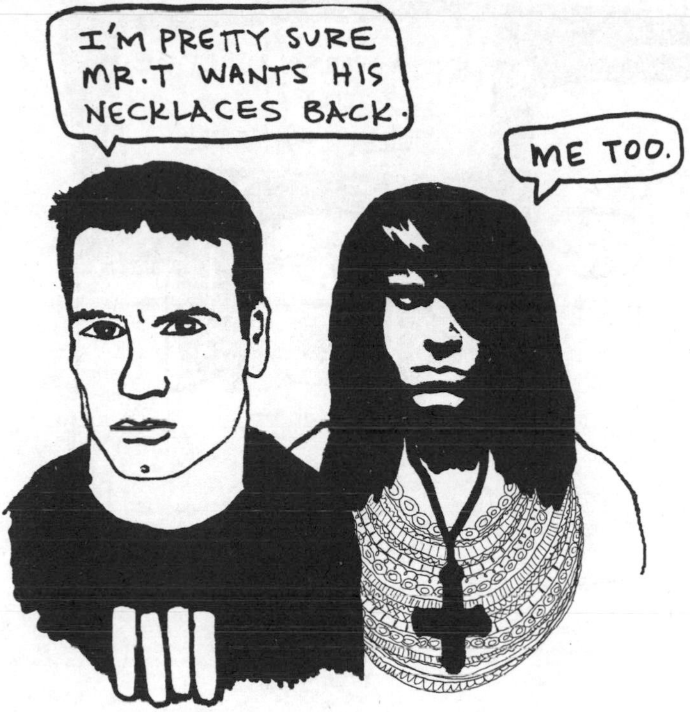
I'M PRETTY SURE MR.T WANTS HIS NECKLACES BACK.
ME TOO.

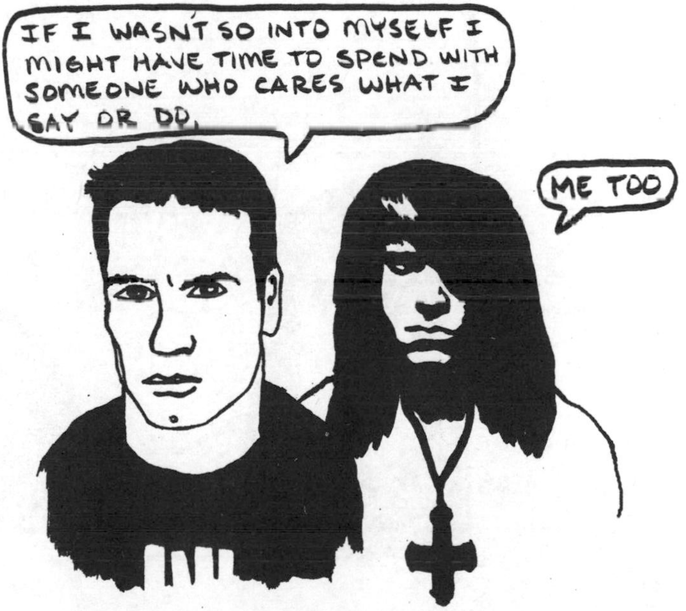
IF I WASN'T SO INTO MYSELF I MIGHT HAVE TIME TO SPEND WITH SOMEONE WHO CARES WHAT I SAY OR DO.
ME TOO

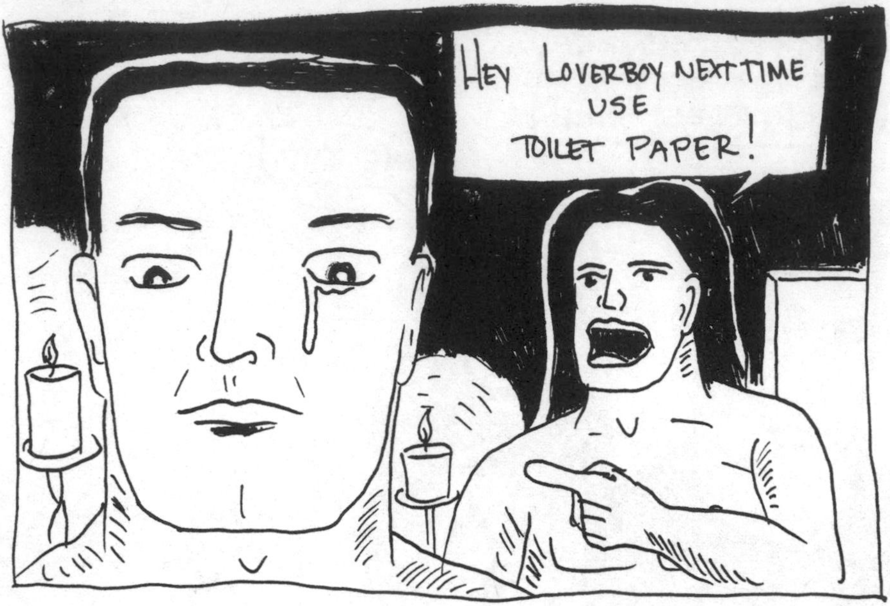
HEY LOVERBOY NEXT TIME USE TOILET PAPER!

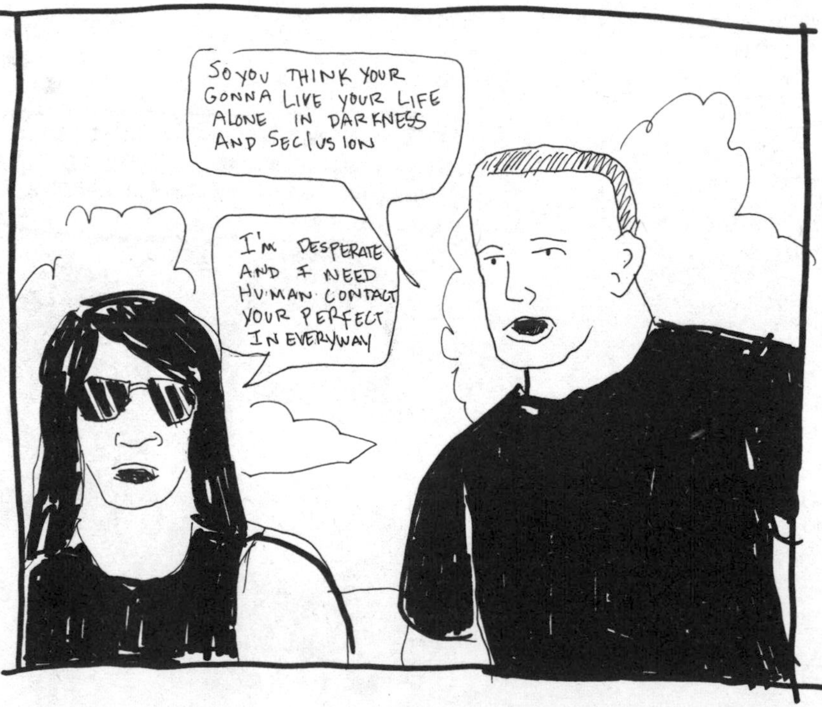
SO YOU THINK YOUR GONNA LIVE YOUR LIFE ALONE IN DARKNESS AND SECLUSION
I'M DESPERATE AND I NEED HUMAN CONTACT YOUR PERFECT IN EVERYWAY

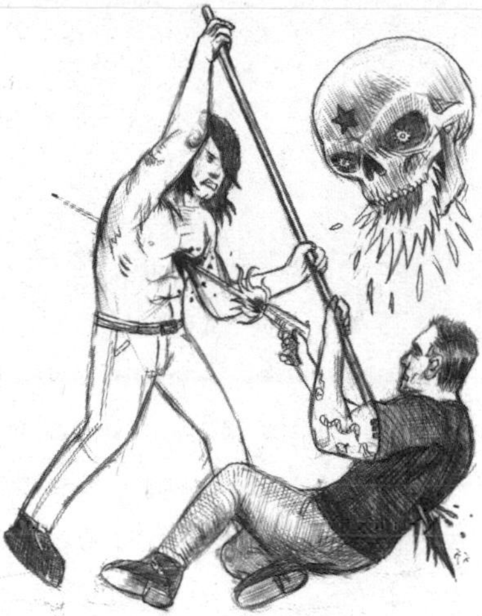

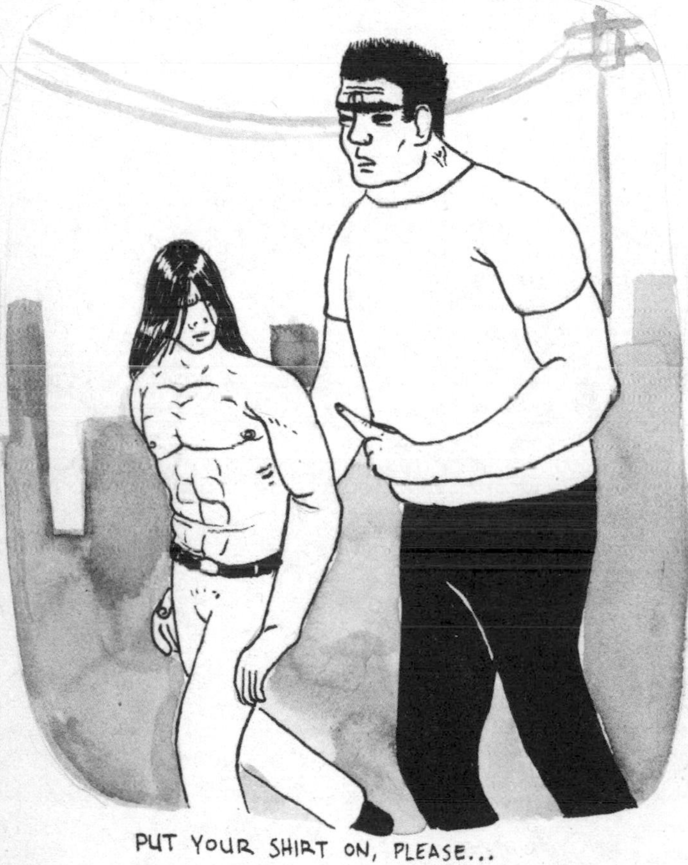

PUT YOUR SHIRT ON, PLEASE...

HEY HALL ITS PARYLL, I FOUND A GREAT APARTMENT, EXCEPT THERE ARE THESE TWO GUYS ONE LITTLE GUY AND A RATHER LARGE OAF. I THINK THEY ARE A LITTLE MORE THEN ROOMATES BUT THEY KEEP THE GARDEN NICE, ANY WAYS SEE YOU AT THE SEANCE LATER TONIGHT

BEEP

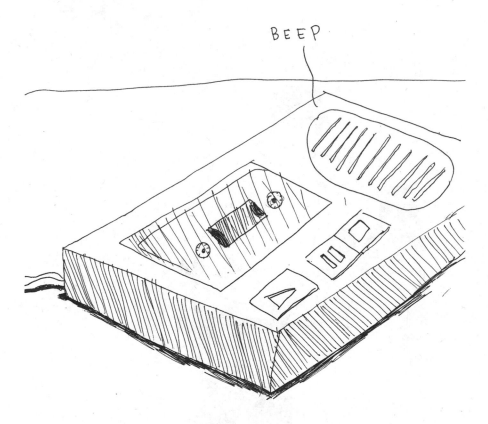

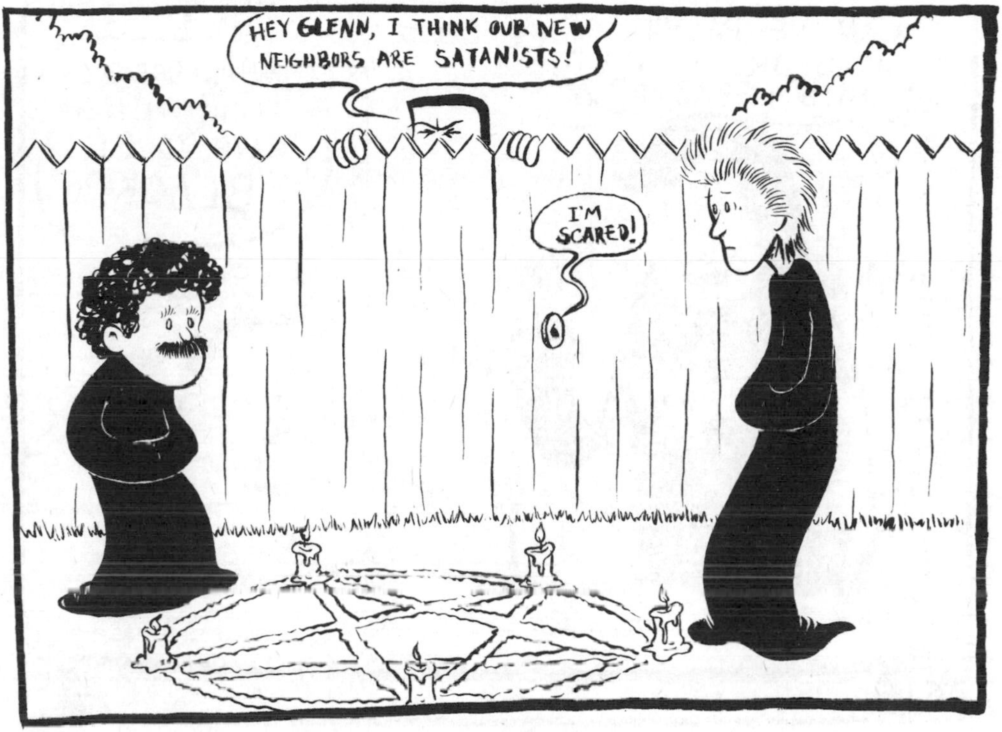
HEY GLENN, I THINK OUR NEW NEIGHBORS ARE SATANISTS!
I'M SCARED!

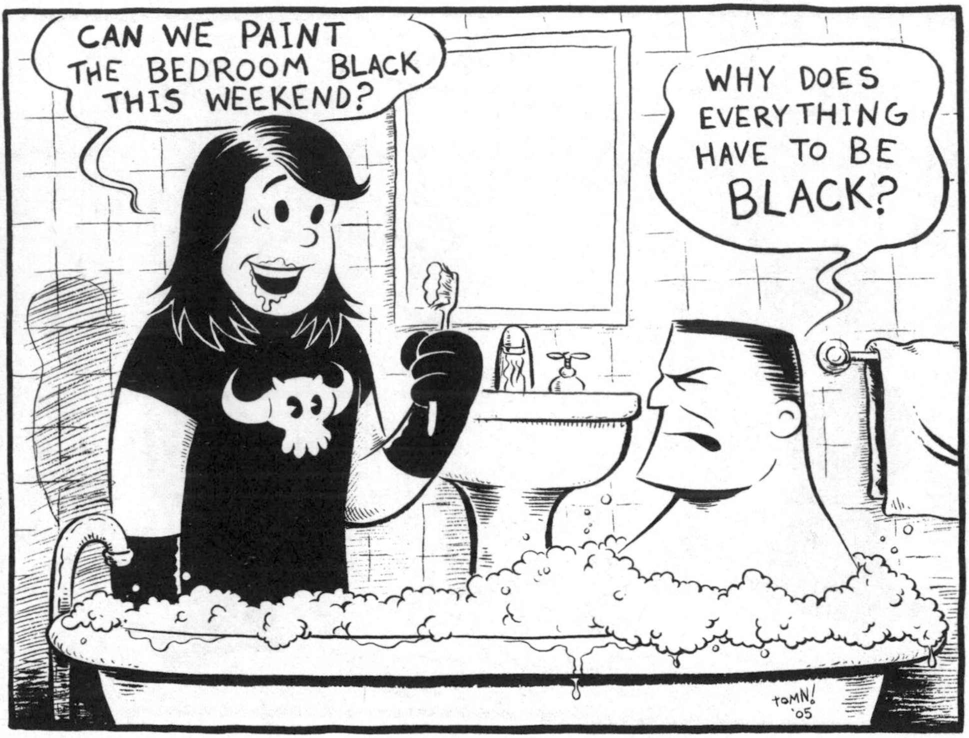
CAN WE PAINT THE BEDROOM BLACK THIS WEEKEND?
WHY DOES EVERYTHING HAVE TO BE BLACK?
TOMN! '05

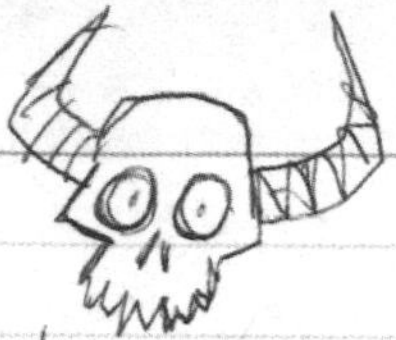

dear diary,

i've been thinking about starting a new band. i was thinking i mite try doing a black metal band because it seems like that's what the kids are into these days. i was trying out some corpse-paint ideas in the bathroom this mourning and HENRY said "WHAT THE HELL ARE YOU DOING?! YOU SHOULD JUST BE YOUR SELF!" i got really mad at him and we had a fight. but i think really i'm just mad at myself 'cause i don't know who i am anymore... when i look at myself in the mirror

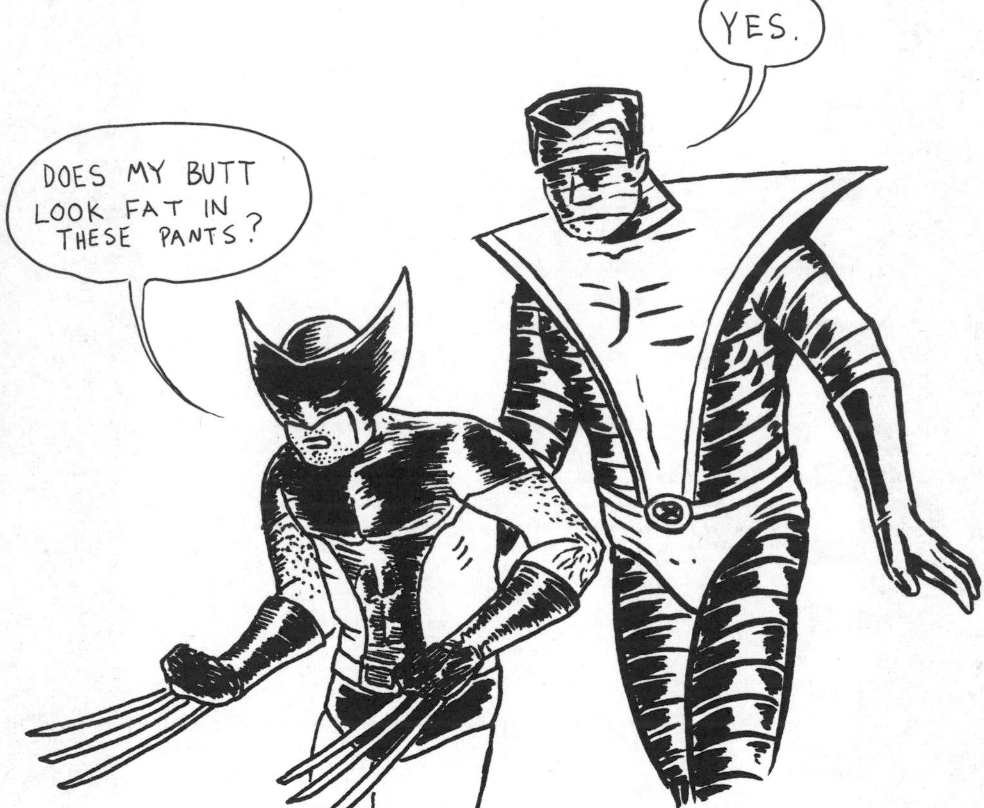
DOES MY BUTT LOOK FAT IN THESE PANTS?
YES.

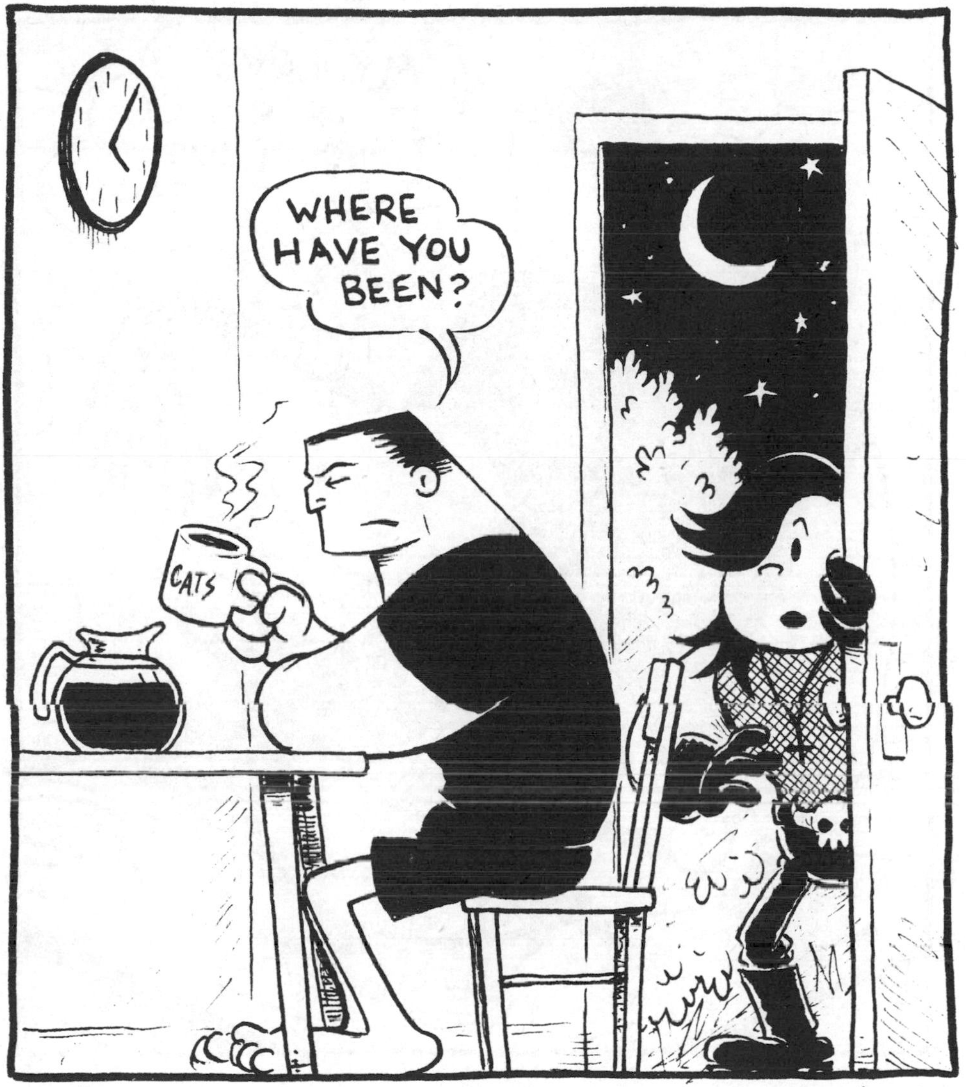
WHERE HAVE YOU BEEN?
CATS
tom N 2013

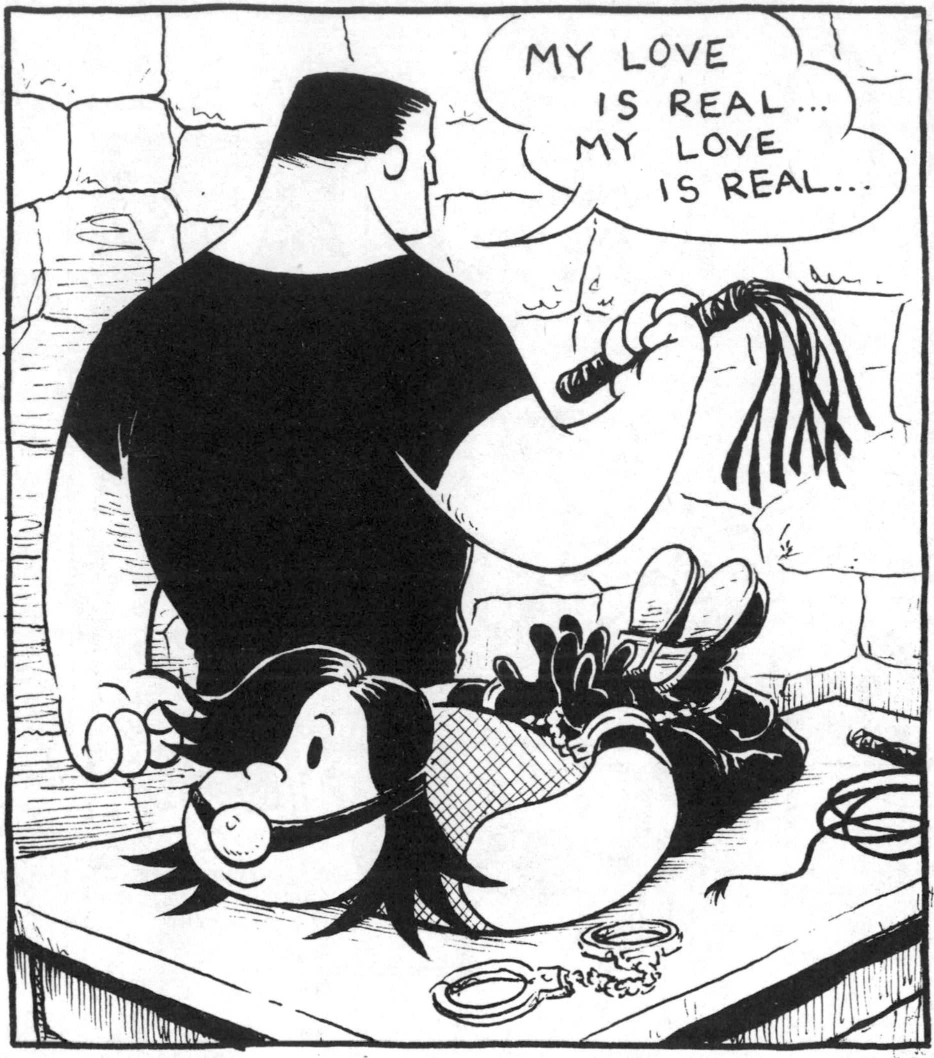
MY LOVE IS REAL... MY LOVE IS REAL...
tom N. 2013

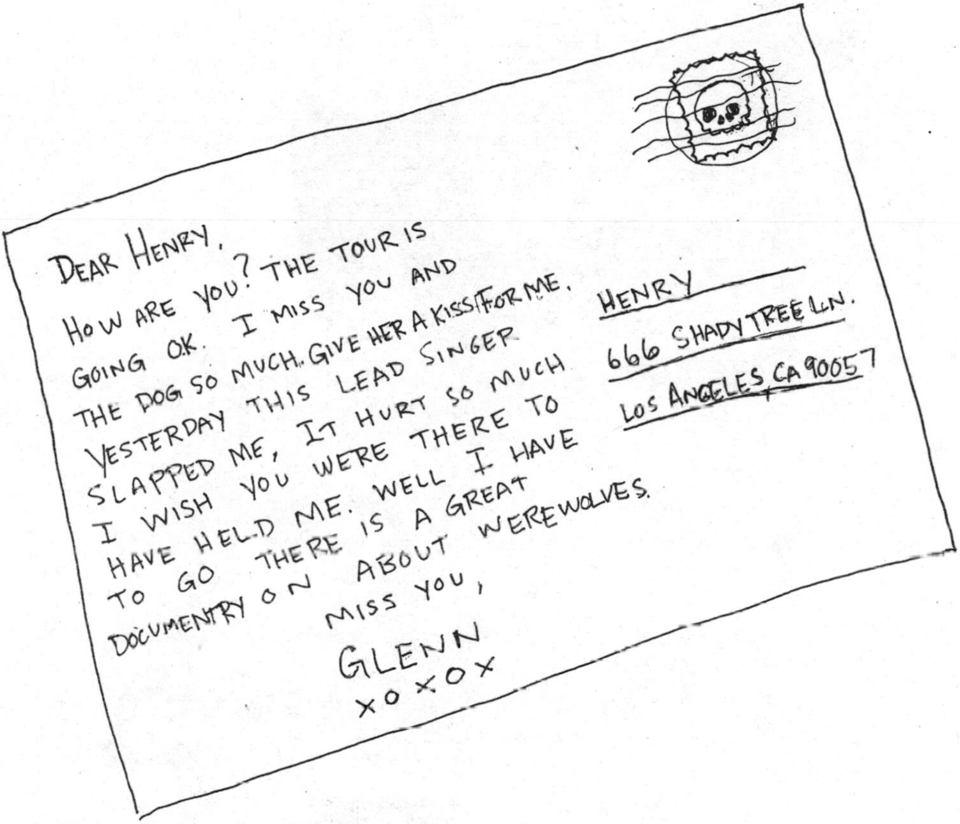
DEAR HENRY,
HOW ARE YOU? THE TOUR IS
GOING O.K. I MISS YOU AND
THE DOG SO MUCH. GIVE HER A KISS FOR ME.
YESTERDAY THIS LEAD SINGER
SLAPPED ME, IT HURT SO MUCH
I WISH YOU WERE THERE TO
HAVE HELD ME. WELL I HAVE
TO GO THERE IS A GREAT
DOCUMENTRY ON ABOUT WEREWOLVES.
MISS YOU,
GLENN
XOXOX
HENRY
666 SHADY TREE LN.
LOS ANGELES, CA 90057

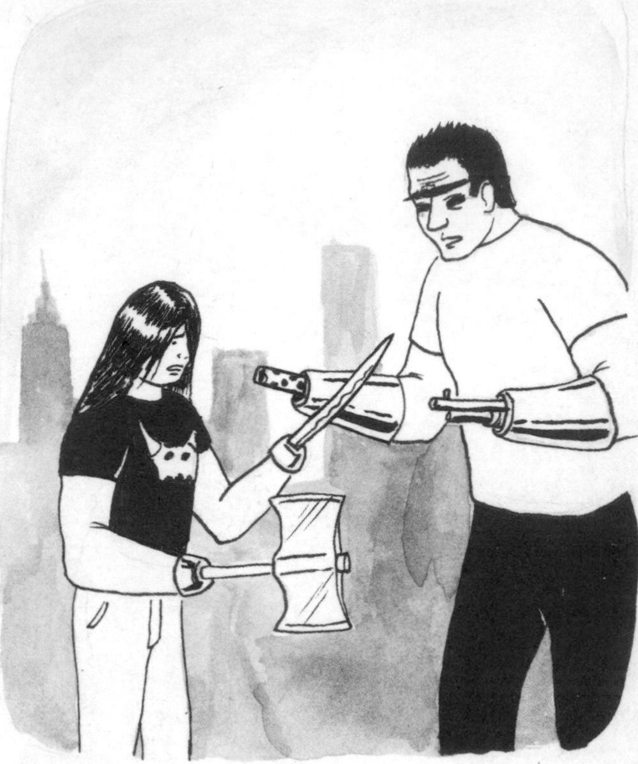

IN HINDSIGHT, MAYBE WE SHOULD HAVE JUST GOTTEN TATTOOS.

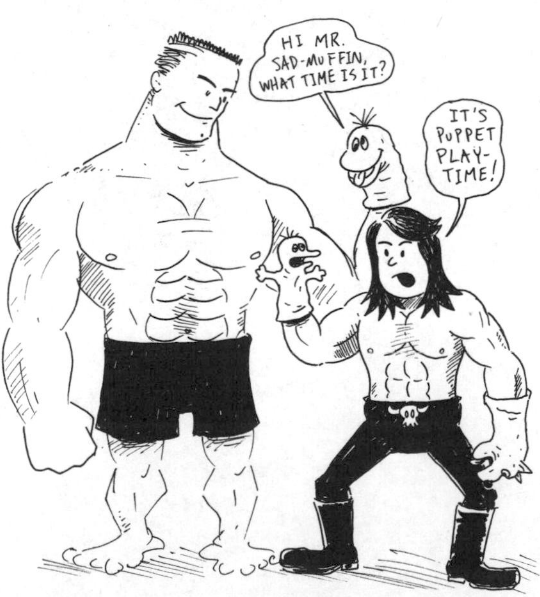
HI MR. SAD-MUFFIN, WHAT TIME IS IT?
IT'S PUPPET PLAY-TIME!

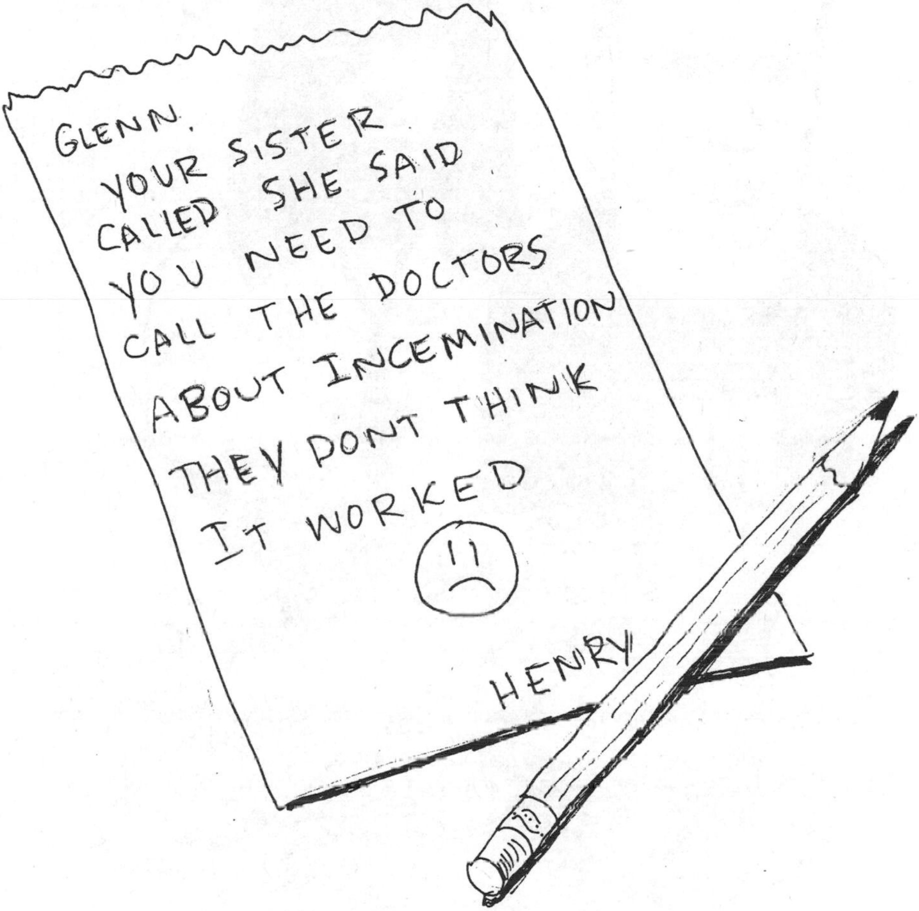
GLENN,
YOUR SISTER
CALLED SHE SAID
YOU NEED TO
CALL THE DOCTORS
ABOUT INCEMINATION
THEY DONT THINK
IT WORKED
HENRY

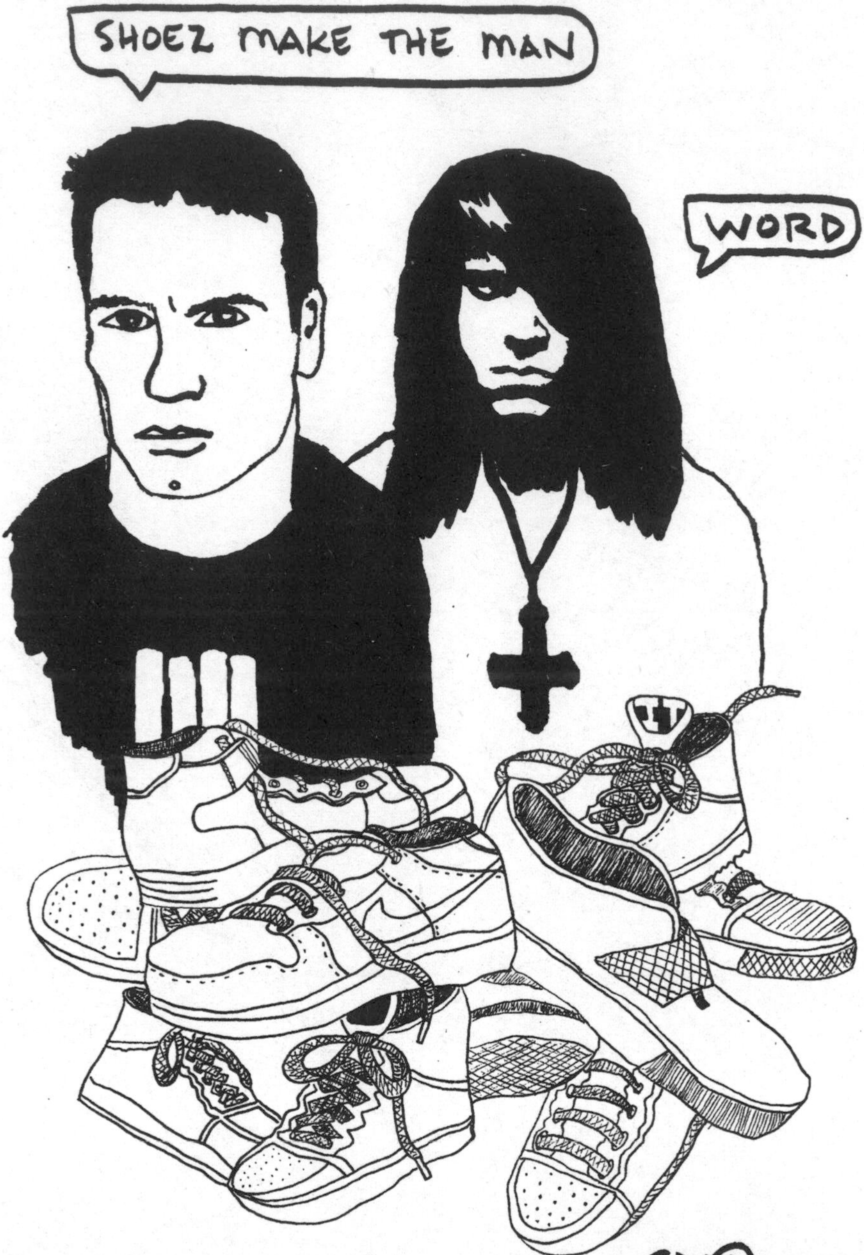
SHOEZ MAKE THE MAN
WORD

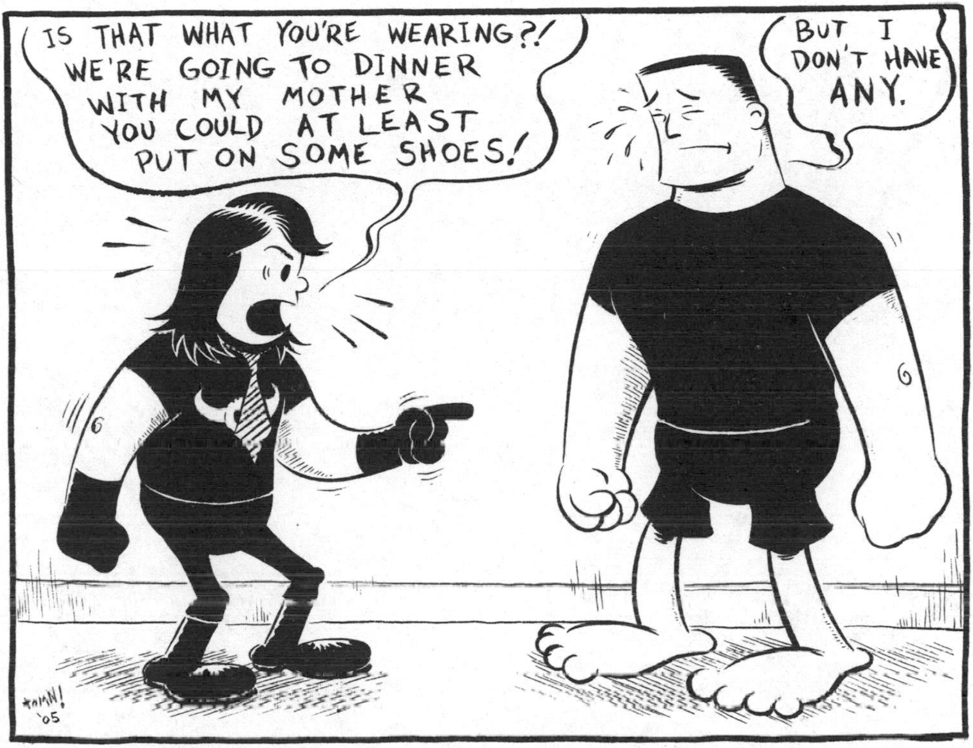
IS THAT WHAT YOU'RE WEARING?! WE'RE GOING TO DINNER WITH MY MOTHER YOU COULD AT LEAST PUT ON SOME SHOES!
BUT I DON'T HAVE ANY.
TOMN! '05

DARYLL,
CAN YOU TALK TO
HENRY AND GLENN WHEN
YOU GET HOME. THEY
ARE VERY UPSET THEIR
DOG IS MISSING.
SEE YOU AT THE
SACRAFICE TONIGHT.
JOHN

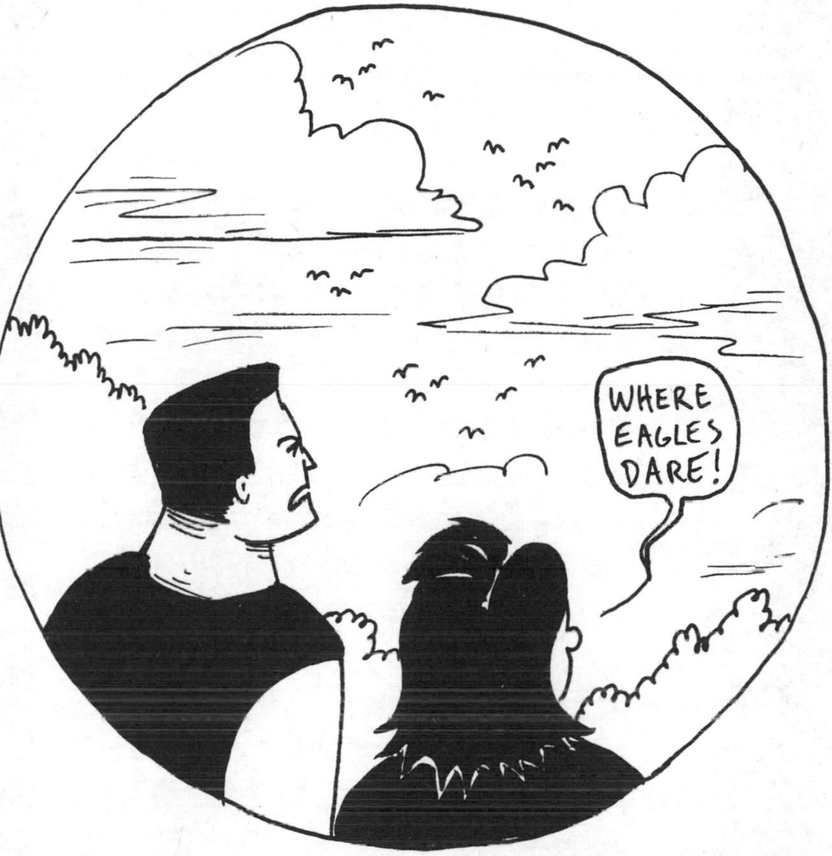
WHERE EAGLES DARE!

"WHEN ANGELS GET TIRED THEY SIT AND REST ON SOFT PILLOWS OF CLOUDS IN THE SKY."

dear diary,

i've been wasting too
much time on twitter again.
but sometimes i get so
lonely when Henry's away.
i don't know what to do
anymore. i feel so alone.
Lost... i keep trying to
write some new songs, and
i even jammed with
Daryl and John in their
garage last nite. but
when i came home to
an empty house all i
wanted to do was eat a
whole tub of mint-chocolate
chip ice cream and watch
re runs of the Golden Girls.

HEY JOHN,
THE NEIGHBORS WANT US TO COME
OVER FOR DINNER AND TO WATCH THE
L WORD I WAS THINKING, YOU COULD
MAKE THAT KILLER DEVIL'S FOOD CAKE TO
BRING. BY. SEE YOU AT THE CHAPEL
LATER. OH THERE STILL LOOKING
FOR THEIR DOG
CONTACTS
MSG
OK
END
SEND

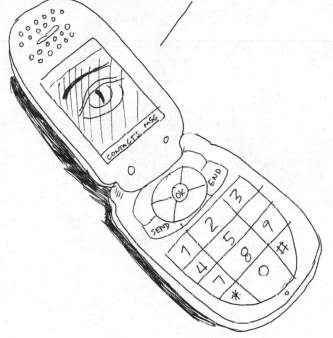

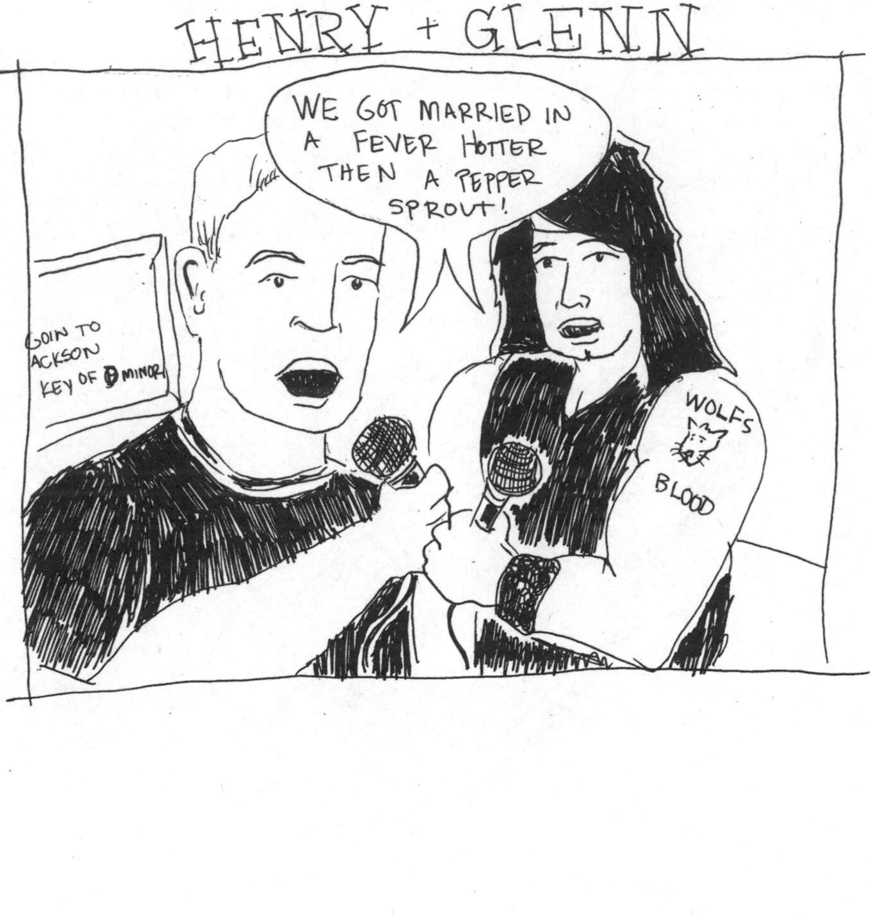
HENRY + GLENN
WE GOT MARRIED IN A FEVER HOTTER THEN A PEPPER SPROUT!
GOIN TO ACKSON KEY OF D MINOR
WOLFS BLOOD

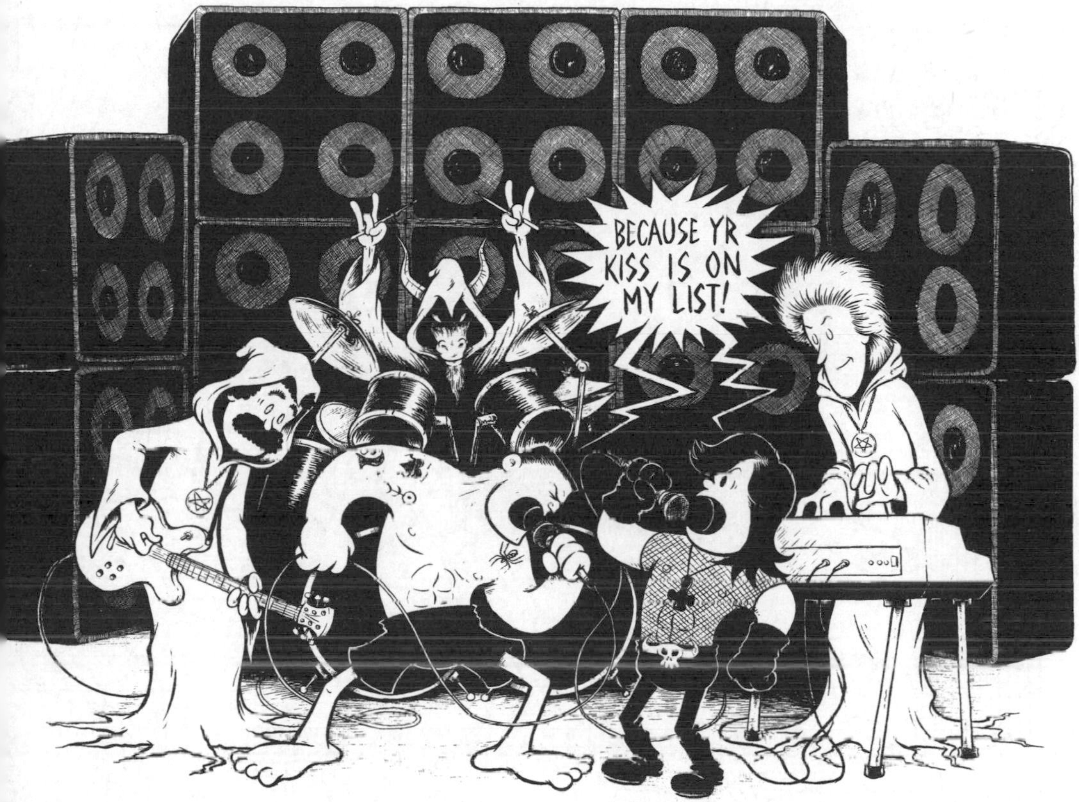
BECAUSE YR KISS IS ON MY LIST!

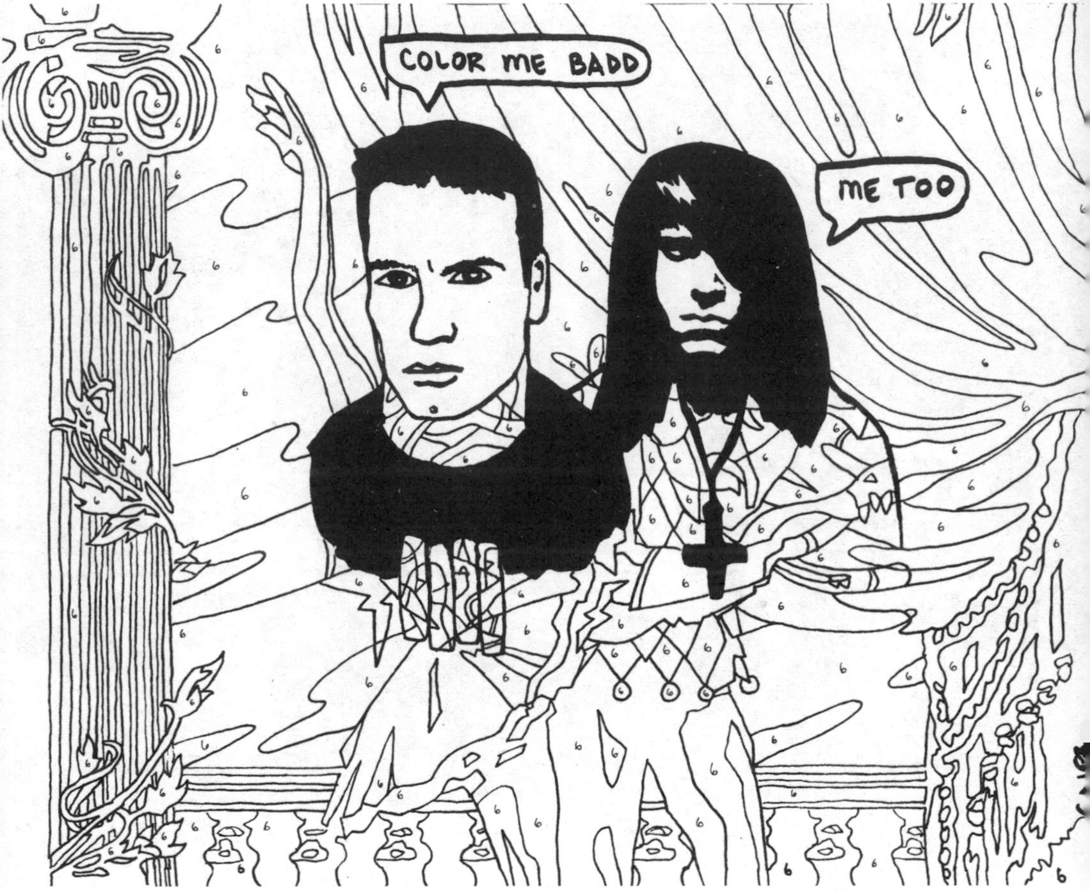
COLOR ME BADD
ME TOO

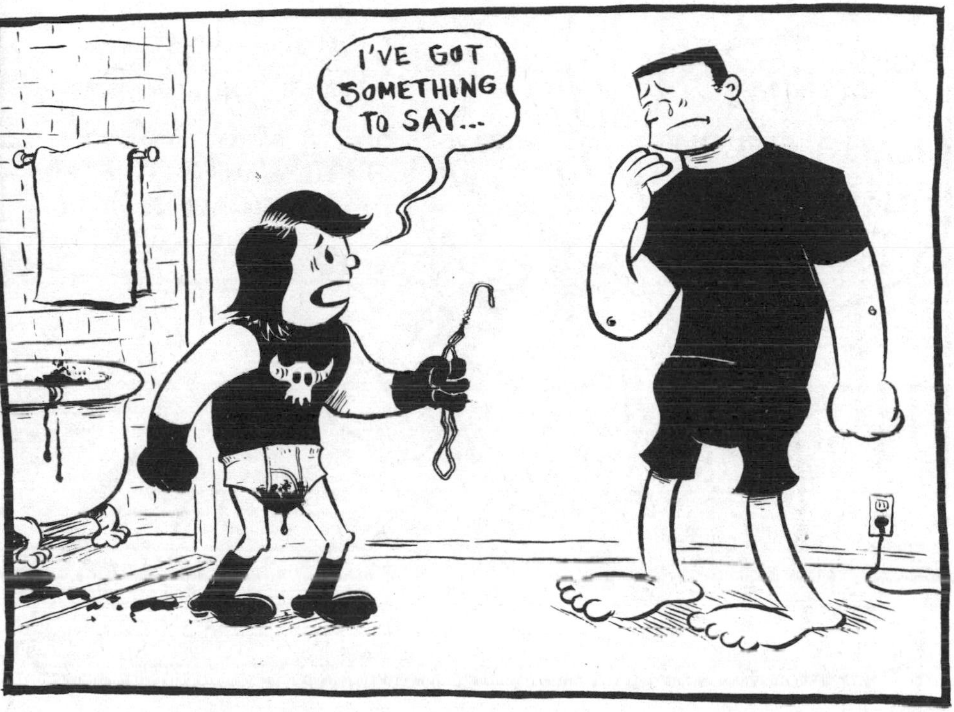
I'VE GOT SOMETHING TO SAY...

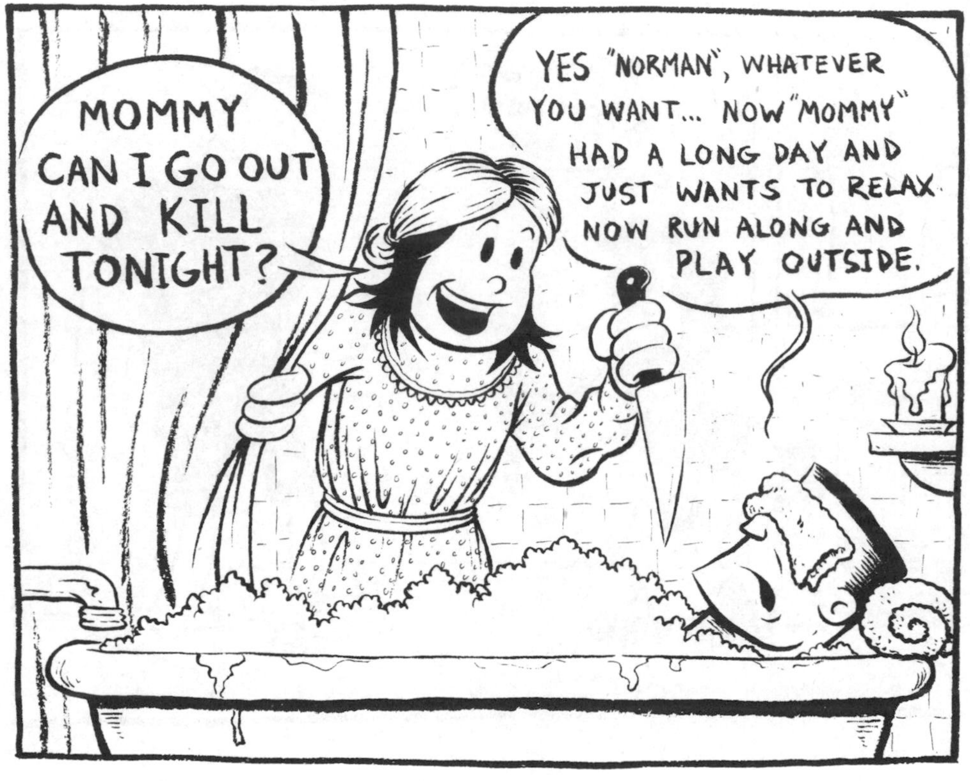
MOMMY CAN I GO OUT AND KILL TONIGHT?
YES "NORMAN", WHATEVER YOU WANT... NOW "MOMMY" HAD A LONG DAY AND JUST WANTS TO RELAX. NOW RUN ALONG AND PLAY OUTSIDE.

HA HA! I WATCHED THAT MOVIE LAST NIGHT!
↓

dear diary of the dead,

HENRY'S on tour again.
i've been feeling kinda down...
but Daryl came over last
nite and brought some pizza
and zombie movies to cheer
me up. he's so cool. we had
so much fun! he even braided
my hair while we watched
RETURN OF THE EVIL DEAD!!!
i gotta go now. John is ~~the~~
holding a seance tonight to
try and talk to Jimi. Daryl
said i could join them. i
wanna get a new outfit to
wear, so i'm off to the
mall for a shopping spree
at Hot topic!!! ♡♡

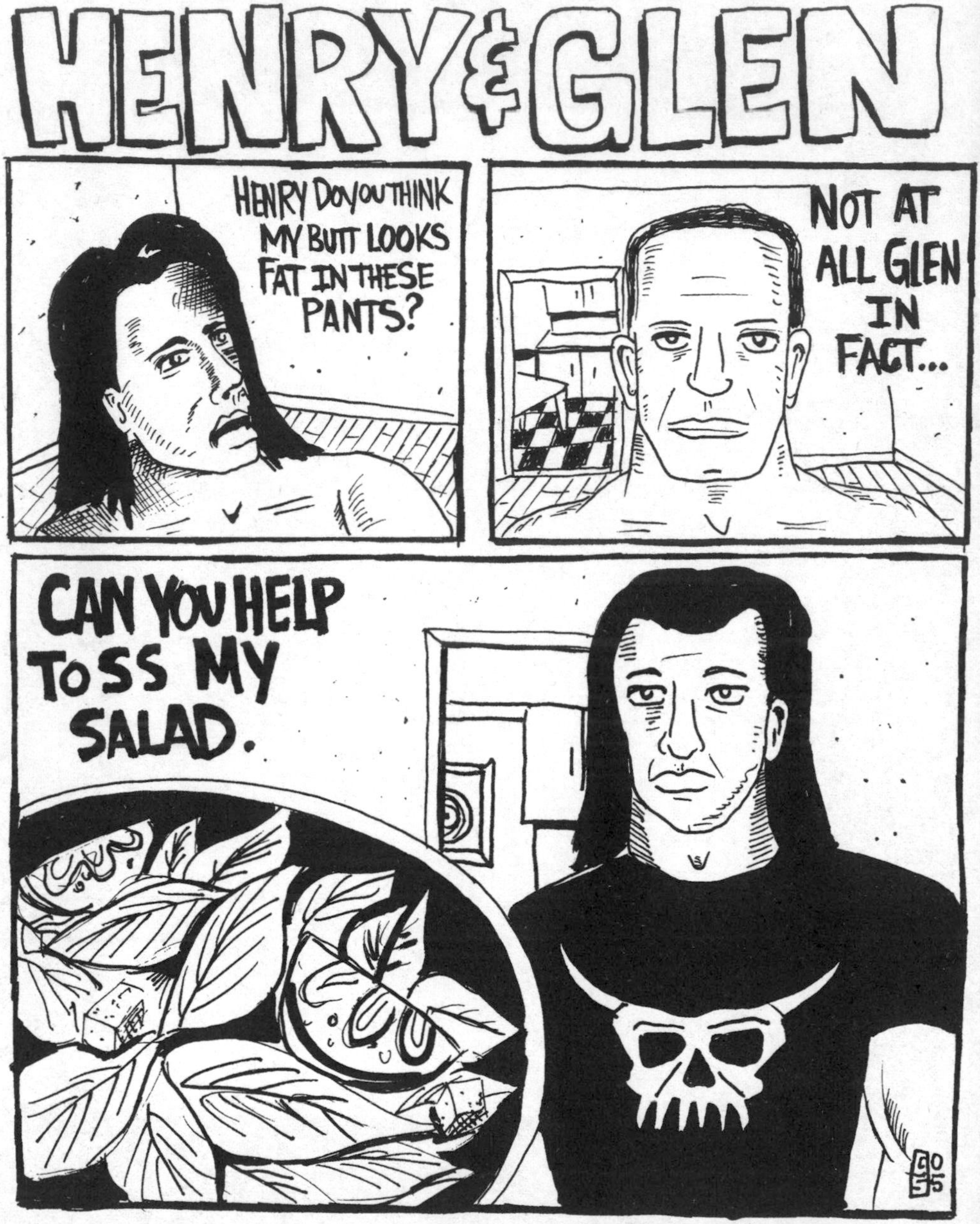
HENRY & GLEN
HENRY DO YOU THINK MY BUTT LOOKS FAT IN THESE PANTS?
NOT AT ALL GLEN IN FACT...
CAN YOU HELP TOSS MY SALAD.

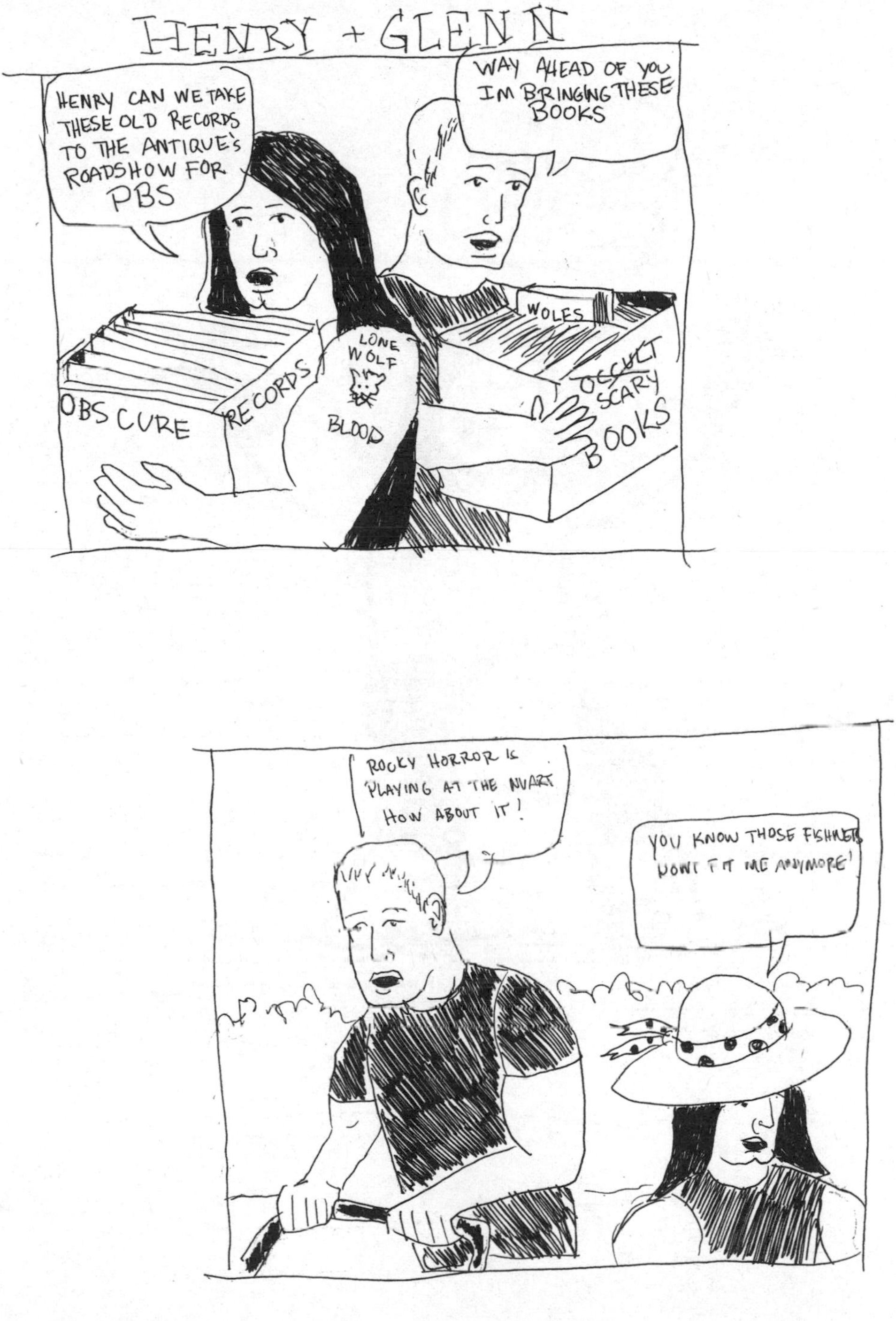
HENRY + GLENN
HENRY CAN WE TAKE THESE OLD RECORDS TO THE ANTIQUE'S ROADSHOW FOR PBS
WAY AHEAD OF YOU IM BRINGING THESE BOOKS
WOLES
LONE WOLF
BLOOD
OBSCURE RECORDS
OCCULT SCARY BOOKS
ROCKY HORROR IS PLAYING AT THE NUART HOW ABOUT IT!
YOU KNOW THOSE FISHNETS DONT FIT ME ANYMORE

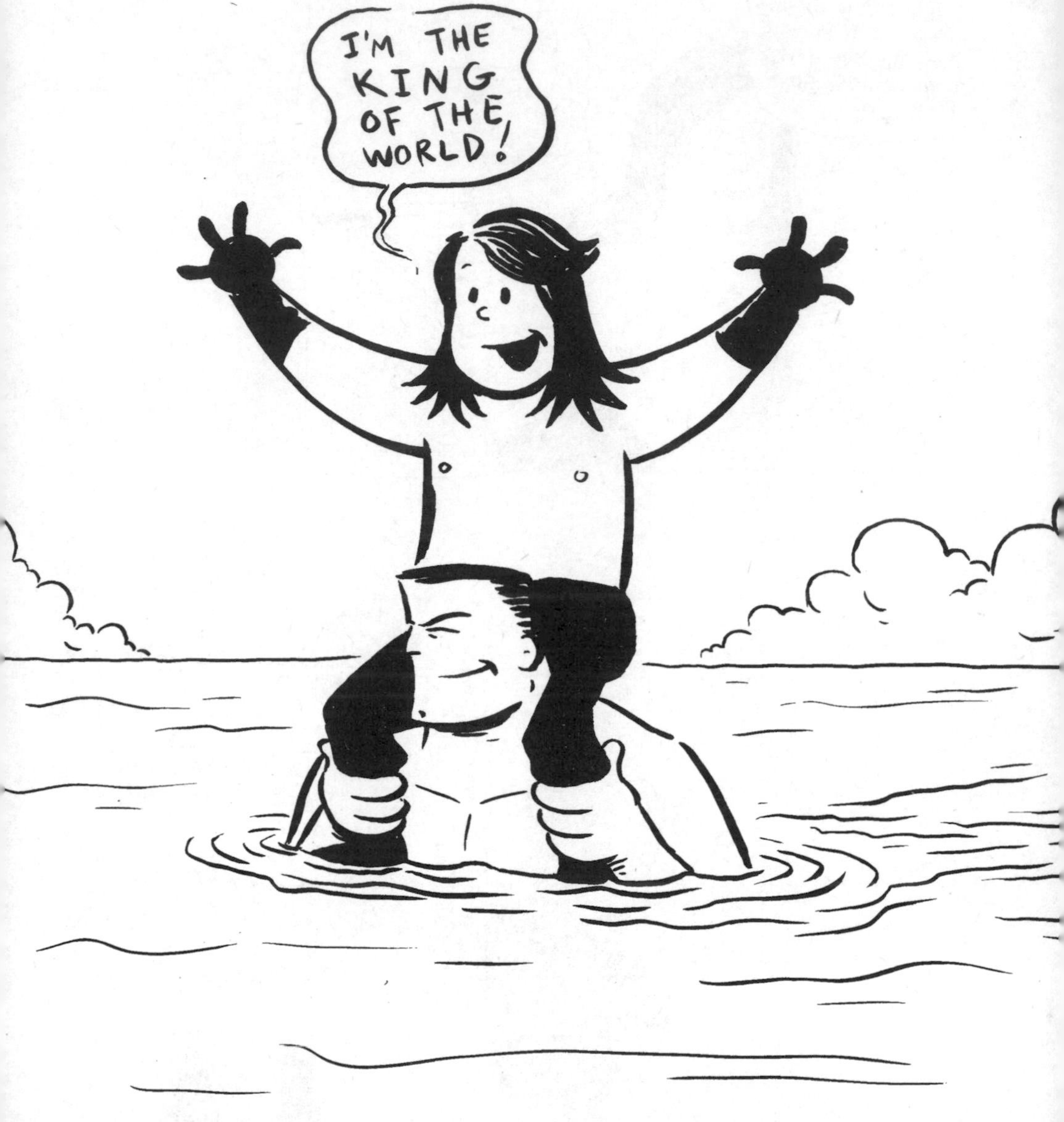
I'M THE KING OF THE WORLD!

Why don't we pay a visit to our neighbors: Henry& Glenn?
Fuck you, Oates.
OH YEAH!!!!!
BREATHE, HENRY.
MOTHERRR...
TATOO
TATOO

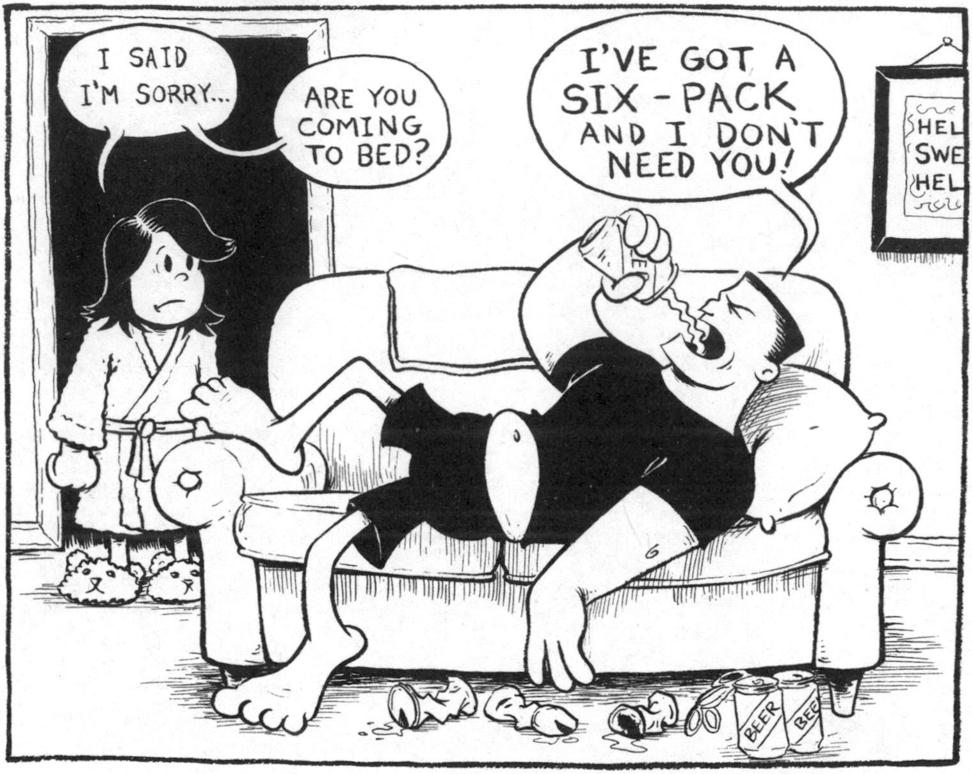
I SAID I'M SORRY...
ARE YOU COMING TO BED?
I'VE GOT A SIX-PACK AND I DON'T NEED YOU!
BEER
BEE

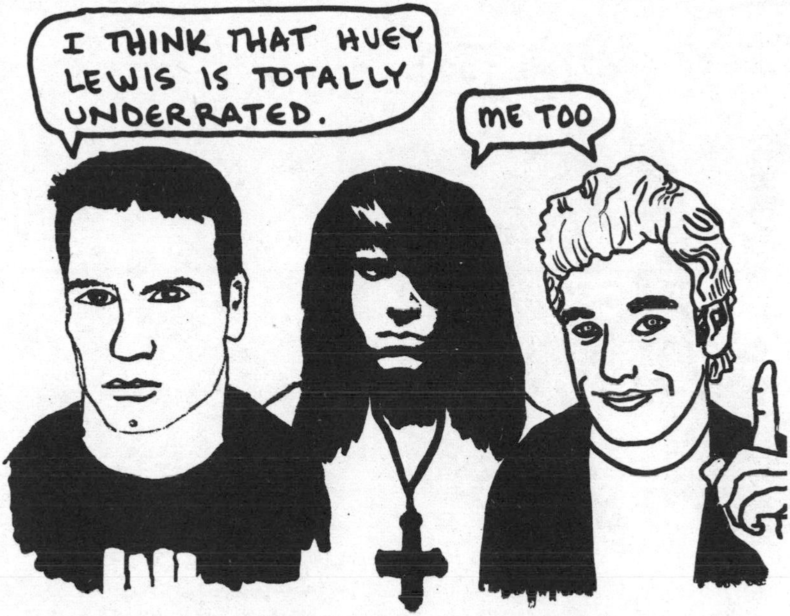
I THINK THAT HUEY LEWIS IS TOTALLY UNDERRATED.
ME TOO

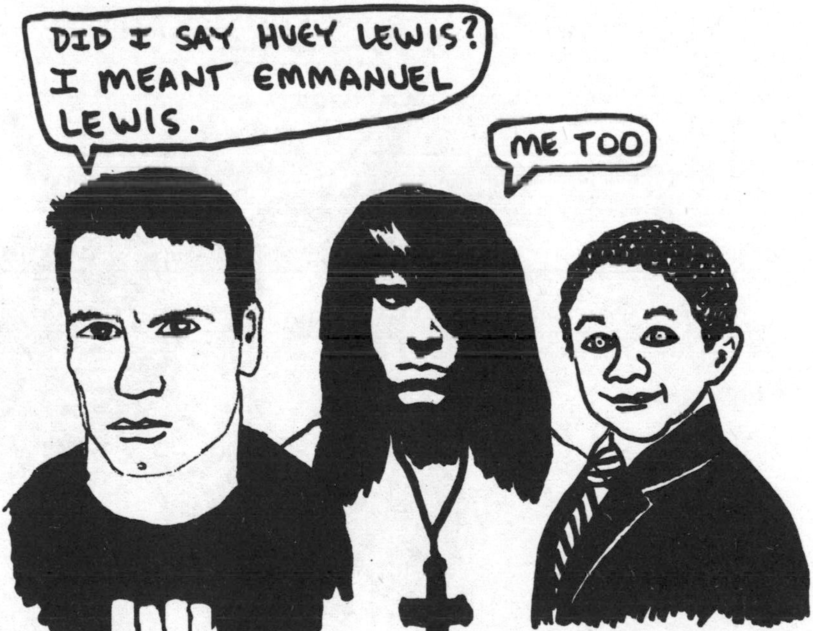
DID I SAY HUEY LEWIS? I MEANT EMMANUEL LEWIS.
ME TOO

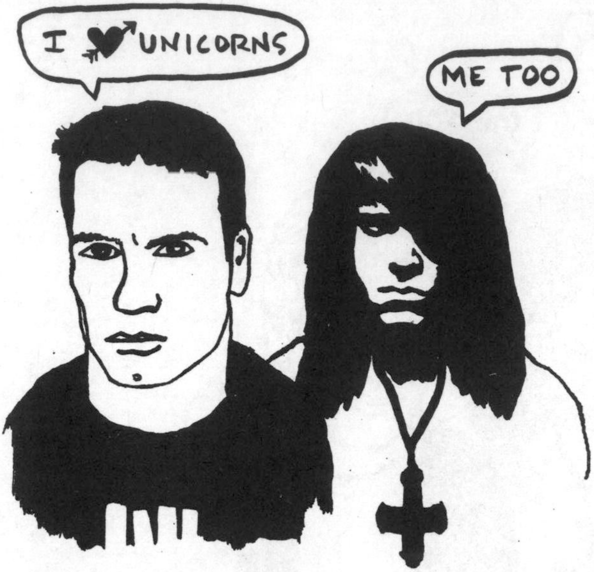
I ♥ UNICORNS
ME TOO

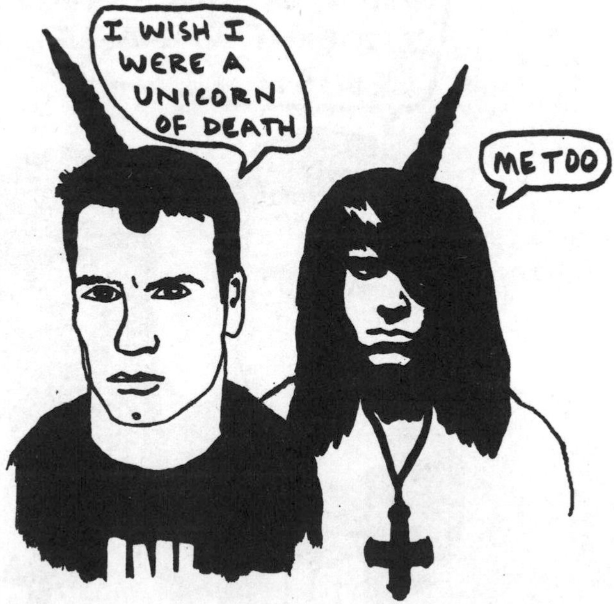
I WISH I WERE A UNICORN OF DEATH
ME TOO

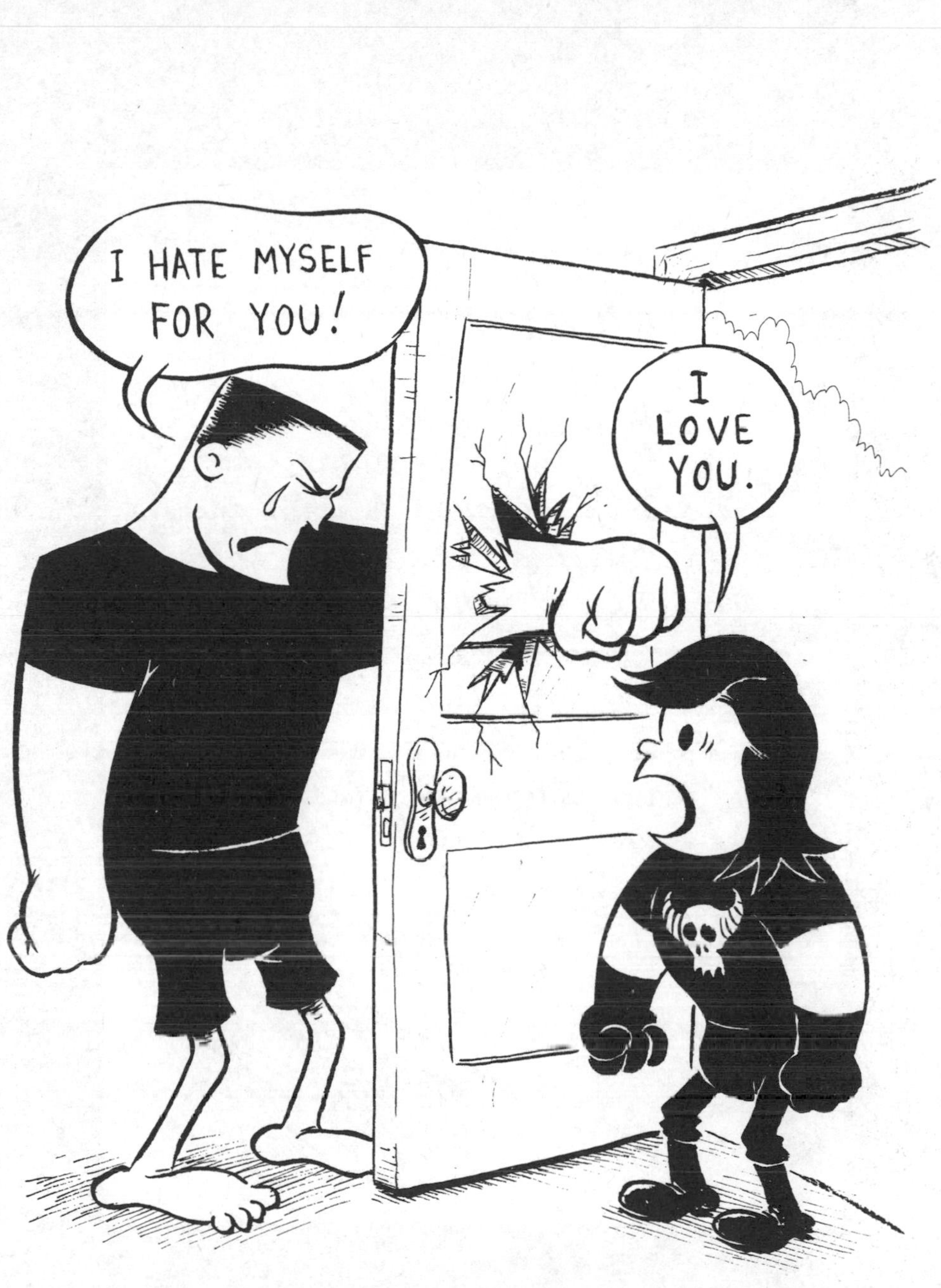
I HATE MYSELF FOR YOU!
I LOVE YOU.

07-08-08

Dear Henry,

It's been a while since I wrote in this diary for a while because I still think it's stupid. But my shrink thinks I need to get more in touch with my emotions. Whatever... I don't know what to do anymore. The radio show is fun. And I guess I still like doing the spoken word tours. But I feel like I'm losing it. I feel like

FUCK
THIS

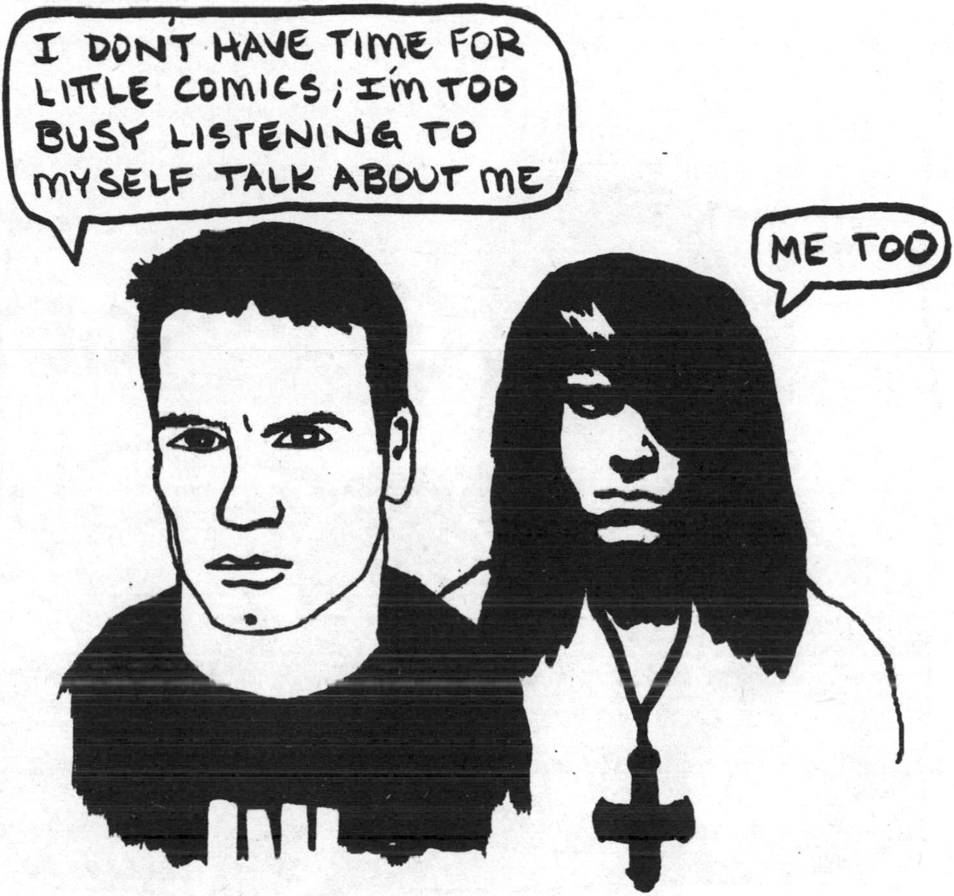
I DON'T HAVE TIME FOR LITTLE COMICS; I'M TOO BUSY LISTENING TO MYSELF TALK ABOUT ME
ME TOO

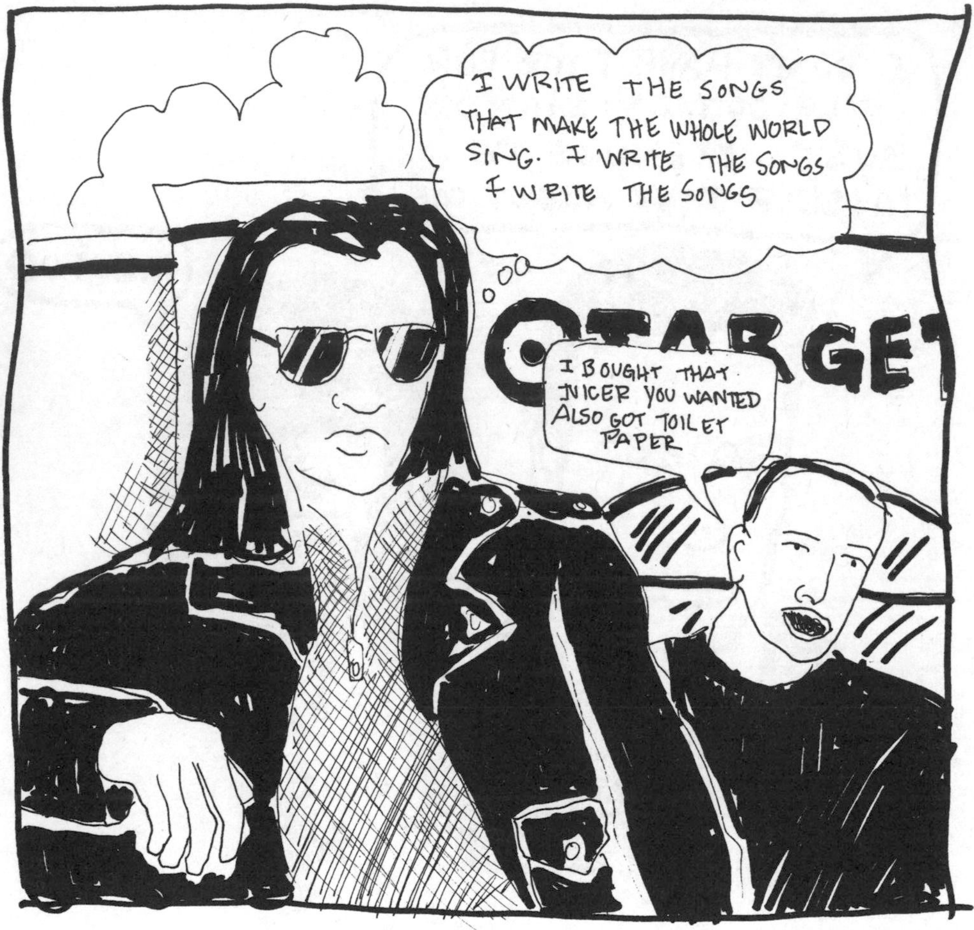
I WRITE THE SONGS THAT MAKE THE WHOLE WORLD SING. I WRITE THE SONGS I WRITE THE SONGS
TARGET
I BOUGHT THAT JUICER YOU WANTED ALSO GOT TOILET PAPER

dear diary,

i saw a dead bird on the sidewalk while i was walking the dog and it reminded me of how cruel this world is and how at any moment we could be crushed by some unstoppable force and we'll be extinguished forever... forgotten... gone... dead. i'm so glad i get to spend my short life here with Henry. i must find a way to become a werewolf so i can live forever and Henry can be one too. i've read all the books, but

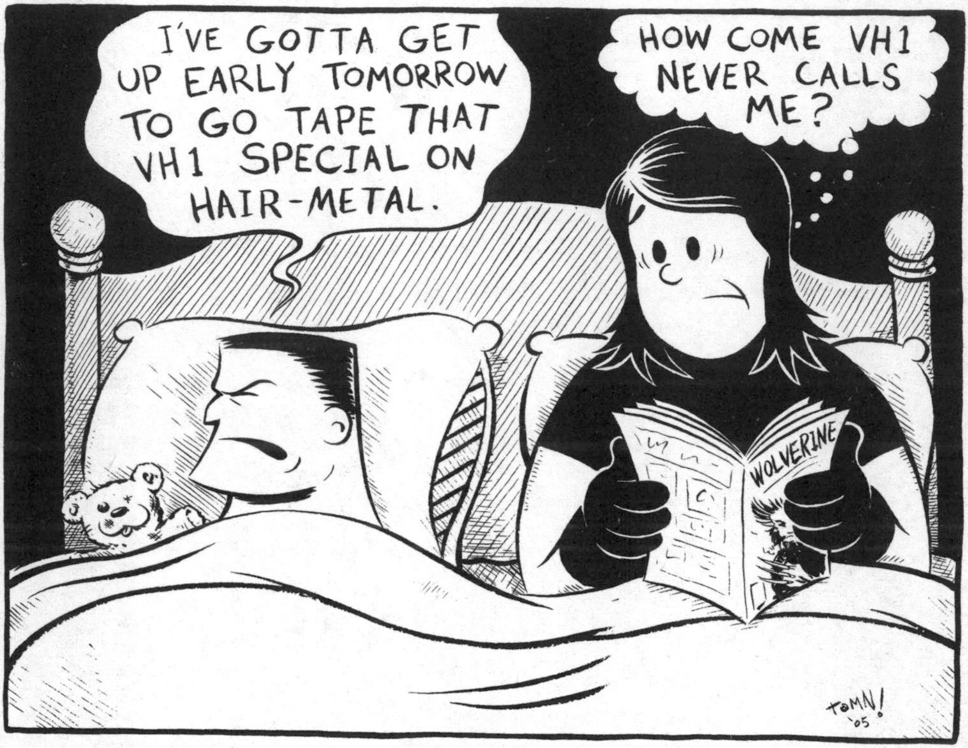
I'VE GOTTA GET UP EARLY TOMORROW TO GO TAPE THAT VH1 SPECIAL ON HAIR-METAL.
HOW COME VH1 NEVER CALLS ME?
WOLVERINE
TOMN! '05

Dear Henry,

I should stop reading Glenn's diary. And I should stop stealing paper from it for my own diary. He might notice I've been reading all of his private thoughts about werewolves and Hitler. He writes about him so much I'm almost jealous... seriously I think he's obsessed. Our therapist says I'm making progress

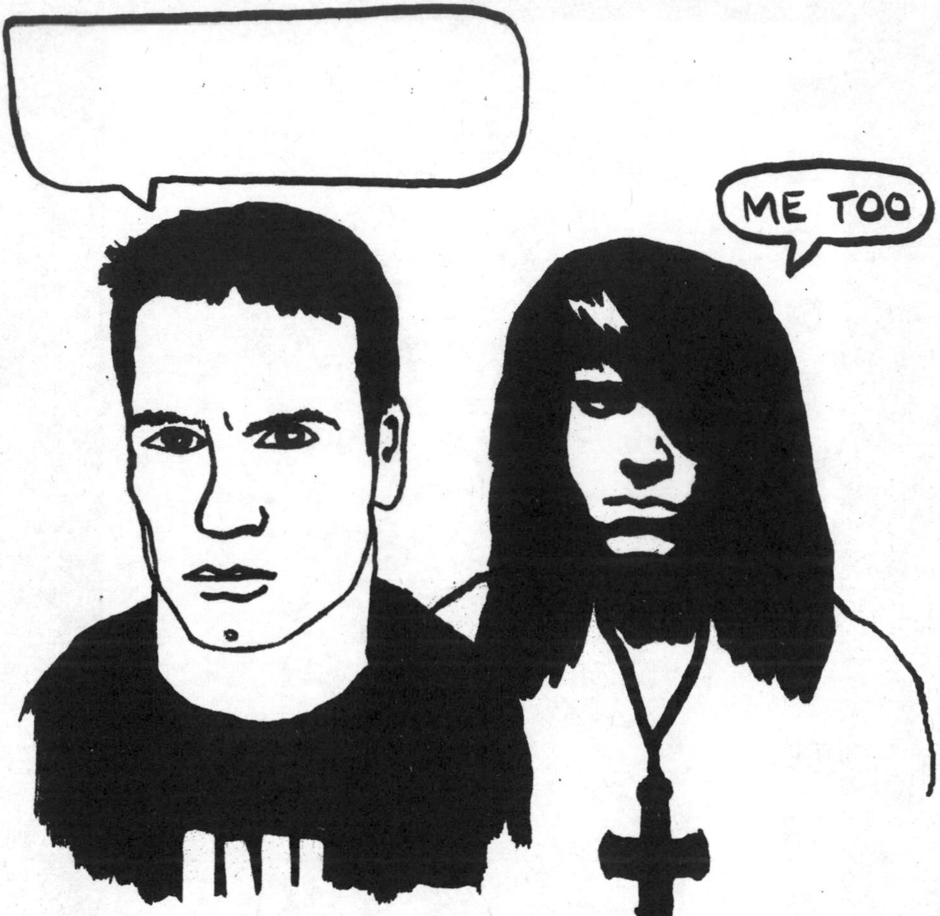
ME TOO

FILL IN YOUR OWN JOKE IF YOU THINK YOU'RE SO DAMN FUNNY

DEAR GLENN,
THE SPOKEN WORD TOUR IS
SO AWESOME. SO MANY GREAT
PEOPLE HAVE COME OUT FOR THE
READINGS AND THE RESPONSE
HAS BEEN SO WONDERFUL. IT's
GREAT THAT ALL THESE PEOPLE
STILL WANT TO SEE ME. THEY
YELL FOR ME TO DO SOME
SONGS WHICH IS GREAT IT
MAKES ME FEEL SO GOOD
INSIDE

HENRY

GLENN

666 SHADYTREE LN.

LOS ANGELES, CA 90057

09-23-08

Dear Henry,

You are an ASSHOLE!

You stupid Liar.

FUCK YOU!

xxoo

Henry

p.s. diaries are still LAME!

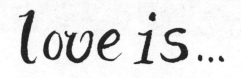

love is...

... an ordinary kind of little angel fuck.

deary diary,

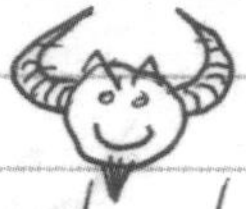

today was a good day! [redacted] Henry and i had an all day date. we went to the museum and saw some dinosaur bones. and then we had a picnic at the beach!!! ♡♡♡ after our picnic we lifted some weights together. I love to get pumped ~~[illegible]~~ [redacted] with Henry!!! but now i'm sad because Henry is leaving tomorrow moorning to shoot some slasher movie. [redacted] i wish i could act so i could be in a horror movie.

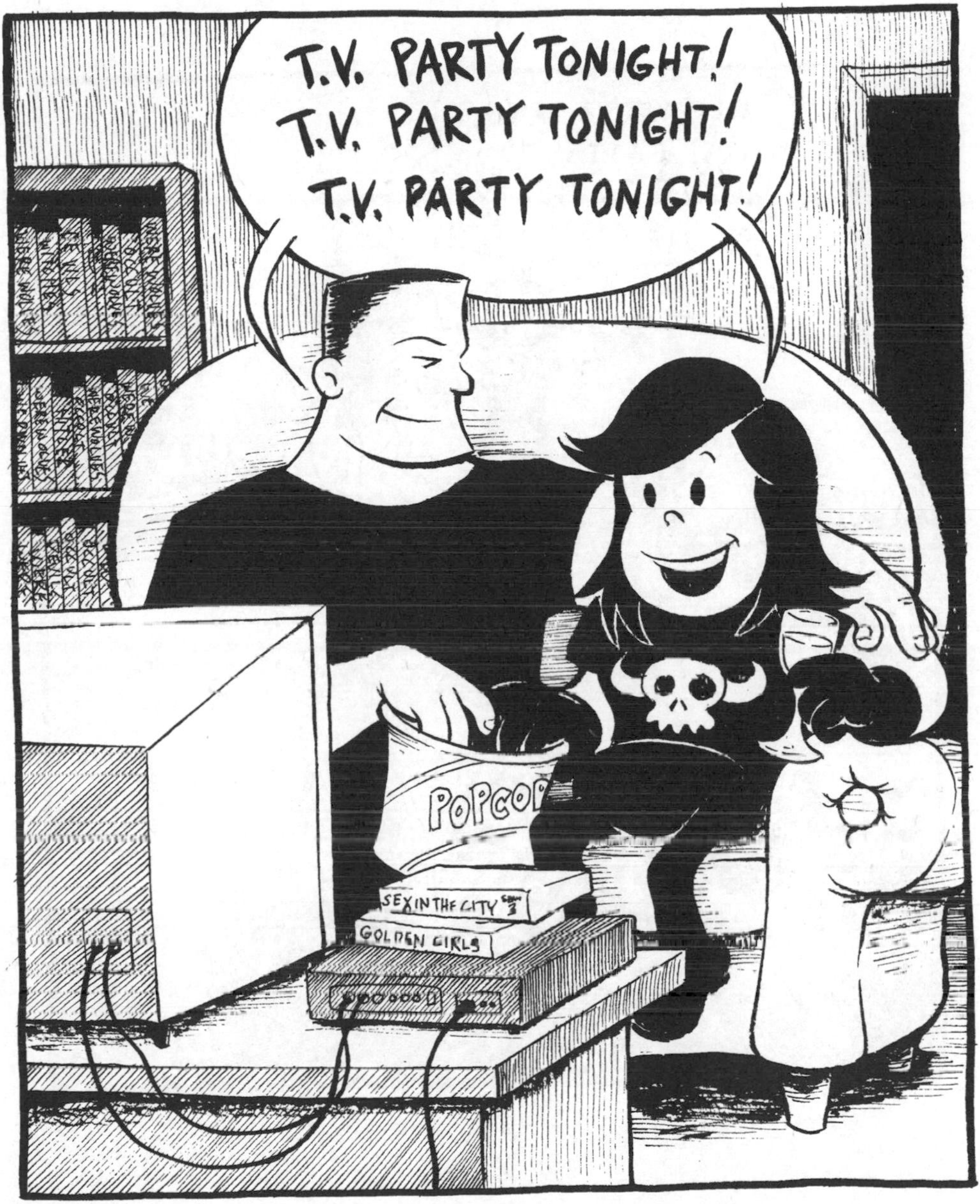
T.V. PARTY TONIGHT!
T.V. PARTY TONIGHT!
T.V. PARTY TONIGHT!
SEX IN THE CITY
GOLDEN GIRLS

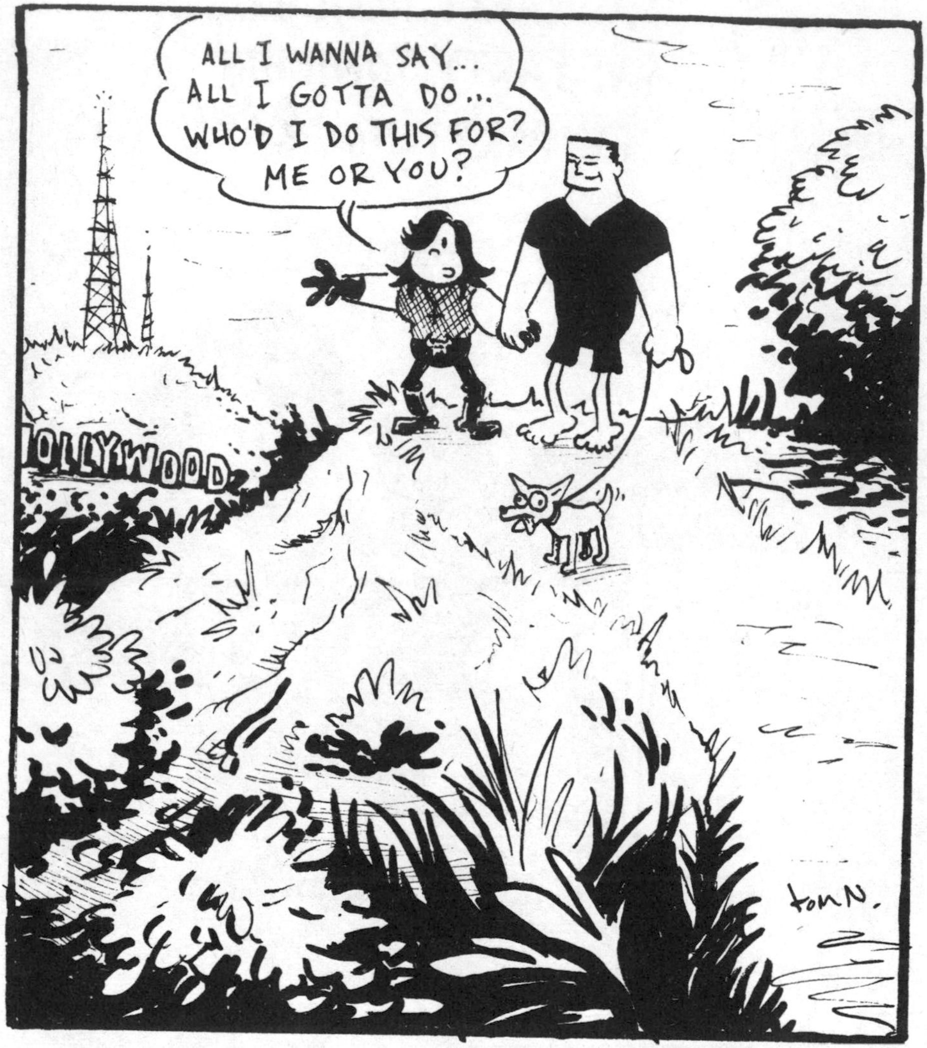
ALL I WANNA SAY...
ALL I GOTTA DO...
WHO'D I DO THIS FOR?
ME OR YOU?
OLLYWOOD
tom N.

"TEXAS IS THE REASON!"

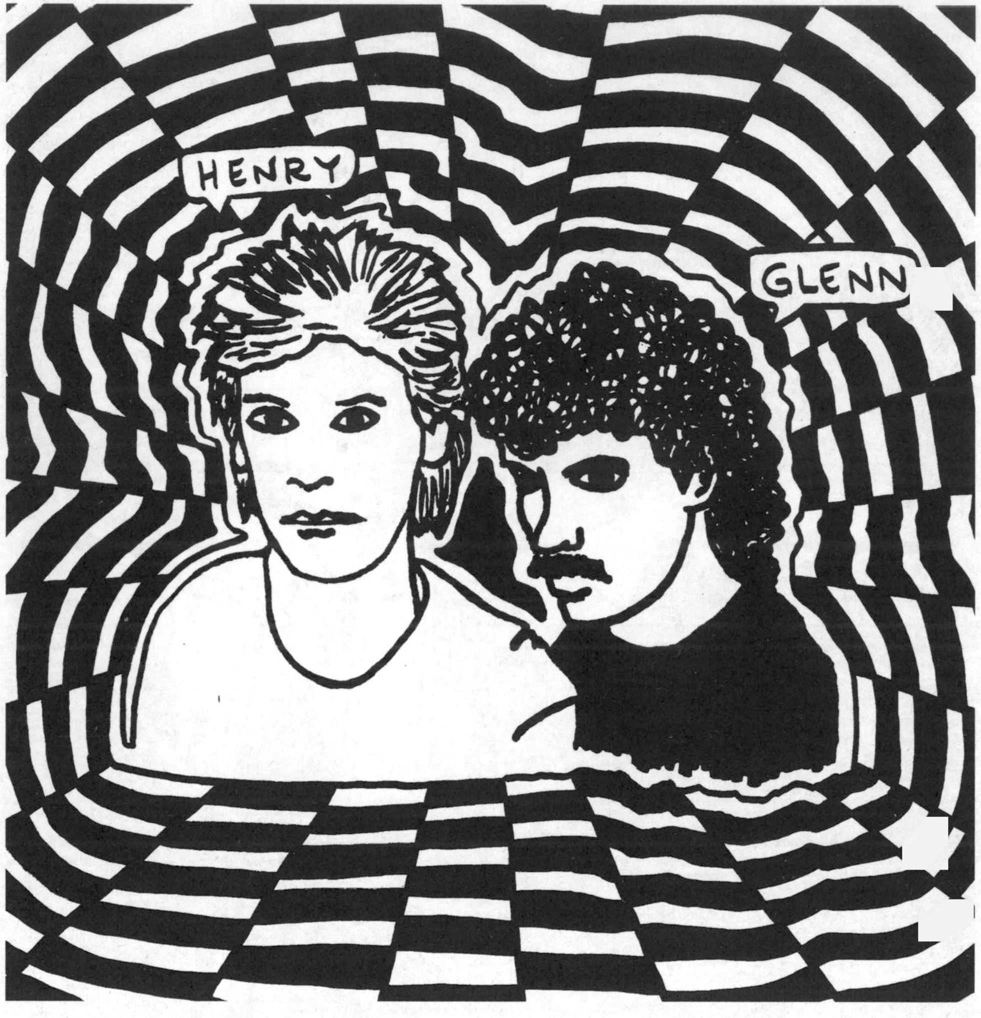
HENRY
GLENN

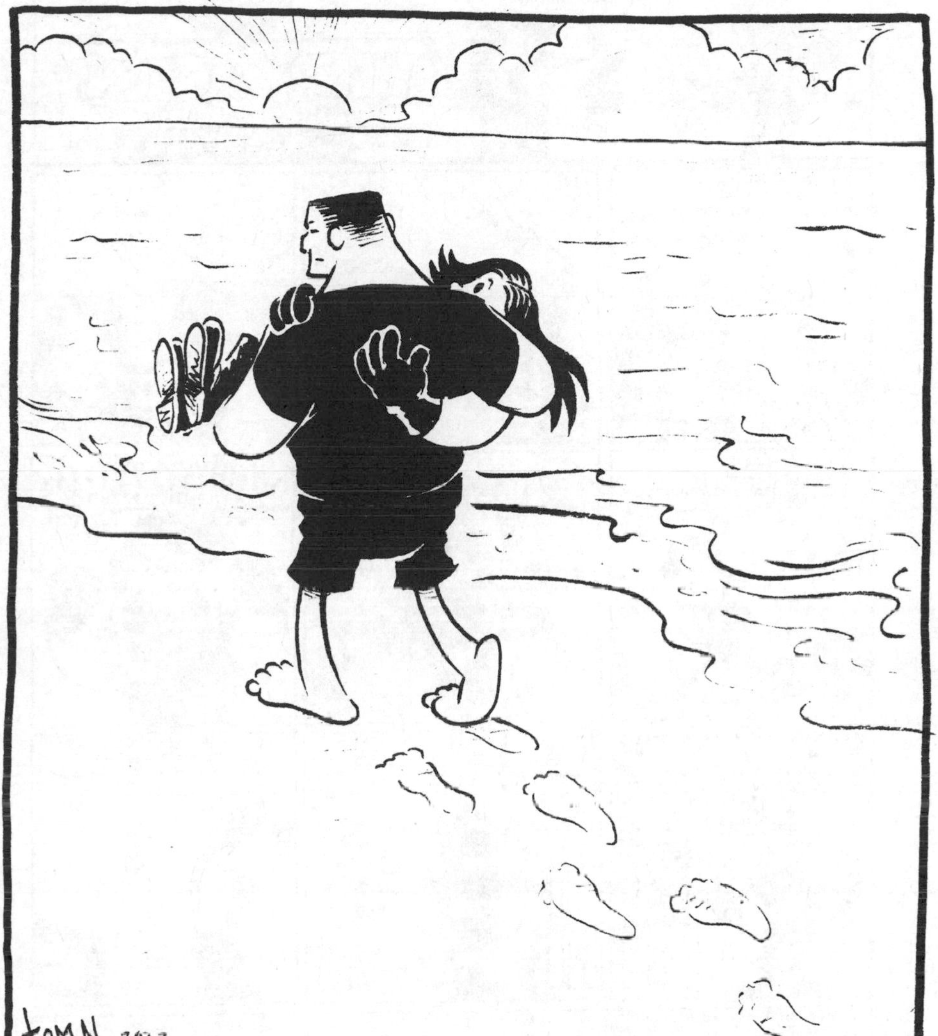
tomN. 2013

WHEN YOU ONLY SEE ONE SET OF FOOTPRINTS, I WAS CARRYING YOU.

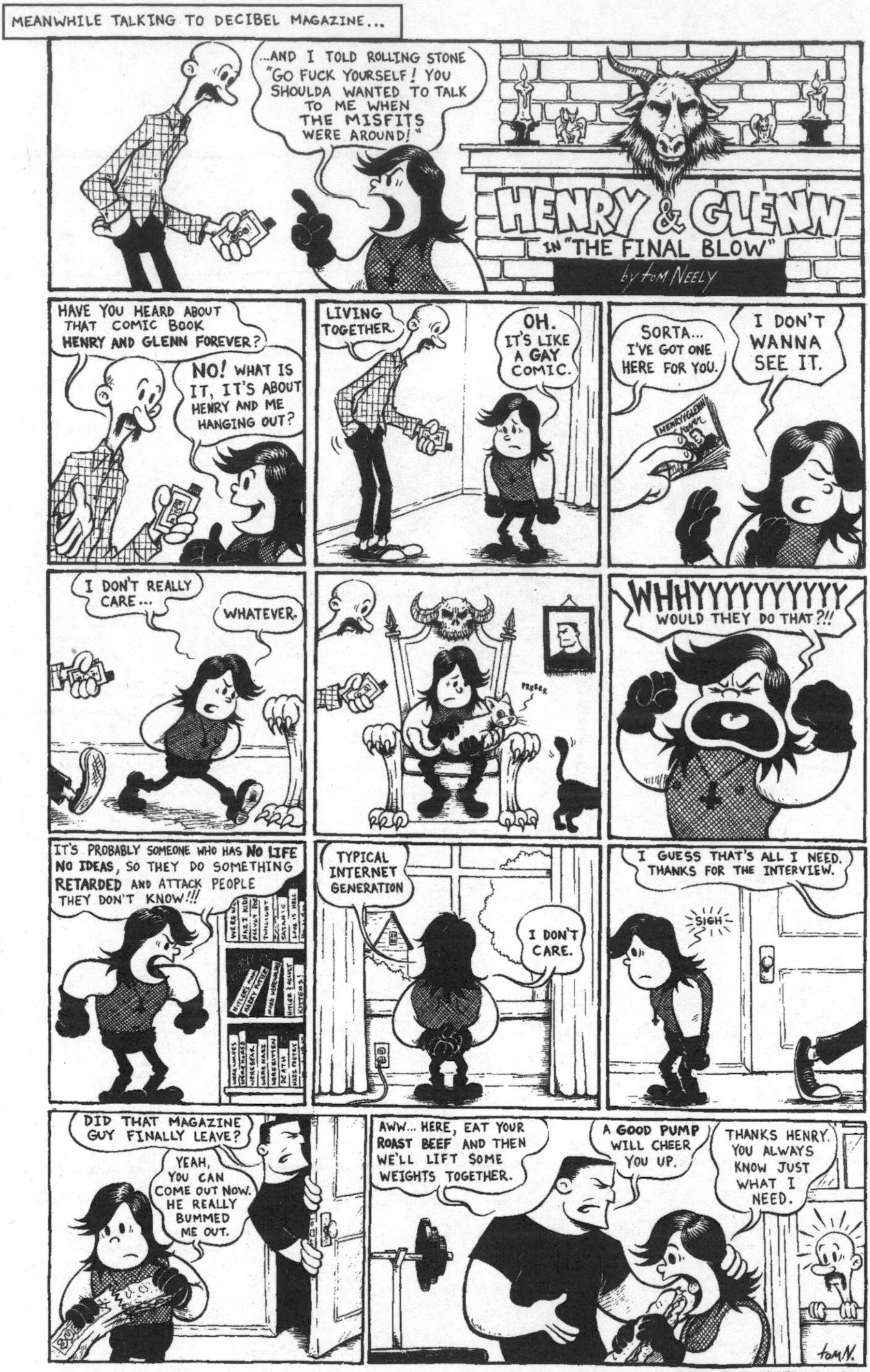
MEANWHILE TALKING TO DECIBEL MAGAZINE...
...AND I TOLD ROLLING STONE "GO FUCK YOURSELF! YOU SHOULDA WANTED TO TALK TO ME WHEN THE MISFITS WERE AROUND!"
HENRY & GLENN
IN "THE FINAL BLOW"
by tom NEELY
HAVE YOU HEARD ABOUT THAT COMIC BOOK HENRY AND GLENN FOREVER?
NO! WHAT IS IT, IT'S ABOUT HENRY AND ME HANGING OUT?
LIVING TOGETHER.
OH. IT'S LIKE A GAY COMIC.
SORTA... I'VE GOT ONE HERE FOR YOU.
I DON'T WANNA SEE IT.
I DON'T REALLY CARE...
WHATEVER.
WHHYYYYYYYYYY WOULD THEY DO THAT?!!
IT'S PROBABLY SOMEONE WHO HAS NO LIFE NO IDEAS, SO THEY DO SOMETHING RETARDED AND ATTACK PEOPLE THEY DON'T KNOW!!!
TYPICAL INTERNET GENERATION
I DON'T CARE.
I GUESS THAT'S ALL I NEED. THANKS FOR THE INTERVIEW.
SIGH
DID THAT MAGAZINE GUY FINALLY LEAVE?
YEAH, YOU CAN COME OUT NOW. HE REALLY BUMMED ME OUT.
AWW... HERE, EAT YOUR ROAST BEEF AND THEN WE'LL LIFT SOME WEIGHTS TOGETHER.
A GOOD PUMP WILL CHEER YOU UP.
THANKS HENRY. YOU ALWAYS KNOW JUST WHAT I NEED.
tomN.

THANKS TO J. BENNETT AND DECIBEL